ROUTLEDGE LIBRARY EDITIONS:
ACCOUNTING

Volume 47

CASH FLOW REPORTING

CASH FLOW REPORTING

A Recent History of an Accounting Practice

Edited by
THOMAS A. LEE

Routledge
Taylor & Francis Group
LONDON AND NEW YORK

First published in 1993

This edition first published in 2014
by Routledge
2 Park Square, Milton Park, Abingdon, Oxfordshire OX14 4RN

and by Routledge
711 Third Avenue, New York, NY 10017, USA

First issued in paperback 2015

Routledge is an imprint of the Taylor & Francis Group, an informa business

British Library Cataloguing in Publication Data
A catalogue record for this book is available from the British Library

ISBN: 978-0-415-53081-1 (Set)
ISBN 13: 978-1-138-96991-9 (pbk)
ISBN 13: 978-0-415-71725-0 (hbk) (Volume 47)

Publisher's Note
The publisher has gone to great lengths to ensure the quality of this book but points out that some imperfections in the original copies may be apparent.

Disclaimer
The publisher has made every effort to trace copyright holders and would welcome correspondence from those they have been unable to trace.

Cash Flow Reporting

A Recent History of an Accounting Practice

Edited by
Thomas A. Lee

Garland Publishing, Inc.
New York and London 1993

Library of Congress Cataloging-in-Publication Data

Cash flow reporting: A recent history of an accounting practice /
edited by Thomas A. Lee.
p.cm.—(New works in accounting history)
Includes bibliographical references.
ISBN 0-8153-1217–2
1. Cash flow—Accounting—History. 2. Accounting—Standards—History. I. Lee, T.A.
(Thomas Alexander) II. Series.
HF5681.C28C367 1993 93-607
657'.72—dc20

All volumes printed on acid-free, 250-year-life paper.
Manufactured in the United States of America.

Design by Marisel Tavarez

CONTENTS

INITIAL AND EXTENDED CASH FLOW REPORTING ARGUMENTS

DEMONSTRATING THE UTILITY OF CASH FLOW REPORTING

INFLUENCING ACCOUNTING POLICY-MAKING

PREFACE

Kuhn's (1970) perception of a scientific revolution in the form of a cyclical sequence of anomaly recognition, insecurity, alternative ideas, schools of thought, and dominating practices is explored in this collection of readings. Its subject-matter is cash flow reporting which, over the last three decades, can be cited as a dominant accounting practice which has emerged from a developmental process of Kuhnian form. The text is constructed around the various stages identified by Kuhn, and selected readings are categorised accordingly. There are also introductory analyses by the editor, and suggested further readings for discussion or essay papers. Cash flow reporting is one of the few significant changes in the financial accounting practices of recent times. This text aims to provide its reader with relevant material to judge and debate this claim. Its general content has been tested over several years at the University of Edinburgh, and I am grateful for the assistance of many Senior honours students at Edinburgh who have given me constructive feedback to improve that content.

ACKNOWLEDGMENTS

The editor, the series editor, and the publisher of this volume wish to thank the following authors, institutions, journals, and publishers for their kind permission to reproduce the copyright materials in this volume. Every effort has been made to trace authors and publishers. The items reproduced are indicated by the numbers by which they are listed in the contents page.

1. Professors M. Bromwich and A. Hopwood (editors), (c) 1981, and Professor T. A. Lee (author).

2. Professor T. A. Lee (author), (c) 1992.

5. **Journal of Accounting Research** and the Institute of Professional Accounting, (c) 1964 and Professor A. R. Drebin (author).

6. Howard Ross (author), (c) 1969 is deceased, and the text from which this reproduction has been taken is out of print.

7. Reprinted with permission from the **Journal of Accountancy**, Copyright (c) 1958 by American Institute of Certified Public Accountants, Inc. Opinions of the author are his own and do not necessarily reflect policies of the AICPA. L. Spacek (author) is deceased.

8. **Abacus**, (c) 1970. Professor E. Stamp (author) is deceased.

11. **Journal of Business Finance and Accounting**, (c) 1976. T. A. Climo (author) could not be traced.

12. Reprinted with permission from the **Journal of Accountancy**. Copyright (c) 1978 by American Institute of Certified Public Accountants, Inc. Opinions of the author are his own and do not necessarily reflect policies of the AICPA. And Professor L. C. Heath (author).

13. Professor G. H. Lawson (author). Reproduced courtesy of Lafferty Publications Ltd., IDA Tower, Pearse Street, Dublin 2, Ireland.
Tel: 353-1-718022 Fax: 353-1-718520.

14. Professor G. H. Lawson (author). Text (c) 1978.

15. Journal of Business Finance and Accounting, (c) 1972 and Professor T. A. Lee (author).

16. Accounting and Business Research, (c) 1981 and Professor T. A. Lee (author).

19. Journal of Business Finance and Accounting, (c) 1988 and A. J. Arnold and R, T. Wearing (authors).

20. American Accounting Association, (c) 1989 and Professors V. L. Bernard and T. L. Stober (authors).

21. Accounting and Business Research, (c) 1989 and J. L. G. Board and J. F. S. Day (authors).

22. Journal of Accounting Research and the Institute of Professional Accounting, (c) 1985. Professor C. J. Casey is deceased and Professor N. J. Bartczak could not be contacted despite several attempts.

23. Financial Analysts Journal, (c) 1980 and Professors J. A. Largay and C. P. Stickney (authors).

24. Professors M. Bromwich and A. Hopwood (editors), (c) 1980 and Professor G. H. Lawson (author).

25. Institute of Investment Management and Research, (c) 1983 and Professor T. A. Lee (author).

26. American Accounting Association, (c) 1987 and Professor G. P. Wilson (author).

29. Journal of Business Finance and Accounting, (c) 1976 and R. Ashton (author).

30. Accounting and Business Research, (c) 1984 and Professor D. Egginton (author).

31. Abacus, (c) 1982 and Professor B. A. Rutherford (author).

32. Accounting and Business Research, (c) 1989 and Professor G. J. Staubus (author).

35. Accounting Standards Board, (c) 1991.

36. Copyright by Financial Accounting Standards Board, 401 Merritt 7, P.O. Box 5116, Norwalk, Connecticut, 06856-5116, U.S.A. Reprinted with permission. Copies of the complete document are available from the FASB.

37. Controller of Her Britannic Majesty's Stationery Office, (c) 1975.

38. Institute of Chartered Accountants of Scotland, (c) 1989.

This book is published on behalf of the Scottish Committee on Accounting History of The Institute of Chartered Accountants of Scotland, and is dedicated to the memory of one of its members, Professor Michael Mepham. Mike was a skilled accounting historian, a fierce debater of accounting issues (particularly, the utility of cash flow accounting!), a good friend, and a very brave and gentle man.

* Lee, T. A., "Cash Flow Accounting and Corporate Financial Reporting," in Bromwich M. and Hopwood A., (eds.), **Essays in British Accounting Research** (London: Pitman Publishing, 1981), pp. 63–78.

* Lee, T. A., "Cash Flow Reporting's Recent History: a Kuhnian Interpretation of a Changing Accounting Emphasis," **Working Paper** (Tuscaloosa: University of Alabama, 1992).

3 Cash flow accounting and corporate financial reporting

T A Lee
Professor of Accountancy and Finance, University of Edinburgh

Approximately 50 writings have been read as preparation for this essay. Three-quarters of them were U.K.-based, and in excess of one-half could be attributed to two U.K. writers—Professors Lawson and Lee. Furthermore, three-quarters of the writings were published in the 1970s. Thus, the subject of cash flow accounting (CFA) is a relatively new one, not attracting many writers to its cause, and being of mainly U.K. interest (at least within the context of corporate financial reporting). However, despite this lack of apparent support in the literature, CFA remains potentially as a serious and viable addition to the corporate financial reporting function, and it is the aim of this essay to review it in order to assess its importance in this context. Inevitably, because of the volume of their contribution to CFA, the work of Lawson and Lee will form the substance of this review. But the work of other accountants will be examined, and a full bibliography is given at the end of the essay.

Nature and Role of CFA

CFA is the term used to denote a system of financial reporting which describes the financial performance of an entity in cash terms. It is based on a matching of periodic cash inflows and outflows, free of credit transactions and arbitrary accounting allocations. Inflows include cash from trading operations and providers of long-term finance; and outflows include payments for replacement and growth investment, taxation, interest, and distributions. As such, it is a measurement and reporting system which avoids time lags and distortions. It concentrates on the liquidity and financial management of the reporting entity, and can be conceived in terms both of actual and forecast cash transactions.

History of CFA

CFA is not a new concept. In fact, as Winjum (1972) has demonstrated, it was the main system of accounting up to the beginning of the 18th century.

Prior to that time, accounting allocations and profit measurements were relatively unimportant; the profit and loss account being used to close off ledger accounts at each period end. However, with the advent of the concept and practice of business continuity, the need grew to produce periodic measures of profit and statements of financial position (Littleton and Zimmerman, 1963). Thus, the basic cash transactions became the foundation for the allocation-based systems of accounting of today.

Although there has been a reasonably sustained interest in funds flow statements (based on allocated accounting data) since the beginning of the 20th century (see Käfer and Zimmerman, 1979), CFA appears to have received little or no support from accountants until the early 1960s. At that time, there was concern over the use of 'cash flow' data in financial analysis—cash flow being interpreted as 'profit plus depreciation' (see Paton, 1963 and Drebin, 1964).[1] The major worry was that such data were being used for decision-making purposes as a substitute for income, and that the cost of durable assets was not being taken into account. Also, at this time, two writers advocated the reporting of pure cash flow data (i.e. CFA)—in the U.S., Coughlan (1960; 1962; 1964) and, in the U.K., Edey (1963).

Coughlan's recommendations were based on a capital budgeting approach involving the reporting of past and expected cash flows as a basis for producing discounted cash flow balance sheets from which measures of income could be derived as a form of internal rate of return. He described these computations of economic income and value as 'industrial accounting', and argued for them because of the distortions caused by conventional accounting allocations, and the need, therefore, to account properly for the influence of time. His pioneering work which, however, appeared to be aimed at internal reporting functions, was apparently not developed further by him.

Edey, on the other hand, advocated the reporting of forecast cash flows because of the difficulties associated with the measurement of profit. He believed such predictive data to be more relevant than profits for the purposes of estimating future dividend levels, evaluating management, and assessing corporate liquidity. Mainly concerned with the provision of relevant information for investors, and with the lack of precision in the meaning of profit, Edey also recommended that investors should be provided with net realizable value-based balance sheets in order to assess potential corporate liquidity, chargeable capacity,[2] and the minimum return to be earned on investment. Edey repeated his recommendations later (1970) but has not developed them since in the literature.

Staubus (1961; 1966) also provided a relatively early contribution to the contemporary CFA debate when reviewing the nature and role of the

1 Confusing CFA with 'cash flow' data which are allocation-based is a common mistake in the accountancy literature—particularly that of the U.S. in the 1960s.

2 Defined as the value of the assets available to act as security for potential borrowings.

funds flow statement for investors. Identifying the importance of assessing corporate liquidity for investment or managerial decisions, he rejected the use of net realizable value data for this purpose and, instead, advocated the reporting of funds statements based on cash or near-cash resources (i.e. including debtors and creditors). In his early work (1961), he envisaged such statements as being of use only to short-term creditors, but in his later writing (1966), he appeared to have widened his views on the relevance of such statements. He particularly emphasized the opinion that cash flow statements ought to distinguish recurrent from non-recurrent flows in order to aid their users in assessing corporate liquidity. Staubus does not appear to have developed his work on CFA since 1966.

Contemporary Contributions

In 1968, Lawson (1968) published his first paper on CFA. Since then he has continued to develop his ideas both conceptually and empirically. Lee (1971) published his first CFA contribution some time later but, together, these writers have provided most of the CFA literature of the 1970s, and this will be examined in detail in later sections. However, Lawson and Lee have not been alone in their support of CFA. In the U.S., the main contributors (other than Coughlan and Staubus) have been Thomas (1969; 1974; 1979), Ijiri (1977; 1978; 1979) and Heath (1978).[3] Briston and Fawthrop (1971), Jones (1975), Climo (1976), and Waldron (1980), have also provided contributions to the CFA debate and literature in the U.K. (in addition to Edey). Their work will be discussed prior to that of Lawson and Lee but, meantime, the U.S. contribution will be reviewed briefly.

U.S. Contributions

Thomas' pioneering work on the frailties of the allocation system in conventional accounting led him to recommend the abandonment of income measurement by accountants, concentrating instead on funds statements using a notion of funds defined in terms of cash plus debtors minus creditors (1969). These net quick asset statements were recommended in addition to statements of monetary and non-monetary assets (1974).

3 The idea of combining CFA and NRVA ought not to be confused with the suggestion by Ronen and Sorter of merging a market rate-determined economic value of the reporting entity with the exit values of its conventionally classified assets and liabilities—see Ronen and Sorter (1972) and Ronen (1974). The Ronen and Sorter proposal was intended to provide investors with (a) means of comparing market values with economic values of the reporting entity and its equity; (b) managerially forecasted cash flows (but in the form of reporting one discounted measure of value); and (c) measurement of the conversion of entity asset economic values into exit values, and vice versa. Nowhere in their system was there a recommendation to specifically disclose either past or forecast CFA data.

However, his relative vagueness with regard to what precise form these statements should take, leaves Thomas' work in a somewhat indeterminate state; he is strongly in favour of reporting allocation-free data (especially related to flow statements) but is less than clear with regard to position statements.[4]

Historic cost accounting is the area for which Ijiri is best known (1967). However, he has recently advocated the use of CFA (1977; 1978; 1979) as a means of enabling the results of managerial decisions to be evaluated on the same basis as they were taken. Ijiri's CFA system, however, is an extension of historic cost, allocation-based accounting. He recommends the reporting of statements reflecting investment flows (changes in historic cost-based assets) and financing flows (changes in sources of finance). The former flows are to be stated before deduction of fixed asset depreciation, and the latter flows are to include such aggregate provisions. Historic costs in this sense are used not to value assets but to describe the entity's investment in them. Ijiri concentrates on what he describes as cash flow recovery (usually profit plus depreciation, interest, and fixed asset sales) and relates this to the total gross investment in assets (before depreciation) in order to determine corporate recovery rates. He recommends these rates as surrogates for discounted cash flow returns in situations where *ex post* measurements of the latter are not possible due to the continuity of the entity concerned. It is not, however, a system which can be regarded as pure CFA; rather, it should be looked upon as an extension of historic cost accounting.

The final U.S. contributor to CFA has been Heath (1978). Writing of the need to provide relevant financial information for investors, creditors and other persons interested in evaluating corporate solvency and liquidity, he has advocated the presentation of a statement of cash receipts and payments (giving a listing of the various sources of cash matched with an equivalent listing of the various uses to which these were put), coupled with a further two statements—one describing the various changes on the assets side of the historic cost-based balance sheet, and the other dealing with the equivalent changes on the liabilities side of the same report. As such, Heath's recommendations do contain an element of CFA but they cannot be taken as advocations of a complete system of financial reporting based on CFA.

U.K. Contributions

A consistent feature of the U.K. accounting literature over the last 10 years or so has been the development of a detailed argument and structure for CFA as a major part of the corporate financial reporting function. Spearheaded by Lawson (1968; 1969; 1970; 1971a; 1971b; 1971c; 1972;

4 In his most recent work, Thomas (1979) advocates cash flow statements coupled with virtually unspecified allocation-free balance sheets.

1973; 1975a; 1975b; 1976; 1978a; 1978b; 1978c; 1979) and Lee (1971; 1972a; 1972b; 1972c; 1974; 1978; 1979a; 1979b; 1979c; 1980a; 1980b), the main argument has been for a logical and coherent reporting framework including statements of past and forecast cash flows, and supported by additional statements concerning, *inter alia*, explanations of variances between actual and forecast data, descriptions of the major assumptions underlying forecast results, audit opinions, and explanations of non-cash transactions. In these respects, the work of Lawson and Lee are reasonably similar, although Lee (1980b) has extended it to include net realizable value-based position statements which relate to the recommended CFA statements.[5]

There have been other contributions to the U.K. debate on CFA. Edey (1963; 1970), as mentioned earlier, provided the initial impetus with his suggestion for the reporting of forecast cash flows. Briston and Fawthrop (1971) also suggested the reporting of such forecasts, supplemented by an audited statement of variances between actual and previously forecast results. Jones (1975) supported the idea of past and forecast cash flow statements as a feasible alternative to the problem of standardizing accounting allocations. The Sandilands Committee on Inflation Accounting (1975), whilst appearing to receive the idea of CFA for corporate financial reporting purposes with some enthusiasm, rejected it on the practical ground that it would not comply with existing company law because of its lack of adherence to statements of profit and financial position.[6] In contrast, Climo (1976) felt that the reporting of CFA data (past and future) would be exceedingly relevant to investors, particularly if the flows concerned were divisionalized, segregated between recurrent and non-recurrent items, and supported by some form of (unspecified) net realizable value-based balance sheet. Waldron (1980) also felt that past CFA reports ought to be supported by forecast data and financial position data—in this case, the former was recommended to be contained in a statement of needs and resources (describing the next 12 months cash receipts and payments), and the latter to take the form of a balance sheet based on (undefined) economic values. On the whole, therefore, these contributions have lent support and added weight to the CFA argument and debate without having the degree of depth and consistency to be evidenced in the work of Lawson and Lee.

The Lawson/Lee Case for CFA

The remainder of this essay is concerned with CFA as advocated by Lawson and Lee. This review will be a general one, examining, first, the

5 The early work on CFA by Lawson and Lee has been reviewed by Ashton (1976), and various similarities and dissimilarities at that time have been examined by him.

6 This appeared to ignore the fact that CFA is usually advocated by its supporters as an addition to the traditional and long-standing system of financial reporting.

structure of the system and, secondly, the considerable advantages which have been claimed for it. References will be made to specific papers when necessary.

Suggested CFA System—Users

The suggestion of a corporate financial reporting system based on cash flows has been underpinned by the fundamental concepts of utility and relevance (Lee, 1971; 1972a; 1972c). This general theoretical base has been operationalized in terms of specific report user groups. Lawson, for example, has been concerned mainly with the use of cash data by investors, CFA containing all the determinants of distributable cash flows—this has characterized most of his writings (as in, for example, 1969; 1971a; 1971b; 1971c; 1972; 1975a; 1978a). However, he has recognized other uses—wage negotiation (1975a; and Lawson and Stark, 1977); bank lending (1978c); and governmental policy-making in relation to corporate taxation (e.g. 1971b; 1973; 1975a; 1975b; 1976; 1978a; 1978c; 1979).

Lee, too, has emphasized the importance of CFA in relation to specific user groups—at first in relation to shareholders (1971; 1972c) but, increasingly, his recommendations for CFA have been given in relation to the needs of a number of specific groups—for example, lenders and creditors, bankers, employees, managers, government agencies, etc. (1974; 1978; 1979b). He has also more recently argued for its general purpose nature in a corporate financial reporting context—i.e. CFA is capable of satisfying a number of different user groups rather than being specifically relevant to a particular group (1980b).

In light of the above comments, as well as a review of the other U.K. papers on CFA, it is clear that such recommendations have been made within the context of an increasing awareness in the 1970s of the need to satisfy the informational needs of corporate report users. Not only is the suggested CFA system seen as being relevant to specific users but is also regarded as having a general relevance. In other words, cash flow data are believed to impinge on most users' behaviour. In this sense, the Lawson and Lee proposals are definitely aimed at aiding user decisions. This underlies all their work, and is made most explicit in their consistent suggestion for the reporting of both past and forecast cash flows. This is not to say that either writer has ignored the use of CFA as a means of making entity management accountable to ownership—the stewardship function (e.g. Lawson, 1975a; and Lee, 1974; 1978). CFA is therefore conceived as a multi-purpose reporting system, compatible with the decision and accountability aims usually associated with the conventional allocation-based reporting systems.

Suggested CFA System—Structure

The system of CFA advocated by Lawson and Lee is all-embracing, containing data related to both actual and predicted business activity, supported (as mentioned previously) by a number of explanatory statements pertaining, *inter alia*, to forecasting assumptions, variances, non-cash transactions, and relevant audit opinions. As his earlier writings indicate (e.g. 1969; 1971a), Lawson has described the reporting entity as a total financial system. Accordingly, his consistent recommendation has been that CFA is an explicit statement of such a system—i.e. the entity receives a net cash flow from its various operational activities (O), and uses this to pay for replacement and growth investment (R), taxation (T), interest on borrowings (I), and distributions to its owners (D). By including new equity receipts (E) and borrowings (B), Lawson's simple tabulated CFA presentation can be reconciled to the periodic change in cash resources of the entity (C). Thus:

$$O - R - T - I + E + B - C = D$$

In other words, the major emphasis is on disclosing the distributed, or distributable, cash flow to the entity's owners and, by deducting E from D, producing a measure of the latter's cash flow which can be used for purposes of discounting to derive a present value of equity. Except for a supplementary statement describing the composition of the operational cash flow, Lawson's system is a relatively simple tabulated one involving 10 years of past data, and between 12 and 18 months of forecast data (1975a). It is also divisionalized, where relevant (1971a).

As will be shown in later sections, the essence of the CFA system described by Lawson is to provide relevant data for a number of measurable tasks—e.g. for determining effective rates of tax, and interest and dividend covers. In other words, he has concentrated on the uses to which CFA could be put rather than on the detail and structure of CFA as a corporate financial reporting system. In contrast, Lee has been mainly concerned with the detail of CFA as a reporting system. Like Lawson, his general recommendations have consistently included the reporting of 10 years of past data, and at least 1 year of forecast data—all suitably audited and supported by a statement of explained variances between actual and forecast results (distinguishing between controllable and uncontrollable differences). However, Lee has also extended this broad framework in a number of ways—first, in relation to statements to support the main CFA data (Lee, 1972c) and secondly, in relation to financial statement data which are compatible with CFA (Lee, 1980b).

Using the above notation, Lee's main CFA statements originally (e.g. 1972c) used the following pattern:

$$O - R - I - T - D + E + B = C$$

This was reasonably similar to that of Lawson above. It assumed that operational cash flows were available to pay, in order of priority, replacement and growth investment (to ensure continuity of the entity), interest on borrowings (deducted before tax as it is allowable for taxation purposes), taxation, and distributions to the entity owners. This would leave a surplus or deficit of cash to be augmented or supplemented by new equity and borrowing receipts. However, as a reporting system, it provided matchings of cash inflows and outflows which suggested new long-term finance was being raised by the reporting entity to pay for dividends (and even taxation) in circumstances where operating cash flows were inadequate to cover these payments in addition to replacement and growth investment. In order to provide a more neutral reporting statement, Lee has recently suggested the formulation (1980b):

$$O - I - T - D + E + B - R = C$$

This effectively leaves the deduction of payments for replacement and growth investment until all available cash resources have been utilized to cover deductions for payments for which some prior commitment or obligation has been recognized by management.

The above basic data in Lee's system are each recommended to be supported by a detailed supplementary statement enabling the report user to comprehend how each figure is composed—e.g. the taxation measure could comprise payments for U.K. and non-U.K. tax; and the replacement and growth investment figure, as well as being derived after making the basic distinction of replacement and growth, could be shown along with receipts for asset disposals and government grants. Furthermore, the operational cash flow statement could be suitably segmented, and all reported statements would require to be audited. A unique feature of Lee's system is the inclusion of a statement to disclose entity transactions which have not involved a cash flow (e.g. the acquisition of assets for equity or loan stock).

Lee (1980b) has extended his CFA system to include statements of financial position based on net realizable values. By combining these potential cash flows with realized cash flows, a measure of total cash flow can be computed. This complete system of CFA can then be tied in with a statement of financial position which describes (in order of realizability) a minimum future cash inflow to be matched against (in order of date of settlement) the various obligations due by the reporting entity. This suggestion is intended as a reasoned answer to the charge that CFA is an incomplete reporting system because it concentrates solely on 'flows' rather than 'stocks'. The combined system appears to provide both, and is, therefore, a practical implementation of the original idea of Edey (1963).

To summarize on the suggested structure of CFA reports, it is clear that there is reasonable agreement in the U.K.—actual and forecast data should be disclosed (segmented where relevant); supplementary disclosure can come from a variety of supporting statements; particular attention ought to be paid to explained forecasting assumptions, and explained variances between actual and forecast results; and auditing of these statements appears to be a priority. Finally, Edey, Climo and Lee (in the U.K.) and Thomas (in the U.S.) have recommended net realizable value position statements in support of CFA. Lee has attempted to implement this suggestion.

However, despite the agreement, there appear to be fundamental differences in the Lawson and Lee proposals. First, Lee conceives of the structure of CFA as an interlocking series of statements for a variety of users. Lawson, on the other hand, is mainly concerned with the provision of cash flow data to improve the information base of investors and financial managers. Secondly, Lawson's system is largely proprietorial in nature because of its attention to distributable flows and investors; Lee's system is enterprise-orientated, intended for a variety of user groups, and concentrating on a reporting of the various cash flows of the entity. The latter approach owes much to the work of Fisher who regarded the entity as a clearing house for various cash flows to creditors, employees, lenders, bankers, government, and owners (Lee, 1979a). This is not to say that Lawson's work has lacked an enterprise approach—his earliest work (e.g. 1969) described CFA as a means of portraying the reporting entity as a total financial system. His later work, however, has concentrated particularly on the needs of investors.

Suggested CFA System—Computation

The computation of CFA data ought to be uncomplicated in an accounting sense. After all, part of its *raison d'etre* is to avoid the complexities and subjectiveness of accounting allocations. Thus, preparing CFA statements from cash transactions should only involve the complications of presentation and disclosure.[7] However, due to the conventional structuring of the credit and allocation-based accounting system, it may not be possible to produce CFA statements directly. In these cases, it should be feasible to take allocated data and, by reversing the effect of the credit transactions and accounting allocations, derive the underlying cash flows. This is particularly feasible when funds statements are available.

Much of the work on adjusting conventional data to their cash flow equivalents is due to the efforts of Lawson (e.g. 1971c; 1976; 1978a; and Lawson and Stark, 1975). By unveiling the hidden cash flows in allocated data, Lawson has been able to highlight the two major shortcomings of the latter, particularly during a period of inflation—i.e. the working capital and depreciation shortfalls in measuring periodic surpluses (e.g. 1975a; 1975b). In conventional accounting, the full cost of working capital is not (and may never be) matched against revenues—e.g. under FIFO systems of stock accounting, there is a base level of stock which will never be

7 There will, of course, also be the problem of forecasting judgements when preparing predicted CFA data.

matched against sales unless the stock is completely consumed (Lawson, 1975b). The same is true of fixed asset costs, assuming continuity of the reporting entity.

Thus, although Lawson's cash flow adjustments to allocated data are, in themselves, relatively obvious and straightforward, his use of them to demonstrate the consistent overstatement of reported entity earnings has been a considerable advance in accounting thinking. In particular, his demonstration that, during periods of inflation, these overstatements become more material, has highlighted the inadequacies of systems of current cost accounting to bridge the gap between the partial costs which are conventionally matched against revenues, and the total costs which, because they have been committed, ought to be so matched (Lawson, 1976; 1978a).

Suggested CFA System—Main Features

CFA has a considerable number of identifiable features which suggest its reporting potential in terms of improving the utility of financial reports. Again, these owe much to the work of Lawson and Lee for their identification. They are given below in no particular order of importance.

1. CFA avoids dubious accounting allocations and thus, unlike periodic income measurements, cash flows provide relatively unambiguous measures of entity financial performance (e.g. Lawson, 1968; 1969; 1970; 1971b; 1971c; and Lee, 1971; 1972c).
2. CFA captures the vital factor in decision-making and valuation of the time value of money; conventional accounting ignores this by allocating data in order to 'smooth' income trends (e.g. Lawson, 1968; 1970; 1971b; 1971c; and Lee, 1971; 1972b).
3. CFA can therefore avoid dubious measures of periodic income which have a variety of meanings depending on the particular measurement contexts and uses to which they are being applied. CFA has a relatively unambiguous meaning, no matter what the measurement context or use is (e.g. Lee, 1974).
4. CFA emphasizes some of the most fundamental and vital features of business activity (cash is the key factor in this long-term issue); the ability of the enterprise to pay its obligations, make distributions, and provide for its future continuity (cash is needed to reinvest, to expand, and to pay for taxation, interest, and distribution commitments, as well as to repay credit and borrowings previously received) (e.g. Lee, 1972c; 1974; 1978).
5. CFA does not require price-level adjustments due to specific inflation as it expresses the cash flow data concerned in the purchasing power of the period in which they were transacted and accounted. However, it may be necessary to convert CFA data of different periods to a base year (by some

form of general price restatement) (e.g. Lawson, 1970; 1971c; 1972; and Lee, 1971; 1978).

6. CFA is capable of producing data which are needed for a variety of decision and control activities both within and without the reporting entity. It, therefore, ought to improve the quality of these matters—e.g. by providing report users with management's views of the future, and data on working capital and depreciation shortfalls, and fiscal drag,[8] there is an argument that the stock market (at least in aggregate) would be more efficient and derive more accurate share values as a consequence (Lawson, 1970; 1971c; 1975a); bankers and lenders would be provided with data relevant to their assessment of the reporting entity's quality of financial (and, particularly, cash) management (Lee, 1980b); and government would learn of the lack of neutrality[9] in its corporate taxation system (Lawson, 1978c; 1979).

7. CFA is the only proper basis for measuring the value of entities as going concerns because of its attention to the time value of money. It is thus capable of providing not only present values of investments but also rates of return which conform with economic principles. CFA is also compatible with Hicksian notions of periodic income and capital valuation (Lawson, 1968; 1969; 1971a; 1978a; and Lee, 1971).

8. CFA as a system of financial reporting is objective, understandable, and simple. It avoids the subjectiveness and language of accounting allocations, and presents the data in a way that is potentially recognizable to its users (Lawson, 1970; and Lee, 1972c; 1974; 1978).[10] It also provides comparable data which are not rendered incomparable because of measurements of different purchasing powers, and subjective allocations (Lee, 1974).

9. CFA conforms to a number of non-accounting theories which, nevertheless, have strong associations with the accounting and reporting function—for example, CFA (as mentioned above) is compatible with economic theories of the time value of money and interest, and of income and capital valuation; it is also consistent with modern capital market theory (Lawson, 1978a).

These are merely a few of the various arguments for, and main features of, CFA which have been highlighted by Lawson and Lee. They cannot really do justice to the case for CFA in financial reporting due to the brevity of description given to each point. Nevertheless, when taken as a whole, they

8 Fiscal drag in this context is the term used by Lawson (1979) to denote the time lag between providing for corporate tax on high levels of accounting profit, and paying for this tax out of considerably smaller cash surpluses in later years (assuming a period of inflation).

9 Tax neutrality is the term used to denote a system of tax which bears equally upon all taxpayers—i.e. it does not favour or discriminate against individual taxpayers.

10 Tweedie (1977), in a pilot study, has produced evidence to suggest that non-accountants may intuitively think of periodic income and financial position in terms of, respectively, cash flows and net realizable values.

provide a formidable case for CFA which is not to be evidenced to such an extent in other systems of financial reporting which have received favour by accountants.

Suggested CFA System—Empirical Evidence

As well as giving conceptual arguments for the introduction of CFA to financial reporting, Lawson and Lee have provided empirical evidence of its utility. In a number of research studies over recent years, both writers have been concerned to back up their assertions with proof of CFA's reporting potential.

In a preliminary study of CFA utility, Lee (1979c) invited shareholders in two medium-sized companies to rank five brewing companies in order of investment preference in accordance with the type of information supplied to them. CFA data comprised one of the information sets provided, and it was found that the companies were ranked considerably differently by shareholders who received CFA data only, compared with those who received historic cost, allocation-based equivalents or a mixture of both. CFA data did not appear to cause any difficulties to its investor-users despite their lack of familiarity with it.

Lee (1980a) has also examined accountants' attitudes towards CFA reporting to external user groups. He evidenced considerable support for the idea—more so for actual cash flow results than for forecast results. CFA data were believed to be useful to most external user groups interested in companies, but especially to bankers and lenders concerned with assessing corporate liquidity. No particular problems were foreseen in preparing past data—several years of audited data being envisaged as the typical reporting format. Forecast statements were not believed to be worthwhile beyond more than one or two years of predicted activity. Most of the respondents' companies utilized CFA systems to a considerable extent for internal management purposes.

Using, alternatively, hypothetical and live data (for individual companies as well as in aggregate), Lawson has documented extensive evidence concerning the utility of CFA data. He has shown that the working capital and depreciation shortfalls for manufacturing companies can be considerable, and can increase substantially as the rate of inflation increases (1975a)—thus, conventional accounting consistently overstates corporate earnings during periods of inflation. He has demonstrated the misleading effects this overstatement may have—e.g. the wisdom of wage claims based on reported income when the effective rates of tax based on CFA are well in excess of the notional rate (Lawson and Stark, 1977).

In more recent times, Lawson has further demonstrated the utility of cash flow data for purposes of economic and financial management. He has revealed (1978c) that, using aggregate data for 1954 to 1976, inclusive, real cash flow returns (net of tax) to shareholders and lenders have typically been negative (particularly between 1964 and 1976). In the same study, Lawson evidences that the market, as a whole, uncovers the cash flows underlying conventional earnings, and impounds these into share prices. His overall conclusions from this data are (a) the market is efficient with regard to cash flow; (b) U.K. companies are consistently paying dividends in excess of cash flow earnings and financing the deficit by borrowings; and (c) company tax rates on a cash flow basis are confiscatory and lack neutrality. These results were further confirmed in a more recent study (Lawson, 1979), although it is not clear that the market is as efficient in unveiling underlying cash flows of individual companies. Suffice to say, however, that Lawson's evidence in the U.K. is of overtaxation, over-distribution, and crisis levels of borrowing to finance this. In this respect, the utility of CFA in the area of corporate taxation has recently been recognized in the report of the Meade Committee (1978), in which it is recommended that company tax in the U.K. be based on measured cash flows. This is the first tangible evidence, other than from the advocates of CFA, of its practical utility and importance.

Conclusions

Although CFA is not as yet a formal part of financial reporting, cash flow data can be derived from conventional allocation-based figures. This can be done relatively easily, and CFA's utility can be reasonably demonstrated at a conceptual level and, increasingly, at an empirical level. A relatively few accountants have achieved this position and, as such, CFA has been argued for at least as consistently as any other system of accounting. Unlike other systems, however, it has not so far suffered from any significant criticism in the published literature.

The argument for CFA has progressed at two levels: conceptually (both in relation to what CFA attempts to describe, and for whom it is addressed); and, more recently, empirically (in terms of utility and feasibility). In other words, CFA is a system which already has a sound theoretical underpinning, a developed measurement and presentation framework, and growing empirical support. Obviously, a great deal of work remains to be undertaken—e.g. in relation to improving the structure and detail of CFA reports (particularly with regard to position statements), forecasting, and avoidance of managerial manipulation of cash flows. Also, there is the very real 'political' problem to be overcome of convincing accounting policy-makers that CFA is a valid, useful and complete reporting system worthy of inclusion in the overall financial reporting package.

That much of this work has been achieved in the U.K. in recent years by so few accountants is a unique contribution to financial reporting. It is to be hoped that their effort will continue to a successful outcome whereby the U.K. can be seen to be the birthplace of the practice of modern CFA for external reporting purposes.

References

Ashton, R., 'Cash Flow Accounting: A Review and Critique,' *Journal of Business Finance and Accounting* (Winter 1976), pp. 63–81.

Briston, R. J. and Fawthrop, R. A., 'Accounting Principles and Investor Protection', *Journal of Business Finance* (Summer 1971), pp. 10–19.

Climo, T. A., 'Cash Flow Statements for Investors', *Journal of Business Finance and Accounting* (Autumn 1976), pp. 3–14.

Coughlan, J. W., 'Contrast Between Financial-Statement and Discounted-Cash-Flow Methods of Comparing Projects', *NAA Bulletin* (June 1960), pp. 5–17.

Coughlan, J. W., 'Accounting and Capital Budgeting', *The Business Quarterly* (Fall 1962), pp. 39–48.

Coughlan, J. W., 'Funds and Income', *NAA Bulletin* (September 1964), pp. 23–34.

Drebin, A. R., ' "Cash-Flowitis": Malady or Syndrome?', *Journal of Accounting Research* (Spring 1964), pp. 25–34.

Edey, H. C., 'Accounting Principles and Business Reality', *Accountancy* (November 1963), pp. 998–1002; (December 1963), pp. 1083–8.

Edey, H. C., 'The Nature of Profit', *Accounting and Business Research* (Winter 1970), pp. 50–5.

Heath, L. C., 'Financial Reporting and the Evaluation of Solvency', *Accounting Research Monograph 3*. American Institute of Certified Public Accountants (1978).

Ijiri, Y., *The Foundations of Accounting Measurement*. Prentice Hall (1967).

Ijiri, Y., 'Corporate Recovery Rate and Cash Flow Accounting', *GSIA Working Paper*. Carnegie-Mellon University (1977).

Ijiri, Y., 'Cash Flow Accounting and Its Structure', *Journal of Accounting, Auditing and Finance* (May 1978), pp. 331–48.

Ijiri, Y., 'A Simple System of Cash Flow Accounting', in R. R. Sterling and A. L. Thomas (eds.), *Accounting for a Simplified Firm*. Scholars Book Co. (1979), pp. 57–71.

Inflation Accounting Committee, 'Inflation Accounting', *Report of the Inflation Accounting Committee*, Cmd 6225 (HMSO, 1975), pp. 156–8.

Jones, C. J., 'Accounting Standards: A Blind Alley?', *Accounting and Business Research* (Autumn 1975), pp. 273–9.

Käfer, K. and Zimmerman, V. K., 'Notes on the Evolution of the Statement of Sources and Applications of Funds', in T. A. Lee and R. H. Parker (eds.), *The Evolution of Corporate Financial Reporting*. Nelson (1979), pp. 133–52.

Lawson, G. H., *Applications of a Business Theory*. University of Liverpool Press (1968).

Lawson, G. H., 'Profit Maximisation Via Financial Management', *Management Decision* (Winter 1969), pp. 6–12.

Lawson, G. H., 'Radical Change in Financial Reports', *Financial Times* (15 July 1970).

Lawson, G. H., 'Measuring Divisional Performance', *Management Accountant* (May 1971a), pp. 147–52.

Lawson, G. H., 'Accounting for Financial Management—Some Tentative Proposals for a New Blueprint', in R. Shone (ed.), *Problems of Investment*. Blackwell (1971b), pp. 36–64.
Lawson, G. H., 'Cash-flow Accounting', *The Accountant* (28 October 1971), pp. 586–9; (4 November 1971c), pp. 620–2.
Lawson, G. H., 'Distributable Profits and Dividends', *Management International Review* (Vol 12 (2–3), 1972), pp. 113–19.
Lawson, G. H., 'Financial Objectives and Annual Financial Targets in the Imputation Tax System', *Journal of Business Finance* (Summer 1973), pp. 1–18.
Lawson, G. H., 'Memorandum Submitted to the Inflation Accounting Committee in July 1974', *Working Paper Series 12* (Manchester Business School, 1975a).
Lawson, G. H., 'The Rationale for Measuring the Cost of Working Capital', *Working Paper Series 15*. (Manchester Business School, 1975b).
Lawson, G. H., 'Initial Reactions to ED18', *Certified Accountant* (December 1976), pp. 357–65 and p. 422.
Lawson, G. H. 'The Rationale of Cash Flow Accounting', in C. van Dam (ed.), *Trends in Managerial and Financial Accounting*. Martinus Nijhoff (1978a), pp. 85–104.
Lawson, G. H., 'The Valuation of a Going Concern on a Cash Flow Basis', *Managerial Finance* (August 1980), forthcoming (1978b).
Lawson, G. H., *Company Profitability and the U.K. Stock Market—An Exercise in Cash Flow Accounting*. Manchester Business School (1978c).
Lawson, G. H., 'The Cash Flow Performance of U.K. Companies: Preliminary Analysis', *paper* to SSRC Conference on Accounting Research (1979).
Lawson, G. H. and Stark, A. W., 'The Concept of Profit for Fund Raising', *Accounting and Business Research* (Winter 1975), pp. 21–41.
Lawson, G. H. and Stark, A. W., 'Does Ford Cash Really Flow?', *Accountancy Age* (12 August 1977), pp. 8–9.
Lee, T. A., 'Goodwill—an Example of Will-o'-the-Wisp Accounting', *Accounting and Business Research* (Autumn 1971), pp. 318–28.
Lee, T. A., 'The Relevance of Accounting Information Including Cash Flows', *The Accountant's Magazine* (January 1972a), pp. 30–4.
Lee, T. A., 'The Nature and Purpose of Cash Flow Accounting', *The Accountant's Magazine* (April 1972b), pp. 198–200.
Lee, T. A., 'A Case for Cash Flow Reporting', *Journal of Business Finance* (Summer 1972), pp. 27–36.
Lee, T. A., 'Enterprise Income: Survival or Decline and Fall?', *Accounting and Business Research* (Summer 1974), pp. 178–92.
Lee, T. A., 'The Cash Flow Accounting Alternative for Corporate Financial Reporting', in C. van Dam (ed.), *Trends in Managerial and Financial Accounting*. Martinus Nijhoff (1978), pp. 63–84.
Lee, T. A., 'The Contribution of Fisher to Cash Flow Accounting', *Journal of Business Finance and Accounting* (Autumn 1979a), pp. 321–30.
Lee, T. A., 'The Simplicity and the Complexity of Accounting', in R. R. Sterling and A. L. Thomas (eds.), *Accounting for a Simplified Firm*. Scholars Book Co. (1979b), pp. 35–55.
Lee, T. A., 'A Test of the Use of Cash Flow Reporting', *Discussion Paper 2*. University of Edinburgh (1979c).

Lee, T. A., 'A Survey of Accountants' Opinions on Cash Flow Reporting', *Discussion Paper 3* (University of Edinbrugh, 1980a).
Lee, T. A., 'Reporting Cash Flows and Net Realizable Values', *Discussion Paper 5*. University of Edinburgh (1980b).
Littleton, A. C. and V. K. Zimmerman, *Accounting Theory: Continuity and Change*. Prentice Hall (1963), pp. 49–71.
Meade Committee, *Structure and Reform of Direct Taxation*. George Allen & Unwin (1978).
Paton, W. A., 'The Cash-Flow Illusion', *The Accounting Review* (April 1963), pp. 243–51.
Ronen, J., 'Discounted Cash Flow Accounting', in J. J. Cramer Jr. (ed.), *Objectives of Financial Statements*. American Institute of Certified Public Accountants (1974), pp. 143–60.
Ronen, J. and Sorter, G. H., 'Relevant Accounting', *Journal of Business* (April 1972), pp. 258–82.
Staubus, G. J., *A Theory of Accounting for Investors*. University of California Press (1961), pp. 134–6.
Staubus, G. J., 'Alternative Asset Flow Concepts', *The Accounting Review* (July 1966), pp. 397–412.
Thomas, A. L., 'The Allocation Problem', *Studies in Accounting Research 3*. American Accounting Association (1969), p. 101 and pp. 108–9.
Thomas, A. L., 'The Allocation Problem: Part Two', *Studies in Accounting Research 9*. American Accounting Association (1974), pp. 119–22.
Thomas, A. L., 'Matching: Up from Our Black Hole', in R. R. Sterling and A. L. Thomas (eds.), *Accounting for a Simplified Firm*. Scholars Book Co. (1979), pp. 11–33.
Tweedie, D. P., 'Cash Flows and Realizable Values: the Intuitive Concepts? An Empirical Test', *Accounting and Business Research* (Winter 1977), pp. 2–13.
Waldron, R., 'Reporting Cash Flow Measurement of Business Achievement and the Statement of Needs and Resources', *Accountancy*, forthcoming.
Winjum, J. O., *The Role of Accounting in the Economic Development of England 1500–1750*. Centre for International Education and Research (1972).

CASH FLOW ACCOUNTING'S RECENT HISTORY: A KUHNIAN INTERPRETATION OF A CHANGING ACCOUNTING EMPHASIS

CFA History to 1980

The previous paper reproduced in this text outlines a brief history of the development of cash flow accounting (CFA) ideas from the late 1960s to 1980 (Lee, 1981b). From the point of view of meaningful analysis, the period covered is exceedingly short and potentially inconsequential in the context of the larger history of accounting and accountants. Yet it has since proved to contain the seeds of what is a significant change of emphasis in financial reporting practice by the late 1980s and early 1990s. The change concerns a requirement to publish a statement of realized cash flows in addition to the conventional set of allocation-based financial statements (e.g., FASB, 1987 in the US; and ASB, 1991 in the UK).

In the late 1970s and early 1980s, US accounting policy-makers and standard-setters initiated a process to provide an addition to the conventional financial reporting set. The new dimension was a disclosure of CFA data free of arbitrary accounting allocations, and emphasizing the reporting entity's liquidity rather than its profitability. In making this change, many of the arguments for CFA which had been made by its academic proponents in the previous decade were implicitly or explicitly acknowledged. As such, this is something that has rarely occurred in financial reporting in modern times. The reason for the change appears to have been a number of spectacular corporate failures in which increasing illiquidity had not been signalled (O'Bryan, 1989, p.317), as well as support for some form of CFA reporting from financial executives and institutions (pp.318-9).

Other CFA developments were also evident during the 1980s. Earlier conceptual arguments were refined and extended by their principal proponents and others. Empirical research into the utility of CFA numbers was expanded and improved. And CFA appeared as a significant component in several main texts on accounting theory. Thus, it can be argued reasonably convincingly that, by the early 1990s, CFA had become an important part of accounting education, practice, and research. This rapid development and implementation of ideas had not been predictable in the 1970s and early 1980s, when CFA was perceived as a research interest of a very small group of academics. It was also inconsistent with the 'market-for-excuses' hypothesis of Watts and Zimmerman (1986).

It is the purpose of this paper to observe and comment on these most recent historical developments in CFA. However, because of the closeness of the writer to the issues concerned, it is not intended as a definitive history of the subject. As Carr (1987, p.23) warns, history is shaped by the objectivity of the historian, and the choices he or she makes of what to observe. In other words, when studying the so-called facts of history, the reader should also study the historian. In this case, the bias in favour of CFA is obvious and freely admitted.

The Kuhnian Progression

The following sections attempt to loosely fit CFA into the historical model proposed by Kuhn (1970) in which scientific ideas progress through several linked stages in an evolving sequence. The Kuhnian revolution (from anomaly recognition to the domination of a particular paradigm to resolve it) is well-known, and has been used previously by accounting historians (e.g. Wells, 1976; and Cushing, 1989). Kuhn's model was explicitly designed for scientific disciplines, not because he felt their historical development was different from that of non-sciences, but because they had been perceived to be so (Kuhn, 1970, p.208). Some writers believe accounting is not a science (e.g. Peasnell, 1978, p.220), and others that it is or could be (e.g. Sterling, 1979, p.3). That is not the issue here. Instead, it is to accept Kuhn's view that all disciplines develop in a revolving way with recognizable phases and breaks in the cyclical progression. In other words, unlike Cushing (1989, pp.9-10), I do not believe I have to establish the scientific nature of accounting for it to be studied from a Kuhnian perspective. Indeed, Kuhn (1970, p.208) would be puzzled at why I should think I needed to make such a case.

The Kuhnian sequence cycles from the recognition to the resolution of an c, and is focused on the establishment of competing schools of thought and, in a Darwinian sense, the eventual domination of one of these schools with respect to the c. When Wells (1976) studied Kuhn's model in relation to competing schools of income determination and asset valuation in the 1960s and 1970s, he ignored the case for the inclusion of CFA in his analysis. His reasons for doing so have to be speculated as CFA was not mentioned in his paper, although he explicitly excluded present value accounting because of its lack of operational support (Wells, 1976, p.478). It has to be presumed that Wells did not consider CFA to be a competing school with regard to anomalies affecting the area of income and capital measurement.

Such a position was not surprising. By the mid 1970s, the main proponents of CFA were either arguing for a substantial demotion in accounting of the importance of income in favour of cash flows (e.g. Lee, 1974), or had just begun to articulate an explicit cash flow-based concept of profit (e.g. Lawson and Stark, 1975). This state of affairs may have created a persistent perception among its critics of CFA as a liquidity-focused system, despite evidence to suggest it was ill-founded (see Egginton, 1984; and Staubus, 1989). Whatever the perception, however, it is the contention of this paper that CFA was one of a number of competing normative paradigms in the 1970s and 1980s with respect to the anomaly of historic cost accounting's utility, and that CFA's Kuhnian development since 1980 is therefore worthy of explanation and discussion in that context.

Pre 1980 CFA Ideas

It is not the intention in this section to repeat what is contained in the previous paper reproduced in this text, other than to remind its reader of several features to be observed in it which are relevant to this paper. These are as follows:

* By 1980, CFA ideas had a relatively short history, with almost all of the conceptual argument coming from the UK generally, and the writings of Lawson and Lee in particular. CFA was therefore a very small school of thought at that time.

* Interest in CFA in the US was spasmodic during the 1960s and 1970s, the main conceptual effort coming from an AICPA-sponsored study of financial reporting and solvency by Heath (1978). Little normative or empirical work in the area was undertaken by US researchers. Thus, the largest financial accounting research community in the world was signalling a predominant lack of interest in CFA by 1980.

* World-wide, empirical testing of the potential utility of CFA ideas had been minimal during the 1970s, and professional accountancy bodies and accounting standard-setters had revealed little specific interest in CFA, either as a complete or partial financial reporting system. However, by the end of the decade, bodies such as FASB and AICPA were beginning to put CFA on their longer-term agendas (O'Bryan, 1989, pp.318-9).

* Accounting textbooks, even of a theoretical nature, were typically devoid of any mention of CFA ideas, thus diminishing their potential impact in the classroom.

The overall conclusion to be drawn from the above brief analysis of the 1980 position is one which is related to the dimension of time. A reporting anomaly appears to have been identified in the late 1960s by a small group of accounting researchers. This concerned the apparent inappropriateness of the conventional financial reporting set to provide information which could relevantly and reliably assist in various report user decision models, particularly with respect to assessing the performance of defined entities and their managements in terms of cash flow returns and liquidity positions. CFA ideas had been initially proposed in the 1970s as a resolution to this anomoly but, by 1980, their exposure had been insufficient to be truly influential in any of the major accounting education, practice, and research communities. This does not mean that their impact was non-existent. Merely that effective diffusion of ideas such as CFA takes time, and a decade may well have been insufficient in this case.

1980 onwards

The period from 1980 to the present time reveals a considerable and, arguably, remarkable activity in CFA. The conceptual efforts of Lawson and Lee continued in the UK. Their writings were mainly directed at extending their original CFA models, and answering the specific challenges of critics. But the most significant events were connected with a measurable expansion in empirical research activity directed at establishing the utility of CFA numbers; the established presence of CFA ideas in the accounting curriculum, particularly in that part dealing with accounting theory; and the adoption of CFA ideas by accounting standard-setters in the form of a required statement describing realized cash flows in suitably decomposed form.

Each of these developments will be discussed in turn. But, prior to doing so, it should be stated that each appears to be reasonably consistent with a history which is following a Kuhnian pattern. The reporting anomoly was identified in the 1960s and 1970s, and alternative CFA strategies formulated for discussion. These strategies were criticised, refined, expanded, tested, and generally defended in the 1980s. Part of an effective defence against challenge comes from empirical testing and part from logical argument. Such evidence and argument appears to have been sufficiently persuasive in the 1980s to cause standard-setters to amend reporting practice to include an element of CFA information. Unsurprisingly, the existence of such new practice has resulted in textbook accounts and explanations of CFA ideas which emphasize the earlier argument and later research and practice. The response of the accounting profession in all these respects has been exceedingly speedy (O'Bryan, 1989, p.320).

Lawson's Conceptual Arguments

Lawson's ideas on CFA have been consistently based on classical economic (finance) theory - specifically, that equity value is based on the equity-holder's perception of the future cash flow returns to be derived from the investment in question. Although developed in a number of papers through the 1970s (see Lee, 1981b for a review of these writings), Lawson's proposed system was clarified in a series of papers in the 1980s (e.g. Lawson, 1980; 1982; and 1985).

The system is now formally described as the *cash flow-market value accounting* (CF-MVA) model, and is explained and articulated fully in a recent text by Lawson in the Garland Publishing *New Works in Accounting History* series (Lawson, 1992, pp.39-108). As in all previous Lawson papers, the fundamental argument is for a system of financial reporting which assists decision makers to predict cash flow returns, and which measures income as a means of assessing entity performance (Lawson, 1992, p.39). The particular focus of CF-MVA is on assessing dividend and debt-equity policies (p.39).

A CF-MVA financial report is based on a number of related *ex post* cash flow and market value identities. Historic cash flows are reported as means of describing the reporting entity's capacity to generate realized cash flows (p.40). Market values are disclosed as an observable collective expectation of unrealized entity cash flows (p.44). The reported cash flows and market values are described in aggregate entity terms, and equated with equity and debt decompositions (pp.41 and 43). Economic income is described by Lawson as a combination of realized entity cash flow and the periodic change in entity market value (p.50).

The significance of the CF-MVA model is argued by Lawson on a number of levels - that is, its ability to assist in determining distributable income, and capital to be maintained (pp.52-8); representing faithfully the relationships between the entity and its equity and debt-holders (pp.58-60); recognizing adequately the accounting elements of assets, liabilities, revenues, expenses, gains, and losses (pp.60-2); and reporting objectively, without allocations, but with price-level effects, and with tax neutrality (p.63).

The main focus which Lawson reveals in his arguments is one concerned generally with debt-equity substitution (pp.65-84) and, particularly, the economic efficiency of managerial decisions related to financing and distribution (p.39). This has been a consistent theme of his CFA writings since the late 1960s - that is, the funding of tax, interest, and dividend payments by borrowing. Throughout his writings, Lawson constantly argues for an information system which demonstrates this effect - sufficient to cause even his supporters to question the political nature of his case (Samuels, 1981, pp.101-2).

Thus, Lawson's arguments are clearly based on an economic philosophy which supports equity funding of projects and other commitments, but questions large-scale debt financing of them. His use of equity and debt market values in CF-MVA demonstrates his view that the market is reasonably efficient in determining expectations of cash flows which reflect managerial performance and policies in these areas (Lawson, 1992, p.45). Indeed, in this respect, he is quite clear in his preference of market values over discounted cash flow valuations as measures of capital (pp.49-50).

When comparing the 1980s with the 1970s, the main change in the CFA system advocated by Lawson, is his *explicit* recognition in the prescribed reporting model of a measure of economic income determined in part by a recognition of an observable change in the market's evaluation of the reporting entity's future cash flows. The basic Lawson CFA argument and focus remain as before.

Lee's conceptual arguments

By the end of the 1970s, Lee (1978; and 1979) was arguing for a CFA system which reported forecast and realized cash flows decomposed into operating, investment and financing activities, together with a statement of financial position based on net realizable values to reflect the current situation. This system was extended and refined into an articulating set of financial statements reflecting realized and unrealized cash flows (using net realizable values as surrogates for potential cash flow), and described as a unified system of cash flow reporting (CFR) (Lee, 1981a; and 1984). Such a system can be interpreted as an attempt to take the common features of the original Lee CFA argument (e.g. as in Lee, 1972) with that of the exit price accounting school of thought (e.g. Chambers, 1966), and merge them into a complete CFA structure based on the realizability of cash flows (Lee, 1981a, p.163).

The specific arguments for this unified extension of CFA were most recently made by Lee in 1984 (Lee, 1984, pp.82-93) - that is, the general relevance and reliability of CFR data; and their specific utility regarding assessments of the reporting entity's cash generating capability and command over resources, and managerial accountability. As such, these arguments are little different from Lee's earlier CFA contributions. The major changes in the advocations are the dropping of a prescription to report forecast CFA data because of its inherent subjectivity (Lee, 1984, p.xi); and the inclusion of income and financial position data to articulate with cash flows.

Comparison of Lawson and Lee

The interesting feature of the above descriptions of the most recent histories of the work of Lawson and Lee is that, despite different CFA orientations, the structure of their system has been changed to, first, exclude *ex ante* data in favour of *ex post* representations of entity cash flows; and, second, construct reports which explicitly link cash flows to measures of income and financial position. Lawson's arguments since the 1960s have been predicated on this linkage as determined in classical economic theory, and was made explicit in his 1990 paper (Lawson, 1992, pp.39-108). Lee, on the other hand, had based his arguments in the 1970s on normative perceptions of user needs, and responded to unwritten criticisms of their lack of attention to income and capital data with respect to entity performance. His response was a unified CFR system in 1980 (Lee, 1981a; and 1984).

The major difference between Lawson and Lee in this respect is that Lawson advocates an aggregate entity measure (debt plus equity market values) as a relevant and representationally faithful means of expressing future cash flows (Lawson, 1992, pp.58-60), whereas Lee prefers the relevance and reliability of market-based exit prices (Lee, 1981a, pp.163-4). These differing views, however, are not in competition - for example, Lawson (1985, pp.106-7) believes market values represent unbiased forecasts of expected cash flows from existing net assets, but also supports the use of exit prices to assess the entity as a going concern.

Influence on Other Theorists

The generic idea of a CFA-type of financial reporting system involving realized cash flow, income and capital appears to have influenced at least two other research groupings. The first relates to the work of Arnold and Wearing (1988). Explicitly acknowledging their debt to earlier research of Lawson and Lee (p.331), Arnold and Wearing have argued for a reporting system (cash flow - exit price accounting) (CaFe), in which realized cash flows are embedded in an exit price framework to emphasize profitability rather than liquidity (p.316). The system is decomposed along the familiar CFA lines of operating, investing, and financing activities (p.318). The main difference between CaFe and Lee's CFR (particularly) is one of emphasis - Lee on cash flows, and Arnold and Wearing on opportunity costs (p.319).

A second influence appears to have been in the work of the research committee of ICAS (McMonnies, 1988). In this still-continuing programme of research, the main statements are prescribed in exit price terms, and include a statement of forecast and realized cash flows (pp.103-4). The argument for this system is similar to both that of Lawson and Lee - particularly with respect to decision relevance and representational faithfulness (p.98). A major difference, however, between the ICAS proposals and those of Lawson, Lee, and Arnold and Wearing is the lack of formal articulation of all the prescribed financial statements into a unified system of CFA.

Influence on Textbook Writers

The influence of the work of Lawson and Lee can be demonstrated by their inclusion in the leading accounting theory texts of the early 1990s. For example, Belkaoui (1993, pp.416-32) has an extensive chapter on the statement of cash flows, citing nine writings of Lawson and eighteen of Lee (pp.430-1). Hendriksen and van Breda (1992, pp.265-79) devote a separate section to CFA in the form of arguments and presentations based on the Lawson CF-MVA model (specifically acknowledging Lawson's assistance, p.273; and citing six of eleven additional readings on CFA from Lawson and Lee). Kam (1990, pp.67-82) also has a separate section on CFA, including a detailed explanation of Lee's CFR system (pp.80-2). Wolk, Francis and Tearney (1989, pp.332-48) have a complete chapter on the statement of cash flows, and specifically acknowledge the prior research of Lawson and Lee in establishing a strong case for CFA (p.342).

These examples demonstrate the effect of CFA arguments on a broader literature. In 1980, CFA ideas existed in the journal literature only. By 1992, most theory texts contain some coverage. Indeed, there are texts solely concerned with providing a student introduction to CFA (Lee, 1984; and 1986), and a recent paper on teaching the statement of cash flows (Dugan, Gup and Samson, 1991). What this means is that, for students of accounting studying the subject at an advanced theoretical level, particularly prior to entry to the accountancy profession, CFA ideas have become a part of the typical educational curriculum. Thus, in the Kuhnian sense of designated schools of thought, CFA has developed sufficiently in the 1980s to at least be considered as such.

Influence on Practice

Although it is not explicitly evident in the relevant literature, it has to be assumed that the conceptual formulations of researchers such as Lawson and Lee in the UK, and Heath in the US, have had some impact on the thinking of accounting policy-makers and standard-setters. The presence of a theoretical literature on CFA, established in the 1970s and honed in the 1980s, cannot have been unknown to the staff researchers of standard-setting bodies such as FASB in the US and ASB (formerly ASC) in the UK. These researchers typically prepare position statements on topics being considered for standards. These statements are essentially literature reviews, and become the foundations for the thinking and debating of working parties and committees charged with drafting a suitable standard (see, e.g., Miller and Redding, 1988, p.68).

The evidence of CFA influence on financial reporting practice can be seen in developments in the 1980s in the US and UK to require disclosure of a statement of realized cash flows. The first sequence is that of the US. Arguably, this started with the FASB (1978, para.25) prescription that potential report users are concerned in the reporting entity's ability to generate favourable cash flows, and that what should be reported to them is information which assists them to assess entity cash flows (paras.37-9). This was followed by two FASB Concepts Statements which advocated a reporting set including a statement of cash flows (FASB, 1980a, para.49; and FASB, 1984, paras.13 and 52-4). In addition, in 1980, FASB had issued a Discussion Memorandum (FASB, 1980b) to discuss the nature of funds reporting. And, in 1981, it issued a further Discussion Memorandum on income, cash flows, and financial position (FASB, 1981). In the latter, it was prescribed that funds statements should be prepared on a cash flow rather than working capital basis. By 1985, FASB had added a cash flow statement project to its agenda and, in 1987, it produced a requirement for such a statement (FASB, 1987). It is clear that there was a growing institutional support (from producers and users) for such disclosure (FASB, 1987, paras.35-43). A recent text on security analysis and cash flow accounting (Hackel and Livnat, 1992) confirms this point.

The US experience was repeated in the UK at the end of the 1980s. Funds statement reporting had been reviewed twice since 1975 in the UK without change to the existing accounting standard (ASC, 1990, para.1.2). However, in 1989, a working party of ASC was charged with the task of a third review, and produced a prescription for cash flow accounting (ASC, 1990) which became a standard in 1991 (ASB, 1991). The required statement of realized cash flows is very similar to its US equivalent - being decomposed into operating, investment, and financing elements, and not requiring the use of actual cash flow data.

The surprising feature of these developments is not just the speed by which CFA ideas have been translated into required practices, but that they have taken place at all. The statement of realized cash flows is based on data disclosure which is reasonably free of arbitrary accounting allocations. It is also structured to reveal aspects of entity liquidity previously hidden from the view of most report users. Resistance to CFA in practice has been minimal both at its introduction and since. It has to be speculated that reporting manager-agents therefore do not perceive any additional political and contracting costs due to the disclosure of realized cash flows. This may be because such costs are associated with accounting practices relating to income numbers rather than cash flows. Whatever the explanation, it is surprising that the capacity of the statement of realized cash flows to reveal previously hidden liquidity positions and problems has not created widespread producer resistance to the relevant accounting standards.

Criticisms of CFA

Prior to 1980 there had been little explicit criticism or even comment on CFA ideas in the literature. Apart from an extensive and relatively uncritical review of the early work of Lawson and Lee by Ashton (1976), the principal advocates of CFA entered the 1980s without challenge. 1982 witnessed the end of that phase in CFA development with the publication of Rutherford's critique of the treatment of the allocation argument in the work of Lee (Rutherford, 1982). Rutherford's fundamental argument was directed at the legitimacy of the CFA argument that cash flow data were allocation-free. A response to this case was made by Lee (1982), concluding that CFA could reasonably avoid accounting allocations relating to time periods, entity segmentations, and data classifications (p.351).

Egginton (1984) criticized the CFA proposals of Lawson and Lee on a number of grounds - that is, that such proposals can never be allocation-free (pp.101-2); the problems associated with reporting cash flow forecasts, particularly with respect to entity performance assessment (pp.102-3); the inability of *ex post* CFA data to assist with performance assessment (pp.104-5); and the inappropriateness of Lee's CFR system for anything other than liquidity assessment (pp.105-7). Both Lawson (1985) and Lee (1985) refuted Egginton's charges in detail, and Lawson (1985, p.107) made explicit his perception of the assistance of these debates in clarifying the rapid evolution of CFA.

The Lee CFR model was further challenged by Staubus (1989) in an essay supporting the utility of reported cash flows for liquidity assessment purposes, but rejecting their appropriateness for performance assessment and reporting on wealth (defined by Staubus in terms of cash flow potential). A reply was formulated by Lee (1990) along the lines that CFR (including net realizable values) is capable of meeting the requirements of Staubus to report on liquidity, profitability, and wealth. In particular, he concluded that the proponents and critics of CFA appeared to have much in common, despite their specific differences, because of a common interest in the reportable business characteristic of cash flow potential (Lee, 1990, p.357).

In other words, what these literature discussions appear to signal is an awareness of the importance of CFA ideas in contemporary accounting thinking, at least sufficient to suggest that a Kuhnian progression is under way. This is encouraging as accountants attempt to respond to criticisms of the relevance and reliability of the conventional financial reporting set. What is less agreeable is the academic dog-fighting by researchers who are in agreement with the basic principles of CFA but who also, for whatever reason, wish to restrict its potential utility to entity liquidity assessments. Such behaviour thus leaves the practical potential of CFA ideas to be judged in terms of less prescriptive and more scientifically based research.

CFA and Empirical Research

The 1980s have witnessed a considerable upsurge in empirical research using CFA-related data. The overall conclusion about the results of this research is that it has not convincingly demonstrated the utility of such information. The signals have been mixed and, perhaps, this is a consequence of the limitations of the research models used rather than a comment on CFA's relevance to user decisions. A point of encouragement, however, is the level of interest in testing CFA data. This can only have come about as a result of the influence of CFA literature arguments over two decades, and the more recent practical introduction of the statement of realized cash flows in the required reporting set. In other words, now that CFA is a practical reality, researchers are concerned to test its credibility generally, and its utility particularly.

The research has been conducted in a number of ways. The first category relates to demonstrations of CFA's utility by means of individual case studies in order to strengthen its conceptual basis. Prior to the existence of CFA statements in published reports, these exercises were based on suitable amendments of funds data, and were a regular addition to the conceptual arguments of both Lawson in the 1970s and 1980s, and Lee in the 1980s. The point of these exercises was to demonstrate with live data the ability of various CFA models to reveal relevant aspects of the cash flow performance and liquidity of the companies concerned. In all cases, these demonstrations were *ex post* and, typically, dealt with a controversial corporate situation (e.g. Largay and Stickney, 1980; Lawson, 1982; Lee, 1982; Arnold and Wearing, 1988; and Wearing, 1989). In other words, they were not designed as research exercises with which to test hypotheses concerned with the decision utility or predictability of CFA data. Indeed, on occasion, they appear to have had a 'political' objective of influencing accounting policy-makers regarding the usefulness of CFA data to inform on key issues such as tax rates, interest cover, and dividend distributions (e.g. Lawson, 1981, pp.94-8). And, prior to the availability of reported CFA statements, they were all subject to measurement inaccuracies (see, e.g., Drtina and Largay, 1985).

Testing of CFA utility and predictability has been undertaken by a number of researchers in a variety of ways. The first concerns the cash recovery rate (CRR) of Ijiri (1978). This attempts to use CFA data derived from reported historic cost figures to derive a firm's internal rate of return (IRR). The CRR datum (with a numerator of a variant of operating cash flow, and a denominator of gross fixed assets) as a surrogate for IRR has been investigated and commented on by a variety of researchers throughout the 1980s and early 1990s (e.g. Salamon, 1982; and Ismail, 1987). The general conclusion drawn from the results of all of these studies is that it is an exercise fraught with difficulty (Stark, 1992, p.21). In any case, like the case study approach, such research does not seek to do anything other than demonstrate that CFA-type data can be used as a surrogate for an unknown but relevant indicator of corporate performance.

Other CFA research has been much more direct in its intention to scientifically determine the relevancy of CFA data as an influence on decisions and, specifically, as a predictor. For example, in the area of bankruptcy prediction, there have been a number of studies, but the evidence of CFA data's utility is relatively indeterminate. Casey and Bartzcak (1985) used operating cash flow data in their prediction model and found that, compared with accrual data, these had no incremental predictive power. This was consistent with the findings of Gentry *et al* (1985a) and Gombola *et al* (1987), and inconsistent with Gentry *et al* (1985b) and certain of the findings of Aziz *et al* (1988). As with all models, the main issue appears to relate to how well the specifications capture the key factors concerning corporate bankruptcy. It may well be that such CFA-based research is at a naive stage in its overall development.

A similar comment may also be pertinent to research into the more general issue of the incremental information content of CFA data. These studies typically tested for CFA utility by observing stock market reaction to published data. Harmon (1984) did so by associating price changes to the publication of accrual-based earnings and funds flow data, and finding the former had a greater association than did the latter. But the funds data were not CFA-based. Bowen *et al* (1987), however, used CFA measures, and concluded that operating cash flow data particularly have significant information content, and have incremental explanatory power beyond accrual data alone (and vice versa) (p.746). This was consistent with Rayburn (1986) who found an association of abnormal security returns with the presence of both operating cash flow and accruals adjustment data (pp.131-2). Wilson (1986) came to a consistent conclusion that the information content of operating cash flow and accruals adjustments taken together is greater than that of the earnings aggregate (p.319). Bernard and Stober's (1989) study, however, does not support these earlier results, and is critical of the naivety of such modelling to capture the complex realities of stock market reaction to a variety of public information sources (p.648). This can also be seen in the work of UK researchers in this area (e.g. Board and Day, 1989; and Board *et al*, 1989).

The major problem with empirical research into CFA to date appears to be the use of accruals data adjusted to provide cash flow surrogates which are not representative of cash flows. In other words, what has been happening in the 1980s is a series of research studies which have attempted to test CFA's utility in relation to information content and predictive power. This work has typically been undertaken using accruals surrogates for cash flows (or accruals-adjusted surrogates), and the 'cash flow' information has been mainly focused on operating cash flows - thereby ignoring the other cash flows inherent in the CFA model. It is hardly surprising under these circumstances that the research results vary and remain inconclusive. Until such time as CFA research models reflect the complexities and interactions of cash flows, the results will be at, best, useless and, at worst, misleading.

Conclusions

This review of the development of CFA over the last decade has revealed an interpretation which does not fit easily into the Kuhnian paradigm. In particular, the sequencing of stages in the progression does not appear in the predicted order. CFA originated in the 1970s as part of a generalized anomaly recognition concerning historical cost accounting. As such, this was a period of intense insecurity in financial accounting. And, despite the development of alternative ideas, it persists to this day because of the continuing dominance of the conventional system over these alternatives. In other words, there may be schools of thought (such as current cost accounting), but none has prevailed over historical cost accounting. That is, except for some elements of CFA (a statement of realized cash flows, and an extended use of current cash equivalents).

What is so remarkable about these CFA reporting intrusions is that they have taken place in the absence of a recognizable CFA school of thought (Lawson and Lee, and the later empiricists hardly constitute a full-blown school of thought). For some non-public reason, CFA ideas are part of practice and the classroom. But they have not resulted from a typical Kuhnian revolution.

Why this is so is hard to say. It may be because Kuhnian revolutions do not apply to the relatively unscientific and highly political function of accounting. Such a conclusion is not particularly strong because the Kuhnian perspective is a familiar individual experience which has been institutionalized by philosophers of science at a collective level (Ziman, 1992). Alternatively, it may be because the CFA addition to historical cost accounting does not constitute a revolutionary change worthy of a Kuhnian perspective because it does not alter the overall reporting model. This argument, too, lacks strength given the fundamental shift in measurement basis which realized cash flows and market prices represent - from allocated to unallocated data.

Occasionally, the seeds of change are sown in imperceptible ways. It is too early to suggest that the statement of realized cash flows, and the increasing use of market prices, are such seeds. However, they do represent change, and they are attracting a wider audience of educators, researchers, practitioners, and regulators. In this sense, it is well worth the time of the accounting historian to monitor this space.

References

Accounting Standards Board, 'Cash Flow Statements,' **Financial Reporting Standard 1** (London: Accounting Standards Board, 1991).

Accounting Standards Committee, 'Cash Flow Statements,' **Exposure Draft 54** (London: Accounting Standards Committee, 1990).

Ashton, R., 'Cash Flow Accounting : A Review and Critique,' **Journal of Business Finance and Accounting**, Winter 1976, pp.63-82.

Arnold, A. J. and Wearing, R. T., 'Cash Flows, Exit Prices and British Airways,; **Journal of Business Finance and Accounting**, Autumn 1988, pp.311-34.

Aziz, A., Emanuel, D. C. and Lawson, G. H., 'Bankruptcy Prediction - An Investigation of Cash Flow Based Models,' **Journal of Management Studies**, September 1988, pp.419-37.

Belkaoui, A. R., **Accounting Theory** (Orlando: Harcourt, Brace Jovanovich, 1993).

Bernard, V. L. and Stober, T. L., 'The Nature and Amount of Information in Cash Flows and Accruals,' **The Accounting Review**, October 1989, pp.624-52.

Board, J. L. G. and Day, J. F. S., 'The Information Content of Cash Flow Figures,' **Accounting and Business Research**, Winter 1989, pp.3-12.

Board, J. L. G., Day, J. F. S. and Walker, M., 'The Information Content of Unexpected Accounting Income, Funds Flow and Cash Flow: Comparative Evidence for the US and UK Economies,' **Research Paper** (London: Institute of Chartered Accountants in England and Wales, 1989).

Bowen, R. M., Burgstahler, D. and Daley, L. A., 'The Incremental Information Content of Accrual Versus Cash Flow,' **The Accounting Review**, October 1987, pp.723-47.

Carr, E. H., **What is History?** (Harmondsworth: Penguin Books, 1987).

Casey, C. J. and Bartczak, N. J., 'Using Operating Cash Flow Data to Predict Financial Distress: Some Extensions,' **Journal of Accounting Research**, Spring 1985, pp.384-401.

Chambers, R. J., **Accounting, Evaluation and Economic Behavior** (Englewood Cliffs: Prentice Hall, 1966).

Cushing, B. E., 'A Kuhnian Interpretation of the Historical Evolution of Accounting,' **The Accounting Historians Journal**, December 1989, pp.1-42.

Drtina, R. E. and Largay, J. A., 'Pitfalls in Calculating Cash Flow From Operations,' **The Accounting Review**, April 1985, pp.314-26.

Dugan, M. T., Gup, B. E. and Samson, W. D., 'Teaching the Cash Flow Statement,' **Journal of Accounting Education**, Spring 1991, pp.33-52.

Egginton, D. A., 'In Defense of Profit Measurement: Some Limitations of Cash Flow and Value Added as Performance Measures of External Reporting,' **Accounting and Business Research**, Spring 1984, pp.99-111.

Financial Accounting Standards Board, 'Objectives of Financial Reporting by Business Enterprises,' **Statements of Financial Accounting Concepts 1** (Stamford: Financial Accounting Standards Board, 1978).

Financial Accounting Standards Board, 'Qualitative Characteristics of Accounting Information,' **Statements of Financial Accounting Concepts 2** (Stamford: Financial Accounting Standards Board, 1980a).

Financial Accounting Standards Board, 'Analysis of Issues Related to Reporting Funds, Flows, Liquidity and Financial Flexibility,' **Discussion Memorandum** (Stamford: Financial Accounting Standards Board, 1980b).

Financial Accounting Standards Board, 'Proposed Statement of Financial Accounting Concepts: Reporting Income, Cash Flows and Financial Position of Business Enterprises, **Exposure Draft** (Stamford: Financial Accounting Standards Board, 1981).

Financial Accounting Standards Board, ' Recognition and Measurement in Financial Statements of Business Enterprises,' **Statements of Financial Accounting Concepts 5** (Stamford: Financial Accounting Standards Board, 1984).

Financial Accounting Standards Board, 'Statement of Cash Flows,' **Statements of Financial Accounting Standards 95** (Stamford: Financial Accounting Standards Board, 1987).

Gentry, J. A., Newbold, P. and Whitford, D. T., 'Classifying Bankrupt Firms with Funds Flow Components, ' **Journal of Accounting Research**, Spring 1985a, pp.146-60.

Gentry, J. A., Newbold, P. and Whitford, D. T., 'Predicting Bankruptcy: If Cash Flow's Not the Bottom Line, What is?,' **Financial Analysts Journal**, September-October 1985b, pp.47-56.

Gombola, M. J., Haskins, M. E., Ketz, J. E. and Williams, D. D., 'Cash Flow in Bankruptcy Prediction,' **Financial Management**, Winter 1987, pp.55-65.

Hackel, K. S. and Livnat, J., **Cash Flow and Security Analysis** (Homewood: Irwin, 1991).

Harmon, W. K., 'Earnings vs Funds Flows: an Empirical Investigation of Market Reaction,' **Journal of Accounting, Auditing and Finance**, Fall 1984, pp.24-34.

Heath, L. C., 'Financial Reporting and the Evaluation of Solvency,' **Accounting Research Monograph 3** (New York: American Institute of Certified Public Accountants, 1978).

Hendriksen, E. S. and Van Breda, M. F., **Accounting Theory** (Homewood: Irwin, 1992).

Ijiri, Y., 'Cash-flow Accounting and Its Structure,' **Journal of Accounting, Auditing and Finance**, Summer 1978, pp.331-48.

Ismail, B. E., 'Some Time Series Properties of Corporate Cash Recovery Rates,' **Contemporary Accounting Research**, Fall 1987, pp.76-88.

Kam, V., **Accounting Theory** (New York: John Wiley and Sons, 1990).

Kuhn, T. S., **The Structure of Scientific Revolutions** (Chicago: University of Chicago Press, 1970).

Largay, J. A. and Stickney, 'Cash Flows, Ratio Analysis and the W. T. Grant Bankruptcy,' **Financial Analysts Journal**, July-August 1980, pp.51-4.

Lawson, G. H., 'The Measurement of Corporate Profitability on a Cash Flow Basis,' **International Journal of Accounting Education and Research**, Autumn 1980, pp.11-46.

Lawson, G. H., 'The Cash Flow Performance of UK Companies,' in Bromwich, M. and Hopwood, A. (eds.), **Essays in British Accounting Research** (London: Pitman, 1981), pp.79-100.

Lawson, G. H., 'Was Woolworth Ailing?,' **The Accountant**, November 4, 1982, pp.612-14 and 632.

Lawson, G. H., 'The Measurement of Corporate Performance on a Cash Flow Basis: A Reply to Mr Egginton,' **Accounting and Business Research**, Spring 1985, pp.99-108.

Lawson, G. H. (ed.), **Studies in Cash Flow Accounting and Analysis** (New York: Garland Publishing, 1992).

Lawson, G. H. and Stark, A. W., 'The Concept of Profit for Fund Raising,' **Accounting and Business Research**, Winter 1975, pp.21-41.

Lee, T. A., 'A Case for Cash Flow Reporting,' **Journal of Business Finance**, Summer 1972, pp.27-36.

Lee, T. A., 'Enterprise Income: Survival or Decline and Fall?,' **Accounting and Business Research**, Summer 1974, pp.178-92.

Lee, T. A., 'The Cash Flow Accounting Alternative for Corporate Financial Reporting,' in van Dam, C., (ed.), **Trends in Managerial and Financial Accounting: Volume 1** (Leiden: Martinus Nijhoff, 1978), pp.63-84.

Lee, T. A., ' The Simplicity and the Complexity of Accounting,' in Sterling, R. R. and Thomas, A. L., (eds.), **Accounting for a Simplified Firm Owning Depreciable Assets** (Houston: Scholars Book Co., 1979), pp.35-55.

Lee, T. A., ' Reporting Cash Flows and Net Realizable Values,' **Accounting and Business Research**, Spring 1981a, pp.163-70.

Lee, T. A., ' Cash Flow Accounting and Corporate Financial Reporting,' in Bromwich, M. and Hopwood, A., (eds.), **Essays in British Accounting Research** (London: Pitman, 1981b), pp.63-78.

Lee, T. A. 'Laker Airways - The Cash Flow Truth,' **Accountancy**, June 1982, pp.115-16.

Lee, T. A., 'Cash Flow Accounting and the Allocation Problem,' **Journal of Business Finance and Accounting**, Autumn 1982, pp.341-52.

Lee, T. A., **Cash Flow Accounting** (Wolkingham: Van Nostrand Reinhold, 1984).

Lee, T. A., 'Cash Flow Accounting, Profit and Performance Measurement: A Response to a Challenge,' **Accounting and Business Research**, Spring 1985, pp.93-7.

Lee, T. A. (ed.), **Towards a Theory and Practice of Cash Flow Accounting** (New York: Garland Publishing, 1986).

Lee, T. A., 'Restricting the Domain and Potential of Cash Flow Accounting,' **Accounting and Business Research**, Autumn 1990, pp.355-8.

McMonnies, P. N. (ed.), **Making Corporate Reports Valuable** (London: Kogan Page, 1988).

Miller, P. B. W. and Redding, R. J., **The FASB: The People, the Process, and the Politics** (Homewood: Irwin, 1988).

O'Bryan, D., 'An Historical Development of Statement of Financial Accounting Standards Number 95: A New Era of Solvency Reporting?,' **Working Paper 78** (Richmond: Academy of Accounting Historians, 1989).

Peasnell, K. V., 'Statement of Accounting Theory and Theory Acceptance: a Review Article,' **Accounting and Business Research**, Summer 1978, pp.217-25.

Rayburn, J., 'The Association of Operating Cash Flow and Accruals With Security Returns,' **Journal of Accounting Research: Supplement**, 1986, pp.112-33.

Rutherford, B. A., 'The Interpretation of Cash Flow Reports and the Other Allocation Problem,' **Abacus**, June 1982, pp.40-9.

Salamon, G. L., 'Cash Recovery Rates and Measures of Firm Profitability,' **The Accounting Review**, April 1982, pp.292-302.

Samuels, J., 'Commentary on Papers by Professors Lawson and Lee,' in Bromwich, M. and Hopwood, A. (eds.), **Essays in British Accounting Research** (London: Pitman, 1981), pp.101-3.

Stark, A. W., 'Problems in Measuring the Cash Recovery Rate and Measurement Error in Estimates of the Firm IRR,' **Working Paper 92/02** (Colchester: University of Essex, 1992).

Staubus, G. J., 'Cash Flow Accounting and Liquidity: Cash Flow Potential and Performance,' **Accounting and Business Research**, Spring 1989, pp.161-9.

Sterling, R. R., **Toward a Science of Accounting** (Houston: Scholars Book Co., 1979).

Watts, R. and Zimmerman, J., **Positive Accounting Theory** (Englewood Cliffs: Prentice Hall, 1986).

Wearing, R. T., 'Cash Flow and the Eurotunnel,' **Accounting and Business Research**, Winter 1989, pp.13-24.

Wells, M. C., ' A Revolution in Accounting Thought?,' **The Accounting Review**, July 1976, pp.471-82.

Wilson, G. P. 'The Incremental Information Content of the Accruals and Funds Components of Earnings After Controlling for Earnings,' **The Accounting Review**, April 1987, pp.293-322.

Wolk, H. I., Francis, J. R. and Tearney, M. G., **Accounting Theory: A Conceptual and Institutional Approach** (Boston: PWS-Kent, 1989).

Ziman, J., 'Subversive Scholar,' **The Times Higher Education Supplement**, November 27, 1992, p.15.

Suggested additional readings:

* Carr, E. H., **What is History?** (Harmondsworth: Penguin Books, 1987).

This is one of the best known and most readable explanations of the nature and role of history and the historian. It is essential reading for students exploring the historical development of ideas in accounting.

* Cushing, B. E., "A Kuhnian Interpretation of the Historical Evolution of Accounting," **The Accounting Historians Journal**, December 1989, pp. 1–42.

This is a detailed and historically extensive examination of accounting from a Kuhnian point of view, revealing the possibility of double-entry bookkeeping as the dominant paradigm.

* Kuhn, T. S., **The Structure of Scientific Revolutions** (Chicago: University of Chicago Press, 1970).

Discussing the development of cash flow accounting from a Kuhnian perspective is enriched by a reading of Kuhn. In particular, the reader is asked to consider the issue of translating Kuhn's ideas from a scientific to a socio-scientific paradigm.

* Previts, G. J., Parker, L. D. and Coffman, E. N., "Accounting History: Definition and Relevance," **Abacus**, March 1990, pp. 1–16.

This is a detailed explanation of and argument for the need for historical studies of accounting issues with respect to assisting teaching, practice and research.

* Wells, M. C., "A Revolution in Accounting Thought?," **The Accounting Review**, July 1976, pp. 471–82.

Wells' paper represents the first attempt by an accounting researcher to explain the development of normative accounting prescriptions within a Kuhnian perspective.

ANOMALY RECOGNITION, INSECURITY, AND INITIAL RESPONSES

Introduction

The period from the late 1950s to the early 1970s was one characterised by a growing insecurity about the strength of the conventional system of historical cost accounting. Although the issue of the subjectiveness of historical cost allocations had been recognised for many decades, the subject became a matter for persistent debate in the academic and professional accounting literatures of the 1960s onwards. The writings reproduced in this section reflect that growing insecurity, as do the additional items in the bibliography.

The major issues were related. For example, the inherent flexibility in conventional accounting practice which lent itself to the possibility of multiple reportings of the same economic events and circumstances (Spa*cek* [1958] and *Drebin* [1964]). The lack of understanding of the accounting issues concerned by so-called expert users (Drebin). The need for reporting comparability (Spacek and Ro*ss* [1969]), consistency (Drebin and *Stamp* [1970]), and uniformity in accounting (Drebin). And failures to disclose economic facts (Ross). In other words, these were issues that remain today, and continue to vex accounting policy-makers and standard-setters. Indeed, the specific problems should be very familiar to current students and practitioners - for example, deferred tax, leases, the capital-revenue expenditure distinction, and inflation accounting (Spacek).

So too are the solutions prescribed - the need to reduce flexibility (Spacek and Drebin), treat the disease rather than the symptoms (Drebin), standardise on an evolutionary basis (Stamp), and relate reported information to the needs of report users (Drebin, Ross and Stamp). In fact, the entire debate encapsulated in these writings can be said to focus on the broadest of prescriptions now contained in the conceptual frameworks of the main accounting standard-setting bodies - that is, the reliable reporting of information relevant to the decision needs of report users. What is also of interest is the genuine concern from both academics and practitioners about the frailties of the conventional financial accounting system.

* Drebin, A.R., "'Cash–Flowitis': Malady or Syndrome?," **Journal of Accounting Research**, Spring 1964, pp. 25–34

* Ross, H., "Present Discontents," in **Financial Statements: A Crusade for Current Values**, Sir Isaac Pitman (Canada), 1969, pp. 5–11

* Spacek, L., "Can We Define Generally Accepted Accounting Principles?," **Journal of Accountancy**, December 1958, pp.40–47

* Stamp, E., "Establishing Accounting Principles," **Abacus**, December 1970, pp. 96–104

"Cash-Flowitis": Malady or Syndrome?

ALLAN R. DREBIN

Financial analysts are devoting attention to a figure they call "cash-flow." As popularly employed, this term describes the sum of net income and the charges for depreciation and amortization originally deducted in calculating income. The Accounting Principles Board has expressed concern with the increasing usage of this calculation, particularly to the extent that it replaces income as a means of measuring corporate performance. Their *Opinion No. 3* states:

> Many of the comments made in connection with "cash flow" analysis leave the reader with the erroneous impression that "cash flow" or "cash earnings" is superior to net income as a measure of a company's real earning power.... In other words, there has been a growing tendency on the part of some people to single out one of the items on the statement of source and application of funds, thereby implying that this figure is more important than other information regarding the flow of funds and often carrying the implication that "net income plus depreciation" is the best measure of the company's profitability.[1]

The CPA does not have any control over the uses which might be made of financial statements, nor of items which might appear in an annual report other than those covered by his opinion. Nevertheless, the APB makes the following recommendations with respect to "cash-flow":

> The amount of funds derived from operations cannot be considered as a substitute for or an improvement upon properly determined net income as a measure of results of operations and the consequent effect on financial position. Misleading implications can result from isolated statistics in annual reports of "cash flow" which are not placed in proper perspective to net income figures and to a complete analysis of source and application of funds. "Cash flow" and related terms should not be used in annual reports in such a way that the significance of net income is impaired, and "cash earnings" or other terms with a similar connotation

---

[1] Accounting Principles Board of the American Institute of CPAs, "Opinion No. 3, The Statement of Source and Application of Funds," *Journal of Accountancy*, November, 1963, p. 66.

> should be avoided. The Board regards computations of "cash flow per share" as misleading since they ignore the impact of cash expenditures for renewal and replacement of facilities and tend to downgrade the significant economic statistic of "earnings per share."[2]

Similarly, Paton points out the dangers in utilizing the "cash-flow" figure as a substitute for income. In essence, he argues that the cost of using durable resources is every bit as real as the cost of labor or raw materials, and thus a company cannot make a profit unless these costs are recovered. He states:

> Security analysts, not always noted for their grasp of accounting principles and procedures, seem to be suffering from an acute attack of "cash-flowitis," manifested especially by their fondness for per-share calculations of "cash-flow," in company with or superseding figures for net earnings per share.[3]

It is indeed apparent that the financial analysts are infected with some sort of malady. But "cash-flowitis" is not the real ailment from which these users of financial statements suffer. "Cash-flowitis" is merely a syndrome of the malignancy which is growing rampant in the financial community. That malady might be called "information anemia."

Symptomatic treatment in this case is not enough. Financial analysts might be persuaded to abandon the use of that deceptive term "cash-flow," but then other symptoms would undoubtedly appear. The only hope for a complete cure is to eradicate the germ which causes this dread disease: inconsistent accounting practice.

There is no question that the cost of fixed assets is an ordinary and necessary cost of doing business which must be recovered before a company can be considered to have earned a profit. In our highly automated society, we are making increasing use of machinery and equipment in all phases of commercial activity; as a consequence, these costs become increasingly important in measuring income. However, the casual and capricious manner in which accountants allocate these costs among economic periods actually impairs the usefulness of financial statements. The depreciation charge often conceals more than it reveals about the real economic progress of a business unit.

Within the framework of "generally accepted principles of accounting" there is a wide range of alternative depreciation procedures. The decision to use double-declining-balance procedure, for example, results in the recognition of twice as much depreciation during the initial year of asset life as is recognized by straight-line. Since in many cases the amount of recorded depreciation exceeds the amount of net income, the choice of procedure can make a very substantial difference in reported earnings.

Yet, income taxes notwithstanding, the depreciation procedure used for financial statement purposes cannot make one whit of difference in the economic progress of a firm. No wonder the security analysts are sick!

[2] *Ibid.*, p. 67.

[3] William A. Paton, "The 'Cash-Flow' Illusion," *The Accounting Review*, XXXVIII (April, 1963), p. 243.

By adding the depreciation deduction back to income, it is often possible to obtain a more clear indication of the economic progress of a company. This is particularly useful when year-to-year or firm-to-firm comparisons are to be made. Certainly, as Paton indicates, this figure does not represent cash-flow in the literal sense of the term; nor does it indicate the real income of a particular company for a given period. However, it does provide a method of reducing the effects of a major inconsistency in accounting practice: discretionary variations in the depreciation charge.

Depreciation accounting has been defined as "a system of accounting which aims to distribute the cost or other basic value of tangible capital assets, less salvage (if any) over the estimated useful life of the unit (which may be a group of assets) in a systematic and rational manner."[4] As long as the method is "systematic and rational" it apparently does not matter what method is used in any company.

But the fact that different companies may choose different methods makes it extremely difficult to compare the operating results of one company with those of another. Not only is there variety of procedure, but their inconsistent application plus the use of "cost" as a base given varying prices make comparisons of results from one year to the next rather hazardous.

Cost allocation under present depreciation procedures may be considered "systematic," but it is by no means uniform. It is not argued here that a uniform method of cost allocation would result in every company's (or for that matter, any company's) recognizing what might be considered "true" income. In economic decisions, however, it is often necessary to consider *relative* performance even though an *absolute* measure may be unobtainable. Thus it might be concluded that, in accounting, it is better to be consistent than right!

A major obstacle to progress in depreciation accounting has been the Federal income tax regulations. The Committee on Accounting Procedure stated that "sound financial accounting procedures do not necessarily coincide with the rules as to what shall be included in 'gross income' or allowed as a deduction therefrom, in arriving at taxable net income."[5] Despite this admonition, the tax tail still wags the accounting dog, and "accepted" accounting procedures seem to change every time Congress meets.

Changes in reporting procedures frequently follow changes in tax regulations. As an example of this practice, consider the recent income reports of United States Steel Corporation. For the year 1962, "Big Steel" reported net income of $163.7 million. This was considerably below the $190.2 million of income reported for the year 1961. From the income statement, 1962 looked like a bad year for U. S. Steel. Robert Tyson,

---

[4] American Institute of CPAs, *Accounting Terminology Bulletin No. 1*, p. 25.

[5] American Institute of CPAs, *Accounting Research Bulletin No. 43*, p. 76.

chairman of the company's finance committee, lamented the "profit squeeze," stating that "the 1962 profit margin was smaller than that of any nonwar year since the depression year of 1938."[6] The company cut its dividend in the final half of 1962, urged the labor unions to restrain their wage demands, and pleaded with the government to allow a price increase.

But careful scrutiny of the income statement reveals that 1962 might not have been such a bad year after all. Sales were up 5 per cent over the previous year and employment costs, which management blames as the primary cause of the "profit squeeze," were somewhat lower.

The other villain which is supposed to be squeezing profits is the Federal income tax: "our Federal income tax structure could scarcely be better designed to extinguish the profit incentive, confiscate capital and paralyze the growth processes."[7] Yet "estimated United States and foreign taxes on income" were actually $29 million lower in 1962 than in 1961.

It turns out that changes in tax procedures were responsible for nearly all of the decrease in net income. It is ironic indeed that the reduction in taxes which presumably *benefited* the company caused the accountants to report lower earnings. The company reported that its "wear and exhaustion of facilities" was $55.4 million greater in 1962 than in 1961. The size of this increase might have been understandable, if it had been due to the utilization of large amounts of new equipment during the year. Certainly the cost of such facilities must be considered in determining net income. This was not the case, however, as the company indicates that the amount of depreciable plant and equipment (at cost) increased by only $4 million during the year. Nor is it apparent that the company suddenly discovered that its facilities were deteriorating at a faster rate than originally anticipated.

The real reason for the increased depreciation charge in 1962 was the easing of Federal income tax requirements. A change in Internal Revenue Service regulations permitted steelmaking equipment to be depreciated for tax purposes in 18 years rather than 25 years. As a result, the company increased its depreciation charges by $44 million, not only for tax purposes but in the financial statements as well. This is explained in notes accompanying the statements:

> U. S. Steel in 1962, for the most part, based its determination of the wear and exhaustion of facilities on the new guideline procedure, as set forth in Revenue Procedure 62-21, which provides guideline lives which are generally shorter than those previously in use.
>
> The investment credit... resulted in a reduction in Federal income tax of $8.2 million.
>
> As a result of the investment credit and the adoption of the guideline procedure wear and exhaustion increased $52.2 million over the basis used prior to 1962.

[6] United States Steel Corporation, *1962 Annual Report*, p. 23.

[7] *Ibid.*, p. 28.

As in previous years wear and exhaustion is, for the most part, related to U. S. Steel's rate of operations.[8]

To the extent that increased depreciation charges are attributable to either more extensive use of existing facilities or to the expansion of these facilities, they may reflect certain economic events which affect the firm. When, however, such increases are merely changes wrought by accountants in deference to the altered views of Congress or the Internal Revenue Service, they do not properly reflect the impact of asset use on the operating results of the firm.

Admittedly, one rationale for the investment credit and faster amortization is to encourage business concerns to replace productive facilities more rapidly. If so, these provisions may actually have some impact on the economic lives of assets. But unless it can be shown that a company does intend to retire assets at an earlier date than would otherwise be economically feasible, the use of tax-oriented depreciation charges can only cause distortions in reported income. If replacement policy is governed solely by "wear and exhaustion" which connote physical deterioration, it is difficult to see how a decision by some Federal official can suddenly cause a blast furnace or a Bessemer converter to wear out at a faster rate.

Until accountants awaken to the responsibility for presenting the economic results of business entities in such manner that the users of financial statements are not misled, the users will continue to make adjustments to suit their particular needs. When too many adjustments become necessary, the users of statements will completely disregard them and rely instead on rumor, intuition and glamour as ways of judging company performance. There is some evidence that this is now occurring in the stock market where reported earnings may bear little relationship to price.

It might be convenient if all readers of financial statements were sophisticated accountants. But, to repeat the Paton observation, "security analysts [are] not always noted for their grasp of accounting principles and procedures." If professional security analysts do not understand accounting procedures, think of the widows and orphans who must rely on these reports when buying or selling securities. It is too much to expect all users of financial statements to make a thorough study of accounting principles. Therefore it seems vital that accountants perform their function: to relate economic events through the financial statements in a manner which does not deceive the readers.

If all accounting reports were printed in Russian or Chinese, very few American readers could understand them. But rather than blaming the readers for not taking sufficient courses in foreign languages, we should make every effort to convey the appropriate information in a language which they can understand.

Changes in accounting procedures which affect income are most difficult

[8] *Ibid.*, p. 33.

for an unwary investor to comprehend. If such changes are deemed essential and appropriate, an attempt should be made to illustrate their impact on income for the period in which the changes occur. In addition to the income determined by use of the newly adopted procedures, the readers should be informed of the amount of income which would have resulted had no changes been made.

For example, in order to compare the 1962 income reported by U. S. Steel Corporation with that of the previous year, the following adjustments might be made with respect to depreciation.

Reported income	$163,679,817
Add: additional depreciation recognized due to adoption of "guideline" lives	44,000,000
Less: taxes applicable to above depreciation	−22,880,000
Adjusted income	$184,799,817

To be sure, the adjusted figure shown above does not necessarily indicate exactly how well U. S. Steel Corporation fared in 1962 relative to 1961. Additional adjustments—for example, for the inconsistent treatment of pension costs—would be necessary to accomplish that. However, the adjusted income recognizes the fact that a corporation does not incur additional expense as a result of regulations permitting faster amortization of property costs for tax purposes.

After making the adjustments for depreciation, adjusted income is found to be $184,799,817. This represents a decrease of less than three per cent from the previous year—not nearly as severe as the 14 per cent decline indicated by the reported income.

Compare these results with those which might have been obtained by a financial analyst calculating "cash-flow." By adding *reported* depreciation to reported income a total "cash-flow" of $429,555,738 is obtained. But the security analyst may have reason to feel insecure even with this figure.

The primary reason for calculating the sum of depreciation charges and income, the figure inappropriately dubbed "cash-flow," is to counteract the effects of discretionary depreciation practices used in determining income. As mentioned above, the choice of depreciation procedure affects reported income but this choice cannot have any real effect on a company's economic progress. Depreciation is simply a device for allocating costs among accounting periods. No matter how you slice it, the total cost must be the same.

Differences in reported depreciation, however, may not be due entirely to variations in the allocation of costs among years. The charge for depreciation may also include some other items in disguise. For example, the depreciation charge reported by U. S. Steel for 1962 includes the amount of income taxes saved because of the investment credit. This is revealed in a note to the financial statements as follows:

The Revenue Act of 1962 provides for an investment credit against Federal income tax of up to 7% of the cost of certain depreciable property acquired and placed in service after 1961. The investment credit applicable to such acquisitions during 1962 resulted in a reduction in Federal income tax of $8.2 million. Since future charges for wear and exhaustion will be reduced by this investment credit, an equal amount has been included in the 1962 cost of wear and exhaustion.[9]

Had U. S. Steel added back the amount of the investment credit to income tax expense (an acceptable alternative accounting treatment), rather than including it in depreciation, the figure computed as "cash-flow" by many analysts would have been $8.2 million lower. It is possible that U. S. Steel will change this method of dealing with the investment credit since, beginning in 1964, total charges for depreciation will no longer be reduced for tax purposes by the investment credit.[10]

The decision to charge depreciation rather than tax expense as a means of deferring the benefits of the investment credit to subsequent accounting periods does not affect reported income. It does not even affect the determination of "funds provided from operations" [11]—one possible meaning of the term "cash-flow." It does, however, affect the computation of the figure that many analysts refer to as "cash-flow"—the sum of reported income plus depreciation.

The varied treatment permitted the investment credit may require further refinement of so-called "cash-flow" to achieve a consistent reckoning among companies or between years. The analyst can accomplish this by subtracting the amount of the investment credit included in depreciation charges from "cash-flow" to calculate what might be called "alternative cash-flow."

The "alternative cash-flow" for U. S. Steel in 1962 would be determined as follows:

Reported income	$163,679,817
Reported depreciation	265,875,921
"Cash-flow"	$429,555,738
Less: Investment credit included in depreciation	8,200,000
"Alternative cash-flow"	$421,355,738

Now consider the manner in which the various income and "cash-flow" figures measure the economic progress made by U. S. Steel in 1962 as

[9] *Ibid.*, p. 33.

[10] The Revenue Act of 1964 does not require that the depreciation basis of property be reduced by the investment credit as was required under the 1962 Act. In addition, it permits the amounts of investment credit taken in 1962 and 1963 to be added back to the depreciation basis of property beginning in 1964.

[11] If the benefits of the investment credit are deferred for statement purposes until subsequent accounting periods, reported expenses are not reduced by the full extent of the credit. A portion of expense currently recognized, then, would not require a current outlay, and thus should be added to reported earnings in determining funds provided from operations. This would be done whether the expense is labeled taxes or depreciation.

compared with 1961. For this purpose, the comparative figures are set forth below:

	(*Millions*) *1962*	*1961*	*Change* (*per cent*)
Reported income	$163.7	$190.2	−13.9
Adjusted income	184.8	190.2	−2.8
"Cash-flow"	429.6	400.7	+7.2
"Alternative cash-flow"	421.4	400.7	+5.2

If the adjusted income is taken as a reasonable indicator of the year-to-year change in economic performance, "cash-flow" comes somewhat closer to showing this change than does reported income. The "cash-flow" adjusted for the spurious charge to depreciation in the amount of the investment credit comes closer still.

It may be concluded, therefore, that in some cases the "cash-flow" calculation provides a convenient way for an investor to compensate for the inconsistent application of depreciation procedures by accountants. As Mason notes:

> ... the significance of net income is impaired if improper or inconsistent methods of accounting for these "non-fund" items is encountered, and if different accounting methods are used by companies in the same industry. The cash-flow figure may then have more stability and comparability than the net income, but it still is not a measure of the increase in the stockholders' equity arising from operations of the period.[13]

It is certainly true that "cash-flow" cannot do an adequate job of portraying operating results. For example, if heavier charges for depreciation are the result of an expansion in plant and equipment, "cash-flow" will conceal this fact and create an illusion of success which may not be justified. And, of course, the layman cannot be expected to recognize the deferral of the investment credit disguised as "wear and exhaustion of facilities." It is a shame that analysts and investors must rely upon such a crude indicator of economic performance while accountants go on preparing statements ostensibly to provide useful information.

Depreciation is only one area of accounting in which inconsistencies abound. For example, a change in U. S. Steel's method of accounting for pension costs resulted in a $43.9 million reduction in that expense for 1962 from the amount which would have been recognized if the same procedure had been used as in 1961. This nearly offset the additional expense recognized because of the change in depreciation procedures, although countervailing errors do not justify each other. Nevertheless, in the auditors' opinion, "the statement of income presents fairly ... the results of the year's operations, in conformity with generally accepted accounting principles applied on a basis *consistent with that of the previous year.*" (Emphasis supplied.)

[13] Perry Mason, *"Cash Flow" Analysis and The Funds Statement*, Accounting Research Study No. 2 (New York: American Institute of CPAs, 1961), p. 39.

Although the report of one company has been singled out here to demonstrate inconsistencies in accounting procedure which do occur, it should be noted that this company is by no means unique in this respect. The 1963 edition of *Accounting Trends and Techniques* revealed that of 600 companies surveyed, 199 had adopted the new depreciation guideline lives for tax purposes. Of these, 76 companies indicated that they had used them for financial reporting purposes as well.[13]

The ambiguous inclusion of the investment credit in depreciation is also very popular. Of 241 companies which disclosed the method of handling the investment credit, 123 companies, slightly more than half, indicated that the tax credit was included with the allowance for depreciation.[14]

The Accounting Principles Board which once showed promise of resolving accounting inconsistencies may actually have contributed to the proliferation of conflicting views on the treatment of fixed assets. With respect to "guideline lives," they state that:

> A taxpayer should carefully review the estimates of useful life of depreciable property adopted for financial accounting purposes, with the objective of conforming them with Guidleline lives to the extent that the latter fall within a reasonable range of estimated useful lives applicable in his business.[15]

The Board thus seems to have relinquished responsibility for determining sound accounting principles to the Internal Revenue Service. They go on to state that, with certain exceptions, "net income for the period should not be *increased* as the result of the adoption of Guideline lives for income-tax purposes only." [16] (Emphasis in the original.) They do not state any objection to a *decrease* in net income as the result of the adoption of Guideline lives; presumably such procedure carries their tacit endorsement.

The Board also supports the inclusion of the investment credit with depreciation:

> ...reflection of income tax provisions in the income statement, in the amount payable (that is, after deduction of the allowable investment credit) is appropriate provided that a corresponding charge is made to an appropriate cost or expense (for example, to the provision for depreciation) and the treatment is adequately disclosed in the financial statements of the first year of its adoption.[17]

It seems clear to me that the Accounting Principles Board has failed to resolve these major issues regarding the treatment of fixed assets. Certified

[13] American Institute of CPAs, *Accounting Trends and Techniques*, Seventeenth Edition (New York: AICPA, 1963), p. 176.

[14] *Ibid.*, p. 123.

[15] Accounting Principles Board of the American Institute of CPAs, "Opinion No. 1, New Depreciation Guidelines and Rules," *Journal of Accountancy*, December, 1962, p. 64.

[16] *Ibid.*

[17] Accounting Principles Board of the American Institute of CPAs, "Opinion No. 2, Accounting for the 'Investment Credit'," *Journal of Accountancy*, February, 1963, p. 71.

public accountants still seem willing to permit glaring changes in accounting practice without any mention in their opinions with respect to consistency.

It is high time for the accounting profession to consider the grave consequences which may result from a failure to heed the early warnings of an epidemic. "Cash-flowitis" is simply the first stage of this disease. As Moonitz observes, a primary factor accounting for the recent emphasis on "cash-flow" has been

> ...the lack of uniformity in accounting procedures, especially in the treatment of the "non-fund" transactions. For example, investment analysts appear initially to have developed "cash-flow" analysis in response to the wide divergence of procedures within specific industries.[18]

As later complications arise, we might find readers of financial statements computing other ersatz income figures. For example they might add back cost of goods sold and employment costs to reported income because they no longer trust the accountants to calculate inventories or pension costs. Finally, in the terminal stage, they will simply disregard all utterances of accountants whether useful or not.

Before it is too late, accountants should take stock of accounting procedures and attempt to provide information which is relevant and useful to the users of these reports. After all, the *readers* of the financial statements, including the financial analysts, have the last word as to whether they will continue to accept and use accounting reports.

---

[18] Maurice Moonitz, "Director's Preface" in *"Cash Flow" Analysis and The Funds Statement*, xi.

from

H. Ross, "Present Discontents," in *Financial Statements: A Crusade for Current Values* (Toronto: Sir Isaac Pitman, 1969), pp. 5–11

CHAPTER 2

Present Discontents

Accountants have never had it so good. Today, no other profession is growing so fast. The big problem facing practitioners now is how to handle the work that pours in on them. How can they recruit and train enough good staff to keep up with the natural growth of their practices? This is not an easy atmosphere in which to develop self-criticism. Nevertheless, there are problems with which we should be concerned.

We have, indeed, the best system of financial communication anyone has ever had. For one thing, other civilizations never had the electronic computer. In fact, they did not even have the ballpoint pen. The financial statements and reporting systems that are commonplace today are incomparably better than were those of the philosophic Greeks, the litigious Romans, the scholarly men of the Renaissance, or the mysterious Chinese. Looking back at even shorter range, the statements published today are more informative and more reliable than were those issued a generation ago. By every sort of comparison, we are doing well—except by the one really vital comparison—namely, the comparison between what we are producing and what is needed. We could not be probing outer space with rockets if it were not for electronic data processing, and this is only the most dramatic illustration of our need for reporting and controls in a society in which the handling of complex problems has become routine work.

Solid accounting textbooks; respectable, well-filled professional journals; the sober, weighty releases of our accounting institutes—all these reflect the attention and concern which are now being given the subject of financial reporting. The accounting profession regards itself (quite properly, I think) as the official custodian of the art of financial reporting. This being the case, the profession should feel committed to a continuing appraisal of the art—but an appraisal made in a judicious spirit, pitched somewhere between the mood of self-congratulation of the after-dinner speeches at gatherings of accountants and the mood of abysmal self-abasement of the General Confession in the Book of Common Prayer.

There is certainly some criticism being made. But is there enough? I believe that criticisms of financial statements tend, most of the time, to run along well below crisis level. When a scandal breaks, there are anguished outcries. Investment analysts and relatively well-informed observers (like the financial page editors), all of whom normally take an indulgent, avuncular view of financial statements, turn suddenly to shrill protest and recrimination. The government security regulatory agencies come out with warlike pronouncements. But the scandal eventually fades, and everyone settles down to low-level grumbling. If the scandal gets enough attention, some new pronouncement may come out (from regulatory agencies or professional institutes) which sharpens a definition here or tightens a regulation there, but which does not produce any improvement that I would describe as basic. The general line of criticism, in a soft key, and normally somewhat sharpened when a financial scandal gets into the headlines, is based on three points:

1) *Complaint of lack of comparability in the statements of similar corporations*

All respectable companies (and some that are not respectable) produce statements that are prepared on what are described as "generally accepted accounting principles." This sounds all right. But because these principles authorize several different treatments of important transactions, it follows that two companies may report their financial results in accordance with accepted principles—and yet compile their figures quite differently. This is regrettable, since comparisons between the statements of different companies are such a basic part of financial analysis that a lack of comparability is extremely serious.

The cure would seem to be simple: just agree on a set of accounting principles which does not countenance different treatments of identical transactions. It must be admitted that the accounting profession has been in deadly earnest in tackling this problem. But its attempts have been marked by a persistent lack of achievement which makes the pursuit of the Holy Grail in chivalric times seem like the instant success story of the TV commercials.

2) *Failure to disclose essential information*

It can be argued that even if different principles are applied in similar circumstances, no serious reader will be misled so long as there is adequate disclosure. Government regulatory agencies have tended to be almost obsessed by this point. It is by no means a complete cure, but it is nevertheless a good thing to keep plugging. In any event, thanks to the long campaign in favour of greater disclosure, this is probably less a problem than it was previously.

3) *Failure to show the "real" position*

There is an uneasy feeling that the profit and loss account does not show "real" income, and that the balance sheet does not show "real" values. Here, we become involved in questions of semantics. Strictly speaking, there is no such thing as "real" or "true" profits, but merely profits which are appropriately calculated for this or that purpose. What is really complained of is that the financial statements produced by accountants do not, in certain important respects, reflect economic facts. This is sometimes explained by claiming that the economist's concept of income is different from the accountant's; but any notion that there are two useful and legitimate ways of looking at the operations of an enterprise simply will not do. The economist and the accountant do have different points of view in financial reporting, because the economist *uses* the statements and the accountant *prepares* them. But it does not follow from this that there should be two types of statement. What does follow is that financial statements must always be a practical compromise between what the user (that is, the economist) would like to have and what the accountant feels he can reliably produce. In this context, the economist should be thought of as the typical statement-user, because, while there is a great variety of statement-users (each of whom may have a distinctive view of his own), the majority of statement-users are nevertheless basically interested in economic factors.

The Accounting Process: A Basic Review

The ineffably simple burden of all three of these criticisms is that financial statements do not tell those who use them what they need to know. What is wrong is not insufficiently-refined concepts, but a basically false starting point—a flaw which is so obvious that it not only escapes attention, but is often not recognized when pointed out. Let us get right back to fundamentals.

Those who study the financial statements of an enterprise want to know (for any one of a variety of reasons) what its financial strength is. This may be because they want to buy it or sell it, to lend it money or borrow from it, to tax it fairly, to estimate its competitive position, to calculate its contribution to the national economy—or for any one of a dozen other reasons. In every case, it is the enterprise's financial strength that must be weighed—not its moral qualities, or its sociability, or its beauty, but its financial stature.

The wealth of any commercial enterprise must be judged from two points of view—and this is true both of large public corporations and of small private corporations, and indeed is true also of partnerships or sole traders. In the first place, the enterprise has a certain amount of wealth; and, in the second place, it has an ability to produce more wealth. Most people dealing with the enterprise want information on both these subjects—how much has the enterprise now, and how much is it likely to have in the future? This point has been put clearly and concisely thus: "Conceptually, the economic position of a company is a composite of the net resources over which the company has control and the prospects for increases or decreases in these net resources."[1]

Balance Sheet and Income Statement

The conventional balance sheet and income statement are supposed to supply the basic information under each of these headings, the balance sheet showing the present wealth of the enterprise and the income statement indicating its earning power. All this seems admirable enough; but there is a serious catch. Largely for historical reasons (and as explained elsewhere in this text), accountants have produced their balance sheets on a basis of cost, rather than on a basis of value. And when this is pointed out, instead of recognizing that a way is being opened up for the production of much more useful statements, they persist in trying to defend that which is clearly indefensible.

It is, of course, a gross oversimplification to suggest that the accountant chooses cost instead of value. The relation between cost and value in accounting is, in fact, subtle and complex. (This relationship

1. John K. Simmons, "A Concept of Comparability in Financial Reporting," *The Accounting Review*, October 1967, p. 681.

will be further explored in the next chapter.) But it is nevertheless true that our present conventional statements are essentially cost-based. And no amount of accounting research, round-table discussion, or fine argument will produce much better statements until we turn our backs resolutely on the double talk and sophistry by which the cost basis, or modified cost basis, is defended.

As a matter of fact, accountants do talk in terms of value (when it suits them) and in certain moods would protest that this was their basic concern. But they do not pursue value consistently. When I wrote *The Elusive Art of Accounting,* I searched out two sharply conflicting pronouncements made by the AICPA. These statements read as follows: "A balance sheet is a statement of the financial condition of the enterprise"; and "A balance sheet does not purport to reflect and could not usefully reflect the value of the enterprise."

It took some looking to find this delightfully parallel wording, but the conflicting claims are common in accounting literature. Accountants argue that they are dealing in values (as indeed they must) when they are trying to describe the purpose of their professional exertions. It would take some pretty sophisticated talk for someone who is preparing a balance sheet to explain his activities in any other terms. What else could he claim to be doing except establishing the current value of the enterprise? On the other hand, when it is pointed out to the accountant that some of his most cherished procedures do not seem even to be aimed at reaching a current value, he replies that they are not intended to.

As suggested above, there are two essential questions relating to an enterprise's wealth: (1) how much has it got, and (2) how much has it the power to produce? The balance sheet is supposed to answer the first of these questions—and goodness knows, current values, and not costs, are what are wanted in that statement. On the other hand, the income statement is supposed to provide a basis on which anyone can inform himself about the enterprise's ability to product wealth—that is to say, its earning power. Here, the cost-value comparison is a little more indirect.

There are all sorts of ways of investigating earning power. But, as talk is cheap and sales pitches can be devastating, there is much to be said for the practice of judging future prospects on the solid facts of past performance. The accountant's objective here is to set down what has happened in the past in a manner which makes it useful in projecting future probabilities. Here, there is, *prima facie,* no obvious reason to prefer value over cost, and the matter must be considered more deeply.

Let us first take the case of an individual. In trying to establish how productive he is likely to be, it is often sufficient to find what his current rate of salary is. In fact, in hiring an individual (which is where this kind of question is likely to arise), his current rate of remuneration will usually be the fact most seriously considered. When the situation is not so simple (for example, where the individual has been running a business), the most likely approach in judging his earning power may be to examine a financial statement for his business. If the business is in the nature of a venture, the statement might be for the most recent venture managed by the individual. This venture might have covered a few weeks or even a period of several years. In either case, a set of statements based on cost might be perfectly satisfactory—for, as explained later, cost is the appropriate basis for venture accounting.

However, if we are dealing not with an individual but with a complex modern public corporation, venture accounting (and the cost basis) is wholly inappropriate. The corporation may well be engaged in all sorts of ventures. But at any given point in time, these will be at various stages of completion, and it will therefore be quite impossible to establish the corporation's earning power by a venture-type financial statement. It is for this reason that the annual-income concept was developed. An income statement purports to show (and should show more unequivocally than do conventional statements) the earnings of the corporation over the past year. As will be argued exhaustively later, this cannot be done satisfactorily other than by statements which are unflinchingly based on current values.

A Matter of Principle or of Utility?

A point of capital significance emerges from this discussion. Accounting is not based on "fundamental principles" in any recognized sense of these words, but on sheer utility or usefulness. A balance sheet must be made up on the basis of current values if it is to make sense to anyone studying the financial stature of an enterprise. But a balance sheet that is prepared on the conventional modified cost basis now in use may be satisfactory for some purposes—for example, in establishing for a banker that he can safely extend a line of credit. Similarly, an income statement may be satisfactory on a cost basis for some purposes—for example, where venture accounting is appropriate. But for the annual statements of a large commercial corporation, current values alone make sense.

Thus, even such a fundamental question as whether to use cost or value as the basis for our statements is not a matter of principle, but simply a question of which provides the more useful information in any given case. It is not the thesis of this book that current-value accounting is intrinsically superior to any other kind—it is simply that current-value accounting is most appropriate for the annual published financial statements of large corporations. Throughout this text, it is the published reports of commercial corporations with which we shall be concerned. These reports present special problems of their own. (Some comments on the accounting problems of other types of enterprise are contained in Chapter 7.)

We may sum up, at this point, by saying that the crucial defect in published statements is that they are based on cost rather than on value—a blunt assertion which will be examined more fully in the next chapter. Two consequences follow from this: (1) statement-users do not get as satisfactory data as they might be provided with; and (2) all attempts to improve financial reporting are frustrated from the start.

By Leonard Spacek

Can We Define Generally Accepted Accounting Principles?

In a provocative challenge to the accounting profession, Mr. Spacek contends that accounting principles can and should be defined to provide substantial comparability between the financial statements of different corporations.

As examples of areas in which he thinks differing accounting treatments should not be permitted, he cites tax allocation, long-term lease obligations, and capitalizing certain items or charging them to expense. He also argues that the effects of inflation should be reflected in depreciation charges.

This is the latest of a number of speeches on accounting principles by Mr. Spacek which have attracted wide attention and comment.

We all prefer to avoid problems that are difficult or unpleasant, or that we believe cannot be solved. I suppose this is just human nature. And in our zeal to avoid facing up to these problems, we are apt to sound like the small boy arguing against going to bed at the proper time—anything to divert attention, delay action or side-step the issues.

Sometimes I am tempted to feel that the public accounting profession is acting the part of this small boy in trying to avoid or delay facing up to the inevitable necessity of defining generally accepted principles of accounting. The reasons advanced may sound plausible to those giving them. But they are not very convincing to those who must rely on the certified statements that are supposed to conform to these undefined principles.

The usual arguments against defining generally accepted accounting principles are that: it would create rigid accounting rules; it would prevent experimentation; and, it would tend to regulate business accounting. Furthermore, the question is asked, "Can we define accounting principles?" Let us see what merit these arguments have.

Rigidity?

The first argument is that clear definitions of accounting principles would establish rules and rigidity in accounting practice. A rule is defined as a "prescribed guide for conduct . . .; uniform or established course; systematic method or practice!" Can accounting rules defined in this manner be objectionable to accountants, to business, to stockholders or to the public? If there is objection to such rules, what could the motive be? Is it a desire to avoid prescribed guides for conduct or for systematic method or practice in accounting?

The purpose of financial reporting is to provide facts for the reader. Doesn't the public, in licensing the public accountant to practice, expect that he will measure the reports he examines against established guides for proper conduct and systematic methods or practices in accounting and reporting? What then is intended to be conveyed by the argument that proper definition of accounting principles would result in rules, as though that were conclusively bad? This objection, in my opinion, is based upon the public accountant's fear that he will be held responsible for consistent accounting treatment of comparable transactions—a standard of performance not observed in the past, but which is required of others in professions having similar responsibilities. We can have no sympathy with this fear, because the responsibility feared is exactly that for which the public accountant is paid and which the public expects him to accept as its licensed representative.

Experimentation?

The next objection frequently cited is that a proper definition of accounting principles would prevent experimentation. Does this mean that we now experiment with the facts which we present to the public? If so, do we tell the public we are experimenting with the business facts and figures to which we certify? If not, is it right to experiment with facts that affect other people's fortunes without telling them? If we are experimenting with some of the facts presented, how do we square this with the certificates in which we say the facts are in accordance with generally accepted principles of accounting?

Actually we do not experiment with facts in financial statements; therefore, no basis exists for this objection. Those who advance this argument are grasping for words to obstruct proper definition of accounting principles; but these objectors know full well that experiments with accounting principles and facts in financial presentations to the public cannot be tolerated.

Where experimentation does occur, as in classification and breakdown of costs, it would continue with greater effect under properly defined principles of accounting. But this experimentation is in the assembly and presentation of data, not in the principles which underlie them. Therefore, this objection, too, is only a red herring thrown across the path of progress to avoid facing up to the requirement for proper accounting. As with other objections, it is without merit. Otherwise, let the profession come forward with illustrations of good experiments that would be prevented if accounting principles were properly defined. The truth is that no desirable experimentation in financial presentation would be prevented by properly defined and understood accounting principles. Let us set this objection aside, therefore, as completely invalid.

Regulatory?

Another objection often raised by businessmen and public accountants alike is that properly defined accounting principles would be regulatory—a bad word. They would regulate business accounting practices. I wonder what these objectors believe is the purpose of accounting reports to stockholders and the public. Those who object to definition of accounting principles on regulatory grounds reveal a misconception of accounting.

If accounting is not regulatory in its result, its objective is not accomplished, and it is useless and should be discontinued. But accounting is regulatory. Even internal accounting reports are regulatory. Reports of management to stockholders and others are regulatory, and the position of the public accountant in certifying them is premised upon his regulatory status. As yet, most of our private and public accounting is not subject to governmental regulation, and this accounting is the best example of nongovernment regulation that we have in our business world. But if the regulatory aspects of our public accounting fail to meet the needs of the stockholders and the public, the only substitute will be government regulation.

It behooves all of us, therefore, to carefully weigh our duties as public accountants and to improve the quality of our performance; otherwise, we will be replaced by government regulators. Business must also join the public accountant in the high-level performance of his work or face the prospect of governmental regulation that makes no pretense of assuming responsibility for the consequence of its decision-making, as the public accountant must do.

Definition?

Now we come to the last question, which is often raised as an objection—can accounting principles be defined?

First, I would like to say in all seriousness that they can be. But, for the sake of discussion, let us assume for a moment that they cannot be defined. Then it must follow that the public has

---

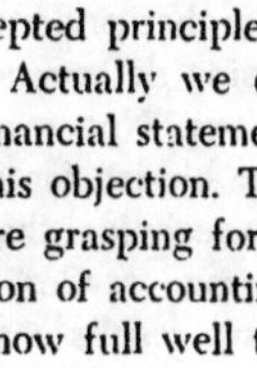

LEONARD SPACEK, *CPA, is managing partner of Arthur Andersen & Co., whose home office is in Chicago. Mr. Spacek is one of nine members of the American Institute's special committee on research program. This paper was presented as a speech at the annual meeting of the Ohio Society of CPAs held in Columbus last September.*

already been misled to such an extent that the whole public accounting profession and business world are guilty of the biggest farce ever perpetrated. Why? Because we have been representing that we have examined the financial statements of business enterprises and found that these statements conform to generally accepted principles of accounting. If we are now to take the position that we cannot possibly define these principles, it follows that we could not have done what we have been representing to the public that we were doing. What excuse have we for this misrepresentation? Are we to say that we did not believe anyone would discover the fact that many of our certifications were without substance?

Accuracy vs. substance?

In some respects, the accounting profession has greatly misled the public. This is in the so-called "accuracy" or "technical" area of accounting. It is difficult to explain why the accountant has always slowed his progress by subordinating the substance of accounting principles to accuracy and preciseness in accounting.

The fact remains, however, that the substance achieved through the years by the public accountant's examination of financial statements has been great indeed. In fact we could not have achieved the great public investor ownership of corporations without the public accountant looking over the shoulder of business. The strides made in accounting since the start of this century have been tremendous. The advance immediately after 1932 was particularly great. It was then that the Securities and Exchange Commission was added to the scene. Even though accounting progress from 1900 to 1930 was great, it was not sufficient to prevent the financial misrepresentations that accumulated and burst in the 1929-1932 crash.

Because accounting progress had not been adequate to prevent the financial statement misrepresentations revealed in the early thirties, the public accountant's role was greatly enhanced by the financial statement registration required by the Securities and Exchange Commission. That development forced a tremendous improvement in accounting for financial statement purposes, and it was accomplished in a very short time in order to catch up with the needs that the public found were not being met. Since then, the requirements for improvement in financial accounting have multiplied manyfold, but our progress in defining and establishing sound accounting principles has continued at a snail's pace. Therefore, we are still at the point where the need for better accounting to meet the requirements that have accumulated in our economic system and in the business world has far outstripped our advances in reporting the facts to the public.

Dangerous delay?

The question therefore arises again—is this lag in accounting progress, in relation to economic and business progress, again to accumulate to such an extent that the deficiencies in accounting will reach a bursting point as they did in 1932 and 1933? We are living in an age when railroad financial statements literally are not worth the paper they are written on, and where the decreasing value of the dollar is making the profit reports of most corporations meaningless except to the specialist. And the specialist uses his knowledge to buy good properties at a fraction of their value because he can analyze the financial reports and adjust them to show up values or liabilities that the average investor has no chance of finding, because the public accountant is doing only half of his job. The specialist, therefore, buys when he finds these hidden values that are unknown to the general reader, and he sells when he finds the hidden liabilities that the general public does not know about.

Again we are in a period like that prior to 1932 when the method of bookkeeping determined the profits reported by corporations. Not even the footnotes always show up these hidden facts; and, when they do, the notes are so technical that they are of little value to the average reader. Thus, while one company's operating results may appear to be good and another's to be bad, a specialist in financial statement analysis may readily determine that the quality is just the reverse.

Reliable comparisons?

In defense of his acceptance of alternate accounting principles chosen by different companies for corresponding transactions, the public accountant argues that he is concerned only with seeing that the individual company maintains its accounts on a consistent basis—not that the accounts of one company are comparable with those of others. This defense of inconsistency in accounting among companies is in itself a form of negligence within the profession. There is no public accountant of importance who does not analyze the financial condition and operations of his clients in relation to other companies. Nor is there a single one who does not know that practically all financial data reported to the public are used for comparative purposes.

In a typical presentation of financial data for

a number of companies in a given industry, earnings per share and other data are tabulated as if they were directly comparable, even though the accounting principles followed may vary widely among the companies listed. These differences, if known and evaluated, probably would materially change the results reported, and would affect the comparative values. Yet we all know that comparison of companies is the purpose of such tabulations.

Another difficulty about comparative tables is that they almost never carry the footnotes which were included in the financial statements from which the figures were drawn. What purpose is served by adding footnotes to explain the accounting or make important disclosures, when the accountant knows that the footnotes usually are lost in the usage of financial data?

The footnotes, however, do serve one purpose—they salve the accountant's conscience. He will say to himself that it is not his fault that the footnote did not go along with the tabulation. True, it is not his fault. But neither should he be satisfied with a footnote explanation instead of requiring the correct accounting in the financial statements themselves. If the statements were corrected, the tabulation would show a true comparison of quality without footnotes, and I am sure it would be far different.

To illustrate, among a large group of oil companies in a comparative table which I have seen recently, there are at least the different accounting practices mentioned below, which could have changed the reported income substantially as compared with the other companies listed, and in one case did change the operating results from a reported loss to a profit.

1. Some companies provide depreciation on the new accelerated declining-balance method at double the normal rates for both book and tax purposes; others use the straight-line basis for both.
2. Some companies claim accelerated depreciation for tax purposes, use straight-line on books, and properly provide for the deferred tax; others do not provide for the deferred tax.
3. Some companies charge intangible drilling costs to expense. (Such costs are deductible for income-tax purposes.) Others properly capitalize intangible drilling costs on the books. Of the companies which capitalize such drilling costs, some properly provide for the deferred tax, while others do not.
4. Some recognize that under retained oil payments they do not own the oil and, therefore, they properly exclude it and the related operations from their accounting. Others disregard the legal aspects and consider the oil payments to be only a means of financing; and they reflect the oil, the related liability and operating results in their accounts. This latter method erroneously increases the profits reported in the early periods and correspondingly reduces the profits in the later periods.

All of these varying accounting practices are excused under the name of "generally accepted principles of accounting"—an excuse that prevents the public from having the facts, but at the same time permits the certifying accountant, the insider and the specialist, to know how far off the information given to the public really is.

Corrective action should be taken by the public accountants to tighten up their ethics and practices to prevent such misleading reporting, so that the individuals who utilize and rely on the statements may have a reasonable chance to be adequately informed on their investments. If the public takes the initiative in forcing improved reporting, the power of supervision will not be left in the hands of our profession, but in government.

Can the principles be defined?

There are those who say that accounting principles cannot be defined. This is only an attempt to avoid their definition. If it were true that we could not define generally accepted principles so the public can understand us, we might as well write our certificate in a foreign language—it would serve our purpose just as well. However, the fact is that it is a simple matter to define generally accepted principles of accounting. The refinements which objectors see in the task are related to minor and unimportant matters which are of no concern to the public.

The fact that theorists see difficulty in achieving minute accuracy is merely a manifestation of the greatest weakness of the accounting mind. It has difficulty in seeing the forest because of the trees. A good illustration of this difficulty is found in the article by the director of research, American Institute of Certified Public Accountants, in the July issue of The Journal of Accountancy.

Effects of inflation

This article complains about businessmen expressing the view that depreciation accounting fails in its purpose by not recognizing price-level changes, and that accordingly the depreciation provisions are not sufficient to meet replacement costs of the plan. The article says that depreciation provisions are not intended to provide funds to cover replacement of the plant. Any businessman knows that the amortization of the cost of a Ford, even adjusted for price level, is not intended to cover the cost of replacing it with a Cadillac. What the businessmen and the public are saying is that the amortization of plant costs (depreciation) that does not recognize changes in price level does not provide them a return of their original capital, in terms of today's purchasing power, to be used toward replacement.

Replacement may mean another business, another building, or a different machine. Even if it is essentially the same machine, it is an improved model. But replacing 1940 dollars with an equal number of 1958 dollars is the same as replacing a bushel of wheat with a half bushel. The replacement in name, but not in kind, is 50 per cent short.

Charging depreciation to operations

The director's response that depreciation charged to income is intended to be an amortization of original cost holds to an outmoded accounting convention. The real reason for charging depreciation to operations is to determine the true net income after a full provision for the fair value of the capital consumed in creating that income. The present practice of providing depreciation based on cost is the rule that is rigid and meaningless as measured against the objective sought.

The public's problems with accounting are just plain everyday "bread and butter" economics. There is nothing complicated, scientific or highly mathematical about the problem.

In refuting the criticisms leveled by the businessmen and the public against original-cost depreciation accounting, which is not adjusted for price-level changes, the director goes on to show why adjustment of price level would be inconsistent with accounting for other costs. He uses the illustration of an insurance premium of $3,000 for which the renewal three years later would be $4,000, or a lease that cost $10,000 per annum for which the renewal ten years later would be $15,000. He asks whether any accountant would contend that the changes in price level of these items should be recognized as they are for depreciation. The answer to his question is yes to the extent that capital is invested in them, and if we are arguing pure theory without considering practical limits. If any accounting practice were carried out with infinite refinement and in full detail, the effort required would far outweigh its usefulness. This is not confined to accounting alone; it applies to every activity of our lives.

Unnecessary detail

The answer to the director is that theoretically all capital costs incurred for the future should be adjusted for the change in price level, but we do not desire to weigh down the substance of such a requirement with extreme detail of application. Theoretically his position would also require that, because we capitalize property costs, we must put into the plant account every picture, desk set, wastebasket and clock in the factory or office. Of course these items are capital, but they are so small we all regard them as expense because the cumulative carry-over benefit from year to year is too small to justify the cost of accounting. The director feels that we cannot recognize price-level changes for depreciation of plant involving millions and billions of dollars, which can and are being computed with a relatively nominal cost, without doing the same thing for each small item classified in deferred charges and elsewhere on the balance sheet. The director, to be consistent, could not support an accounting principle capitalizing the cost of a $25 million plant unless the principle was also applied to a $5 wastebasket.*

Accounting principles can be defined if we stop trying to make accounting into a world of its own for a group of highly trained technicians and instead, mold it into a tool to convey to the public salient and important facts which will serve them as a guide for establishing a course to follow. Accounting principles can easily be defined if we address ourselves to the purposes of accounting and not to its nonessential cost-creating details. Public accountants can write and speak eloquently about accounting principles in textbooks, brochures and speeches, and then resort to some inner urge known only to them in applying these principles.

The facts are that the judgment required should apply primarily to the presentation and in determining when detailed procedures have gone far enough and the cost of bookkeeping outweighs its usefulness. It just doesn't make sense to tell the public that professional skill is required to determine that Fifo presents the financial position better in one company and Lifo in another;

---

* Ed. Note: *Comment on the foregoing paragraphs referring to the American Institute's director of research will to be found in* Accounting and Auditing Problems, *p. 73.*

or that one company should capitalize intangible drilling cost but another should charge it to expense; or that one company should provide for deferred tax and another does not have to; or that all companies except railroads should capitalize major property costs but railroads do not have to. The decisions as to which of these accounting practices are followed are made by the client (company), and the public accountant must approve them or lose his client. There is no independence of position by the public accountant in such cases. Let us not read into the profession some self-serving lingo that makes us feel as if we are possessed with some divine knowledge of accounting principles, when it is not so.

Basic concepts

If we were to examine the concepts adopted by our profession as the basis for accounting principles, we could be well satisfied. Let us take Accounting Research Bulletin 43, for instance. Here are the definitions of accounting as published by the profession, with which no one could find substantive objection. (Italics supplied.)

> 1. Accounting is essential to the effective functioning of any business organization, particularly the corporate form. The test of the corporate system and of the special phase of it represented by corporate *accounting ultimately lies in the results which are produced. These results must be judged from the standpoint of society as a whole—not merely from that of any one group of interested persons.*

Then the first sentence of item 2 reads:

> 2. The uses to which the corporate system is put and the controls to which it is subject change from time to time, and all parts of the *machinery must be adapted to meet changes as they occur.*

Item 3, same page, says:

> 3. *The fairest possible presentation of periodic net income, with neither material overstatement nor understatement, is important, since the results of operations are significant not only to prospective buyers of an interest in the enterprise but also to prospective sellers.*

Then item 4 reads as follows:

> 4. *This evolution has also led to a demand for a larger degree of uniformity in accounting.* Uniformity has usually connoted similar treatment of the same item occurring in many cases, in which sense it runs the risk of concealing important differences among cases. Another sense of the word would require that different authorities working independently on the same case should reach the same conclusions. Although uniformity is a worthwhile goal, it should not be pursued to the exclusion of other benefits. Changes of emphasis and objective as well as changes in conditions under which business operates have led, and doubtless will continue to lead, to the adoption of new accounting procedures. Consequently diversity of practice may continue as new practices are adopted before old ones are completely discarded.

These objective standards or postulates of accounting principles are good, and if they were followed, 95 per cent of the misstatement of fact in financial statements would disappear. The other 5 per cent is less than the degree of accuracy that can be obtained under any principles. However, these standards must have been written only for the record and for window dressing, because nowhere in the decisions on principles followed is it stated that these were the guides used, nor does it say how the decisions arrived at were obtained from or based on these guides. Even if these standards could not be applied in all cases, the committee on accounting procedure could have stated in its decisions where the standards were not followed, and why not. Let me analyze two situations.

Tax allocation

After more than a year's work, the American Institute's Research Bulletin 44, recently issued on a revised basis, requires the recognition of deferred taxes (if material) in those cases where companies take advantage of accelerated depreciation for tax purposes, but provide lesser amounts on the books. This bulletin replaces the original ARB 44 issued in 1954 when the problem originally arose under the 1954 Internal Revenue Code.

The original bulletin approved several practices that were contrary to the basis of accounting defined above under standards Nos. 1, 2, 3 and 4; and original bulletin ARB 44 was in contravention of chapter 10(b), paragraph 4. As recently revised, ARB 44 was brought into agreement with these objective standards on which it should have been based in the first instance. As originally issued, it avoided saying how it could possibly conform to the standards of accounting principles contained in ARB 43. As a consequence, it misled many businesses into adopting reporting practices which misrepresented earnings available for dividends for several years. Now these companies are having to change their accounting and many are doing it retroactively. Thus, a system of decision-making within the profession, set up to narrow the alternative practices, was used to establish alternative methods. We cannot achieve properly defined accounting principles if we deliberately set out to define them incorrectly.

ARB 44, as revised, carries the dissents of some members of the accounting procedure committee who are opposed to deferred tax accounting. They should dissent from the premises of accounting principles quoted above rather than from the accounting set forth in the bulletin that conforms to these premises. Like a judge, it is the duty of the committee members to make decisions in accordance with the law (in this case, the premises) not how they think the law (or the premises) should be written.

But this is not the end of the road of inconsistencies traveled by ARB 44. As revised, it contains an exception (paragraph 8) which says in substance that utilities need not provide for deferred taxes "if it may reasonably be expected" that such deferred taxes can be collected from customers in the future. This exception violates each of the premises listed above, and it violates the basic premise of utility rate making that the ratepayers of the future cannot be required to pay costs attributable to serving present consumers. Furthermore, the above standard (reasonable expectancy of future collection) in ARB 44 (Revised) for omitting provision for deferred taxes cannot be met, because it is in fact *not* reasonable to expect future customers to pay the cost of serving present consumers, and no regulatory commission can so bind future commissions as to give reasonable assurance of future collection.

It is appropriate, however, under these circumstances to ask why this exception (paragraph 8) was included in ARB 44 (Revised). Here again we have a failure in professional responsibility by the committee members who assented to its issuance. This exception was inserted in the bulletin at the last moment and the committee had no opportunity to study or investigate its meaning or import; no statement of the reasons for its insertion has been made and justifiable reasons for the inclusion of this exception are not apparent.

Defining accounting principles

This exception with respect to utilities in the bulletin's requirements further facilitates overstatement of profits, and it again encourages alternative accounting practices. But what is even more serious is that this exception opens the way for the contention that this bulletin establishes the principle that if, in future selling prices, a company can "reasonably expect" to collect the costs applicable to present sales, no provision need be made for present costs on an annual basis. There is no reason why these special-privilege departures in defining accounting principles could not be avoided, if the profession is in fact independent and desires to report the truth to the public. If the profession is independent and wants to speak the truth, accounting principles can be defined.

So long as the accounting profession cannot recognize accounting principles where they are highly important to the public welfare and at the same time ignore their application to immaterial items, the professional accountant will continue to stumble over his own feet.

Long-term lease obligations

Another illustration of this adherence to technical details and outmoded practices within the profession is its failure to recognize the corporate obligation imposed by long-term leases. Leases originally were not important in corporate affairs; usually they related to office space or to small plants or equipment and ran for relatively short periods. In recent times, however, long-term leases have come to be used as a means of financing plant expansion and additions. These leases carry enormous commitments payable over long periods of time. And of course there also exists the related asset—the right of occupancy or use.

There is no more reason to omit this asset and the corresponding liability in the case of a long-term lease than there is to omit both the plant and the debt when the plant is financed by borrowed money. However, since it was accepted practice not to record lease obligations when they were unimportant, the profession continued the same practice when the lease obligations became significant.

These lease obligations have become so important to financial institutions which loan money for long periods that loan agreements and trust indentures are now being written to require that, in computing indebtedness for measuring indenture restrictions, the rents under such leases must be capitalized and included in long-term debt. Yet the accounting profession goes along ignoring these lease obligations completely except for an occasional footnote that is meaningless.

Here again judgment must be used by the accountant in the computation, but the decisions in such cases are directly related to the importance of the item involved. While accountants with their technical point of view argue about difficulties and dilemmas, the borrower and the lender solve the problem in a practical way, as illustrated in Exhibit I. But the public stockholder who should also be informed of these obligations, which are senior to the equity, and who relies on his representative, the public accountant, to advise him, continues to remain in the dark as to what these obligations are.

While the public accountant looks for reasons why accounting principles cannot be defined, others less qualified go ahead and do the job; therefore, the job can be done when the desire and the will to do it exist.

Exhibit I

Extracts from Indenture

Limitation on funded indebtedness. The company will not create, guarantee or otherwise become liable for any funded indebtedness if, after giving effect thereto, the funded indebtedness will exceed 50 per cent of net tangible assets.

Definition of "funded indebtedness." "Funded indebtedness" shall include, at any date, all indebtedness which has a final maturity more than one year after such date, and shall also include capitalized rent under all restricted leases.

Definition of "restricted lease." "Restricted lease" shall mean any arrangement with any lender or investor, providing for the leasing by the company of any property which (a) has been sold or transferred by the company to such lender or investor, or to any person to whom funds have been advanced by such lender or investor on the security of such property, or (b) has been acquired from another person by such lender or investor, or by any person to whom funds have been advanced by such lender or investor on the security of such property, for the purpose of leasing such property to the company.

Definition of "capitalized rent." "Capitalized rent" under any restricted lease shall mean, at any time as of which the amount thereof is to be determined, fifteen times the maximum aggregate amount of the net rental obligations under such lease in respect to which the company will be liable in any period of twelve consecutive months subsequent to such time; provided, however, that, in case the aggregate of the net rental obligations provided for in said lease to be paid during the original term thereof discounted at the rate of 6 per cent shall be at least equal to the value of the leased premises at the beginning of such term (as determined at any time by the board of directors) capitalized rent may, at the option of the company, be deemed to be the aggregate of the remaining net rental obligations under said original term of the lease discounted at the rate of 6 per cent.

Definition of "net tangible assets." "Net tangible assets" shall mean (1) the value of all property both real and personal (exclusive of patents, trademarks, copyrights, goodwill, etc.) after deducting all proper reserves, less (2) the current liabilities and any reserves for deferred taxes on income provided, however, that in computing net tangible assets there shall be included as an asset the capitalized rent on all restricted leases.

Definition of "current liabilities." "Current liabilities" shall include, at any date, all liabilities which would, in accordance with generally accepted accounting principles, be classified as current liabilities, but in any event including all indebtedness, whether secured or unsecured, payable on demand or maturing not more than one year after such date (other than capitalized rent).

EDWARD STAMP

Establishing Accounting Principles

An essential preliminary to a rational discussion of this topic is the definition of what is meant by 'accounting principles'. Before attempting to define the term, it may be useful to indicate what is specifically excluded. Thus, at least for the purposes of this paper, the term 'accounting principles' is not regarded as meaning

(a) the rules, systems, procedures, etc., associated with the processes of book-keeping;

(b) the rules and procedures associated with a National Code of Accounts, despite the fact that in some European countries such rules and procedures *are* regarded as an integral part of the principles of accounting;

(c) professional codes of ethics, however important these may be in the practice of accountancy;

(d) commonly accepted requirements, which may vary from one jurisdiction to another, governing accounting presentation and disclosure. Such requirements are of course extremely important, and indeed 'full disclosure' must be regarded as a fundamental prerequisite to the presentation of 'a true and fair view';[1]

(e) questions of terminology. Once again, such matters are of considerable importance and it is plainly necessary to define concepts with precision. 'Accounting principles' are clearly involved with concepts, but presumably once the principles have been established the concepts will necessarily have been defined.

In the context of this paper 'accounting principles' are thought of as *that corpus of logically self-consistent concepts which form the basis of measurements used in accounting reports which are to be relevant to the needs of users.*

This definition is concerned with the output of an accounting information system and it specifies that that output should be relevant to the needs of its users. It is this aspect of the problem upon which attention ought to be focused, not on the nature or the type of information system employed by the accounting entity. Thus, although the electronic computer gives accountants added capacity and flexibility in designing information systems, the existence of the computer cannot and will not solve the accounting principles problem. Accounting principles are concerned with ends rather than with means.

It is clear that the definition given is not merely concerned with financial

1. It should be noted that present practice generally involves 'full disclosure' on the historical cost basis. There is no 'full disclosure' of current values. This surely begs a fundamental question of principle, and it is difficult to reconcile such disclosure practices with the alleged presentation of 'a true and fair view'.

PROFESSOR STAMP is Head of the Department of Accounting and Business Method in the University of Edinburgh.

accounting. It is a peculiarity of modern accounting thought that financial accounting and management accounting are frequently segregated, as if they existed in two separate and watertight compartments. Yet both branches of the discipline ought to be based upon the same set of principles, and concepts such as present value and opportunity cost are, or ought to be, as fundamental to the solution of financial accounting problems as they are to the solution of problems in management accounting. A dichotomy does exist in practice however, and, all too frequently, soundly based proposals made by management accountants (e.g., in the field of replacement decision-making) are rejected by a (senior) financial accountant employing concepts that are quite irrelevant to the decision which has to be made.

Bearing all of this in mind, we shall nevertheless concentrate on the problems of financial accounting (i.e., of reporting to outsiders rather than to insiders) since this is the general orientation of this conference.

As stated earlier, it is presumed that the accountant is operating in an environment where full disclosure is an accepted policy. This is the case in most English-speaking countries, but it should be noted that in many European countries concealment rather than disclosure is the general rule in the preparation of financial accounting reports, even of public companies. Secret reserves are common in Switzerland and Germany, consolidated accounts are virtually unknown in France, and in Italy the process of profit determination and disclosure is flexible indeed.

It should also be noted that the definition of accounting principles implies a concern with the process of *measurement*. Accountants are concerned with the problems of the determination of the value parameters implied by any given concepts of value, income, etc. In making such determinations or measurements accountants are inevitably involved with the process of estimation, since in the final analysis the value of any asset is dependent upon what will happen to it in the future. Measurement processes also involve problems of allocation, and in some cases (for example in the costing of joint products) the process of allocation may be arbitrary.[2] One must also consider, when making accounting measurements, the problems of objectivity and verifiability of the measurements made. The profession will have to accept that if there is to be an improvement in the relevance of accounting measurements to the needs of users there may have to be a trade-off with objectivity and verifiability. As one American writer has noted, it is better to be approximately right than to be precisely wrong. This suggests the desirability of disclosing the estimated precision and reliability of accounting measurements, instead of encouraging the reader to assume that the figures in financial statements contain no 'margin of error'.[3]

2. Whether allocation should be attempted in such cases is another matter.

3. It has become the practice in Britain recently for leading practitioners to complain that laymen fail to realize that accounting measurements are not exact. Such remarks are intended as a defence against criticisms of the shortcomings of financial accounts. The fault surely lies not in the eyes of the lay beholders but in the published financial accounts, which fail to disclose the existence of inexactitudes of measurement.

The development of contemporary 'principles'

It was stated above that management accounting and financial accounting ought properly to be based upon the same set of fundamental accounting principles. Yet, whereas the development of management accountancy has been a relatively tranquil process, developments in the field of financial accounting have been surrounded by great controversy over the years. It is perhaps instructive to consider briefly why this is so.

The information needs which are supposed to be supplied by modern financial accountancy have evolved as a result of the rapid growth of enterprises since the Industrial Revolution. The vast appetite of the modern corporation for capital has resulted in the well-known phenomenon of the divorce of ownership from management, and the development of capital and securities markets. Since the average shareholder is neither entitled to see nor competent to understand the books of the enterprises in which he owns shares, and since he clearly has a right to know how 'his' enterprise is being managed and how it fares financially, he is entitled, under the law, to receive periodic reports on its financial condition and progress from the management. Reports made by management to shareholders in this way are normally examined by auditors in order to lend credibility to their contents.

It is not necessary to dwell at any length on the reasons why the reports might lack credibility, in the absence of an auditor's examination and report. The matter has been thoroughly discussed elsewhere.[4] Suffice it to say that the interests of management are often in conflict with those of outsiders, in particular with those of shareholders. However, although the auditor reports his opinion of the financial accounts, the responsibility for the preparation of such accounts rests entirely with the management, and management has been given a very free hand in determining the accounting measurement rules employed in preparation of financial accounts. As new situations develop management generally decides for itself how best to measure and report the changed conditions, and the auditor has traditionally adopted the passive role of accepting management's measurements provided he thinks they present 'a true and fair view'. As a result, numerous different, and often inconsistent, accounting measurement rules have been adopted and accepted in practice. The role of the professional accounting bodies has largely been to codify such rules from time to time and attempt to generalize them, as best they can, into 'principles'.

Thus the development of financial accounting principles has, in its active phase at least, been the prerogative of management. The rules and measurement techniques employed by management accountants have developed in a similar fashion, but in this case the rules are employed in the preparation of internal reports which are directed to and used exclusively by the management itself. No conflict of interest is involved, and it is therefore not too surprising that there has not been a great deal of controversy over the development of management accounting rules.

4. *See*, for example, Charles E. Johnson, 'Management and Accounting Principles', *Law and Contemporary Problems*, Autumn 1965.

Nor is it surprising, perhaps, that such rules have employed concepts, such as opportunity cost, which are clearly relevant to the needs of the user — since the user is management itself. Although the same concepts are appropriate in the development and preparation of financial accounting reports, the incentive to use them is lacking, since management is generally much less concerned with the relevance of its reports to shareholders than it is with the relevance of reports prepared for management itself. Thus whilst management, in its own decision-making processes, might well employ estimates of current values, it is quite content to continue submitting reports to shareholders (and other outsiders) based upon historical cost, a basis which in many cases is supremely irrelevant to the needs of the shareholders.

Professional recommendations and their value

The result of this process over the years has been the accumulation of a large set of pragmatically developed measurement rules and procedures, coupled with attempts to formulate generalizations known as 'generally accepted accounting principles'. The multiplicity of the rules, and their general irrelevance,[5] has inevitably led to the present situation where the whole structure of financial accounting is falling into disrepute. Professional bodies of accountants in the English-speaking countries have been attempting to deal with this situation for over a generation, and they seem as far from a solution now as they did when they began. Most of the attempts have consisted of the issuance of recommendations, bulletins, or opinions, which have attempted to 'narrow the areas of difference' and hence reduce the multiplicity of accounting principles. Such an approach has been strongly criticized by Professor W. T. Baxter, notably in an article published in *The Accountant*.[6] Baxter's main grounds for objecting to the issuance of recommendations seem to be as follows:

(1) He fears that participation by 'authority' in the process of determining accounting principles will restrict freedom of thought and experiment in the development of principles.

(2) He feels that there is, in any event, no sure way of recognizing the truth. Thus as he points out, the Royal Society does not solve the problems of physics by setting up committees and making pronouncements on what the laws of physics are or should be.

(3) The issuance of recommendations inevitably narrows the scope for individual thought and judgment on the part of the accountant.

Although I have sympathy with some of Baxter's apprehensions, I am afraid that freedom of thought and experiment in developing accounting principles has, in the hands of management, often been treated as a licence to disregard the information needs of investors. It is not at all clear that a *laissez-faire* approach is necessarily the best way of reaching truth in financial reporting.

I also believe that one can fall into error if one attempts too close an analogy

5. Based, as they almost invariably are, upon historical cost measures.

6. 'Recommendations on Accounting Theory', *The Accountant*, 10 October, 1953, pp. 405-10.

between the development of accountancy and the development of one of the natural sciences such as physics. The natural sciences deal with an objective and lifeless world where consent and agreement are unnecessary in establishing the theories or principles governing the behaviour of atoms etc. It seems to me that a better analogy is with the development of the principles of legal jurisprudence. The law is concerned essentially with the evolutionary development of human situations in which consent and agreement between parties are sought within the framework of a general sense of values. Lawyers attempt to secure their objectives in part by defining a basic conceptual structure of jurisprudence. It seems to me that accounting principles are also likely to be developed on an evolutionary rather than upon an axiomatic basis. Even the most basic concepts, such as those of profit and of value, will, I suspect, be found to depend to some degree on environmental conditions — e.g., on whether one is concerned with entities operating in a capitalist or in a communist frame of reference.

To say this is not to deny the importance of logic in the development of accounting principles, any more than one can deny the place of logic in the development of the principles of jurisprudence. It is clearly necessary that accounting principles should be internally consistent amongst themselves, and logic will be necessary to ensure that accounting principles lead to reports which are relevant to the real world, and which enable valid comparisons to be made between companies and over extended time periods.

The form of future developments

How then should one go about establishing accounting principles?

In the first place I believe that this task cannot be performed by a government committee, or even by a government commission operating on a permanent basis, although each may sometimes play a useful role in prodding the profession into action. Nor do I believe that accounting principles can or should be established, or even consolidated, in the form of legislation. In my view the establishment of accounting principles is the responsibility of the accounting profession.[7]

Although measurement problems will be important, as we have already noted, they should not be allowed to dominate the scene. Measurement problems are essentially practical and empirical in nature, whereas the important and fundamental problem is to define what it is that one is trying to measure. Deciding this involves mental abstractions, speculative thought, the construction of concepts, and the process of disputation. Indeed, we must first of all settle whether or not we believe that accounting principles are axiomatic or evolutionary in their nature. Until this point has been settled the task can scarcely begin.[8]

As I have already made clear, I believe that accounting principles are evolutionary in nature since they deal with the measurement of conditions in a changing,

7. These points are argued at length in Edward Stamp and Christopher Marley, *Accounting Principles and the City Code: The Case for Reform*, Butterworth, London 1970, especially Chapter 15.

8. This of course implies, in one sense at least, an axiomatic approach!

evolving world. Accordingly, I believe that a teleological approach is necessary in their development. The needs of the user of financial reports must be dominant in determining what goes into such reports, and clearly user needs will vary with time and place. It is necessary to define who are the users of financial reports, and what decisions they are reasonably likely to make on the basis of such reports. In this way one ought to be able to determine the general information needs of users and hence the required information content of the reports submitted to them. This may entail the preparation of different reports for different users. This already accounts for the distinction between management accounting and financial accounting reports.

Clearly a wide range of information is necessary for most users, and it is necessary to define the spectrum of information which is likely to be required. It is also desirable to define how much of this information can be presented in its 'raw' form, and how much of the information should be processed before presentation and in what manner. The dominant requirement is surely that the reports should provide information *relevant* to the needs of the user; it seems obvious that current financial accounting reports, based on historical cost, are not relevant.

In my opinion a single-value approach to financial accounting reports will be found to be insufficient. Indeed, quite apart from anything else, the problems of measurement (already referred to above) seem to make it essential to indicate, in accounting reports, the probable range of values within which the 'true' value lies. Even if one supplied several different sets of accounts drawn up on different bases, e.g., replacement costs, net realizable value, etc., a 'range' would be necessary for most figures contained in the several reports simply because of the difficulties of measurement and estimation.

It is quite clear that, if accounting principles are to be developed and established in accordance with such a pattern, a considerable amount of research will be necessary, and much of this research will have to be of a behavioural nature. We must attempt to define the *utility* of accounts if we are to construct them properly. In the meantime the general inutility of financial accounts is evident from the following statements by the Institute of Chartered Accountants in England and Wales.

> A balance sheet does not purport to show the realisable value of assets. . . . A balance sheet is not a statement of the net worth of the undertaking. . . .[9]
> The results shown by accounts prepared on the basis of historical cost are not a measure of the increase or decrease in wealth in terms of purchasing power; nor do the results necessarily represent the amount which can prudently be regarded as available for distribution, having regard to the financial requirements of the business. Similarly the results shown by such accounts are not necessarily suitable for purposes such as price-fixing, wage negotiations and taxation, unless in using them for these purposes due regard is paid to the amount of profit which has been retained in the business for its maintenance. . . .[10]

9. The Institute of Chartered Accountants in England and Wales (hereafter ICAEW), *Recommendations on Accounting Principles N 18.*

10. ICAEW *Recommendation N 15.*

> The purpose for which annual accounts are normally prepared is not to enable individual shareholders to take investment decisions. . . .[11]

These quotations make it clear that the senior professional body in Britain has been engaged for years in recommending 'accounting principles' which produce financial accounts having little if any relevance to some of the more obvious needs of users. The process is reminiscent of Greek science; the philosophers speculated without reference to the facts of the real world, which they regarded as irrelevant to their speculations.

At the same time, if accountancy must concern itself more with the facts of the environment, it must also be more concerned with the value of speculative thought. The conceptual structure of conventional accountancy shows very little evidence of any recognition of the value either of abstract, theoretical, speculative reasoning power, or of the pragmatic utility of tying down one's concepts to the needs of the workaday world.

Evolutionary development

It seems therefore that, for the establishment of accounting principles,

(a) empirical research is necessary in order to determine the nature of the information which financial accounts should contain;

(b) a conceptual framework must be constructed, including concepts of income and value which will result in measurements relevant to the observed needs of users;

(c) there must be a continual testing of the environment so as to detect inadequacies of accounting thought and practice, along with changes in environmental conditions, necessitating evolutionary changes in principles so that accounting adapts to the changed circumstances.

Steps (a) and (b) have yet to be taken, let alone completed. It might perhaps be argued that the current conventional structure of accountancy represents a completed structure developed to meet the needs of a bygone age. Indeed, there is probably a good deal of truth in such a contention since historical cost accounts were probably quite adequate for the purposes of owners and creditors in the days of small-scale 'cottage' industry. But if accountancy is not to suffer the fate of the Brontosaurus, it must learn to adapt to changing conditions, and an evolutionary mechanism must be built into the process of establishing and evolving accounting principles. In my view a mechanism which might perform this function very effectively is the institution of an 'Accounting Court'. I have argued the case for this elsewhere[12] and the reasoning will not be developed here. But if such an institution, in one form or another, is accepted, then it is possible to visualize the life-cycle of an accounting principle somewhat in the following form.

11. ICAEW *Miscellaneous Technical Statements S 8.*

12. Edward Stamp, 'The Public Accountant and the Public Interest', *The Journal of Business Finance* Vol. 1, Spring 1969. Also dealt with by the author in Australian Society of Accountants Endowed Lecture, University of Sydney, 30 August, 1966.

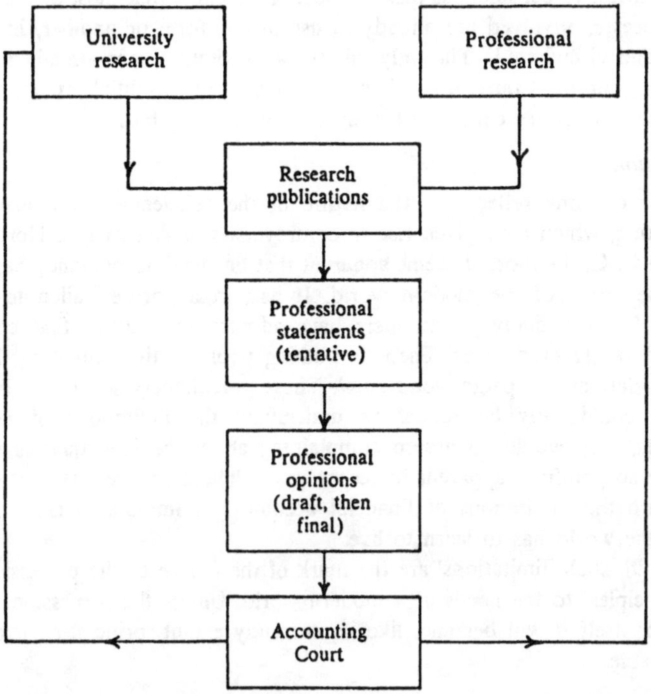

Empirical and speculative research would be conducted in the universities and in the research divisions of the professional institutes. As a result of such research, studies would be published and these would form the basis of debates within the professional and academic communities. Eventually the designated committee of the professional body (e.g., the Accounting Principles Board in the United States) would issue a tentative statement on the various issues under debate, and this statement would then be followed by an Opinion, in the form of an exposure draft, setting out the manner in which the problems should be dealt with in practice (supported by a statement of the theoretical principles underlying the recommendation). Once the exposure draft had been properly discussed a full-scale Opinion would ensue and this would then constitute the most up-to-date authoritative recommendation on the subject. As time passed the merits and demerits of the Opinion, and the underlying theoretical principles, would be tested by experience. In all contentious cases this experience would be funnelled through the Accounting Court which would have the function of interpreting Opinions, and of commissioning further research by the Research Division and the universities when it appeared that principles and practice were getting out of line with changing environmental conditions. And so the cycle would begin once more.

It seems to me that it is only by a process such as this that one can hope to produce a framework of accounting principles which is capable of evolutionary development. A conspicuous merit of such a system is that most of the institutions and processes involved are already in use in one form or another, in the United States and elsewhere.[13] The only additional institution, not already in existence, is the Accounting Court. It is this which provides the essential process of feedback from the environment into the system on a continuing basis.

Conclusion

The more one reflects on the nature of the deficiencies in modern financial accounting, which have given rise to controversies in Australasia, North America, and the U.K., the more it seems apparent that financial accountancy has lost touch with the needs of the modern world. It has, in a phrase, failed to adapt and evolve. Far too many practitioners have adopted an attitude that can be summarized rather crudely as 'There is nothing wrong with accounting that a good public relations campaign won't cure'. These practitioners seem to believe that, if laymen could only be taught to understand the limitations of conventional accounts, they would soon stop complaining about the inadequacies which have become so painfully apparent in recent years. These professional apologists seem to regard the 'limitations of financial accounts' as immutable facts of life with which the world has to learn to live.

In truth such 'limitations' are the mark of the failure of the profession to adapt its 'principles' to the needs of a modern world. Unless the profession soon learns to adapt itself it will become, like its currently extant 'principles', irrelevant and dispensable.

13. Mainly in the United States. British research is still only minimal, and the British equivalent of the Accounting Principles Board (the 'Accounting Standards Steering Committee') has only recently been set up.

Suggested additional readings

* Chambers, R. J., "Measurement and Misrepresentation," **Management Science**, January 1960, pp. 141–48.

If there is any work that typifies the normative response to accounting anomalies in the conventional system, it is that of Chambers. This particular paper concentrates on the ability of conventional accounting to misrepresent the financial performance and position of reporting entities.

* Coughlan, J. W., "Accounting and Capital Budgeting," **The Business Quarterly**, Fall 1962, pp. 39–48.

Coughlan is one of the first writers to be concerned with the anomaly of *ex post* financial reporting not being in cash flow terms compatible with the *ex ante* basis for taking investment decisions in business.

* Garner, P., "The Development of Accounting Principles and Standards," in Garner, P. and Berg, K. B. (eds.), **Readings in Accounting Theory** (Boston: Houghton Mifflin, 1966), pp. 95–109.

This is a very readable paper which deals with the development of generally accepted accounting principles, and the issues which relate to their formulation and interpretation. It is a good example of the concern in the accountancy profession over anomalies which are noticed only gradually in accounting practice.

* Moonitz, M., "The Basic Postulates of Accounting," **Accounting Research Study 1** (New York: American Institute of Certified Public Accountants, 1961).

This study represents one of the first institutional responses to the unease in the 1950s and 1960s regarding the lack of a theoretical structure to support generally accepted accounting principles.

* Thomas, A. L., "The Allocation Problem," **Studies in Accounting Research 3** (Evanston: American Accounting Association, 1969).

This is a classic study of one of the most persistent of accounting anomalies— the need to decompose specific transactions over several periods or entities according to perceptions of service received. This anomaly is the stimulus for many of the arguments for cash flow accounting.

INITIAL AND EXTENDED CASH FLOW REPORTING ARGUMENTS

Introduction

One of the least discussed responses to the initial period of unease about the conventional financial reporting system was cash flow accounting. Most of the literature concerning theories and prescriptions to resolve the problems of historical cost accounting has focused on matters relating to accounting for general and specific price changes. Cash flow accounting has occupied a less prominent but none-the-less important place in the so-called golden age of accounting theory.

Cash flow accounting theory was originally argued by Lawson and Lee at the end of the 1960s and beginning of the 1970s. Working independently and, in the case of Lawson, publishing in predominantly non-accounting sources, the idea of reporting cash flows ex ante and ex post emerged. *Lawson*'s (1970) ideas can be seen to be firmly based in classical economic theory and, specifically, the investment decision model. His reporting system is aimed at disclosing actual and forecast cash flows sufficient to assist the investor to predict a future dividend stream. In fact, Lawson specifies the reporting company as a cash flow model, emphasising residual cash flow after deductions of new investment and tax payments. This residual was to become a focal point for his later arguments on the merits of cash flow accounting. The most important factor in his work, however, is the specification of reporting priorities in terms of the needs of the anticipated information consumer.

Lee (1972) also took this approach, arguing the need for both past and forecast data, and for cash flow accounting to be in addition to rather than instead of the conventional reporting system. Lee also tended to make more of the opportunity to specify a normative theoretical argument based on a wide range of decision needs (not just investment), the importance of cash and cash flow to the survival of the reporting entity, and the need for reliable (objective) information. Lee's system is specified as including forecast and actual data, decomposed financial statements, and explanations of reporting assumptions and variances.

These early ideas were commented on by a relatively few researchers. *Climo* (1976) is one such case, again emphasising the importance of satisfying report user needs. Thus, if anything consistent can be found in the early cash flow accounting ideas, it is that the major anomaly of the failure of conventional accounting to satisfy the information needs of users (particularly, as in the case of Climo, investor needs). He especially points out the need for forecast data, and the isolation of recurrent and non-recurrent cash flows.

The second paper of *Lawson* (1978) is an example of how he developed his arguments for cash flow accounting in the 1970s and 1980s. The framework is still based and dependent on economic argument and theory, and largely concerned with investors. However, he is also seen to be concerned with entity valuation, the dividend versus retention question, the tax burden on entities, and the need to avoid financial crises in business. He sees cash flow accounting providing information to assist in each of these areas.

Lee (1981) also extended his original ideas on cash flow accounting, largely as an attempt to respond to (usually) oral comment regarding the need for performance reporting, but also because of further thinking about the need for an improved theory of cash flow accounting. The second Lee paper reproduced below outlines the results of that further thinking, and defines a system of financial reporting which is based on the compatibility of the arguments underlying the original cash flow accounting prescriptions and exit price systems of reporting. The consequence of this melting of ideas is a cash flow-based system which links actual cash flows with cash flow equivalents, and provides measures of liquidity, profitability and financial position sufficient to allow a full financial performance assessment of the reporting entity.

The ideas of both Lawson and Lee appear to have had some impact on thinking outside the UK by the late 1970s. The AICPA study by *Lloyd* (1978) is a significant example of this. It concerns a detailed investigation of the nature, role and utility of the conventional accruals-based funds statement. He criticises the confusing and misleading nature of such a statement, particularly with respect to the common confusion between profit and cash flow. Consistent with previous writings reproduced in this text, Lloyd prescribed a system of cash flow reporting based on user needs for information relating to the reporting entity's operating, investing and financing activities. In other words, what can be seen at this point in the evolution of cash flow accounting ideas is the transformation by accounting standard-setters of the original prescriptions into more practical proposals for reporting reform. The precise nature of this reform will be discussed in a later section of this text.

* Climo, T. A., "Cash Flow Statements for Investors," **Journal of Business Finance and Accounting**, Autumn 1976, pp. 3-16

* Heath, L. C., "Let's Scrap the 'Funds' Statement," **Journal of Accountancy**, October 1978, pp. 94-103.

* Lawson, G. H., "Cash Flow Accounting," **The Accountant**, 28 October and 4 November, 1970, pp. 386-69 and 620-22

* Lawson, G. H., "The Rationale of Cash Flow Accounting," in C. van Dam (ed.), **Trends in Managerial and Financial Accounting** (Boston: Martinus Nijhoff, 1978, Vol.1), pp. 85-104

* Lee, T. A., "A Case for Cash Flow Reporting"' **Journal of Business Finance**, Summer 1972, pp. 27-36

* Lee, T. A., "Reporting Cash Flows and Net Realisable Values," **Accounting and Business Research**, Spring 1981, pp. 98-105

CASH FLOW STATEMENTS FOR INVESTORS

T.A. CLIMO*

Beginning from the current emphasis that the usefulness of accounting information is contingent on the identification of a specific group of receivers, their objectives and decisions, cash flow statements are examined in the context of the investor in Limited Companies. An investor's decision model is used which clarifies the type of information a cash flow statement should contain. A major departure from other literature on cash flow statements is its non-interlocking but meaningful relationship with the income and financial position statements.

INTRODUCTION

Recently, there have been three related and hopeful signs for financial accounting. Accounting standards are thought to demand recognition that:

(1) prior to their issue, agreement is reached on "the fundamental objects and principles of periodic financial statements";[1]

(2) the fundamental object must be the communication of information;[2]

(3) information "must be appropriate to its expected use by the potential users".[3]

Accounting statements are not now thought to be adjudged by as vague a criterion as truth and fairness. Statements are either useful or not useful for the purpose for which they are prepared. This purpose is to communicate information about an organisation to interested parties (users) so that they may make decisions commensurate with satisfying their objectives. Accounting, like any service activity, has as its objective the provision of a service designed to satisfy someone else's objectives.

This criterion of usefulness has two strands : information that is used and information that is useful. The accountant should attempt to ensure that the information used is useful, but this may not be the case.[4] The accountant should investigate the user's needs and give him information which is relevant to satisfy those needs. Ideally, the user will use that amount of information without which a rational decision could not be made.[5] Such is the upper limit of information provided by the accountant.[6]

**The author is Lecturer in Accounting at the University of Kent at Canterbury.*
(Paper received May 1975, revised August 1975)

Journal of Business Finance & Accounting, 3,3(1976) 3

It is therefore a prerequisite of any examination of cash flow statements or any other proposed formal statement that the expected users of these statements are specified along with their objectives and the decisions they are likely to make. A necessary preliminary is to specify the type of entity being examined and the groups of individuals interested in its activities. It is erroneous to infer either that one group of individuals is indicative of the others or useful information for one group is necessarily useful to the others. Usefulness must stand the test of the particular informational demands of a particular group of interested individuals.

CASH FLOW STATEMENTS FOR INVESTORS

With this in mind, we begin by delineating our enquiry to examine the requirements of existing and/or potential investors in Limited Companies incorporated under the United Kingdom Companies Acts. Investors are parties who provide finance for companies. Specifically, they include equity and preference shareholders, debenture holders, and loan creditors. This is not to exclude recognition of interested parties other than investors; rather it specifies one particular group of users. Although most of the examples below will be drawn from shareholders, similar – yet different – examples could be used that are relevant to other types of investors.

The objective of investors is to consume in a manner which suits their particular wants (buying a second house, providing for a son's education, leaving a large estate, etc.). Fundamental to this consumption is the receipt of cash flows from various sources – employer, government and investment. Cash flows from the latter will be through periodic payments and/or realisation of the investment.

The investor, following this reasoning, makes decisions regarding the acceptability of cash flows arising from an investment. These decisions take the form of investment – whether to buy, subscribe, loan or grant credit – or disinvestment – whether to sell or claim repayment. It may also involve decisions as to the appointment of directors, receivers or liquidators.

The acceptability of a cash flow is determined by the investor (and not the accountant) according to whether he will be able to obtain the satisfaction he wants with it. A man who wants £10,000 to retire on in twenty years is ill-advised to invest his £1,000 in anything which earns a compound interest of less than 12%.[7] A need becomes established for information to be communicated to investors which informs them of the cash flows they may expect to receive from investment in a company.

It is always convenient, after citing a group of users, their objectives and the decisions they are likely to make, to impute a decision model to depict the user's decision-making process.[8] This enables the type of information that is needed to be clarified and the range of such information to be delimited.

We impute that investors invest when $P \leqslant V$ and disinvest when $P \geqslant V$, where P is the current price of the investment and V the investor's valuation of the investment. The price includes the market or issue price, or the amount offered in repayment of shares or loans in settlement of debts. The valuation is assumed to be determined by discounting the future cash flows expected by the investor at a rate of interest acceptable to him. Therefore, in the valuation model below, although the accountant should provide the investor with information relating to C, he should not provide information relating to r or n.

$$V = \sum_{j=1}^{n} \frac{C_j}{(1+r)^j}$$

where V = the investor's valuation of the investment;
C = the future cash flow from the investment expected by the investors;
r = the investor's acceptable rate of interest;
n = the time horizon of the investor.

The expected cash flows are thus equivalent to a return on V equal to annual interest at the rate r and with the repayment of V at time n.[9]

It is important here to distinguish the cash flows expected by the investor (C) from the cash flows expected to be paid to the investor by management. Ideally, the two will be the same. However, as I said above, the accountant attempts to provide information relating to C, and this may not be C itself. Management's expectations of payments to investors is as close to C as the accountant may come. If an investor prefers to apply, say, some certainty-equivalent factor to management's forecast (based, let us also say, on management's inability to achieve forecast in the past) this is perfectly proper, indeed is to be encouraged. The C is the investor's own. The accountant attempts to give the relevant information available that is needed for the investor's determination of C. The accountant does not determine C for the investor.

Variability in the cash flows which the investor expects to receive and the cash flows he actually receives defines the risk of the investment to the particular investor. Variability between the cash flows which the company expects to pay to investors and the cash flows they actually pay indicates the proficiency of management in forecasting. Since the accountant presents managements's forecasts, the investor may obtain some idea of his risk by knowing this latter variability. Figure 1 suggests the manner in which this information is intended to be useful.

FIGURE 1

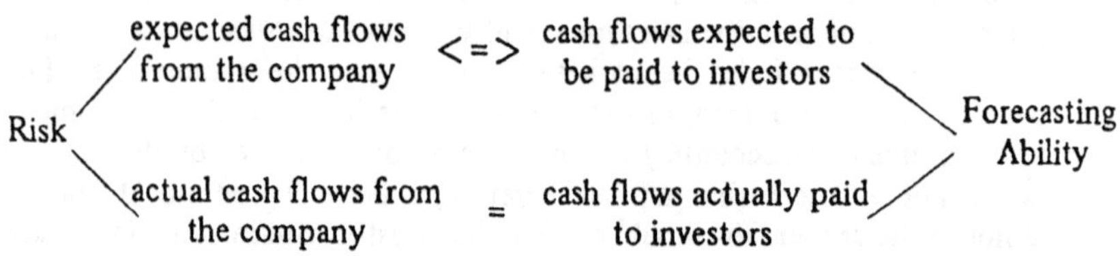

Investors' and management's expectations may differ, or be the same. Investors' actual receipts and management's actual payments must be identical. The variance between management's expectations and actual payments is a forecasting variance; but it is not the variance that defines the investor's risk. The investor's risk is the variance between his expected and actual receipts. Just as the accountant cannot measure C, the investor's expectations from the investment, he also cannot measure the investor's risk. Again, the accountant only gives information that relates to this risk, here the forecasting variance.

MINIMAL CONTENT OF CASH FLOW STATEMENTS FOR INVESTORS

It is now time to describe a framework for providing the information deemed necessary in the previous section. We know that there must be both a past and a future cash flow. The cash flow for past periods (PCF) should show the forecast and actual payments by the company to its investors enough periods back to give the investor a reasonable idea of management's forecasting ability. The cash flow for future periods (FCF)[10] should show the payments which management expects the company to make to its investors.

The monitoring of FCF is only partially met by noting major discrepancies in PCF. There is clearly a case for making known the components that go to make up FCF, and by implication, PCF. Expected payments may be made as forecast by the company to investors without arising as anticipated. An "acceptable" cash receipt at the expense of substantial debt funding or sale of assets may prevent investors from appropriately estimating r, n and, subsequently, V. Where the investor is made aware of the potential loss in earnings from the sale of an asset, or the potential cash drain from excessive debt funding, two inclusive possibilities arise:

(1) he may wish to shorten his time horizon, n;

(2) he may wish to revise the return, r, which he finds acceptable, so as to incorporate the additional risk factor.

Since it is all the future cash flows from the present point in time which affect his evaluation of V, a cash flow statement must show any change in the asset or debt structure of the firm. To do otherwise would be misleading. PCF is of use in informing the investor of the reliability of management's forecast. It does not afford him the guarantee of similar payments into the future.

A need, therefore, becomes established, for FCF to show the manner in which cash is expected to come into and go out of the company. The future investment plans of the company and the extent to which they rely on the company's ability to raise external finance will thus be shown. In this way, the investor will be able to make some judgement as to whether there will be sufficient finance to support a forecast level of trading, and the likelihood of payments to him were trading to suffer a cutback.

The cash flow statement should, therefore, inform the investor, according to his class, of the amount and reliability of management's forecast of the future cash flows from the company to him in the context of all the company's cash flows. It should show the manner in which cash has been or is expected to be received for the past three periods and the future three periods, and the forecasts made of past periods. There is no inherent reason why three years be chosen; this seems a minimal requirement.

In order to report on the full cash flow of a company, it is necessary to distinguish one set of cash flows from another. It is sensible to categorise cash flows in such a way as to aid investors' understanding and ability to make different or further predictions. As such, there are three types of cash flows, categorised according to the nature of their associated transactions, that is, the different expectations of their recurrence.

1. RECURRENT CASH FLOWS are those associated with transactions expected to recur in the normal course of business at least once in each accounting period. Specifically included are trading flows, taxation outflows associated with other recurrent cash flows, and distributions to investors other than realisation of their investment (that is, including dividend and interest payments but excluding repayment of loans and share capital). Trading flows should be classified by principal activities and within each such classification fixed outflows should be shown separately from net variable flows. Where fixed outflows are not attributable to a particular class of activity they should be shown separately. Fixed outflows are those relating to transactions, the volume of which does not vary with the volume of trading.

2. NON-RECURRENT CASH FLOWS are those associated with transactions expected to occur and possibly recur in the normal course of business but not regularly in each accounting period. Specifically included are flows not classed

as recurrent and associated with the realisation, acquisition, and provision of capital resources; finance provided by investors; and the realisation of the investments of investors.

3. EXTRAORDINARY CASH FLOWS are those associated with transactions not expected in the normal course of business. Specifically included are payments or receipts for damages and tax repayments resulting from losses.

The assumptions upon which the forecast of cash flows for future periods have been made should be stated. Where there are any material differences between either forecast and actual flows, or previously and presently forecast flows, an explanation should be noted with an indication of whether or not the variation is owing to factors within the control of the management of the company.

In Table 1, a format for a cash flow statement is given which is in keeping with the spirit of the above recommendations. The following conventions have been adopted : + stands for a positive cash flow, – a negative cash flow, ± the net of positive less negative cash flows, X the most recent past year, F the latest forecast cash flow, P the previous year's forecast and A the actual cash flow. Table 2 is a supplementary statement of trading cash flows. (Totals for PCF and FCF are not provided since investors will value each period's flow according to their own acceptable rate of interest.)[11]

ANALYSIS OF CURRENT YEAR RESULTS WITH FORECASTS FOR THOSE RESULTS AS STATED IN PREVIOUS YEARS

The forecast that lines up next to the most recent past year result (Year X) is a revised forecast. And quite rightly. It is an assessment error to expect someone to satisfy a performance standard that was set up under either vastly different or additional constraints from those which actually held. (This is one budgeting anomaly that Bromwich (4), for example, attempts to eradicate.) Nonetheless, it is an essential skill of management not only to revise erroneous forecasts with accuracy, but to make fairly accurate three-year estimates in the first place. There is a qualitative difference in the calibre of a good one-year forecasting management, and a good two- or three-year one. An example will illustrate this meaning.

Suppose two companies, On and Off, with identical net trading inflow before tax in year X had made precise estimates for these inflows in year X – 1. In year X, the cash flow statement for the two companies appear the same.

	Company On Cash Flow Statement X	
	F	A
Net Trading Inflow before tax	10	10

TABLE 1

CASH FLOW STATEMENT FOR A COMPANY WITH THREE PRINCIPAL TRADING ACTIVITIES

	X - 2 F	X - 2 A	X - 1 F	X - 1 A	X F	X A	X + 1 P	X + 1 F	X + 2 P	X + 2 F	X + 3 F
RECURRENT CASH FLOWS											
Net Trading Inflow before tax (see Table 2)	±	±	±	±	±	±	±	±	±	±	±
Non-Trading Inflow (by source)	+	+	+	+	+	+	+	+	+	+	+
Non-Trading Outflow	-	-	-	-	-	-	-	-	-	-	-
Taxation	-	-	-	-	-	-	-	-	-	-	-
(sub total 1)											
NON-RECURRENT CASH FLOWS											
Realisation of Capital Resources	+	+	+	+	+	+	+	+	+	+	+
Investment by Investors	+	+	+	+	+	+	+	+	+	+	+
Acquisition and Provision of Capital Resources	-	-	-	-	-	-	-	-	-	-	-
(sub total 2)											
EXTRAORDINARY											
(sub total 3)											
TOTAL CASH FLOWS FOR THE PERIOD (1+2+3)	±	±	±	±	±	±	±	±	±	±	±
CASH RETAINED b/f	±	±	±	±	±	±	±	±	±	±	±
CASH AVAILABLE	±	±	±	±	±	±	±	±	±	±	±
DISTRIBUTIONS TO INVESTORS											
Recurrent (by class)	-	-	-	-	-	-	-	-	-	-	-
Non-Recurrent (by class)	-	-	-	-	-	-	-	-	-	-	-
CASH RETAINED c/f	±	±	±	±	±	±	±	±	±	±	±

TABLE 2

CASH FLOW STATEMENT FOR A COMPANY WITH THREE PRINCIPAL TRADING ACTIVITIES

STATEMENT OF TRADING CASH FLOWS

	X − 2		X − 1		X		X + 1		X + 2		X + 3
	F	A	F	A	F	A	P	F	P	F	F
DIVISION A											
Net Variable Trading Inflow	±	±	±	±	±	±	±	±	±	±	±
Less: Fixed Trading Outflow	−	−	−	−	−	−	−	−	−	−	−
(sub total 1)											
DIVISION B											
Net Variable Trading Inflow	±	±	±	±	±	±	±	±	±	±	±
Less: Fixed Trading Outflow	−	−	−	−	−	−	−	−	−	−	−
(sub total 2)											
DIVISION C											
Net Variable Trading Inflow	±	±	±	±	±	±	±	±	±	±	±
Less: Fixed Trading Outflow	−	−	−	−	−	−	−	−	−	−	−
(sub total 3)											
NET TRADING INFLOW BEFORE TAX AND FIXED OUTFLOWS COMMON TO ALL TRADING (1+2+3)	±	±	±	±	±	±	±	±	±	±	±
LESS: FIXED OUTFLOWS COMMON TO ALL TRADING	−	−	−	−	−	−	−	−	−	−	−
NET TRADING INFLOW BEFORE TAX	±	±	±	±	±	±	±	±	±	±	±

	Company Off Cash Flow Statement X	
	F	A
Net Trading Inflow before tax	10	10

Let us suppose, however that the previous estimates applicable to the year X result were as follows:

	X - 3	X - 2	X - 1	X
	F	F	F	A
Company On	11	10	10	10
Company Off	50	10	10	10

The proficiency of these two managements in forecasting are far from identical. Even though both made adjustments to their forecasts in X - 2, the amount of the adjustment was different, and hence the consequences for assessing their three-year forecasting ability are different. No mention of the adjustment will have been made in the previous two cash flow statements. To rectify this, Table 3 could be included as another supplementary statement monitoring all the previous forecasts made in the context of the current year's flows. It is important to emphasise that this would not be additional information to four years of cash flows, rather it places that information in a more readily available format.

OTHER STATEMENTS REQUIRED BY INVESTORS

Although there has been a suggestion[12] that cash flow statements represent an alternative to the provision of income and financial position statements, this is not the view taken here. Nor is the view taken that these other two statements merely represent "stewardship accounting information".[13] In my opinion, a conscious effort needs to be made to co-ordinate the cash flow, income, and financial position statements in such a way as to provide the investor with a full understanding of the range of possibilities open to the company. The income and financial position statements should inform the investor of, firstly, a measure of income on which he can base his expectation of the future market value of investments in the company; and, secondly, the capacity of the company to change resources held as a result of past and planned investment, and undertake alternative investment. As such, the income statement would assume the planned use of resources as shown by the cash flow statement, whilst the financial position statement would assume the cessation of the use of present resources.[14]

A subtle difference between the cash flow and income statements is that the latter depicts the maximum amount the company could pay to investors in a period while maintaining the expectation of being able to continue to pay that

TABLE 3

CASH FLOW STATEMENT FOR A COMPANY WITH THREE PRINCIPAL TRADING ACTIVITIES

ANALYSIS OF CURRENT YEAR RESULTS WITH FORECASTS FOR THOSE RESULTS AS STATED IN PREVIOUS YEARS

	X – 3 F	X – 2 F	X – 1 F	X A
RECURRENT CASH FLOWS				
Net Trading Inflow before Tax	±	±	±	±
Non-Trading Inflow	+	+	+	+
Non-Trading Outflow	–	–	–	–
Taxation	–	–	–	–
(sub total 1)				
NON-RECURRENT CASH FLOWS				
Realisation of Capital Resources	+	+	+	+
Investment by Investors	+	+	+	+
Acquisition and Provision of Capital Resources	–	–	–	–
(sub total 2)				
EXTRAORDINARY				
(sub total 3)				
TOTAL CASH FLOWS FOR THE PERIOD (1+2+3)	±	±	±	±
CASH RETAINED b/f	±	±	±	±
CASH AVAILABLE	±	±	±	±
DISTRIBUTION TO INVESTORS				
Recurrent	–	–	–	–
Non-Recurrent	–	–	–	–
CASH RETAINED c/f	±	±	±	±

amount in the future; that is, the amount that could be paid and not merely that which is or is expected to be paid.[15] The financial position statement represents to the investor that opportunity available to the company as evidenced by its ability to enter the market and realise the financial interest in it. Such a liquidation or break-up value can act as another monitor of V, the investor's valuation of the investment. If the financial position statement reflects a value greater than V, the investor is inclined to initiate liquidation proceedings.[16]

NOTES

1 The topic, eight standards and fifteen exposure drafts later, of a "current" investigation by the Accounting Standards Steering Committee.

2 See (11), Exposure Draft No.0 (U.K.C. Series), "The Fundamental Objectives of Accounting Statements". This is the first of five Exposure Drafts prepared by the financial reporting group at the University of Kent at Canterbury.

3 From (5), loc. cit., p.168 where credit is given to (1). The Manchester School have gone into this in a big way : see (2).

4 Surveys, such as that carried out in (5) suffer from just this point. They tell us what people use, and not what is useful. This latter notion must come from an intellectual investigation which may involve usurping the conceptual scheme implied in the information people use. Satisfying users' stated needs isn't the entire answer either : they may think they need some information which is not useful even to their own stated objectives. For example, the primary ranking of EPS by security analysts in (12), see Table 2, p.25, is mysterious to me. See (13). Kahneman and Tversky (7) go some of the way to explaining the use made of existing financial reports, viz. that people are more confident making inferences on the basis of redundant information than independent information.

5 Of course, rational decisions, those which maximally utilise all available information, may have bad outcomes. The information which would lead to a better decision may not be available when the decision is, and needs to be, taken. For the insights of a research psychologist in this regard : see (6).

6 The accountant exercises his judgement in the selection of this information, and this judgement may be suspect. This does not detract from our information model, rather it points the direction to which behavioural considerations become significant for financial reporting.

7 This is not to say that the accountant qua financial accountant offers this advice.

[8] See (3).

[9] See (11), Exposure Draft No.1 (U.K.C. Series), "Financial Reporting to Investors in Companies – The Accounting Statements Required", the second of the drafts cited in Note 2.

[10] This is not to be confused with the FCF (Free Cash Flow) model of Joel Stern; see (13).

[11] See page 4. If follows, therefore, that each column is either a forecast of both events and price levels or the actual occurrence of the two, i.e. cash flow figures are in money terms applicable to that year. To the extent that deviation from forecast is owed to wrong assumptions about the change in prices, this will be stated separately in the statement of assumptions and subsequent explanation.

[12] See (8).

[13] T.A. Lee, (9), loc. cit., p.27.

[14] To see the working of these two statements, see Drafts nos. 3 and 4 referred to in note 2. Implied in this approach is the rejection of interlocking balances between financial statements. See (10).

[15] A more obvious difference is that not all cash flows are relevant when discounting in order to determine the measure of income. For this purpose we can think of there being direct cash flows – those resulting from operations – and indirect cash flows – resulting from the reinvestment of any retained cash from operations for capital maintenance or growth. It is only after a measure of income is formulated that indirect cash flows may take their place in a cash flow projection. Income truly is primary.

[16] Such an inclination, which stems from a "rational man" economic argument, appears debatable in light of the recent drop in share prices to one-third of asset values.

REFERENCES

(1) American Accounting Association, A STATEMENT OF BASIC ACCOUNTING THEORY (1966).

(2) Arnold, J. and Hope, A., "Reporting Business Performance", ACCOUNTING AND BUSINESS RESEARCH (1975), 96–105.

(3) Bird, Peter, "Objectives and Methods of Financial Reporting : A Generalised Search Procedure", ACCOUNTING AND BUSINESS RESEARCH (1975), 162–167.

(4) Bromwich, Michael, "Standard Costing for Planning and Control", THE ACCOUNTANT, April–May 1969.

(5) Carsberg, B., Hope, A. and Scapens, R.W., "The Objectives of Published Accounting Reports", ACCOUNTING AND BUSINESS RESEARCH (1974), 162–173.

(6) Fischhoff, Baruch, HINDSIGHT : THINKING BACKWARD?, Oregon Research Institute Monograph, vol.14, no.1, 1974.

(7) Kahneman, D., and Tversky, A., "On the Psychology of Prediction", PSYCHOLOGICAL REVIEW (1973), 237–251.

(8) Lawson, G.H., "Some Arguments for Cash-flow Accounting", CERTIFIED ACCOUNTANT, April–May 1973.

(9) Lee, T.A., "A Case for Cash Flow Reporting", JOURNAL OF BUSINESS FINANCE (1972), 27–36.

(10) Macdonald, Graeme, PROFIT MEASUREMENT: ALTERNATIVES TO HISTORICAL COST. Accountancy Age, 1974.

(11) Macdonald, G., Bird, P., and Climo, T., STATEMENTS OF OBJECTIVES AND STANDARD PRACTICE IN FINANCIAL REPORTING. Accountancy Age, 1975.

(12) Pankoff, Lyn D. and Virgil, Robert L., "Some Preliminary Findings from a Laboratory Experiment on the Usefulness of Financial Accounting Information to Security Analysts", EMPIRICAL RESEARCH IN ACCOUNTING (1970), 1–48.

(13) Stern, Joel, "Earnings Per Share is a Poor Indicator of Performance", OMEGA, (1974), 11–32.

LET'S SCRAP THE "FUNDS" STATEMENT

The profession should identify the objectives of the funds statement and then design new statements that achieve those objectives.

by Loyd C. Heath

Funds statements found in practice today are a hodgepodge of miscellaneous information presented in a confusing and misleading way.

Many accountants see the problem as one of defining "funds." They attribute the confusion over the funds statement to confusion over what is meant by the term "funds." R. A. Rayman, for example, argued:

"The fact that funds analysis has not made more headway may be attributable to the absence of a definition of funds which is generally accepted. There is, in fact, a variety of definitions ranging over the whole spectrum of liquidity, from cash at one extreme to total resources at the other, with compromises like working capital somewhere in between."[1]

In my opinion, the fundamental problem is not a definitional one. Confusion over what is meant by the term funds is merely a symptom of a more basic problem: confusion over the objectives of the funds statement. The solution does not lie in redefining funds; it lies in scrapping the funds statement, identifying the objectives it tries but fails to meet and designing statements that achieve those objectives.[2]

Specious Objectives

The stated objectives of funds statements in Accounting Principles Board Opinion no. 19, *Reporting Changes in Financial Position*, are specious. Superficially they appear to be reasonable but when analyzed and applied in practice they are unclear, misleading and unattainable. According to the opinion, the objectives are "(1) to summarize the financing and investing activities of the entity, including the extent to which the enterprise has generated funds from operations during the period, and (2) to complete the disclosure of changes in financial position during the period."

The meaning of the first objective is unclear. It begs the question of what effects of financing and investing activities should be summarized. Financing and investing activities, like all business activities, have many different effects. A single transaction may affect cash, working capital, total assets, capital structure, net assets and so forth. Obviously not all of those effects can be portrayed in a single statement, but the opinion is silent as to which one or ones are the object or objects of attention in the statement. Paragraph 8 says only that the statement "should be based on a broad concept embracing all changes in financial position" without even saying a broad concept of what! The problem reflects more than just poor draftsmanship; it reflects the absence of an underlying concept.

The second objective is unattainable. As noted, business activities have many effects. No statement can possibly "complete the disclosure of changes in financial position" (par. 4) or "disclose all important changes in financial position for the period covered" (par. 11). A meaningful statement must focus on

[1] R. A. Rayman, "Is Conventional Accounting Obsolete?" *Accountancy*, June 1970, p.423.

LOYD C. HEATH, Ph.D., is associate professor of accounting at the University of Washington, Seattle, Washington. He is a member of the American Accounting Association and the author of several articles that have appeared in professional publications.

[2] The analysis and recommendations that follow are based on my forthcoming research monograph, *Financial Reporting and the Evaluation of Solvency*, to be published by the accounting standards division of the American Institute of Certified Public Accountants.

a specific aspect or dimension of financial position such as cash, working capital, net assets, monetary assets and so forth. The possibilities are almost limitless. No statement can portray in an understandable way all effects of all activities on all possible measures of financial position. As Arthur Stone Dewing observed:

"But no representation of anything in this world can be perfect. It must portray one or more aspects or attributes of the thing represented and neglect or throw into insignificance the other aspects or attributes. This observation is conspicuously true when we are dealing with . . . accounting statements. Such statements must select one or at most a very few aspects of the objects represented and neglect all others—as vital statistics consider only the length of years of a man, neglecting every other aspect of his life or characteristics as a human being."[3]

Many of the alleged objectives of funds statements described in accounting literature are even more confusing than those in Opinion no. 19. For example, one widespread belief is that fund statements are somehow supposed to show what "happened" to a company's profits or "where its profits went."[4]

Profits are not a physical "thing" that can be disposed of, retained or paid out. Profit is simply the name given to the change in a company's net assets that results from selected operating, financing and investing activities during a period of time, or, as the APB defined it, "the net increase (net decrease) in owners' equity (assets minus liabilities) of an enterprise for an accounting period from profit-directed activities. . . ."[5] It is a *change* in net assets, not an asset. It is measured in money but it is not money. One could, of course, show what became of a company's *cash*—part of which may have been received as a result of its profit-directed

activities. A statement of cash receipts and payments would show that. Similarly, one could also prepare a statement that explains changes in some group of assets, say, its quick assets, part of which may have been received as a result of its profit-directed activities. But to try to show what "happened" to a company's profits is a meaningless objective; no statement can possibly show that.

Implicit Objectives

Although the APB's stated objectives in Opinion no. 19 are unclear, a careful reading of the opinion suggests that the board was concerned with reporting the effects of *all* business activities (not just financing and investing activities) on at least two and perhaps three different measures of financial position.

The first was to report changes in some measure of the cash or near-cash resources of a company, that is, changes in some measure of its debt-paying ability. A number of specific provisions of the opinion support that view. Paragraph 10 requires that "the Statement should prominently disclose working capital or cash provided from or used in

[3] Arthur Stone Dewing, *The Financial Policy of Corporations*, 5th ed., vol. 1 (New York: The Ronald Press Co., 1953), p.517.

[4] Perry Mason stated that a funds statement "contributes materially to . . . the answers to such questions as . . . Where did the profits go?" (Perry Mason, *"Cash Flow" Analysis and the Funds Statement*, Accounting Research Study no. 2 [New York: AICPA, 1961], p.49). Paton and Paton stated that a funds statement "is designed to . . . indicate what disposition has been made of earnings." (William A. Paton and William A. Paton, Jr., *Corporation Accounts and Statements* [New York: Macmillan Co., 1955], p.440). A. B. Carson maintains that "among other things it supplies an answer to the question: 'What happened to the profit?'" (A. B. Carson, "A Source and Application of Funds' Philosophy of Financial Accounting," *Accounting Review*, April 1949, p.160). Roy A. Foulke argues that it "gives a clear answer to the question of what has become of the net profits." (Roy A. Foulke, *Practical Financial Statement Analysis*, 6th ed. [New York: McGraw-Hill Book Co., Inc., 1968], p.474).

For other similar examples, see Donald A. Corbin, "Proposals for Improving Funds Statements," *Accounting Review*, July 1961, p.398; National Association of Accountants Research Report no. 38, *Cash Flow Analysis for Managerial Control*, (New York: NAA, 1961), p.58; David F. Hawkins, *Corporate Financial Reporting*, rev. ed. (Homewood, Ill.; Richard D. Irwin, Inc., 1977), p.125; Donald E. Kieso and Jerry J. Weygandt, *Intermediate Accounting*, 2nd ed. (New York: John Wiley & Sons, 1977), p. 983; and Jay M. Smith, Jr., and K. Fred Skousen, *Intermediate Accounting*, 6th ed. (Englewood Cliffs, N.J.: Prentice-Hall, Inc., 1977), p.682.

[5] APB Statement no. 4, *Basic Concepts and Accounting Principles* (New York: AICPA, 1971), par. 134.

operations for the period." Paragraph 11 states, "The Statement may be in balanced form or in a form expressing the changes in financial position in terms of cash, or cash and temporary investments combined, of all quick assets, or of working capital." Paragraph 14 further specifically requires that "outlays for purchase of long-term assets . . . proceeds from sale (or working capital or cash provided by sale) of long-term assets" and "dividends in cash" all be disclosed.

The second type of change that the board appears to have been concerned with having reported was capital structure changes. Capital structure refers to the claims on the resources used to operate a business enterprise, including both debt and equity claims. Changes in the size of a company's capital structure result from activities such as the borrowing and repayment of debt, sale and repurchase of capital stock, profit-directed activities and cash or property dividends. Changes in the composition of a company's capital structure result from activities such as the conversion of convertible securities into common stock and refinancing operations including the "swapping" of one type of financial instrument for another in a financial reorganization.

Many changes in the size and composition of a company's capital structure also affect its cash, it working capital and other measures of debt-paying ability, but some of them do not. Evidence that the board was concerned with having changes in the size and composition of a company's capital structure as well as changes in its debt-paying ability reported is found in the requirement in paragraph 14 that "the Statement should clearly disclose" activities such as "conversion of long-term debt or preferred stock to common stock . . . issuance, redemption, or purchase of capital stock . . . for assets other than cash" and "dividends . . . in kind or other distributions to shareholders." Other evidence of the board's concern with changes in a company's capital structure is found in paragraph 6:

"However, a funds statement based on either the cash or the working capital concept of funds sometimes excludes certain financing and investing activities because they do not directly affect cash or working capital during the period. For example, issuing equity securities to acquire a building is both a financing and investing transaction but does not affect either cash or working capital. To meet all of its objectives, a funds statement should disclose separately the financing and investing aspects of all significant transactions that affect financial position during a period. These transactions include acquisition or disposal of property in exchange for debt or equity securities and conversion of long-term debt or preferred stock to common stock."

The third type of change that the board seems to have been concerned with having reported is changes in a company's long-term assets such as plant and equipment and long-term investments. Many of the increases in those assets would, of course, be revealed by a statement that shows only changes in cash or working capital. Some, however, such as those resulting from the issuance of debt or equity securities, would be excluded from that type of statement.

The requirement to show the issuance of securities for consideration other than cash or working capital as sources and uses of funds appears to have been motivated in part by the desire to disclose changes in long-term assets as well as the desire to disclose changes in a company's capital structure. However, the opinion does not contain similar requirements for transactions that increase long-term assets but do not either decrease working capital (or other measure of debt-paying ability) or increase total capital. Such transactions are undoubtedly unusual but do occur. The exchange of a long-term investment in securities for plant and equipment or the exchange of land for securities are examples. The opinion requires that outlays for the purchase of long-term assets be disclosed but whether the term "outlays" embraces or excludes exchanges of the kind mentioned is not clear.

In summary, the APB may have intended to require the disclosure of all increases in long-term assets, but its intentions are not clear. It certainly gave no indication of any desire to show decreases in long-term assets; only the "proceeds from sale (or working capital or cash provided by sale) of long-term assets," not the book value of assets sold, is required to be disclosed.

Relevant Objectives

Changes in all three of the measures of financial position discussed in the last section are clearly of interest to investors, creditors and other external users of financial statements. Changes in debt-paying ability are of such obvious interest to creditors and investors that the matter hardly requires comment; the only real issue is which measure of debt-paying ability is likely to be most useful. Changes in the size and composition of a company's capital structure are also clearly of interest. One of the most widely used financial ratios in credit analysis is the ratio of debt to equity. That ratio would obviously be affected by changes in the composition of a company's capital structure such as the conversion of debentures into common stock and various kinds of refinancing operations. The nature of those activities and a report of how they affect a company's capital structure would, therefore, also be of interest. Changes in the amount or composition of long-term assets are likely to signal changes in a company's future profits and future cash needs so that they, too, are likely to be of interest to investors and creditors.

Conflicting Objectives

The basic problem with Opinion no. 19 is not, therefore, that it requires disclosure of unimportant or irrelevant information but that it requires too many different types of information to be disclosed on the same statement. The result is a confusing statement.

Financial statements are maps of economic territory; they portray the financial characteristic of business enterprises. Different maps are needed for different purposes because only a limited amount of information can be portrayed on a single map. A single geographic map designed to portray changes in annual rainfall, changes in educational level of the population, changes in agricultural crops and changes in unemployment is not likely to portray any of that information clearly. Similarly, a single financial statement designed to portray many different types of changes in the financial position of a business enterprise is not likely to portray any of that information clearly. That, however, is exactly what Opinion no. 19 requires of the funds statement. To achieve the multiple and disparate objectives of that statement, the term funds was defined so broadly that it has become meaningless, and a funds statement based on a meaningless concept of funds does not communicate information effectively. That is the heart of the problem of the confusing funds statements found in practice today.

Recommendation

Once the basis of the confusion over the funds statement is diagnosed, the general nature of a solution becomes obvious; several different statements are needed to communicate clearly the information now crammed into a single statement. Specifically, three

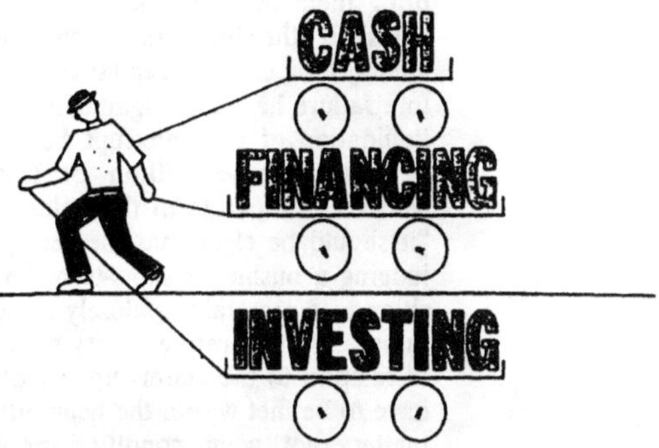

statements are needed to replace the funds statement and achieve its objectives: a statement of cash receipts and payments, a statement of financing activities and a statement of investing activities.

Statement of Cash Receipts and Payments

One of the relevant objectives of funds statements is to report changes in some measure of debt-paying ability. Both historically and currently the measure of debt-paying ability used most frequently in funds statements has been working capital. That measure is rejected here in favor of cash.

The principal reason for recommending a change from working capital as a measure of debt-paying ability to cash is that the approach to evaluation of a company's solvency, or "credit analysis" as it is often called, has changed and the information needs of financial statement users have therefore also changed. During the 1920s when funds statements based on working capital changes were developed, the adequacy of a company's working capital position, particularly as measured by its current ratio, was considered the "alpha and omega" of credit analysis.[6] It was argued that current liabilities are paid with current assets and current

[6] Foulke, p.178.

assets must therefore exceed current liabilities by an "adequate margin."

During the 1950s there was a searching reappraisal of working capital as a measure of debt-paying ability. Arthur Stone Dewing wrote in 1953 that "bankers learned by tragic experience that there was no mystical significance in the two-to-one ratio. They observed that in many types of business, under the stress of general disaster, inventories could not be sold, and if such an attempt should be made, not a two-to-one or even a three- or four-to-one ratio would bring them the immediate payment of their debts. If the business failed, the relative amounts of current capital in the days before failure had little significance in the final liquidation of the bankrupt business."[7]

That same year Bion B. Howard and Miller Upton wrote in their classic text that "it should be clear that the real problem in judging a business's short-term financial position is to ascertain as closely as possible the future cash-generating ability of the business in relation to the claims upon cash that will have to be met within the near future. . . . It matters not what condition prevails at a given time; the important thing is whether the business in performing its regular operating functions can continue to generate cash in sufficient quantity and in satisfactory time to meet all operating and financial obligations."[8]

More recently, John B. Coughlan observed ironically that "working capital has been thought of as a 'pool' of resources available to satisfy the claims of short-term creditors. But it is unlikely that any banker or creditor will slake his thirst from any part of the pool other than the cash portion. Many a firm has been known to pay its debts with cash, but not one has drawn a check on working capital. Working capital, *per se*, has no bearing on short-term credit standing and it is only useful for whatever implications it may have for cash and cash flow."[9]

Those views are widely accepted by financial analysts today. The emphasis in credit analysis has shifted from analysis of current working capital position to dynamic analysis of future cash receipts and payments in much the same way that the emphasis in security analysis shifted from static analysis of balance sheet values to dynamic analysis of net income some thirty or forty years earlier.[10]

The central question in credit analysis today is not whether a company's working capital is "adequate" but whether the cash expected to be received within a given time period will equal or exceed required cash payments within that same period. Analysis of working capital position does not provide that information. A company's principal sources of cash are from sale of its products or services to its customers, from borrowing and from issuance of stock to investors. Its principal uses are payments to employees, suppliers and governments, repayment of debt and purchase of plant and equipment. Most of the cash a company will receive within the following year is not represented by assets classified as current, and most of the obligations it will have to pay are not represented by liabilities classified as current.

The old concept of current assets as the source from which current liabilities will be paid is meaningless under this framework of analysis. Current liabilities are not paid with current assets; they are paid with cash. Whether a company's current or its noncurrent assets were the source of its cash is an unanswerable question. One can no more determine whether current or noncurrent assets provided the cash generated by a company's operations than he can determine which blade of the scissors cut the cloth, because both were clearly necessary.[11]

The rationale for recommending a statement of cash receipts and payments as one of the statements to replace the funds statement is implicit in the above discussion. If a financial statement user's primary object of attention is the future cash receipts and payments of a company, then it follows that a statement of past cash receipts and payments would be useful for the same reason that historical income statements are useful in predicting the future income of a company: both provide a basis for predicting future performance.

7 Dewing, pp.708-09.

8 Bion B. Howard and Miller Upton, *Introduction to Business Finance* (New York: McGraw-Hill Book Co., Inc., 1953), p.135.

9 John W. Coughlan, "Funds and Income," *NAA Bulletin*, September 1964, p.25.

10 For a discussion of this shift in security analysis, see Benjamin Graham, David L. Dodd and Sidney Cottle, *Security Analysis: Principles and Technique*, 4th ed. (New York: McGraw-Hill Book Co., Inc., 1962), p.214.

11 The role of current–noncurrent classification of assets and liabilities in the evaluation of a company's solvency is discussed more fully in the monograph referred to in footnote 1. That study concludes that the present practice of identifying certain assets and liabilities as current on a company's balance sheet is misleading and recommends that it be discontinued.

Reporting cash receipts and payments is widely advocated today by many financial statement users, particularly bankers. For example, Walter B. Wriston, chairman of the board of Citibank, N.A., stated in a recent speech before Peat, Marwick, Mitchell & Co. personnel, "When I came into the banking business, we were asset-conscious and we loaned money on that basis. Well, assets give you a warm feeling, but they don't generate cash. The first question I would ask any borrower these days is, 'What is your break-even cash flow?' That's the one thing we can't find out from your audit reports and it's the single most important question we ask. It's important that you figure out a way to present the difference between real cash flow and accrual cash flow."[12]

An example of the form of cash receipts and payments statement recommended, together with a recommended supporting schedule showing details of cash provided by operations, is presented for Example, Inc., in exhibit 1, page 100.

Only business activities that affected cash are shown on the statement of cash receipts and payments. If financing and investing activities that did not affect cash are shown on statements of cash receipts and payments as if they did, users will become confused over the purpose of the statement and what it shows. Financing transactions that did not affect cash are shown on the recommended statement of financing activities; investing transactions that did not affect cash are shown on the recommended statement of investing activities.

For the purpose of clarity of presentation, details of cash provided by profit-directed activities or what are called operations (to simplify terminology on the statement) are shown on a separate schedule rather than on the face of the statement of cash receipts and payments. Both the absolute magnitude of many of the cash receipts and payments from operations (such as the amount of cash collected from customers and the amount paid for merchandise) as well as the many types of cash payments would tend to overshadow some of the other items on the statement of cash receipts and payments (such as cash borrowed and fixed assets purchased), which may be of greater significance to the financial statement user in estimating future cash receipts and payments.

The schedule of the cash provided by operations illustrates the direct (as opposed to the indirect) method of calculating that amount. When the direct method is used, the schedule shows the actual sources and uses of cash. If the indirect method was used, the schedule would start with net income and adjust that figure for all revenues and expenses that did not affect cash. Those are the two alternative methods of presenting funds provided by operations in statements of changes in financial position that the APB described as acceptable in Opinion no. 19.

The indirect method is basically a set of worksheet adjustments rather than an explanation of how operating activities affected cash. It is analogous to calculating income by subtracting stockholders' equity at the beginning of the year from stockholders' equity at the end of the year and then adjusting the difference for nonincome items, such as dividends and purchases and sales of capital stock. This method, of course, will always "work" if the proper adjustments are made, but if accountants were to prepare income statements in this way, many financial statement users would be confused. They would begin to describe dividends, for example, as a "source" of income in the same way they now describe depreciation as a "source" of funds because they are both "add-backs" when the indirect method of calculation is used. The indirect method of calculating cash provided by operations is pernicious because it is almost certain to continue to confuse financial statement users by reinforcing the incredible belief that profits and depreciation are sources of cash. The direct method, on the other hand, is likely to be useful in dispelling some of the confusion that now exists over the relationship between business activities and cash receipts and payments because it shows clearly that profits are neither cash nor a source of cash, that cash comes from customers, that it is paid for merchan-

"A statement of cash receipts and payments alone would not accomplish all of the objectives of Opinion no. 19."

[12] *World* (Peat, Marwick, Mitchell & Co.), Spring 1974, p.49.

Exhibit 1

Example, Inc.
Cash receipts and payments statement
Year ending December 31, 1977

Cash balance December 31, 1976		$15,666
Sources of cash:		
Cash provided by operations (schedule 1)	$27,537	
Sale of marketable securities	3,062	
Sale of land, buildings and equipment	12,793	
Net amount borrowed	31,092	
Received from sale of common stock	7,495	81,979
Cash available		97,645
Uses of cash:		
Land, buildings and equipment purchased	62,119	
Dividends paid	13,558	75,677
Cash balance December 31, 1977		$21,968

Schedule 1

Calculation of cash provided by operations

Cash collected from customers		$783,545
Interest and dividends received		1,417
Total cash receipts from operations		784,962
Cash payments:		
For merchandise inventories	$457,681	
For administrative and selling expenses	264,577	
For interest	6,941	
For other expenses	14,953	
For taxes	13,273	757,425
Cash provided by operations		$ 27,537

dise, administrative and selling expenses, taxes and so forth and that depreciation is neither a source nor a use of cash.

Statement of Financing Activities

A statement of cash receipts and payments alone would not accomplish all of the objectives of Opinion no. 19. The APB was concerned with the effects of business activities on the size and composition of a company's capital structure and on its long-term assets as well as how those activities affected its debt-paying ability. The second statement recommended in this article, the statement of financing activities, is designed to achieve the second of those objectives: disclosure of the effects of business activities on the capital structure of a firm.

Before describing and discussing the recommended form of the statement of financing activities, it is necessary to clarify what is meant by the term "capital structure." As noted earlier, that term is used to refer to the claims on a company's resources. Typically, however, only equity and long-term debt are considered parts of a company's capital structure; short-term debt is excluded. Some short-term debt, however, such as bank loans and commercial paper, is analogous to long-term debt in the sense that it requires conscious effort or specific negotiation on the part of owners or managers to obtain. Other short-term debt does not require conscious effort or negotiation to obtain; it is "spontaneous" or "self-generating" and grows "out of normal patterns of profitable operations without especial effort or conscious decision on the part of owners or managers."[13] Examples of spontaneous debt include trade accounts payable, wages payable and taxes payable. Debt that requires negotiation, whether short or long term, may be referred

[13] Pearson Hunt, Charles M. Williams and Gordon Donaldson, *Basic Business Finance*, rev. ed. (Homewood, Ill.: Richard D. Irwin, Inc., 1961), p.116.

to as financing liabilities. Debt that does not require negotiation may be referred to as spontaneous liabilities.[14]

Although both short-term financing liabilities and spontaneous liabilities are usually classified as current, the distinction is useful in preparing a statement of financing activities because different underlying considerations affect the amount of credit available from those two different sources. The amount available from spontaneous sources depends on considerations such as the volume of purchases of inventories and supplies, normal credit terms of a company's suppliers and conventional practices as to frequency of payment of salaries and wages. Credit available from spontaneous sources tends to increase as sales rise and fall when sales decline. Credit available from short-term financing sources, on the other hand, depends on the same basic consideration as credit available from long-term sources, that is, lenders' evaluations of a company's ability to repay a loan when due. Furthermore, financial statement users tend to regard commercial paper and short-term bank loans (which may, in fact, be short term in name only) as financing sources in the same sense that bonds and long-term bank loans are financing sources. Consequently, the term "capital structure" as used in this article refers to both equity capital and financing liabilities regardless of whether those financing liabilities are short or long term.[15] A statement such as the current form of funds statement that purports to report financing activities but excludes by definition a class of financing activities that most businessmen regard as major sources of financing is misleading.

[14] R. K. Mautz made a similar distinction. He referred to "primary financing interests" and "incidental financing interests." He argued that incidental financing interests including, for example, trade creditors and employees "provide financing, but this is neither the primary intent of the particular interest nor the basic reason for the transaction." (R. K. Mautz, *An Accounting Technique for Reporting Financial Transactions*, Special Bulletin no. 7 [Urbana, Ill.: University of Illinois, Bureau of Economic and Business Research, 1951], pp.21-22.)

[15] Other implications of the distinction between financing and spontaneous liabilities are discussed in the monograph referred to in footnote 1. That study recommends that liabilities be classified as financing, operating and tax. Operating and tax liabilities are two types of spontaneous liabilities.

A statement of financing activities for Example, Inc., is shown in exhibit 2, page 102. This statement is similar in form to the recommended statement of cash receipts and payments. It explains changes in a company's capital structure in much the same way that a statement of cash receipts and payments explains changes in its cash position. However, it includes changes in the composition of a company's capital structure (conversion of securities into common stock) as well as changes in its size. Profits and dividends as well as financing activities more narrowly defined, such as borrowing and repayment of debt and purchase and sale of capital stock, all affect a company's capital structure and should therefore be shown on the statement of financing activities.

Many business activities that affect a company's capital structure, such as borrowing money, repayment of debt, sale of capital stock and payment of dividends, also affect its cash position and should therefore appear on its statement of cash receipts and payments as receipts and payments of cash as well as on its statement of financing activities. While this might appear to be duplicate reporting of those activities, it really is not. Different effects of them are reported on each of the two statements. The statement of cash receipts and payments reports their effects on cash, whereas the statement of financing activities reports their effects on capital structure. That is necessary to keep both statements clear, simple and understandable. The alternative, of course, is to design a statement that reports both types of effects on a single statement. That is what the APB tried to do in Opinion no. 19. It cannot be done in such a way that both the objectives of the statement as well as the information reported on it are clear and understandable to financial statement users.

Both increases and decreases in each type of debt instrument are shown on the recommended statement of financing activities rather than only net changes. The fact that a company engaged in extensive short-term financing, for example, during the year may be regarded as significant by some financial statement users even though there was little or no net change in that liability. It indicates a dependence on credit that, if jeopardized, could have important implications. Although not illustrated in exhibit 2, the rate of interest and other significant terms of any new financing might usefully be described briefly either on the face of the statement or in notes to the statement. Other details of financing might also be usefully shown. Divorcing the statement from cash or working capital changes allows both the preparer and user to focus attention on financing activities and may open the door to several additional types of disclosure not illustrated in exhibit 2.

Statement of Investing Activities

A statement of investing activities is the third of the three statements recommended to replace the funds statement. The rationale for such a statement is that long-term investment in plant and in securities acquired for the purpose of control have special significance to financial statement users because they represent relatively inflexible long-term commitments and all changes in those assets should therefore be reported.

A statement of investing activities for Example, Inc., is presented in exhibit 3, page 103.

The statement of investing activities should disclose all acquisitions of long-term investments (including plant and equipment, investments in other controlled companies and deferred charges of various types) regardless of whether they were acquired for cash, for debt or equity securities or in exchange for other real assets. The statement of cash receipts and payments, of course, would show the cash paid for long-term investments, and the statement of financing activities would show the securities issued, but only the statement of investing activities would disclose all acquisitions. Retirements and other decreases of long-term investments, on the other hand, would appear only on the statement of cash receipts and payments to the extent they were sold for cash, and they would rarely appear on the statement of financing activities, but they would appear on the statement of investing activities.

Conclusion

In 1964 John B. Coughlan observed that the funds statement based on working capital changes has "baffled a generation of accounting students" and "it is therefore hardly conceivable that it has enlightened stockholders and other lay readers."[16] In the years since Coughlan wrote, two APB opinions on the

[16] Coughlan, p.24.

Exhibit 2

Example, Inc.
Statement of financing activities
Year ending December 31, 1977

	Increase or (decrease)
Debt financing	
Notes payable to banks	
Borrowed	$ 50,000
Repaid	(16,908)
Net amount borrowed	33,092
Mortgage repaid	(2,000)
Net increase in debt financing	31,092
Equity financing	
Convertible preferred	
Conversion of 300 shares $100 par value 5% convertible preferred for 1,500 shares $10 par value common stock	(30,000)
Common stock and capital in excess of par	
Issued 1,500 shares on conversion of 300 shares 5% convertible preferred	30,000
Issued 500 shares for $7,495 cash	7,495
Retained earnings	
Net increase	3,983
Net increase in equity financing	$11,478

Exhibit 3

Example, Inc.
Statement of investing activities
Year ending December 31. 1977

Plant and equipment

Land, buildings and equipment,	
December 31, 1976	$319,101
Plus purchases	62,119
	381,220
Less cost of properties disposed of	31,595
Land, buildings and equipment,	
December 31, 1977	$349,625

subject of funds statements have been issued. They have baffled another generation of accountants by casting the funds statement in the role of a statement with no clear goal or purpose but merely as a dumping ground for reporting heterogeneous transactions not reported elsewhere. The result should have been predictable: these statements do not enlighten either lay or sophisticated users.

The solution to the problem of the enigmatic funds statement does not lie in searching for a new definition of funds that will enable all of the objectives of the statements to be achieved. It lies in identifying clearly the financial reporting objectives that need to be achieved but are not achieved by the balance sheet and income statement and designing new statements that achieve those objectives. ■

Cash-flow Accounting

by Professor G. H. LAWSON, M.A.(Econ.), A.C.C.A.

There is a fairly widespread, but erroneous, belief that advocacy of cash-flow accounting is equivalent to the assertion that the disclosure of a company's summarized bank statement for the last twelve months is the best method of reporting financial performance.

IT is indeed perhaps a little unfortunate that the expression cash-flow accounting should have passed into common usage, though I must admit that a name more accurately describing the nature of the beast does not readily suggest itself – at least not to me.

What is cash-flow accounting?

As I understand things, or perhaps more precisely as I have hitherto attempted to argue the case for cash-flow accounting, it constitutes the analytical framework for linking past, present, and prospective financial performance. It is, therefore, a vehicle which may be used to disclose the past development of the finances of business and therefore the determinants of the true return actually received by proprietors or shareholders in the past. (Hereafter I shall refer to company and shareholders rather than to a business and its proprietors.) Alternatively it may be used as a system for disclosing the determinants of the true return shareholders are likely to receive in the future. Cash-flow accounting may therefore also be regarded as an aid to investor decision-making.

Thus, because the logic of the method, which derives from financial and economic theory, dictates that all financial transactions be specified as cash-flows to facilitate an allowance for the time-value of money as one of the costs of resource utilization (or, alternatively, as a prerequisite to the incorporation of an allowance for shareholder time-preference), there is quite clearly no valid reason for the inference that cash-flow accounting is synonymous with receipts and payments accounting in the traditional sense of that expression.

In the light of these introductory remarks it should now be apparent that most of my subsequent comments will be concerned little with the specification of a company as a total cash-flow model, but mainly with the nature, use, derivation, and disclosure of the data which should be enshrined within a cash-flow system. It may nevertheless be useful to have a company depicted as a cash-flow model in front of us (Illustration 1).

I take it I am on pretty firm ground in suggesting that one of the desiderata of a satisfactory method of disclosure is that the method should be capable of revealing the components of the true past and prospective return to shareholders and that, notwithstanding statement V 8 [formerly S 8[[*The Accountant*, August 7th, 1965], the purpose for which annual accounts are normally prepared ought to be to enable individuals to take investment decisions. Thus the true return obtainable by shareholders is directly and obviously related to the financial relationship subsisting between a company and its shareholders which is *par excellence* an example of the investment decision. A shareholder who commits capital now, thereby foregoing current consumption, obtains the opportunity to consume and/or reinvest an uncertain stream of benefits or net disposable receipts in the future.

In the case of a limited company, which enjoys a potentially indefinite life, the stream of net disposable receipts obtainable by the chain of successive generations of shareholders is an infinite stream of dividends (net of new injections of external equity finance). It is in this infinite stream of dividends that the return to shareholders truly resides and this applies equally to shareholders who do not propose to retain their shares indefinitely or, indeed, who propose to sell now. Individuals who invest for a finite time-period obtain an exit share price, the magnitude of which (assuming rational and informed investor behaviour), will depend upon the incoming shareholders' estimates of the dividend stream to be received thereafter.

Now it is easy to argue that, if companies were obliged to disclose their prospective dividend streams and the expected inflows and outflows of cash whence that dividend stream will ultimately emerge, investors would be able to deduce more accurate and objective share values, and simultaneously would be more capable of assessing relative financial efficiency. In addition to more rationally-based share prices, we might also expect the latter to become inherently more stable and, as a further consequence, a more accurate relationship between equity returns and the structure of fixed interest rates. Thus, with a much more efficient capital market it is not unreasonable to conclude that there would be an improvement in the whole process of economic organization in our market economy.

In a much more realistic mood, one is perhaps compelled to concede that an obligation to disclose all the information to which I have just referred – that is, future plans and estimates in full financial detail – would create an impossible situation for the majority of companies. But, accepting that it may not be possible to have fully detailed and quantified estimates of the components of an infinite dividend stream, one should not then leap to the inference that in the absence of complete information about the future, there is little point in having any more than we currently receive. Nor should we give up the attempt to develop new methods of presenting current information and managerial intentions, thus enabling investors to infer much more than is currently possible about the magnitudes and time-profile of a company's future dividend stream.

Determinants of the future dividend stream

Whilst it may be difficult, not to say impossible, to quantify all the determinants of a company's future dividend stream, they can, however, be specified. Such a specification, which is exemplified by the cash-flow model in front of you, is illuminating because it clearly suggests the manner in which all available

This is the first part of a paper delivered to this year's Cambridge Summer Conference of The Institute of Chartered Accountants in England and Wales. The author is Professor of Finance at the Manchester Business School.

Illustration 1

FRAMEWORK FOR A TOTAL CASH-FLOW FINANCIAL SYSTEM

End Year	1	2	3	etc.	etc.
(1) Increase or decrease in	+	+	+	+	+
bank balance or overdraft	−	−	−	−	−
(2) Net operating cash-flows	+	+	+	+	+
(3) Corporation taxes on (2)	−	−	−	−	−
(4) Capital expenditure (including portfolio investment)	−	−	−	−	−
(5) (i) cash grants; and	+	+	+	+	+
(ii) tax rebates resulting from tax depreciation allowances on (4)	+	+	+	+	+
(6) Long term debt flows (in and out)	+	+	+	+	+
including interest payments on debt	−	−	−	−	−
(7) Tax rebates on debt interest	+	+	+	+	+
payments	−	−	−	−	−
(8) External equity finance	+	+	+	+	+
(9) Sales of surplus assets	+	+	+	+	+
(10) Tax rebates on existing assets and losses brought forward	+	+	+	+	+
(11) Distributable equity cash-flows	$D_1(1-d)$	$D_2(1-d)$	$D_3(1-d)$	etc.	etc.
(12) *Less* External equity finance	E_1	E_2	E_3	etc.	etc.
(13) Shareholders' cash-flow stream	$D_1(1-d)-E_1$	$D_2(1-d)-E_2$	$D_3(1-d)-E_3$	etc.	etc.

Operating cash-flow statement (subheading (2))

End Year	1	2	3	etc.	etc.
(i) Sales receipts	+	+	+	+	+
(ii) Materials	−	−	−	−	−
(iii) Labour	−	−	−	−	−
(iv) Works overhead	−	−	−	−	−
(v) Administrative overhead	−	−	−	−	−
(vi) Selling overhead	−	−	−	−	−
Transfer to (2) above	+	+	+	+	+

$$W_0 = \frac{D_1(1-d)-E_1}{1+k} + \frac{D_2(1-d)-E_2}{(1+k)^2} + \ldots$$

Here the objective function allows for the contribution by equity shareholders of any new external finance ($E_1, E_2, \ldots$).

information ought to be presented if the shareholder is to be helped to infer the maximum about the level and growth of future dividends.

The dimensions of a future dividend stream clearly depend upon a number of factors of which, leaving aside taxes, investment incentives, and additional injections of equity finance, the following are perhaps the most important:

(*a*) the level of earnings generated by existing assets net of any capital expenditure (hereafter referred to as replacement expenditure) necessary to maintain the trading and productive capacity of those assets intact;

(*b*) the allocation of that earnings level between dividends and retentions, i.e., the pay-out ratio or plough-back ratio;

(*c*) the average rate of return which can be obtained by reinvesting retentions in new capital projects, i.e., capital expenditure over and above replacement expenditure, within the firm or, for that matter, in investments outside it;

(*d*) the time-profile of cash-flows expected from new capital projects;

(*e*) the level of debt-financing and debt-raising capacity.

Assuming for the moment that the foregoing information was available for the latest and previous accounting years, it would be possible to draw a set of logically-based numerical inferences about a company's future dividend stream.

Now it may be tempting to argue that, apart from two or three magnitudes which can be sensibly estimated, namely, (i) capital expenditure necessary to maintain trading and productive capacity intact and (ii) the expected rate of return on new capital projects including their expected cash-flow time profiles, most of the foregoing information can already be derived from the conventional profit and loss account (or a series thereof) and balance sheets, and that it is entirely open to whomsoever wishes to have this information to undertake the necessary analysis for himself.

Such a contention ought to be challenged for at least two reasons. First, if it is the case that published accounting data needs first to be further analysed before they can be used by investors to facilitate further inferences for decision-making purposes, the accountant has not completed his task.

A second and much more pertinent consideration is that even among accountants themselves, to say nothing of the armies of other professionals who lack the accountant's technical skill but nevertheless analyse accounts as a matter of daily routine, there is nothing like unanimity as to what further analysis ought to be undertaken. The simple, but nevertheless vital, point I am leading up to is this: if, as seems to be widely accepted, earnings are taken to be the funds which can be allocated between dividends and the finance to be utilized for *new* investment from which future earnings and dividend growth can be expected, earnings must necessarily be measured on a cash-flow basis.

Contrary to widespread belief, the measurement of earnings on a cash-flow basis is not merely a matter of adding back depreciation to conventional profit before deducting replacement capital expenditure. Converting conventional profit back to cash-flow earnings is in fact quite a detailed operation involving adjustments in respect of so-called working capital changes, between one accounting period and the next, i.e., changes in trade debtors, trade creditors, inventories, debtors, and creditors in respect of overheads and so on. In a situation in which there is turnover growth in money terms, a failure to make working capital adjustments to conventional profit can result in very significant and seriously misleading deviations between true cash-flow and what is popularly believed to be cash-flow.

In an inflationary world, that is in the real world, for any given rate of growth of output the deviation between true and 'conventional' cash-flows is magnified to the extent that a company is able to pass on price increases into selling prices. Hence the higher the rate of 'shifted' cost escalation, the higher is the inflationary contribution to the deviation. At this juncture it is perhaps important to give a real world example of the deviation to which I have just referred (Illustration 2).

In Illustration 2, retained earnings conventionally measured overstate retentions truly available for redeployment in new investments by a factor of approximately 4½. Had the company made a dividend payment of (say) £3,000 – superficially a very modest or conservative proportion of post-tax profits over the 10-year period in question – true retentions would have been overstated by a factor of about 8. It is also of significance, for a reason to which I shall refer in a moment, that in this particular case the year-by-year percentage deviation between 'conventional' cash-flow and true cash-flow was by no means consistent.

The relevance of the fact that the application of the conventional rules of accounting will generally result in a very serious overstatement of earnings truly retained for re-investment should now be apparent. It is this: if an accounting system does not provide an accurate measure of the earnings truly retained by a company on behalf of its shareholders it follows that the appraisal or estimation by shareholders of the effect of the plough-back decision on future earnings and dividend levels is systematically undermined from the start.

I strongly suspect that this state of affairs, conjoined with the fact that the deviation between 'conventional' and 'true' cash-flows is not a consistent percentage, explains why more than one member of the academy has found little or no positive correlation between plough-back and future earnings growth. Thus, using conventionally measured retentions as an implicit or explicit proxy for new capital investment, these researchers have correlated the former with future earnings levels, in an attempt to determine *inter alia* how profitably funds had been reinvested within the firm. But, as the accountant may prefer to put it, in so far as in circumstances of turnover growth (measured in money terms), some proportion of these (conventional) retentions has already been absorbed in the form of extra working capital in supporting a past turnover increase, this proportion is clearly not available for investment once again. It is in my view a major weakness of the accruals system of accounting that it facilitates this kind of confusion between capital and revenue; or, in other words, that it falsely gives the impression that certain funds which effectively have already become fixed capital investment are still available for distribution or r investment. As already stated, this possibility clearly has important implications for individuals who attempt to draw inferences about the growth of future earnings and dividends.

Sources and applications of funds

Now it will doubtless be objected that I am making too much of a song and dance about the extent to which the conventional system of accounting overstates the funds truly available for reinvestment in projects that will contribute to future earnings growth, and that the position can, in any event, be clearly elucidated by the 'appropriate' use of the source and application of funds statements. Whilst this latter assertion is absolutely correct, it is obviously important that the nature of the 'appropriate' use of source and application of funds statements should be clearly understood. There is also the pertinent but unresolved question as to how the investing public might be given sufficient guidance about the 'appropriate' usage of source and application of funds statements – and it is hardly necessary to add that at present companies are not legally obliged to disclose source and application of funds statements.

Supplemented by further actual data, an enlarged version (Illustration 3) of the previous illustration clearly suggests that the appropriate use of a source and application of funds statement requires, in effect, that it be converted into a cash-flow statement.

Thus, referring to the source and application of funds statement on the left-hand side of Illustration 3 and again assuming replacement expenditure to be £25,000 (this, as explained earlier, is probably a conservative estimate of the capital expenditure which was necessary to maintain trading and productive capacity intact) the amount of retentions truly available for re-investment in new capital projects is evidently equal to 'conventional' cash-flow *minus* replacement expenditure *minus* taxes provided *minus* increase in working capital, i.e. £69,266−£25,000−£19,171−£18,313=£6,782. This latter number is clearly given by operating cash-flows *minus* replacement expenditure *minus* taxes paid, i.e., £45,333−£25,000−£13,551=£6,782.

Given the importance which is almost universally attached to the conventional profit figure, the lay reader of the accounts of the company in question could, even if fortunate enough to be provided with a source and application of funds statement, be

Illustration 2

TEN-YEAR PERIOD ENDED SEPTEMBER 30th, 1969

Conventional accounts (i.e., accounting flows)	£	£	Cash-flows
Profit before depreciation (i.e., conventional cash-flow)	+69,266	+45,333	Pre-tax operating cash-flow
Historical cost depreciation	−20,020	−25,000	Estimated replacement capital expenditure (see note)
Taxation charged in profit and loss account	−19,171	−13,551	Taxes paid
Cumulative post-tax retained profit	+£30,075	+£6,782	Distributable cash-flow

As the following illustration suggests, £25,000 is probably a very conservative estimate of depreciation calculated on a current cost basis.

Assumptions

(i) Average asset life: seven years.

(ii) Weighted average cost of finance in money terms (i.e., company employs a mixture of debt and equity): 10 per cent per annum.

To recover current capital expenditure of £1,000 over a period of seven years it would be necessary to make a (constant) annual depreciation charge, *a*, of £205·4 given by:

$$£1{,}000 = a\left[\frac{1-(1+0{\cdot}1)^{-7}}{0{\cdot}1}\right]$$

whence, $a =$ £205·4.

On a fixed instalment basis, annual depreciation of £1,000÷7=£143 would be charged. The latter constitutes approximately 70 per cent of the £205·4 annual depreciation calculated on a current cost basis whereas the historical cost depreciation embodied in the 10-year illustration represents 80 per cent of the (£25,000) current cost depreciation estimate. To this extent the £25,000 estimate is conservative.

Illustration 3

TEN-YEAR PERIOD ENDED SEPTEMBER 30th, 1969

Source and application of funds statement					*Source and application of cash statement*
Source of funds	£	£	£		***Source of cash***
Share capital		500	500		Share capital
Bank overdraft		24,822	24,822		Bank overdraft
Short-term loan		6,263	6,263		Short-term loan
Hire-purchase credit		4,013	—		
'Conventional' cash-flow:					
Pre-tax profit	49,246				
Depreciation	20,020				
		69,266	45,333		Operating cash-flow
Total		£104,864	£76,918		Total
Application of funds	£	£	£	£	***Application of cash***
Capital expenditure:					*Capital expenditure:*
Replacement	25,000			25,000	Replacement
New projects	40,272			36,259	New projects
		65,272	61,259		
Investment in associated company		1,894	1,894		Investment in associated company
Taxes on profit		19,171	13,551		Taxes paid
Increase in working capital		18,313	—		
Increase in cash balance		213	213		Closing cash balance
Total		£104,864	£76.918		Total

forgiven for assuming that the company had earned (net of tax) £49,246—£19,171=£30,075 for its shareholders, but proposed to retain this profit for re-investment on their behalf in order to raise the future level of earnings. In general the lay reader would not be told that two correctives, one in respect of depreciation and the other in respect of working capital, usually need to be applied to (conventionally-measured) retentions before the finance truly available for raising the earnings level can be ascertained.

Had the company in question paid a dividend in excess of £6,782, as would have been legally possible, more would have been distributed to shareholders than had actually been generated from trading and production. In these circumstances the dividend would obviously have been subvented from non-equity cash which was probably intended as finance for fixed-capital formation – though again shareholders would not normally be informed of such a state of affairs. Furthermore, this situation could continue for as long as a company had access to external debt or equity cash sources. Thus the fact that it would not continue indefinitely would be due not to the operation of any inbuilt safeguard within the accruals system of accounting but because, in the long run, creditors and shareholders would, in the absence of a commensurate return on capital invested, refuse to provide further finance.

The fact that in a situation of indefinite turnover growth it is possible for 'conventional cash-flow' consistently to exceed 'true cash-flow' (and therefore to mask an uncovered dividend situation) also raises the presumption that for a particular rate of growth of turnover and selling price level, 'true cash-flow' may be persistently negative. In that case, trading and production are permanently subsidized by some other source of cash, whilst 'conventional profits' (net of depreciation) are persistently positive.

Again, it can be said that such a situation would not continue indefinitely because external sources of finance would sooner or later dry up. But once more the crux of the matter is the absence of a safeguard within the accruals system of accounting. In this case there is nothing, apart from the ultimate sanction just mentioned, to prevent the system disclosing a situation which on common-sense grounds alone ought to be rejected, namely, one in which a persistent negative operating cash-flow is apparently consistent with truly profitable business activity.

It is clearly necessary to emphasize that the duration and extent to which the accruals system of accounting may mask an adverse situation may be such that a substantial amount of capital may be eroded before the reality of the situation becomes patently obvious.

It is now perhaps important to state quite explicitly that the substance of the foregoing remarks amounts to a contradiction of the commonly held view that the difference between the cash-flow and accruals bases of measuring profits is merely a question of a difference in timing, and that both systems will disclose the same total profits in the long run. Apart from the fact that the question of timing is by no means a trivial consideration, the sum of cash-flow profits can only equal the sum of accrued profits in virtually only one very special case – namely, when on the winding-up of a business all assets and liabilities are realized at balance sheet values. For all practical purposes this, and one or two other highly restricted situations, can be ignored.

In summing up my comments under the first two sub-headings of this lecture, I would merely like to suggest that cash-flow accounting, as I understand it, constitutes the analytical framework in which should be embodied all financial information about the past, present, and future whence a company's proprietors can attempt to infer the magnitudes and time-profile of a potentially infinite dividend stream.

As I have attempted to show, in order to estimate the shareholders' expected cash-flows and especially the growth therein, it is necessary to infer another set of cash-flows, namely, a company specified as a cash-flow model. Whether one cares to admit it or not, the analysis of conventional accounting data as a prerequisite to the inferring of a future dividend stream amounts to the conversion of accounting flows into cash-flows. It is a curious paradox that whereas when engaging in forward planning the accountant will readily allow for extra working capital but then, in disclosing data to investors who fundamentally are engaging in the same forward planning exercise, acts as though he no longer believes that the working capital corrective is necessary. Thus, in the latter case the accountant effectively shifts the line of demarcation between revenue and capital thereby overstating the former and understating the latter.

(*To be concluded.*)

Cash-flow Accounting – II

by Professor G. H. LAWSON, M.A.(Econ.), A.C.C.A.

THE main purpose of the first part of this paper was to suggest that cash-flow accounting, as I have attempted to describe it, is justifiable in its own right in the logic of economics and finance.

As should now be apparent, and unlike the conventional accruals system of accounting, cash-flow accounting explicitly recognizes that a company's cash-generating and profit-making abilities are integrally related. Indeed, if we first allow for the time-value of money using a discounting or compounding procedure, the ability to generate cash and the capacity to earn profit are not merely integrally-related considerations but are in fact synonymous. If this is so, and in so far as inflation contributes to the deviation between 'conventionally-measured' (i.e., accrued) profits and profits measured on a cash-flow basis, the conventional method of accounting becomes increasingly less useful for managerial purposes in an inflationary world. The higher the rate of inflation the more acute the managerial problem, and the greater the motivation to switch to cash-flow accounting. This is my diagnosis of the causes of the recent renaissance of cash-flow accounting in its new forward-looking guise.

Is cash-flow accounting an alternative to accounting for inflation, or merely a reaction to it? In offering a brief answer to this question, I would say that cash-flow accounting is logically defensible in any circumstances but that as a managerial tool it is inherently more capable of demonstrating or accounting for the impact of inflation on company profits and finances than any other system. Hence, whilst the recent revival of interest in cash-flow accounting may have been stimulated by the present alarming rate of inflation which I suppose really began in 1969, cash-flow accounting *per se* is, in my view at least, much more than a mere pragmatic reaction to what I sincerely hope will soon be seen as a transient phenomenon.

Perhaps I may now refer to some of the wider aspects of inflation which have implications for the accounting process, that is to say, the accounting process as I understand it.

Future dividends

The actual return provided for a shareholder is delivered in actual money terms. The successive dividends in which this return truly resides are therefore not directly comparable in an inflationary world. Should a shareholder wish to ascertain whether a dividend is being maintained in terms of purchasing power, he must in some way correct for the rise in the general level of prices, or perhaps more accurately, for the rises in the prices which are relevant to his own pattern of expenditure.

It is in my view a mistake to conclude that because we live in a world characterized by endemic inflation, we must abandon accounting in money terms. (It is, of course, important that we should be in accord on matters of definition, though by now my own interpretation of accounting in money terms ought to be pretty clear.) It is not obvious to me that, in order to provide a shareholder with the information from which he can attempt to infer the magnitude and growth rate of future dividends, it is necessary to correct an array of magnitudes in the latest set of accounts with index numbers. Provided replacement expenditure is reasonably accurately measured in terms of current prices and, additionally, provided operating earnings have been calculated on a cash-flow basis (i.e., in the jargon of the accountant, working capital adjustments have been effected), the fund which is truly divisible between (*a*) dividends and (*b*) finance for redeployment in new investments, can always be measured in terms of current prices, that is, in actual money prices.

Something which, in my view, ought readily to suggest itself is that explicit attempts should be made to inform shareholders about the nature of the impact of inflation on a company's finances and how, in consequence, future dividends are likely to be affected.

In speaking of (say) 5 per cent annual inflation or a 5 per cent rise in the general level of prices between one year and the next, we are in fact making use of a weighted arithmetic average. Thus, if the average annual increase is 5 per cent, there must be many prices, of which wages and salaries are a notable example, that are rising at a faster annual rate than 5 per cent. Concurrently, other prices in the economy must, by definition, be increasing at less than 5 per cent annually. As an example of the latter, one can perhaps point to the unit capital costs of successive generations of fixed assets. In general it is to be expected that technological advance will cause a continuous decline in asset prices in real terms. Indeed one can go further and legitimately suggest that, generally speaking, for any given shareholder expectations about future inflation, escalating wage rates constitute a long run bias in favour of capital intensive manufacturing processes.

The extent to which the individual company is affected by inflation and price changes *vis-à-vis* other companies will obviously depend upon at least three things. First, the relative proportions of wage, salary, materials, overhead, and capital costs in the structure of its total annual cash outflows; secondly, the ability and inclination of the company to vary the ratio of the aforementioned factor costs; and thirdly, the ability and inclination of the company to pass on inflationary and other cost increases into selling prices. All three of these factors represent important considerations for any management which attempts to forecast the future development of its company's finances, or, in other words, the determinants of the cash-flow stream ultimately available for shareholders.

Equally they are considerations which ought to be held clearly in view by shareholders who attempt to deduce their future dividend streams. In the absence of an obligation to publish detailed and fully quantified financial plans, explicitly allowing for anticipated price changes, the impact of the latter on company finances should at least be the subject of a commentary in a company's annual report and accounts. Such a commentary would attempt an economic analysis along the lines I have just proposed and, contributing information about expected relative price changes would be of importance not only to shareholders but also from the standpoint of resource allocation at the macroeconomic level. Until the problems of inflation and rising prices are first explicitly and universally recognized for what they are, namely phenomena which ought to be taken into account in all current decisions and estimates by both management and shareholders, the whole process of resource allocation is less than efficient because all are attempting to optimize in relation to the wrong set of prices.

It would also follow from what I have been saying about the

The first part of this paper appeared in *The Accountant* of October 28th.

relative impact of inflation as between one company and the next, that the problem cannot be handled merely by the application of a corrective in the form of a single index number.

Extra cash for replacement

My previous suggestion that escalating wage rates constitute an effective long-run bias in favour of capital-intensive manufacturing processes is entirely consistent with the fact that the replacement cost of an asset may substantially exceed its historical cost. If the rise in the general level of prices is accompanied by changes in the relative prices of labour and capital goods, the technological possibilities of (capital-labour) substitution will always offer advantageous financial opportunities. The fact that asset replacement costs may, in absolute terms, exceed their historical costs is a financial problem which, to a greater or lesser extent, characterizes all economically-valid investment decisions.

The important distinction which therefore needs to be held clearly in view is the difference between relative and absolute price changes. All this is perhaps best described with the use of an example which, as will be shown, can also be used to draw out important implications from an accounting standpoint.

Illustration 4

Assumptions

(i) In a non-inflationary world investors require a discounted cash-flow rate of return of 5 per cent per annum from the ordinary shares of company X. (For illustrative convenience personal taxes are ignored.)

(ii) The shareholders of company X anticipate annual inflation at the rate of 5 per cent per annum, i.e., they expect their initial (money) capital invested to be eroded at the annual rate of 5 per cent.

(iii) Given the shareholders' required rate of return and their expectations about future inflation, the directorate of company X aims to provide its shareholders with a rate of return of at least 10 per cent per annum in money terms.

(iv) Company X has the opportunity to invest shareholders' capital in Project Y which has the following (expected) characteristics:

Capital cost in terms of 1971 prices – £3,352 (outflow)
Expected life – five years
Annual wage savings resulting from this investment in terms of 1971 prices – £1,000 (annual end-year inflow).

(v) Wage rates are expected to rise at an annual rate of 8 per cent.

Analysis

(*a*) In terms of 1971 prices, the discounted cash-flow rate of return provided by project Y is given by the value of r which satisfies the equation:

$$£3{,}352=\frac{1{,}000}{1+r}+\frac{1{,}000}{(1+r)^2}+\frac{1{,}000}{(1+r)^3}+\frac{1{,}000}{(1+r)^4}+\frac{1{,}000}{(1+r)^5}$$

$$=1{,}000\left[\frac{1-(1+r)^{-5}}{r}\right]$$

whence, using tables to solve for r,

$$r=15 \text{ per cent per annum.}$$

(*b*) In the absence of inflation and rising wage rates, and given the requirement of a shareholders' (minimum) rate of return of 5 per cent per annum, shareholders' capital would be maintained intact if project Y were capable of generating an annual cash-flow, a, given by:

$$£3{,}352=\frac{a}{1+0{\cdot}05}+\frac{a}{(1+0{\cdot}05)^2}+\frac{a}{(1+0{\cdot}05)^3}+\frac{a}{(1+0{\cdot}05)^4}+\frac{a}{(1+0{\cdot}05)^5}$$

$$=a\left[\frac{1-(1+0{\cdot}05)^{-5}}{0{\cdot}05}\right]$$

whence, again using tables,

$$a=£3{,}352\div4{\cdot}3295$$
$$=£774.$$

(i.e., a five-year annuity of £774 (paid in arrears) purchased at a price of £3,352 provides a rate of interest of 5 per cent in addition to the full recovery of capital).

If, in this case, depreciation disclosed in the accounts were based on the assets' historical cost and calculated on a fixed instalment basis, the annual charge would be £3,352÷5 = £670.

Annual depreciation actually charged would therefore represent only 670÷774 = 87 per cent of the provision which would be necessary to maintain the shareholders' initial capital of £3,352 intact.

(*c*) Taking into account the expected annual increases in wages, the discounted cash-flow rate of return provided by project Y is given by the value of r^* which satisfies the equation:

$$£3{,}352=\frac{1{,}000}{1+r^*}+\frac{1{,}000(1+0{\cdot}08)}{(1+r^*)^2}+\frac{1{,}000(1+0{\cdot}08)^2}{(1+r^*)^3}+\frac{1{,}000(1+0{\cdot}08)^3}{(1+r^*)^4}+\frac{1{,}000(1+0{\cdot}08)^4}{(1+r^*)^5}$$

$$=\frac{1{,}000}{r^*-0{\cdot}08}\left[1-\frac{(1+0{\cdot}08)^5}{(1+r^*)^5}\right]$$

whence, $r^*=22$ per cent per annum.

(*d*) Taking into account shareholder expectations about future inflation, in addition to their required rate of return, shareholders' capital would be maintained intact if project Y was capable of generating an annual cash-flow, a^*, given by:

$$£3{,}352=a^*\left[\frac{1-(1+0{\cdot}1)^{-5}}{0{\cdot}1}\right]$$

whence, $a^*=£3{,}352\div3{\cdot}7908$
$=£884.$

Assuming the same conventional depreciation charge as in (*b*) namely, £670, the latter would, in this case, represent only 670÷884 = 76 per cent of the provision which would be necessary to maintain the shareholders' initial capital of £3,352 intact.

(*e*) The nature of the bias in favour of capital intensive assets can now be drawn into sharper perspective. With reference to (*a*) to (*d*) above, and assuming again (i) that wage rates will continue to rise at an annual rate of 8 per cent, (ii) that shareholders continue to entertain the expectation of 5 per cent annual inflation (i.e., a required money return of 10 per cent), the proposition is that so long as the annual rate of increase in capital costs is less than 8 per cent, the generations of assets which succeed project Y will, *ceteris paribus*, become more profitable. This may be demonstrated in the following manner.

Given 8 per cent (expected) annual wage rate escalation and a shareholder (minimum) required rate of return of 10 per cent per annum, in money terms, the net present value of project Y is given by:

$$\frac{£1{,}000}{0{\cdot}1-0{\cdot}08}\left[1-\frac{(1+0{\cdot}08)^5}{(1+0{\cdot}1)^5}\right]-£3{,}352 \qquad (1)$$

Assuming the capital cost, of such a project as this, increases at the annual rate of 6 per cent, its net present value if adopted one year later would, other things being the same, be equal to:

$$\frac{£1{,}000(1+0{\cdot}08)}{0{\cdot}1-0{\cdot}08}\left[1-\frac{(1+0{\cdot}08)^5}{(1+0{\cdot}1)^5}\right]-£3{,}352(1+0{\cdot}06) \qquad (2)$$

Given that the value of (1) is positive, which necessarily follows from part (c), mere inspection shows that the value of (2) exceeds the value of (1).

Assuming, as seems to be suggested by what evidence there is, that the previous assumptions are realistic, it would follow, as already stated, that the level of economically viable capital-intensive projects in the economy as a whole will tend to rise in relation to the level of viable labour-intensive projects.

Conclusion

Perhaps I may now conclude this section, and indeed the paper itself, by drawing your attention to the fact that I have not attempted a direct answer to the question of how to provide the extra cash for the replacement of fixed assets at prices exceeding acquisition cost. It seems to me that the crux of the matter must, given that the relationship between a company and shareholders is *par excellence* an example of the investment decision, be concerned with the prevention of the erosion of shareholders' capital. As I understand things, it is this particular concept of the inviolability of proprietors' capital which ought to suggest the basis for measuring the cost of maintaining earning-power intact. In other words, in attempting to lay down a theoretical basis for company accounting, attention should be focused pre-eminently on the economic relationship between a company and its shareholders. There is no reason whatsoever for assuming that because a joint stock enterprise is endowed with a separate legal personality that a company directorate is accountable to that person as such or, perhaps more to the point, that in attempting to measure profits we may adopt an entity concept which allows us to pretend that shareholders no longer exist.

As I have attempted to show, if we start from the assumption that before earnings can be reckoned shareholders' capital must first be maintained intact, it is then clearly necessary for company decision makers to ensure that rising prices are correctly allowed for in investment decisions, that shareholder expectations about future inflation are also sensibly embodied in the analysis, and, last but not least, that due recognition is given to the time-value of money – which is another way of saying that we should explicitly recognize from the outset that shareholders have time-preferences.

V. THE RATIONALE OF CASH FLOW ACCOUNTING

Gerald H. Lawson

1. Introduction

As a method of measuring financial performance, cash flow accounting is concerned with most, if not all, of the traditional purposes of accounting and with many of the problems, notably inflation, prospective financial performance (Lawson, 1969), etc., to which accounting is now seeking to adapt.

Whereas virtually all variations of the historic, current and replacement cost bases of accounting studiously adhere to the principle of disclosing financial information through the profit and loss account and balance sheet media, developments in cash flow accounting in the last decade have emphasised (Lawson, 1969; Lee 1972) the income aspect of financial performance alone.

There are convincing reasons, well rooted in economic theory, why the axiomatic connection between the balance sheet and profit and loss account, which has often been too readily assumed in the past, should be severed. Thus, it might be argued, the proprietorship of a company quoted in the stock market can dispense with the balance sheet because it can observe the market value of its wealth on a daily basis. Moreover, a proprietorship desirous of the enjoyment of its full periodic income in the celebrated Hicksian[1] sense must anyway, as this paper explains, trade some proportion of its shares in the market. Market value criteria cannot therefore be ignored. But none of this implies that the balance sheet should be abandoned.

If the value of proprietorship wealth (value of a business in use) representing capitalised future dividends, which, in turn, derive from current and future earning power, is quoted in the market place, it is arguable that the balance sheet should reveal the market or exchange value of the net assets of the business (break-up or disposable value). A comparison of a company's value in use with its value in exchange yields important information from a resource allocation standpoint, not to mention the interests of its owners.

1. '... we ought to define a man's income as the maximum value which he can consume during a week, and still expect to be as well off at the end of the week as he was at the beginning' (Hicks, 1946).

The cash flow method of reporting past or prospective financial performance on a going-concern basis avoids any confusion between the functions of the income statement and balance sheet and certainly does not imply that all variants of the balance sheet concept should be cast overboard. Though this paper ignores the balance sheet and concentrates on comparisons between historic cost, current cost and cash flow bases of reporting annual income, a statement of financial affairs which is completely consistent with cash flow accounting can readily be devised.

Apropos some of the other principal purposes which accounting data are normally expected to serve, a number of important claims for cash flow accounting may be made. These include:

1. Whilst cash flow accounting is no more than receipts and payments accounting it is, contrary to what many accountants and others seem to have supposed, backed by sound economic principles (Lawson and Stark, 1975). Indeed, it is entirely consistent with both classical capital theory and modern capital market theory.[2]
2. Cash flow accounting is completely consistent with the principles of tax neutrality. Put more strongly; cash flow accounting is the only way of giving operational effect to the principles of tax neutrality (Lawson and Stark, 1975; Sumner 1975).
3. On a more pragmatic level, cash flow accounting is the only basis of corporate taxation which effectively has inbuilt safeguards that can prevent the kind of financial crisis suffered by British industry in 1974. This crisis resulted from an interesting combination of technical factors which, even now, have not been properly understood (Lawson and Stark, 1975; Lawson, 1974b).
4. Cash flow accounting is the only system of accounting that correctly captures relative price changes. It therefore succeeds in measuring periodic financial performance in terms of periodic purchasing power. That is to say, it compares like with like and also satisfies the necessary conditions for handling changes in the general level of prices (Lawson, 1974a).

The impression should by now have been given that cash flow accounting is a somewhat involved subject and that its protagonists are willing to have it judged against stringent criteria. This said, we may now turn to some of the details of the subject.

2. It is probably because accountants and others have failed to appreciate the relevance of the equilibrium assumptions of capital market theory that such irrelevant methods of accounting for financial performance in conditions of inflation have recently been proposed.

2. Cash flow accounting and shareholders

Cash flow accounting (CFA) is an accounting model which measures the return to shareholders in precisely the manner in which that return is enjoyed. The CFA model therefore explicitly allows for the existence of the individuals who are entitled to the proprietorship income which the historic cost-based conventional accruals accounting model (CAAM) allegedly measures. One of the most perplexing features of the CAAM is that it does not have shareholders in it and does not therefore specifically allow for the financial relationship between them and their company. Nor does the CAAM allow for the existence of capital markets.

Unless the financial relationship between a company and its shareholders is made explicit in, or as an adjunct to, the corporate income accounting process, there must at least be a strong presumption that, whatever the accounting model employed actually does measure, it is unlikely to reveal the (observable) manner in which consumable or reinvestable income is actually transferred to or received by shareholders. A realistic accounting model must also take cognisance of capital markets and share prices.

The foregoing propositions and some of their implications are elaborated in the following pages.

3. Return to shareholders

In defining the return which individuals or institutions obtain from *any* investment bought in the market place, it is useful to distinguish between the single period return (or periodic income) and the multiperiod return. The distinction between investment returns and the *disposal* (i.e. consumption and/or reinvestment) of those returns is also a matter of some consequence in the interpretation of periodic returns.

3.1. Single period return

The single period *rate of return*, r_e, obtained by an equity shareholder is the value of r_e which satisfies the equation

$$P_0 = \frac{D_1 + P_1}{1 + r_e} \tag{1}$$

whence

$$P_0 r_e = D_1 + (P_1 - P_0) \tag{1a}$$

(P_0 and P_1 are the entry and exit prices of the share at end-years 0 and 1 respectively; and, D_1 is a dividend received at the end of year 1.)

Both the L.H.S. and R.H.S. of (1a) define the single period return (as opposed to rate of return) to the investor.[3] The R.H.S. is however of *greater importance* in that it defines the *components* of the single period return and, in turn, raises a major category of considerations about the corporate income measurement process.

The single period return obtained by a shareholder is represented by a dividend paid directly to him[4] by his company *plus* the change in the market price of his share.[5] Assume that $P_1 > P_0$ and that the shareholder desires to consume (or reinvest elsewhere) the *whole* of his periodic income. If so, he must realise the proportion of his end-year 1 shareholding given by $P_1 - P_0$. He thereby maintains his initial (money) capital intact and therefore disposes of a periodic income measured in the classical Hicksian economic sense.

It must be emphasised that in order to realise (i.e. consume and/or reinvest) his *full* (Hicksian) income, the shareholder *must* transact in the market place. It is in this way, and only in this way, that the second component of the full periodic (Hicksian) income can be obtained. To state that the single period return to a shareholder is the sum of a component delivered directly by the company to shareholders, i.e. dividend, and a capital gain (or capital loss) which can only be obtained by making use of the capital market, is not to assert that capital gains (or capital losses) must necessarily be realised by shareholders annually. *What it does however imply is that, contrary to what has often been advocated, the Hicksian concept of periodic income cannot be applied by companies in determining shareholders' total periodic income.* All that companies can ever determine is the 'directly delivered' component of periodic income, the expected future values of which are at the root of the complex market capitalisation process which results in observable share prices.

As the writer has pointed out elsewhere (Lawson, 1975), the Sandilands Inflation Accounting Committee was wholly in error in stating that it is because a company's capitalisation rate and its expected future dividend stream both defy

3. L.H.S. and R.H.S. denote left and right-hand sides respectively.

4. A policy of zero dividends in no way negates the analysis which follows.

5. Should the shareholder provide further capital, B_1, for his company, equation (1a) needs to be adjusted to:

$$P_0 r_e = D_1 - B_1 + (P_1 - P_0). \tag{1b}$$

quantification that the Hicksian concept of income cannot be applied *by companies* (*Inflation Accounting*, 1975). The share prices which can be observed in the market place are the consequence of an automatic market capitalisation process and are precisely the values which are needed by investors (as opposed to companies) to give effect to the Hicksian concept of periodic income. The Hicksian concept of periodic income cannot generally be fully implemented by companies because the periodic income given by $D_1 + (P_1 - P_0)$ can only be paid out by companies when $P_1 = P_0$. In all other cases, i.e. in general, the company can only pay out D_1. The Sandilands Committee's suggestion that a company cannot pay out $D_1 + (P_1 - P_0)$ because P_1 and P_0 cannot be quantified is not only observably false; it is, conceptually speaking, also an error of double-counting (Lawson, 1975).

3.2. Multiperiod return

The familiar geometric mean *rate of return* obtained by a shareholder who holds for n years is given by the value of r_e which satisfies (2).

$$P_0 = \frac{D_1}{1 + r_e} + \frac{D_2}{(1 + r_e)^2} + \ldots + \frac{D_n + P_n}{(1 + r_e)^n} \tag{2}$$

The sequence of single period rates of return: $r_1, r_2, \ldots, r_3$, from which the geometric mean rate, r_e, is derived, is defined by equation (2a), namely,

$$P_0 = \frac{D_1}{1 + r_1} + \frac{D_2}{(1 + r_1)(1 + r_2)} + \ldots + \frac{D_n + P_n}{(1 + r_1)(1 + r_2)\ldots(1 + r_n)} \tag{2a}$$

whence,

$$P_1 = \frac{D_2}{1 + r_2} + \frac{D_3}{(1 + r_2)(1 + r_3)} + \ldots + \frac{D_n + P_n}{(1 + r_2)(1 + r_3)\ldots(1 + r_n)} \tag{2b}$$

$$\vdots$$

$$P_{n-1} = \frac{D_n + P_n}{1 + r_n}, \tag{2c}$$

and,

$$r_n P_{n-1} = D_n + (P_n - P_{n-1}). \tag{2d}$$

Since an n-period investor does not realise any of his shares until end-year n, the sequence of periodic incomes corresponding to the n-year holding period is therefore:

$$D_1, D_2, \ldots, D_{n-1}, D_n + (P_n - P_{n-1}). \quad \text{(2e)}^6$$

Except for the terminal period, the (finite) multiperiod sequence of periodic returns corresponds to the sequence of periodic income components i.e. dividends, delivered directly to the shareholder by the company. In the multiperiod situation, it is much more obvious that the company cannot distribute the full amount of the Hicksian periodic income since, in effect, such a periodic payment would violate the assumptions whence all subsequent dividends emerge. That is to say, any higher level of distributions could only be made possible either by resort to debt financing which is effectively a trade-off of future dividends for higher current dividends, i.e. a mere change in the time-profile of a dividend stream.[7] Alternatively, a company which, in attempting to distribute the full Hicksian periodic income, gradually realised its assets would contravene the ground rules in that it would quickly erode itself out of existence. Such a strategy would *in general* be non-optimal for shareholders since they would receive a stream of cash flows having a lower present value than that which could be provided by maintaining their company as a going concern.

It is worth emphasising that, whereas the terminal periodic income in the (finite) multiperiod case is by definition realised in full, it is, like the fully realisable periodic income of any other period, partly delivered by the company and partly obtainable from capital market transactions.

For completeness, the sequence of periodic incomes obtained by shareholders who realise the full periodic income each year may be considered. It is represented by:

$$D_1 + (P_1 - P_0),\ P_0/P_1[D_2 + (P_2 - P_1)],\ P_0/P_2[D_3 + (P_3 - P_2)], \ldots \quad (3)$$

Thus, in all three of the cases represented by (1a), (2e), and (3) respectively, the total periodic income which may be realised or disposed of by shareholders is the sum of a component delivered directly by the company and a second component which may – or may not – be realised by the selling (or buying) of shares in the market place. Except for the limiting case of share prices which are constant in

6. In (2), (2b), (2c), (2d), (2e) and (3) new capital, B_t, contributed by shareholders is ignored.

7. This strategy would effectively force shareholders to realise the (indirect) share appreciation component of periodic income since it amounts to the substitution of debt for equity capital which, in turn, will cause a decline in the value of equity shares by precisely the amount of the debt-financed component of the total dividend.

perpetuity, a company in any of the three above situations cannot provide shareholders with the full Hicksian periodic income. Since a company can only deliver the dividend part of the disposable periodic income, the corporate income measurement process can, to the extent that it is proprietorship-oriented in the sense described above, report no more than the determinants of current and future periodic dividend payments or, in the case of zero dividend payments, the determinants of plough-back alone.

4. The determinants of dividend and retentions

The determinants of a company's dividend payments are by definition periodic cash inflows and periodic cash outflows. Ignoring the peculiarities of the advance corporation tax, which is a feature of the U.K. imputation tax system,[8] the determinants of a company's dividends may be expressed[9] as:

$$D_j = k_j - h_j - A_j - F_j - t_j - R_j \pm M_j \pm N_j \pm B_j \tag{4}$$

The R.H.S. of (4) represents a company specified as a total cash flow statement. The symbol $\pm B_j$ stands for new capital raised (+) from shareholders or capital repaid (−). The shareholders' periodic cash flow is therefore $D_j \pm B_j$ and, assuming the company continues in perpetuity, the (geometric mean) rate of return on the *original* equity investment is given by the value of r_e which satisfies the equation:

$$B_0 = P_0 = \sum_{j=1}^{\infty} \frac{D_j + B_j}{(1 + r_e)^j} \tag{5}$$

An examination of equation (4) readily suggests the manner in which it (or part of it) may be applied as a criterion of financial performance. If a company is financially viable, the following condition will 'on average' be satisfied:[10]

$$k_j - h_j - A_j - F_j - t_j > 0 \tag{6}$$

8. Cash grants for which particular categories of capital expenditure may qualify are also ignored.
9. A full glossary of symbols is given at the end of this chapter.
10. The expression 'on average' or, alternatively, 'taking one year with another' really means:

$$\sum_{j=1}^{\infty} \frac{k_j - h_j - A_j - F_j - t_j}{(1 + r_e)^j} > 0$$

However, financial performance *is* measured annually so the problem of annual performance must be

The L.H.S. of (6) can be regarded as post-tax earnings measured on cash flow basis.

To the extent that:

$$k_j - h_j - A_j - F_j - t_j - D_j > 0 \tag{7}$$

a company's directorate has exercised a discretion to reinvest some proportion of internally-generated funds (which might otherwise have been distributed as dividends) in growth capital projects. The L.H.S. of (7) therefore defines plough-back or *internally-financed* capital formation. Total new capital formation is represented by R_j in (4), and may be partly financed by net externally-raised finance: $\pm M_j \pm N_j \pm B_j$.

Whilst a company's directorate is, to the extent that annual cash flow earnings are positive, able to exercise some discretion over the allocation of $k_j - h_j - A_j - F_j - t_j$ between dividends, D_j, and new capital formation, R_j, care needs to be exercised in the interpretation of the annual cash flow *earnings* criterion. This point is valid regardless of the accounting basis on which annual earnings are to be measured. The fact of the matter is that annual earnings *are only of significance for an individual year examined in isolation.* Thus, denoting $k_j - h_j - A_j - F_j - t_j$ with CFE_j, the sequence of earnings CFE_j, CFE_{j+1}, $CFE_{j+2}, \ldots$, is, even aside from the impact of inflation, not amenable to inter-period comparison. It is only possible for shareholders to enjoy each of the periodic earnings CFE_j, CFE_{j+1}, $CFE_{j+2}, \ldots$, if those earnings are distributed in full.[11] If earnings are less than fully distributed, a time series of earnings data is a misleading series from a financial performance measurement standpoint. In other words, there is an interdependence between the level of plough-back, no matter how small, and future earnings which, as stated, means that each of a sequence of earnings cannot be enjoyed by shareholders in full. In fact, plough-back represents a sacrifice of current earnings in return for higher future dividends.

There is, thus, virtually no logical escape from the proposition that the dividend payment (or the determinants thereof) is the critical focal point in the corporate periodic income measurement process. However, since the plough-back level represents the measure of the amount that is currently sacrificed by shareholders in return for higher future dividends, it (the current plough-back level) is obviously a number of some considerable relevance to shareholder financial welfare. That is to say, the true current plough-back level is also, or at least

faced. Hence the attempt to measure annual earnings on a cash flow basis and the possible need of a little subjective judgement as implied by 'on average'.

11. A somewhat similar point has recently been cogently argued by A. J. Merrett (1975); it is considered at greater length by Lawson and Bean (n.d.).

arguably, an important piece of information in relation to the complex capitalisation process already mentioned, viz., the estimation and capitalisation of future dividends.

A cash flow system of accounting is the one and only method of disclosing accurate plough-back data. This is not to say that a cash flow earnings measure of plough-back will always be perfectly accurate. This is not so. The accuracy of the plough-back measure depends essentially upon the accuracy with which the dividing line between replacement investment, A_j, and growth investment, R_j, can be drawn. This may not always be easy. In defining plough-back as the funds that can be used to finance *new* capital formation, the pre-empted component of 'conventionally measured' earnings represented by periodic working capital investment must explicitly be allowed for. A genuine cash flow measure of earnings automatically includes the periodic working capital corrective.

5. Comparison with other accounting systems

The foregoing analysis represents at least part of the logical basis of a corporate accounting model which is consistent with observable reality and which has as its main aim the reporting of financial performance from a proprietorship standpoint. If this aim is accepted as the paramount objective of accounting, the cash flow earnings equation can be taken as a yardstick for evaluating other accounting models in that it can be used to indicate the extent to which the latter over- or understate the earnings which may truly be divided between plough-back and dividends in an individual year.[12]

5.1. CAAM versus CFA model

Earnings, $E_j^{(H)}$, measured in accordance with generally-accepted (historic cost-based) accounting principles are given by:

$$E_j^{(H)} = d_j - (a_{j-1} + b_j - a_j) - L_j - F_j - t_{j+1} - t_{j+1}^* \tag{8}$$

12. An especially interesting aspect of this problem concerns the effect of overestimated earnings on the measure of plough-back and, in turn, the possible correlation between the latter and future earnings growth. For example, if earnings of 100 embody a 25 per cent overstatement, i.e. should be 80, a 40 per cent pay out ratio will cause plough-back to be overstated by 50 per cent. That is to say, plough-back would be stated as 100 − 40 = 60 instead of 80 − 40 = 40. As the writer has shown elsewhere (Lawson, 1974a; 1974b), this kind of overstatement can provide a complete explanation for the low to zero correlations between plough-back and future earnings growth which have been reported by a number of researchers during the last decade or more.

Cash flow earnings, CFE_j, have already been defined as:

$$CFE_j = k_j - h_j - A_j - F_j - t_j \tag{6}$$

Deducting (6) from (8) we obtain:

$$\begin{aligned} E_j^{(H)} - CFE_j &= (d_j - k_j) - (b_j - h_j) + (a_j - a_{j-1}) + \\ &\quad + (A_j - L_j) + (t_j - t_{j+1} - t^*_{j+1}) \quad (9)^{13} \\ &= l_j - i_j + f_j + \text{ditto} + \text{ditto} \\ &= \Delta \text{ debtors} - \Delta \text{ creditors} + \Delta \text{ inventories} + \text{ditto} + \text{ditto} \end{aligned}$$

$= p_j$ (periodic working capital investment) $+ A_j - L_j$ (depreciation shortfall) $+ t_j - t_{j+1} - t^*_{j+1}$ (difference between tax paid and total tax provided).[14]

Thus, in order to convert *pre-tax* conventionally-calculated profits into earnings measured on a cash flow basis, the former needs to be adjusted by p_j and $A_j - L_j$. That is to say,

$$CFE_j(\text{pre-tax}) = d_j - (a_{j-1} + b_j - a_j) - L_j - F_j - p_j - (A_j - L_j) \tag{10}$$

Consequently, the implementation of a full-blooded system of external reporting on a cash flow basis in no way interferes with a company's internal accounting and data processing. It merely necessitates the application of two simple correctives to the profit and loss account.

5.2 CAAM versus Sandilands current cost accounting (CCA) model

The comparison in this case is equation (8) with equation (11), i.e.

$$E_j^{(H)} = d_j - (a_{j-1} + b_j - a_j) - L_j - F_j - t_{j+1} - t^*_{j+1} \tag{8}$$

$$E_j^{(S)} = d_j - (a_{j-1} + b_j - a_j) - \alpha_j - L_j^{(S)} - F_j - t_{j+1}^{(S)} - t_{j+1}^{*(S)} \tag{11}$$

$$E_j^{(H)} - E_j^{(S)} = \alpha_j + L_j^{(S)} - L_j + t_{j+1}^{(S)} + t_{j+1}^{*S} - t_{j+1} - t^*_{j+1} \qquad (8)\text{–}(11)$$

13. The symbol t^*_{j+1} stands for a transfer to a tax equalisation account.

14. In recent years $E_j^{(H)}$ has, in the U.K., exceeded CFE_j by very substantial margins at the company sector level. Indeed, in 1974 a positive $E_j^{(H)}$ was associated with a negative CFE_j. This situation was

Equation (11) differs from (8) in two fundamental respects and in two further respects which are a consequence of the corporate tax implications of the Sandilands CCA prescriptions (Inflation Accounting Steering Group, 1976).

The term α_j in equation (11) represents the Sandilands cost of sales adjustment and is given by:

$$\alpha_j = \frac{(y_j - y_{j-1})(x_j + x_{j-1})}{2} \tag{12}$$

where, y_{j-1}, y_j are opening and closing unit inventory costs respectively (measured on a F.I.F.O. basis); and x_{j-1}, x_j are opening and closing inventory volumes respectively. (Thus, $x_{j-1}y_{j-1} = a_{j-1}$ and $x_j y_j = a_j$.)

The term $L_j^{(S)}$ stands for depreciation calculated in accordance with the indexation method proposed by the Sandilands Committee. Indexed depreciation, $L_j^{(S)}$, can readily be compared with the historic cost-based depreciation charge L_j in equation (8). For example, if a company has a stock of assets, each of which has a life expectancy of w years, acquired at prices of $A_{-z}, A_{-z+1}, \ldots, A_{-1}$, $z, z-1, \ldots, 1$ year ago, L_0, is given by:

$$L_0 = \sum_{j=-z}^{-1} A_j/w \tag{13}$$

By contrast, the Sandilands indexed depreciation, $L_0^{(S)}$, at end-year 0 is given by:

$$L_0^{(S)} = I_0 \sum_{j=-z}^{-1} A_j/wI_j \tag{14}$$

where $I_{-z}, I_{-z+1}, \ldots, I_0$ is the sequence of values of the index of asset prices at end-years $-z, -z+1, \ldots, 0$.

In conditions of endemic inflation, that is, in general, $L_j^{(S)} > L_j$. Similarly, in an inflationary world, α_j will usually be positive for the majority of companies and the cumulative cost of sales adjustment $\sum_{j=1977}^{j} \alpha_j$ will be positive for an even larger majority.

The corporation tax charge, t_{j+1}, under the existing U.K. corporation tax regime, included in equation (8) differs from the 'Sandilands' tax charge, $t_{j+1}^{(S)}$. If, as is often the case in the U.K., total capital expenditure, $A_j + R_j$, incurred in

mainly due to the high periodic working capital investment, p_j, the main determinants of which were relative price changes. (See Lawson, 1974b, page 6 et seq.)

period j qualifies for a 100% tax depreciation allowance,[15] t_{j+1} is given by:

$$t_{j+1} = T_j[d_j - (a_{j-1} + b_j - a_j) - F_j - A_j - R_j - STA_j] \tag{15}$$

where T_j stands for the nominal rate of corporation tax in period j. By comparison, the Sandilands tax charge, $t^{(S)}_{j+1}$, is given by:

$$t^{(S)}_{j+1} = T_j[d_j - (a_{j-1} + b_j - a_j) - F_j - A_j - R_j - \alpha_j] \tag{16}$$

The difference between t_{j+1} and $t^{(S)}_{j+1}$ is obviously given by:

$$t_{j+1} - t^{(S)}_{j+1} = T_j(\alpha_j - STA_j) \tag{17}$$

Whereas α_j is the previously-defined Sandilands cost of sales adjustment, STA_j represents the stock appreciation allowance for which companies are eligible under the existing U.K. corporation tax regime and is given by:

$$\begin{aligned} STA_j &= (a_j - a_{j-1}) - 0.15\{d_j - (a_{j-1} + b_j - a_j) - F_j - A_j - R_j\} \\ &= 0.85(a_j - a_{j-1}) - 0.15\{d_j - b_j - F_j - A_j - R_j\} \end{aligned} \tag{18}$$

If unit inventory costs (measured on a FIFO-basis) tend to increase over time, the Sandilands cost of sales adjustment, α_j, will reasonably approximate the stock appreciation allowance, STA_j, taking one year with another.[16] If so, the Sandilands corporation tax charge, $t^{(S)}_{j+1}$, is a tolerable approximation of the tax, t_{j+1}, charged under the present tax system.

The transfer, t^*_{j+1}, to a tax equalisation account shown in equation (8) is intended to adjust the tax charge, t_{j+1}, such that the total tax provision, $t_{j+1} + t^*_{j+1}$, expressed as a percentage of pre-tax profit, $d_j - (a_{j-1} + b_j - a_j) - L_j - F_j$, is equal to the nominal rate of corporation tax, T_j. That is to say, t^*_{j+1} satisfies the equation:

$$\frac{t_{j+1} + t^*_{j+1}}{d_j - (a_{j-1} + b_j - a_j) - L_j - F_j} = T_j \tag{19}$$

15. For simplicity, possible tax depreciation allowances at lower rates on capital expenditure incurred in previous periods are ignored here.

16. This proposition is based upon results yield by a computer-based, multiperiod total financial model. Note, however, that if unit inventory costs fall, that is, if $y_{j-1} > y_j$, the Sandilands cost of sales adjustment will take on a negative value. (See section 5.3.1.).

Similarly, the 'Sandilands' tax equalisation account transfer is the value of $t^{*(S)}_{j+1}$ which satisfies the equation:

$$\frac{t^{(S)}_{j+1} + t^{*(S)}_{j+1}}{d_j - (a_{j-1} + b_j - a_j) - \alpha_j - L^{(S)}_j - F_j} = T_j \tag{20}$$

Since

$$\frac{t_{j+1} + t^{*}_{j+1}}{d_j - (a_{j-1} + b_j - a_j) - L_j - F_j} = \frac{t^{(S)}_{j+1} + t^{*(S)}_{j+1}}{d_j - (a_{j-1} + b_j - a_j) - \alpha_j - L^{(S)}_j - F_j} \tag{21}$$

and

$$d_j - (a_{j-1} + b_j - a_j) - L_j - F_j > d_j - (a_{j-1} + b_j - a_j) - \alpha_j - L^{(S)}_j - F_j \tag{22}$$

then

$$t_{j+1} + t^{*}_{j+1} > t^{(S)}_{j+1} + t^{*(S)}_{j+1} \tag{23}$$

But if, as seems to be the case,

$$t_{j+1} \simeq t^{(S)}_{j+1} \tag{24}$$

then

$$t^{*}_{j+1} > t^{*(S)}_{j+1} \tag{25}$$

The last four equations viz., (19), (20), (21) and (22), constitute a precise juxtaposition of the CAAM and CCA earnings measures and are worthy of emphasis. They may be summarised as follows. The pre-tax CAAM earnings measure will usually exceed its CCA counterpart. The CAAM total tax provision will usually exceed the corresponding CCA total tax provision. However, since the tax charge, $t^{(S)}_{j+1}$, implicit in the CCA earnings measure will approximate the tax charge, t_{j+1}, payable under the existing corporation tax regime, the Sandilands (profit) transfer, $t^{*(S)}_{j+1}$, to the tax equalisation account will be less than the corresponding transfer under the CAAM in conjunction with the existing tax regime. It also follows, as is the explicit intention of the Sandilands CCA proposals, that $E^{(S)}_j < E^{(H)}_j$. To that extent, the CCA earnings measure, $E^{(S)}_j$, can be regarded as an improvement on earnings, $E^{(H)}_j$, measured in accordance with generally-accepted historic cost principles. In the present context 'improvement' means superior proxy of the earnings which may truly be allocated between dividends and plough-back.

5.3. Sandilands CCA model versus CFA model

To determine whether the CCA earnings measure is a reasonable proxy for the cash flow earnings, CFE_j, which may truly be divided between plough-back and dividends *in an individual year*, it is merely necessary to compare equations (6) and (11), i.e.,

$$E_j^{(S)} = d_j - (a_{j-1} + b_j - a_j) - \alpha_j - L_j^{(S)} - F_j - t_{j+1}^{(S)} - t_{j+1}^{*(S)} \quad (11)$$

$$CFE_j = k_j - h_j - A_j - F_j - t_j \quad (6)$$

$$E_j^{(S)} - CFE_j = (p_j - \alpha_j) + [A_j - L_j^{(S)}] + [t_j - t_{j+1}^{(S)} - t_{j+1}^{*(S)}] \quad (11)\text{–}(6)$$

If $E_j^{(S)} - CFE_j$ is positive, the CCA earnings measure overstates the amount which may truly be divided between plough-back and dividends in an individual year and *vice versa*. An examination of the three components of $E_j^{(S)} - CFE_j$, each of which is basically a different problem-area, facilitates inferences as to the conditions under which $E_j^{(S)} - CFE_j > 0$.

5.3.1. Periodic working capital investment, p_j, versus the cost of sales adjustment, α_j

As already indicated, periodic working capital investment, p_j, is given by:

$p_j = l_j - i_j + f_j$ [i.e., periodic change in (debtors *minus* creditors *plus* inventories)]

and

$f_j = a_j - a_{j-1}$ [periodic change in inventories]

$= x_j y_j - x_{j-1} y_{j-1}$.

But,

$\alpha_j = \frac{1}{2}(y_j - y_{j-1})(x_j + x_{j-1})$ [Sandilands cost of sales adjustment]

$$\therefore f_j - \alpha_j = \tfrac{1}{2}(y_j + y_{j-1})(x_j - x_{j-1}). \quad (26)$$

In conditions of endemic inflation, both f_j and α_j will usually take on positive values because of rising unit inventory costs and/or increasing physical inventory volumes. However, if f_j and α_j are generally positive, then, as the above analysis shows, f_j will usually exceed α_j. Moreover, in inflationary conditions, the probability that f_j is positive must be higher than the probability of a positive α_j since an occasional decline in unit inventory costs i.e. a situation such that $y_{j-1} > y_j$, can be countervailed by rising inventory volumes (i.e. $x_j > x_{j-1}$) such that $a_j > a_{j-1}$ (that is $f_j > 0$). By contrast, α_j will take on negative values whenever $y_{j-1} > y_j$ regardless of the values of x_{j-1} and x_j. In sum, the Sandilands cost of sales adjustment, α_j, will, in inflationary conditions, generally fall short of the full 'stock appreciation' corrective, $f_j = a_j - a_{j-1}$, which must be applied to the CAAM if it is desired to express earnings as the amount which can truly be allocated between plough-back and dividends.

As already indicated, f_j is one of the three components of p_j. The CCA method takes no cognisance of the other two, namely, l_j and i_j. Although l_j and i_j may, to a large extent, cancel out for companies in aggregate, the ratio of l_j to i_j at the level of the individual firm is characterised by a significant degree of (observable) dispersion and should therefore be treated as a separate corrective to the CAAM. In that the CCA model takes no cognisance of l_j and i_j, it is deficient by comparison with the CFA model.

5.3.2. Capital investment and indexed depreciation, $L_j^{(S)}$

The computation of the Sandilands depreciation charge, $L_j^{(S)}$, is a rather crude exercise in the use of index numbers in that such a calculation will eliminate much of the dispersion about the average of asset costs. This dispersion across companies is precisely the kind of information that ought to be captured by the accounting process in order to reveal different degrees of company profitability.

Rather more to the point is the question of what the Sandilands indexed depreciation method actually achieves in relation to crucial distinction between the earnings of an individual period *viewed in isolation* and the earnings of a *sequence* of periods.

Consider a purely equity-financed company[17] which has acquired identical assets at prices of $C_{-z}, C_{-z}(1+g), C_{-z}(1+g)^2, \ldots, C_{-z}(1+g)^{w-1}$ at end-years $-z, -z+1, -z+2, \ldots, -z+w-1$. Assume that each of these assets has a life expectancy of w years and, that after end-year $-z+w-1$, when asset prices continue to increase at the rate g, one asset is replaced annually. Hence, after end-year $-z+w-1$ the company operates with an asset stock represented by w

17. The choice of a purely equity-financed company is a simplifying assumption which immediately obviates provisos concerned with such tangential matters as long term money gains, etc.

identical assets. The respective investment and Sandilands-type depreciation policies of the company are thus:

End-year j	$-z$	$-z+1$	$-z+2$	...	$-z+w-1$	$-z+w$	$-z+w+1$
Investment, C_j	C_{-z}	$C_{-z}(1+g)$	$C_{-z}(1+g)^2$	...	$C_{-z}(1+g)^{w-1}$	$C_{-z}(1+g)^w$	$C_{-z}(1+g)^{w+1}$
Depreciation, $L_j^{(S)}$	—	$\frac{C_{-z}(1+g)}{w}$	$\frac{2C_{-z}(1+g)^2}{w}$	...	$\frac{(w-1)C_{-z}(1+g)^{w-1}}{w}$	$C_{-z}(1+g)^w$	$C_{-z}(1+g)^{w+1}$

As the above table shows, it is only in conditions of zero investment growth that Sandilands-type depreciation, $L_j^{(S)}$, will coincide with total investment, C_j. Given any degree of growth, the *present* value of a sequence of Sandilands depreciation charges will, assuming continuously rising asset prices, generally be lower than the present value of the corresponding sequence of investments. It is therefore only in continuing conditions of zero investment growth that Sandilands depreciation is correct from the standpoint (a) of periodic earnings measured in isolation; *and* (b) of a time-series of earnings. In these conditions, periodic earnings and periodic dividends will, or should, coincide and the CCA model will also give full effect, in terms of the purchasing power of the period in which it was incurred, to total capital expenditure, C_j.

Given any degree of investment growth, the Sandilands depreciation charge will, ignoring the indivisibility problem,[18] always be equal to the cost of replacing the number of plant years consumed in the previous period. Hence, the CCA model is, like most other methods of accounting, unsuitable for disclosing a sequence of annual earnings, since it generally fails fully to give effect to total capital expenditure, C_j. Unless the serial dependence between the growth capital expenditure, R_j, in any individual year and future earnings growth is recognised, the CCA model will therefore repeat the classic error of most other accounting models and, even in a world free of inflation, will rarely generate a time-series of earnings which are amenable to inter-period comparison.

18. For example, at end-year $-z+1$ in the above table, $C_{-z}(1+g)/w$ is an arbitrary allocation representing the current cost of one plant year. It is arbitrary in the sense that assets cannot be decomposed into plant years simply by dividing their current costs by their expected lives. Second-hand assets with one-year expected lives may however be available in the market place. By contrast, at end-year $-z+w$, $C_{-z}(1+g)^w$ is the current cost of replacing w plant years and in no sense constitutes an arbitrary allocation.

5.3.3. Taxes paid, t_j, versus total taxes provided, $t^{(S)}_{j+1} + t^{*(S)}_{j+1}$, under the Sandilands proposals

Given the present U.K. basis of corporation tax, and recalling the time-lag between tax charges and tax payments, actual taxes, t_j, *currently* paid in any year j will generally be less than the total tax, $t^{(S)}_{j+1} + t^{*(S)}_{j+1}$, which would be provided in accordance with the Sandilands proposals.[19] Hence, whereas in general *pre-tax* $E^{(S)}_j >$ *pre-tax* CFE_j, the relative post-tax position is much less obvious.

That is to say, if, in general

$$t_j < t^{(S)}_{j+1} + t^{*(S)}_{j+1},$$

and

$$k_j - h_j - A_j - F_j < d_j - (a_{j-1} + b_j - a_j) - \alpha_j - L^{(S)}_j - F_j,$$

it is not clear whether

$$k_j - h_j - A_j - F_j - t_j < d_j - (a_{j-1} + b_j - a_j) - \\ - \alpha_j - L^{(S)}_j - F_j - t^{(S)}_{j+1} - t^{*(S)}_{j+1}$$

i.e., whether $CFE_j < E^{(S)}_j$.

It can however be safely suggested that the absolute deviation between $E^{(S)}_j$ and CFE_j will, as a rule, be less than the absolute deviation between *pre-tax* E_j and *pre-tax* CFE_j. Thus, because the Sandilands post-tax measure of earnings, $E^{(S)}_j$ includes a transfer, $t^{*(S)}_{j+1}$, to a tax equalisation account, not to mention the possibility that $t^{(S)}_{j+1} > t^{(S)}_j$, earnings, $E^{(S)}_j$, may somewhat fortuitously turn out to be a reasonable proxy for CFE_j.

In concluding these comments on corporate taxation, two crucial qualifications must be made. Because U.K. corporate tax payments, tax charges and profit transfers to tax equalisation accounts are not based upon a pre-tax cash flow measure of earnings, both U.K. corporate tax policy and tax equalisation accounting are at odds with the principles of tax neutrality (Sumner, 1975). Moreover, since both the existing U.K. basis of taxation and the basis proposed in the Sandilands Report do not allow for the full tax deductibility of periodic working capital, p_j, both will inevitably cause the effective rate of tax

19. In the interests of clarity, it is emphasised that in this comparison CFE_j embodies the existing tax regime whereas $E^{(S)}_j$ includes the existing tax regime with I_j substituted for STA_j. However, as already explained in section 5.2, these two regimes closely approximate each other and therefore $t^{(S)}_{j+1} \simeq t_{j+1}$.

paid on cash flow earnings, CFE_j, to exceed the nominal rate of corporation tax (Lawson, 1974b).

5.3.4. Sandilands CCA model versus CFA model: conclusion

As the comparison of equations (6) and (11) shows, there are three significant differences between the bases of the Sandilands CCA model and the CFA model respectively. Viewing the earnings of an individual period in isolation, the first of these differences will generally result in an overstatement of the earnings truly available for allocation between plough-back and dividends. The third difference, namely, that between taxes paid and total taxes provided, will tend to countervail the first two. That is to say, *post-tax* cash flow earnings, CFE_j, will usually be more closely aligned with the *Sandilands post-tax* measure, $E_j^{(S)}$, than is the case with the corresponding pre-tax magnitudes.

Even though the Sandilands post-tax *periodic* earnings measure, $E_j^{(S)}$, should, by and large, prove to be a reasonable proxy for CFE_j – a testable assumption which must be subject to very considerable doubt – the Sandilands CCA model cannot be regarded as a theoretically satisfying basis for measuring the amount of earnings which are truly available for allocation between dividends and funds available for the financing of new capital formation. Any earnings measure which relies on a combination of the dubious logic of tax equalisation accounting and the time-lags between tax payments and total tax provided to countervail a failure fully to allow for the cost of periodic working capital investment and a depreciation shortfall must be suspect.

The inability of the CCA model to cope with the serial dependence problem is an even greater indictment of the method and probably resides in the failure on the part of the Sandilands Committee to understand the relevance of the Hicksian concept of personal income to the measurement of company financial performance.

Finally, it is interesting to ponder whether the inaccuracy of accounting earnings measures is correctly detected by markets and whether such inaccuracy has implications for resource allocation. I incline to the view that, whereas the U.K. stock market may be efficient, the process of resource allocation by managerial decision-making may be much less so; and, that the Government's management of the economy including its fiscal policy has been disastrously misled by accounting data in the past. Judging from what one hears at the moment, there seems every chance that the same thing could happen again, though perhaps in a much less acute form. I would however speculate that bank managers will not be caught out the next time round and that henceforth they will rightly do their accounting in cash flow terms.

List of symbols

a_j	inventory at *end of year j* valued on a FIFO basis $(= x_j y_j)$
A_j	replacement capital expenditure paid in year j
α_j	Sandilands cost of sales adjustment for year j
b_j	revenue expenditure incurred by a company in year j
B_j	external equity finance received (+) or repaid (−) by a company in year j
c_j	cost of sales in year j
C_j	total capital expenditure incurred in year j $(= A_j + R_j)$
CFE_j	post-tax earnings measured on a cash flow basis in year j
d_j	sales recorded in year j (invoiced sales *plus* cash sales)
D_j	dividend paid to shareholders in year j
$E_j^{(H)}$	net profit (i.e. less depreciation, interest and total tax provided) measured on an historic cost basis in year j
$E_j^{(S)}$	net profit (i.e. less depreciation, interest and total tax provided) measured on a CCA basis in year j
f_j	*additional* inventory investment in year j $(= a_j - a_{j-1} = b_j - c_j)$
F_j	interest charged (and paid) in year j
h_j	cash paid to suppliers in year j on revenue accounts
i_j	*additional* credit taken in year j $(= b_j - h_j)$
I_j	index of asset acquisition costs at end-year j
j_j	total credit taken at *end of year j* $(= \sum i_j)$
k_j	cash collected from customers in year j on account of sales (including cash sales)
l_j	*additional* credit given in year j $(= d_j - k_j)$
L_j	accounting depreciation (historic-cost basis)
$L_j^{(S)}$	accounting depreciation calculated in accordance with the Sandilands indexation method
M_j	year j increase in bank overdraft or reduction in bank balance (+); or, decrease in bank overdraft or increase in bank balance (−)
N_j	medium and/or long term debt raised (+) or redeemed (−) in year j
p_j	additional working capital invested in year j $(= l_j + f_j - i_j)$
P_j	share price at end-year j
r_e	geometric mean cost of equity capital (shareholder rate of return)
$r_1, r_2, \ldots, r_n$	sequence of single period costs of equity capital
R_j	growth investment in year j
STA_j	stock appreciation allowance in year j
t_j	corporation tax payment due in year j
t_{j+1}	tax charge in year j payable in year $j+1$ (CAAM in conjunction with the existing tax regime)
$t_{j+1}^{(S)}$	tax charge in year j payable in year $j+1$ (Sandilands CCA proposals)
t_{j+1}^{*}	profit transfer to tax equalisation account (CAAM in conjunction with the existing tax regime)
$t_{j+1}^{*(S)}$	profit transfer to tax equalisation account under the Sandilands CCA proposals
T_j	nominal rate of corporation tax charged in year j

w	expected life of an asset
x_j	physical inventory volume at end-year j
y_j	unit inventory cost at end-year j
z	age of first asset acquired with expected life of w

References

Hicks, J. R., 1946, *Value and Capital*, (Oxford University Press), p. 172.

Inflation Accounting: Report of the Inflation Accounting Committee, Cmnd. 6225, H.M.S.O., 1975, September, pp. 28–30.

Inflation Accounting Steering Group, 1976, *Guidance Manual on Current Cost Accounting*, December.

Lawson, G. H., 1969, 'Profit Maximisation via Financial Management', First published in *Management Decision*, Winter. Revised version published in *Handbook for Managers* (Kluwer-Harrap Handbooks, Installment 4), 1972, London.

Lawson, G. H., 1974a, 'Memorandum Submitted to the Inflation Accounting Committee', Working Paper 12, Manchester Business School, July.

Lawson, G. H., 1974b, 'The Rationale for Measuring the Cost of Working Capital', Working Paper 15, Manchester Business School, July.

Lawson, G. H., 1975, 'Initial Reflections on Sandilands – I', *Certified Accountant*, November.

Lawson, G. H. and Bean, n.d., *Enterprise Valuation – a Cash Flow Approach*. Forthcoming.

Lawson, G. H. and Stark, A. W., 1975, 'The Concept of Profit for Fund Raising', *Accounting and Business Research*, no. 21, Winter.

Lee, T. A., 1972, 'A Case for Cash Flow Reporting', *Journal of Business Finance*, vol. 4, no. 2, Summer.

Merrett, A. J., 1975, 'Measuring Trends in Profitability', *Lloyds Bank Review*, October.

Sumner, M. T., 1975, 'Neutrality of Corporate Taxation, or on Not Accounting for Inflation', Manchester School of Economic and Social Studies, December.

A case for cash flow reporting

by T. A. Lee
Department of Accounting and Business Method
University of Edinburgh

A RELUCTANCE TO CHANGE?

INVARIABLY, over the years, whenever there has been a sustained demand for better accounting information[1] for investors, the traditional response has been an increased disclosure of items of the existing type of reported information—that is, stewardship information.[2] This somewhat illogical principle of attempting to equate quantity with quality has failed to combat (at least in this writer's opinion) the increasing doubt with regard to the relevance and utility of stewardship accounting information for investors who are concerned mainly with making decisions.[3] It is a problem which has caused numerous writers to look for alternative types of reportable accounting information, hopefully more relevant to the decision-making investor. The main effort to date in this area has been concerned with expressing the traditional stewardship information in contemporary terms, by adjustment of its original monetary value measurements [1]. However, what has either been forgotten or ignored in this drive for improvement in financial reporting is the question of whether stewardship information (adjusted or unadjusted) is the most relevant and, therefore, the most useful type available for reporting to persons primarily concerned with making investment decisions. Surprisingly, despite a mounting debate about the needs of information users, those who have advocated monetarily adjusted stewardship statements have rarely, if indeed ever, questioned their fundamental relevance to the user. The implication to be drawn from this is that those who seek to make such technical adjustments are quite satisfied with the information's basic relevance and utility. They therefore do not advocate a major change in the *nature* of the accounting information being supplied to investors. Instead they look for refinements in the *technical* process of valuation. This gives an impression that there is a deep-seated, if unwitting, reluctance to change the nature of reported information when there appears to be a pressing need for change.

THE NEED FOR CHANGE

Utility and relevance are, in the opinion of the writer, *the* primary concepts of accounting. They should govern the measurement and communication of all types of accounting information; the logic being that information can be useful to its user only if it is likely to influence or have a bearing on his decisions and actions. If utility and relevance are accepted as such important parts of accounting thought, it follows that all accounting information, whatever its nature or measurement process, should be capable of satisfying the informational needs of its potential user. Those persons who support the production of stewardship accounting information for what are basically decision-making activities, either consciously or unwittingly are assuming that the needs of the investor are thereby satisfied. A study of the available literature reveals that they appear to think it unnecessary even to argue in support of this assumption, despite the conflicting fact that stewardship accounting information, in either its monetarily adjusted or unadjusted form, looks back in time, whereas the investor is predominantly interested in the future. In contrast to this school of thought there is another, much more recent and very much smaller, which has suggested the measurement and communication of past and forecast cash flow information as relevant sources of knowledge about the

[1] Accounting information, in the sense it is used throughout this paper, refers to that which is communicated by companies to their shareholders.

[2] For an authoritative acknowledgment of stewardship as the main purpose of present-day company financial statements, see "Accountants' liability to third parties", *Statement S8*, ICAEW, p. 2.

[3] For purposes of this paper, the term "investors" is intended to include both the "average prudent investor" and the "investment manager", although it is recognized that detailed accounting information is probably more extensively and intensively used by the latter person than by the former.

company for the investor [2]. Advocacy of this type of information for decision-makers has so far appeared to meet with little support, despite the fact that the arguments both for and against such a proposal have been put forward in detail by those concerned. So far as can be seen, only Lawson has advocated the complete abolition of conventional stewardship financial statements, the other writers advocating cash flow statements as supplements to them. In this connection it should not be forgotten that stewardship accounting information is extremely useful for accountability purposes and, consequently, should be available to fulfil such a role—that is, as a means of making management accountable for the custodianship of the resources entrusted to it by the shareholders. In addition, so far as profit is a measure of the use made of these resources, then the reporting of such a measure is an important part of any stewardship function. However, when it comes to the question of decision-making, stewardship information *appears* less relevant and less useful to the investor than cash flow information in either its historic or projected form. The following sections attempt to support this observation.

THE KEY FACTOR OF CASH

The proposition being made in this section is that cash is *the* key resource of a company and, consequently, it is suggested that investors should have a much better knowledge about company cash than they do at present by means of the conventional profit statements, balance sheets and funds statements. As Hendriksen has stated (italics added), "In the final analysis, cash flows into and out of the business enterprise are *the most fundamental events* upon which accounting measurements are based and upon which investors and creditors base their decisions" [3].

The business activity of a company is normally on a "cash to cash" basis, most transactions involving some cash movement either in the short or in the long term. Without cash the company could not survive in the economic world today, no matter how good its products, no matter how bright its public image, no matter how skilled its managers and workers. Cash, at the end of the day, determines its fate; indeed, cash may be likened to the life blood of the company. This raises the question that if cash is so important to corporate economic survival, then why should not investors (and, consequently, interested creditors and lenders) be given detailed accounting information about it? After all, they should be concerned with the vital question of the company's survival, for the value (both present and future) of their existing or potential interest in the company is quite definitely linked with this factor.

In addition, looking at the company's cash position specifically from the point of view of the interested investor, it is reasonable to suggest that cash is also the key factor so far as his expectations of dividends are concerned. The company's ability to provide the shareholder with a return on his investment is obviously geared to its cash position, both present and future. If there is no cash, there can be no dividends, and so far as can be reasonably observed, investment values are at least partly influenced by the dividend factor. As well as the question of dividends, the investor's expectations of recovering his investment are equally geared to the survival and, thus, to the cash position of the company, for if the company fails he may very well lose part or all of his investment in it.

Summarizing, therefore, it appears that the investor's interest in the survival of the company, together with its ability to provide a stream of dividends for him, demands far more accounting information about its current and anticipated cash positions than is required to be communicated at present.

DECISIONS CONCERN THE FUTURE

Investors who are interested in the business activities and affairs of companies should be regarded first and foremost as decision-makers, for they periodically have to make decisions affecting their existing or potential interests in the company. These decisions, by definition, require consideration of alternative courses of action, and the main factor in this process is the future. Questions about the future of the company, and of investments in it, must be asked and to some extent answered by the investor if he is to take investment action in a rational and reasonable manner. Thus it can be safely said that in almost every decision he has to make, the investor must inevitably take cognizance of forecasts—whether these are his own or someone else's. These forecasts should be as formal and credible as possible, and avoidance of uninformed guesswork must be aimed for at all times. It therefore appears to be very important that the investor should have some form of information relating to the future of the company. In the opinion of the writer, it is extremely doubtful whether historic accounting information, of the type contained in either monetarily adjusted or unadjusted stewardship financial statements, is the most relevant and useful for purposes of helping the investor to predict (a) future dividends and other benefits receivable by him from the company; (b) its future survival, maintenance or expansion; and (c) the degree of risk and uncertainty connected with his existing or potential investment in it. This, however, should not be taken as a statement of absolute denial of the relevance and usefulness of historic accounting information for decision-making purposes. Such information is ***known*** to be used by investors (exact research will have to be carried out to determine the extent of this usage), and it is also accepted that historic data is an essential ingredient in the techniques of quantitative forecasting, including time series analysis and causal models [4]. Nevertheless, it appears to be reasonable to suggest that forecast accounting information, projecting the activity of the company into the future, should prove to be more beneficial than historic data to the investor when he makes decisions. It relates to the future, and it is that dimension of time, despite its inherent uncertainty, which corresponds most with the investor's needs and requirements in the decision-making process. In addition, if cash is such an important key factor to the investor (as explained in the previous section), it would seem logical to provide forecast information relating to the cash flows and cash position of the company. The further into the future these forecasts go, the better equipped the investor should be to make his decisions. However, it must be remembered that the usefulness of forecasts undoubtedly diminishes the more they extend into the future, until such time as they have little relevance because of the degree of uncertainty attached to them. In other words, forecasts should not reflect time periods which are unrealistic to predict. Despite this constraint, which effectively is acknowledging the constantly and rapidly changing society of which the company is a part, it appears that the general propositions being put forward in this section hold true in business investing today—that is (a) the existence of a future creates a need to make decisions concerning that future; (b) these decisions require some formal information about the expected future; and (c) accountants should be concerned with satisfying this informational need (despite the possible high degree of uncertainty, and despite the views of those who, like Chambers, are concerned solely with accountants measuring and reporting factual information about business activity which has already taken place [5].

THE IMPORTANCE OF OBJECTIVITY

It has long been recognized by accountants that one of the main concepts of accounting is objectivity—that is, whenever possible, bias or lack of objectivity should be avoided in the accounting process by those persons responsible for it. Chambers has summed it up well in his concept of neutrality where he states that accounting information should be relevant to its user, no matter what decision or action he takes related to it [6]. In other words, the processor of the information[4] should not bias it toward any one potential decision or action of the decision-maker. This is quite clearly a fundamental aspect of accounting thought, and one which should underlie all accounting practice. It is therefore not surprising

[4] The term "processor" will be used from now on throughout the remainder of this paper to cover collectively all those persons in company management who are in some way involved in or responsible for the production of accounting information.

to learn that critics of published forecast accounting information find it largely unacceptable because of its supposed lack of objectivity. Objectivity however, in the sense they are using the term, concerns not so much the attitude of mind of the information processor but more the availability of verifiable evidence to support the information. What is being forgotten in this apparent conflict between objectiveness and subjectiveness in accounting is that there are two distinct, albeit related, concepts of objectivity. The first concerns the neutrality of the processor—his attitude of mind to the information and its potential user. The second concerns a technical characteristic of the information. Mental objectivity is an essential aspect of *all* accounting and should be adhered to at all times, whatever the nature of the information being produced. On the other hand, technical objectivity cannot possibly be achieved in all areas of accounting and this fact should be recognized and accepted. Personal judgment and opinion is a fundamental part of the accounting process. It applies just as much to stewardship accounting information on the accrual basis (because of the underlying allocation and valuation procedures involved) as it does to forecast accounting information on a cash basis (because this is based on an uncertain future). It is therefore suggested that so long as mental objectivity is being adhered to by the information processor, technical objectivity (or the lack of it) should not be used as an excuse for not producing forecast accounting information when this is *technically feasible*—the overriding criteria should always be the relative relevance and usefulness of the information to the investor. If there is any doubt about mental objectivity on the part of the processor, then the audit function goes some way towards establishing the credibility of the accounting process and, indirectly, of the processor. A 1966 American Accounting Association Committee supported this view that accounting information (whether past or future) should be verified whenever possible, in order to retain the confidence in it of its potential user [7]. The same Committee, however, also acknowledged the fact that there are varying degrees of verifiability, depending on the type of accounting information concerned. Both the writer [8] and Tomkins [9] have acknowledged the importance of information verification and have suggested that forecast accounting information should be independently audited and reported on. Edey, on the other hand, has stated that the audit of such information is not necessary [10], whilst Briston and Fawthrop have elaborated on this latter opinion, seeing little point in verification when there is such uncertainty underlying the information [11]. What these "no audit" writers appear to neglect is the fact that the audit function can be regarded as a behavioural study of the information processor as well as a technical exercise to prove the validity of certain accounting procedures.

Taking the above points collectively, it is proposed in this section that, if objectivity is accepted as an important criterion of accounting, production of the type of accounting information which appears to present the most reasonable balance of relevance *and* objectivity should be aimed for at all times—because of its overall utility to the user. Cash flow information appears to the writer to satisfy these conditions best. Firstly, in its historic form, it is perhaps the most objective information possible, avoiding most of the subjectiveness which enters into the technical adjustments involved in the traditional accrual accounting; it is also the most relevant information for purposes of comparison with forecast information should this be measured on a cash basis. Secondly, forecast cash flows, although involving a great deal of uncertainty (however, no more so than budgeted profits on the accrual basis), clearly avoid the necessary subjectiveness of accrual judgments and opinions. Therefore, they appear to be far less subjective in a *total* sense than profit forecasts.

CASH FLOW STATEMENTS

The above points appear to the writer to be several of the main arguments in favour of preparing and presenting past and forecast cash flows for investors. The main advantages and disadvantages of such a reporting system have already been discussed by him in a previous paper [12], and therefore it is not intended to repeat them here. What will be looked at in greater detail at this stage are the nature and content of the proposed cash flow statements. This is done in order to give interested readers an opportunity of seeing what these reports could look like in practice. It is hoped that their presentation may generate further suggestions for amendment and improvement.

One or two general points about the statements should be noted before going any further: (a) It is recommended by the writer that conventional stewardship financial statements, portraying past business activity, measured on the accrual basis and described in contemporary money terms, should be published in addition to the cash flow statements, not so much for decision-making but more as information for an entirely different purpose—that of stewardship; (b) The forecast cash flows ideally should reflect several years' anticipated activity within the company—say, four or five years at the most. The earlier years, because of their proximity to the present, would naturally tend to be more accurate than the later years. But each forecast year would be subject to continuous reassessment, and this process should ensure that account is being taken of significant events likely to alter an original forecast. For the purposes of the following illustrations, only three years of forecasts are shown, as this is thought to represent the maximum which companies should be asked to disclose, at least until such time as management becomes more skilled and experienced with available forecasting techniques. As Chambers *et al.* have stated, "The need today, we believe, is not for better forecasting methods, but for better application of the techniques at hand" [13]; (c) Both past and forecast cash flow information published for the benefit of investors should be subject to independent audit. Past cash flows should reasonably be expected to be audited by professional accountants, but as far as future cash flows are concerned, these would in all probability require to be verified and reported on by experts in specialist management fields, including business forecasting.

The composition of both past and future cash flows for external reporting purposes should be made up of the following elements:

a) Manufacturing and/or Trading Transactions Flow—giving details of revenues received and expenditure paid for, both relating to the operational activity of the company. This data would be analysed according to significant economic unit groupings, and would exclude any exceptional or relatively non-recurrent items.

b) Exceptional or Non-recurrent Transactions Flow—giving details of those cash transactions, connected with the company's operational activity, which can reasonably be described as either exceptional or relatively non-recurrent.

c) Financial Transactions Flow—giving details of monies received and repaid by the company to its shareholders, lenders and bankers, but excluding interest and dividend payments.

d) Capital Transactions Flow—giving details of the cash movements resulting from the purchase and sale of "profit-contributing" resources by the company, including land, buildings, plant, equipment, investments and sums expended in the area of research and development.

e) Taxation Transactions Flow—giving details of taxation payments made by the company, as well as the receipt of any refunds from the tax authorities.[5]

f) Interest and Dividend Transactions Flow—giving details of interim and final dividends paid by the company to its shareholders, as well as interest payments to lenders.

In addition to the above statements, it is also suggested that the following supplementary statements should be published for use by investors:

g) Non-cash Transactions Statement—giving details of those transactions incurred by the company which in themselves will not cause any immediate move-

[5] It should be noted that, unless the government of the day changed the basis of computing company taxation liabilities, the payment of these liabilities would continue to be arrived at with reference to accounting profits measured on the accrual basis. This, obviously, is one very good reason for retaining stewardship statements until such time as government can be convinced of the merits of measuring tax on a cash basis.

ment of cash, but which should have a significant bearing on cash flows in the future. Examples include the purchase of shares in another company when satisfied in part or in whole by the issue of shares or loan stock in the acquiring company; the purchase and sale of goods and services between companies which are settled by contra accounting entry in the respective books of account; and the issue of bonus shares to shareholders. Failure to include this type of data in cash reports (because it does not directly affect cash) would, in the opinion of the writer, fail to provide all the information required by the investor to assess the survival prospects of the company, his dividend expectations, etc.

h) *Statement of Basic Assumptions*—giving details, at least in relatively general terms, of the main assumptions which management has had to make in order to compute the figures contained in the forecast cash flow information mentioned above. Such assumptions could be classified as follows:

1) *Business Assumptions*—that is, assumptions specifically connected with the operational and related activity of the company. These would include those relating to estimations of sales demand (including consumer behaviour), production levels, pricing, capital projects, financing schemes, etc, over which the company and its management should have some degree of control and influence.

2) *Economic, Political and Social Assumptions*—that is, assumptions, unlike those in (1) above, which mainly reflect matters completely outside the control and direction of the company and its management. Examples include governmental policy regarding industrial development; the general economic and social climate, including rates of inflation and interest, unemployment levels, the state of the Balance of Payments, and so on.

In a fully developed system of reported cash forecasts it is possible to envisage the publication of a range of expectations reflecting possible variations in the underlying assumptions. At first, however, the forecasts should reflect "reasonable" expectations rather than the extremes of optimism or pessimism.

i) *Statement of Material Variations*—giving details, again in relatively general terms, of the major variations between actual and forecast cash flows. This would help to give the investor some idea of differences due to (1) factors within the control of the company's management; and (2) factors outside such control. It would also provide him with some knowledge of the dependability of forecast information in the type of business activity the company is in. This would be helpful in assessing the degree of uncertainty and risk applicable to an investment in such a company. It also satisfies the stewardship function between management and ownership in a relatively obvious and meaningful way.

DRAFT CASH FLOW STATEMENTS

The main statement, outlined below, reflects the overall cash flow of the company (both actual and forecast), and follows the pattern of a related form of stewardship financial statement—the source and application of funds statement. In the case of cash flow statements, the "funds" are described in terms of cash. In the case of funds statements, the "funds" are measured in terms of accounting accruals.

From the above type of statement, the investor could obtain the following specific information, *inter alia*, about the company he was assessing for investment purposes, and which he could then compare with similar data for other companies. (Each comment is applicable to both actual and forecast information.)

a) The company's ability to generate sufficient cash resources to survive in the long term is conveyed in the overall picture portrayed in the statement, particularly in the individual and total figures in items 1, 7 and 9.
b) The company's ability to generate sufficient cash resources to distribute satisfactory dividends, as well as to pay its interest obligations to lenders, is also conveyed in the statement as a whole, but

TABLE 1: Statement of total cash flow of company
Statement of total cash flow—year to 31 July 1971

Cash Flows	*Appendix*	*Year to 31 July* 1967 *F A*	1968 *F A*	1969 *F A*	1970 *F A*	1971 *F A*	Total *F A*	1972 *F*	1973 *F*	1974 *F*	Total *F*
1) Bank and Cash Balances Brought Forward		+ + − −	+ + − −	+ + − −	+ + − −	+ + − −	+ + − −	+ −	+ −	+ −	+ −
2) Operational Transactions Flow	A	+ + − −	+ + − −	+ + − −	+ + − −	+ + − −	+ + − −	+ −	+ −	+ −	+ −
3) Exceptional Transactions Flow	B	+ + − −	+ + − −	+ + − −	+ + − −	+ + − −	+ + − −	+ −	+ −	+ −	+ −
4) Financial Transactions Flow	C	+ + − −	+ + − −	+ + − −	+ + − −	+ + − −	+ + − −	+ −	+ −	+ −	+ −
5) Capital Transactions Flow	D	+ + − −	+ + − −	+ + − −	+ + − −	+ + − −	+ + − −	+ −	+ −	+ −	+ −
6) Taxation Transactions Flow	E	+ + − −	+ + − −	+ + − −	+ + − −	+ + − −	+ + − −	+ −	+ −	+ −	+ −
7) *Net Distributable Flow*		+ + − −	+ + − −	+ + − −	+ + − −	+ + − −	+ + − −	+ −	+ −	+ −	+ −
8) Interest and Dividends	F	− −	− −	− −	− −	− −	− −	−	−	−	−
9) *Undistributed Bank and Cash Balances*		+ + − −	+ + − −	+ + − −	+ + − −	+ + − −	+ + − −	+ −	+ −	+ −	+ −

Note: In this and subsequent Tables column "*F*" contains forecast data, and column "*A*" contains actual data; + is a cash inflow and − is a cash outflow.

with particular reference to the figures given in items 7 and 8.

c) The investor should be interested in the dividend *and* interest "covers" applicable to the company, and these can be obtained from the above statement by comparing the related figures in items 7, 8 and 9.

d) Following the comments made in (b) and (c), it is possible to calculate figures for *distributable* cash per share, as well as for *distributed* cash per share, both being measures of the worth of the shares compared with other alternative investments. It should be noted, however, that as individual annual figures for cash flows can be materially affected by periodic movements in cash due to financial or capital transactions, then it would perhaps be more reasonable to use five-yearly averages for this purpose to eliminate the "ups and downs" of individual years.

e) The cash available and used for capital transactions, which are designed to ensure the company continues as a going concern, should be considered by the investor, and items 1 to 4 inclusive, when related to item 5, should be of assistance to him in this respect.

f) The relative contribution of cash generated from operational activity and from external finance, in order to meet capital, tax and dividend requirements, can be gained from the individual and total figures.

The appendices A to F in the above statement are intended to refer the investor to additional statements which contain the detail of the total figures given in the overall statement. B, E and F are relatively self-explanatory, but the remainder merit some further explanation and illustration. Table 2 (below) outlines the Statement of Operational Transactions Flow, and supports the figures in item 2 in the overall statement in Table 1.

The main advantage of this supporting cash flow statement appears to be that it supplies the investor

TABLE 2: Appendix A to total cash flow statement
Statement of operational transactions flow—year to 31 July 1971

Cash Movements	*Year to 31 July*									
	1967 *F A*	*1968* *F A*	*1969* *F A*	*1970* *F A*	*1971* *F A*	*Total* *F A*	*1972* *F*	*1973* *F*	*1974* *F*	*Total* *F*
Economic Unit A										
1) *Sales Revenues*	+ +	+ +	+ +	+ +	+ +	+ +	+	+	+	+
2) Materials Costs	− −	− −	− −	− −	− −	− −	−	−	−	−
3) Labour Costs	− −	− −	− −	− −	− −	− −	−	−	−	−
4) Allocable Overhead Costs	− −	− −	− −	− −	− −	− −	−	−	−	−
5) *Net Cash Contribution*	+ +	+ +	+ +	+ +	+ +	+ +	+	+	+	+
1−(2+3+4)	− −	− −	− −	− −	− −	− −	−	−	−	−
Economic Unit B										
6) *Sales Revenues*	+ +	+ +	+ +	+ +	+ +	+ +	+	+	+	+
7) Materials Costs	− −	− −	− −	− −	− −	− −	−	−	−	−
8) Labour Costs	− −	− −	− −	− −	− −	− −	−	−	−	−
9) Allocable Overhead Costs	− −	− −	− −	− −	− −	− −	−	−	−	−
10) *Net Cash Contribution*	+ +	+ +	+ +	+ +	+ +	+ +	+	+	+	+
6−(7+8+9)	− −	− −	− −	− −	− −	− −	−	−	−	−
11) Non-allocable Overhead Costs	− −	− −	− −	− −	− −	− −	−	−	−	−
12) *Net Operational Cash Flow*	+ +	+ +	+ +	+ +	+ +	+ +	+	+	+	+
5+10−11	− −	− −	− −	− −	− −	− −	−	−	−	−

with information concerning the contribution to total cash flow of each of the company's economic units. It does so without revealing individual profit margins, a point which is often put forward as the reason for not disclosing detailed costs of production in conventional stewardship financial statements. The emphasis of the statement, therefore, is not on the relative profit contribution of each unit, but on the relative contribution each makes to the continuing survival of the company as a whole—a much more fundamental, and in many ways, more important issue to the investor.[6]

Table 3 outlines the Statement of Financial Transactions Flow, reflecting the movements of cash to and from persons outside the company who are partly financing the activity.

The last illustration, Table 4, outlines the Statement of Capital Transactions Flow, which is perhaps the most vital of all as far as the future continuance of the company is concerned. It depicts the "sunk" costs which the company has paid for in order to maintain and expand its business activity. It includes purchases of profit-contributing resources such as land, buildings, plant and investments in other companies paid for by cash. These latter investments would include any controlling interests in subsidiary companies, purchased wholly or partly for cash. If the purchase has been wholly in cash then a full analysis of the resources and liabilities taken over should be made in this statement. If, on the other hand, only part of the investment is paid for in cash, then the statement should contain the payment, and a footnote should refer the reader to the Statement of Non-cash Transactions which should contain details of the full transaction. One further heading to be included in this statement warrants additional explanation at this stage, and that is the cost of research and development expenditure. This mainly reflects the company's commitment to the future, and gives some indication of the anticipated revenues which must flow into the company in the long term if it is to recover these "sunk" costs

[6] The extreme difficulty of convincing management of the need to disclose this analysis is recognized by the writer.

TABLE 3: Appendix C to total cash flow statement
Statement of financial transactions flow—year to 31 July 1971

Cash Movements	Year to 31 July 1967 F	1967 A	1968 F	1968 A	1969 F	1969 A	1970 F	1970 A	1971 F	1971 A	Total F	Total A	1972 F	1973 F	1974 F	Total F
1) *Loans Received*	+	+	+	+	+	+	+	+	+	+	+	+	+	+	+	+
2) Loan Repayments	−	−	−	−	−	−	−	−	−	−	−	−	−	−	−	−
3) *Share Issue Receipts*	+	+	+	+	+	+	+	+	+	+	+	+	+	+	+	+
4) *Total Net Contribution*	+	+	+	+	+	+	+	+	+	+	+	+	+	+	+	+
1−2+3	−	−	−	−	−	−	−	−	−	−	−	−	−	−	−	−

TABLE 4: Appendix D to total cash flow statement
Statement of capital transactions flow—year to 31 July 1971

Cash Movements	Year to 31 July 1967 F	1967 A	1968 F	1968 A	1969 F	1969 A	1970 F	1970 A	1971 F	1971 A	Total F	Total A	1972 F	1973 F	1974 F	Total F
1) Outright Purchase of Physical Resources:																
Land and Buildings	−	−	−	−	−	−	−	−	−	−	−	−	−	−	−	−
Plant and Vehicles	−	−	−	−	−	−	−	−	−	−	−	−	−	−	−	−
2) Instalment Purchasing of Physical Resources:																
Plant and Vehicles	−	−	−	−	−	−	−	−	−	−	−	−	−	−	−	−
3) Hire Rental of Plant	−	−	−	−	−	−	−	−	−	−	−	−	−	−	−	−
4) *Sale of Physical Resources:*																
Land and Buildings	+	+	+	+	+	+	+	+	+	+	+	+	+	+	+	+
Plant and Vehicles	+	+	+	+	+	+	+	+	+	+	+	+	+	+	+	+
5) Net Cost of Acquiring	+	+	+	+	+	+	+	+	+	+	+	+	+	+	+	+
Physical Resources	−	−	−	−	−	−	−	−	−	−	−	−	−	−	−	−
1+2+3−4																
6) Purchase of Investments:																
In Subsidiary Companies	−	−	−	−	−	−	−	−	−	−	−	−	−	−	−	−
In Associated Companies	−	−	−	−	−	−	−	−	−	−	−	−	−	−	−	−
In Quoted Companies	−	−	−	−	−	−	−	−	−	−	−	−	−	−	−	−
7) *Sale of Investments:*																
In Quoted Companies	+	+	+	+	+	+	+	+	+	+	+	+	+	+	+	+
8) Net Cost of Acquiring Investments	+	+	+	+	+	+	+	+	+	+	+	+	+	+	+	+
6−7	−	−	−	−	−	−	−	−	−	−	−	−	−	−	−	−
9) Research and Development Costs	−	−	−	−	−	−	−	−	−	−	−	−	−	−	−	−
10) Net Capital Transactions Flow	+	+	+	+	+	+	+	+	+	+	+	+	+	+	+	+
5+8+9	−	−	−	−	−	−	−	−	−	−	−	−	−	−	−	−

and survive. The delay between incurring the expenditure and later recovering it through sales is of vital interest to the investor.

These, then, are some suggestions put forward by the writer in support of cash flow reporting. The next stage is to test their acceptability in the "market-place". It is hoped to be able to report the results of such research in the near future.

REFERENCES

[1] For example, see *Accounting for Stewardship in a Period of Inflation*, ICAEW, 1968 (for general adjustments): and E.O. Edwards and P.W. Bell, *The Theory and Measurement of Business Income*, California University Press, 1961 (for specific adjustments). For a detailed account of this extremely complex problem, see Edward Stamp, "Income and Value Determination and Changing Price-Levels: An Essay Towards a Theory", *The Accountant's Magazine*, June 1971, pp. 277–92.

[2] See for example, H.C. Edey, "Accounting Principles and Business Reality", *Accountancy*, November 1963, pp. 998–1002 and December 1963, pp. 1083–88; Gerald Lawson, comments in *Accountancy Age*, 24 July 1970, pp. 1–2 and 6 November 1970, pp. 10–11; and in "Cash-Flow Accounting", *The Accountant*, 28 October 1971, pp. 386–89; and T.A. Lee, "Goodwill—An Example of Will-O-the-Wisp Accounting", *Accounting and Business Research*, Autumn 1971, pp. 318–28; and in "The Relevance of Accounting Information Including Cash Flows", *The Accountant's Magazine*, January 1972, pp. 30–4.

[3] Hendriksen, Eldon S., *Accounting Theory*, Irwin, 1970 (revised edition), p. 237.

[4] See for example, John C. Chambers, Satinder K. Mullick and Donald D. Smith, "How to choose the right forecasting technique", *Harvard Business Review*, July–August 1971, pp. 45–74.

[5] See his views on this matter in Raymond J. Chambers, "The Role of Accounting", *The Accountant*, 22 February 1969, pp. 255–60; and in *Accounting, Evaluation and Economic Behaviour*, Prentice Hall, 1966, p. 98.

[6] Raymond J. Chambers, *Accounting, Evaluation and Economic Behaviour*, Prentice Hall, 1966, pp. 154–56 and 164.

[7] The Committee to Prepare a Statement of Basic Accounting Theory, *A Statement of Basic Accounting Theory*, American Accounting Association, 1966, pp. 10–11 and 53.

[8] Lee, "Goodwill—An Example of Will-O-the-Wisp Accounting", *op. cit.*, p. 327.

[9] Tomkins, C.R., "The Development of Relevant Published Accounting Reports", *Accountancy*, November 1969, pp. 817–18.

[10] Edey, *op. cit.*, p. 1088.

[11] Briston, R.J. and Fawthrop, R.A. "Accounting principles and investor protection", *Journal of Business Finance*, Summer 1971, pp. 15–17.

[12] Lee, *op. cit.*, pp. 326–28.

[13] Chambers, Mullick and Smith, *op. cit.*, p. 74.

Reporting Cash Flows and Net Realisable Values*

T. A. Lee

Several arguments have been advanced for financial reporting to be based on cash flow accounting (CFA).[1] The literature also contains many items explaining the case for net realisable value accounting (NRVA).[2] Typically, however, these systems of reporting have been examined and presented separately, and rarely has any detailed attempt been made to link them.[3] The purpose of this paper is to make such a connection, in the hope of revealing to the interested reader that CFA and NRVA are parts of a single system of reporting which concentrates on the importance and accessibility of cash in business enterprise activity. As such, it is concerned particularly with describing how CFA and NRVA data can be brought together in a series of articulating financial statements which provide more relevant information for the report user about cash and cash management than can be given in either a CFA or NRVA system on its own.

It is not concerned with advancing individual arguments for the reporting of either CFA or NRVA data. These have already been well rehearsed in the accountancy literature, and should be familiar to the interested reader. Equally, it is not concerned with demonstrating that CFA is a particular sub-set of NRVA, or vice versa. Such artificial distinctions are futile if, as is suggested in this paper, both are parts of a single cash-orientated system of financial reporting. In other words, the writer is concerned that advocates of CFA and NRVA have been working separately, and may well have ignored the possibility that their arguments and recommendations are similar but incomplete without each other, and could be strengthened through unification.

Points of similarity

Before proceeding to the main part of the paper, it would appear to be relevant to describe briefly the main points of similarity in CFA and NRVA as they are presently and separately constituted. These are made in order to demonstrate that linking the two systems within one reporting framework is not a casual *ad hoc* exercise, and that they are compatible.

1. CFA and NRVA are both based firmly on the importance of cash as a business resource. CFA describes in detail cash flows to and from various sources, and NRVA describes the adaptability of the reporting enterprise in terms of its command over money (resources being valued using net realisable values, or 'current cash equivalents').

*This paper is based on an earlier one presented to the annual conference of the European Accounting Association, Amsterdam, March 1980. It has benefited considerably from comments on the earlier paper by Professors R. J. Chambers and M. C. Wells and an anonymous referee.

[1]For a summary of CFA arguments, and a full bibliography on the subject, see T. A. Lee, 'Cash Flow Accounting and Corporate Financial Reporting,' *Discussion Paper 6*, University of Edinburgh, 1980.

[2]For a full bibliography on the case for NRVA, particularly as expounded by R. J. Chambers and R. R. Sterling, see T. A. Lee, *Income and Value Measurement*, Nelson, 2nd. ed. 1980, pp. 185–7.

[3]Only in a casual way has it been attempted before: see R. Edwards, 'The Nature and Measurement of Income,' in *Studies in Accounting*, W. T. Baxter and S. Davidson (eds.), Institute of Chartered Accountants in England and Wales, 3rd. ed. 1977, pp. 126–38; H. C. Edey, 'Accounting Principles and Business Reality,' *Accountancy*, December 1963, p. 1087; T. A. Climo, 'Cash Flow Statements for Investors,' *Journal of Business Finance and Accounting*, Autumn 1976, pp. 11 and 13; T. A. Lee, 'The Cash Flow Accounting Alternative for Corporate Financial Reporting,' in *Trends in Managerial and Financial Accounting*, C. van Dam (ed.), Martinus Nijhoff, 1978, p. 84; and T. A. Lee, 'The Simplicity and Complexity of Accounting,' *Accounting for a Simplified Firm*, in R. R. Sterling and A. Thomas (eds.), Scholars Book Co., 1979, pp. 47–50. Edwards' contribution was originally published in 1938 and appears to have been the first, although it must be noted that his recommendations relating to cash flow and net realisable value were effectively limited to what he described as merchanting businesses (that is, retail concerns). In fact, he specifically excluded total valuations for industrial businesses, with a recommendation that only individual assets ought to be valued where this would produce relevant information. Additionally, his cash flow recommendations were vague, being based on cash receipts and expenditures with certain unspecified adjustments, and lacking any illustration or numerical example. The cash flow accounting recommended appears to have been based for industrial businesses on the nineteenth century double-account system of accounting and reporting.

2. CFA and NRVA are both allocation-free systems. Neither contains arbitrary allocations due to short-term periodic reporting, and thus both are free of such accounting interference.

3. The condition of enterprise survival is greatly emphasised in CFA and NRVA—the former being concerned with the way in which cash has been generated to meet its obligations and requirements, and the latter with the availability and accessibility of cash for future activity and needs.

4. Both systems concentrate on reporting on the activity of the enterprise and its management. Neither assumes continuity of this activity, and both appear capable of providing essential information on the financial management of the reporting entity (particularly that pertaining to its liquidity).

5. Cash, current cash equivalents, and cash flows are matters which appear to underlie most of the decision models to which financial reporting is directed—for example, shareholders concerned about dividends; lenders, bankers and creditors concerned about interest and capital repayments; employees concerned about wages and security of employment; and so on. Both CFA and NRVA would therefore appear to be of relevance to these potential report users.[4]

Linking CFA and NRVA

In its historic form, CFA describes the realisation and utilisation of cash—that is, the conversion of non-cash resources into cash, and the use of cash funds generated from various sources to acquire resources and meet obligations. NRVA, on the other hand, describes, within aggregate totals, a mixture of both the realisation and utilisation of cash (as in CFA), and the pre-realisation changes in the net realisable values of non-cash resources and the amounts due on various obligations. The 'linking' of the two systems can be achieved relatively easily by the segregation of NRVA data into realised cash flows and unrealised cash flows—the former described in detail in CFA terms, and the latter represented by the aforementioned changes in the net realisable values of reported assets, and changes in the amounts of reported obligations. In this way, it can be argued that CFA-based financial statements would thereby cease to be incomplete because of their present failure to deal with unrealised cash flows (and thus with statements of financial position); and NRVA-based statements would provide much greater information on the realised cash flows which presently are contained, but not separately identified, in its measures of realisable income. The exact formulation required for the 'linking' can be described as follows:

$$\Delta C + \Delta N = \Delta O$$

where ΔC represents the net realised change in the total cash resources of the reporting enterprise for a defined period—that is, sales revenues received minus total operational payments, minus total payments for new and replacement investment, minus loan interest, taxation, and dividend payments, plus or minus cash transactions relating to long-term financing (such as loans and share capital).

ΔN is the total unrealised net cash flow representing the periodic change in the net realisable value of the non-cash assets of the reporting enterprise (including those assets which are readily-realisable, those which are not-so-readily realisable, and those which are non-realisable). ΔO is the total change in the various obligations or liabilities of the reporting enterprise (including its short, medium and long-term debts, and its owner's capital measured in net realisable value terms). This aggregation of periodic realised and potential cash flows from the use and holding of assets provides the report user with a total cash flow figure which is equivalent to the net increase (or decrease) during the period in taxed and undistributed, actual and potential, cash funds in the enterprise. It is an expression of the change in its total measured command over money, and reveals the increment (or decrement) in the enterprise's potential for repaying its financial obligations, maintaining and changing its operations and activities, meeting wage claims and making distributions. In other words, it represents financial information which ought to be of interest to most report users.

Because of the flow nature of this data, they should be contained within a statement which reconciles with position statements at the beginning and end of the period concerned. Thus, using assumed figures for purposes of demonstration, the overall reporting system described above could be summarised as in Figure 1.

This outline contains several features which ought to be described at this stage before proceeding further:

1. The opening and closing position statements

[4] This has been recognised in at least one major study of financial reporting: Accounting Objectives Study Group, *Objectives of Financial Statements*, American Institute of Certified Public Accountants, 1973, pp. 17–20.

Figure 1

Opening Cash Resources Statement	£000	*Total Cash Flow Statement*	£000	*Closing Cash Resources Statement*	£000
Realised cash	5	Realised cash flow	39	Realised cash	44
Readily-realisable assets	43	Increase in potential cash flow	17	Readily-realisable assets	60
Not-readily-realisable assets	18	Increase in potential cash flow	12	Not-readily-realisable assets	30
Non-realisable assets	–	Increase in potential cash flow	–	Non-realisable assets	–
	66		68		134
Short-term obligations	32	Additional credit received	18	Short-term obligations	50
Long-term obligations	10	Additional borrowings received	8	Long-term obligations	18
Indefinite obligations	24	Additional funds accruing	42	Indefinite obligations	66
	66		68		134

are described as 'cash resources' statements rather than as conventional balance sheets. They treat all measurable assets of the enterprise as cash or potential cash—through the use of net realisable values. Thus, its command over money is emphasised by measuring its assets in current cash equivalent terms.

2. The assets are ordered for purposes of the position statements in order of realisability—from the already-realised to the non-realisable. This provides the user with some idea of the degree of certainty associated with the enterprise's command over money (such command being more absolute with certain assets than with others). It also means a rethinking of asset classification from either the traditional fixed and current or monetary and non-monetary categories.[5] If a system of reporting is being advocated which emphasises the realisation or potential realisation of the reporting enterprise's resources, it appears only sensible to ensure that the latter are described in a way which accords with the notion of realisability. The above formulation does this; the traditional classification, although intended originally to do so in terms of fixed and current assets, does not.

3. The liabilities of the enterprise (including its ownership interests) are also ordered—in this case in terms of order of potential repayment (from the most to the least immediate obligation). Again, this will require rethinking as to classification, but should provide report users with some impression of the timing of repayments of obligations for which cash resources will be required (and are available as described in the earlier part of the cash resources statement).

4. The total cash flow statement reflects all actual and potential cash flow changes affecting the assets and obligations of the enterprise over a defined period—that is, the total net increase or decrease in its command over money. The separate parts of this total cash flow are attributable to the various actual and potential cash and cash equivalent resources and obligations in the cash resources statement. Thus, the entire emphasis in the system is on cash flow and cash resources (actual and potential). It is essentially one concerned with the cash management function within the enterprise although, as will be seen later, it can also be used for purposes of income assessment as a means of evaluating the success or failure of enterprise management in terms of returns on capital employed, etc.

5. It is possible to derive a measure of income from the reported data, this being based on net realisable values. The datum describing additional funds accruing to indefinite obligations forms the basis for this, as it represents (assuming no new

[5]This is not entirely a new idea—a somewhat different variation of it can be seen in M. C. Wells, 'Costing for Activities,' *Management Accounting* (USA), May 1976, pp. 35–6; and in S. G. Gray and M. C. Wells, 'Corporate Liquidity and Disclosure of Financial Position: A Comment on European Developments and a Counter Proposal,' *Journal UEC*, 3/1977, pp. 156–8.

capital issued or capital repayments) the income retained for the period after taxation and distribution. Thus realisable income (Y_r) could be formulated as follows:

$$Y_r = \Delta R + t + d \pm I$$

where ΔR represents the additional funds accruing to capital in net realisable value terms; t represents taxation provided for the period; d represents dividends provided for the period; and I represents capital repayments (+) or new capital (−).

6. The non-realisability of certain specialised assets, and therefore their lack of potential in providing cash from sale as distinct from use, is recognised in this scheme with nil values and value changes being attributed to these items.

Outline financial statements

The above outline is obviously insufficient for financial reporting purposes. It requires to be expanded and presented in such a way as to be comprehensible and meaningful to its readers. Thus, as a first step, the undernoted outline statements have been prepared—that is, a Statement of Realised Cash Flow; a Statement of Total Cash Flow Movements (realised and potential); a Statement of Net Cash and Cash Equivalent Resources (again, realised and potential); and a Statement of Realisable Income (see Figures 2, 3, 4 and 5).

Figure 2 provides its reader with a portrayal of the actual cash inflow and outflow for the defined period. It could be supported by detailed schedules analysing the composition of individual figures given in it. As such, it describes the cash flow underlying the retained income measure based on net realisable values, and represents the factual and incontrovertible part of the latter datum (although the ordering and presentation of data are open to debate). The next statement looks beyond the point of realisation, and describes potential increases and decreases in cash resources which, with varying degrees of certainty, could be converted into actual cash movements.

If reported, Figure 3 would provide an explanation of the total potential increase in the reporting enterprise's command over money during the period. It is a general statement of the cash management exercised within the enterprise, resulting in a net realisation of cash flow and a net increase in potential cash flow. In particular, it reveals the incremental changes in cash and cash-equivalent resources available to cover the incremental changes in financial obligations—in the case of resources, highlighting the range of potential realisability; and, in the case of obligations, the range of possible repayment timing.

As such, it provides more information concerning the realisability of assets, and repayment of obligations, than does the equivalent NRVA-based income statement. The latter does not

Figure 2
CF Ltd.
Statement of Realised Cash Flows
Period t_1—t_2

	£000
Cash receipts from customers	187
Less: cash payments for materials, wages and overheads	124
Cash Operating Margin	63
Less: loan interest paid	2
Pre-tax Cash Flow	61
Less: taxation paid	13
Distributable Cash Flow	48
Less: dividends paid	10
Operating Cash Flow Available for Investment	38
Add: long-term loans received	8
Total Cash Flow Available for Investment	46
Less: cash payments for new buildings	7
Total Increase in Cash Resources	39

Figure 3
CF Ltd.
Statement of Total Cash Flow Movements
Period t_1—t_2

	£000	£000
Realised Cash Flows		
Net realised cash flow for the period (as per Statement of Realised Cash Flows)		39
Readily-Realisable Cash Flows		
Potential cash flows represented by an increase (decrease) in the net realisable values of readily-realisable assets:		
Amounts due by customers	7	
Stocks of finished goods	8	
Motor vehicles	(6)	
Land and buildings	8	17
	—	—
		56
Not-Readily-Realisable Cash Flows		
Potential cash flows represented by an increase (decrease) in the net realisable values of not-readily-realisable assets:		
Work-in-progress	15	
Plant and machinery	(3)	12
	—	—
Total Potential Increase in Cash Resources		68
		—
Change in Short-Term Obligations		
Potential cash outflows in the near future resulting from increases in:		
Amounts due to suppliers	9	
Taxation due to Inland Revenue	7	
Distributions due to owners	2	18
	—	
Change in Long-Term Obligations		
Potential cash outflows in the long-term resulting from increases in:		
Borrowings from merchant bank		8
Change in Indefinite Obligations		
Indeterminate future cash outflows resulting from increases in:		
Funds pertaining to owners (see Statement of Realisable Income)		42
		—
Total Potential Increase in Obligations		68
		—

reveal specific details of cash or cash equivalent movements in individual asset categories, and it also fails to report changes in many of the obligations of the reporting enterprise. In other words, the Statement of Total Cash Flow Movement is effectively a funds statement based on net realisable values; its data are rearranged to be compatible with the position statement—the Statement of Total Net Cash and Cash Equivalent Resources—which is based on a reasoned ordering of the enterprise's assets and liabilities.

The next statement supporting these descriptions of cash flow is the end-of-period 'cash resources' report—the Statement of Net Cash and Cash Equivalent Resources (Figure 4). Together with corresponding figures relating to the beginning of the period, it contains descriptions of the total resources of the enterprise in cash or cash equivalent terms. As such, it provides a total reporting of the actual and potential cash resources and obligations of the reporting enterprise. Thus, it not only describes the assets and liabilities of the enterprise in current value terms which are understandable and not subject to the arbitrariness of periodic data allocations; it also reveals the financial resources currently available to management to meet existing financial obligations and future commitments. The uniqueness of this 'balance sheet' is that it is a statement of financial position which attempts to reflect the liquidity of the reporting enterprise in reasonably clear and understandable terms which do not

Figure 4
CF Ltd.
Statement of Net Cash and Cash Equivalent Resources
as at t_1 and t_2
Resources

	t_1 £000	t_2 £000
Realised Cash Resources		
Bank, cash and deposit balances	5	44
Readily-Realisable Non-Cash Resources		
Amounts due to customers	11	18
Stocks of finished goods	10	18
Motor vehicles	10	4
Land and buildings	12	20
	43	60
Not-Readily-Realisable Non-Cash Resources		
Work-in-progress	9	24
Non-specialist plant and machinery	9	6
	18	30
Non-Realisable Non-Cash Resources		
Specialist plant and machinery	–	–
	66	134
Obligations		
Short-Term Obligations		
Amounts due to suppliers	9	18
Taxation due to Inland Revenue	13	20
Distributions due to owners	10	12
	32	50
Long-Term Obligations		
Borrowings from merchant bank	10	18
Indefinite Obligations		
Funds pertaining to owners (see Statement of Retained Income)	24	66
	66	134

Figure 5
CF Ltd.
Statement of Retained Income
Period t_1 to t_2

	£000
Realised income	74
Less: taxation provided	20
Distributable Income	54
Less: dividends provided	12
Retained Income for Period	42
Add: retained income of previous periods	24
Total Retained Income (as per Statement of Net Cash and Cash Equivalent Resources)	66

adhere to the rather misleading fixed and current asset categories of traditional accounting, and are compatible with the cash flow analysis contained in the previous cash-based funds statement. It is therefore a rearranged NRVA-balance sheet, and provides a position statement which has for so long been missing from CFA systems of reporting.

The final Statement of Retained Income (Figure 5) also provides a means of filling a gap in CFA—in this case, the lack of a measure of income in the latter.

This statement thus completes the combined CFA and NRVA system by providing the NRVA-based measure of income which reconciles with the equivalent position statement. Thus the complete system comprises a realised cash flow statement, a cash-based funds statement, a realisable income statement, and a net realisable value position statement.

Advantages of the combined system

The above outline statements contain the following advantageous features which appear to strengthen the case for reporting in such a way:

1. The two cash flow statements clearly separate and identify the objectively measured realised cash flow data from the far more subjective potential cash flow data described by the unrealised movements in the enterprise's assets and liabilities. The idea of distinguishing factual from judgmental data in accounting statements in this way should be capable of aiding their users in assessing the varying degrees of credibility inherent in such information. In addition, the 'ranking' of actual and potential cash flows in order of realisability and repayment provides them with indications of what cash is or will be available for future activities and commitments of the enterprise.

2. Although it can be argued that there is no need to ensure the articulation of the 'surplus' and 'position' statements, the above scheme of reporting ensures a proper reconciliation of actual with potential cash flows. It is thus intended as a complete cash-orientated system with all reported data being capable of being matched, compared and justified. In this way, these cash-based statements are available for an assessment of the extent and quality of the reporting enterprise's cash management. If the managing of cash flow is regarded as a vital ingredient in the survival of the enterprise in both the short-term and long-term, it appears to be sensible to report on such matters.

Thus, it can be anticipated that these statements would be useful primarily for, for example, (a) bankers, lenders and suppliers concerned with evaluating the liquidity of the enterprise in connection with the amount and risk associated with their existing and potential cash claims on it; (b) investors anxious to predict the amount and risk associated with the future cash distributions by the enterprise which are such a vital ingredient in their investment decisions; (c) employees desiring to assess the financial position of the enterprise in connection with future job and pay prospects; and (d) government monitoring the effects of its taxation policies and procedures on the cash flow of business enterprises. Each of the decision models inherent in the above descriptions of users relies to a considerable extent on the short or long-term availability of cash within the reporting enterprise. The recommended system provides information likely to meet these requirements. Income is there as well, but this system destroys the notion of the all-embracing importance of income in relation to such matters as interest and capital repayments, credit settlements, dividend distributions and wage claims.[6] With respect to each of these matters, cash appears to be just as, if not more, important.

In addition, it does not appear unreasonable to presume that enterprise management would find such statements useful when involved in the process of managing cash flow and resources—for example, when comparing with previously forecast activity, determining distribution levels, and deciding on borrowing requirements. Indeed, as has been recently suggested, the aims of enterprise management should be compatible with those persons interested in its financial reports, and thus the information needs of management and external interests should be just as compatible.[7]

3. The accounting practices used in the above statements are simple and straightforward—no complex data allocation procedures have been undertaken, and no extensive explanation of such procedures is necessary to the report user.

4. The combined system ought to satisfy the advocates of both CFA and NRVA. It contains all the data normally required in each of these systems, but in such a way as to highlight the crucial feature of both—cash and its accessibility.

[6]This was originally suggested by Edwards, *op. cit*, p. 135, and more recently implied in H. C. Edey. 'The Logic of Financial Accounting.' *The Deloitte, Haskins and Sells Lecture*, Cardiff University College Press, 1980, pp. 8–11.

[7]This idea has been most elegantly explored in Edey, *op cit*, pp. 6–7.

Conclusion

The above points have been put forward as matters for debate by those who regard improvements to the financial reporting function to be essential. In particular, they are presented as a means of extending CFA and NRVA to the point at which it can be said that the reported data are complete so far as liquidity management assessment at least is concerned. It is not a case of adding CFA and NRVA data together; it is an admission that each is incomplete without the other, and that financial reports are irrelevant without both. Finally, it might be suggested that this cash-orientated system may only have a limited application to certain types of enterprise whose asset structure is mainly composed of readily-realisable assets (such as banks, property and insurance companies).[8] To limit the system in this way is to deny that liquidity matters, generally, and cash flow and cash accessibility, particularly, are of no concern to industrial organisations. The non-realisability of assets in the latter due to their specialised nature is recognised in the system outlined in this paper—they have no sale value, and therefore do not add to the reporting entity's command over money until such time as they generate cash flows from use.

[8]As suggested in Edwards, *op cit*, pp. 132–3.

Suggested additional readings

* Ijiri, Y., 'Cash Flow Accounting and Its Structure,' **Journal of Accounting, Auditing and Finance**, May 1978, pp. 331-48.

Ijiri is best known for his axiomatic arguments in defence of historical cost accounting. However, in the late 1970s, he developed normative arguments to derive cash flow accounting data from historical cost financial statements. He main cash flow proposal is for a cash recovery rate with which to approximate the reporting entity's internal rate of return.

* Jones, C. J., 'Accounting Standards: A Blind Alley?,' **Accounting and Business Research**, Autumn 1875, pp. 273-79.

Jones perceived the standardisation of historical cost accounting in the early 1970s as a recipe for perpetuating the anomalies of that system. He advocated cash flow accounting as a reasonable alternative to the accounting standards process because of the relevance of cash flow data for performance assessment.

* Lawson, G. H., 'Measuring Divisional Performance,' **Management Accounting**, May 1971, pp.147-52.

This is an early prescriptive piece by Lawson, in which he demonstrates the utility of his cash flow accounting proposals in the context of better assessing the performance of separable parts of the reporting entity.

* Lee, T. A., 'Goodwill - an Example of Will-O'-the-Wisp Accounting,' **Accounting and Business Research**, Autumn 1971, pp. 318-28.

This paper by Lee identifies the origins of his cash flow accounting prescriptions in a detailed analysis of the accounting anomalies associated with reporting on goodwill and other intangibles.

* Staubus, G. J., 'Alternative Asset Flow Concepts,' **The Accounting Review**, July 1966, pp. 397-412.

Staubus' work represents one of very few US attempts to articulate a conceptual argument for cash flow accounting statements as part of financial reporting.

DEMONSTRATING THE UTILITY OF CASH FLOW REPORTING

Introduction

The next part of the Kuhnian sequence involves a relatively sophisticated empirical testing of the prescriptive claims made for them by normative theorists. Several studies were undertaken in the 1970s and 1980s. They fall into different categories, but the overall effect has been to conclude that more research needs to be done (using more sophisticated and realistic models), and that the jury is still out regarding a verdict on cash flow accounting's utility.

The different categories of empirical research are represented in the following reproduced papers. *Largay* and *Stickney* (1980), *Lawson* (1981), *Lee* (1983), and *Arnold* and *Wearing* (1988) each use the technique of a detailed analysis of the past cash flow results of well-known companies - either to demonstrate how to use the available data (particularly Lee), or to provide evidence of how specific corporate situations are better revealed by the use of cash flow analyses (particularly, Largay and Stickney). The major point of interest in these analyses is the primary focus on operating cash flow generation and its relation to other cash flows and to earnings. Lawson, for example, reveals issues concerning interest and dividend covers, effective tax rates, and the debt-equity substitution which takes place in cash flow terms. Largay and Stickney, on the other hand, look to cash flow accounting's potential to predict corporate failure. Lee describes the problems, in the absence of cash flow data, of adjusting accruals figures to cash flow equivalents, and then the further adjustments needed to put the derived cash flow data in a form suitable for sensible analysis.

Certain of the remaining studies fall into a general research category of using publicly-available data to empirically test modelled relationships. Typically, these are designed to demonstrate whether there is statistically significant support for the notion that cash flow accounting data contain information incrementally beyond that contained in conventional earnings. In the case of *Wilson* (1987), by separating earnings into two different sets of accounting components, the answer was a muted result that the operating cash flow component did, indeed, contain additional information. *Bernard* and *Stober* (1989), on the other hand, extending the time frame and, using an independent sample of firms, reported that they could not replicate the Wilson effect over a longer period. Indeed, their general conclusion was that they could not find the economic logic by which the market assimilates either cash flow or accrual data. In other words, a great deal more research needs to be done with respect to theory and model specification in relation to the testing of the potential utility of reported cash flows.

Board and *Day* (1989) were not so reticent when they concluded from their study of share price reaction to the publication of accounting information that cash flow data had no effect. Instead, they preferred to prescribe it for non-investment uses.

Interestingly, this conclusion is similar to that of *Casey* and *Bartczak* (1985) with respect to their study of the incremental power of cash flow data over earnings when distinguishing failed from non-failed firms. Arnold and Wearing, on the other hand, were content to stick with individual company analysis to argumentatively demonstrate the utility of cash flow accounting. In this case, they analysed the results of a well-known entity on a cash flow and exit price basis (using a model adapted by them from earlier work of Lee).

Thus, what can be seen from the reproduced studies in this section is a gradual exploration of the idea of cash flow accounting. This exploration is taking different directions and meeting new problems. It is also helping to identify the nature and role of cash flow accounting, generally, and the claims which can or cannot be made for it, particularly.

* Arnold, A. J. and Wearing, R. T., "Cash Flows, Exit Prices and British Airways," **Journal of Business Finance and Accounting**, Autumn 1988, pp. 311-33.

* Bernard, V. L. and Stober, T. L., "The Nature and Amount of Information in Cash Flows and Accruals," **The Accounting Review**, October 1989, pp. 624-52.

* Board, J. L. G. and Day, J. F. S., "The Information Content of Cash Flow Figures," **Accounting and Business Research**, Winter 1989, pp. 3-11.

* Casey, C. J. and Bartczak, N. J., "Using Operating Cash Flow Data to Predict Financial Distress: Some Extensions," **Journal of Accounting Research**, Spring 1985, pp. 384-401.

* Largay, J. A. and Stickney, C. P., "Cash Flows, Ratio Analysis and the W. T. Grant Bankruptcy," **Financial Analysts Journal**, July-August 1980, pp. 51-54.

* Lawson, G. H., "The Cash Flow Performance of UK Companies," in Bromwich, M. and Hopwood, A. (eds.), **Essays in British Accounting Research** (London: Pitman Publishing, 1981), pp. 79-100.

* Lee, T. A., "Funds Statements and Cash Flow Analysis," **The Investment Analyst**, July 1983, pp. 13-21.

* Wilson, G. P., "The Incremental Information Content of the Accruals and Funds Components of Earnings After Controlling for Earnings," **The Accounting Review**, April 1987, pp. 293-322.

Journal of Business Finance & Accounting, 15(3) Autumn 1988, 0306 686X $2.50

CASH FLOWS, EXIT PRICES AND BRITISH AIRWAYS

A.J. ARNOLD AND R.T. WEARING*

INTRODUCTION

The benefits to be obtained from reporting cash flows and exit prices in external reports have been extensively discussed in the literature in the last twenty years, notably by Lawson and Lee, and Chambers and Sterling, but almost entirely as alternatives.

Both focus on cash, or cash equivalence, and both seek to avoid or minimise accruals adjustments whereby assumptions about future events are incorporated in reported results and position statements, but each is incomplete. Cash flow accounting lacks a position statement that would enable the magnitude of cash flows to be evaluated, and exit price accounting has not satisfactorily segregated realised and unrealised gains and losses.

Their conjunction, other than in a casual way, was first made by Lee in 1981, even though they have been seen as intuitive accounting concepts.

The use of an accounting system based on cash flow-exit information would represent a radical departure from conventional financial reporting practice. It is fair to question such a change on two grounds. Firstly, it could be argued that if stock markets are strong form efficient then the additional information which we propose should be incorporated into published financial statements will already have been impounded into share prices. Secondly, it might be thought that the incremental costs involved in providing the additional information would outweigh any potential benefits.

We would answer these objections as follows. To take the efficient markets objection first, we would argue that the market on present evidence is probably not strong form efficient and that while investors represent an important group of accounts users, there are other well defined user groups, for instance employees, loan creditors and government who would benefit from our proposed reporting system. Even in the case of investors, it is reasonable to argue that while the market may estimate the information we propose, the reporting of this information would provide an important role in validating these estimates. Thus, even if the fact of reporting the extra information did not directly result in a significant movement in the company's share price this should

* The authors are Lecturers in Accounting, in the Department of Economics, at the University of Essex. This is a revised version of a paper presented at the British Accounting Association annual conference at Aberystwyth in April 1986. The authors gratefully acknowledge the helpful comments of participants. (Paper received June 1986, revised October 1986)

not be taken as evidence that the information is redundant. On the contrary, it could be argued that the market is thereby shown to be efficient and that the extra information has performed a useful function in validating the market's previous estimates.

To counter the argument that the incremental costs of providing the additional information would exceed any possible benefits, we would contend that most companies already generate cash flow information for internal management accounting purposes. As regards exit prices, we think that most managements would be aware of the importance of having access to this information in order to take decisions on an opportunity cost basis. For these reasons we would argue that the incremental costs in reporting CaFE information externally would be relatively small.

British Airways has been chosen for comparing accruals accounting and cash flow-exit information for several reasons. Firstly, unlike most other nationalised industries, British Airways is subject to some international competition from other airline operators and its financial results are highly dependent upon cyclical variations in airline traffic. Secondly, accounting treatments have been adopted in recent years which have had significant effects on reported profits in particular years. Focusing on cash flows may provide useful insights into the economic performance of British Airways and may provide useful information for predicting future trends. Thirdly, a high proportion of British Airways' assets consists of aircraft, a standardised asset for which we could obtain reasonably reliable exit prices from published data and trade sources. Finally, the Government was committed to privatising British Airways. In this context, additional information on cash flows and exit prices should contribute to the debate over whether privatisation is likely to have improved the future performance of British Airways.

The purpose of this paper is to support the proposition that the reporting of cash flows and exit prices in external reports would provide benefits to users, to put forward an integrated cash flow-exit price model for reporting practice and to apply it to the affairs of British Airways since 1974 so that its information content can be appraised and contrasted with the information contained in the external reports as published.

CASH FLOWS AND EXIT PRICES

Cash and price are two of the most basic notions in an exchange economy, yet neither have achieved a central role in financial reporting. The benefits to be obtained from reporting cash flows and exit prices to those outside the reporting entity have been extensively discussed in the literature in the last twenty years and occasionally applied, but with the exception of Edey (1963a) and Lee (1981a and 1984c) they have been conceived as alternative approaches rather than natural complements.

Cash Flows

Early accounting concentrated on reporting the cash outcomes of transactions, but as accounting developed, the pattern of cash inflows and cash outflows was modified by the accruals or matching concept to yield a profit figure supposedly indicative of business performance. The 'creative' possibilities presented by accounting concepts were revealed in the 1920s and 1930s but it was not until 1963 that Edey suggested that the financial reports should focus on cash not profit as 'in the end it is money that buys things and not figures of profit' (1963a, p.999); and 'for the investor, whether he be owner-manager or minority shareholder, the type of accounting statement that would be most useful would be a cash forecast' (1963a, p.1001).

Thomas (1969) declared it was time to consider the possibility of ultimate failure in our efforts to determine income and suggested the substitution of allocation-free funds statements for income statements since allocation assertions did not reflect anything that existed in the external world.

Rayman (1970) criticised the conventional system for failing to differentiate between the results of actual events and the effects of accounting procedures' and suggested a segregated system of funds accounting, but it is Lawson and Lee who have consistently made the case for cash flow accounting in a series of writings since 1968.

Cash flow accounting involves the reporting of a classified list of last year's cash flows, and a set of forecast cash flows, with supporting analyses of the variances between last year's actual and forecast flows, (see Briston and Fawthrop, 1971). It therefore emphasises the most fundamental events in business activity, cash flows into and out of the enterprise, and by the segregation of past (cash) facts from future estimates, accounting time period allocations, based on estimates of consumption, are avoided.

The result is a set of statements that is objective, understandable and simple, and which meets the needs of a variety of users concerned with stewardship, liquidity, performance appraisal and investment. In particular, cash flow accounting meets one of the fundamental accounting objectives, 'to provide information useful to investors and creditors for predicting, comparing and evaluating potential cash flows to them in terms of amount, timing and related uncertainty' (American Institute of Certified Public Accountants, 1973).

Cash flow provides data which, because it is properly dated, can be discounted at a rate selected by the user, and which does not require price level adjustment, although comparisons over time require, and the data permit, general price level adjustment to a base period.

Finally, the use of a flow statement integrates trading activities and investment, dividend and financing policies, unlike information presented in profit and loss account and balance sheet format.

A restricted version of cash flow accounting, involving depreciation and working capital correctives to published data, has been used in aggregated form to reveal that, due to reliance on conventional data, 63 per cent of dividend payments by quoted companies over the period 1954–1976 had been financed by lenders (Lawson, 1979). Cash flow accounting has also been used to analyse the operations of a number of individual companies.[1]

Critics have shown that cash flow reports can be distorted, for example, by delaying payments to creditors, and that they ignore non-cash changes in assets and liabilities, including holding gains and losses, so that no estimate is provided 'of the extent to which these flows were obtained by consumption of assets' (Egginton, 1984, p.104). Operating cash flows have also been found to be poor predictors of failure (Casey and Barkczak, 1984).

It is not unduly difficult to make a case for cash flow information as a supplement to the main accounts, perhaps in place of funds flow statements, which retain many of the accruals adjustments inherent in conventional profit determination, but harder to support them as an acceptable measure of performance as they do not reflect holding gains or losses, do not identify the surplus that should (as opposed to could) be viewed as available for distribution, and do not enable the construction of performance, position and failure appraisal ratios as no satisfactory capital stock[2] is identified that can be related to the flows.

Exit Prices

Conventional financial accounting records the conversion of input costs to exit prices for every completed (i.e., cash to cash) transaction, but utilises potential exit prices for incomplete transactions only as a byproduct (e.g., as 'residual value' when calculating depreciation to be allocated) or as a form of prudence (e.g., lower of cost or market value for stock). Although Canning (1929) gave some support to the relevance of net realisable values, and Edey called for a movement towards providing shareholders with the fundamental data of financial decisions including 'estimates of the realisable value locked up in their companies' assets' (1963b, p.1086), advocacy of the systematic use of exit prices is generally associated with Sterling, and, in a modified form (CoCoA), with Chambers.

Exit (or NRV) price accounting involves the construction of balance sheets by means of estimated current market prices, 'values that could currently be realised if the assets were sold at the best prices immediately available' (Edwards and Bell, 1961, p.79). The Income Statements articulate with Balance Sheets in the usual manner, although allocation based charges such as depreciation are replaced by 'price-variation' charges.

Exit prices produce a dated money-equivalent asset figure which does not require any time period allocations or assumptions about the future, use current prices and produce figures which are all in current £s, and avoid mixing factual statements (calculations of actual past events) and hypothetical statements (calculations of the expected consequences of possible future events), two forms of calculation that are 'logically and technically different' (Chambers, 1976).

All differences between costs or book values of assets at the end of a period and their independently discovered money equivalents are charged to profit and loss and monetary amounts are identified that possess 'additivity' in the sense that 'numbers of monetary units designating the same kinds of prices in monetary units of the same kind are additive' (Chambers, 1970, p.51).[3] The use of exit prices results in properly financial position statements. Finance means money, cash or its substitutes, and 'things which have no money equivalent, no price, have no present financial characteristic' (Chambers, 1970, p.49). Such statements provide 'the acid test of financial capacity to meet financial commitments' (Egginton, 1980, p.14) relevant to creditor protection, and provide users with the balance sheet information they expect to get (Chambers, Hopwood and McKeown, 1984).

Exit price based approaches have received limited empirical testing, due to the difficulty of obtaining such information if it is not reported, but on two occasions CoCoA has been applied empirically, leading to conclusions that it represents a feasible approach (Gray, 1976), that produces figures substantially different from conventional balance sheets, and which 'compare favourably' in terms of accuracy (as indicated by dispersion measures) with conventional figures (McKeown, 1971).

There have been four main criticisms of the use of exit prices. The inclusion in the Income Statement of upward price variations (holding gains) on stock and fixed assets as readily as downward price variations has been viewed as an imprudent basis for dividend policy.

Secondly, the use of exit prices implies to some an assumption that the entity, or its assets both fixed and current, are to be liquidated.

When exit prices are applied to highly specific assets the result is an accelerated pattern of charge against profits which does not reflect physical usage of and benefit from that asset.[4]

Finally, Whittington has argued that exit prices lack relevance to a continuing business 'where continuity is assumed either to be axiomatic or to be the most profitable option open to the firm' since net realisable value does not then represent the consequences of a course of action that will be taken (1983, p.125), and that exit prices are not the opportunity cost (the best alternative foregone) merely the cost of one of several alternative courses of action.

We do not find many of these arguments very convincing. The 'value of the unexpired benefits of a firm's past capital expenditure is represented either by the values that would be released if its assets were to be sold in the second-hand markets, or by the cash flows that a combination of assets is expected to generate in the future' (Lawson, 1985, p.102), and although a business has multiple disposition possibilities within the firm, for the business as a whole, which is the province of financial reporting, there is no third choice beyond hold or sell.

Which of these two decisions are taken will presumably affect future cash flows, both in amount and timing, but for the purposes of a detailed position statement the assets by definition are held and the opportunity foregone is to have sold, at the best prices immediately obtainable, so the exit price foregone is the opportunity cost to the firm as a whole.

Moreover, position statements do not conventionally attempt to 'value' the firm as a whole, a function of its future and yet to be revealed ability to generate cash flows, but to attach monetary amounts to its separate constituent parts; thus the bases of figures used for these parts cannot imply the fate of the entity as a whole, and the opportunity cost argument negates the claim that the liquidation of even some of its assets is contemplated.

The attachment of a low or zero figure to specialised assets certainly does not identify the pattern of usage/benefit, because this cannot be ascertained without knowledge of the future, but does indicate that it has a reduced property base for borrowing and that the 'firm's original cash is locked-in' (Chambers, 1970, p.48) both of which are highly relevant to risk and investment appraisal.

The one serious weakness of exit price accounting concerns its apparent anticipation of income, or more generally its failure to delineate realised from unrealised gains/losses, a distinction which is necessary both for the appraisal of performance and risk, and for the determination of a dividend ceiling in accordance with company law.

An Integrated Cash Flow-Exit Price (CaFE) System

Tweedie (1977) and Lee (1984b) have found that cash flow and net realisable values are the 'intuitive accounting concepts'. Interestingly, Tweedie found an 'apparent contradiction between a preference for cash flow reporting combined with support for recording assets in the balance sheet' (1977, p.9) in respondents who wished to write off the asset in the cash flow statement yet record it at realisable value in the balance sheet, and Lee found that 43 per cent of his respondents (with no prior experience of accounting) used a cash flow basis in the Income Statement and a net realisable basis on the Balance Sheet (1984b, p.135).

A suitably combined cash flow-exit price system would, we think, offer users a form of reporting which focuses on the range of financial policy decisions, and in particular avoids emphasising 'profit' at the expense of liquidity; includes operating and investment decisions and performance as clearly delineated parts of the same report, and pays proper attention to temporal aspects by providing a statement of past flows and changes, a position statement in current terms (both for assets and liabilities), and estimates of future flows. This avoids interperiod allocations based on estimates of resource consumption.

It provides a position statement with a consistent valuation method that identifies the opportunity cost of assets and liabilities to the firm as a whole, identifies holding gains and losses and segregates them into realised and unrealised, which in turn provides the basis for the chosen dividend policy. Such a combined system provides properly dated flows and position statements, the latter in current cash equivalents. This facilitates indexation (to reflect purchasing power changes), and performance and position appraisal by means of ratio analysis.

Only Edey in narrative form (1963a), and Lee (1981a) and in extended form (1984c) have supported the reporting of cash flows and exit prices jointly as a means of meeting user needs. Lee originally supported the reporting of cash flows alone, but has gradually increased the role of net realisable values; vis. in 1978 exit value balance sheets were appended to his cash flow reports because 'there are convincing arguments to suggest they complement it rather well and prevent the loss to report users of statements of financial position' (1978, p.80). In 1981 they had 'become part of a single system of reporting which concentrates on the importance and accessibility of cash in business enterprise activity' (Lee 1981a, p.163), while in 1984 'the vital importance of sale prices as a means of describing such conversions ex ante is relatively obvious' (1984c, p.65).

Although we, and Lee, advocate accounting systems that integrate cash flows and exit prices we do not see their integration taking place in the same manner, nor to achieve the same ends. The system is not defined by the flow but by the periodic use of exit prices; the conjunction is not a 'unified system of cash flow reporting' in which 'cash flows and sale price accounting are essentially subjects of cash flow reporting' (Lee, 1984c, p.50) but a framework in which exit price changes are analysed into their realised (i.e. cash flow) and non realised components. Thus under CaFE accounting there is no description of exit prices as either cash or flows, no attempt to classify into 'readily realisable' or 'not readily realisable' cash flows, nor any description of profit as a combination of 'realised and unrealised cash flows' (Lee, 1984c, p.65), since exit prices are seen not as a 'reflection of potential cash' (Lee, 1984c, p.51) but as a measure of the opportunity cost at balance sheet date of asset retention.

The CaFE system of reporting past events and present positions is essentially a 4*4 matrix for each year. (In addition a statement of estimated future flows would be provided and related to subsequent outturns by means of variance analysis; we have not detailed this here since British Airways did not make such estimates available).

	S1	S2	S3	S4
D1				
D2				
D3				
D4				

Statement 1 (S1) is the Exit Price Balance Sheet at the start of the year, and Statement 4 (S4) is the Exit Price Balance Sheet at the end of the year. The Balance Sheets are linked by two statements of equal importance, a Statement (S2) of Realised (Cash Flow) Annual Changes and a Statement (S3) of Non-realised Annual Changes.

Unlike conventional Balance Sheets and Income Statements, each of the four statements is classified under consistent decison-related headings.

D1 Finance
D2 Investment
D3 Operations (subdivided into, I Interest, II Other Operations, III Taxation, IV Dividends)
D4 Cash

Each statement adds vertically, and each decision area adds horizontally, since it is the aggregation of realised and non-realised effects that accounts for changes between successive balance sheets. (Realised is used in its everyday meaning of 'converted into money').

The results, as applied to British Airways 1975–85 are set out in Table 1, Table 2 and Table 3. In Table 1, D4 (Cash) does not include bank overdrafts, since financing is shown as D1. Operations are subdivided and include taxation paid and dividends paid, not proposed. D3.2 (Other Operations) is shown without supporting detail as a consequence of preparing the information from external sources; a company operating the approach themselves could supply suitably classified detail. Share capital is grouped with other forms of finance and thus separated from operating surplus, and deficits are also included in the finance section.

Table 2 by definition omits D4 (Cash). D3 (Operations) shows the increased obligation consequent on an increase in finance received, and holding losses on assets. Because of a lack of information, stores were valued at cost, and do not provide any holding gains or losses. The holding gains represent the change in long term asset figures between successive balance sheets, other than those due to cash payments or receipts, being the change in the realisable value. No attempt has been made, or should be made, to allocate this between a consumption element and a non-consumption element, since any such division is arbitrary, and indeed pointless to external users since both elements derive from continued ownership (as opposed to realisation) of the asset. A reconciliation of the operations movement on the Balance Sheet is given at the foot of Table 2.

Under this approach the three alternative accounting flows (Staubus, 1966) can then be identified; the cash flows are the realised annual changes; the funds flows are the cash flows adjusted for the credit component of the non realised annual changes, and the income flows are the funds flow added to or subtracted from the second part of non realised annual changes, holding gains.

Table 1

British Airways Realised (Cash Flow) Annual Changes (£m)

	1974/75	*1975/76*	*1976/77*	*1977/78*	*1978/79*	*1979/80*	*1980/81*	*1981/82*	*1982/83*	*1983/84*	*1984/85*
DI FINANCE											
Issue of public dividend capital	80.0	63.7	10.0	10.0	10.0	10.0	10.0	10.0			
Issue of loan capital	14.7	84.5	48.8	130.6	133.3	182.9	325.8	196.9	64.1	47.5	
Loans repaid	(57.4)	(79.1)	(54.8)	(57.4)	(77.1)	(21.0)	(32.4)	(38.6)	(98.1)	(213.3)	(328.6)
	37.3	69.1	4.0	83.2	66.2	171.9	303.4	168.3	(34.0)	(165.8)	(328.6)
D2 INVESTMENT											
Sale of fixed assets	9.2	4.6	12.3	5.0	1.7	5.7	37.4	17.5	110.3	11.4	48.2
Purchase of fixed assets	(141.0)	(127.7)	(138.5)	(208.5)	(225.4)	(295.7)	(271.0)	(153.0)	(172.7)	(250.2)	(119.2)
	(131.8)	(123.1)	(126.2)	(203.5)	(223.7)	(290.0)	(233.6)	(135.5)	(62.4)	(238.8)	(71.0)
D3 OPERATIONS											
.1 *Interest*											
Interest received	5.5	3.9	8.1	7.1	10.8	13.4	8.1	5.0	11.7	15.1	18.7
Interest paid	(16.2)	(14.0)	(18.9)	(23.0)	(25.0)	(38.1)	(73.1)	(111.2)	(120.3)	(108.7)	(113.0)
	(10.7)	(10.1)	(10.8)	(15.9)	(14.2)	(24.7)	(65.0)	(106.2)	(108.6)	(93.6)	(94.3)
.2 *Other Operations*	90.4	74.9	145.7	158.7	214.0	136.6	15.0	72.1	223.3	496.8	547.0
.3 *Taxation paid*	(4.5)	1.4	(2.8)	(8.5)	4.8	(19.1)	(7.9)	(2.0)	(14.9)	(3.3)	(1.5)
.4 *Dividends paid*				(16.7)	(24.2)	(15.0)	(7.0)				
(D3.1 + D3.2 + D3.3 + D3.4)	75.2	66.2	132.1	117.6	180.4	77.8	(64.9)	(36.1)	99.8	399.9	451.2
D4 INCREASE (DECREASE) IN CASH (D1 + D2 + D3 = D4)	(19.3)	12.2	9.9	(2.7)	22.9	(40.3)	4.9	(3.3)	3.4	(4.7)	51.6

Table 2

British Airways Non-Realised Annual Changes (£m)

	1975/76	1976/77	1977/78	1978/79	1979/80	1980/81	1981/82	1982/83	1983/84	1984/85
DI FINANCE										
Decrease in share capital				160.0						
(Increase) decrease in government tax credit	4.2	(33.4)	(2.8)	(41.1)	4.0	54.8	71.9	0.7	(9.2)	(72.8)
(Increase) decrease in other credit received	(85.1)	(57.4)	(58.6)	(103.7)	(35.5)	1.1	(309.5)	(16.1)	(106.4)	(333.3)
Increase (decrease) in trade credit received	47.4	50.0	47.3	47.2	41.7	11.8	86.0	9.4	6.1	145.1
	(33.5)	(40.8)	(14.1)	62.4	10.2	67.7	(151.6)	(6.0)	(109.5)	(261.0)
D2 INVESTMENT										
Longterm assets	(49.8)	(47.2)	(117.0)	(52.1)	(69.4)	(93.1)	167.3	(48.4)	(70.9)	476.1
D3 OPERATIONS										
(Increase) decrease in finance received	(33.5)	(40.8)	(14.1)	62.4	10.2	67.7	(151.6)	(6.0)	(109.5)	(261.0)
Holding gains (losses) on longterm assets	(49.8)	(47.2)	(117.0)	(52.1)	(69.4)	(93.1)	167.3	(48.4)	(70.9)	476.1
	(83.3)	(88.0)	(131.1)	10.3	(59.2)	(25.4)	15.7	(54.4)	(180.4)	215.1
OPERATIONS MOVEMENT RECONCILIATION										
Accumulated surplus at start of year	226.4	209.3	253.4	239.9	430.6	449.2	358.9	338.5	383.9	603.4
Realised surplus (deficit)	66.2	132.1	117.6	180.4	77.8	(64.9)	(36.1)	99.8	399.9	451.2
Non-realised surplus (deficit)	(83.3)	(88.0)	(131.1)	10.3	(59.2)	(25.4)	15.7	(54.4)	(180.4)	215.1
Accumulated surplus at end of year	209.3	253.4	239.9	430.6	449.2	358.9	338.5	383.9	603.4	1269.7

Table 3

British Airways Exit Price Balance Sheets (£m)

	31.3.75	*31.3.76*	*31.3.77*	*31.3.78*	*31.3.79*	*31.3.80*	*31.3.81*	*31.3.82*	*31.3.83*	*31.3.84*	*31.3.85*
DI FINANCE											
Share capital	216.3	280.0	290.0	300.0	150.0	160.0	170.0	180.0	180.0	180.0	180.0
Government tax credit	62.9	58.7	92.1	94.9	136.0	132.0	77.2	5.3	4.6	13.8	86.6
Longterm liabilities	185.7	218.2	221.6	297.6	337.0	492.8	782.4	1010.6	1053.2	899.1	625.9
Current liabilities	164.3	224.8	275.0	333.8	458.9	506.2	511.0	751.9	673.3	768.1	1048.2
Less Debtors	(115.4)	(162.8)	(212.8)	(260.1)	(307.3)	(349.0)	(360.8)	(446.8)	(456.2)	(462.3)	(607.4)
	513.8	618.9	665.9	766.2	774.6	942.0	1179.8	1501.0	1454.9	1398.7	1333.3
D2 INVESTMENT											
Fleet	449.0	505.0	564.0	634.0	750.0	897.0	1011.0	1302.0	1350.0	1488.0	2036.0
Land and property	141.2	147.3	155.0	168.0	193.0	238.0	263.0	269.0	244.0	258.0	252.2
Equipment	90.1	99.5	107.3	116.8	141.8	164.5	176.9	180.3	173.2	185.7	208.1
Interest in other companies	16.9	18.7	23.2	17.2	22.8	28.7	17.8	20.2	18.3	21.7	4.2
Stores	11.6	14.1	16.3	19.3	23.9	29.6	31.7	33.0	14.9	15.0	17.2
	708.8	784.6	865.8	955.3	1131.5	1357.8	1500.4	1804.5	1800.4	1968.4	2517.7
D3 OPERATIONS											
Accumulated surplus	226.4	209.3	253.4	239.9	430.6	449.2	358.9	338.5	383.9	603.4	1269.7
D4 CASH (D1 + D3 – D2 – D4)	31.4	43.6	53.5	50.8	73.7	33.4	38.3	35.0	38.4	33.7	85.3

BRITISH AIRWAYS

There are two factors which make an objective appraisal of the performance of any nationalised industry difficult when based on its financial accounts alone.

Firstly, the intention of the original statutes which set up the nationalised industries was that they should operate in the 'public interest'. Because they pursue objectives other than pure profit maximisation, the Income Statement of a nationalised industry cannot give a complete picture of the 'success' or otherwise of that industry over time. Given that the nationalised industries were originally required to break even taking one year with another, the use of the term 'Profit and Loss Account' rather than 'Income Statement' is somewhat incongruous. Moreover, there is always the temptation for governments to intervene in the affairs of nationalised industries in order to promote their own political and economic objectives, for instance with regard to levels of employment and inflation. More recently, the government has been criticised for interfering in the pricing policies of the nationalised gas and electricity industries in order to increase government revenues. The effects of such interventions cannot be adequately captured in the Income Statement alone.

These problems have been recognised by many observers, although the media invariably tend to report some figure of financial profit as the most suitable indicator of a nationalised industry's performance for a particular year. In 1976 the National Economic Development Office produced a report (NEDO, 1976) which suggested that one way of overcoming these difficulties would be for the nationalised industries to report 'performance indicators' in their annual accounts. In addition they should report any instances where government has intervened in their affairs. These suggestions were taken up in a subsequent White Paper published in 1978 (HMSO, 1978).

Secondly, it is speculated that nationalised industries may adopt accounting policies which further their own objectives. 'Excessive' profits earned by nationalised industries are likely to provoke a reaction from the public and the media that they are abusing their privileged monopoly position. Hence the reporting of an unduly high profit figure could be as embarrassing as a financial loss and it is speculated that the more 'successful' industries may, for instance, introduce current cost accounting with the aim of reducing reported profit figures. Likierman (1983) has addressed this issue although he finds that the evidence that nationalised industries may manipulate their accounts is not conclusive.

Over the years British Airways has been subject to a great deal of interference by governments in pursuit of their own political and economic objectives. Such intervention by government ministers can have serious, and long term, consequences for the industry involved. Pressure from the Government has been evident in investment decisions taken by the predecessors of British Airways, i.e. British European Airways and British Overseas Airways (see, for instance, Pryke, 1981). 'The (Select Committee) 1964 Report on BOAC revealed the influence which had been used to persuade BOAC to buy the VC10 against its commercial judgement' (Foster, p.106). The decision to order Concorde by the Board of British Airways was reluctantly taken after the Government confirmed that it would partially compensate the airline for losses incurred in operating Concorde.

Such intervention tends to be typical for the nationalised industries generally, and it could be argued that provided this information is given to users of accounts they will not be misled. The 1978 White Paper (1978, p.19) reported that the government of the day had asked each of the nationalised industries to include in the annual report a statement summarising the government's main instructions and guidance. Likierman found that some nationalised industries referred to ministerial intervention in the text of their annual report and accounts, but 'because industries did not make it clear when there were *no* directions, it was difficult to know whether this requirement had been complied with or not' (Likierman, 1979, p.31). It is quite likely that government ministers are reluctant to have details of their intervention brought out into the open and Rees claims that they will only issue directives as a last resort and admission of failure (Rees, 1979, p.4).

We should also note that, with regard to British Airways, accounting treatments have been adopted in recent years which have been regarded by some commentators as an attempt to make the industry more saleable to the private sector. During the financial year ended March 1982, more than £400m was written off as extraordinary items relating to severance schemes and to write offs of fixed assets. The effect of these treatments was to produce a 'bottom line' deficit of £545m compared with a deficit of £145m for the previous year. One interpretation of the motivation for making these write offs at such a time was that the asset base would be reduced so that in the next and subsequent financial years, operating profits would be enhanced by lower depreciation charges and the fact that virtually all the redundancy costs had been effected in the financial year 1981/82. The combined effect of these two factors would be to make the future reported profits of British Airways more attractive to future private investors.

Two desirable characteristics of accounting reports referred to in the Corporate Report (ASSC, 1975,) relate to comparability and timeliness. The accounting reports of British Airways can be questioned in terms of comparability for the reasons given above. In terms of timeliness it interesting to note that the 1981/82 accounts (year end 31 March, 1982) were not published until October 1982 and that the 1984/85 accounts were not published until December 1985. Delays of this order would be unusual for a quoted company in the private sector and would raise serious doubts in investors minds about the future viability of such a company.

The use of a CaFE reporting system would not completely eradicate such difficulties. However, we would argue that such a system would at least restrict the scope for introducing debatable accounting treatments, which tend to distort the pattern of net profit in selected years and consequently create difficulties in making intertemporal and interindustry comparisons. Where delays in publishing the annual accounts have arisen through difficulties in assessing the future costs of legal actions (as has happened with British Airways) our proposed CaFE system would not reduce such delays. But where delays have occurred over difficulties in deciding which accounting treatment to adopt for writing off fixed assets or allocating the cost of severance schemes over more than one accounting period, then we would argue that our proposed CaFE system does offer a well defined path for resolving such difficulties and would clearly reduce such delays.

Preparing the Cash Flow Data

The cash flow data was calculated on the basis of the published balance sheets, profit and loss accounts and source and application of funds statements of British Airways for the financial years 1974/75 to 1984/85 inclusive: 1974/75 was chosen since BEA and BOAC were dissolved and merged under the name British Airways on 1 April, 1974. A number of difficulties were encountered in converting this information to a cash flow basis.

For example, SSAP 10 (ASC, 1978) suggests that dividends paid and taxation paid should be shown as an application of funds. However, the British Airways source and application of funds statement takes profit after tax and dividends as its starting point. Hence, the tax payments or refunds shown in our cash flow statement were estimated on the basis of the breakdown of liabilities in the notes to the accounts and the profit and loss account data. Because of the nature of the published information, we stress that they are only estimates. However, in relation to the other cash flows they are relatively small so that any differences between our estimates and the true tax flows are unlikely to affect the overall picture.

Changes in accounting treatments between years had to be adjusted for. The description of fixed asset and investment disposals changes from 'Disposal of fixed assets and investments' (1980/81) to 'Net book value of fixed asset and investment disposals' (1981/82) to 'Net proceeds from tangible asset and investment disposals' (1983/84). In the case of the 1980/81 accounts it is not clear whether the term 'Disposal of fixed assets and investments' refers to net book value written off or to sale proceeds.

Preparing the Exit Price Data

For most businesses it would be difficult to identify exit prices if one had to rely solely on the publicly available information. In the case of British Airways, however, a very high proportion of total assets consists of aircraft and details of the company's aircraft fleet at each balance sheet date were readily available.

Aircraft are standardised assets, 'which are quite negotiable. From time to time there is a glut of aircraft, but they can be stored; there is a well established secondhand market' (Institute of Fiscal Studies, 1984, p.101). The value of an aircraft depends on its ability to make money in a competitive market, a function of its unit costs, which in turn are size related — large aircraft have a lower cost per seat but cost more per mile to fly, and airlines attempt to balance these two factors in each individual market.

The rising cost of new aircraft has slowed technical development, but the demand for travel has outpaced the growth in world GNP, and marginal operators in the airline business provide a demand for used aircraft which has overturned the conventional wisdom that jet aircraft are obsolete after 16 to 18 years; the resale price for used aircraft is buoyant.[5] Aircraft are not, therefore, a simple wasting asset with a predictable life of 16 to 18 years (see British Airway's depreciation policy); they represent, depending on their unit costs, an asset with investment and resale potential.

There are trade agencies which monitor the secondhand market both as an investment aid, and to assist in insurance claims, and for most aircraft we have obtained figures which represent the average half-life market value of a typically equipped airline aircraft in average condition of the same type, variant and age as the British Airways fleet. For some turboprops used by British Airways to a decreasing extent in recent years, Tridents and VC 10s, figures were imputed by reference to comparable aircraft.

Concorde presented special difficulties as no market in these aircraft has been established. British built planes tend to be inefficient and have higher fuel costs than American built aircraft. As we have referred to above, at one stage British Airways would not have purchased Concorde but for Government assurances of financial support. During 1977/78 Concorde made a net loss of £178m and its 'cost per seat mile was roughly three times that of the Boeing 747' (Pryke, 1981, p.132). (Aviation fuel cost 75 cents per gallon in 1979 compared with only 11 cents in 1972).

Concorde first earned reported profits in 1982/83 (Allen, 1986) and the stabilisation of fuel costs and the growth of charter flights have increased its profitability. The growth of charter and small parcel freightage possibilities have also increased its marketability.

Accordingly we have valued Concorde by reference to a Boeing 747 as follows: ten per cent until 1982 and one hundred per cent in 1982 and thereafter. The resulting figures are inevitably approximate, however, and will yield results that must be treated with considerable caution.

The valuation of other assets presented fewer problems. Market values were noted in the accounts for trade and other investments, and land and property. Debtors should be at their potential sale price to a commercial factor (Ma, 1974) but their balance sheet figure was taken as a fairly close approximation. No information is available for the exit price of equipment and stores so we used undepreciated cost as a proxy; any inaccuracies in these assumptions will be limited in their impact on the results due to consistency of application and the relatively small size of the assets concerned (6 per cent and 0.5 per cent of total assets respectively). They will also be less distorting to time series analysis than the depreciation write-offs, supplementary charges, asset write-downs and write-ups, and extraordinary provisions adopted in the published accounts.

The conversion of capital and liabilities to an exit basis is in general straightforward; reserves are considerably affected by the change and deferred tax has been included on a full, not partial basis, utilising supplementary information in the accounts, both for reasons of consistency and to ensure that future 'obligations' have been identified. The decline in called up share capital consequent on the 1978/79 write off is also included as it represents a decrease in eventual obligation to the government.

DISCUSSION

In Table 4 and Figure 1 we have shown a published indicator of performance together with three based on CaFE accounting. In Column I is set out historic cost return on net assets, the main indicator of performance listed in British Airways' Ten Year Results and Statistics, and in Columns II, III and IV are cash flows, funds flows and profits as returns on net assets, in each case on as comparable a basis as possible with the published accounts.

Over the period 1975–85 all four indicators generally move in the same direction, with the published indicator being lower than those based on CaFE accounting until 1982/83 and notably so in 1980/81.

Table 4

British Airways Performance Indicators

	I	II	III	IV
	%	%	%	%
1975/76	2.2	11.1	6.4	(1.9)
1976/77	20.7	20.1	14.8	8.6
1977/78	12.4	19.8	18.1	4.1
1978/79	14.7	24.5	31.3	25.6
1979/80	6.3	13.6	14.5	8.2
1980/81	(6.6)	1.8	6.9	(0.2)
1981/82	1.0	5.0	(4.9)	6.1
1982/83	23.2	14.5	14.2	11.2
1983/84	29.9	30.4	23.9	19.7
1984/85	28.7	27.3	14.7	37.6

I Historic cost return on net assets (published data)
II Cash flow on operations before tax and interest to net assets (CaFE basis)
III Cash flow on operations before tax and interest less/(plus) increase/(decrease) in finance received to net assets (CaFE basis)
IV As III plus/(less) holding gains/(losses) to net assets (CaFE basis)

The results confirm a 'turnaround' in British Airways in 1980/81 but support suggestions that the published results for that year exaggerated the deterioration and subsequent recovery. Cash flows are strongly supportive of the historic cost returns, but if these cash flows (Column II) are adjusted to allow for the considerable increase in short term credit, both from trade and other creditors and from sales in advance of carriage (Column III) the downturn in CaFE based funds flows to net assets since 1983/84 is far more pronounced. If, however, holding gains are included in the returns (Column IV) 1984/85 has been British Airways' most successful year to date.

Figure 1

British Airways Performance Indicators

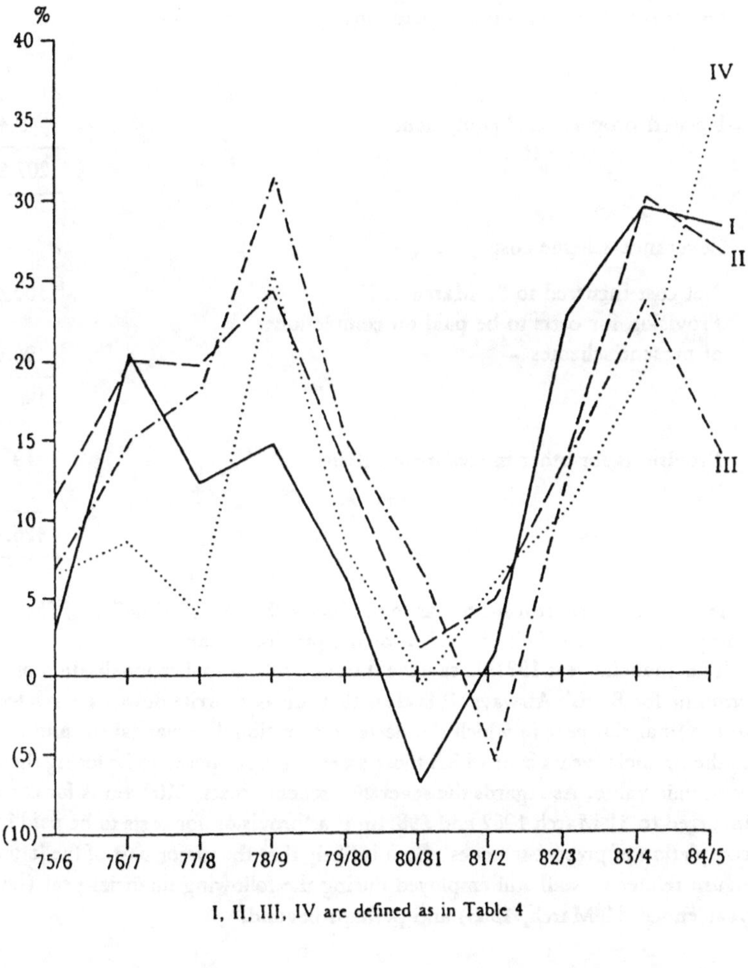

I, II, III, IV are defined as in Table 4

As we have mentioned above, accounting treatments have been adopted in recent years which might be regarded as an attempt to make the industry more saleable to the private sector. We referred to the fact that during the financial year ended March 1982, more than £400m was written off as extraordinary items relating to the implementation of severance schemes and to reductions in the book values of fixed assets.

The extraordinary charges (amounting to £426.4m) which were put through the Profit and Loss Account for the year ended 31 March, 1982 were described in the annual accounts (British Airways, 1982, p.22) as follows:

Supplementary amortisation	
Provisions to write down the unamortised cost of fleet and other assets to the amount estimated to be recoverable from future operations	
	£m
Fleet	198.5
Related property and equipment	9.4
	207.9
Severance scheme costs	
Net cost incurred to 31 March 1982	100.4
Provision for costs to be paid on completion of present schemes	98.4
	198.8
Provisions for other miscellaneous items	19.7
	426.4

The effect of these treatments was to produce a 'bottom line' deficit of £545m compared with a deficit of £145m for the previous year.

The financial year 1981/82 saw the start of a substantial rationalisation programme for British Airways. It is clear that the asset write downs are related to the financial year in which the decision to rationalise was taken, and not to the financial years over which those assets were supposed to be losing their economic value. As regards the severance scheme costs, £100.4m is for costs incurred to 31 March 1982 and £98.4m is a 'provision for costs to be paid in completion of present schemes'. So it is likely that the major part of the latter figure relates to staff still employed during the following financial year (i.e. year ended 31 March, 1983) and perhaps beyond.

In fact, so severe were the provisions for future severance costs that in the financial years 1983/84 and 1984/85 amounts of £33.2m and £10.7m respectively were added back in the published profit and loss accounts. Of course, if by 1983/84 British Airways had been privatised (as the Government originally intended) the results of the newly privatised concern would have been better than anticipated.

The effect of the 1981/82 extraordinary write offs is twofold. Firstly, the asset base is immediately reduced in value. Secondly, the operating costs in future years are reduced through lower depreciation charges and also through the fact that a substantial proportion of severance costs is diverted into the financial year 1981/82. The effect on return on net assets (defined as profit before interest and tax/average net assets) in years subsequent to 1981/82 is unambiguous. Return on net assets will be enhanced since the numerator increases whilst the denominator decreases. As can be seen from Figure 1, comparing indicator I with indicators, II, III and IV it can be seen that for 1982/83 the improvement is greatest for indicator I which is in line with our previous comments on the accounting treatments adopted by British Airways.

The following year (i.e. 1983/84) shows an improvement for all four indicators and the improvement for the published indicator I is the least pronounced of the four. In fact 1983/84 compared to 1982/83 was a very successful year for British Airways. In 1983/84 British Airways repaid £213.3m of long term loans (compared with £98.1m for the previous year) and raised less by way of capital borrowings compared to the previous year. British Airways was also able to spend more on fixed assets in 1983/84 (£250.2m) compared to the previous year (£172.7m).

When comparing 1983/84 and 1984/85, holding gains have a major effect on the results, and the conclusions to be drawn about British Airways' position and performance. Orthodox accounting emphasises operational performance and gives little indication of how well or badly management has used the assets at its disposal; under CaFE accounting the profit figure (Column IV) includes holding gains (based on changes in exit prices) as unrealised but relevant and thus gives some indication of the opportunity cost involved in the organisation continuing to hold its assets. British Airways foregoes an opportunity by not realising for cash the high value assets (i.e. aircraft) at its disposal.

The increase in the accumulated surplus from £603.4m at 31 March, 1984 to £1,269.7m at 31 March, 1985 gives an indication of the rapidly changing fortunes of this particular company and, by implication, of the airline industry in general. It thereby gives an indication of the risk factors which need to be taken into account by management. By contrast, inspection of the balance sheets prepared on the conventional basis for those two dates gives little indication of the most interesting features of the assets operated by British Airways.

We are not suggesting that British Airways should take this course of action, since no decision about investment or disinvestment can possibly be taken on the basis of one financial indicator, but we are saying that there are tangible costs and benefits involved in investing in and operating high value assets.

The size of the holding gains in 1984/85 is a consequence of the recent policy to buy (more efficient) American aircraft, and the $:£ exchange rate used to obtain exit prices for aircraft in £ sterling. If holding gains continue to be made, then British Airways should be able to perform even better in the future; if they are viewed as essentially temporary and fragile then British Airways will probably continue to decline from a peak in 1984/85. The permanence of holding gains and other aspects of company performance is a matter for the markets to evaluate; the identification of holding gains is a matter for the accounting system to address, rather than ignore or confuse.

CONCLUSIONS

We have shown in this paper how it is possible to construct a comprehensive reporting system which combines cash flows and exit prices within an exit price framework, and we have applied this to published data for British Airways from 1975 to 1985. We have not been able to apply the full system we have proposed as no estimates of future cash flows were available, but comparisons can be made between the past/present time dimensions of CaFE accounting, and the conventional information set.

We believe that the statements which are presented as Tables 1 to 3 incorporate to a substantial degree the advantages of a combined cash flow-exit price system which has been outlined above. Exit prices have been used and yield a position statement which is both consistent in valuation basis across the full range of assets and liabilities, and which identifies the opportunity cost of these assets to the firm as a whole. No assumptions about future usage patterns are required as part of attaching a present monetary figure to assets, and of identifying past costs; valuation replaces cost allocations based on estimates of resource consumption. Holding gains and losses are computed and included as annual changes, but the overt categorisation of the annual change into its realised and unrealised components allows users to make their own judgements on the reliability of the results. We would hesitate to suggest that any system could shackle 'creative accounting', but CaFE accounting does, we think, combine a comprehensive approach with a clear segregation of factual and estimated results.

The statements of realised (cash flow) and non-realised annual changes link successive balance sheets; all three have been reordered so that a consistent classification is followed in each, which in a sense is chronologically appropriate. That is, they deal firstly with the question of how an organisation raises its finance, secondly the question of how those resources are used, thirdly operational aspects of the organisation and fourthly the resulting increase or decrease in cash. We believe that this layout has more intuitive appeal, especially to managers and others without extensive financial training. We suggest that future research could usefully attempt to identify whether our approach does possess greater explanatory power than conventional financial statements.

Earnings through more sophisticated money management are now becoming an important part of the trading results of many multinationals. Some of the larger multinationals, through their treasury operations, are virtually taking on the role of mini banks, and fuller information about cash flows and opportunity costs is as important as it has ever been.

We believe that this paper, which owes a great deal to earlier research by Chambers, Lawson, Lee and others, can provide a sound basis from which to approach complex and interesting issues such as the identification and quantification of goodwill and dividend distribution policy. Certainly we would argue that our system is better able to tackle such issues than the existing reporting system which can only deal with these issues in an arbitrary and ad hoc manner. Fuller information disclosure which relates directly to all the opportunities facing organisations is long overdue.

NOTES

1 British Leyland (Lee, 1981b), Laker Airways (Lee, 1982a), Marks and Spencer, Dunlop Holdings, ICL (Lee, 1982b), Lonrho (Lee, 1983a), Sears Holdings (Lee, 1983b), The Hongkong and Shanghai Banking Corporation (Lee, 1983c), Barratts (Lee, 1984a), Pergamon Press (Arnold and Webb, 1982), Woolworths (Lawson, 1982), UDS (Lawson, 1983), Royal Dutch Shell (Egginton, 1984; Lee, 1985; Lawson, 1985) and the nationalised industries (Lee and Stark, 1984).

2 The only stock revealed is cash held, which is too narrow to be a satisfactory position statement.

3 The criticism that the asset values are not additive in the sense that if all were realised at the same time a lesser sum would be realised is a confusion of 'aggregation' and 'additivity'; additivity relates to the consistency of the valuation approach and not the way that a seller may or may not approach any given sale.

4 'By the sale price canon, the whole investment might well need to be written off in its first year, with absurd results on trends of reported earnings' (Baxter 1967).

5 In 1972 a new Boeing 747 cost $25m and in 1985 that same aircraft could be sold for $25.3m.

REFERENCES

Accounting Standards Committee (ASC), (1978), 'Statements of Source and Application of Funds', *Statement of Standard Accounting Practice No. 10,* (Accounting Standards Committee, 1978).

Accounting Standards Steering Committee (ASSC), (1975), *The Corporate Report,* (Institute of Chartered Accountants in England and Wales, 1975).

Allen, R. (1986), 'Concorde', *Airline Executive* (January 1986), pp. 30–41.

American Institute of Certified Public Accountants (1973), 'Objectives of Financial Statements' (1973).

Arnold, A.J. and B.J. Webb (1982), 'Cash, Profits and Pergamon', *The Accountant* (8 July, 1982), pp. 28–30.

Baxter, W.T. (1967), 'Accounting Values: Sale Price versus Replacement Cost', *Journal of Accounting Research* (1967), pp. 208–214.

Briston, R.J. and R.A. Fawthrop (1971), 'Accounting Principles and Investor Protection', *Journal of Business Finance,* Vol. 3, No. 2 (1971), pp. 10–19.

British Airways, *Annual Report and Accounts,* 1975–1985.

Canning, J.B. (1929), *The Economics of Accountancy* (Ronald Press, 1929).

Casey, C.J. and N.J. Barkczak (1984), 'Cash Flow — It's Not the Bottom Line', *Harvard Business Review* (July/August 1984), pp. 61–66.

Chambers, R.J. (1970), 'Second Thoughts on Continuously Contemporary Accounting', *Abacus,* Vol. 6, Part 1 (September 1970), p. 49.

——— (1976), 'The Functions of Financial Statements', *Accounting and Business Research* (Spring 1976), p. 85.

———, W.S. Hopwood and J.C. McKeown (1984), 'The Relevance of Varieties of Accounting Information: A USA Survey', *Abacus*, Vol. 20, Part 2 (1984), pp. 99–110.

Edey, H.C. (1963a), 'Accounting Principles and Business Reality', *Accountancy* (November 1963), pp. 998–1002.

——— (1963b), 'Accounting Principles and Business Reality — II', *Accountancy* (December 1963), pp. 1083–1088.

Edwards, E.O. and P.W. Bell (1961), *The Theory and Measurement of Business Income* (University of California Press, 1961).

Egginton, D.A. (1980), 'Distributable Profit and the Pursuit of Prudence', *Accounting and Business Research* (Winter 1980), pp. 3–14.

——— (1984), 'In Defence of Profit Measurement: Some Limitations of Cash Flow and Value Added as Performance Measures for External Reporting', *Accounting and Business Research* (Spring 1984), pp. 99–111.

Foster, C.D. (1971), *Politics, Finance and the Role of Economics* (George Allen and Unwin, 1971).

Gray, S.J. (1976), 'Accounting for Price Changes: A Case Study of a Multinational Company', *Journal of Business Finance and Accounting* (Spring 1976), pp. 1–13.

HMSO, (1978), *The Nationalised Industries*, Cmnd. 7131 (HMSO, 1978).

Institute of Fiscal Studies (1984), *Civil Aviation Policy and the Privatisation of British Airways* (Institute of Fiscal Studies Report Series No. 12, 1984).

Lawson, G.H. (1979), 'Company Profitability and the UK Stock Market 1954–76: An Exercise in Cash Flow Accounting', *Manchester Business School Discussion Paper* (1979).

——— (1982), 'Was Woolworth Ailing?', *The Accountant* (4 November, 1982), pp. 12–32.

——— (1983), 'Why the Current UDS Takeover Bids Became Inevitable', *The Accountant* (10 February, 1983), pp. 13–16.

——— (1985), 'The Measurement of Corporate Performance on a Cash Flow Basis: A Reply to Mr Egginton', *Accounting and Business Research* (Spring 1985), pp. 99–108.

Lee, T.A. (1978), 'The Cash Flow Accounting Alternative for Corporate Financial Reporting' in C. Van Dam (ed.), *Trends in Managerial and Financial Accounting: Income Determination and Financial Reporting* (Martinus Nijhoff, 1978).

——— (1981a), 'Reporting Cash Flows and Net Realisable Values', *Accounting and Business Research* (Spring 1981), pp. 163–170.

——— (1981b), 'What Cash Flow Analysis Says About BL's Finances', *Financial Times* (23 October 1981), p.15.

——— (1982a), 'Laker Airways — The Cash Flow Truth', *Accountancy* (June 1982), pp. 115–116.

——— (1982b), 'Towards A Practice of Cash Flow Analysis', *University of Edinburgh Discussion Paper 13* (July 1982).

——— (1983a), 'The Lonrho Phenomenon' *The Accountant* (19 May, 1983) pp. 11–12.

——— (1983b), 'Funds Statements and Cash Flow Analysis', *The Investment Analyst* (July 1983), pp. 13–21.

——— (1983c), 'The Financial Statements of the Hongkong and Shanghai Banking Corporation 1865–1980', in F.H.H. King (ed.), *Eastern Banking: Essays in the History of the Hongkong and Shanghai Banking Corporation* (Athlone Press, 1983), pp. 77–92.

——— (1984a), 'SSAP 10 and Cash Flow Analysis', *The Accountant's Magazine* (June 1984), pp. 232–233.

——— (1984b), 'Cash Flows and Net Realisable Values: Further Evidence of the Intuitive Concepts', *Abacus*, Vol. 20, No. 2 (1984), pp. 125–137.

——— (1984c), *Cash Flow Accounting* (Van Nostrand Reinhold, 1984).

——— (1985), 'Cash Flow Accounting, Profit and Performance Measurement: A Response to a Challenge', *Accounting and Business Research* (Spring 1985), pp. 93–97.

——— and A.W. Stark (1984), 'A Cash Flow Disclosure of Government-Supported Enterprises' Results', *Journal of Business Finance and Accounting* (11, 1, 1984), pp. 1–11.

Likierman, A. (1979), The Financial and Economic Framework for Nationalised Industries, *Lloyd's Bank Review* (October 1979, pp. 16–32).

——— (1983), 'Evidence on Accusations of Manipulating Profitability: Adjustments for Inflation by the Nationalised Industries 1976–81', *Accounting and Business Research* (Winter 1983), pp. 29–34.

Ma, R. (1974), 'On Chambers' Second Thoughts', *Abacus* (December 1974), pp. 124–128.

McKeown, J.C. (1971), 'An Empirical Test of a Model Proposed by Chambers', *Accounting Review* (January 1971), pp. 12–29.

National Economic Development Office (1976), *A Study of UK Nationalised Industries* (HMSO, 1976).
Pryke, R. (1981), *Nationalised Industries: Policies and Performance Since 1968* (Martin Robertson, 1981).
Rayman, R.A. (1970), 'Is Conventional Accounting Obsolete?', *Accountancy* (June 1970), p. 422–429.
Rees, R. (1979), 'The Pricing Policies of the Nationalised Industries', *The Three Banks Review* (122, June 1979).
Staubus, G.J. (1966), 'Accounting Flows: Income, Funds and Cash', *The Accounting Review* (July 1966), pp. 397–412.
Thomas, A.L. (1969), 'The Allocation Problem in Financial Accounting Theory', *Studies in Accounting Research No. 3* American Accounting Association (1969).
Tweedie, D.P. (1977), 'Cash Flows and Realisable Values: The Intuitive Accounting Concepts: An Empirical Test', *Accounting and Business Research* (Winter 1977), pp. 2–13.
Whittington, G. (1983), *Inflation Accounting: An Introduction to the Debate* (Cambridge University Press, 1983).

THE ACCOUNTING REVIEW
Vol. LXIV, No. 4
October 1989

The Nature and Amount of Information in Cash Flows and Accruals

Victor L. Bernard and Thomas L. Stober

ABSTRACT: Based on stock price behavior around the release of annual reports in 1981 and 1982, Wilson [1987] concludes that for a given amount of earnings, the market reacts more favorably the larger (smaller) are cash flows (current accruals). The goals of this paper are to assess the generality of Wilson's finding and to assess alternative economic arguments that would manifest themselves as a "preference" for cash flows over current accruals. For the overall period, 1977–1984, there is no evidence of the simple relation observed by Wilson in his two-quarter test period. We then examine progressively more contextual models of the implications of cash flows and accruals. These models are also unsuccessful in explaining stock price behavior around the release of detailed financial statements. We conclude that either (1) the security price reactions to the release of cash flow and accrual data in financial statements are too highly contextual to be modeled parsimoniously, or (2) important uncertainties about the contents of detailed financial statements are resolved prior to their public release.

Based on a sample of observations from the fourth quarters of fiscal years 1981 and 1982, Wilson [1987, table 1] finds evidence that for a given amount of earnings, the stock market reacts more favorably the larger (smaller) is the cash flow (accrual) component. Wilson's tests are based on stock price behavior during the nine days surrounding the release of the annual report, when detailed earnings information (including cash flows and accruals) is publicly disclosed for the first time.

This paper extends the work of Wilson in two ways. The first is to assess the generality and robustness of Wilson's result by conducting the same tests over 32 quarters using a largely independent sample of firms. The results do not contradict Wilson's for the two quarters that he examined, but there is no evidence of a similar result for the overall period, 1977–1984.

Financial support for this project was provided by the Michigan Business School. We thank Curt Coffer and Carol Frost for their help as research assistants and Peter Easton and Mark Zmijewski for providing the financial statement release dates used in this study. We are also grateful for the suggestions of Dan Collins, Susan Chaplinsky, Dick Dietrich, Robert Holthausen, Bruce Johnson, Robert Lipe, Robert Magee, Jerry Salamon, Katherine Schipper, Abbie Smith, Peter Wilson, Mark Zmijewski, and the workshop participants at Alabama, Arizona State, Chicago, Duke, Florida State, Harvard, McMaster, Michigan, Northwestern, and Texas.

Victor L. Bernard is Professor, and Thomas L. Stober is Assistant Professor, both at Michigan Business School, University of Michigan.

Manuscript received January 1988.
Revisions received July 1988 and February 1989.
Accepted April 1989.

Given the failure to confirm the simple relation observed by Wilson, the second step is to examine progressively more contextual models of the implications of cash flows and accruals. We argue that it is not obvious that cash flows should be "preferred" to accruals on average. However, motivated by Wilson [1987, p. 320], we hypothesize that such a "preference" might arise under certain macroeconomic conditions. No support for that hypothesis is found. An alternative hypothesis under which the nature of information conveyed by cash flow and accrual data varies according to which specific accrual accounts are unexpectedly high or low is offered but, again, we fail to find support for the hypothesis.

In sum, we are unable to identify the economic logic underlying how the market assimilates information about cash flows and accruals. That is, we find no systematic difference between the implications of cash flows and accruals, as reflected in stock price behavior surrounding the release of detailed financial statements.

There are at least two possible interpretations of the evidence. One is that the differential price implications of the cash flow and accrual components of earnings are so highly contextual that they are not amenable to parsimonious modeling. An alternative interpretation is that it is inherently difficult to detect reactions to the release of detailed financial statements, in part because any important uncertainties about their contents may have been resolved prior to their publication. Note that although the latter explanation is inconsistent with the results of Wilson [1987], it may warrant attention, given how brief was the time period he examined, and how modest was the explanatory power of his model (R^2 less than .03; see Wilson [1987, table 1]). Moreover, others have been unable to detect unusual variance in stock prices around the release of detailed financial statements.[1]

The rest of the paper is organized as follows. Section I discusses prior research and outlines reasons why the valuation implications of cash flows and accruals might differ. Section II describes the present data and Section III applies the tests of Wilson [1987] to the data. In Sections IV through VI, we test more contextual models of the security price implications of cash flows and accruals. Conclusions are offered in Section VII.

I. The Potential Information in Cash Flows and Accruals

Existing Evidence

Prior studies of the information in cash flows and accruals [Wilson, 1986 and 1987; Rayburn, 1986; and Bowen et al., 1987] can be interpreted within a common framework. Each decomposed accounting earnings as follows:

Cash Flow from Operations
+Current Accruals

=Working Capital from Operations
+Noncurrent Accruals

=Accounting Earnings.

Here, current accruals include such items as increases in inventories and receivables and decreases in payables, while depre-

[1] Foster et al. [1986] find no unusual price volatility in the week of annual report releases (the annual report may or may not have been preceded by a 10-K release, as in Wilson [1987]). Foster et al. [1983] find no evidence of higher-than-average price volatility in the week of a 10-K release, given that the annual report has already been released (this represents a reversal of the conclusion in Foster and Vickrey [1978]). To our knowledge, there is currently no evidence on the price volatility surrounding the release of the *earlier* of the 10-K or the annual report.

ciation and deferred income taxes are (negative) noncurrent accruals.

Each of the studies involves regressions of stock return metrics against the unexpected portions of the above components of earnings (or combinations thereof). Writing the abnormal return on security j in period t (R_{jt}) as a function of unexpected operating cash flows (UCF_{jt}), unexpected current accruals (UCA_{jt}), unexpected noncurrent accruals ($UNCA_{jt}$), and a disturbance term, u_{jt} yields:

$$R_{jt}=b_0+b_1(UCF_{jt})+b_2(UCA_{jt}) +b_3(UNCA_{jt})+u_{jt}. \quad (1)$$

An alternative representation of the same equation denotes unexpected working capital from operations as $UWCO_{jt}$(thus $UWCO_{jt}=UCF_{jt}+UCA_{jt}$), and unexpected accounting earnings as UE_{jt}(thus $UE_{jt}=UWCO_{jt}+UNCA_{jt}$). Substituting $(UWCO_{jt}-UCF_{jt})$ for UCA_{jt} and $(UE_{jt}-UWCO_{jt})$ for $UNCA_{jt}$, in equation (1), yields:

$$R_{jt}=b_0+(b_1-b_2)UCF_{jt} +(b_2-b_3)UWCO_{jt} +b_3UE_{jt}+u_{jt}. \quad (2)$$

In Wilson [1987], the event window is centered around the publication of the annual report, at which time earnings have already been announced. Therefore, in that design, unexpected earnings must be zero ($UE_{jt}=0$). Wilson also obtains evidence [Wilson, 1986, secs. 5.2 and 5.4] consistent with working capital from operations being known by that time ($UWCO_{jt}=0$); this may simply indicate that noncurrent accruals are relatively predictable. Under these conditions, equation (2) can be rewritten as:

$$R_{jt}=b_0+(b_1-b_2)UCF_{jt}+u_{jt}. \quad (3)$$

The major results of recent research can be discussed within the framework of equations (1), (2), and (3).[2] Wilson [1987, table 1] estimates the equivalent of equation (3), and obtains a significantly positive coefficient. Wilson's estimates imply that $(b_1-b_2)>0$.[3] Since b_1 and b_2 represent the "response coefficients" on unexpected cash flows and unexpected current accruals, respectively, in equation (1), this result can be interpreted to indicate that the market responds more favorably to one dollar of cash flow than to one dollar of current accruals.

Wilson [1986, secs. 2 and 3] points out that the Wilson [1987] result is subject to two alternative interpretations. Given that total working capital from operations is already known, either (1) cash flows may be informative while current accruals are not ($b_1>0$; $b_2=0$), or (2) both cash flows and current accruals are informative, but differentially so ($b_1>0$; $b_2>0$; $(b_1-b_2)>0$). To distinguish between these two alternatives, Wilson [1986] reestimates equation (3), with returns data from the period surrounding the financial statement release date, simultaneously with a constrained version of equation (1), with returns data for the period surrounding the earnings announcement date.[4] Wilson [1986, sec. 5.4] finds evidence consistent with the market responding favorably to both un-

[2] Jennings [1987] considers such alternative representations of equations used to assess information in earnings components.

[3] Wilson [1987] moves immediately to a simple regression like equation (3), and so it never becomes necessary to express the coefficient in terms of differences between coefficients on earnings components, as is done here. However, the coefficient in equation (3) does have this interpretation, as shown above and in Wilson [1986, eq. (8)]. Therefore, the Wilson [1987, table 1] t-test on the coefficient (b_1-b_2) in equation (3) corresponds to the Wilson [1986, sec. 5.4] chi-square test of differences between coefficients (b_1 vs. b_2).

[4] Equation (7) in Wilson [1986] corresponds to our equation (1); however, Wilson groups all accruals into a single category, or (alternatively) excludes noncurrent accruals from the analysis. Wilson's equation (8) corresponds to our equation (3).

expected cash flows ($b_1>0$) and unexpected current accruals ($b_2>0$), but more favorably to the former ((b_1-b_2) >0).[5]

In summary, Wilson [1987], in combination with Wilson [1986], implies that the market responds favorably to both unexpected cash flows and unexpected current accruals, but more favorably to the former. However, there is mixed evidence on the extent to which this "preference" for cash flows over current accruals holds across other research designs. That same implication can be drawn from Bowen et al. [1987], who estimate an equation that takes on the form of equation (2), using annual returns data for 1972–1981.[6] Their results indicate that $(b_1-b_2)>0$ and $(b_2-b_3)>0$, which implies that the market responds more favorably to cash flow than to current accruals, and more favorably to current accruals than to noncurrent accruals. On the other hand, different implications can be drawn from Rayburn [1986, tables 7 and 9], who estimates a form of equation (1), using annual returns data for 1962–1982.[7] Rayburn obtains positive but approximately equal estimates of b_1 and b_2, implying no difference in the market response to cash flows and current accruals, with mixed results on noncurrent accruals.

We argue below that it is not obvious that a more favorable response to cash flows than to current accruals should necessarily hold. It is possible to construct an argument in which such a result would obtain only under certain conditions and also possible to construct other arguments in which the opposite result would be obtained. Doubts about the generality of the results are also raised by its failure to hold in Rayburn [1986], and by Wilson's own speculation [1986, pp. 188–189; 1987, p. 320] that the result might be specific to his test period.

Below, we consider alternative explanations for possible differences in the security price implications of cash flows and accruals. Some of the explanations are unconditional, and predict that the reaction to unexpected cash flows would always be larger than the reaction to accruals, or vice versa. Other explanations are less parsimonious, and permit the sign of the difference to vary across time, or across firms.

Alternative Explanations

A common basis offered for expecting differential security price implications for cash flows and accruals could be labeled a "quality of earnings" explanation.[8] A second is based on the speculation in Wilson [1986 and 1987], in which the differential price impacts vary according to macroeconomic conditions. Finally, a third explanation, in which the price impacts vary according to the specific mix of components of unexpected current accruals, is proposed.

The "Quality of Earnings" Explanation. Under the "quality of earnings" explanation, accruals have a smaller impact on prices than cash flows (or no impact at all) since accruals are either subject to manipulation (e.g., inven-

[5] To reconcile the Wilson [1986] results with our interpretation, note that Wilson's unexpected current accruals have the opposite sign of UCA_{jt}. Thus, our b_2 corresponds to Wilson's $-\delta_{CA}$; our b_1 corresponds to Wilson's δ_{CO}.

[6] Bowen et al. [1987] estimate an equation that includes the three measures of performance listed in equation (2), plus unexpected cash flow after investment. In most specifications, the latter is not significant (for example, see table 7 of that paper).

[7] Rayburn [1986] segregates noncurrent accruals into two components, deferred taxes and depreciation.

[8] References on this point include: Brealey and Myers [1981] and Healy [1985] (in Rayburn [1986]); Brealey and Myers [1981], Treynor [1972], and a Chase Financial Brochure (in Wilson [1986 and 1987]).

tories), or represent only very indirect links to future cash flows (e.g., depreciation).[9] Alternatively, O'glove [1987, p. 107] argues:

> Obviously, higher trending inventories in relation to sales can lead to inventory markdowns, write-offs, etc. In addition, it is important to note that an excess of inventories, time and time again, is a good indicator of future slowdown in production.

O'glove [1987, p. 107] also argues that an excess of accounts receivable

> . . . may provide a clue as to whether a company is merely shifting inventory from the corporate level to its customers because of a "hard sell" sales campaign or costly incentives. In such an instance, this type of sales may constitute "borrowing from the future."

The "quality of earnings" explanation leads to a simple, unambiguous prediction: that market prices will react more to a given amount of unexpected cash flows than the same amount of unexpected accruals. Despite its simplicity, the prediction has appeal, at least with respect to the difference between cash flows and *noncurrent* accruals. The link between future cash flows and noncurrent accruals (such as depreciation and deferred taxes) are tenuous at best. Moreover, the evidence in Wilson [1986, sec. 5.2] is consistent with the possibility that noncurrent accruals have a small or zero impact on price.

With respect to the difference between cash flows and *current* accruals, however, the logic is much less compelling. First, the link to future cash flows is much more direct for current accruals than for noncurrent accruals. Second, although the incentives and ability of managers to manipulate accounting accruals is debatable and the frequency of such manipulations is an empirical issue, it seems doubtful that systematic manipulations of current accruals are widespread.[10] Third, competing explanations predict that, under certain conditions, the sign of the difference between the coefficients of cash flows and current accruals would be the opposite of that predicted by the "quality of earnings" explanation.

To test the validity of the "quality of earnings" explanation as it applies to cash flows and current accruals, one hypothesis to be tested with the extended sample is:

$$b_1 > b_2 \text{ (coefficient on cash flows} > \text{coefficient on current accruals).}$$

There are other explanations that yield an unambiguous predictions about the sign of the difference. For example, Wilson [1987, p. 295] mentions a "liquidity" argument under which the market responds more favorably to cash flows than accruals because high liquidity is a signal of a smaller likelihood of financial distress. Our purpose here is not to provide an exhaustive list of these potential explanations; instead, we will test to see

[9] The term "quality of earnings" is often used in the financial press, but is difficult to define. One detailed discussion of the term is presented in Harvard Business School Note 9-178-126, by David Hawkins and Leslie Pearlman (revised April 1985). Other sources of discussion are O'glove [1987, esp. Chap. 8], and Bernstein [1978, pp. 617–629].

To the extent that the "quality of earnings" depends on the proportion of earnings derived from recurring sources, the quality of earnings argument is related to Lipe's [1986] demonstration that the reaction to earnings components depends on their "persistence," or the strength of the relation between a shock in a given earnings component and future values of the same and other earnings components.

[10] DeAngelo [1988], Healy [1985], and Jones [1988] provide evidence consistent with management manipulation of current accruals. However, a question in these and similar studies is whether the research design properly controls for the nondiscretionary portion of accruals. McNichols and Wilson [1988] attempt to do this with one current accrual—the provision for bad debts—and conclude that only a small portion of the variation in this account is discretionary.

if any of the explanations with unambiguous directional predictions are consistent with the data.

The Macroeconomic Conditions Explanation. Wilson [1986, pp. 188–189; 1987, p. 320] noted that the 1981–1982 period during which he found a greater impact on security prices for unexpected cash flows than for unexpected current accruals was a period of economic downturn. He then speculated that perhaps these differential security price reactions are attributable to how well firms anticipate and adjust to changing economic conditions. As the economy contracts, the market would react favorably when management liquidates noncash working capital, which would manifest itself as a "preference" for cash flow over current accruals. Thus, the prediction is:

$b_1 > b_2$ (coefficient on cash flow > coefficient on current accruals) in an economic contraction.

In contrast, during an expansion, the market would react favorably when management uses cash to increase noncash working capital, and we have:

$b_1 < b_2$ (coefficient on cash flow < coefficient on current accruals) in an economic expansion.

A second hypothesis tests whether the sign of $(b_1 - b_2)$ depends on the unexpected component of GNP. Since economic expansion and contraction is also related to interest rates, the unexpected component of interest rates is considered as an alternative conditioning variable.

The Mix of Components of Unexpected Current Accruals Explanation. Under this explanation, the relative security price impact of cash flows versus accruals is generally indeterminate; that is:

$b_1 > b_2$ *or* $b_1 < b_2$ (coefficient on cash flow is greater *or* less than coefficient on current accruals) depending on the specific mix of current accruals.

Consider the following decomposition of current accruals:

current accruals =
increases in inventories
+ increases in receivables
− increases in payables.

Using this identity, an alternative to equation (1) decomposes the term pertaining to unexpected current accruals, $b_2(UCA)$, so as to explicitly identify unexpected changes in inventories, receivables, and payables (denoted *UINV*, *UREC*, and *UPAY*) as follows:

$$R_{jt} = b_0 + b_1(UCF_{jt}) + b_{2I}(UINV_{jt}) + b_{2R}(UREC_{jt}) + b_{2P}(UPAY_{jt}) + b_3(UNCA_{jt}) + w_{jt}. \quad (4)$$

Abstracting from the competing theories described above, the maintained hypothesis would be that all the coefficients in equation (4) are the same.[11] Below, we consider whether the coefficients on these components of unexpected current accruals should differ from one another, from the coefficient on unexpected current accruals, and from the coefficient on unexpected operating cash flows (i.e., whether $b_{2I} = b_{2R} = b_{2P} = b_2 = b_1$).

Just prior to the release of financial statements, net earnings are already known. Thus, the unexpected components of cash flows and accruals that become known at the financial statement release date must sum to zero or:

$$UCF_{jt} + UINV_{jt} + UREC_{jt} + UPAY_{jt} + UNCA_{jt} = 0 \quad (5)$$

[11] Our maintained hypothesis also abstracts from other reasons why stock price response coefficients might vary across earnings components, such as Lipe's [1986] notion of persistence.

where expectations for each are based on information revealed through the earnings announcement date.

Substituting equation (5) into equation (4) yields:

$$R_{jt}=b_0+(b_{2I}-b_1)UINV_{jt} +(b_{2R}-b_1)UREC_{jt} +(b_{2P}-b_1)UPAY_{jt} +(b_{2R}-b_1)UNCA_{jt}+w_{jt}. \quad (6)$$

Since inventories, receivables, and payables support the ongoing operations of the firm, there should be a relation between the balances in such current operating accounts and future sales levels. Section V considers how such a relation might arise from a simple model of the operating cycle, and describes the factors that would determine the signs of $(b_{2I}-b_1)$, $(b_{2R}-b_1)$, and $(b_{2P}-b_1)$. This model suggests that the differences in security price implications of cash flows and current accruals may be due to what they reveal about managers' beliefs concerning future sales levels (or the demand for a firm's products). Because the directional prediction for the stock price reaction to the inventory component of current accruals in equation (6) differs from that of the two explanations above, it can be empirically distinguished from competing explanations.

The three arguments presented in this section are not the only possible reasons why valuation implications could differ between cash flows and current accruals or why they could vary across the components of current accruals. Other possible explanations could be based, for example, on more refined notions about "earnings quality" under alternative accrual accounting methods (e.g., LIFO vs. FIFO). Alternatively, the context might be important (e.g., a decrease in inventories may have favorable security price implications if it results from attempts to improve the inventory system).[12] If the security price implications of cash flows and accruals are too highly dependent on the specific context in which they occur, then the tests summarized in this paper will be unlikely to provide evidence consistent with the predictions summarized above.

II. Data and Expectations Models

Sample Selection

The sample consists of all corporations that filed quarterly and annual reports with the SEC from 1976 (when SEC registrants were first required to furnish quarterly balance sheet data in addition to quarterly income statement data) through 1985 and for which the required data were available. The required data fell into three categories.

1. *Quarterly earnings, sales, funds flow, and balance sheet data.* Data for the 1976–1984 period were available on COMPUSTAT II, and provided a quarterly time-series of 36 observations for each firm which, due to differencing, allowed estimation of expectations models for accounting variables over the test period 1977–1984.

2. *Earnings announcement dates and information release dates for 10-Qs, 10-Ks, and annual reports.* Release dates for these reports were obtained from *The Wall Street Journal* and from computer files maintained by the SEC.[13]

To maintain a clear separation between the effects of earnings announce-

[12] Another example is provided by Stober [1986], who describes how information from financial statement notes about LIFO inventory liquidations might be used to assess the "quality of earnings" previously reported. Consistent with the above predictions, this explanation leads to the view that unexpectedly low inventory balances for LIFO firms are "bad news."

[13] We appreciate the efforts of Peter Easton and Mark Zmijewski, who obtained this data from the SEC and made a portion of it available to us. We conducted a series of reasonableness tests on the financial statement release dates, but excluded only 0.5 percent of the data from consideration on that basis.

ments and the effects of financial statement releases, Wilson [1987, p. 299] used only observations with at least eight days separating these two events. He reports that for over 90 percent of his observations, at least eight days separated the earnings announcement date and the first date that either the annual report or the 10-K arrived at the SEC. For the fourth quarter releases in our sample, 89.7 percent of these dates were separated by at least eight trading days (90.3 percent in Wilson). Following Wilson, observations are excluded if there were fewer than eight days between the two dates. For the observations remaining, the mean and the median number of trading days between those dates in the fourth quarters of firms fiscal years were 25 and 24, respectively, both in the full 1977–1984 sample period and in the 1981–1982 subperiod. The mean and the median were 17 and 15 days, respectively, for all observations, including fiscal quarters one through three, indicating that 10-Q reports follow earnings announcements more closely than is the case for year-end reports.

3. *Daily stock returns data.* These data were obtained from the CRSP database.

There were 177 firms for which the required COMPUSTAT II data for the period 1976–1984 were available, and which were also listed on CRSP for the period 1977–1984. Of these firms, 170 were located on the SEC computer file of financial statement release dates. For some of these firms, CRSP returns were missing for some days during 1977–1984. Also, financial statement release dates were not available for some quarters. Thus, while 170 firms potentially represent 5,440 quarterly observations over an eight-year period, the actual number of usable observations was fewer. Approximately ten percent of the firms were also included in the Wilson [1986 and 1987] sample of the fourth quarters of 1981 and 1982 only.

Measures of Funds from Operations

The tests required measures of cash flow from operations and working capital from operations, but these data were not available on COMPUSTAT II for years before 1984. Thus, these amounts were constructed by using income statement and balance sheet data as follows:

Working capital from operations
=Operating income before depreciation
−Interest expense
−Current portion of income tax expense.

Cash flow from operations
=Working capital from operations
−Increase in net working capital other than cash and securities, net of short-term debt.

The correlations between our measures of working capital from operations (scaled by total assets), and those actually reported by the firms for the four quarters of fiscal 1984 are .80, .75, .81, and .75.[14] Except for the inability to segregate current income tax expense into operating and nonoperating segments, the measure used is one that could have been reported by firms as working capital from operations, in accordance with GAAP. The benefit of our measure is that it is calculated consistently across firms, while the measures actually reported by firms are not (see Ketz and Largay [1987]). In fact, inconsistency in

[14] Four alternatives yielded similar results. They were: (1) income before special items, nonoperating items, and extraordinary items, plus depreciation and deferred taxes; (2) income before nonoperating items and extraordinary items, plus depreciation and deferred taxes; (3) income before special items and extraordinary items, plus depreciation and deferred taxes; and (4) operating income before depreciation.

reporting practices across firms is a likely explanation for our inability to approximate the reported numbers with greater precision.

Firms' Information Release Policies

Although the first date on which cash flow and accrual data are publicly available typically coincides with the financial statement release date, some firms reveal these data in news releases at some prior time. These firms should be excluded from tests on the period surrounding the financial statement release date.

To ascertain when the sample firms first released financial statement information to the public, a news release survey similar to that of Wilson [1987] was conducted. Because it would be difficult to obtain news release copies for the entire 1977–1984 period, only news releases announcing earnings for firms' most recent fiscal years were requested: one announcing fourth quarter earnings and one pertaining to a quarter other than the final quarter of the fiscal year. For the final sample, 137 out of 170 (81 percent) responded. This identified the firms that, in 1986, furnished data sufficient to calculate funds flow measures prior to financial statement release, and excluded those firms from tests that focus on the period surrounding the financial statement release date, on the assumption that the same disclosure policy had been in effect since 1977.[15,16]

Identification of the date at which interim financial statement data first became available presented a special problem, since the sample firms issued both 10-Qs and quarterly reports to shareholders (QR/Ss), but release dates are available only for the former. Firms were asked to indicate whether they released the QR/S prior to the week during which the 10-Q was released. The 38 firms that answered in the affirmative (27.7 percent) were eliminated from tests which focus on the period surrounding the release of interim financial statements.

Expectations Models

To replicate Wilson [1987], we estimate expectations models for cash flow and working capital from operations (after the earnings announcement date) using Wilson's method. Wilson applied OLS estimation to a pooled cross-section of firms, which assumes that model parameters are the same for all firms. The independent variables used in these expectations models are listed in Table 1. Since we have more data than Wilson, we modified his approach by estimating the same models not only in a single pooled cross-section but also in industry-based pools, which permit the model parameters to vary industry-by-industry. This was implemented by grouping the sample into 33 industries primarily on the basis of two-digit COMPUSTAT industry codes.

Table 1 also contains summary statistics on the goodness of fit for the expectations models and compares their performance here to that in Wilson's [1987] sample. Where the expectations models

[15] Since our understanding is that early disclosure of these data were less common in prior years, we view this assumption as conservative. However, following Wilson [1986 and 1987], we assumed that any firm not responding did not reveal detailed financial statement data prior to the release of the financial statements.

[16] For the release of annual financial statements, the date at which financial statement information is first publicly available would ordinarily be the earlier of the release date of the annual report to shareholders (AR/S) or the date at which the 10-K report is received at the SEC. We were able to identify dates that the SEC received 10-K reports and annual reports (as well as the dates it received definitive proxy statements, which must be accompanied by an annual report). However, of the firms responding to the news release survey, 37 (27.0 percent of the sample) stated that they typically mail a separate fourth-quarter report to shareholders prior to mailing the annual report; we excluded these firms from tests which focus on the period surrounding the AR/S release.

TABLE 1

SUMMARY OF EXPECTATIONS MODELS USED IN REPLICATION OF WILSON [1987]

Independent variables used in prediction of quarter* t *values of cash from operations, or working capital from operations (all variables scaled by total assets).

Values already announced for quarter t:	Sales Net Earnings
Values reported previous quarters: (values for quarter $t-1$; sum of values for quarters $t-2$ and $t-3$; values for quarter $t-4$)	Sales Cash from operations Current accruals Noncurrent accruals
Value for annual period including quarter t:	Capital expenditures

Summary Statistics for Estimation of Expectations Models:

Dependent Variable:	*Cash from Operations*			*Working Capital from Operations*		
	Wilson[a]	*This Study*		*Wilson*[a]	*This Study*	
	1981–1982 4th Qtr.	*1981–1982 4th Qtr.*	*1977–1984 All Qtrs.*	*1981–1982 4th Qtr.*	*1981–1982 4th Qtr.*	*1977–1984 All Qtrs.*
Expectations Models Estimated in Pooled Cross-Section:						
Number of Observations	463	209	2,594	463	209	2,594
R-squared	.47	.52	.40	.66	.74	.65
Residual autocorrelations:						
lag 1	—	—	.04	—	—	−.00
lag 2	—	—	.02	—	—	.00
lag 3	—	—	−.00	—	—	−.05
lag 4	—	—	−.15	—	—	−.03
Expectations Models Estimated in Time-Series, Industry-by-Industry:						
Number of observations						
Minimum:	N/A	N/A	32	N/A	N/A	32
Maximum:	N/A	N/A	480	N/A	N/A	480
R-squared (median across industries):	N/A	N/A	.48	N/A	N/A	.83
Residual autocorrelations (estimated in pooled data set):						
lag 1	—	—	.05	—	—	−.03
lag 2	—	—	.01	—	—	.01
lag 3	—	—	−.03	—	—	−.03
lag 4	—	—	−.05	—	—	−.02

[a] Results reported in Wilson [1987, p. 307].

are estimated in pooled cross-section (the approach used by Wilson), the R^2s of these models in our sample during the time periods studied by Wilson [1987] are higher than those reported by Wilson. The explanatory power of these pooled cross-sectional models falls off somewhat when estimated over the entire 1977–1984 time period; however, the expectations models estimated on an industry-by-industry basis exhibit a greater degree of explanatory power, on average, than those estimated in pooled cross-section. Table 1 also shows that there is very little residual autocorrelation under either approach, indicating that these expectations models are efficient forecasters of funds from operations. Finally, note that the functional form of the expectations models used here is precisely the same as that used in Wilson [1986 and 1987] so that this feature of our design should not create any differences between our results and those of Wilson.

III. Replication and Extension of Wilson [1987]

The empirical tests to replicate and extend the work of Wilson [1987] assume that any difference between the stock price implications of cash flows and current accruals is the same for all firm-periods. Thus, the tests can be viewed as emanating from the "quality of earnings" explanation and others in which the sign of the difference is unconditional.

Following Wilson, the event period is the nine-day interval surrounding the release date of reports to shareholders. The procedures used to identify event dates and estimate key variables mimic those used by Wilson as closely as possible. The primary differences were as follows. First, while Wilson's tests were based only on fourth quarter data taken from the annual reports to shareholders (AR/S), our tests were based on data from all fiscal quarters, taken from both interim and annual reports.[17] Second, while Wilson's sample was restricted to firms with SIC codes 1000–4800, 20 percent of the present sample includes firms from wholesaling, retailing, and services (SIC 5000–8900). Third, our measures of funds from operations were constructed from income statement and balance sheet data, whereas Wilson's were taken directly from the statement of changes in financial position.

In this section the primary interest is in the following equation, which corresponds to equation (3) of Section I:

$$R_{jt}=c_0+c_1 UCF_{jt}+z_{jt}, \qquad (7)$$

where:

R_{jt} = the accumulated market model prediction error[18] for firm j during the nine-day window surrounding the release of financial statements for quarter t, and

UCF_{jt} = unexpected cash flow from operations for firm j, quarter t, scaled by total assets at the end of quarter $t-1$, where expectations are conditional on information released through the earnings announcement date (see Table 1 for the expectations model).

Except for differences in the notation, equation (7) above is the identical to equation (2) of Wilson [1987] when he uses unexpected cash from operations as the independent variable. If we assume, based on Wilson's evidence [1986, sec. 5.2] that working capital from operations is essentially known by the market as soon as earnings are announced, c_1 is equal to (b_1-b_2) in equation (3).

On the other hand, if we allow for the

[17] Following Wilson, we use the AR/S release date as the financial statement release date in our replication. We also conducted tests using the earlier of the AR/S release date and the date the 10-K report is received at the SEC as the financial statement release date.

[18] To maintain comparability with Wilson [1987], market model parameters were estimated during a 120-day estimation period, from trading day $t-210$ to $t-91$, where t denotes the last trading day in the quarter for which earnings and funds flow information is reported. Thus, the market model estimation period does not overlap with any of the period to which the accounting data used to compute unexpected funds flow pertains.

possibility that there is some uncertainty about working capital from operations after earnings have been announced, there is motivation for using unexpected working capital from operations in an equation like Wilson's. In the present notation, this equation would be:

$$R_{jt}=d_0+d_1UWCO_{jt}+z_{jt}, \qquad (8)$$

where $UWCO_{jt}$ is the unexpected working capital from operations for firm j, quarter t, scaled by total assets at the end of quarter $t-1$, and expectations are conditional on information released through the earnings announcement date.

Although Wilson finds no evidence of uncertainty about working capital from operations once earnings have been announced, we present estimates of equation (8) for completeness. The coefficient d_1 in equation (8) should be interpreted as the difference between the price response coefficients on working capital from operations and its complement, noncurrent accruals. However, if the value of $UWCO_{jt}$ (excluding measurement error) is close to zero for all firms, we will be unable to estimate this coefficient with precision.

Table 2, panel A presents the results of Wilson's estimation of equations (7) and (8). He obtained a significantly positive regression coefficient on unexpected cash flow from operations, suggesting that the market reacts favorably upon learning that the amount of earnings that arrived in the form of cash flow (rather than accruals) is higher than expected. Wilson obtained an even larger positive coefficient on unexpected working capital from operations but, given that it was estimated so imprecisely, he was unable to reject the hypothesis that the underlying parameter equals zero at conventional levels.

Panels B and C of Table 2 summarize the portion of the replication that includes only data from the fourth quarters of 1981 and 1982 used in Wilson [1987]. Panel B contains the results based on the statistical method used by Wilson. Under that approach, the expectations models for cash flows and working capital from operations are estimated by pooling all sample firms together. The approach in panel C differs, in that expectations models are estimated within industry pools.

In general, although the results reported in panel B are not as strong as Wilson's, they do not contradict his results. In the regression of market model prediction errors against unexpected cash flow from operations, the coefficient is about three-fourths as large as Wilson's. The difference in significance levels reflects, in part, less precision in our estimate, which in turn is partially due to the smaller sample size. If all else remained constant while the sample size was expanded to the size of Wilson's, our t-statistic would be 1.68; if our coefficient remained constant while attaining Wilson's degree of precision in estimation, the t-statistic would be 2.43.

In the regression of market model prediction errors against unexpected working capital from operations, the coefficient estimate is nearly identical to Wilson's, and like Wilson's coefficient, it is not statistically significant at conventional levels. Finally, in panel C, our results based on industry-specific expectations models indicate an even weaker relation between unexpected funds flow and stock returns than those based on expectations models estimated over the entire sample.

Our use of income statement and balance sheet data (rather than data from the statement of changes in financial position) to calculate cash flow from operations could explain why the esti-

TABLE 2

REGRESSIONS OF ABNORMAL STOCK RETURNS DURING THE FINANCIAL STATEMENT RELEASE PERIOD AGAINST UNEXPECTED FUNDS FLOW

Test period: Fourth Quarters of 1981 and 1982

Panel A. Results as Reported in Wilson [1987][a]:

	Funds Flow Variable: Cash Flow from Operations	*Funds Flow Variable: Working Capital from Operations*
Coefficient	.23	.26
t-statistic	3.26	1.10
R-squared	.029	.001
n	325	325

Panel B. Results of Wilson's Method Applied to New Sample—Expectations Models Estimated in Pooled Cross-Section:

	Funds Flow Variable: Cash Flow from Operations	*Funds Flow Variable: Working Capital from Operations*
Coefficient	.17	.25
t-statistic	1.17	.62
R-squared	.009	.002
n	158	158

Panel C. Results Based on New Sample—Industry-Specific Expectations Models:

	Funds Flow Variable: Cash Flow from Operations	*Funds Flow Variable: Working Capital from Operations*
Coefficient	.13	.10
t-statistic	0.89	.22
R-squared	.005	.000
n	158	158

[a] As originally reported, Wilson's coefficients were based on a regression where the dependent variable is the average daily abnormal return. To make the coefficient comparable with our results, where the dependent variable is a nine-day cumulative abnormal return, Wilson's coefficients are multiplied by nine.

mated coefficient is smaller than Wilson's. However, as discussed in Section II, our approach conforms closely to that which firms could follow under GAAP and our measure (unlike Wilson's) has the virtue of not being influenced by the frequent inconsistencies in how firms measure cash flows from operations. Note also that, although Wilson's coefficient is significant while ours is not, the difference between Wilson's coefficient and ours is statistically insignificant at conventional levels.

It is also possible that we were unable to replicate Wilson's result more closely because we have included nonindustrial firms, while Wilson did not. To ascertain whether restricting the sample to industrial firms would alter these comparisons, we conducted supplemental analyses analogous to those in panel B on only those firms from industries with

TABLE 3

REGRESSIONS OF ABNORMAL STOCK RETURNS DURING THE FINANCIAL STATEMENT RELEASE PERIOD AGAINST UNEXPECTED FUNDS FLOW (1977–1984)

Panel A. Results of Wilson's Method Applied to New Sample—Expectations Models Estimated in Pooled Cross-Sections:

	Funds Flow Variable: Cash Flow from Operations			*Funds Flow Variable: Working Capital from Operations*		
	All Quarters	*Fourth Quarters Only*	*Fourth Quarters 1981–1982*	*All Quarters*	*Fourth Quarters Only*	*Fourth Quarters 1981–1982*
Coefficient	−.05	−.02	.17	−.02	.11	.25
t-statistic	−1.42	−.31	1.17	−.19	.69	.62
R-squared	.001	.000	.009	.000	.001	.002
n	2,401	662	158	2,401	662	158
t-*statistics by Firm Size Quintile:*						
1 (smallest)	−1.59	−1.18	.65	−.11	1.28	1.62
2	−.84	1.46	1.87	.27	.29	−.10
3	1.30	−.03	−.33	.57	−.02	−1.40
4	−1.64	−.35	−.21	−.15	−.40	−2.30
5 (largest)	0.44	−.18	.27	−.72	.26	2.28

Panel B. Results Based on New Sample—Industry-Specific Expectations Models:

	Funds Flow Variable: Cash Flow from Operations			*Funds Flow Variable: Working Capital from Operations*		
	All Quarters	*Fourth Quarters Only*	*Fourth Quarters 1981–1982*	*All Quarters*	*Fourth Quarters Only*	*Fourth Quarters 1981–1982*
Coefficient	−.06	−.03	.13	−.08	.02	.10
t-statistic	−1.63	−.39	.89	−.62	.10	.22
R-squared	.001	.000	.001	.000	.000	.000
n	2,399	662	158	2,400	662	158
t-*statistics by Firm Size Quintile:*						
1 (smallest)	−2.24	−1.99	−1.17	.06	.84	1.05
2	−.96	1.26	2.05	−1.20	−.96	−.87
3	1.22	.61	.08	.62	.23	−.30
4	−.96	.07	.38	−.14	.13	−.64
5 (largest)	0.12	−.15	1.25	−.63	.18	1.95

SIC codes 1000–4800, resulting in 29 fewer observations. The coefficients and degree of explanatory power in these regressions were similar to those in panel B and the *t*-statistics declined in accordance with the reduction in sample size.

Although the tests for the fourth quarters of 1981 and 1982 are based on fewer firms than those in Wilson [1987], the database permits examination of whether Wilson's results are specific to the time period that he examined. A set of results for the entire time period 1977 through 1984 is presented in Table 3. Wilson's method (expectations models estimated over the entire sample) is applied in panel A, while expectations models estimated on an industry-by-industry basis are used in panel B. Results are presented for all firm-quarters combined, separately for the fourth quarters of firms' fiscal years,[19] and for the 1981–1982 fourth quarters. In Table 3, even in regressions with over 2,400 firm-quarters of observations, none of the coefficients on unexpected funds flow in the 1977–1984 period is significantly different from zero. Note also that, if the market responds more favorably to unexpected funds flow than to the complementary unexpected accruals, one would expect the coefficients reported in Table 3 to be positive but, in fact, most of the coefficients for periods other than the 1981–1982 fourth quarters are negative.

Wilson's tests were also extended by considering firm size. Freeman [1987] and Atiase [1985] indicate that, for large firms, there exist private information sources more timely than accounting reports; thus, one would not expect the published financial statements of large firms to convey as much new information to the market as those of smaller firms. The *t*-statistics for results stratified by firm size are also presented in Table 3. There is no obvious pattern in the results across the different size classes.[20] In particular, there is no evidence that information about unexpected cash flows/accruals was more likely to be impounded in market prices for small- and medium-sized firms than for large firms during the period surrounding the release of the annual report.

Finally, these tests were modified in several other ways—deletion of outliers,[21] use of market-adjusted returns instead of market model prediction errors, and centering the event window around the earlier of the 10-K or the AR/S release dates, instead of around AR/S release dates. None of these modifications altered the conclusions. Thus, in general, we found no systematic evidence that unexpected funds flows or accruals would explain stock price behavior in short windows surrounding the release of financial statements outside of the fourth quarters of 1981 and 1982.

IV. Tests of Whether Valuation Implications Vary According to Macroeconomic Conditions

This section describes tests of Wilson's conjecture that his result might extend only to periods of economic downturn, and that the opposite result would be obtained in periods of economic improvement. The 1977–1982 period was partitioned into three regimes, using each of two proxies for unexpected changes in the state of the economy. The proxies used are the unexpected components of real GNP and of short-term interest rates (on 90-day Treasury bills). The prediction is that when GNP growth is unex-

[19] There are two motivations for reporting separate results for the fourth quarters of firms' fiscal years. First, whereas fourth-quarter accruals are audited, interim accruals are not. Second, we have more confidence in our financial statement release dates for the fourth quarter. For the vast majority of observations, we have both annual report and 10-K release dates, but for interim releases, we have only 10-Q dates. We rely on questionnaires to exclude firms that tend to issue quarterly reports before 10-Qs are released (see Section II).

[20] Significant *t*-statistics for the largest firms would be contrary to our expectations about the effects of firm-size on the amount of new information conveyed by financial statements. Although there are some significant negative *t*-statistics for the smallest sized firms, a negative relation between unexpected funds flow and abnormal stock returns would be inconsistent with the results reported in Wilson [1987, p. 308, note 32].

[21] For these tests, we deleted observations where the absolute value of *UCF* was greater than eight percent of total assets (representing approximately three percent of the sample) and observations where the absolute value of *UWCO* was greater than four percent of total assets (representing approximately one percent of the sample). These cutoffs were determined after visual inspection of distributions of these variables; the lower value of the cutoff for *UWCO* reflects the relatively greater predictability of working capital from operations.

pectedly low, or interest rates are unexpectedly high for the quarter just ended, the market would respond favorably around report release dates to those firms that contemporaneously liquidated current working capital accounts and, thus, generated more cash from operations. Thus, during such a regime, we would expect a positive coefficient on unexpected cash flows from operations in equation (7). In contrast, when GNP is unexpectedly high, or interest rates are unexpectedly low, we would expect that same coefficient to take on a negative sign.

The unexpected components of real GNP and interest rates were identified by fitting time-series models to the data.[22] The 11 quarters with the most negative unexpected components were placed in one regime; the 11 with the most positive make up another and the remaining 10 quarters constitute a third regime. We then followed the same estimation approach used in Table 3, except that both the expectations models for cash from operations and the final regressions were estimated within regimes.[23]

Because Wilson's [1987, p. 320] conjecture arose from observing that the fourth quarters of 1981 and 1982 he studied were part of a period "when the economy was in a severe downturn (1981–1982)," it is of interest to know how these two quarters would be classified on the basis of our proxies for the state of the economy. For the partition based on unexpected interest rates, both these quarters fall in the regime where we would expect a positive coefficient in equation (7), meaning that interest rates were unexpectedly high in both of these quarters. In contrast, for the partition based on real GNP, only the fourth quarter of 1981 falls in the regime where we would expect a positive coefficient (meaning that real GNP growth was unexpectedly low in this quarter); in the fourth quarter of 1982, unexpected real GNP growth was near zero, thus allowing no prediction as to the coefficient's sign.

Table 4 summarizes the results based on partitioned data. There is clearly no support for the predictions. The coefficients take on the "wrong" signs as frequently as the "right" ones; they are never statistically significant and the R^2s are all less than .01. Similar conclusions are reached using an event window centered around the earlier of the 10-K or annual report date for fourth quarter reports (as opposed to using annual report dates only), or when market-adjusted returns are substituted for market model prediction errors.[24]

In Table 4, contemporaneous values of unexpected GNP growth were used to partition time periods according to the present state of the economy. However,

[22] The time-series models were estimated with quarterly data. For the short-term interest rate series, a simple random walk model fits well. For real GNP, the raw series used was already seasonally adjusted and a Box-Jenkins IMA(1,2) model eliminated most of the remaining serial dependence. For GNP, observations are available only for quarters ended in March, June, September, and December. Firms with fiscal quarters ended in other months were matched with the nearest calendar quarter available. Since an interest rate for a 90-day T-bill is available at the end of any month, it was always possible to match an observation to any given fiscal quarter.

[23] The improvement in fit obtained from permitting the coefficients of the expectations models for cash flow from operations to vary by regime is small; the overall R-squared for expectations models estimated in pooled cross-section rises from .40 to .42 when we partition on either unexpected GNP or unexpected interest rates.

[24] We also attempted another partition, based on levels of interest rates. Motivation for this approach is provided by Collins and Kothari [1988], who show that earnings response coefficients vary inversely with the level of interest rates. If the coefficient c_1 in our model depends on the level of interest rates, then equations (7) and (8) are random coefficients models and pooling observations across different interest rate regimes would reduce the efficiency of the estimators. However, results of using this partition did not alter the conclusions.

TABLE 4
REGRESSIONS OF ABNORMAL STOCK RETURNS DURING THE FINANCIAL STATEMENT RELEASE PERIOD AGAINST UNEXPECTED FUNDS FLOW: EFFECTS OF PARTITIONING ON MACROECONOMIC CONDITIONS (1977–1984)

Panel A. Expectations Models Estimated in Pooled Cross-Sections—Within Economic Regimes:

Predicted Sign of Coefficient:	*Positive*		*No Prediction*		*Negative*	
State of Economy:	*Unexpected GNP Growth Low*	*Unexpected Interest Rates High*	*Unexpected GNP Growth Near Zero*	*Unexpected Interest Rates Near Zero*	*Unexpected GNP Growth High*	*Unexpected Interest Rates Low*
Coefficient	−.06	−.07	.00	−.01	−.10	−.01
t-statistic	−.94	−1.26	.06	−.13	−.49	−.23
R-squared	.001	.002	.000	.000	.003	.000
n	846	883	748	666	807	852

Panel B. Industry-Specific Expectations Models—Estimated within Economic Regimes:

Predicted Sign of Coefficient:	*Positive*		*No Prediction*		*Negative*	
State of Economy:	*Unexpected GNP Growth Low*	*Unexpected Interest Rates High*	*Unexpected GNP Growth Near Zero*	*Unexpected Interest Rates Near Zero*	*Unexpected GNP Growth High*	*Unexpected Interest Rates Low*
Coefficient	−.10	−.06	−.12	−.00	−.13	−.06
t-statistic	−1.38	−.86	−1.47	−.00	−1.70	−.79
R-squared	.002	.001	.003	.000	.004	.001
n	817	848	719	645	775	819

Fama [1981] observes that common stock returns tend to lead measures of real output such as GNP. To the extent that stock prices react to the future course of the economy, partitions based on realized future GNP growth rates may provide better tests of the Wilson conjecture. Tests were conducted with the partitions based on unexpected real GNP for quarter $t+1$, but the conclusions did not change. Neither did they change the data partitioned on the basis of realized annual growth rates in real GNP for the year ended in quarter $t+4$.

Despite the failure to find support for the Wilson conjecture, it is possible that the coefficients of equation (7) do vary according to the state of the economy but that we have improperly partitioned the time periods into economic regimes. To assess the likelihood of that possibility, one final test was conducted. Here, the null hypothesis is that the coefficients for *each* quarter are the same. The approach used is a standard test of linear restrictions on a coefficient vector (see Theil [1971, eq. 7.23]). The resulting test statistic should be distributed as an $F(62, 2337)$ under the null hypothesis. The observed value of the test statistic is .99; a value at least this large would be observed by chance approximately 50 percent of the time. This failure to find any significant differences in the coefficients of equation (7) across time suggests that further attempts to document time-varying coefficients are not likely to be fruitful.

V. Potential Links Through Future Sales: A Simple Model of the Information in Current Accrual Components

The third explanation to be considered is that the stock price implications of cash flows and current accruals vary across firms according to their specific mix of current accrual components. A simple model of the operating cycle permits prediction of the signs of the coefficients in equation (6). Because current period sales are always disclosed prior to or at the time information on current accruals is released, we consider whether (and how) current accruals could provide information about *future* period sales incremental to that in *current* period sales. A formal description of this model is provided in the Appendix. This section describes the model's essential features, its empirical implications, and some evidence on the predictive links.

Changes in Inventory Balances

The model in the Appendix segregates inventory into two components: (1) the optimal inventory balance, given management's expectation of future sales, and (2) the deviation from this balance. The second component includes inventory "buildups" and "liquidations" that arise as a function of deviations of prior sales from expectations. Now consider investors who have already received announcements of earnings and sales for the period, and who are awaiting disclosure of the inventory balance in the published financial statements. Since sales are known, the market is already aware of the second component's magnitude: the deviation from the optimum due to imperfectly anticipated sales volume. The market also has some (imperfect) estimate of management's expectation of period $t+1$ sales, and uses that to form its own (imperfect) estimate of the optimum, given management expectations. Upon publication of the actual inventory balance, the market can determine this remaining component with certainty, and can infer management's beliefs about future sales. Higher than expected inventory signals higher future sales, which should typically have favorable implications for firm value. In other words, given that sales and earnings are already known, the market would react favorably upon learning that the portion of earnings coming in the form of inventory (rather than cash) is higher than expected. This implies that in equation (6):

$b_1 < b_{2I}$ (coefficient on cash flow < coefficient on inventories).

It is important to note that the expected inventory balance is conditioned on knowledge of current period sales. If it were not, higher than expected inventory could simply reflect an inventory buildup resulting from an unanticipated decline in customer demand, which would presumably be a negative signal. That would stand in direct contrast to the prediction made here, and would be consistent with predictions based on the "quality of earnings" explanation.

Changes in Receivables Balances

Upon receipt of sales and earnings information, the market can form expectations for the receivables balance. The subsequent announcement of end-of-period receivables reveals unexpected receivables (*UREC*). If *UREC* is negative (because collections were unexpectedly low, and/or receivables unexpectedly high), it could imply either of the following. First, it may reveal that management was able to generate the previously announced sales volume only by relaxing credit policy and/or "borrowing sales from the future" (as argued by O'glove [1987, p. 107]). Second, it may reveal that customers have become less willing or able to pay quickly. We would view both of these as negative signals about the value of the firm; *however, these implications for firm value may or may not operate in terms of changes in expected future sales*. Nevertheless, contrary to the case of unexpected inventories, this leads to the prediction that, in equation (6):

$b_1 > b_{2R}$ (coefficient on cash flow > coefficient on receivables).

In this case, the directional prediction of our model is the same as that under the "quality of earnings" explanation.

Changes in Payables Balances

The third major remaining component of current accruals consists of changes in accounts payable. The payables balance could reveal information about two things. First, since payables are a function of inventory purchases, changes in payables balances provide a (redundant) signal about management's expectations of future sales. Second, payables balances provide a signal about unexpected changes in the pace of "retiring" this form of debt. The possible implications of the second signal for share values are unclear to us . Thus, we conduct tests on the full model (eq. (6)), and a version of the model including only changes in inventory and receivables balances, excluding payables.

The Importance of Segregating the Components of Current Accruals

Prior studies may have lost much of the information available in current accruals by treating them collectively. Our analysis suggests that changes of the same sign in receivables and inventory may have opposite impacts on share values. Also, unexpected changes in inventory and unexpected changes in payables may both provide information about future sales, but that information may be lost when the two accounts are offset against each other by grouping current accruals. Thus, if the components of current accruals convey information about future sales, then holding working capital from operations constant, *aggregate* current accruals may have ambiguous implications for valuation.

Evidence on Links in the Model

Tests of our model require expectations models for sales, inventories, receivables, and payables. These expectations models, described in Table 5, were estimated from data pooled within industries and include some firm-specific parameters to take care of within industry variation. The unexpected components of the inventory and receivables balances as of the end of quarter t are defined as those not predictable on the basis of inventory and receivables balances through quarter $t-1$ and sales through quarter t; the models allow for seasonality in sales and in the relation of inventory and receivables to sales.[25]

[25] Due to concerns about efficiency of the parameter estimates, we also reestimated the expectations models for inventories and receivables assuming the seasonal adjustment parameters k_{1q} and p_{3q} (see Appendix) were the same for all four quarters with no change in the results.

TABLE 5

SUMMARY OF EXPECTATIONS MODELS USED IN SECTIONS V AND VI

Dependent Variable:	*Sales* (S_t)	*Inventory* (I_t)	*Receivables* (R_t)	*Payables* (P_t)
Model estimated in:	Seasonal differences ($S_t - S_{t-4}$)	Levels	Levels	Levels
Independent variables:	($S_{t-1} - S_{t-5}$)	I_{t-1} $E_t(S_{t+1})$ $E_{t-1}(S_t)$ $S_t - E_{t-1}(S_t)$ (See Appendix)	R_{t-1} S_t (See Appendix)	P_{t-1} P_{t-4} I_t R_t
Approach to pooling:	Data pooled within industries[a]	Data pooled within industries[b]	Data pooled within industries[c]	Data pooled within industries
Approach to scale specific firms' data to mitigate heteroscedasticity	Two-stage Weighted Least Squares	Scale all data by sales	Scale all data by sales	Scale all data by sales
R-squared (for median industry):	.58	.92	.77	.71
Residual autocorrelations (estimated in pooled data set):				
lag 1	.06	.10	−.06	−.05
lag 2	.10	−.00	−.02	.11
lag 3	.07	−.00	.06	.03
lag 4	−.32	.13	−.06	.28

[a] Intercept (drift term) is permitted to vary by firm; slope coefficient is assumed constant across firms within industry.

[b] Coefficient on $E_t(S_{t+1})$ reflects firm-specific and seasonal variation (see Appendix). Otherwise, all coefficients are assumed constant across firms within an industry.

[c] Coefficient on R_{t-1} reflects firm-specific and seasonal variation (see Appendix). Otherwise, all coefficients are assumed constant across firms within an industry.

Table 6 examines the relation between the unexpected components of inventory and receivables at the end of quarter t, and unexpected sales for quarter $t+1$, where expectations are conditional on sales for quarter t. We adopt the perspective of an investor who has received a sales announcement (along with an earnings announcement) for quarter t, but does not yet know the inventory and receivables balances for the end of quarter t. The investor has predicted sales for period $t+1$ using information about sales through quarter t with the time-series forecasting model developed by Foster [1977].[26] We then ask how much of the investor's sales forecast error could be explained by the unexpected changes in inventory and receivables balances reported for the end of quarter t.

Table 6 presents the regression equation used to assess whether inventory and receivables balances are incrementally useful in predicting sales. The results in panel A suggest that positive

[26] This model assumes that quarterly sales follow a first-order autoregressive process in seasonal differences. See Table 5 for details.

TABLE 6

INCREMENTAL USEFULNESS OF INVENTORY AND RECEIVABLE BALANCES AS PREDICTORS OF FUTURE SALES, GIVEN THAT PRIOR SALES ARE ALREADY KNOWN

Explanation: Unexpected sales of quarter $t+1$ (where the expectation includes information about quarter t sales) are regressed against unexpected inventory and receivables balances of quarter t. The latter are intended to represent those portions of inventory and receivables that are not predictable, given that sales for quarter t are already known.

Pooled time-series, cross-sectional regression estimates for:

$$\frac{S_{t+1}-E(S_{t+1}|S_t)}{E(S_{t+1}|S_t)}=a_0+a_1\frac{I_t-E(I_t|S_t,I_{t-1})}{E(S_{t+1}|S_t)}+a_2\frac{R_t-E(R_t|S_t,R_{t-1})}{E(S_{t+1}|S_t)}+e_{j,t-1},$$

where:

S_t=Sales for quarter t;
I_t=Inventory, end of quarter t;
R_t=Receivables, end of quarter t;
and expectations models are as described in Table 5.

Panel A. Full Sample of Individual Securities:

Independent Variable:	*Unexpected Inventory*	*Unexpected Receivables*
Coefficient	.24	−.19
t-statistic	6.55	−11.04

R-squared=.028 n=5,585

Panel B. Sample of Individual Securities, Excluding "Outliers" (Observations excluded where absolute value of regressor exceeds 30 percent):

Independent Variable:	*Unexpected Inventory*	*Unexpected Receivables*
Coefficient	.18	−.01
t-statistic	4.70	−.23

R-squared=.004 n=5,431

Panel C. Full Sample, Grouped into 25 Portfolios Based on Quintiles of UINV, *then on Quintiles of* UREC *within Each of the Original Quintiles*[a]:

Independent Variable:	*Unexpected Inventory*	*Unexpected Receivables*
Coefficient	.38	.08
t-statistic	5.51	1.50

R-squared=.601 n=25

[a] No exclusion of outliers; when outliers excluded, results are similar.

sales forecast errors are associated with unexpectedly high prior-quarter inventory levels (t=6.55) and unexpectedly low prior-quarter receivables levels (t= −11.04).[27] Thus, revelation of the inven-

[27] There are more observations available in Table 6 than in Tables 1 and 2 because we need not restrict attention to firm-quarters for which detailed earnings compo-

tory and receivables balances could have served to improve the prediction of sales, even after prior sales had already been taken into account. However, in panel B, when outliers are excluded from the sample, the significance of receivables is lost.[28] Furthermore, the R^2's for the regressions in both panel A and panel B are extremely low (.028 and .004), indicating that improvements in sales forecasting ability are modest, even though statistically significant. In panel C, following an approach like that used in Beaver et al. [1979], firms are grouped into 25 portfolios based on rankings of their independent variables,[29] to determine the effect of diversifying some of the firm-specific "noise." After grouping, the R^2 rises (as expected) to .601 and unexpected inventory balances remain good predictions of future sales[30] (t=5.51); however, the coefficient on unexpected receivables switches sign.

On the basis of the evidence in Table 6 we conclude that there is modest support for the model. Specifically, inventory balances do appear to be incrementally useful in predicting future sales, after controlling for information about current and prior sales. Moreover, this supports the link in our model which differentiates its predictions from a simple "quality of earnings" story. But, receivables balances do not generally have similar predictive ability; so if unexpectedly high receivables balances are "bad news," the data do not support the existence of a link through future sales, as argued by O'glove [1987].

VI. Tests of the Information in Earnings Components Based on the Links Between Inventory, Receivables, and Future Sales

Since the model predicts that the security price implications of cash flows and accruals vary across firms, in addition to over time, it is possible that tests based on current accrual components could explain stock price behavior even when the tests previously discussed could not. Having established at least some support for the economic links between inventory, receivables, and future sales, we now seek to determine whether the current accrual components can explain stock price behavior around the release of quarterly and annual reports.

Our tests are based on a modified version of equation (6). Since Wilson [1986, sec. 5.2] presents evidence to show that noncurrent accruals are either uninformative, or already known prior to the financial statement release date, we drop $UNCA_{jt}$ as a regressor to obtain:

$$R_{jt}=b_0+(b_{2I}-b_1)\,UINV_{jt}+(b_{2R}-b_1)\,UREC_{jt}+(b_{2P}-b_1)\,UPAY_{jt}+w_{jt}. \qquad (9)$$

The model discussed in Section V predicts that $(b_{2I}-b_1)$ is positive, and that $(b_{2R}-b_1)$ is negative. Our model suggests that unexpected payables convey (in a noisier fashion) the same information conveyed by unexpected inventory. Thus, given that $UINV_{jt}$ is already included in the regression, the model provides no motivation for including $UPAY_{jt}$. However, since the portion of unexpected payables that is not redundant with unexpected inventory could

nent data are available for the first time upon release of the financial statements, and because missing CRSP data is not an issue here.

[28] Observations where the absolute value of *UINV* and *UREC* exceeded 30 percent of sales were classified as outliers. A casual examination of the data indicates that some of these outliers are caused by events such as acquisitions and the initial offering of credit cards to customers.

[29] First, we rank all observations (firm-quarters) on unexpected inventory and form five groups. Then, within each of those groups, we rank firm-quarters on unexpected receivables, and again form five groups.

[30] This result is qualitatively insensitive to the exclusion of outliers.

conceivably have security price implications, we present estimates of equation (9) both with and without $UPAY_{jt}$. The expectations for payables are conditioned, in part, on the contemporaneous values of inventory and receivables, so that any information reflected in $UPAY_{jt}$ is intended to be incremental to that in $UINV_{jt}$ and $UREC_{jt}$ (see Table 5 for details).

There are two procedural differences between the tests summarized here and those used in the replication and extension of Wilson [1987]. First, for the vast majority of fourth quarter observations where both the 10-K and annual report date are available, we use the *earlier* of the two, rather than just the annual report date.[31] Second, whereas our earlier tests used market model prediction errors to maintain comparability with Wilson, here we report results based on market-adjusted returns.[32] However, our results are qualitatively insensitive to both of these procedural differences, with one exception, as discussed below.

Estimates of equation (9) appear in Table 7. Panel A presents results of estimating equation (9) while using only the two regressors (*UINV* and *UREC*) for which the model offers predictions. Panel B presents estimates of the full equation, including *UINV*, *UREC*, and *UPAY*. The estimates in panel A provide little support for the predictions of our model: the coefficients on unexpected inventories all take on the predicted positive sign, but none is significant, and coefficients on unexpected receivables are generally of the wrong sign and insignificant. Overall, the explanatory power of these regressions is quite low; the R^2 is never higher than .02.

In panel B, we again find no support for predictions concerning *UINV* and *UREC*.[33] In contrast, *UPAY* does take on significant coefficients using data from only fourth quarters. However, it is not clear why unexpectedly high payables balances should reveal favorable information about the value of the firm, after controlling for the level of inventory.[34] Also, although the result (and all others in Table 7) is insensitive to the treatment of outliers,[35] all *t*-statistics are below 1.7 when market model prediction errors are substituted for market-adjusted returns, or when Wilson's approach and only annual report dates are used. Finally, the result is insignificant at the .10 level in the full sample.

Our final attempt to find support for the model involved focusing on a subset of the sample industries. We identified ten of 33 industries where unexpected inventory balances provided statistically significant incremental explanatory power (at the .01 level, using a one-tailed

[31] Because we also use 10-K dates in cases where no annual report date is available, there is a slight increase in sample size.

[32] That is, we simply subtract the market index return from raw returns since we were concerned that "noise" in the market model intercepts from short (90-day) estimation periods used in our replication of Wilson [1987] would offset any advantages of using the market model. Brown and Warner [1985] indicate there is no clear gain in power from using market model prediction errors instead of market-adjusted returns even though their market model is estimated with 250 observations. Others share this concern (see Penman [1988], esp. note 3).

[33] Some may wonder why inclusion of *UPAY* affects the estimates of coefficients on the other regressors, given that *UPAY* is designed to capture only information incremental to inventory and receivables. One reason is that since expectations for the three regressors are created in time-series, industry-by-industry, they would not necessarily be orthogonal in the final, pooled cross-sectional regression. The second reason is that the expectations for payables are conditioned on contemporaneous levels of inventory and receivables, not on *UINV* and *UREC per se*.

[34] One possibility is that unexpectedly high payables arise when the firm builds raw materials inventory near the end of the quarter. If that action is taken in anticipation of higher demand, it could be viewed as a good signal by the market.

[35] As in Table 7, outliers are defined as observations where at least one of the regressors (prior to scaling) has an absolute value greater than 30 percent of sales.

TABLE 7

REGRESSIONS OF MARKET-ADJUSTED STOCK RETURNS DURING THE FINANCIAL STATEMENT RELEASE PERIOD AGAINST UNEXPECTED INVENTORY, RECEIVABLES, AND PAYABLES, CONTROLLING FOR CONTEMPORANEOUS SALES AND EARNINGS (1977–1984)

Pooled time-series cross-sectional regression estimates for equation (9):

$$R_{jt}=b_0+(b_{2I}-b_1)UINV_{jt}+(b_{2R}-b_1)UREC_{jt}+(b_{2P}-b_1)UPAY_{jt}+e_{jt},$$

where:

R_{jt}=Market-adjusted return for firm j, during nine days surrounding release of financial statements for quarter t;
$UINV_{jt}$=unexpected inventory at end of same quarter;
$UREC_{jt}$=unexpected receivables at end of same quarter; and
$UPAY_{jt}$=unexpected payables at end of same quarter.

(Expectations for all independent variables are conditioned on quarter t sales and earnings and all regressors are scaled by market value of equity prior to the event window.)

Panel A. Estimation Excluding UPAY *as Regressor:*

	Coefficients (t-statistics)				
Sample	$b_{2I}-b_1$	$b_{2R}-b_1$	$b_{2P}-b_1$	R^2	n
All firm quarters	.01 (.38)	−0.1 (−.43)	—	.000	2,589
Fourth quarters only	.03 (1.25)	.01 (.37)	—	.002	858
Fourth quarters, 1981–1982	.06 (1.34)	.09 (1.64)	—	.020	206

Panel B. Estimation of Full Model:

	Coefficients (t-statistics)				
Sample	$b_{2I}-b_1$	$b_{2R}-b_1$	$b_{2P}-b_1$	R^2	n
All firm quarters	−.00 (−.13)	−.01 (−.64)	.02 (1.52)	.001	2,589
Fourth quarters only	.01 (.41)	−.00 (−.15)	.06 (2.58)	.010	858
Fourth quarters, 1981–1982	.03 (.62)	.05 (.94)	.10 (2.53)	.051	206

test) in the sales prediction equation of Table 6. We then reestimated regressions like those summarized in Table 7. Again, the estimated coefficients were not reliably different from zero.

We conclude that there is little support for the stock price predictions derived from consideration of the separate effects of the components of unexpected current accruals. As in previous sections, we are unable to explain stock price behavior around the release of financial statements by using detailed information about cash flows and accruals.

VII. Concluding Remarks

This paper has reexamined recent research concerning the valuation implications of detailed components of earnings (in particular, cash flows and current accruals) and has attempted to develop some economic logic for why the valuation implications should differ across these components.

Our approach was to attempt to confirm one simple relation observed in prior research, and then to examine progressively more contextual models of the valuation implications of cash flows and accruals. We were unable to confirm that the relation observed by Wilson [1986 and 1987]—a larger price reaction to cash flows than to accruals—extends beyond his test period of the fourth quarters of 1981 and 1982. When we allowed the relative impacts of cash flows and accruals to vary according to the state of the economy, we were again unable to explain a significant fraction of stock price behavior. Moreover, our failure to find evidence of any significant variation over time in the relative impacts of cash flows and accruals suggests that other partitions of the data according to time periods are not likely to overturn this conclusion. Finally, we introduced a model in which the relative price impacts of cash flows and accruals depend on what the accruals reveal about management expectations of future sales. Although we found modest support for the economic logic underlying the model, we were unable to detect any empirical support for its stock price predictions.

Whenever one fails to reject the null hypothesis in research of this nature, there are several potential explanations. We have conducted a number of supplemental analyses in an effort to eliminate some of these explanations. We believe the remaining explanations fall into two categories. One maintains that financial statement release dates may not represent important events for pricing, because the essential information included therein has already been made available through alternative channels. This explanation is consistent with our previous interpretation of Bowen et al. [1987], whose results imply that cash flows and current accruals have different associations with returns measured over annual intervals. However, Rayburn [1986] finds no such difference, and even in Bowen et al., the result is sensitive to treatment of outliers, and is significant in only two of ten years (see Bowen et al. [1987, table 7, pgs. 744–745], in conjunction with our discussion in Section I). A second explanation maintains that differences in the valuation implications of cash flows and the various accrual accounts are more contextual than any of the models examined here.

Our conclusion is that further progress in this line of research will require a better understanding of the economic context in which the implications of detailed earnings components are interpreted. In addition, any research based on short-run association tests will require more knowledge of the process by which information is transmitted from firms to the public. In the meantime, we suggest that it is possible that the links between detailed earnings components and valuation are so highly contextual that no parsimonious model could ever capture more than a small portion of the story.

APPENDIX

A SIMPLE MODEL OF THE LINKS BETWEEN CURRENT ACCRUALS AND FUTURE SALES

We consider a model of the operating cycle of the firm, in order to identify what valuation-relevant signals might be conveyed by information about current accruals. Two of the three major components of current accruals are considered: changes in inventory and changes in receivables.

Changes in Inventory Balances

Assume that inventory at the end of period t, denoted by I_t, consists of two components. The first is I_t^*, representing the optimal balance of inventory, given management's expectation of future sales $E_t(S_{t+1})$. The second component is D_t, representing the deviation from the optimal balance. This component depends on not only the deviation of period t sales (S_t) from management's expectations at the end of period $t-1$ ($E_{t-1}(S_t)$), but also on the previously existing deviation from the optimal balance (D_{t-1}). Thus:

$$I_t = I_t^* + D_t, \tag{A1}$$

where (by assumption):

$$I_t^* = k_{1_q} E_t(S_{t+1}), \tag{A2}$$

and:

$$D_t = k_2 D_{t-1} + k_3[E_{t-1}(S_t) - S_t]. \tag{A3}$$

The behavioral assumption underlying equation (A2) is that the optimal inventory balance is a constant fraction of management's expectation of next quarters' sales, where this fraction may vary only with the quarter (q) of the firm's fiscal year.[1] Equation (A3) assumes that, if actual sales levels differ from expectations, then an unplanned inventory buildup or liquidation, in the amount $k_3[E_{t-1}(S_t) - S_t]$, would occur by the end of period t. In addition, equation (A3) posits that if a deviation from the optimum (D_{t-1}) already existed at the beginning of the period, a fraction k_2 of that deviation would still remain at the end of the period.

Noting that $D_{t-1} = I_{t-1} - I_{t-1}^* = I_{t-1} - k_{1_q} E_{t-1}(S_t)$, we can combine equations (A1), (A2), and (A3) to obtain:

$$I_t = k_{1_q} E_t(S_{t+1}) + k_2 I_{t-1} - k_2 k_{1_q} E_{t-1}(S_t) + k_3[E_{t-1}(S_t) - S_t]. \tag{A4}$$

After earnings and sales have been announced, but before the inventory balance is revealed in the published financial statements, the market is already aware of how large an "inventory buildup" or "inventory decline" should have occurred as a result of sales deviating from expectations. Those effects are captured in the last three terms in equation (A4). What the market does not know (with certainty) is the first term, which depends on management's expectation of future sales, $E_t(S_{t+1})$. Publication of

[1] We recognize that more sophisticated models of optimal inventory balances exist. Our simple specification in equation (A2) is motivated primarily by a desire for parsimony and to specify the model in terms of observable variables.

the inventory balance in the complete financial statements permits the market to infer what management expectations must be.

The empirical tests require an estimate of expected inventory from the point of view of the market, after the announcement of sales but before the release of financial statements. For that purpose, we use the sales forecast model in Foster [1977] to proxy for the market's expectation of future sales, and estimate the following analog of equation (A4):[2]

$$I_t = m_1 k_{1q} E_t(S_{t+1}) + m_2 I_{t-1} - m_3 k_{1q} E_{t-1}(S_t) + m_4[E_{t-1}(S_t) - S_t] + e_t, \qquad (A5)$$

where:

k_{1q} = seasonal adjustment factor, equal to the mean inventory-to-expected-sales ratio for each firm and each of the four quarters of the fiscal year; and

m_1, m_2, m_3, m_4 = coefficients to be estimated, assumed identical within industries, but permitted to vary across industries.

In estimation, all left-hand and right-hand side variables are scaled by sales, to permit pooling across firms within the same industry.

Changes in Receivables Balances

Letting R_t, S_t, and C_t denote receivables at the end of period t (net of allowances for bad debts), sales for period t, and collections for period t, respectively, we have the accounting identity for receivables:

$$R_t = R_{t-1} + S_t - C_t. \qquad (A6)$$

We model collections as a function of the beginning balance of receivables, the current period's sales, and a disturbance term, u_t:

$$C_t = p_1 R_{t-1} + p_2 p_{3q} S_t + u_t. \qquad (A7)$$

The term $p_2 p_{3q} S_t$ captures the portion of current sales that are expected to be collected within the same period, in accordance with management's long-run credit policy (the term p_{3q} is permitted to be seasonal, as in the inventory model). The term u_t captures transitory deviations from expected collections, due to changes in credit policy, or customers' willingness or ability to pay. Combining equations (A6) and (A7) yields:

$$R_t = (1 - p_1) R_{t-1} + (1 - p_2 p_{3q}) S_t - u_t. \qquad (A8)$$

After sales (S_t) are announced, but before the end-of-period receivables balance (R_t) is revealed, the market already knows the first two terms on the right-hand side of equation (A8). Revelation of R_t permits the market to infer u_t, the deviation from the expected collection experience.

[2] While k_1 appears twice in equation (A4), we do not impose this restriction in estimation. The reason for this is to let the parameters on I_{t-1} and $k_{1q}E_t(S_{t-1})$ remain free to help eliminate sources of nonstationarity not identified in the derivation of the model. This is equivalent to permitting the error term to be a function of those terms. Also note that permitting the coefficients in equation (A5) to vary across industries can mitigate potential problems arising from the use of different inventory costing methods, such as LIFO and FIFO.

The empirical tests require an expectation of R_t from the market's perspective. Our expectation model is based on an estimate of equation (A8). In estimation, we assume that p_{3_q} is equal to the mean collections-to-sales ratio for each firm and each of the four quarters of the fiscal year. We also assume that p_1 and p_2 are identical within industries, but permit them to vary across industries. To permit pooling within industries, we scale all variables by sales.

REFERENCES

Atiase, R. K., "Predisclosure Information, Firm Capitalization, and Security Price Behavior Around Earnings Announcements," *Journal of Accounting Research* (Spring 1985), pp. 21–36.

Beaver, W. H., R. Clarke, and W. F. Wright, "The Association Between Unsystematic Security Returns and the Magnitude of Earnings Forecast Errors," *Journal of Accounting Research* (Autumn 1979), pp. 316–340.

Bernstein, L. A., *Financial Statement Analysis: Theory, Application and Interpretation*, Revised Edition (Richard D. Irwin, Inc., 1978).

Bowen, R. M., D. Burgstahler, and L. A. Daley, "The Incremental Information Content of Accrual Versus Cash Flows," The Accounting Review (October 1987), pp. 723–747.

Brealy, R. A., and S. Myers, *Principles of Corporate Finance* (McGraw-Hill, Inc., 1981).

Brown, S. J., and J. B. Warner, "Using Daily Stock Returns: The Case of Event Studies," *Journal of Financial Economics* (March 1985), pp. 3–31.

Collins, D. W., and S. P. Kothari, "A Theoretical and Empirical Analysis of the Determinants of the Relation Between Earnings Innovations and Security Returns," Unpublished working paper (University of Rochester, July 1988).

DeAngelo, L. E., "Managerial Competition, Information Costs, and Corporate Governance: The Use of Accounting Performance Measures in Proxy Contests," *Journal of Accounting and Economics* (January 1988), pp. 3–36.

Fama, E. F., "Stock Returns, Real Activity, Inflation, and Money," *American Economic Review* (September 1981), pp. 545–565.

Foster, G., "Quarterly Accounting Data: Time-Series Properties and Predictive-Ability Results," The Accounting Review (January 1977), pp. 1–21.

Foster, T. W., III, and D. Vickrey, "The Incremental Information Content of the 10-K," The Accounting Review (October 1978), pp. 921–934.

———, D. R. Jenkins, and D. W. Vickrey, "Additional Evidence on the Incremental Information Content of the 10-K," *Journal of Business Finance and Accounting* (U.K.) (Spring 1983), pp. 57–66.

———, ———, and ———, "The Incremental Information Content of the Annual Report," *Accounting and Business Research* (U.K.) (Spring 1986), pp. 91–98.

Freeman, R. N., "The Association Between Accounting Earnings and Security Returns for Large and Small Firms," *Journal of Accounting and Economics* (July 1987), pp. 195–228.

Healy, P. M., "The Effect of Bonus Schemes on Accounting Decisions," *Journal of Accounting and Economics* (April 1985), pp. 85–107.

Jennings, R., "Interpreting Incremental Information Content: A Components Perspective," Unpublished working paper (University of Texas at Austin, December 1987).

Jones, J. J., "The Effect of Foreign Trade Regulation on Accounting Choices and Production and Investment Decisions," Unpublished Ph.D. dissertation (University of Michigan, 1988).

Ketz, J. E., and J. A. Largay III, "Reporting Income and Cash Flows From Operations," *Accounting Horizons* (June 1987), pp. 9–17.

Lipe, R. C., "The Information Contained in the Components of Earnings," Supplement to *Journal of Accounting Research* (1986), pp. 37–64.

McNichols, M., and G. P. Wilson, "Evidence of Earnings Management from the Provision for Bad Debts," Supplement to *Journal of Accounting Research* (1988), pp. 1–31.

O'glove, T. L., *Quality of Earnings: The Investor's Guide to How Much Money A Company Is Really Making* (The Free Press, 1987).

Penman, S., "Earnings Reporting and the Evolution of Stock Market Prices," Unpublished working paper (University of California at Berkeley, May 1988).

Rayburn, J., "The Association of Operating Cash Flow and Accruals with Security Returns," Supplement to *Journal of Accounting Research* (1986), pp. 112–133.

Stober, T. L., "The Incremental Information Content of Financial Statement Disclosures: The Case of LIFO Inventory Liquidations," Supplement to *Journal of Accounting Research* (1986), pp. 138–160.

Theil, H., *Principles of Econometrics* (John Wiley & Sons, 1971).

Treynor, J. L., "The Trouble with Earnings," *The Financial Analysts Journal* (September/October 1972), pp. 41–43.

Wilson G. P., "The Relative Information Content of Accruals and Cash Flows: Combined Evidence at the Earnings Announcement and Annual Report Release Date," Supplement to *Journal of Accounting Research* (1986), pp. 165–200.

———, "The Incremental Information Content of the Accrual and Funds Components of Earnings After Controlling for Earnings," The Accounting Review (April 1987), pp. 293–322.

Accounting and Business Research, Vol. 20, No. 77, pp. 3–11, 1989

The Information Content of Cash Flow Figures

J. L. G. Board and J. F. S. Day*

Abstract—This paper investigates the link between earnings and share prices for a sample of UK companies for the years 1961 to 1977. Three measures of earnings were used: the traditional historical cost accounting return and two which were closer to cash flow measures. The strength of the link between earnings and cumulative abnormal returns was investigated relative to the level of inflation. The results indicate that, while there is substantial information content in the traditional historical cost rate of return, there is very little information conveyed by the measure closest to pure cash flow. No support was therefore found for the use of cash flow based reports. Evidence was found showing substantial changes in the nature of the relationship between accounting and stock returns, but this could not be explained by the effects of inflation.

This paper complements the study by Board, Day & Walker (1989) which examined the link between inflation and company profit for a large sample of US companies. The paper examines the link between earnings and share prices for a sample of UK companies, making use of three measures of earnings (two of which are closer to cash flow based measures than historical cost earnings). The strength of this link relative to the rate of inflation is also considered. Section I contains some discussion of the hypotheses under examination, sections II and III contain discussion of the techniques and sample, and sections IV to VII discuss the results of the tests. Section VIII contains some concluding remarks.

I. Theoretical framework

It now seems generally agreed that, although accounting numbers are not the only source of information about companies' prospects, accounting earnings do provide information to the stock market which is used in the setting of prices. A crude rationale for this belief might be that increased profits indicate an increased likelihood of that company being in a good trading position. A more sophisticated view, following from the implications of the efficient market hypothesis, which highlights the linkages between share prices and earnings, is given below.

Rational shareholders are assumed to be concerned only with their eventual wealth, which is derived from gains made from dividend payments and capital gains. Thus the price of a share should reflect the present value of a stream of expected future dividends. Changes in expectations about this stream will cause the price to change, enabling shareholders to make gains or losses on sale. As the following equation shows, the dividend stream is based on the pattern of expected future cash flows, and so we would expect information which is used to form expectations about the future pattern of cash flows to be useful.

$$P_t = \sum_{t=0}^{\infty} E(D_t)/(1+r)^t = \sum_{t=0}^{\infty} E(CF_t)/(1+r)^t$$

where

D_t represents the dividend paid at time t,

CF_t represents the cash flow at time t, and

r represents an appropriate discount rate.

This will be indicated by a change in share prices when such information is released into the market.

The role of earnings rather than cash flows in this valuation process is an important issue. Accounting earnings might be used as a surrogate for future cash flows.[1] A simple justification for this is that historical cost accounting earnings is the standard reported earnings measure and is the most common variable to be analysed in the press and accounting literature. This suggests that, other things being equal, in a rational market there should be an observable link between earnings and share prices. Furthermore, as current earnings also provide information about future earnings (and hence dividends), in an efficient market only the unexpected component of an earnings announcement will provide new information because prices

*The authors are members of the Department of Accounting and Finance, London School of Economics and Political Science. They are most grateful to the referees of this paper, whose suggestions have resulted in a much improved paper.

[1]This issue is discussed in Watts and Zimmerman (1986).

will already reflect any expected level of earnings. Available evidence suggests that, in both the UK and US, prices reflect publicly available information.

A more complex justification for the use of accounting earnings as a surrogate for cash flows comes from the use of unexpected earnings in tests which examine the link between earnings and abnormal returns. If unexpected earnings are a better indication of the change in expected future cash flows than unexpected cash flows then it is possible that unexpected earnings could have a higher association with abnormal returns than unexpected cash flows. It has been argued that the accruals process by which cash flows are transformed into accounting earnings can mean that accounting earnings are a better guide to 'maintainable' future cash flows than are current cash flows. Easton (1985) shows that accounting earnings are a good predictor of the future stream of cash receipts from an equity investment, and that there is a high correlation between security prices and the present value of receipts. The two measures have operating cash flows in common and several studies have tested the strengths of the links between unexpected earnings and unexpected cash flows and abnormal returns, e.g. Ball and Brown (1968) and Beaver and Dukes (1972). These studies suggest that accounting earnings are a better predictor of future cash flows than are current cash flows. However, the possibility that earnings are used as a surrogate for current cash flows should be investigated. If this is the case, the relation between accounting earnings and share prices will be expected to be weaker than the comparable relation involving actual cash flows.

Essentially, the current announcement has two effects. Firstly, one term in the discounting process is resolved, i.e. $E(CF_t)$ becomes CF_t, and, secondly, knowledge of CF_t allows modification of the stream of expected future cash flows $E(CF_{t+1}) \ldots E(CF_T)$. Given the role of cash flows in valuation and the imperfect correlation between historical cost accounting profit, HC, and cash flow, it is possible that direct revelation of CF_t will provide clearer information to investors than would HC earnings (from which an estimate of CF_t would have to be made). The counter argument is that, although the stream $CF_t \ldots CF_T$ is of primary interest, it is HC_t which provides the basis for a better estimate of future cash flows than the current period's cash flow. If true, the results presented below will show that HC dominates cash flow in terms of information content.

The question then arises of the measurement of earnings. Traditional historical cost accounting profit is the usual measure. However, it is well known that under some conditions, notably inflation, use of a traditional HC system, with its adherence to financial capital maintenance, tends to overstate profits and understate asset values (unless increments in asset values are passed through income) thus exaggerating the accounting rate of return. Other measures such as replacement cost (which formed the basis for some of the adjustments proposed in SSAP16), constant purchasing power (proposed in PSSAP7) or cash flow figures could be used instead. This paper examines the usefulness of two measures of cash flow.

One test of the usefulness of alternatives to HC is to examine the nature of the link between alternative earnings measures and share prices during periods of varying inflation. A measure whose information content is greater than that of HC will:

(a) convey more information than HC in any period (i.e. exhibit a stronger link between it and share price movement), and
(b) be such that the strength of any link between the measure and share prices will be affected by the rate of inflation to a lesser extent than the comparable relationship using HC.

II. Techniques used

The methods adopted in this paper are based on the well known method of assessing the relevance of accounting information for investors by examining cumulative abnormal returns (CARs), whose use in this context was examined by Ball and Brown (1968). Their study investigated the question of the association of accounting earnings with share price movements and found such an association. Other researchers have since replicated and extended Ball and Brown's work both using their data and using data relating to other than the US countries.[2] Ball and Brown also considered whether accounting earnings convey information to the stock market and found that, although not very timely, some information is revealed by the annual announcement.[3]

The argument is that share prices or returns are affected by two classes of information: market wide, and firm specific. The former can be controlled by using a market index (e.g. the FT Actuaries) to remove these effects from individual firms' returns. Any remaining variation can then be attributed to firm specific factors. To do this, it is conventional to use a time series regression of the following form:

$$R_{it} = a_i + b_i M_t + e_{it} \qquad (1)$$

[2] Beaver, Lambert and Morse (1980), for example, considered the relation between the magnitude of unexpected earnings and the magnitude of the abnormal rate of return.

[3] If they do, then unexpected earnings should have the same sign as the mean abnormal rate of return in the month in which the earnings were announced. Later studies have confirmed this result (e.g. Benston and Watts, 1978).

where:

R_{it} is the return on company i's shares in period t,
M_t is the return on the market index in period t,
a_i and b_i are coefficients, estimated in a previous period, and
e_{it} measures firm specific effects.

Thus, by focusing on e_{it}, rather than R_{it}, one can make at least partial allowance for systematic market wide effects.

To avoid bias, rather than use the e_{it} values directly it is appropriate to use values of a_i and b_i which have been estimated over a different (usually immediately preceding) period, and to form predicted returns for company i for the months of interest. The difference between actual and predicted returns can then be used as unbiased estimates of the firm specific effects. For example, we might use the period 1976–1980 to form estimates of a_i and b_i which are then used to predict returns for the months around the 1981 earnings release date.

The use of the market model is not above criticism. Although it is used in almost every study of information content, studies such as that by Brown and Warner (1980) indicate that it is not a particularly sensitive model. Nevertheless, it is part of the dominant approach to these studies and as the purpose of this paper is to compare different accounting numbers, as long as the method is consistent between cash flow and HC earnings the results are unlikely to be substantially affected.

If an earnings figure is announced in one month, any effect of the announcement on expectations about next year's earnings will be observed in the e_{it} values for the months leading up to the release. A summary measure of the effect is simply to compound these values for the twelve months between announcements (after which the next year's announcement takes place).[4] Thus:

$$CAR_{it} = \prod_{k=t}^{t+11} [(1 + e_{ik})]^{(1/12)}$$

Repeating this adjustment for all companies in the sample will result in a set of CARs, to use in the tests.

All that remains is to define a measure of unexpected earnings. As discussed in section I, the figure used should reflect the unexpected component of this year's earnings. In the absence of a well specified model of investors' expectations, a simple model was used: the market is hypothesised to expect the firm to earn the same this year as it did last. Unexpected earnings are then the difference between this year's earnings and last, i.e. $E_{it}—E_{it-1}$. This definition of unexpected earnings is essentially that of a random walk. In a related study (Board, Day and Walker, 1988) two alternative models of predicted income were used: the average of that company's income over the last six years, and the value predicted from a time series regression of this company's income on the average income for the companies in the simple. Application of these three models indicated that the sample random walk model used in this paper was clearly superior to the other two. Of course, this does not mean that earnings are random but, rather, that no simple model seems better able to describe the pattern.

This model of investor expectations is naive. Recent work in the USA examines the use of directly observed expectations (e.g. Brown, Hagerman, Griffin and Zmijewski 1987a and 1987b), and from this it appears possible that more sophisticated models or direct observations of expectations would permit different conclusions to be drawn. Of course there are problems with directly observed expectations data, not least that this is not available in the UK for the long sample period considered in this paper.

For any year we now have for each company a figure for CAR and three for unexpected earnings (one for each earnings measure used). The test used is a cross-sectional regression of the form:

$$CAR_{it} = a_t + b_t E_{it} \qquad (2)$$

where the subscript t indicates that the test takes place in year t, and E_{it} is the unexpected earnings figure. There will be one equation of the form of (2) for each earnings measure. There will be a significant information effect if the coefficient b_t, or equivalently the R^2, is significantly different from zero.

III. Dataset

Monthly share price data were taken from the London Share Price Database distributed by the London Business School. Accounting data were obtained from the Cambridge/DTI data and verified against the EXSTAT files. The following selection criteria were used. Firms should:

(i) be publicly quoted and be in the first 800 of *The Times* top 1000 UK firms (firms lower than this are likely to suffer from estimation problems associated with thin trading). The sample numbered 416 after firms without a stock exchange quotation had been removed.
(ii) have an accounting year end of December 31 (this is the most common year end date). 233 firms remained in the sample after this stage.
(iii) be in the manufacturing, non-oil, sector (it was felt desirable to keep to manufacturing companies and exclude others in order to

[4] The reason for the cumulation over a full 12 months is to attempt to capture the entire effect of the earnings values. The use of 12 month cumulation is conventional in this type of study in which it is the amount of information rather than the method of transmission which is of primary interest. To assess the effect of this, 1 and 3 months cumulation were also used in the tests for information content. It was found that 12 months cumulation yielded by far the strongest results.

avoid earnings streams which might otherwise be unduly influenced by circumstances which did not have a market-wide impact). This reduced the sample to 130 companies.

(iv) have a full set of accounting data for the years 1961–1977 (the years covered by this paper). The main cause of incomplete data was companies incorporating, merging, or liquidating during this period. This left 68 companies.

(v) have not more than 10 missing share returns over the period 1961–1977 (more than this and the construction of abnormal return indices becomes difficult).

These criteria produced a sample of 44 companies. Of these 5 were excluded because inspection and comparison with alternative data sources led to the conclusion that their accounting data, as recorded, contained errors and were not completely reliable, leaving a sample of 39 manufacturing companies.

Three aspects of this research design give cause for concern: the data, the models of investor expectations and the use of the market model. The sample is both small and biased in that only manufacturing companies which traded over the 18 year sample period are considered. It is possible that cash flow data is of greater value in non-manufacturing or new companies, in which case the value of cash flow data is underestimated in this sample. Statistically, although small, the sample is quite large enough to permit 'normal' tests and analysis.

Three measures of earnings were used:

(a) ROI = Net Income/NBV
(b) WCAP = (Net income + Depreciation + Deferred Taxation)/NBV
(c) NETQ = WCAP + (Change in Stock and Work in Progress)/NBV

where:

Net Income
= operating profit + dividends + interest
+ other income received
− interest paid − tax paid
− transfers to deferred taxation reserve,

and

NBV = opening net book value of shareholders' funds.

Measure (a) is the HC return on investment measure, (b) is based on working capital and (c) on net cash (quick) assets. WCAP corresponds closely to a measure used by Beaver and Dukes (1982), but NETQ, which incorporates an adjustment of the change in stocks, does not seem to be a measure yet tested by other researchers. All three are then expressed as accounting rates of return and, as discussed above, the unexpected earnings for each measure is simply the first difference of that measure. Although Christie (1987) concludes that market value rather than book value is the correct deflator in returns studies, book values have been used in many previous studies and are used here in the calculation of all three measures.

For each company, the values of the cumulative abnormal returns were estimated as follows:

(i) Regress R_{it} on M_t (equation (1)) using 6 years (initially January 1955 to December 1960) of the sample data. As a balance between the desire for estimates based on a long time series and the requirement for stability over the estimation and prediction periods, six years was chosen as the length of the estimation period.

(ii) Use the estimated a_i and b_i coefficients to calculate the predicted R_{it} values for the 12 months leading up to the announcement. The difference between actual and predicted values form the abnormal returns for the period.

(iii) Use the 12 abnormal returns to find the cumulative abnormal return for the year.

(iv) 'Roll' the sample frame on by 12 months and repeat steps (i) to (iii) for January 1956 to February 1963, January 1957 to February 1964, and so on until the final period from January 1971 to February 1978.

After this process, we have four numbers (CAR, ROI, WCAP and NETQ) for each of the 39 companies for each of the 17 years of the sample period.

IV. The information content of different earnings measured

This section is concerned with the examination of the information content of the three measures of unexpected earnings. The test used (see section II) was based on a regression model of the form of (2) and treated each year as independent of the others. The results are summarised in Table 1.

Table 1
Information Content of Three Accounting Measures

Year	*RPI*	*ROI*	*WCAP*	*NETQ*
1962	0.041	0.401*	0.275*	0.242*
1963	0.021	0.179*	0.118*	0.099
1964	0.033	0.015	0.005	0.006
1965	0.048	0.015	0.020	0.017
1966	0.038	0.024	0.029	0.011
1967	0.025	0.026	0.010	0.017
1968	0.048	0.215*	0.150*	0.028
1969	0.054	0.317*	0.010	0.001
1970	0.064	0.128*	0.154*	0.001
1971	0.094	0.064	0.107*	0.007
1972	0.071	0.139*	0.112*	0.000
1973	0.091	0.121*	0.071	0.020
1974	0.160	0.208*	0.030	0.029
1975	0.242	0.039	0.009	0.055
1976	0.165	0.060	0.058	0.012
1977	0.159	0.136*	0.276*	0.001

*Significant at 5% level.
For explanation of column headings see Table 2.

Table 2
Variable Names Used in Tests for Incremental Information

RPI	Rate of inflation (retail price index)
ROI	Information content of historical cost based rate of return
WCAP	Information content of working capital based rate of return
NETQ	Information content of quick asset based rate of return
WCRO	Information content of WCAP over ROI
NQRO	Information content of NETQ over ROI
ROWC	Information content of ROI over WCAP
NQWC	Information content of NETQ over WCAP
RONQ	Information content of ROI over NETQ
WCNQ	Information content of WCAP over NETQ

The first two columns of the table show, respectively, the year and the rate of inflation, measured by the proportionate change in the retail price index (RPI), over that year. The following three columns show the results for ROI, WCAP and NETQ respectively. The entries in the column show the 'explanatory power' of the regression, as measured by the coefficient of determination, R^2. An asterisk indicates that the coefficient was significant at the 5% level. Thus, marked entries indicated statistically significant relationships between unexpected earnings and share prices.

It can be seen that there is a substantial information content to the ROI measure. Significant information is observed in 9 of the 16 years and the WCAP measure produces a significant result in 7 years. However, NETQ apparently contains very little information which helps investors in their evaluation of companies.

V. Tests for incremental information content

An additional test for the year by year impact of earnings figures is to examine not whether one measure is reflected in the abnormal returns but whether one measure contains more information than is contained in another. To examine the incremental information content of, say, NETQ over ROI the following procedure is used:[5]

(i) Regress CAR on ROI:

$$CAR_{it} = a_t + b_t ROI_{it} + w_{it}$$

(ii) Regress NETQ on ROI:

$$NETQ_{it} = a_t + b_t ROI_{it} + z_{it}$$

The test of section IV can then be repeated using w_{it} instead of CAR_{it} and z_{it} instead of $NETQ_{it}$:

(iii) Regress z_{it} on w_{it}: $w_{it} = a_t + b_t z_{it} + x_{it}$.

The first regression removes all influence of ROI from CAR, while the second removes any influence of ROI from NETQ earnings. If NETQ is to be judged superior to ROI, it should be able to explain at least part of the variation in CAR which is unexplained by ROI. Note that it is, in principle, possible both for NETQ to have incremental information content over ROI and, simultaneously, for ROI to have incremental information content over NETQ. The interpretation of such a finding would be that each reflects different information from the other. Consequently, although both remain useful, neither dominates the other. Table 2 shows the naming conventions used in the tests for incremental information content.

The results are shown in Table 3. It seems that both ROI and WCAP contain substantial information content over NETQ. This is as expected from the earlier discussion in which the absence of any significant information content of NETQ was noted. Similarly, there is no suggestion that NETQ contains information that is not already contained in the ROI and WCAP figures. Comparing now ROI and WCAP, it seem that ROI has incremental information over WCAP in 5 of the 16 years, while WCAP conveys incremental information in 2. Since ROI is the existing accepted measure, any replacement for it would have to be demonstrably superior to it. Therefore, these results do not provide strong support for the replacement of ROI by WCAP, nor do they suggest that the WCAP figures provide particularly valuable information.

VI. Time series tests

In the light of the widespread view that HC, and hence ROI, becomes unreliable during periods of inflation, it is to be expected that its information

[5] As discussed in Christie *et al.* (1984), this two stage procedure is no different to a single, bivariate regression of the form:

$$CAR_{it} = a_t + b_t HC_{it} + c_t WCAP_{it} + v_{it}.$$

As the two methods are equivalent, the choice between them is arbitrary. We chose the two stage method to aid comparison with earlier work.

Table 3
Incremental Information Content Results

Year	*WCRO*	*NQRO*	*ROWC*	*NQWC*	*RONQ*	*WCNQ*
1962	0.059	0.063	0.222*	0.122*	0.259*	0.160*
1963	0.039	0.133*	0.106*	0.126*	0.210*	0.144*
1964	0.023	0.028	0.033	0.017	0.038	0.016
1965	0.003	0.016	0.001	0.016	0.010	0.012
1966	0.006	0.044	0.002	0.056	0.057	0.072
1967	0.058	0.007	0.073	0.011	0.016	0.003
1968	0.041	0.112*	0.114*	0.114*	0.283*	0.225*
1969	0.212*	0.001	0.457*	0.000	0.317*	0.009
1970	0.033	0.008	0.004	0.007	0.134*	0.159*
1971	0.060	0.008	0.016	0.012	0.066	0.112*
1972	0.000	0.000	0.030	0.001	0.138*	0.112*
1973	0.001	0.030	0.054	0.009	0.130*	0.061
1974	0.091	0.013	0.258*	0.032	0.195*	0.033
1975	0.012	0.046	0.041	0.051	0.029	0.004
1976	0.012	0.004	0.014	0.008	0.052	0.054
1977	0.162*	0.010	0.001	0.027	0.144*	0.295*

The column headings indicate results for:

WCRO Information content of WCAP over ROI
NQRO Information content of NETQ over ROI
ROWC Information content of RQI over WCAP
NQWC Information content of NETQ over WCAP
RONQ Information content of ROI over NETQ
WCNQ Information content of WCAP over NETQ

content would decline during such times.[6] One very simple way of looking for such a decline is to compare the rate of inflation, measured by the retail price index RPI, for each year with the goodness of fit of regression (2). The raw data for these regressions comes from column 1 of Table 1 which shows the rate of inflation, and the R^2 values resulting from the information content tests (i.e. the application of regression (2) to each of the earnings measures) which are reported in the remaining columns of Table 1 and, for incremental information content, in Table 4. The first panel of Table 4 shows summary results for regression of the form:

$$R^2_{Et} = a + b\,RPI_t \qquad (3)$$

where R^2_{Et} represents the appropriate R^2 value for a particular earnings figure in a particular year.[7]

Table 4
Time Series Tests

Dependent	*Constant*	*Slope*	R^2
ROI	0.154*	−0.276	0.025
WCAP	0.093*	−0.042	0.001
NETQ	0.046	−0.137	0.021
WCRO	0.046	0.565	0.004
NQRO	0.047	−0.172	0.077
ROWC	0.108	−0.222	0.013
NQWC	0.051	−0.150	0.048
RONQ	0.157	−0.322	0.043
WCNQ	0.097	−0.059	0.002

Significant at 5% level.

[6]Since HC is adversely affected by inflation, it would be expected that, in periods of high inflation, the link between reported earnings and abnormal returns would change. The nature of the change depends on the effect of inflation on expectations. Suppose inflation was perfectly anticipated and all companies were equally affected by inflation then both the slope coefficient and the R^2, our measure of the above link, would be unaffected by inflation. Since investors would simply divide all earnings figures by the inflation rate, the only effect would be a shift downwards of the intercept. If inflation was perfectly anticipated but the effect was not constant across companies, the cross-sectional nature of the regressions would be expected to produce a shift in the intercept (by the average effect of inflation) and also a change in the slope coefficient reflecting the differing effect of inflation on each company. The R^2 need not be affected, since the 'correct' forecast of future cash flows can still be made for each company. However, to the extent that inflation is unanticipated, its effect on earnings cannot be fully calculated *ex ante* and a decline in the goodness of fit of the earnings/excess returns relation would be expected. In the extreme case in which inflation is completely unexpected and its effect on individual companies unknown, the reported HC earnings figure would yield no information and the effect of the announcement of such earnings would have no effect on share prices.

[7]Because we are interested in the relationship between the link between inflation and information content, the tests reported in Table 3 are based on 2 tailed tests. The null hypothesis is that the coefficients are significantly different to zero (either positive or negative).

We would expect the link between R^2_{ROIt} and RPI to be stronger than those between RPI and R^2_{WCAPt} or R^2_{NETQt}, because WCAP and NETQ, being cash flow measures, should be less sensitive to the effects of inflation than HC (if only because of the distortion induced by items such as HC depreciation, which are excluded from WCAP and NETQ). There is some indicative support for this hypothesis in that the link between inflation and earnings is strongest when earnings are measured by ROI and that in all cases there is a negative relation between inflation and information content. This relation is weakest for WCAP, the earnings definition which has information content as well as being based on cash flows. However, the effects are slight and not statistically significant. There is, therefore, no formal support for the hypothesis that inflation has a material effect on the information content of the various income numbers.

The second part of Table 4 shows the results of similar regressions in which the dependent variable is the R^2 value from the incremental information tests. Although the link between these figures and inflation is slightly greater, a statistically significant relation does not exist.[8]

VII. Direct time series tests

A more direct approach to the examination of the time series pattern of information content is to include time explicitly in the information content tests. This can be achieved either by addition of an inflation term to equation (2), or by modelling the effect of inflation on the slope and intercept of (2). The two approaches are shown in equations (4) and (5), the derivation of which is discussed in the appendix. Alternatively, a set of dummy variables could be used to capture time, rather than specific inflationary, effects. Such a model appears as equations (6) and (7) below.

$$CAR_{it} = a + bE_{it} + cEPI_t \quad (4)$$

$$CAR_{it} = a + bE_{it} + cRPI_t + dE_{it}RPI_t \quad (5)$$

$$CAR_{it} = \sum_{j=1}^{16} a_j D_{jt} + bE_{it} \quad (6)$$

$$CAR_{it} = \sum_{j=1}^{16} a_j D_{jt} + bE_{it} + dE_{it}RPI_t \quad (7)$$

The variables D_{jt} in (6) and (7) represent a set of sixteen dummy variables each taking the value 1 for each month in one of the sample years and 0 otherwise, and E_{it} represents one of the three earnings measures (ROI, WCAP or NETQ). Thus, in these models, the intercept is replaced by sixteen new variables. The appendix to this paper shows the derivation of these models.

The results are shown in Table 5. It is clear that there does seem to have been an important relation between stock returns and both inflation and published earnings. In the equations of model (4), both earnings and inflation have a positive effect on returns. When the cross product terms, $E_{it}RPI_t$, are included to allow for the indirect impact of inflation through its effect on earnings, it tends as expected to reduce returns. However, the lack of statistical significance on these coefficients means that firm conclusions should not be drawn from this.

When time is explicitly included through the series of dummy variables, the explanatory power of the regressions increases. The increased significance of the time variables, used in (6) and (7), over the simple RPI measure, used in (4) and (5),

[8]Inspection of the residuals from these regressions revealed some autocorrelation. However, when maximum likelihood procedure was used to control for this, no change in the pattern of the results was observed.

Table 5
Direct Time Series Tests

Model	*Earn*	*const*	*E*	*RPI*	*E.RPI*	*D*	R^2
(4)	ROI	−0.072*	2.232*	0.630*			0.097*
	WCAP	−0.079*	1.653*	0.676*			0.067*
	NETQ	−0.056*	0.208*	0.509*			0.020*
(5)	ROI	−0.072*	2.565*	0.622*	−3.166		0.097*
	WCAP	−0.079*	2.314*	0.653*	−5.953		0.070*
	NETQ	−0.055*	0.165	0.496*	0.352		0.020*
(6)	ROI		2.646*			6	0.157*
	WCAP		2.088*			8	0.129*
	NETQ		0.121			4	0.065*
(7)	ROI		3.210*		−5.137	6	0.158*
	WCAP		2.854*		−6.759	7	0.132*
	NETQ		0.070		0.450	4	0.065*

Significant at 1% level.
Column D indicates the number of dummy variables significant at 5% level.

suggests that the effect is not caused by inflation alone.[9]

VIII. Conclusions

In this paper we have examined the information, as reflected in stock market returns, contained in earnings figures based on historical costs and two measures of cash flow. No previous UK studies have examined changes in the information content of earnings figures over time. The results presented here compare data for the years 1961 to 1977. The results can be summarised as follows:

(a) There is considerable evidence of a consistent information content both in the traditional return on investment measure and in the working capital based measure of cash flow. There is no evidence of information content in the net cash assets earnings figures (section IV).

(b) There is some evidence that the return on investment figures yield more information than either of the others, and that the working capital measure is superior to the net cash assets measure (section V).

(c) There is little evidence that the information content of any of the earnings figures is substantially influenced by inflation. In particular, the historical cost values, which are most in error during inflation, do not appear to be regarded as more unreliable during inflationary than during non-inflationary periods.

(d) There is some evidence of a time effect on the information content of earnings measure, and this does not appear to be wholly caused by inflation. The causes of this effect deserve further investigation.

Although the findings of this study do not support the notion that historical cost earnings should be replaced (or indeed supplemented), it must be remembered that there are other uses to which published accounts may be put.[10] While it is beyond the scope of this paper to examine such aspects of cash flow accounting,[11] it is likely that the real value of cash flow information will be found in these areas.

Irrespective of the efficient markets hypothesis it is possible that, even if cash flow data are economically more meaningful than HC, investors will continue to base their decisions on HC. Empirically, this would mean that the dominance of cash flow over HC data would not be revealed. Possible reasons why investors may behave in this way are individuals are used to HC and, while it is still available, see no reason to change their behaviour especially as they are likely to believe that other investors, and thus the market, base their decisions upon HC earnings. Secondly, as dividend payouts are statutorily based upon HC earnings (realised profits calculated using the accruals convention), HC is seen as a more relevant basis for decision-making than cash flow measures.

[9]The significant dummy variables are shown in the following Table;

Year	65	66	67	68	69	70	71	72	73	74	75	76	77
ROI	*		*	*				*	*		*		
WCAP	*		*	*				*	*		*	*	*
NETQ	*					*	*		*				

[10]See, for example, the references in Carsberg and Page (1985).

[11]For a summary of this literature see Lee (1981).

References

Ball, R. and P. Brown (1968), 'An Empirical Evaluation of Accounting Income Numbers', *Journal of Accounting Research*, 7, pp. 300–323.

Ball R. and R. Watts (1972), 'Time Series Properties of Accounting Income', *Journal of Finance*, 27, pp. 663–682.

Beaver, R. L. and R. E. Dukes (1972), 'Interperiod Tax Allocation Earnings Expectations, and the Behavior of Security Prices', *Accounting Review*, 48, pp. 320–333.

Beaver, R. L., Lambert and Morse (1980), 'The Information Content of Security Prices', *Journal of Accounting and Economics*, 2, pp. 3–28.

Benston, G. and R. Watts (1978), unpublished working paper, *University of Rochester*.

Board, J. L. G. and M. Walker (1985), 'The Information Content of SSAP16 Earnings' in Carsberg, B. V. and Page, M. (eds), *Current Cost Accounting: the Benefits and the Costs*, Prentice Hall International.

Board, J. L. G., J. F. S. Day and M. Walker (1989), 'The Information Content of Unexpected Accounting Income, Funds Flow and Cash Flow', *Institute of Chartered Accountants in England and Wales*.

Brown, L., R. Hagerman, P. Griffin and M. Zmijewski (1987a) 'Security Analyst Superiority Relative to Univariate Time Series Models in Forecasting Quarterly Earnings', *Journal of Accounting and Economics*, pp. 61–87.

Brown, L., R. Hagerman, P. Griffin and M. Zmijewski (1987b), 'An Evaluation of Alternative Proxies for the Market's Assessment of Unexpected Earnings', *Journal of Accounting and Economics*, pp. 159–193.

Brown and Warner (1980), 'Measuring Security Price Performance', *Journal of Financial Economics*, 8, pp. 205–258.

Christie, A. (1987), 'On Cross Sectional Analysis in Accounting Research', *Journal of Accounting and Economics*, 9, pp. 231–258.

Christie, A., M. Kennelly, T. King and T. Shaeffer (1984), 'Testing for Information Content in the Presence of Multicollinearity', *Journal of Accounting and Economics*, 6, pp. 205–217.

Easton, P. (1985), 'Accounting Earnings and Security Valuation: Empirical Evidence on the Fundamental Links', *Journal of Accounting Research*, Supplement, pp 54–77.

Johnston (1983), *Econometric Methods*, Prentice Hall International.

Lee, T. A. (1981), 'Cash Flow Accounting and Corporate Financial Reporting' in M. Bromwich and A. Hopwood (eds), *Essays in British Accounting Research*, Pitman, pp. 63–78.

Watts, R. L. and J. L. Zimmerman (1986), *Positive Accounting Theory*, Prentice Hall International, Chapter 3, pp. 65–66.

White, H. (1980), 'A Heteroskedasticity-Consistent Covariance Matrix Estimator and a Direct Test for Heteroskedasticity', *Econometrica*, May, pp. 817–828.

Appendix

The time series formulation of section VII, and particularly of model (5), is obtained as follows. Assume that the basic relationship between abnormal returns and earnings used in sections IV to VI holds, i.e.

$$CAR_{it} = a_t + b_t E_{it} + u_{it} \quad \text{(A1)}$$

which applies cross-sectionally in each year.

Now assume that inflation has an indirect effect on CAR_{it} through its effect on a_t and b_t. Thus:

$$a_t = a_1 + RPI_t + v_{it} \quad \text{(A2)}$$

$$b_t = b_1 + b_2\, RPI_t + w_{it} \quad \text{(A3)}$$

This assumes that there are simple linear, but possibly differing, effects of RPI_{it} on a_t and b_t. Substituting (A2) and (A3) into (A1) yields:

$$CAR_{it} = a_1 + a_2 RPI_t + b_1 E_{it} + b_2 RPI_t E_{it} + w_{it} E_{it} + v_t + u_{it} \quad \text{(A4)}$$

In this, a_1, a_2, b_1 and b_2 can be readily identified with a, c, b and d in (5) above. However the final three terms cannot be directly associated with the residual from the estimated form of (5). This is because the use of ordinary least squares requires, among other things, that the residual terms be uncorrected with the explanatory variables (Johnston 1983). Clearly, as E_{it} appears both as an independent variable and in the residual, this requirement cannot be met.

The general problem of heteroskedasticity has been considered by White (1980), who suggests a method of adjusting the estimation method to yield consistent estimates of the coefficients' standard errors (the coefficient estimates themselves will, in any case, be unbiased). These estimation methods were applied in the regressions of (5), and the reported significance levels reflect the corrected standard errors. In the event, the correction made little difference to the 'naive' values, which suggests that the heteroskedasticity may not have been particularly severe in this case. Because the White procedure is a large sample method, errors in our rather small sample are likely to remain in the adjusted standard errors on which the results in Table 4 are based. However, given the marginal impact of the adjustments in this case, we have no reason to suspect that heteroskedasticity was at all severe in the present context.

Journal of Accounting Research
Vol. 23 No. 1 Spring 1985
Printed in U.S.A.

Using Operating Cash Flow Data to Predict Financial Distress: Some Extensions

CORNELIUS CASEY* AND NORMAN BARTCZAK†

1. *Introduction*

Recently, financial statement users and regulators of publicly reported financial accounting data have argued in favor of the disclosure of detailed information on firms' current operating cash flows (Harris et al. [1980], FASB [1981], Smith [1982], and Thomas [1982]). The FASB suggests that such disclosures will allow users to assess better the amount, timing, and uncertainty of future cash flows. It states that "the greater the amount of future net cash inflows from operations, the greater the ability of the enterprise to withstand adverse changes in operating conditions" [1981, p. 11]. The presumption that historical operating cash flows enable better assessments of future cash flows, however, is based on intuition rather than on empirical evidence (Griffin [1982]).

Our study was conducted to assess whether operating cash flow data and related measures lead to more accurate predictions of bankrupt and

* Associate Professor, Dartmouth College—the Editors of the *Journal of Accounting Research* were saddened to learn of the death of Professor Casey in October 1984; † Lecturer, Harvard University. The authors gratefully acknowledge the helpful comments of participants in accounting workshops at several universities. Suggestions made by E. Altman, P. Griffin, J. Horrigan, W. Mikkelson, T. Selling, J. Shank, C. Stickney, and P. Williamson are appreciated, as is the computing assistance rendered by D. Bower, S. Hare, D. Roberts, and G. Peterson. J. Ohlson kindly provided many of the financial statements for the bankrupt firms. Funding for this project was provided by the Tuck Associates, Dartmouth College, and the Division of Research, Harvard Business School. [Accepted for publication September 1984.]

nonbankrupt firms.[1] Recent studies (Gombola and Ketz [1983] and Gombola et al. [1983]) found that ratios based on operating cash flow load on a separate statistical factor, suggesting that operating cash flow variables may be useful in descriptive and predictive studies involving financial ratios. Our results suggest otherwise, at least with respect to bankruptcy prediction.

In another study (Casey and Bartczak [1984]) we reported that accrual-based multivariate discriminant models forecasted corporate bankruptcy more accurately than any single operating cash flow ratio. The focus of the present study is on the *marginal* predictive content of the operating cash flow ratios, in contrast to our previous study which examined their univariate predictive value. The poor performance of the operating cash flow ratios in the previous study does not preclude their ability to enhance predictive power when used in combination with accrual-based ratios. Previous accounting studies have been unable to document the existence of incremental information content in operating cash flow data (Bowen, Burgstahler, and Daley [1984]). Unlike the present study, these studies have used restrictive surrogates for measuring cash flow from operations, and thus the issue of whether operating cash flow data have incremental information value is unresolved.

In section 2 we review prior bankruptcy studies that have examined the potential usefulness of operating cash flow data. Section 3 describes the methodology employed in the present study, including selection of sample firms and analyses applied to the firms' accounting data. Results are presented in section 4, followed by some limitations of the study and possible directions for future related research in section 5.

2. *Previous Research*

Most accounting and finance studies of corporate financial distress define "cash flow" as net income plus nonworking capital expenses, so they omit items such as changes in current assets and current liabilities which may have a significant impact on a company's actual cash flow from operations. This has led to suggestions for broader measures of cash flows (e.g., Largay and Stickney [1980] and Gombola and Ketz [1983]). Our definition of cash flow from operations (*CFO*) is essentially the same

[1] Bankruptcy was selected as the specific form of financial distress and as the criterion event for three primary reasons: (1) the direct and indirect costs of bankruptcy are significant in relation to the value of the firm (Altman [1983*a*]): (2) results from this study can be compared with previous studies of bankruptcy prediction; (3) the costs of data gathering and the problem of interpreting the economic significance of other events (e.g., loan default) were viewed as greater than the benefits of using events whose occurrences are arguably less subject to noneconomic factors than is bankruptcy. Thus, while bankruptcy prediction per se is not the main focus of this study, bankruptcy is nonetheless a convenient event for assessing one aspect of the information value of operating cash flow data.

as theirs: working capital provided by operations, plus or minus changes in the noncash working capital accounts except for short-term indebtedness (seasonal bank loans, nontrade notes payable, and the current portion of long-term debt). This concept of operating cash flow is also consistent with the recent FASB *Exposure Draft* [1981].

Empirical research on the relationship between *CFO* and financial distress has provided only limited evidence that such data are useful in discriminating between troubled and healthy firms (table 1). None of the studies listed there was validated using separate holdout samples of bankrupt companies. Moreover, the proportion of failed firms in all of the studies except that of Largay and Stickney [1980], which involved only one company, was close to or equal to 50%. This is likely to lead to artificially low overall error rates (Deakin [1977]).[2]

Some basic differences between our study and those of previous studies are: (1) a focus on the potential *marginal* improvement in classification accuracy using *CFO*; (2) a larger number of sample firms and a smaller proportion of failed firms; (3) a validation of the results based on a holdout sample; (4) a preliminary canonical correlation analysis of the amount of variance in the operating cash flow ratios already accounted for by accrual-based ratios; and (5) the inclusion of first-order interactions between the operating cash flow and accrual-based ratios.

The expectation of the FASB (and others) that the level of operating cash flow will serve as a useful indicator of the likelihood of financial distress does not derive from any formal theory. It is merely consistent with an apparent shift in preference by many analysts to use cash flow data for assessing a firm's financial performance (Hawkins [1977]). The present study neither proposes nor tests any theory of the probability of financial distress. While such theories do exist (see Scott [1981] for a survey; also Emery and Cogger [1982]), no one theory is generally accepted (Ball and Foster [1982]) and none gives specific attention to our measure of operating cash flow.

3. *Method*

3.1 SAMPLE FIRMS

The sample firms are the same companies used in our previous study on operating cash flows (Casey and Bartczak [1984]). Sixty firms were selected that had petitioned for bankruptcy during the period 1971–82. The bankrupt firms were a subset of the 105 failed firms used in a previous study (Ohlson [1980]) and included firms listed by Dun and Bradstreet and the *Wall Street Journal Index*. Criteria for inclusion in

[2] Type II error is the classification of a nonfailed firm as failed; Type I error is the classification of a failed firm as nonfailed; overall error rate is a weighted combination of Type I and Type II error rates.

the present study were: (1) the stock of the company was publicly traded, and (2) at least five, and in some cases six, years of published financial statements were available prior to the failure date. The first criterion was imposed in order to undertake a related study involving market value data. The second allowed for the inclusion of a trend variable in the analyses. We also made sure that the data for the first year prior to failure were actually publicly available prior to the bankruptcy petition date (Ohlson [1980]) by requiring all audit opinions for the first year data to be dated prior to the bankruptcy petition date. The average time between the date of the financial statements for the first year prior to bankruptcy and the bankruptcy filing date was 11.6 months. This compares to 7.5 months in Altman's [1968] study and 13 months in Ohlson's [1980] study. Of course, a survival bias was unavoidably injected into the analysis as a result of the second criterion. In addition, complete financial statements for some firms were not available in our libraries, which further reduced the sample to 60 companies. The failed firms spanned a wide range of sizes and industry classifications.

A sample of 230 nonfailed firms was chosen from the *Compustat Industrial Tape*. The nonfailed firms were selected to match the industrial classifications of the failed firms, to the extent possible. Industry classification was controlled for explicitly rather than included as an independent variable for three reasons. First, the discriminatory power of industry membership was not an issue in the present study; rather, the focus was on the marginal information value of operating cash flow data relative to only other financial data. Second, many different industries were represented in the study which would have required numerous categorical independent variables, one for each industry. This would have seriously reduced our degrees of freedom in estimating the parameters of the statistical estimation models. Third, analysts are less inclined to make comparisons of ratio values across industries since they are generally aware that the distributions of ratios are frequently industry specific. Consequently, there is little loss of generalizability due to controlling explicitly for industry membership.

The firms were not matched on size, nor was size included as an independent variable, even though it has been found to be a significant discriminator in previous bankruptcy prediction research. Matching on size would have limited the generalizability of the study's findings to firms of equal size. More important, the discriminatory power of size was not an issue of particular interest in the present study. Finally, any potential dispersion resulting from not controlling for size was mitigated by the scaling effect inherent in the financial ratios used as independent variables.

The financial data for the nonfailed firms were taken from time periods contemporaneous with the failed firms. The sample size of 230 resulted from applying two selection criteria in addition to those used in selecting

TABLE 1

Empirical Studies of the Relationship Between CFO Variables and Financial Distress

Study	Number and Type of Firms	Time Period	Cash Flow Variables	Methods	Findings
Raja, Nosworthy, and Goureia [1980]	15 "growth" and 21 "problem" companies; categories defined by a commercial bank holding loans to these firms	Data from 1972 to 1978 used to construct models; only most recent year's classification results presented	*CFO*/Sales *CFO*/Total Assets *CFO*/Net Worth *CFO*/Total Debt Means of *CFO* ratios above Number of years of negative cash flow	Stepwise linear discriminant analysis No holdout sample Unpaired analysis	Error Rates Type I / Type II / Overall 21% / 35% / 28% Cash flow/total debt was the most significant univariate discriminator
Largay and Stickney [1980]	One firm only, the W. T. Grant Co.	1966 to 1974	*CFO* only	Comparisons of the levels and trends of *CFO* with other traditional financial statement ratios and W. T. Grant's stock price	*CFO* provided a more accurate and timely signal of W. T. Grant's impending failure than the other measures
Gentry, Newbold, and Whitford [1985]	35 failed and 35 nonfailed firms; failed firms located in *Compustat Annual Industrial Research File*	Data from specific three-year periods during 1970 to 1981 used to build models for individual firms; only most recent year's results presented based on (a) most recent year's data and (b) a three-year average	Total cash flow segmented into seven components: —operating flows —working capital flows —financial flows —investment flows —dividend flows —fixed coverage flows —other flows Each component is divided by total net cash flow. (The sum of operating and working capital flows equals *CFO*)	Three separate techniques: linear discriminant, probit, and logit analyses, with each analysis considering all cash flow variables simultaneously Paired analysis by size and industry classification No holdout sample, but rather a secondary sample of "weak" and "nonweak" companies as defined by various financial services	*MDA* classification accuracy and predicted probabilities of failure were marginally better than probit and logit analyses for original sample firms: *MDA Error Rates for Original Sample* (accounting data from one year prior to failure) Type I / Type II / Overall 26% / 17% / 21% (accounting data based on a three-year average) 23% / 11% / 17% Best results for secondary sample were achieved with logit and probit analyses: *Logit Error Rates for Secondary Sample* (accounting data from one year prior to failure) 22% / 35% / 28% (accounting data based on a three-year average) 22% / 30% / 26%

Gombola et al. [1983]	52 failed and 52 nonfailed firms; failed firms taken from Dun and Bradstreet's *Business Failure Record*	Data from 1965 to 1977 used to construct individual models for each year; results presented for each of the most recent four years prior to failure	*CFO*/Sales *CFO*/Total Assets *CFO*/Total Debt [*CFO* is defined to include changes in current liabilities related to short-term financing activities]	Factor analysis applied to an independent set of firms' data taken from 1965 to 1977 in order to compute factor scores. Resulting factor scores used in linear discriminant and probit analyses No holdout sample Paired analysis by size and industry classification	*CFO* ratios load on a separate factor during 1973 to 1977 period Scores on *CFO* factor are significantly different between failed and nonfailed firms only in first year prior to failure during 1973 to 1977, and probit model is significant only for first year prior to failure Decrease in predictive accuracy upon deletion of *CFO* factor is not statistically significant

the bankrupt firms. First, firms with missing values on the *Compustat* tape were eliminated. Second, to control for a possible industry bias, nonfailed firms were randomly eliminated from those industries with disproportionately large numbers of firms relative to other industries in the sample. The resulting ratio of approximately four nonbankrupt firms to one bankrupt firm was also the median ratio of nonfailed firms to failed firms over all industries.

To avoid including nonfailed firms that might be viewed as near bankrupt, which could lessen the potential incremental discriminating power of the operating cash flow variables, we searched *Predicasts' F and S Index of Corporate Change* for the years 1971–82. Based on its review of multiple sources, this publication highlights significant company events, including unfavorable financial occurrences (e.g., omission of a preferred dividend). We established that none of the nonfailed firms was listed by *Predicasts* for any such reasons.

3.2 INDEPENDENT VARIABLES

The operating cash flow variables examined in this study were *CFO*, as previously defined, *CFO* divided by current liabilities, or *CFCL*, and *CFO* divided by total liabilities, or *CFTL*. Multivariate models (described below) that did not include operating cash flow ratios were employed as convenient standards for assessing the marginal discriminatory power of the operating cash flow variables. These models are identical to the accrual-based models employed in our previous study in which the related classification accuracy proved significantly greater than accuracy based on the univariate operating cash flow ratios (Casey and Bartczak [1984]).

CFO was selected for analysis because its supposed predictive value has been highlighted recently in the accounting literature and financial press more than any other measure of cash flow. *CFCL* and *CFTL* were included since *CFO* by itself abstracts from indebtedness, a factor which a priori is likely to be related to the occurrence of bankruptcy. Separate measures for current and total indebtedness were included, since it was not evident which measure was more likely to be related to bankruptcy, although technical insolvency (i.e., the inability to meet current obligations) has been cited as a frequent cause of formal bankruptcy declaration (Altman [1983*b*]). The multivariate models used as standards consisted of six ratios (hereafter, accrual-based ratios): cash/total assets, current assets/total assets, current assets/current liabilities, sales/current assets, net income/total assets, and total liabilities/owners' equity. These ratios have generated high loadings on orthogonal dimensions in previous studies (Chen and Shimerda [1981]). Each of the first five ratios also loaded highest on a statistical factor in a prior bankruptcy study (Libby [1975]).

3.3 ANALYSES

All analyses described in this and later sections were conducted both with and without outliers, where an outlier was defined as a company for which any ratio in any year was more than four standard deviations from its group mean. Because the vast majority of results were not affected significantly by inclusion or exclusion of outliers, results are presented for all 290 firms.

Canonical correlation analyses were first performed for each year on the two sets of six accrual-based and three operating cash flow ratios in order to ascertain their canonical roots and indices of redundancy. If the two sets of ratios were highly positively correlated, the value of an analysis of the marginal discriminatory power of the operating cash flow variables would be a moot point.[3]

Both linear multiple discriminant analysis *(MDA)* and conditional stepwise logit analyses were conducted for each year. We decided to employ linear as opposed to quadratic *MDA*, even though the variance/covariance matrices of financial ratios of the bankrupt and nonbankrupt firms were unequal (Box's F-test, $\alpha < .01$ for all analyses). We did so because previous research (Lachenbruch [1975]) has shown linear *MDA* to be robust to violations of this assumption, especially when large sample sizes are used (see also Altman, Haldeman, and Narayanan [1977] who found that linear *MDA* significantly outperformed quadratic *MDA*). Logit analysis was employed because of its frequently cited conceptual advantages relative to multiple discriminant analysis (e.g., Zavgren [1983]).

4. Results

4.1 MULTIPLE DISCRIMINANT ANALYSES (MDAs)

Eight *MDAs* were run using the Cooley and Lohnes [1971] program. Classifications were performed using a chi-square procedure, as well as one based on a Euclidean distance measure. The classification results were essentially insensitive to the choice of the classification procedure, so only the chi-square classifications are reported. The eight *MDA* models were run using the six accrual-based ratios alone and using the six ratios plus one or more of the operating cash flow ratios. For the first year prior to failure, the average annual first differences in the cash flow ratios for the preceding four years were also included.

Each of the *MDAs* was constructed with standardized, log-transformed ratios, using a proportionately stratified random sample of 50% of the total sample of 290 firms. Classification results were based on the 50% holdout sample. All discriminant analyses assumed equal prior probabilities of group membership. These assumptions are consistent with most previous studies. Moreover, using real-world-based prior probabilities of

[3] The first canonical roots were statistically significant (Bartlett's approximate chi-square, $\alpha < .01$) in all five years. A redundancy index, the equivalent of R^2 in multiple regression, was also computed for each year and indicated that the accrual-based ratios could explain no more than 30% of the variance in the set of operating cash flow ratios. This finding justified a further investigation of the potential marginal information value of the cash flow ratios.

bankruptcy and asymmetric loss functions has a canceling effect that has not led to improved results in previous bankruptcy studies (Altman [1983*b*]).

Because of statistically significant levels of multicollinearity in each year, no attempt was made to assess the relative contributions of the individual independent variables to their respective multivariate models. Multicollinearity aside, the value of such assessments is questionable at best and misleading at worst. A survey of previous bankruptcy studies (Altman [1983*b*]) indicates that the relative contribution of individual financial ratios is very sample specific.

All *MDA* models were statistically significant ($\alpha < .05$) for the first three years prior to bankruptcy. The univariate F-ratios for the operating cash flow variables did not exhibit a consistent pattern. *CFCL* was statistically significant ($\alpha < .05$) for the first three years, *CFTL* for the first two years, and *CFO* for the first, fourth, and fifth years prior to bankruptcy. The group means for *CFO*, *CFCL*, and *CFTL* are displayed in figure 1. None of the differences between group means of the average annual first differences in the operating cash flow variables was statistically significant.

The main issue here is whether a *marginal* increase in classification accuracy can be achieved by including operating cash flow ratios. Classification results by year for the *MDA* model based on the six accrual-based ratios alone and for the best performing *MDA* model that contained one or more cash flow ratios are presented in table 2.[4] Two observations can be made. First, classification accuracy was not improved by the addition of the operating cash flow variables, either in a practical or a statistically significant sense for the bankrupt, nonbankrupt, or total groups of firms. The reason was the high level of within-group dispersion on the operating cash flow ratios. Figure 2, which is representative of all five years, makes this clear. The exception was the fourth year prior to failure for the bankrupt group of firms, but this result was one of the few cases sensitive to the inclusion of outliers. When the outliers (17 nonbankrupt, 9 bankrupt firms) were removed, no significant differences in classification accuracy between models remained. Second, the results in terms of the level and trend of accuracy across years are generally consistent with the findings of previous bankruptcy studies. The relatively lower accuracy rates in the first year were probably caused by the use of "older" data for the first year for those firms whose most recently issued financial statements were unavailable prior to the date of the bankruptcy petition filing.

4.2 LOGIT ANALYSES

Several stepwise logistic regressions were run for each year based on the same ratios and a stratified random sampling procedure used in the

[4] Details of the results based on the other models are available upon request from the authors.

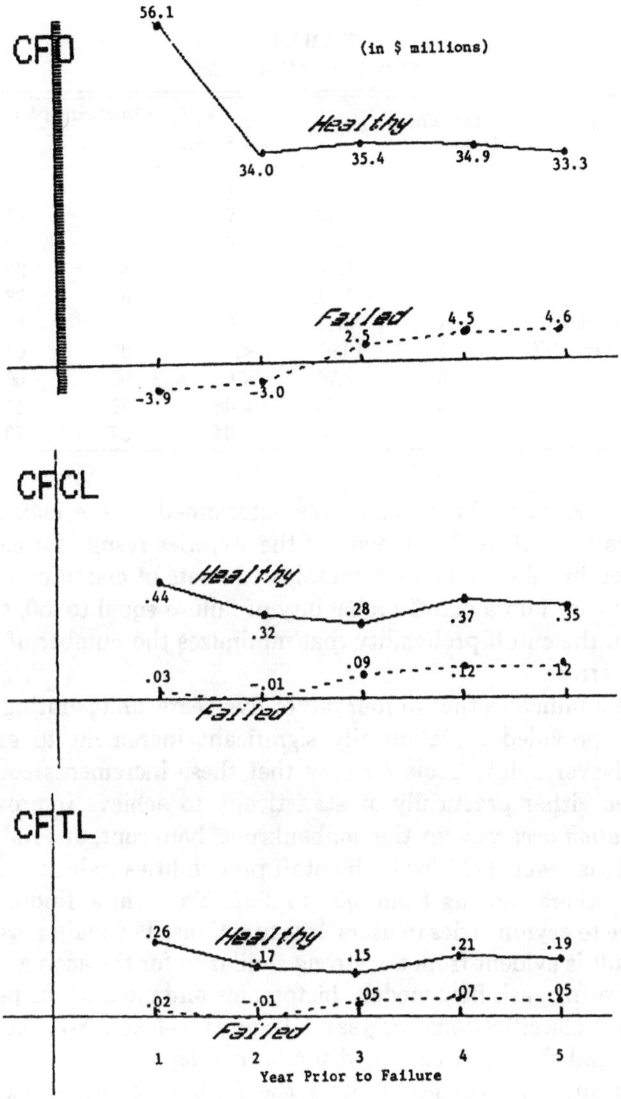

FIG. 1.—Means of healthy (nonbankrupt) and failed (bankrupt) firms.

MDA models. First-order interaction effects between the respective operating cash flow variable and the six accrual-based ratios were also allowed to enter the models. The results did not vary significantly across the logit models that incorporated one or more of the operating cash flow variables, so only the results for the marginally best-performing operating cash flow model and the accrual-based ratio model are shown here.

The "best-performing" operating cash flow model allowed entry of the six accrual-based ratios, the three operating cash flow ratios, and the interactions between *CFO* and *CFCL* and between *CFO* and *CFTL*, based on α-levels for entry and removal of variables of .10 and .20, respectively.

TABLE 2
Results for MDA Models

Model	Year Prior to Bankruptcy	F-Ratio	Critical α-Level (Rao's F-Test)	Classification Accuracy		Total
				Bankrupt	Nonbankrupt	
Six Accrual-Based Ratios Alone	1	10.34	<.01	87	83	86
	2	12.40	<.01	89	63	84
	3	4.31	<.01	90	57	84
	4	2.19	<.05	83	30	72
	5	1.34	<.25	58	73	61
Six Accrual-Based Ratios and *CFTL*	1	8.87	<.01	87	87	87
	2	10.97	<.01	87	67	83
	3	3.76	<.01	90	60	83
	4	1.98	<.06	76	47	70
	5	1.15	<.34	57	70	60

Entry or removal of a variable was determined by the maximum likelihood ratio method. A summary of the stepwise results for each year is presented in table 3. Table 4 contains two sets of classification results, the first based on a cutoff probability of failure equal to .50, the second based on the cutoff probability that minimizes the number of misclassification errors.

Table 3 indicates that in four out of five years, an operating cash flow variable provided a statistically significant increment to *explanatory power*. Nevertheless, table 4 shows that these increments could not be exploited either practically or statistically to achieve improvement in *classification accuracy* for the nonbankrupt, bankrupt, or total groups of firms. This result held for both cutoff probabilities indicated in table 4, and for others ranging from .008 to .992. Thus these findings are not sensitive to asymmetries in users' loss functions. The main reason behind this result is evident from the strong similarity for the accrual-based and the operating cash flow models' histograms and plots of the percentages of correct classifications for year 1 (figures 3–4 and 5–6, respectively). Years 2 and through 5 exhibited similar overlaps.

Our results are consistent with the findings of other studies (e.g., Kaplan and Urwitz [1979], Ohlson [1980], and Gentry, Newbold, and Whitford [1985]), which have found that *MDA* and either logistic or probit regression generate similar results, notwithstanding the assumed advantages of the latter. The findings support Ohlson's conclusions that "many 'reasonable' [statistical estimation] procedures will lead to results which will not differ too much" [1980, p. 129].

5. *Summary and Directions for Future Research*

This study provides evidence on whether operating cash flow data can increase the accuracy of accrual-based multiple discriminant and logit models to distinguish between bankrupt and nonbankrupt firms. Our

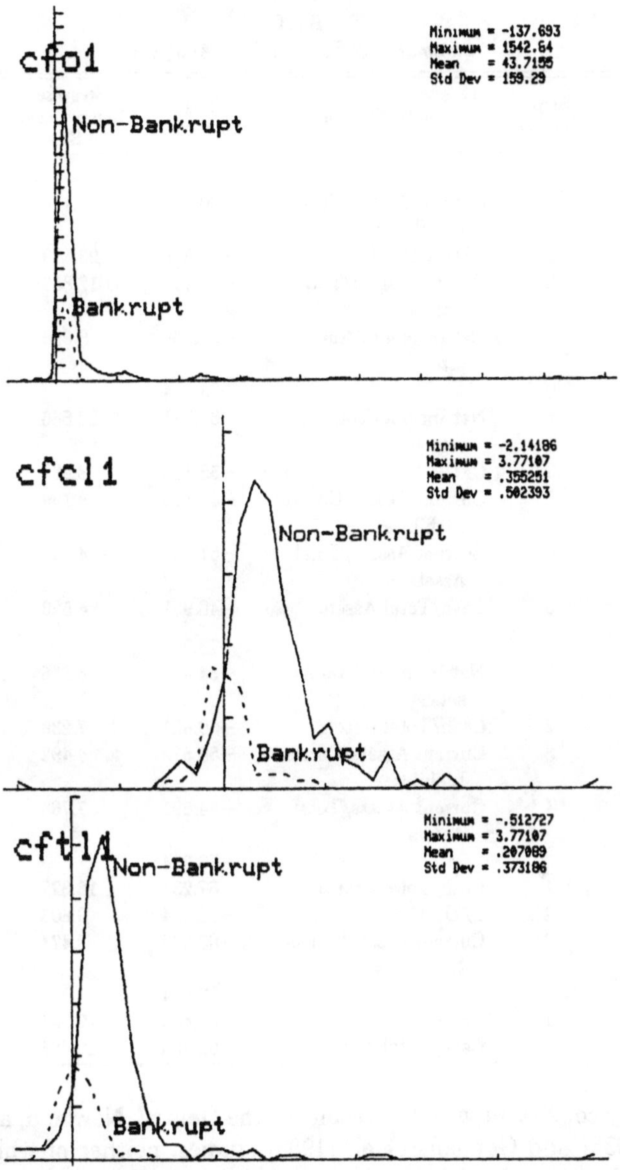

FIG. 2.—Distributions of operating cash flow variables one year prior to bankruptcy.

results suggest that operating cash flow data do not provide incremental predictive power over accrual-based ratios. Hence, the results fail to support the conclusion by some (e.g., Gombola et al. [1983]) that the omission of cash flow ratios in bankruptcy studies by Altman [1968] and others may have been inappropriate. These finding are consistent with those of our previous study (Casey and Bartczak [1984]) and are also

TABLE 3
Summaries of Stepwise Logit Analyses

Year	Step Number	Ratio Entered	Log Likelihood	Stepwise Improvement Chi-Square	Critical α-Level
1	0		−73.924		
	1	Current Assets/Current Liabilities	−60.368	27.110	0.000
	2	*CFO* × *CFCL*	−48.629	23.479	0.000
	3	Current Assets/Total Assets	−42.199	12.859	0.000
	4	Net Income/Total Assets	−37.366	9.666	0.002
2	0		−73.924		
	1	Net Income/Total Assets	−62.581	22.686	0.000
	2	*CFCL*	−58.113	8.935	0.003
	3	Current Assets/Current Liabilities	−53.514	9.199	0.002
	4	Current Assets/Total Assets	−51.211	4.605	0.032
	5	Cash/Total Assets	−48.951	4.520	0.034
3	0		−73.924		
	1	Net Income/Total Assets	−64.440	18.966	0.000
	2	Cash/Total Assets	−60.821	7.239	0.007
	3	Current Assets/Current Liabilities	−58.575	4.492	0.034
	4	Current Assets/Total Assets	−54.691	7.768	0.005
4	0		−73.924		
	1	Cash/Total Assets	−67.235	13.377	0.000
	2	*CFO*	−62.334	9.803	0.002
	3	Current Assets/Current Liabilities	−60.597	3.474	0.062
5	0		−73.924		
	1	*CFCL*	−67.432	12.984	0.000
	2	Cash/Total Assets	−62.189	10.486	0.001

generally consistent with the results of the Gentry, Newbold, and Whitford [1985] and Gombola et al. [1983] studies, neither of which found *CFO* to improve classification accuracy significantly.

Notwithstanding our findings, other possible uses of operating and nonoperating cash flow data should be explored. For example, operating cash flows may provide improved predictions of other events of interest—for example, corporate acquisitions, loan defaults, and dividend omissions. Similarly, a broader definition of cash flows, for example, total cash flows, might lead to improved classification accuracy.

No attempt was made in this study to explore the predictive ability of operating cash flow data when used in conjunction with nonfinancial

TABLE 4

Classification Accuracy of Stepwise Logit Models (%)

	INDEPENDENT VARIABLE SET*					
	Six Accrual-Based Ratios			Nine Ratios Including *CFO* *CFCL* *CFTL*		
Firm Category	NB	B	T	NB	B	T
Year Prior to Bankruptcy						
1	95	63	88	96	53	87
	95	63	88 (.50)	94	63	88 (.425)
2	95	40	84	96	40	84
	93	53	85 (.425)	97	37	85 (.608)
3	95	40	84	95	40	84
	98	37	86 (.542)	97	40	86 (.542)
4	98	20	82	95	40	84
	97	30	84 (.46)	96	40	84 (.50)
5	97	13	80	98	13	81
	100	10	81 (.575)	97	27	83 (.425)

* The first row of accuracy rates in each year is based on a cutoff probability of failure equal to .50. The second row of accuracy rates in each year is based on the cutoff probability which maximizes total classification accuracy.

```
        Histogram of Predicted Probabilities of Failure for
           Group Bankrupt Using Accrual-Based Ratios
         "M" Marks the Median, "Q" Marks the Quartiles

         X        XX      X          X                X X
  X      XX   X   XXX X   X X  X X X XX   X X    X   XXXXX
+----+-----+-----+--Q-+-----+-----+M---+-----+-----+Q-----+-----+
0          .17       .33       .50        .67        .83        1.0
```

```
   Histogram of Predicted Probabilities of Failure for Group Non-bankrupt
  Each "X" Represents 2 Responses, "*" Represents Fewer than 2 Responses
             "M" Marks the Median, "Q" Marks the Quartiles

*
X
X
XX
XX
XX
XX
XX
XX
XXX
XXXX
XXXX*X    *
XXXXXX * *X           *
XXXXXXXXXXX ***XX    *X*X* **  *      *        **  *
+QM--+---Q+-----+-----+-----+-----+-----+-----+-----+-----+-----+-----+
0        .17        .33        .50       .67        .83          1.0
```

FIG. 3.—Six accrual-based ratios.

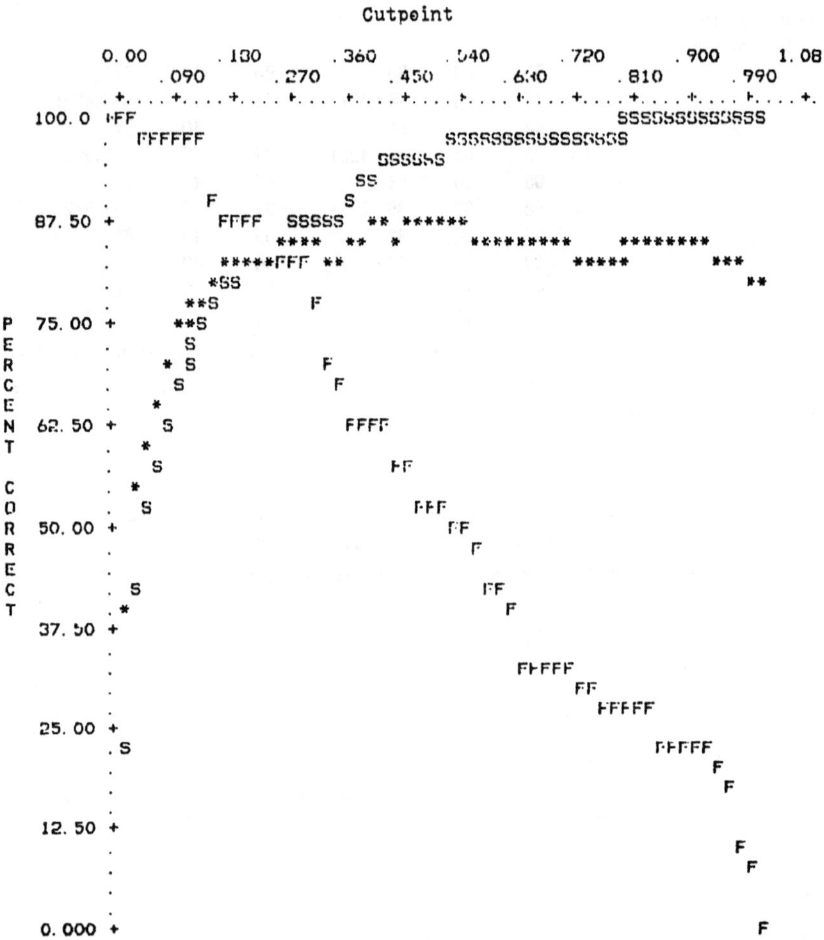

FIG. 4.—Percentage of correct classification as function of the cutpoint for accrual-based model. Plot characters are first characters of group names and * = total. F = failure (bankrupt) and S = success (nonbankrupt).

```
          Histogram of Predicted Probabilities of Failure
       for Group Bankrupt Using Operating Cash Flow Ratios

           "M" Marks the Median, "Q" Marks the Quartiles

                         X                  X     X  X                   X X
     X       X        X X XX    XX   XX     X X   X   XXXX XX X        X XXX
+----+-----+-----+-----Q-----+-----+-----+--M--+-----+Q----+-----+-----+
0          .17         .33         .50         .67         .83         1.0
```

```
           Histogram of Predicted Probabilities of Failure
                       for Group Non-bankrupt

Each "X" Represents 2 Responses, "*" Represents Fewer than 2 Responses
           "M" Marks the Median, "Q" Marks the Quartiles

*
X
X
X
X
X
X
X
X
X
X
X
X
X
X
X
X
X*
XX
XX
XX
XX*
XXX* *
XXXX X* *
XXXXXXX*XX X***X* X X *   *  *X     X      * *    X
QM---+-Q--+-----+-----+-----+-----+-----+-----+-----+-----+-----+-----+
0          .17         .33         .50         .67         .83         1.0
```

FIG. 5.—Nine ratios.

information, or with financial data other than the six ratios included in the multivariate empirical model. Thus, model misspecification could be an issue. Also, the specific characteristics of the operating cash flow variables examined in this study (i.e., their levels and interactions) by no means exhaust their total statistical properties. For example, Emery and Cogger [1982] posit the variance of total cash flows to be a significant determinant of a firm's viability. Future research might investigate the possible predictive ability of higher-order moments of the distributions of operating cash flow variables.

The time period studied here spanned more than a decade, and it is possible that the predictive ability in operating cash flow data varied over this period. Gombola et al. [1983] found that the coefficient attached

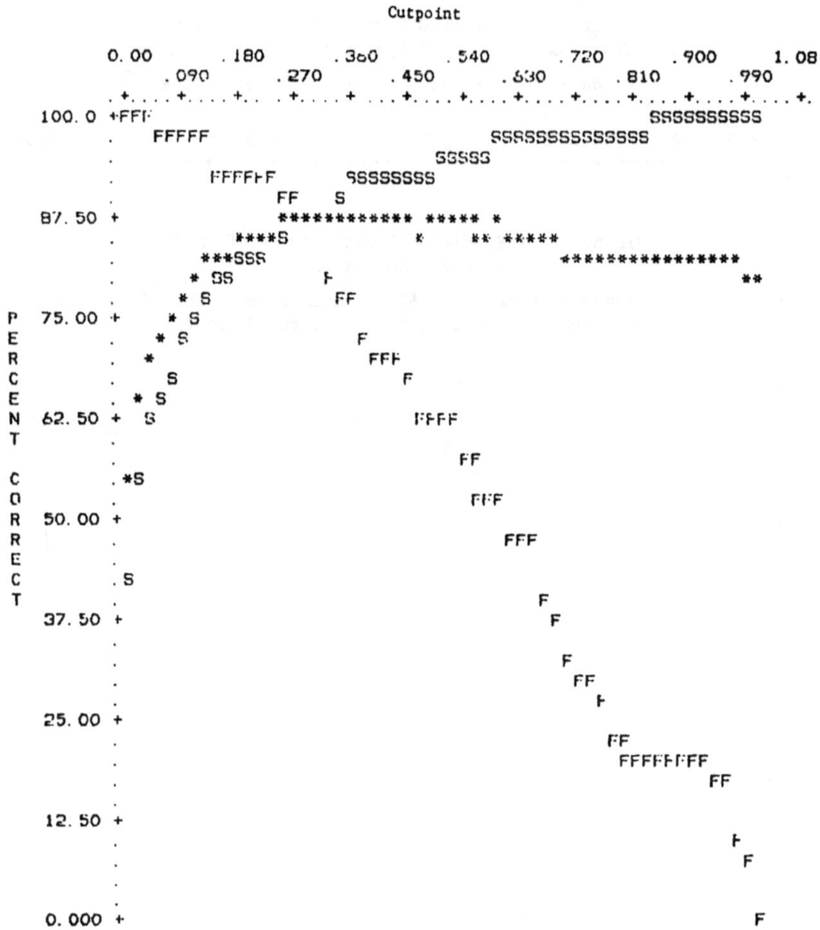

FIG. 6.—Percentage of correct classification as function of the cutpoint for operating cash flow model. Plot characters are first characters of group names and * = total. F = failure (bankrupt) and S = success (nonbankrupt).

to an operating cash flow factor score was statistically significant for the first year prior to failure during the period 1973 to 1977, but not prior to 1973.[5] Accordingly, research which investigates the potential sensitivity of this study's findings to variation in time periods might be useful.

[5] The practical significance and generalizability of this finding is unclear, since the authors did not validate their finding on an independent holdout sample.

REFERENCES

ALTMAN, E. I. "Financial Ratios, Discriminant Analysis, and the Prediction of Corporate Bankruptcy." *Journal of Finance* (September 1968): 589–609.

———. "A Further Empirical Investigation of the Bankruptcy Cost Question." *Journal of Finance* (1983*a*).

———. *Corporate Financial Distress.* New York: Wiley, 1983*b*.

———, R. HALDEMAN, AND P. NARAYANAN. "ZETA Analysis: A New Model to Identify Bankruptcy Risk of Corporations." *Journal of Banking and Finance* (June 1977): 29–54.

BALL, R., AND G. FOSTER. "Corporate Financial Reporting: A Methodological Review of Empirical Research." *Journal of Accounting Research* (Supplement 1982): 161–234.

BOWEN, R. M., D. BURGSTAHLER, AND L. DALEY. "Empirical Evidence on the Relationship Between Earnings, Cash Flow, and Cash Flow Surrogates." Working paper, University of Washington, June 1984.

CASEY, C., AND N. BARTCZAK. "Cash Flow—It's Not the Bottom Line." *Harvard Business Review* (July/August 1984): 60–66.

CHEN, K. H., AND T. A. SHIMERDA. "An Empirical Analysis of Useful Financial Ratios." *Financial Management* (Spring 1981): 51–60.

COOLEY, W. W., AND P. R. LOHNES. *Multivariate Data Analysis.* New York: Wiley, 1971.

DEAKIN, E. "Business Failure Prediction: An Empirical Analysis." In *Financial Crises: Institutions and Markets in a Fragile Environment,* edited by E. Altman and A. Sametz. New York: Wiley, 1977.

EMERY, G. W., AND K. O. COGGER. "The Measurement of Liquidity." *Journal of Accounting Research* (Autumn 1982, pt. I): 290–303.

FINANCIAL ACCOUNTING STANDARDS BOARD. *Reporting Income, Cash Flows and Financial Position of Business Enterprises: Exposure Draft.* Stamford, Conn.: FASB, 1981.

GENTRY, J. A., P. NEWBOLD, AND D. T. WHITFORD. "Classifying Bankrupt Firms with Funds Flow Components." *Journal of Accounting Research* (Spring 1985): 146–60.

GOMBOLA, M. J., AND J. E. KETZ. "A Note on Cash Flow and Classification Patterns of Financial Ratios." *The Accounting Review* (January 1983): 105–14.

GOMBOLA, M. J., ET AL. "Cash Flow as a Predictor of Failure." Working paper, Pennsylvania State University, July 1983.

GRIFFIN, P. A. *Usefulness to Investors and Creditors of Information Provided by Financial Reporting: A Review of Empirical Accounting Research.* Stamford, Conn.: FASB, 1982.

HARRIS, L., ET AL. *Study of the Attitudes Toward and an Assessment of the Financial Accounting Standards Board.* Stamford, Conn.: Financial Accounting Foundation, 1980.

HAWKINS, D. "Toward an Old Theory of Equity Valuation." *Financial Analysts Journal* (November/December 1977): 48–53.

KAPLAN, R. S., AND G. URWITZ. "Statistical Models of Bond Ratings: A Methodological Inquiry." *Journal of Business* 52, no. 2 (1979): 231–61.

LACHENBRUCH, P. A. *Discriminant Analysis.* New York: Hafner Press, 1975.

LARGAY, J. A., AND C. P. STICKNEY. "Cash Flows, Ratio Analysis and the W. T. Grant Company Bankruptcy." *Financial Analysts Journal* (July/August 1980): 51–54.

LIBBY, R. "The Use of Simulated Decision Makers in Information Evaluation." *The Accounting Review* (July 1975): 475–89.

OHLSON, J. A. "Financial Ratios and the Probabilistic Prediction of Bankruptcy." *Journal of Accounting Research* (Spring 1980): 109–31.

Predicasts' F & S Index of Corporate Change. Cleveland: Predicasts, 1971–82.

RAJA, A., M. NOSWORTHY, AND D. GOUREIA. "Diagnosis of Financial Health by Cash Flow Analysis." Working paper, London Business School, 1980.

SCOTT, J. "The Probability of Bankruptcy: A Comparison of Empirical Predictions and Theoretical Models." *Journal of Banking and Finance* 5 (1981): 317–44.

SMITH, R. "Cash Flow Adequacy." *Standard and Poor's Creditweek* (November 8, 1982): 445–46.

THOMAS, B. "Reporting Cash Flow Information." *Journal of Accountancy* (November 1982): 98–103.

ZAVGREN, C. V. "Corporate Failure Prediction: The State of the Art." *Journal of Accounting Literature* (1983).

James A. Largay, III and Clyde P. Stickney

Cash Flows, Ratio Analysis and the W.T. Grant Company Bankruptcy

Although they surfaced as a gusher rather than a trickle, the problems that brought the W.T. Grant Company into bankruptcy and, ultimately, liquidation, did not develop overnight. Whereas traditional ratio analysis of Grant's financial statements would not have revealed the existence of many of the company's problems until 1970 or 1971, careful analysis of the company's cash flows would have revealed impending doom as much as a decade before the collapse.

Grant's profitability, turnover and liquidity ratios had trended downward over the 10 years preceding bankruptcy. But the most striking characteristic of the company during that decade was that it generated no cash internally. Although working capital provided by operations remained fairly stable through 1973, this figure (which constitutes net income plus depreciation and is frequently referred to in the financial press as "cash flow") can be a very poor indicator of a company's ability to generate cash. Through 1973, the W.T. Grant Company's operations were a net user, rather than provider, of cash.

Grant's continuing inability to generate cash from operations should have provided investors with an early signal of problems. Yet, as recently as 1973, Grant stock was selling at nearly 20 times earnings. Investors placed a much higher value on Grant's prospects than an analysis of the company's cash flow from operations would have warranted.

The W.T. Grant Company was the nation's largest retailer when it filed for protection of the Court under Chapter XI of the National Bankruptcy Act on October 2, 1975. Only four months later, the creditors' committee voted for liquidation, and Grant ceased to exist. The collapse of Grant is a business policy professor's dream—ambiguous marketing strategy, personnel compensation based on questionable incentive schemes, financially and administratively unsound credit operations, centralization versus decentralization issues and poorly conceived and poorly executed long-range plans. Problems of this magnitude do not develop overnight, although they often surface as a gusher rather than a trickle.

As we will show, a traditional ratio analysis of Grant's financial statements would not have suggested the existence of many of these problems until approximately 1970 or 1971. As recently as 1973, Grant stock was selling at nearly 20 times earnings. Perhaps investors believed that Grant would continue to prosper despite many years of consistent but lackluster performance; after all, the company had been in existence since the turn of the century, paying dividends regularly from 1906 until August 27, 1974. But Grant's demise should not have come as a surprise to anyone following its fortunes closely; a careful analysis of the company's cash flows would have revealed the impending problems as much as a decade before the collapse.

James Largay is Professor of Accounting at the College of Business and Economics, Lehigh University. This article was written while he was Coopers & Lybrand Visiting Associate Professor of Accounting at The Amos Tuck School of Business Administration, Dartmouth College. Clyde Stickney is Associate Professor of Accounting at The Amos Tuck School of Business Administration, Dartmouth College.

The authors thank the Tuck Associates Program for its financial support.

Exhibit I W.T. Grant Company Stock Prices and Selected Ratios For the Fiscal Years Ending January 31, 1966 to 1975

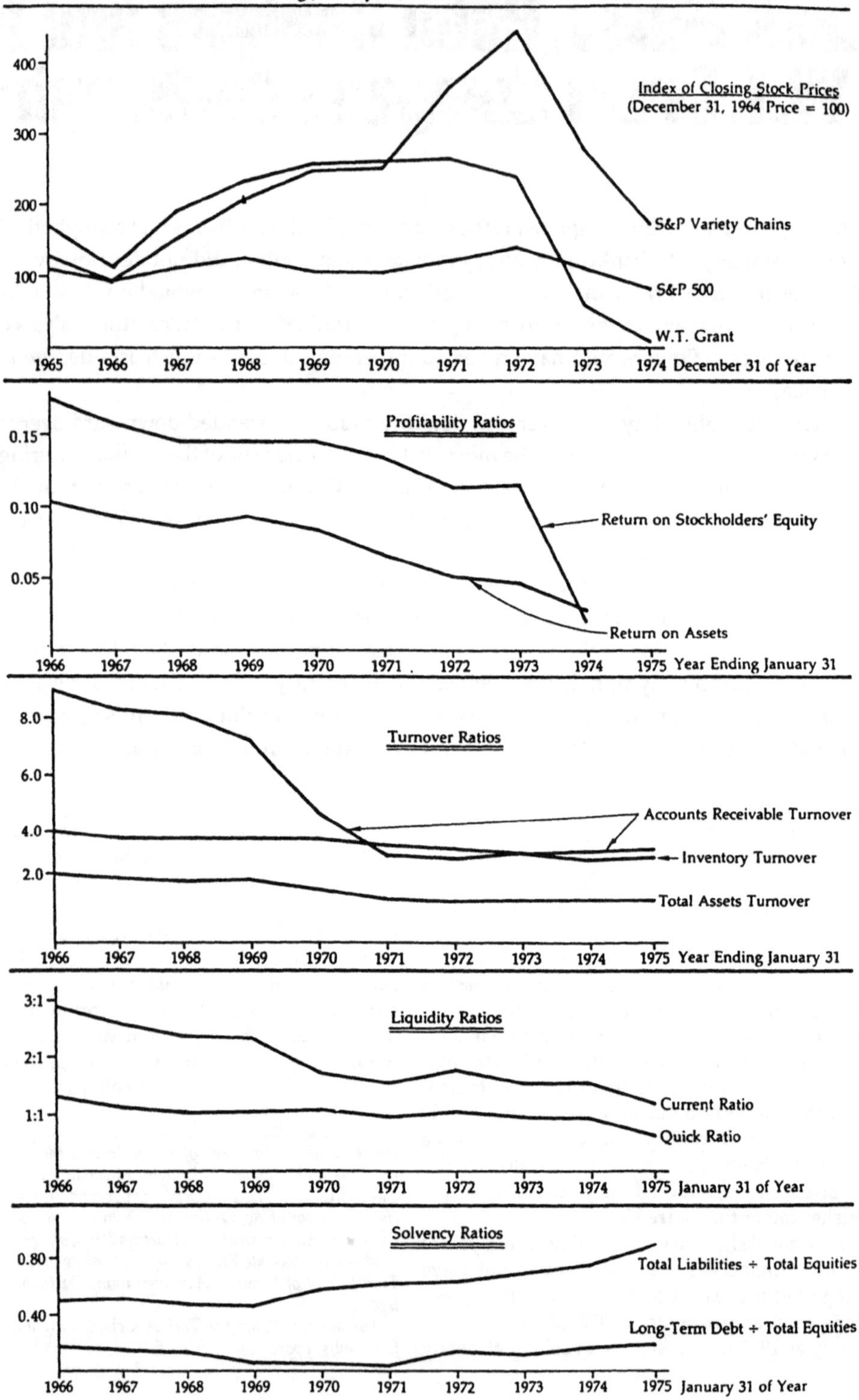

Stock Prices and Ratio Analysis

Prior to 1971, Grant's stock had tended to perform like other variety store chain stocks. Beginning in June or July of 1971, however, the stock price performance of Grant and the other variety chains parted ways.

Exhibit I presents data on monthly closing prices and various ratios from Grant's financial statements for the 10 years preceding bankruptcy in 1975. The top panel shows the December 31 closing price for Grant's stock for each year expressed as a ratio of the closing price on December 31, 1964 (i.e., the December 31, 1964 closing price equals 100). It also shows the values of the Standard & Poor's Variety Chain Stock Price Index and the Standard & Poor's 500 Composite Stock Price Index at the end of each year, each expressed as a ratio of its value on December 31, 1964.

The bottom four panels in Exhibit I show the trends in Grant's profitability, turnover, liquidity and solvency ratios over the fiscal periods between 1966 and 1975 (ending January 31 of each year). The profitability, turnover and liquidity ratios tended downward over this 10-year period. The solvency ratios reflect increasing proportions of liabilities in the capital structure. The most significant deterioration in these ratios, however, occurred during the 1970 and 1971 fiscal periods, leading the stock market's recognition of Grant's problems by approximately one year.

Net Income and Cash Flows

The most striking characteristic of the Grant Company during the decade before its bankruptcy was that it generated virtually no cash internally. The company simply lost its ability to derive cash from operations. After exhausting the possibilities of its liquid resources, it had to tap external markets for funds. As the failure to generate cash internally continued, the need for external financing snowballed.

Most textbooks in corporate finance, investments and financial statement analysis devote little attention to computing or using cash flow from operations. Yet the calculations are straightforward enough. One starts with working capital provided by operations from the statement of changes in financial position, adds changes in current asset accounts (other than cash) that decreased and current liability accounts that increased and subtracts changes in current asset accounts (other than cash) that increased and current liability accounts that decreased. In accounting terms, the calculation is equivalent to adding credit changes in working capital accounts and subtracting debit changes. Exhibit II summarizes the process of converting working capital provided by operations to cash flow provided by operations.

Exhibit III graphs Grant's net income, working capital provided by operations and cash flow provided by operations for the 1966 to 1975 fiscal periods. Note how poorly working capital provided by operations correlates with cash flow from operations. The financial press frequently refers to "cash flow," defined as net income plus depreciation. This measure of cash flow approximates working capital provided by operations, which (as Exhibit III shows) may prove a very poor surrogate for the cash flow actually generated by operations.

Exhibit II Computing Cash Flow Provided by Operations from Published Financial Statements

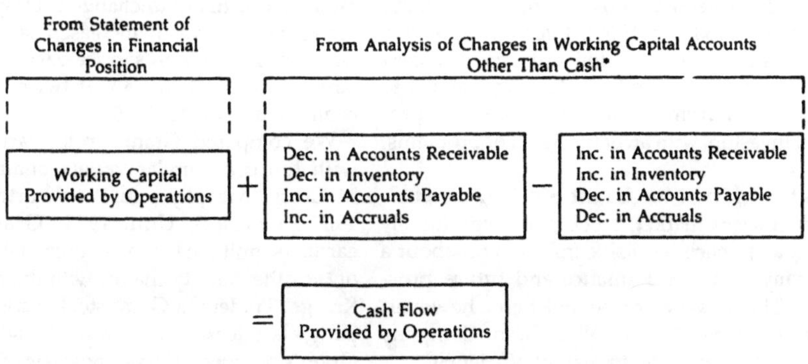

*Accounts such as "Bank Loans" and "Current Portion of Long-Term Debt" must be excluded from the analysis. Even though treated as current liabilities, they represent neither cash provided nor cash used by operations.

Exhibit III W.T. Grant Company Net Income, Working Capital and Cash Flow From Operations For Fiscal Years Ending January 31, 1966 to 1975

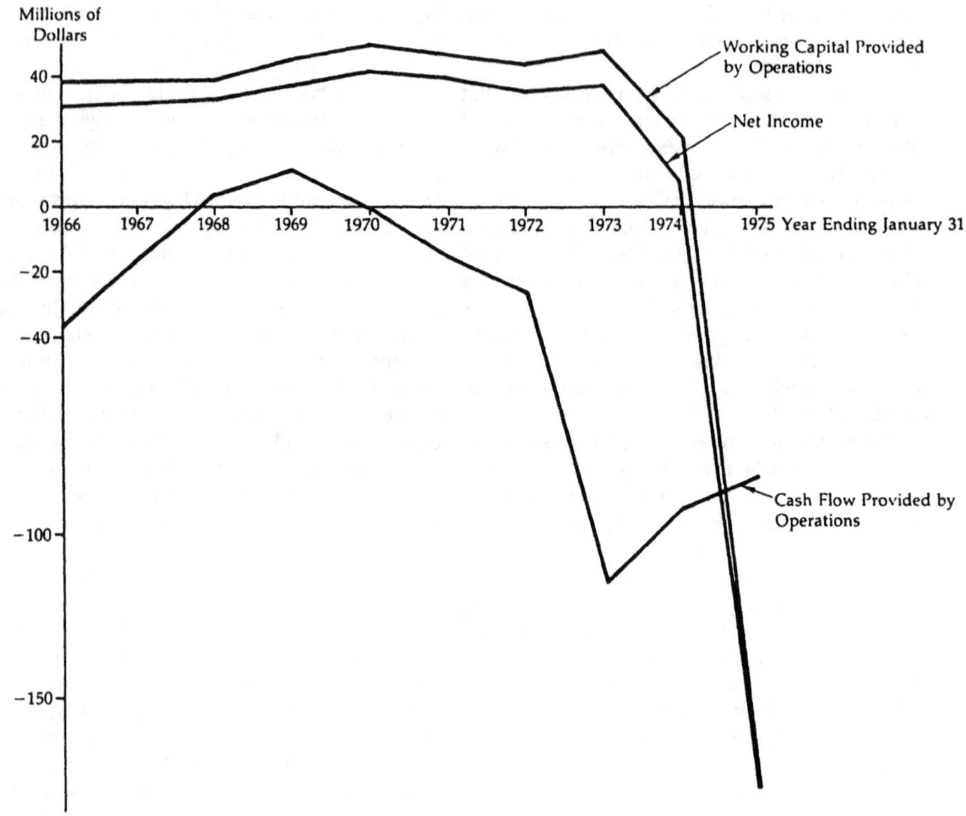

While Grant's net income was relatively steady through the 1973 period, operations were a net user, rather than provider, of cash in all but two years (1968 and 1969). Even in these two years, operations provided only insignificant amounts of cash. Grant's continuing inability to generate cash from operations should have provided investors with an early signal of problems.

Was the Market for Grant Stock Efficient?

In an efficient market, stock prices continually reflect all publicly available information about a company's past performance and future prospects. The evidence presented here, however, seems to suggest that the W.T. Grant Company was a counterexample to market efficiency.

Operations were a net user of cash in eight of Grant's last 10 years. Between January 31, 1966 and January 31, 1973, Grant's sales nearly doubled, but its earnings and earnings per share remained virtually unchanged. Despite its failure to translate vastly increased sales into additional profits, Grant's price-earnings ratio on January 31, 1973 was about twice what it had been on January 31, 1966.

We compared Grant's price-earnings ratios with those of similar variety chains (Kresge, McCrory, Murphy and Woolworth) over the 1965-75 period. Until 1973, Grant's price-earnings multiple tended to exceed the multiples of the other variety chains, with the exception of Kresge. Traders in Grant stock during the company's last decade placed a much higher value on Grant's prospects than an analysis of the company's cash flow from operations would have warranted. ■

4 The cash flow performance of U.K. companies[1]

G H Lawson
Professor of Business Finance, Manchester Business School

Introduction: Cash Flow Accounting and Summary of Aggregate Data Analysis

This section outlines the rudiments of cash flow accounting and summarizes aggregate data analysis that is reported in detail elsewhere.[2]

The historic cost accounting performance of quoted companies in the U.K. manufacturing sector during the period 1954 to 1976 can be juxtaposed with their cash flow performance as in Table 4.1.

Table 4.1 *U.K. quoted Manufacturing Companies: Weighted Average Profits and Weighted Average Cash Flows 1954 to 1976 (see note (i)).*

	Historic cost	*Cash flows*	
Pre-tax profit	690	407	Entity earnings (see note (ii))
less interest	97	97	*less* interest
Pre-tax profit	593	310	Pre-tax equity earnings
Tax @ 44%	260	260	Effective equity tax burden @ 84% (see note (iii))
Post-tax profit	333	50	Post-tax equity earnings
Dividends (40%)	133	133	Dividends (net of new equity capital)
		26	Liquidity change
Retained earnings	200	(109)	(Debt-financed deficit)

Notes

(i) 23-year averages of profits and cash flows initially restated at base-year prices.
(ii) Operating cash flow minus net capital investment (see identity (2), page 81).
(iii) The effective entity tax burden in this example is 64%, namely, 260/407.

1 I am grateful to Professor J. M. Samuels for his criticisms of the previous draft of this paper which is based on work at the Manchester Business School during 1979 for the Cash Flow Accounting Sub-Committee of The Association of Certified Accountants. The main burden of the individual company analysis reported was undertaken by Keith Thompson and Kian Chin (MBS). Financial support from the SSRC, The Esmée Fairbairn Charitable Trust and The Association of Certified Accountants is gratefully acknowledged.

2 See Lawson (1979).

As virtually all the conclusions which emerge from this paper are concerned with the deviation between pre-tax historic cost profit and entity earnings, it is as well to mention the two components of this deviation at the outset. They are: (a) periodic working capital investment, that is, periodic change in (receivables plus inventories less payables) and; (b) a depreciation shortfall equal to periodic capital investment (net of displacements) *minus* periodic depreciation (including accounting profits or losses on assets displaced). The customary objection that this definition of a depreciation shortfall ignores the unexhausted benefits of periodic capital expenditure is accommodated in the analysis which follows.

In emphasizing that Table 4.1 is a multiperiod caricature of aggregate performance, at least two further qualifications should be entered. First, the twelve months' average time-lag between the charging of corporate taxes and the payment thereof has been ignored in Table 4.1 in order to draw the possible decision-making consequences of the deviation between pre-tax profit and entity earnings into sharper focus. In all analysis which follows this time-lag has been explicitly taken into account.

Secondly, and more important, the effective equity and entity rates of tax on cash flow earnings defined by Table 4.1 are approximations which tend to *understate* the average multiperiod rates of tax on pre-tax equity and entity (cash flow) earnings respectively. Since this proposition has such profound implications from both a corporate and public policy standpoint, and is also pertinent to most of the findings reported here, the basis of the true effective rate of tax on both entity and equity cash flow earnings first needs to be described in detail. It should also be noted that if, as depicted by Table 4.1, dividends persistently exceed post-tax equity earnings, the effective equity tax rate will, typically, be lower than the effective entity tax rate. This follows from the definitions of effective tax rates that are derived later in this section.

Cash Flow Accounting: Cash Flow Statements Expressed in Money Terms

A total cash flow statement for any year j can be expressed as:

$$(k_j - h_j) \pm B_j \pm N_j \pm M_j \equiv (A_j + R_j - Y_j) + F_j + t_j + D_j \pm H_j \tag{1}$$

that is,

total cash inflows ≡ total cash outflows (including liquidity change)

where, in year j,

$k_j - h_j$ stands for operating cash flow, that is, cash, k_j, collected from customers *minus* cash, h_j, paid out to suppliers of all goods and services other than capital goods;

B_j is new capital received (+) from equity shareholders or repaid (−) thereto;
N_j is new medium/or long-term loans raised (+) or repaid (−);
M_j is the increase (+) or decrease (−) in bank overdrafts and/or short-term loans;
$A_j + R_j - Y_j$ represents net cash outlays on capital investment comprising replacements, A_j, growth investment, R_j, and displacements, Y_j;
F_j represents interest payments;
t_j is the corporate tax payment;
D_j is the dividend paid to shareholders; and,
H_j represents the increase (+) or decrease (−) in liquidity.

Any cash flow concept of periodic earnings must evidently be wholly, or partly, represented by some variant of the basic cash flow identity represented by (1) above. For example, re-arrangement of expression (1) gives

$$(k_j - h_j) - (A_j + R_j - Y_j) - t_j \mp H_j \equiv (F_j \mp N_j \mp M_j) + (D_j \mp B_j) \qquad (2)$$

that is,

operating cash flow	− net capital investment	− tax payments	∓ liquidity change	≡ lenders' cash flows	+ shareholders' cash flows

or,

periodic post-tax entity earnings[3] ≡ total distributions

Alternatively, and by analogy with the equity basis of accounting,

$$(k_j - h_j) - (A_j + R_j - Y_j) - F_j - t_j \mp H_j \equiv (D_j \mp B_j) \mp N_j \mp M_j \qquad (3)$$

that is,

periodic post-tax equity earnings adjusted for periodic liquidity change	≡	periodic shareholder cash flows	∓	periodic external debt transactions

For completeness, periodic equity cash flows, $D_j \mp B_j$, that is, dividends minus (or plus) equity capital raised (or repaid) may be defined as:

$$D_j \mp B_j \equiv (k_j - h_j) - (A_j + R_j - Y_j) - F_j - t_j \mp H_j \pm N_j \pm M_j \qquad (4)$$

Cash Flow Accounting: Rates of Return and Effective Tax Rates

Making use of the foregoing identities; the respective 23 year *ex post*

3 Periodic pre-tax entity earnings can obviously take on positive or negative values depending upon the sizes (and signs) of the operating cash flow, $k_j - h_j$, and net investment, $A_j + R_j - Y_j$.

(aggregate) equity (r_e), debt (r_d) and entity (r) rates of return for the period covered by Table 4.1, p. 79, namely, 1954–76, may be defined as:

$$V_{53}^{(e)} = \sum_{j=1}^{23} \frac{D_j \pm B_j}{(1+r_e)^j} + \frac{V_{76}^{(e)}}{(1+r_e)^{23}} \quad (5)$$

$$= \sum_{j=1}^{23} \frac{(k_j - h_j) - (A_j + R_j - Y_j) - F_j - t_j \mp H_j \pm N_j \pm M_j}{(1+r_e)^j} + \frac{V_{76}^{(e)}}{(1+r_e)^{23}} \quad (5a)$$

$$V_{53}^{(d)} = \sum_{j=1}^{23} \frac{F_j \pm N_j \pm M_j}{(1+r_d)^j} + \frac{V_{76}^{(d)}}{(1+r_d)^{23}} \quad (6)$$

and,

$$V_{53}^{(e)} + V_{53}^{(d)} = \sum_{j=1}^{23} \frac{(D_j \pm B_j) + (F_j \pm N_j \pm M_j)}{(1+r)^j} + \frac{V_{76}^{(e)} + V_{76}^{(d)}}{(1+r)^{23}} \quad (7)$$

$$= \sum_{j=1}^{23} \frac{(k_j - h_j) - (A_j + R_j - Y_j) - t_j \mp H_j}{(1+r)^j} + \frac{V_{76}^{(e)} + V_{76}^{(d)}}{(1+r)^{23}} \quad (7a)$$

where,

$$V_{53}^{(e)},\ V_{53}^{(d)}, \text{ and } V_{76}^{(e)},\ V_{76}^{(d)}$$

represent the end-year 1953 and end-year 1976 aggregate market values of equity and debt respectively.[4]

It follows from the previous five equations, which represent the universally acknowledged methods of calculating (observable) proprietorship rates of return, that the effective *ex post* rates of tax on entity and equity cash flow earnings (for the 23-year period in question) are defined by T and T_e in equations (8) and (9) respectively.

$$V_{53}^{(e)} + V_{53}^{(d)} = \sum_{j=1}^{23} \frac{[(k_j - h_j) - (A_j + R_j - Y_j) \mp H_j](1 - T)}{(1+r)^j} + \frac{V_{76}^{(e)} + V_{76}^{(d)}}{(1+r_e)^{23}} \quad (8)$$

4 The end-year 0 and end-year 23 entity values may be assumed to embody the unexhausted benefits of assets (and outstanding debt) at those respective year ends. This argument is developed at length in Lawson (1979). (See p. 83 *et seq.*).

$$V_{53}^{(e)} = \sum_{j=1}^{23} \frac{[(k_j - h_j) - (A_j + R_j - Y_j) - F_j \mp H_j \pm N_j \pm M_j](1 - T_e)}{(1 + r_e)^j} + \frac{V_{76}^{(e)}}{(1 + r_e)^{23}} \quad (9)$$

The entry and exit values, $V_{53}^{(e)}$ and $V_{76}^{(e)}$, can be regarded as 'net of tax' market values since they represent the (observable) present value of a taxed expected equity cash flow stream at end-years 53 and 76 respectively.[5]

Equation (8) can be re-written:

$$V_{53}^{(e)} + V_{53}^{(d)} = (1 - T) \sum_{j=1}^{23} \frac{(k_j - h_j) - (A_j + R_j - Y_j) \mp H_j}{(1 + r)^j} + \frac{V_{76}^{(e)} + V_{76}^{(d)}}{(1 + r)^{23}} \quad (8a)$$

Substituting $\sum_{j=1}^{23} [(k_j - h_j) - (A_j + R_j - Y_j) \mp H_j - t_j](1 + r)^{-j}$

for $V_{53}^{(e)} + V_{53}^{(d)} - \{V_{76}^{(e)} + V_{76}^{(d)}\}(1 + r)^{-23}$

$$T = \frac{\sum_{j=1}^{23} t_j(1 + r)^{-j}}{\sum_{j=1}^{23} [(k_j - h_j) - (A_j + R_j - Y_j) \mp H_j](1 + r)^{-j}} \quad (10)$$

5 Although not needed for the analysis which follows, the corresponding pre-tax entry and exit values may be defined as:

$$V_{53}^{(e)}/\{1 - \bar{T}_e^{(53)}\} \quad \text{and} \quad V_{76}^{(e)}/\{1 - \bar{T}_e^{(76)}\}$$

where $\bar{T}_e^{(53)}$ and $\bar{T}_e^{(76)}$ denote expected tax rates as at end-years 1953 and 1976 respectively. This proposition can be elaborated as follows. In the absence of taxes, the observable end-year 0 market value, P_0, of an expected perpetual income stream, $\bar{x}_1, \bar{x}_2, \ldots$, may be defined as:

$$P_0 = \sum_{j=1}^{n} \frac{\bar{x}_j}{(1 + \bar{r})^j} + \frac{\bar{P}_n}{(1 + \bar{r})^n} \text{ where } \bar{P}_n = \sum_{j=n+1}^{\infty} \frac{\bar{x}_j}{(1 + \bar{r})^j}$$

and $\bar{r}$ denotes a cost of capital that is commensurate with the risk characterizing the income stream in question. If the expected cash flows, $\bar{x}_j$, are now assumed to be taxable, the position changes to:

$$V_0 = \sum_{j=1}^{n} \frac{\bar{x}_j(1 - \bar{T})}{(1 + \bar{r})^j} + \frac{\bar{V}_n}{(1 + \bar{r})^n}$$

where, $V_0 = P_0(1 - \bar{T})$ and $\bar{V}_n = \bar{P}_n(1 - \bar{T})$ and $\bar{T}$ is the expected rate of tax.

Similarly, equation (9) can be re-written as:

$$V_{53}^{(e)} = (1 - T_e) \sum_{j=1}^{23} \frac{D_j \pm B_j + t_j}{(1 + r_e)^j} + \frac{V_{76}^{(e)}}{(1 + r_e)^{23}} \tag{9a}$$

which, after substituting $\sum_{j=1}^{23} (D_j \pm B_j)(1 + r_e)^{-j}$ for $V_{53}^{(e)} - V_{76}^{(e)}(1 + r_e)^{-23}$

yields

$$T_e = \frac{\sum_{j=1}^{23} t_j(1 + r_e)^{-j}}{\sum_{j=1}^{23} (D_j \pm B_j + t_j)(1 + r_e)^{-j}} \tag{11}$$

Generally speaking, the expressions for T and T_e that are defined by equations (10) and (11) are very accurately approximated by:

$$T = \frac{\sum_{j=1}^{23} t_j}{\sum_{j=1}^{23} [(k_j - h_j) - (A_j + R_j - Y_j) \mp H_j]} \tag{12}$$

and,

$$T_e = \frac{\sum_{j=1}^{23} t_j}{\sum_{j=1}^{23} (D_j + B_j + t_j)} \tag{13}$$

This is an important result[6] since it facilitates the calculation of T and T_e when, because of (sufficiently strong) multiple sign-changes, equations (8) and (9) yield multiple or indeterminate real values for r and r_e. In the latter

6 Its robustness can readily be tested by computing equations (10) and (11) for a large range of positive and negative values for r and r_e, respectively. The rare cases in which the values of T and T_e yielded by equations (12) and (13) do not accurately approximate the respective values yielded by (10) and (11) are due to multiple sign changes in cash flows which ultimately result in inconsistencies between the signs of the right-hand sides of equations (10) and (12) and between those of the right-hand sides of (11) and (13).

A clue as to why (12) and (13) are good approximations of (10) and (11) respectively, is to be found in equations (5a) and (7a). Using equation (7a); if $V_{53}^{(e)} + V_{53}^{(d)} = V_{76}^{(e)} + V_{76}^{(d)}$

circumstances, equations (10) and (11) can obviously not be solved for T and T_e.[7]

The effective tax rates T, T_e, of the companies whose performances are reported in this paper are, in fact, computed on two bases. First, as illustrated in Table 4.1 and, thereafter, in accordance with equations (12) and (13) respectively.[8] The tendency for the former method of calculation to understate the latter is ascribable to the fact that the cash flow earnings defined by Table 4.1 ignore periodic liquidity changes, $\pm H_j$. As indicated by equations (8) to (11) (inclusive), such changes should clearly be taken into account.

Aggregate Data: Analysis and Conclusions

If, as is indeed the case, Table 4.1 accurately reflects the main features of the 1954–76 financial performance and financial behaviour of U.K. manufacturing companies then, at this level of aggregation:

(i) effective interest covers were much lower than those perceived by lenders;
(ii) companies suffered enormous fiscal drag;
(iii) dividends were significantly uncovered; and,
(iv) the resultant deficit-financing by lenders caused a substantial increase in debt levels, i.e. debt-equity substitution has taken place.

Other things being equal, the substitution of debt for equity will result in an increase in the value of debt and, tax effects aside, an equal reduction in the market value of equity. The substantial decline in the (real) market value of equity that has taken place in the U.K. since April 1965 has not been offset by an equal increase in the market value of debt.[9] The debt-equity substitution argument therefore needs to be supplemented with something else, for example, a decline in the quality of entity earnings[10] and/or confiscatory taxation.

---

and if $\{(k_j - h_j) - (A_j + R_j - Y_j) \mp H_j\}$ and t_j are all constants then,

$$r = \frac{(k_j - h_j) - (A_j + R_j - Y_j) \mp H_j - t_j}{V_{53}^{(e)} + V_{53}^{(d)}}$$

$$= \frac{[(k_j - h_j) - (A_j + R_j - Y_j) \mp H_j](1 - T)}{V_{53}^{(e)} + V_{53}^{(d)}}$$

whence, $$T = \frac{t_j}{(k_j - h_j) - (A_j + R_j - Y_j) \mp H_j}$$

7 It may also be noted that since (12) and (13) are approximations for (10) and (11) respectively, T and T_e explicitly allow for the unexhausted benefits of capital expenditure.

8 See p. 95.

9 See Lawson and Stark (1981).

10 Lawson (1979).

The enormous deviations between the historic cost and cash flow magnitudes shown in Table 4.1 prompts one to question whether, like lenders, the British Treasury and company directorates, the market has also been fooled by the historic cost accounting model.

The time-series relationship between income gearing[11] and equity earnings on the one hand, and the behaviour of the de Zoete Equity Index (expressed in real terms) on the other, suggests that a combination of low equity earnings and high income gearing is, relatively speaking, usually associated with a low end-year equity index value and vice versa. This raised the presumption that the data may afford at least a rough-and-ready statistical test of the following semi-strong version of the efficient market hypothesis.[12]

In forming its expectations about future dividends, the market uncovers a company's past and current underlying cash flow situation and, using all other relevant known and knowable information, derives estimates of *ex ante* cash flows. This, in turn, leads to the determination of share prices.

To test this hypothesis, the following multiple regression (adaptive expectations) model was used:

$$EI_j = x_1 + x_2\ ECFE_j + x_3\ ECFE_{j-1} - x_4\ CV_{(j,j-3)} \qquad \text{(I)}$$

where,

EI_j denotes the (January 1) level of the de Zoete cost of living-adjusted equity price index for year j;

$ECFE_j$ denotes post-tax equity cash flow earnings as defined by Table 4.1 in year j;[13] and,

$CV_{(j,j-3)}$ represents the coefficient of variation of the past four years equity cash flow earnings about their four-year mean.

The previous year's *ECFE* is used as a proxy for the expected value of equity cash flow earnings estimated by the market in the individual year in question. The coefficient of variation, *CV*, is a proxy for the degree of risk which characterizes expected equity cash flow earnings which, in turn, may be assumed to be a function of the volatility of post-tax entity income and of the expected income gear ratio.

11 Interest divided by entity earnings (as defined in Table 4.1).

12 The test is rough-and-ready because aggregate data are basically unsuitable for the task. Thus, the accounts for each individual company included in the sample are for accounting years which end between 6 April of the year shown and 5 April in the following year. The aggregated accounts for the years shown therefore span a period of 24 months. For example, a company making up its accounts to 10 April 1954 would be included in the year 1954, as would a company reporting on a financial year ending 31 March 1955. Each individual sample year therefore includes accounts for the last nine months of the previous calendar year and for the first three months of the succeeding calendar year.

13 Whereas *EI* is the level of the index on 1 January, *ECFE* denotes earnings aggregated over a two-year period ending three months later (see previous footnote).

A trend in both the *EI* and *ECFE* series could give spurious correlation in the data and lead to misleading statistical results. To avoid this, the raw data were differenced[14] and the resultant series was used for statistical testing. Differencing does not change the model—the model indicates the change over the year which, together with last year's absolute figure, gives this year's actual value for the series.

In that the suggested model explains about 60 per cent of the movements in *EI*, it stands up quite well to the data. The results (using the backshift operator) are:

$$(1-B)EI_j = 3.142 + 0.0744(1-B)ECFE_j + 0.0385(1-B)ECFE_{j-1} - 19.15(1-B)CV_{(j,j-3)}$$

(st. errors)	0.0159	0.0163	15.13
(t ratio)	4.675	2.364	1.266

R-squared = 0.6012; Durbin-Watson statistic = 2.043;
Degrees of freedom 18–3; F test = 8.70.

Having established the model, it was further tested on random samples of the data points. The results were encouraging in that only the constant varied substantially (its range was 32 to −4) and the R-squared was always above 0.58.

The above cash flow hypothesis may be tested indirectly by regressing an equity price index expressed *in money terms* on the historic cost accounting variables corresponding to those included on the right-hand side of equation (I). Such a model is:

$$EI(\mathrm{m})_j = x_1 + x_2\, HCP_j + x_3\, HCP_{j-1} - x_4\, CV_{(j,j-3)} \qquad \text{(II)}$$

where,

$EI(\mathrm{m})_j$ denotes the level of de Zoete equity price index (on January 1) expressed in money terms for year j;

HCP_j stands for actual historic cost profit (i.e. not re-expressed at base year prices) for year j; and,

$CV_{(j,j-3)}$ represents the coefficient of variation of the past four years' historic cost profits about their four-year mean.

The results yielded by model II are counter-intuitive. That is to say, the signs preceding the second, third and fourth coefficients are the wrong way

14 Differencing means that the change in the series over the year is used instead of the absolute value. This is represented by the backshift operator, B, where $(1-B)X_j = X_j - X_{j-1}$, the difference over the year in series X_j.

about. They are:

$$(1-B)EI(m)_j = 106.94 - 0.085\,(1-B)HCP_j - 0.701\,(1-B)HCP_{j-1} + 777.02(1-B)CV_{(j,j-3)}$$

(st. errors)	0.1955	0.21404	1118.1
(t-values)	0.433	3.276	0.695

R-squared = 0.3162; Durbin-Watson statistic = 2.836;
Degrees of freedom 18 – 3; F test = 3.62.

It is tempting to conclude that cash-flow data re-expressed in terms of a base-year price level constitute highly relevant information for stock market investors, and that historic cost accounts *per se* are apparently ignored by the market whilst being taken seriously by lenders, company directorates and the tax authorities.

Analysis of Individual Company Data

As already noted, the relative orders of magnitude shown in the right-hand column of Table 4.1 reveal the weighted average cash flow performance of U.K. quoted manufacturing companies during 1954–76. The extent of the dispersion about this average across companies is clearly of interest. To reveal dispersion, the accounts of nine of the companies that are included in the F.T. 30 share index were restated on a multiperiod cash flow basis in both money and real terms. The companies selected and the inclusive years covered are:

Blue Circle	(1959–77)	Bowater	(1961–78)	John Brown	(1965–79)
Coats Patons	(1962–78)	Dunlop	(1960–78)	E.M.I.	(1961–78)
I.C.I.	(1961–78)	Plessey	(1963–79)	Tesco	(1960–79)

The analyses of their cash flows, restated at December 1978 prices, are summarized in Table 4.2.

To supplement the individual company (multiperiod) cash flow analyses, their annual (equity) market values were ascertained and, like the cash flows, restated at a base-year price level. The ultimate aim was the formulation of a multiple regression model which, it was hoped, would explain the serial behaviour of a company's equity market value in terms of its equity cash performance.

An indication of the behaviour of the total (real) market values (debt plus equity) of the nine companies over the respective observation periods is provided by Table 4.3, which also shows the real rates of return they generated for their lenders and shareholders.

Digression on the Specification Problem

In formulating a model that is intended to relate a company's stock market performance to its cash flow performance, at least two problems are

Table 4.2 *Average Annual Cash Flow Performance of 9 U.K. Companies Restated at December 1978 Prices*

	Bowater 1961/78 £m	John Brown 1965/79 £m	Coats Patons 1962/78 £m	Dunlop 1960/78 £m	E.M.I. 1961/78 £m	I.C.I. 1961/78 £m	Plessey 1963/79 £m	Tesco 1960/79 £m	Blue Circle 1959/77 £m	
1. Entity earnings	+21.98	+4.65	+38.97	+30.73	+ 4.79	+203.55	+15.07	+11.79	+26.73	$(k_j-h_j)-(A_j+R_j-Y_j)$
2. *Less* interest	−25.82	−2.74	−10.26	−26.31	− 8.97	− 84.94	− 8.30	− 0.08	− 6.82	F_j
3. Pre-tax equity earnings	− 3.84	+1.91	+28.71	+ 4.42	− 4.18	+118.61	+ 6.77	+11.71	+19.91	
4. Tax paid	−26.90	−2.60	−31.38	−32.89	−18.78	−169.78	−21.41	− 7.87	−19.83	t_j
5. Payments to minorities	− 2.14	−0.49	− 0.47	+ 1.42	− 1.19	− 0.22	+ 0.27	+ 0.18	− 1.19	
6. Post-tax equity earnings	−32.88	−1.18	− 3.14	−27.05	−24.15	− 51.39	−14.37	+ 4.02	− 1.11	
7. Dividend payments*	+ 8.26	−0.70	−12.28	− 1.41	+ 9.22	− 42.83	+ 7.04	− 1.87	− 7.01	$D_j \mp B_j$
8. Increase in cash	− 7.86	−1.72	− 0.51	− 3.27	− 3.58	− 67.72	− 1.73	− 2.75	− 2.65	H_j
9. Deficit(−) surplus(+)	−32.48	−3.60	−15.93	−31.73	−18.51	−161.94	− 9.06	− 0.60	−10.77	
Financed by:										
10. Bank overdraft	+12.82	+2.56	+ 7.85	+14.19	+ 4.06	+136.33	+ 5.06	+ 0.07	+ 3.13	M_j
11. Loan capital	+19.65	+1.07	+ 8.05	+17.55	+14.42	+ 25.66	+ 3.98	+ 0.53	+ 7.65	N_j

* Net of equity capital raised or repaid.

Table 4.3 *Market Values and Internal Rates of Return at December 1978 Prices*

	Opening values			*Closing values*			*Rates of Return*[1]		
	Debt	*Equity*	*Entity*	*Debt*	*Equity*	*Entity*	*Debt*[2]	*Equity*[3]	*Entity*
	£m	*£m*	*£m*	*£m*	*£m*	*£m*	%	%	%
Bowater	228	468	696	258	293	551	−5.3	− 5.4	− 5.2
John Brown	0	89	89	12	98	110	*	+ 1.6	+ 0.6
Coats Patons	27	460	487	57	203	260	−8.3	+ 3.0	− 2.4
Dunlop	87	224	311	236	103	339	−2.4	− 3.5	− 2.9
E.M.I.	17	179	196	146	156	302	−5.0	− 6.1	− 5.7
I.C.I.	281	3670	3951	750	2205	2955	−9.9	− 1.3	− 3.0
Plessey	61	230	291	56	195	251	−4.1	− 1.9	− 2.8
Tesco	1	10	10	10	221	231	−6.6	+18.5	+18.0
Blue Circle	8	416	424	86	202	288	−2.6	− 1.4	− 1.6

1. Computed in accordance with equations (5), (6) and (7).
2. Net of tax on interest payments at the rate of 23 per cent.
3. Net of tax on dividend payments at the standard rate of income tax.
* Indeterminate.

encountered which do not appear to arise in the analysis of aggregate data. The one problem concerns the unexhausted benefits of capital expenditure whereas the other relates to the distinction between portfolio risk and individual company risk.

Total Risk and Market Risk

Following the capital-asset pricing model, the total and market risks of the market portfolio (or some sensible proxy therefor) are synonymous. It is reasonable to measure multiperiod market portfolio risk with the (moving) coefficient of variation of its (cash flow) earnings stream (as illustrated by model I above, p. 86) which by definition will not include market value changes. Hence, if this coefficient of variation is seen to change over time, it is being assumed that portfolio risk is changing over time.

In the case of the individual company, the distinction between total risk and market risk is, according to the CAPM, of the essence. Thus, share prices will apparently only compensate for the risk which cannot be diversified away. Now in that a company's market risk (beta) coefficient is dimensionless, i.e. measured in relation to a normalized market portfolio risk of unity, a substantial change in the variance of the returns to the market portfolio may have little effect on a company's beta coefficient.

Recall the CAPM formulation of a company's (single-period) cost of capital, $\bar{r}_e$, namely:

$$\bar{r}_e = i + (\bar{r}_m - i)\beta_e$$

where (everything measured in real terms)

i is the single-period risk-free interest rate,
$\bar{r}_m$ is the expected one-period rate of return on the market portfolio, and,

β_e is the covariance of the rates of return on the market portfolio and company e divided by the variance of the expected rate of return on the market portfolio.

It would therefore appear that a change in the market portfolio risk will primarily affect an individual security's risk and, therefore, its price, by changing the magnitude of the excess return, $\bar{r}_m - i$. This mechanism would involve a change in the level of share prices in response to the market's view that earnings had undergone a quality change and, in turn, would, given the market portfolio expected earnings stream, result in a change in the expected rate of return on the market portfolio.

Whereas the derivation of 'moving' coefficients of variation from *ex post* market portfolio earnings data is realistic, the derivation of a sequence of excess returns, $r_m - i$, is not. Portfolio price adjustments in response to continuous serial changes (in the same direction) in portfolio earnings risk result in *ex post* periodic rates of return, r_m, which are seemingly perverse. Hence, *ex post* values of $r_m - i$ ought not to be used for proxying $\bar{r}_m - i$. A way around this problem does, however, suggest itself.

In that the expected excess, $\bar{r}_m - i$, is a function of market portfolio risk, the coefficient of variation of market portfolio earnings can reasonably be used as a proxy therefor. This still leaves the question of what to do about the company's beta coefficient itself. If betas are stable over time, there would appear to be no problem. Here we use the betas that are published by the London Business School (1979).

Unexhausted Benefits of Capital Expenditure

The unexpired benefits of capital expenditure are apparently ignored when, as in Table 4.1, equity cash flow earnings, $ECFE_j$, are defined either as:

$$ECFE_j = (k_j - h_j) - (A_j + R_j - Y_j) - F_j - t_j \text{ [15]}$$

or in accordance with identity (3), p. 81, *ante*.

The unexpired benefits of capital expenditure are expectations which can be assumed to be impounded in the market values of a company's debt and equity. In measuring multiperiod *ex post* performance on a cash flow basis the latter values should therefore be taken into account.[16] In using an adaptive expectations model to explain the serial relationship between cash flow performance and market value, growth capital expenditure, R_j, is an

15 These symbols were defined earlier in section 1.

16 As already noted, equations (5) to (9) (inclusive) exemplify rate of return calculations which account for the unexpired benefits of capital expenditure via entry and exit values. Corresponding absolute performance measures are elaborated in Lawson (1979), which contains a fuller discussion of the treatment of capital expenditure in cash flow accounting.

appropriate proxy for the effect on market value of the unexpired benefits of capital expenditure. Thus, it can be argued, replacement expenditure, A_j, is primarily intended to maintain existing earning power intact whereas growth expenditure creates additional earning power. If R_j is invested in new projects promising positive net present values, a company's market value will, in efficient stock markets, respond immediately thereto.

At the aggregate level, the distinction between A_j and R_j is possibly of much lesser importance because total capital expenditure is, under the effect of cross-section averaging, much more stable over time.

Individual Company Regression Model

In attempting to explain an individual company's share price behaviour in terms of its cash flow performance, whilst allowing for both risk and unexpired capital expenditure, models III and IV were used.

$$P_j = x_1 + x_2 ECFE_j + x_3 ECFE_{j-1} - x_4 CV^{(m)}_{(j,j-3)} \cdot \beta_e \pm x_5 H_j + x_6 R_j \qquad \text{(III)}$$

where,

P_j is the level of the company's share price in year j restated at a base-year price level;

$ECFE_j$ denotes the company's cash flow earnings for year j;

$CV^{(m)}_{(j,j-3)}$ represents the coefficient of variation of the past four years' 'market portfolio' equity earnings about their four-year mean;

β_e stands for the beta coefficient of the individual company in question;

H_j denotes change in the company's cash balance in year j; and

R_j represents the company's growth capital expenditure in year j which was in turn estimated from $A_j + R_j - 1.25\ L_j$, where L_j is the depreciation charge published in year j.

The results for I.C.I. derived from model III are:

variable	*coefficient*	*st. errors*	*t ratio*
$ECFE_j$	0.031	1.45	0.02
$ECFE_{j-1}$	−1.743	1.24	−1.40
$CV^{(m)}_{(j,j-3)}\beta_e$	−1.42	48.09	−2.98
H_j	−0.371	1.76	−0.211
R_j	0.462	1.30	0.357
constant	1713.8	116.94	14.655

R-squared 0.39; Durbin-Watson statistic 1.183
degrees of freedom 16; F test = 3.04.

These results show that only the constant and the coefficient of variation were significant and even then the R^2, Durbin-Watson and F-values suggest that their relevance may be slight.

As both $CV^{(m)}_{(j,j-3)}$ and P_j display trends that are strong enough to render the series unusable for statistical purposes, it was necessary to introduce a dummy variable (0 to 1972 and 1, thereafter) to cause P_j to be stationary. The H_j, $ECFE_j$ and R_j series are sufficiently stationary and need not be transformed. The results with the dummy variable were:

variable	*coefficient*	*st. errors*	*t ratio*
$ECFE_j$	0.588	1.23	0.48
$CV^{(m)}_{(j,j-3)}\beta_e$	−28.4	85.54	0.34
H_j	2.06	1.38	1.497
R_j	0.704	1.03	0.69
constant	1709.3	87.03	19.64
dummy	−764.6	246.35	3.104

R-squared 0.59; Durbin-Watson statistic 1.691.

These results represent no improvement and the $CV^{(m)}_{(j,j-3)}$ has become virtually unimportant.

Model IV was the same as model III except that $CV^{(m)}_{(j,j-3)}$ was replaced with the corresponding coefficient of variation for the individual company in question. In this case, all series were stationary except the P_j series itself.

As with model III, the regressions were tried with and without dummy variables in an attempt to reveal the effects of non-stationarity. The results are:

without dummy: *R*-squared = 0; Durbin-Watson statistic = 0.834; all *t*-values less than 1.

with dummy:

variable	*coefficient*	*st. errors*	*t ratio*
ECF_j	0.967	1.29	0.752
$CV^{(m)}_{(j,j-3)}\beta_e$	−0.312	14.33	0.022
H_j	1.427	1.22	1.165
R_j	0.857	1.12	0.765
constant	1719.0	116.21	14.792
dummy	−777.9	169.38	4.59

R-squared 0.60.

The low *t*-values indicate that the model is unusable in its present form. This being the case, it was not tested with the data for the other companies.

Alternative specifications are to be tried in the future. As there is a stronger visual correlation between the equity cash flows of individual companies and their equity market values than between the latter and historic cost profits, there is a presumption that the appropriate model will be a cash flow specification. But if any model is to provide a convincing explanation of the relationship between performance measured in accordance with some accounting method and stock market performance, it will need to take cognizance of post-tax earnings, risk and debt-equity substitution.

Financial Analysis of the Data

Interest Cover

The interest cover ratios (reflecting legal commitments to lenders) that may be derived from Table 4.2 show that, over the periods in question, effective interest covers fell well short of what is regarded as normality among lending institutions (see Table 4.4, below). To the extent that the decisions to lend to the nine companies in question were based on historic cost interest cover yardsticks, this outcome was virtually inevitable.

In that the stock appreciation tax reliefs that were introduced in November 1974 have lessened the pressure on corporate financial viability, the interest cover ratios that have emerged since that date are of particular significance. These are separately indicated in Table 4.4.

Table 4.4 *Interest Cover Ratios*

Inclusive years		*% of Interest Covered (see note)*	*% of Interest Covered since 1974*
1961–78	Bowater	85	159
1965–79	John Brown	170	280
1962–78	Coats Patons	380	482
1960–78	Dunlop	117	105
1961–78	E.M.I.	53	158
1961–78	I.C.I.	240	204
1963–79	Plessey	182	304
1960–79	Tesco	∞	∞
1959–79	Blue Circle	392	528

Note
Derived from Table 4.2 (row 1 divided by row 2).

In six of the nine cases, interest cover ratios have strengthened since 1974. Those of I.C.I. and Dunlop have deteriorated. Except for Coats Patons and Blue Circle, the post-1974 values shown in Table 4.4 are much lower than the conventional interest cover yardsticks derived from the published accounts. Moreover, as discussed in the concluding section, the joint effect of interest and tax commitments is the crucial consideration in assessing a company's financial viability.

Effective Tax Rates

As the analysis outlined at the beginning implies, (effective) corporate tax rates may reflect either equity or entity concepts of cash flow income. The equity approach treats interest payments as a tax-deductible expense and, holding clearly in view the legal nature of loan commitments, provides some indication of the effect of taxes on corporate financial viability.

Columns (2) and (3) of Table 4.5 show the average effective rates of tax (calculated in accordance with Table 4.1 and equation (13) respectively) on

Table 4.5 *Effective Rates of Tax on Equity Earnings*

				Since 1974	
(1) Inclusive years		*(2) (see note i)* %	*(3) (see note ii)* %	*(4) (see note iii)* %	*(5) (see note iv)* %
1961–78	Bowater	∞	144	177	109
1965–79	John Brown	136	79	16	1766
1962–78	Coats Patons	109	72	66	76
1960–78	Dunlop	744	96	1816	104
1961–78	E.M.I.	∞	196	282	140
1961–78	I.C.I.	143	80	146	94
1963–79	Plessey	316	149	91	89
1960–79	Tesco	67	81	51	59
1959–79	Blue Circle	100	74	53	71

Notes

(i) Computed in accordance with Table 4.1 and derived from Table 4.2 (row 4 ÷ row 3).

(ii) Computed in accordance with equation (13) and derived from Table 4.2 [row 4 ÷ (row 4 + row 7)].

(iii) Computed as in column (2) above using only the post-1974 data included in Table 4.2.

(iv) Computed as in column (3) above using only the post-1974 data included in Table 4.2.

the equity cash flow earnings of the nine companies in the sample for the inclusive years indicated in column (1). Columns (2) and (3) both suggest that the U.K. corporate tax system virtually confiscated equity earnings.[17] If so, dividends (net of new equity raised) could only have been paid out of new debt.

Although the tax burden on equity cash flows may have fallen slightly since 1974, it still appears to be confiscatory at the equity level in the cases of Bowater, Dunlop, E.M.I. and I.C.I.

It is arguable that if company cash flow performances are restated at a base-year price level, i.e. in real terms, the (gross) interest payments

17 In that all nine companies generated a significant proportion of their income abroad, this proposition should be qualified accordingly.

disclosed in Table 4.2 mainly represent the repayment of lenders' capital. Thus, leaving aside the fact that corporate debt is not risk free and that interest payments therefore embody a risk premium, corporate taxable capacity should, so the argument runs, be measured on an entity basis. There is, however, a counter-argument, namely, that an effective equity tax rate calculated in accordance with equation (11) fully allows for repayments of lenders' capital which amounts are reflected in share values.[18] Be this as it may, an entity concept of taxable capacity is justifiable in its own right. That is to say, an undertaking's taxable capacity ought to be independent of the manner in which that undertaking is financed.

The proposition that (gross) interest payments represent the repayment of lenders' capital should be qualified in respect of personal taxes. The evidence suggests that lenders shift their personal taxes forward into the interest rate.[19] If so, such taxes become a charge on entity earnings and should be added to corporate tax payments. Such an adjustment, using a 23 per cent personal tax rate, is included in Table 4.6.[20]

Table 4.6 *Effective Rates of Tax on Entity Earnings (Corporate Tax adjusted for Tax on Interest)*

				Since 1974	
(1) Inclusive years		*(2) (see note i)* %	*(3) (see note ii)* %	*(4) (see note iii)* %	*(5) (see note iv)* %
1961–78	Bowater	149	233	80	95
1965–79	John Brown	69	110	19	352
1962–78	Coats Patons	86	88	57	63
1960–78	Dunlop	127	142	105	143
1961–78	E.M.I.	435	1723	118	143
1961–78	I.C.I.	93	139	86	146
1963–79	Plessey	155	175	68	80
1960–79	Tesco	67	87	51	76
1959–79	Blue Circle	80	89	47	72

Notes

(i) Computed in accordance with Table 4.1, note (iii), and derived from Table 4.2, i.e., [row 4 + (0.23) (row 2)] ÷ row 1.

(ii) Computed in accordance with equation (12) and derived from Table 4.2, i.e., [row 4 + (0.23) (row 2)] ÷ (row 1 − row 8).

(iii) Computed as in column (2) above using only the post-1974 data included in Table 4.2.

(iv) Computed as in column (3) above using only the post-1974 data included in Table 4.2.

18 See Lawson (1979).

19 Stapleton and Burke (1978).

20 Judging from the evidence cited in Stapleton and Burke, 23 per cent is a conservative estimate of the tax shifted forward into interest rates.

The effective entity tax rates shown in columns (2) and (3) of Table 4.6 provide compelling evidence of the confiscatory character of the corporate tax regimes that have operated in the U.K. in the last two decades. Moreover, the values in columns (4) and (5) of this table strongly contradict the new conventional wisdom to the effect that the 1974 stock appreciation relief has roughly eliminated the effects of inflation on taxable earnings.[21]

In concluding this discussion of corporate taxes, reference is made to the popular view that the only corporation tax paid by companies is the advance corporation tax that is simultaneously payable with dividends. As Table 4.2 suggests, and as is confirmed by an examination of the individual years' data since 1974, the ACT paid by all nine companies has represented only a small fraction of their total corporate tax burdens.

Dividend Cover

A comparison of lines 6 and 7 in Table 4.2 suggests that Tesco alone succeeded in covering its average dividend payment over the years in question. The shareholders of Bowater, E.M.I. and Plessey were net cash flow contributors over the respective 18-, 18- and 17-year periods analysed. Assessing dividend cover on the assumption that 77 per cent of interest paid represented the repayment of lenders' capital, John Brown and Tesco covered their dividends from internally-generated finance.

In assessing the degree of debt-equity substitution that resulted from uncovered dividends, periodic liquidity changes are also a pertinent consideration. To the extent that periodic liquidity changes reflect transactions and precautionary motives, they constitute an investment (or disinvestment) of the same character as inventory changes. Like the unexhausted benefits of capital expenditure, inventories and cash balances can be assumed to be impounded in a company's market value. It may, therefore, be contended that liquidity changes should be accounted for in a multiperiod cash flow statement in much the same manner as capital investment. On this argument, all nine companies engaged in (dividend-induced) debt-equity substitution (on average every year) over the respective periods considered and, except for Tesco, whose average dividend was only 32 per cent debt-financed, wholly financed their dividends with debt.[22] If dividend policy is an active decision variable and is based on historic cost profits, such debt-equity substitution is the predictable outcome mentioned at the outset. Whilst the level of debt-raising was trivial in Tesco's case, the changes in the relative market values of debt and equity (shown in Table 4.3 above) are generally consistent with a signifi-

21 This view was recently reiterated by the Governor of the Bank of England (1979).

22 Treating 77 per cent of interest as the repayment of lenders' capital and taking dividends net of new equity raised.

cant degree of debt-equity substitution stemming from uncovered dividend payments.

Since 1974, the shareholders of Bowater, John Brown, Dunlop and E.M.I. have been net cash contributors and these companies have, on average, also raised debt in each year during the period. The dividends paid to the shareholders of Coats Patons, I.C.I., Plessey, Tesco and Blue Circle were debt-financed to the extent of 29, 100, 100, 41 and 89 per cent respectively.

Market Values

The entity market values of Bowater, Coats Patons, I.C.I., Plessey and Blue Circle declined in real terms over the periods considered. In the cases of Coats Patons, I.C.I. and Blue Circle real debt levels rose significantly causing a reverse leverage effect on their equity market values. The percentage declines in the latter were 28, 54 and 40 per cent for Coats Patons, I.C.I. and Blue Circle respectively. Notwithstanding net cash flow contributions from their respective shareholders, there were real declines in the market values of both debt and equity in the cases of Bowater and Plessey.

The real increase in the entity market value of E.M.I. must be qualified by the fact that its shareholders were net cash contributors over the 18 year observation period. Notwithstanding this equity cash injection, its equity market value declined by 13 per cent in real terms.

The entity market values of the three remaining companies, namely, John Brown, Dunlop and Tesco, increased in real terms. In the cases of John Brown and Tesco, the real market values of both debt and equity showed increases. In Dunlop's case, an increase in entity market value was associated with a 271 per cent increase in the market value of its debt and a 54 per cent decline in the market value of its equity which, in 1978, constituted 30 per cent of its total market value.

Taking cognizance of the debt ratios of Bowater, Dunlop and E.M.I., expressed on a market value basis, it is reasonable to question whether these companies may not be geared to precarious levels. Their debt levels constituted 47, 70 and 48 per cent of their respective entity values at their 1978 financial year ends.

Implicit in the foregoing paragraphs, and in the discussion in the earlier sections, is the proposition that (real) multiperiod cash flow analyses and (real) changes in market values are integrally related. Viewed on its own, the multiperiod cash flow analysis understates the financial performance of four of the companies in the sample and overstates it in the case of the other five. The degree of profitability achieved by the nine companies over the respective (roughly 18-year) periods considered is more decisively indicated by the real rates of return shown in Table 4.3 above. On these criteria, shareholders did slightly better than lenders, and only Tesco and John Brown were profitable as entities over the period as a whole.

Conclusions

It should finally be questioned whether the combination of interest and taxes that is borne by U.K. companies is a dangerous threat to their financial viability. Notwithstanding the obligation under debt contracts to pay interest payments which effectively provide for the return of lenders' capital *as a prior charge on equity cash flow earnings*, the interpretation of Table 4.2 represented by (row 1, minus 23 per cent of row 2, minus row 4), provides the most appropriate statement of corporate financial viability in a fundamental economic sense. Over the respective (roughly 18-year) observation periods, four companies, namely, Bowater, Dunlop, E.M.I., and Plessey were, judged by the latter criteria, not financially viable.

Since 1974 the position has improved. Only Dunlop and E.M.I. seem, on average, to have satisfied the above definition of corporate bankruptcy.[23] It is, however, noteworthy that both these companies generated positive pre-tax entity earnings in three of the four years between 1974 and 1978. Their annual averages for this four-year period were £39.2m and £23.45m respectively compared with the £30.73m and £4.79m shown in Table 4.2 (for periods of 19 and 18 years, respectively). It may therefore be concluded that the U.K. corporate tax system still lacks the inbuilt safeguards that would prevent it from converting financial viability into corporate bankruptcy.[24]

It must also be added that companies cannot rely on the possibility that lenders will always modify debt contracts in accordance with the above notion of 'corporate financial viability in a fundamental economic sense', and will usually be more impressed by lines 1 and 2 of Table 4.2. When gross interest payments exceed adjusted taxes, financial viability is obviously more stringently evaluated by this comparison.

There is also the point that taxable capacity is measured independently of cash flow interest cover. Thus, the combined, legally-enforceable, burden of interest and taxes may be potentially overwhelming in many cases in practice. If Table 4.4 (column 4) is anything to go by, this would appear to be true of Bowater, Dunlop, E.M.I., I.C.I. and Plessey. It says much (or little) for the U.K. lending mechanism that such companies do not encounter serious financial trouble.

Finally, one may question the implications of the results presented in this paper for the formation of expectations by businessmen. If, intuitively or

23 See Table 4.6, column (4).

24 As shown elsewhere (see Lawson (1979)), the U.K. system of corporation tax also increases the volatility of post-tax company earnings.

otherwise, businessmen are aware of the effect of a hostile fiscal environment on the returns to investment they will respond accordingly. There seems little point in examining the efficiency of the U.K. lending mechanism in seeking explanations for a low level of investment in circumstances in which dividends are habitually debt-financed because the returns to equity investment are confiscated by the tax system.

References

Henfrey, A. W., Albrecht, B. and Richards, P., 'The U.K. Stockmarket and the Efficient Market Model: A Review', *The Investment Analyst* (No. 48, 1977).

Ijiri, Y., 'Cash-Flow Accounting and Its Structure', *Journal of Accounting Auditing and Finance* (1978, No. 4).

Lawson, G. H., 'Accounting for financial management: some tentative proposals for a new blueprint' in Sir Robert Shone (ed.), *Problems of Investment*. Blackwell (1971).

Lawson, G. H. and Stark, A. W., 'The Concept of Profit for Fund Raising', *Accounting and Business Research* (Winter 1975).

Lawson, G. H., 'The Rationale of Cash Flow Accounting' in Cees van Dam (ed.), *Trends in Managerial and Financial Accounting*. Martinus Nijhoff, Leiden/Boston (1978).

Lawson, G. H., *Company profitability and the U.K. stock market—an exercise in cash flow accounting* (Manchester Business School, Research Report, March 1979).

Lee, T. A., 'A Case for Cash Flow Reporting', *Journal of Business Finance* (Summer 1972).

Lee, T. A., 'The cash flow accounting alternative for corporate financial reporting' in Cees van Dam (ed.), *Trends in managerial and financial accounting*. Martinus Nijhoff, Leiden/Boston (1978).

Lawson, G. H. and Stark, A. W., 'Equity values and inflation: dividends and debt financing' *Lloyds Bank Review* (January 1981, No. 138).

London Business School, *Risk Measurement Service*. LBS Financial Services (January–March 1979).

Richardson, G., The Rt. Hon., 'Companies, Inflation and Taxation', *Bank of England Quarterly Bulletin* (December 1979).

Stapleton, R. C. and Burke, C. M., *Tax Systems and Corporate Financing Policy*, Monograph Series in Finance and Economics, N.Y.U. (1978).

Funds Statements and Cash Flow Analysis

T. A. Lee, Professor of Accountancy and Finance University of Edinburgh

Companies fail because of lack of cash flow and cash resources. Although there be many reasons for this point being reached, the life of a company ends when its cash flow ceases, and its sources of cash disappear.

It is doubtful if many investment analysts would disagree with this conclusion, and presumably few would not be interested in receiving and using financial information relating to cash flow and cash resources. But recent research evidence suggests otherwise.

The Lee and Tweedie Studies

In a series of studies, Lee and Tweedie have sought to demonstrate that investors generally have a relatively small interest in reported information which would be helpful in assessing and predicting corporate liquidity. In 1975, for example, in a study of both private and institutional investors,[1] they found that only 16% of respondents indicated liquidity data to be the most significant part of annual financial statements. A later study in 1977 of private shareholders[2] revealed that only 7% of respondents classified liquidity data as particularly relevant to their investment needs. Indeed, 43% did not read the funds statement (which is arguably the single most valuable information source on liquidity matters). 18% read its content thoroughly, and it was typically classified as of slight importance.

Institutional investors were reported on similarly in 1981,[3] and the results were somewhat more encouraging. 67% of respondents read the funds statement thoroughly (although 7% failed to read it at all). It was generally considered to be of moderate to considerable importance in investment matters. But only 27% of respondents believed liquidity data to be particularly important; 7% predicted liquidity data; and an alarming 64% appeared to have no understanding of the content of funds statements.

Profit and Cash Flow

In all three studies, profitability and profit statements were the focal point for most investors. Thus, this general pattern of behaviour appears to ignore a vital and elementary financial lesson concerning the relationship between profits and cash flows.

Realised profit before depreciation (defined in terms of historic costs) is a product of two separable measurements – first, the operating cash flow (defined as operating cash receipts minus operating cash payments); and, second, the associated periodic change in working capital (defined restrictively in terms of stocks and work-in-progress plus debtors and minus creditors – each such item relating to operational receipts and payments, and debtors and creditors including prepayments and accruals, respectively). Thus, the conventionally reported profit can be described as operating cash flow ± the periodic change in working capital (+ if it is a decrease, and – if it is an increase). Alternatively, operating cash flow can be derived by netting the realised profit and working capital data.

Put more basically, operating cash flow can be seen to be an expression of the realised profit of a company after maintenance of its working capital at levels determined by its financial management. It is therefore a description of the cash flow which is available from its trading operations for purposes of such matters as capital expenditure (possibly including research and development), taxation, distribution, and borrowing repayments.

Investment analysts ought to be concerned to receive information not just about realised profits but also about the underlying operating cash flows – the former to inform him of corporate profitability and the latter to "fine tune" profits data in liquidity terms. A company, for example, will consume cash from realised profits whenever it increases its stocks or debtors, or decreases its creditors. Likewise, realised profits can be augmented by financial management which results in decreased stocks or debtors, or increased creditors.

Thus, operating cash flow is the product of the actions of financial management as well as profitable activity, and it is information about this which aids the investment analyst in assessing whether or not a company is viable in terms of *both* profitability and liquidity. The latter, particularly, is the key to corporate survival, although each interacts with the other. The problem with conventional corporate accounting and reporting is that related data are so articulated as to hide the liquidity information within the reported data on profitability.

For example, suppose realised profit before depreciation for a defined period is £560,000. When received, this figure can be related for analysis purposes to others such as capital employed, total assets, turnover, etc. in order to assess its quality and meaning by means of familiar ratios. But suppose also that, over the same period, stock has increased by £305,000, debtors by £211,000, and creditors by £100,000 (a net increase in these working capital items of £416,000). By definition, this means that the underlying operating cash flow is £560,000 – 416,000 or £144,000, a decidedly less inspiring figure in terms of the cash flow available to fund capital expenditure, taxation, dividends and borrowing repayments. Equally, if the change in the stated working capital items had been a net decrease of £416,000, the operating cash flow equivalent would have been nearly double the profit as £560,000 + 416,000 or £976,000. Both operating cash flow figures reflect the results of profitable operations coupled with financial management.

It is therefore being argued in this paper that the combination of profitability and liquidity data in this way provides the investment analyst with a view of both sides of the same coin when assessing corporate viability over time – business survival depending on both profits from operations and sound financial management. In addition, this approach to investment analysis has the considerable advantage of avoiding many of the subjective judgments involved in profit measurements which tend to cast doubt on the latter's reliability. The netting of profit and the working capital change negates all such judgements concerning the accounting for stocks and work-in-progress, debtors and prepayments, and creditors and accruals. If they exist in working capital, they must also exist in realised profit. Netting therefore cancels them, and leaves the investment analyst with objective cash flows.

The remainder of this paper is concerned to develop the above-mentioned points by introducing a method of cash flow analysis which is based on profit and related data, minimises the accounting problem of subjective judgment, provides needed information on the liquidity situation underlying profitability, and makes specific use of the funds statement. In fact, the latter document is the key to such analysis given the lack of reporting of actual cash flow information by companies.

Using the Funds Statement

Since 1975 in the UK,[4] the funds statement has become a familiar part of corporate financial reporting – the relevant provision being applicable to all companies with an annual turnover of £25,000 or more. The usual presentation format is the reconciliation of various sources of funds (such as profit before depreciation, share capital issues, and fixed asset disposal proceeds) with various uses of these funds (including capital expenditure, increases in working capital, and tax and dividend payments), and often balancing with movements in defined monetary resources or borrowings. Thus, a typical funds statement might appear in an annual report as follows:

Source of Funds	£	£
Trading profits after interest and depreciation		383,000
Add: adjustments for depreciation and other non-fund items		177,000
Funds from operations		560,000
Rights issue proceeds		100,000
Long-term loan		110,000
Investment grants		15,000
Disposal of fixed assets		16,000
		801,000
Application of Funds		
Capital expenditure		156,000
Increase in working capital:		
Stock and work-in-progress	305,000	
Debtors	211,000	
(Creditors)	(100,000)	
		416,000
Taxation paid		209,000
Dividends paid		168,000
Repayment of loan		30,000
		979,000
Increase in bank overdraft		178,000

The above financial statement contains much useful data for the investment analyst but arguably it is not in a form which easily aids his understanding of the liquidity position of the company as it has progressed over the period concerned. Much of the reported funds data are already in a cash form, and a modest rearrangement provides the analyst with information which is on a relatively pure cash basis. The steps involved in this rearrangement are as follows:

1. Net the funds from operations with the increase in working capital to obtain an operating cash flow for the period of £144,000 (£560,000 – 416,000). The profit and the working capital change would be added if the latter represented a decrease.

2. Net the flows for capital expenditure, asset disposals and investment grants to get the total net cash flow on new investment. For liquidity purposes, the analyst is concerned to know how much cash was spent by the company on the latter, and in this case the figure is £125,000 (£156,000 – 16,000 – 15,000).

3. Net the borrowing flows to obtain the aggregate change in total borrowing for the period as this will reflect the additional cash received or repaid by the company. The above funds statement reveals an aggregate additional borrowing of £258,000 (£178,000 + 110,000 – 30,000).

4. The remaining figures require no further adjustment usually, and are now available with those in 1, 2 and 3 above to produce a cash flow statement for the period which can be the basis for further analysis. It would take the following format:

Cash Inflows	**£**
Operating cash flow	144,000
Share capital	100,000
Additional borrowing	258,000
	502,000
Cash Outflows	**£**
Capital expenditure	125,000
Taxation paid	209,000
Dividends paid	168,000
	502,000

In this way, the detail of the funds statement has been reduced to a relatively few key datum, each expressed in cash terms, and devoid of subjective accounting practices. It reflects the contribution to the cash needs of the company from operations, shareholders, and lenders and bankers. In particular, it provides a cash flow-based portrayal of changes in the gearing of the company – by comparing operational cash flow and share capital issues with additional borrowing (in this case, £144,00 + £100,000 or £244,00 related to £258,000). In addition, the cash uses can be typically split between "plough back" expenditure in the form of new net investment (in this case, £125,000) and "distributional" payments such as tax and dividends (in this case, £209,000 + 168,000 or £377,000). In other words, the inflow section describes the company's reliance on internal and external generation of cash, and the outflow section also makes a similar distinction in terms of expenditure. In the above example, the company has required more external cash funding than could be generated internally. It has used a minority of the available cash on new investment.

Further Adjustments and Aggregations

It would be wrong for any analyst to judge the profitability and financial position of a company solely on the basis of an isolated year's results. To do so would be meaningless because it would not allow for comparability generally, and the assessment of trends particularly. The issue of liquidity analysis is no different. In fact, due to the inevitable lumpiness of cash flows (which conventional accounting sets out to defeat by smoothing practices), it is essential that the analyst examines cash flow data in the form of a multi-period trend analysis.

The length of these period aggregates will depend on what the analyst regards as a normal operational cycle for the company concerned. With retail concerns such as stores, a trend using single-year results may be perfectly adequate to detect long-term changes and movements. On the other hand, for a civil engineering contracting company, the use of four or five-year aggregates may be more appropriate if significant trends are to be spotted, and if the distortions of the cash results of individual years are to be avoided.

The first step in this process of meaningful aggregation prior to interpretation is to obtain the requisite number of years' cash flow results laid out as described in the previous section (that is, equating cash inflows with outflows). For example, assuming that the normal operating cycle of the company is judged to be three years (which would be a usual manufacturing situation), the following cash flow data have been prepared from available funds statements. In order to obtain a minimum of three multi-period aggregates, at least five years of individual results are required for example, 1978, 1979, 1980, 1981 and 1982 provide aggregates of 1978–9–80, 1979–80–1, and 1980–1–2. Four multi-period aggregates require six years of results.

Five aggregates need seven years; and so on. In this case, four three-year aggregates have been prepared from six sets of individual cash flow dȧta (in addition to a six-year summary):

	1977	*1978*	*1979*	*1980*	*1981*	*1982*	*Total*
Cash Inflows	£000	£000	£000	£000	£000	£000	£000
Operating cash flow	532	501	144	80	90	178	1,525
Share capital	—	—	100	—	—	—	100
Additional borrowing	50	113	258	306	365	49	1,141
	582	614	502	386	455	227	2,766
Cash Outflows							
Capital expenditure	222	214	125	138	267	105	1,071
Taxation paid	240	260	209	101	54	62	926
Dividends paid	120	140	168	147	134	60	769
	582	614	502	386	455	227	2,766

The above single period results are reduced in the first instance to three-year "rolling" totals:

	1977–9	*1978–80*	*1979–81*	*1980–2*	*1977–82*
Cash Inflows	£000	£000	£000	£000	£000
Operating cash flow	1,177	725	314	348	1,525
Share capital	100	100	100	—	100
Additional borrowing	421	677	929	720	1,141
	1,698	1,502	1,343	1,068	2,766
Cash Outflows					
Capital expenditure	561	477	530	510	1,071
Taxation paid	709	570	364	217	926
Dividends paid	428	455	449	341	769
	1,698	1,502	1,343	1,068	2,766

And these data can be further reduced to a simpler form by conversion to percentages of the total flow for each multi-period aggregate:

	1977–9	*1978–80*	*1979–81*	*1980–2*	*1977–82*
Cash Inflows	%	%	%	%	%
Operating cash flow	69	48	24	33	55
Share capital	6	7	7	—	4
Additional borrowing	25	45	69	67	41
	100	100	100	100	100
Cash Outflows					
Capital expenditure	33	32	39	48	39
Taxation paid	42	38	27	20	33
Dividends paid	25	30	34	32	28
	100	100	100	100	100

The analyst has thus reduced the relevant data to manageable proportions which can be updated as each new year's results are received – that is, when the results for 1983 are available, those for 1977 could be left out of the analysis.

Interpreting Cash Flow Data

Producing cash flow data from funds statement, and aggregating them into multi-period totals, are only first steps in the direction of assessing corporate liquidity. The next stage is to take the data and interpret them within the context of the particular company and the other available sources of information about it. Interpretation in this context is not a matter where specific rules or guidelines can be laid down. Much depends on the expert judgment of the analyst but general principles can be stated:

1. Companies with liquidity problems will tend to be those with a diminishing operating cash flow contribution, and increasing reliance on external funding such as additional borrowing. In other words, a failing company is one which is not generating sufficient cash flow from its realised profits in the long-term. This may be due to inadequate profitability, and this can be best judged through conventional profit-based analyses using profit margins and returns on capital employed. However, another reason may be the quality of financial management which is allowing working capital to exceed minimum required levels. Increased working capital must be converted into cash flow eventually otherwise it remains as, for example, costly and unsaleable stock and uncollected debts. Equally, decreased working capital results in cash flows additional to those represented by the realised profits of the period.

Successful companies in cash flow terms are therefore those which over a considerable period, convert their reported profits into cash flows, and thereby minimise their need for external funding. Unsuccessful companies fail to maximise on operating cash flow, and inevitably increase their dependence on borrowings to compensate. A comparison of operating cash flows to additional borrowings provides the analyst with a useful measure of this additional gearing in cash terms – that is, devoid of the subjective judgments affecting conventional gearing calculations which are based on equity data containing retained profits. An increasing and continuous cash-based gearing is a sure indicator of liquidity problems due to poor profitability and/or poor financial manage-

This general principle can be reasonably seen in the admittedly exaggerated example used earlier in this section. Using three-year rolling totals, the trend has been quite clear – the contribution from operating cash flow has dropped steadily from a 1977–9 figure of 69% to a 1980–2 equivalent of 33%; and this has been compensated for by an equal and opposite rise in the additional cash funding from borrowing – from 25% in 1977–9 to 67% in 1980–2.

2. The total cash flow pool available to a company from such sources as operations and borrowings mentioned above is usually required in the first instance to provide for the cost of capital expenditure representing either a maintenance or a change in the physical structure of the company. It is this new investment which is the key to the generation of operating cash flows in the future. Without an adequate investment in the past, operating cash flows are bound to decline as such things as plant and equipment deteriorate and the company loses its competitiveness in a rapidly-changing technological age.

What is therefore of crucial importance in cash flow analysis in this respect is the degree to which available cash is being invested in needed capital expenditure. In particular, the analyst ought to be concerned to learn of the balance over time between capital expenditure and distributions. The less cash which is being spent on the former and the more on the latter may be a clue to predictions of operating cash flows (and, thus, borrowings) in the future.

Of course, much will depend on the individual circumstances of the company and the nature of its activities and operations. For example, manufacturing companies may have a considerably greater use of available cash for replacement and new fixed assets than, say, retail concerns such as stores and supermarkets. Also, companies may reinvest by selling off assets such as land and buildings and use the proceeds to acquire needed alternative assets. In these cases, the net cash investment may appear relatively small, and the analyst ought to take care in his interpretation of the detailed figures. Likewise, the analyst will require to exercise caution in this respect with companies funding capital expenditure by leasing.

This topic will be dealt with later as will the entire question of assets acquired by non-cash funding. Meantime, the CFA figures provided in the example in this section reveal a growing use of cash for investment – from 33% in 1977–9 to 48% in 1980–2 – although much of the latter contribution was due to the surge of expenditure in 1981 to £267,000 (a level similar to those of 1977 and 1978 and roughly twice as much as in 1979, 1980 and 1982). By contrast, the level of cash spending on taxation was falling – from 42% in 1977–9 to 20% in 1980–2. Distributions, on the other hand, were at a relatively high level throughout the six years concerned – averaging 28% of the available cash.

3. One further interpretative principle also concerns the use of available cash and that is the level of taxation paid by the company being analysed on a cash basis. Apart from the considerable advantage for the analyst of using a tax figure which is devoid of the largely uninterpretable adjustments of accountants using deferred tax practices, the overall tax payment as a percentage of the total cash "pool" available in particular periods provides him with an indication of the effective cash rate of taxation which can be expected for the company concerned. Corporate taxation is not neutral in the sense that all companies are treated by tax provisions in the same way – for example, with regard to such matters as capital allowances. Thus, by taking operating cash flow minus capital expenditure, and relating this with tax payments, it is possible to obtain a tax rate on a cash basis which can be compared with similar companies. In the previous example, the tax rate for each of the years is as follows:

	1977	*1978*	*1979*	*1980*	*1981*	*1982*	*Total*
	%	%	%	%	%	%	%
Cash tax rate	77	91	1100	(174)	(31)	98	204

Thus, it can be seen that tax rates can become very high and, in cases when capital expenditure exceeds available operating cash flow, they become negative. In order to avoid these distorting single-period results, the use of three-year totals reveals the following data:

	1977–9	*1978–80*	*1979–81*	*1980–2*
	%	%	%	%
Cash tax rate	115	230	(169)	(83)

The company in this case would appear to be suffering confiscatory levels of taxation, and this (not unusual) situation would be revealing to an analyst concerned to identify problem areas affecting the company.

Cash Flow Analysis Problems

The above explanations of the use of cash flow data derived from funds statements to analyse corporate liquidity would be incomplete unless some mention was made of the problems of judgement which exist in such analyses.

1. The natural "lumpiness" of cash flows is difficult to deal with unless some attempt is made to "smooth" them by trend analysis techniques as explained above. This requires judgments to be made concerning the appropriate operating cycle to apply but this will probably be detectable from other sources of information available to the analyst – for example, reviews of operations. However, it must be remembered that, despite such available information, cash flow analyses depend on judgments by the analyst (rather than by the information producer).

2. The setting off of realised profits against working capital changes makes an assumption that all working capital items relate to profit and operating cash flow. The analyst must therefore be vigilant in detecting items within the working capital context which may relate to other matters (for example, creditors applicable to capital expenditure). Not to make these corrections can distort the operating cash flow and other data. However, company report disclosures may not be sufficient to make these distinctions – in which case the analyst must cope with the data as best he can, remembering that multi-period rolling totals may well minimise the effects of such errors.

3. In a similar vein the analyst may require to deal with non-cash transactions – for example, assets purchased and financed by the issue of share capital or loan stock. On these occasions, there are two schools of thought – either to leave these simultaneous but quasi-cash transactions in the CFA analysis as if they were cash inflows and outflows (because they would have been such if negotiated at different times); or to exclude them but note their existence (because they did not result in a cash movement, and because much depends on the valuation judgments made in relation to the assets and the funding). Because of the latter problems, it may be thought to be prudent to exclude rather than include such non-cash items unless the valuation issue is one about which there is little doubt. One of the biggest examples of this problem area concerns the matter of long-term

leasing of assets. The individual analyst will require to interpret such data in a cash flow analysis context as he see fit.

4. A crucial classification problem affects cash flow-based analysis, and that is the question of what should be regarded as capital expenditure. If funds statements are used to derive cash flow data, the analyst is dependent on the company's classification of capital expenditure. It may well be that items which could be defined as the latter have been written off to profit (for example, as on research and development). In these instances, if sufficient disclosure of the relevant items has been made by the company in its annual financial statements, then some adjustment can be made to the capital expenditure item and the operating cash flow (appropriately increasing both items by the same amount). If no disclosure is made, the analyst has to rely on the company's classification of capital expenditure.

5. In relation to cash flow-based analysis, the crucial matter of investment in capital expenditure can be described in net terms – that is after deduction of the proceeds of the sale of fixed assets and the receipt of investment grants. The net cash outflow is the significant feature. However, this may mean that such an aggregation may hide information, particularly in circumstances where disposal proceeds are large in relation to acquisitions. In these cases, the analyst must take care to note the simultaneous investment and disinvestment which is taking place in the company concerned.

6. One of the most vexed accounting problems is that concerning the translation of foreign currencies when the company concerned has business operations and net assets overseas. In these circumstances, translation normally takes place in order to render the overseas data compatible with its home-based equivalent. In particular, however, there is a difficulty with funds statements in that movements in funds (whether sources or uses) may be shown which are nothing more than currency restatements – that is, they do not represent actual sources or uses of funds.

In these circumstances, the funds statement ought to eliminate such restatements and thereby reflect funds movements at the time of the appropriate transactions. Some companies do this; others do not. If the latter is the case, the analyst who makes use for cash flow purposes of a funds statement which contains restatement surpluses and/or deficits may find his computation of such matters as operating cash flow, borrowings and capital expenditure to be seriously distorted. On the basis of whatever is disclosed about foreign exchange translation in the financial statements, the analyst must make some adjustment to avoid these distortions. If he does not, an increase in borrowing in a cash flow statement or an increase in operating cash flow may appear to be cash inflows when, in part, they represent translation "surpluses". If there is inadequate disclosure of these matters then cash flow analysis must be regarded as subject to unquantifiable distortions. That this should be possible reflects badly on the present state of funds statement practice which makes no mention of the translation problem.

An Example of Cash Flow Analysis

The above sections have attempted to outline the structure and form of cash flow-based financial

	1975	*1976*	*1977*	*1978*	*1979*	*1980*	*1981*	*1982*
Cash Inflows	£m	£m	£m	£m	£m	£m	£m	£m
Operating cash flow	43.6	52.8	45.0	50.4	85.6	92.7	94.2	123.9
Additional borrowing	—	—	—	4.3	—	—	—	10.6
Decrease in cash assets	7.8	—	—	—	—	—	—	—
	51.4	52.8	45.0	54.7	85.6	92.7	94.2	134.5
Cash Outflows								
Extra-ordinary items	—	—	—	—	—	2.0	6.6	5.3
Capital expenditure	19.2	22.8	17.5	11.6	25.6	43.7	3.2	62.6
Taxation paid	20.0	17.4	14.4	18.9	20.2	21.7	30.6	28.4
Dividends paid	8.5	9.2	10.2	11.2	16.9	15.5	18.8	21.4
Borrowing repayments	3.7	2.1	0.1	—	4.2	7.0	5.9	—
Increase in cash assets	—	1.3	2.8	13.0	18.7	2.8	29.1	16.8
	51.4	52.8	45.0	54.7	85.6	92.7	94.2	134.5

analysis. They have also provided explanations of the main reasons for and problems associated with the latter activity. In order to complete this exposition, the reader may find it useful to examine the cash flow results of a large U.K. public company and its subsidiaries – Sears Holdings PLC. The undernoted data have been taken from the available funds statements of the group for the last eight years. The data are free of foreign exchange distortions, and the trend analysis uses three-year rolling aggregates to avoid the peaks and troughs of Sears' very diverse operations. The results are first given as those of individual years, then these are aggregated and shown as percentage contributions to total cash inflow or outflow.

Although, in this case, a review of the above figures may be reasonably straighforward because of the relatively steady increase in most of the inflows and outflows, it has been argued in this paper that the analyst ought to use simple trend analysis techniques to aid the interpretation of cash flows. In this case, the use of three-year totals has been judged to be sufficient to smooth the lumpiness of individual years' results, and to reflect the diverse retail and manufacturing activities of Sears Holdings.

	1975–7	*1976–8*	*1977–9*	*1978–80*	*1979–81*	*1980–82*	*1975–82*
Cash Inflows	£m	£m	£m	£m	£m	£m	£m
Operating cash flow	141.4	148.2	181.0	228.7	272.5	310.8	588.2
Additional borrowing	—	2.1	—	—	—	—	—
Decrease in cash assets	3.7	—	—	—	—	—	—
	145.1	150.3	181.0	228.7	272.5	310.8	588.2
Cash Outflows							
Extra-ordinary items	—	—	—	2.0	8.6	13.9	13.9
Capital expenditure	59.5	51.9	54.7	80.9	72.5	109.5	206.2
Taxation paid	51.8	50.7	53.5	60.8	72.5	80.7	171.6
Dividends paid	27.9	30.6	38.3	43.6	51.2	55.7	111.7
Borrowing repayments	5.9	—	—	6.9	17.1	2.3	8.1
Increase in cash assets	—	17.1	34.5	34.5	50.6	48.7	76.7
	145.1	150.3	181.0	228.7	272.5	310.8	588.2

The above figures now enable the analyst to discern more clearly the trends underlying the single-period figures. In this case, the group is clearly funding itself from its operations – available cash being used increasingly on capital expenditure, tax, dividends and cash assets. Borrowing has also been decreased over the eight-year period. However, the relativity of the various inflows and outflows cannot be easily examined until the above data are further converted into percentage form to provide a picture of ratio-based contributions.

	1975–7	*1976–8*	*1977–9*	*1978–80*	*1979–81*	*1980–82*	*1975–82*
Cash Inflows	%	%	%	%	%	%	%
Operating cash flow	97	99	100	100	100	100	100
Additional borrowing	—	1	—	—	—	—	—
Decrease in cash assets	3	—	—	—	—	—	—
	100	100	100	100	100	100	100
Cash Outflows							
Extra-ordinary items	—	—	—	1	3	4	2
Capital expenditure	41	35	30	35	27	35	35
Taxation paid	36	34	30	27	27	26	29
Dividends paid	19	20	21	19	19	18	19
Borrowing repayments	4	—	—	3	6	1	2
Increase in cash assets	—	11	19	15	18	16	13
	100	100	100	100	100	100	100

The cash flow analysis is now a matter of interpretation of relatively unambiguous data presented in a simple format. In the case of Sears, the stability of inflows and outflows throughout the eight-year period is obvious. The almost single inflow has been operating cash flow (the three-year aggregate increasing by 120% from 1975–7 to 1980–82's figure of £310.8m.

Capital expenditure has accounted for 35% of cash outflow (relatively consistently throughout the period), but has varied considerably through the eight years. It has averaged £25.8m per annum – that is, 35% of the equivalent figure for operating cash flow. Although this figure may appear to be relatively low, the level of new investment has been considerably higher at £330m for the eight years – sale disposals for the period totalling £123.8m.

Taxation payments have amounted to approximately 30% of outflow between 1975 and 1982, and 20% approximately of the outflow has met dividend payments (in both cases consistently throughout). Thus, about 50% of total outflow has accounted for cash outgoings for which little direct benefit is received in return. Despite this, the company has increased its cash assets considerably – by £76.7m in total (13% of outflow), and reduced its borrowings by a net £8.1m.

A Final Comment

The above admittedly brief analysis of the cash flow of Sears Holdings is given solely for illustrative purposes. In cash terms, it has been a successful group of companies during the last decade. In some sense, it is relatively cash rich and a major criticism may be made that not enough has been done with the cash flow which has been available. This having been said, however, analysts will find it a much easier case for cash flow analysis than many other companies, particularly where there is a lack of operating cash flow over the long-term.

The latter is the key to a company's business survival. Unless, over a number of years, it is capable of generating cash flow from its operations to meet its needed capital expenditure, tax and dividends, it will require to seek external funding which, in turn, will tend to diminish future operating cash flows – a trend which can develop into an uncontrollable spiral despite the existence of reported realised profits. The latter are only an intermediate accounting step to the cash flows needed to survive.

References

(1) T. A. Lee and D. P. Tweedie, "Accounting Information: An Investigation of Shareholder Usage," *Accounting and Business Research*, Autumn 1975, pp. 280–91.

(2) T. A. Lee and D. P. Tweedie, *The Private Shareholder and the Corporate Report*, Institute of Chartered Accountants in England and Wales, 1977.

(3) T. A. Lee and D. P. Tweedie, *The Institutional Investor and Financial Information*, Institute of Chartered Accountants in England and Wales, 1982.

(4) "The Funds Statement," *Statement of Standard Accounting Practice 10*, 1975.

THE ACCOUNTING REVIEW
Vol. LXII, No. 2
April 1987

1986 Competitive Manuscript Award

The Incremental Information Content of the Accrual and Funds Components of Earnings After Controlling for Earnings

G. Peter Wilson

ABSTRACT: This study investigates whether the accrual and funds components of earnings have incremental information content beyond earnings itself. The research design is motivated by the insight that earnings and revenues are announced in the *Wall Street Journal* before the annual report, which contains both accrual and funds items, is released. This allows a direct measurement of the incremental information content of the accrual and funds components of earnings which is not possible when these releases are treated contemporaneously. This study finds evidence of an association between stock returns, measured over a short interval covering the date the annual reports arrive at the SEC, and new information about the cash and noncash components of earnings released at that time. By itself, this result implies that at least one of these components has information content. After controlling for earnings, incremental information about the cash and noncash components of earnings is precisely the same.

This paper investigates the incremental information content[1] of the accrual and funds components of earnings beyond earnings itself. Several authors have considered this and similar issues using a variety of funds definitions and methodologies. Ball and Brown [1968] and Beaver and Dukes [1972] each compared the dependence of stock returns on earnings and cash flows defined as earnings plus depreciation and amortization. Although both studies found a larger dependence on earnings, their results were not statistically significant. Kaplan and Patell [1977] tried to measure the incremental effect of working capital from operations after con-

This paper is based on my dissertation at Carnegie-Mellon University which was partially supported by the Deloitte Haskins & Sells Foundation. I am indebted to my dissertation committee, Bob Kaplan, Katherine Schipper (chairman), and Ken Singleton for their assistance and to others who have provided helpful comments, notably Stan Baiman, Bill Beaver, Mark Fichman, George Foster, Yuji Ijiri, Laurentius Marais, Maureen McNichols, Jim Noel, Jim Patell, Gerald Salamon and Carolyn Wilson. In addition, I appreciate the suggestions made by two anonymous reviewers, the members of the American Accounting Association's Competitive Manuscript Committee, and participants at the 1985 Stanford Summer Camp.

G. Peter Wilson is Assistant Professor of Accounting, Stanford University.

Manuscript received November 1985.
Revision received July 1986.
Accepted October 1986.

trolling for an earnings effect. However, because of the high correlation between earnings and working capital from operations, they could not separate this incremental effect. Other papers that have investigated issues related to the information content of earnings and cash flow measures include Beaver, Griffin, and Landsman [1982]; Easton [1983]; Rayburn [1986]; and Bowen, Burgstahler, and Daley [1986b].

As in Kaplan and Patell, the hypothesis considered in this study is that, conditional on knowing earnings, investors do not change their assessment of share value when they observe funds from operations. The tests performed here are motivated by the insight that earnings and revenues are announced in the *Wall Street Journal* before the annual report, which contains both accruals and funds, is released. This allows a direct measurement of the incremental information content of the accrual and cash components of earnings which is not possible when these releases are treated contemporaneously.

This paper considers two ways to decompose earnings. Each alternative splits earnings into two parts: a funds from operations component and a corresponding accrual component. In one case, the funds component is working capital from operations, and the accrual component is the *noncurrent accruals* variable, which is defined here as working capital from operations less earnings.[2] In the other case, the funds component is cash from operations and the accrual component is the *total accruals* variable, which is defined here as cash from operations less earnings. The term "accruals" will be used when it is not necessary to distinguish between the noncurrent and total accruals. Similarly, "funds" and "cash flow" are used interchangeably when it is not necessary to distinguish between working capital and cash from operations.

For both decompositions, earnings is the difference between funds from operations and the corresponding accrual component. Thus, in the interval between the earnings and funds announcements, when no new information is learned about earnings, new information about the accrual and funds components of earnings is the same.[3] Accordingly, at the funds announcement date, it is impossible to determine the *individual* contributions of accruals and funds to the magnitude of the stock price reaction. In this case, information content implies that the accrual and funds components of earnings, taken together, have incre-

[1] Strictly speaking, the expression "incremental information content" is used differently here than in other studies. Typically, C is said to have incremental information content over E if $f(R|E,C) \neq f(R|E)$, where f is a probability density function and R is a stock return measured over an interval which contains the dates when E and C are released. In this study, information about an earnings component, C, is said to have incremental information content over earnings, E, if $f(R|C) \neq f(R)$, where R is measured over an interval subsequent to the earnings announcement. Thus, there is an assumption that earnings are fully impounded in share price before the start of the interval over which R is measured. Evidence presented later supports this assumption for the sample used here. There is not a significant association between earnings and stock returns at the date the annual report arrives at the SEC.

[2] Working capital from operations is defined here as earnings after extraordinary items plus noncurrent accruals (i.e., discontinued operations + deferred taxes + depreciation and amortization + unremitted earnings of unconsolidated subsidiaries + adjustments for other noncurrent accruals used in the determination of earnings). Cash from operations is defined here as working capital from operations plus *current accruals* (i.e., the net changes in all of the working capital accounts except for changes in cash, marketable securities, and short-term debt). These definitions were adopted here because they were used most frequently in the financial statements of the sample firms. However, there is no universal acceptance of these definitions.

[3] Here the terms "new information" or "unexpected information" are used interchangeably to denote the change in expectations about a variable over an interval.

mental information content beyond earnings.

There are several reasons why this study is investigating these particular funds items: (1) They have been central to an "earnings versus cash flow" debate which has expanded from a focus on working capital from operations versus earnings to a more recent interest in cash from operations. (2) From an informational "usefulness" perspective they are associated with qualitatively different measures of a firm's financial status. Working capital from operations is more closely related to long-run profitability, whereas cash from operations is more closely related to recent operations and liquidity. (3) There seems to be a demand by investors for information about these particular funds items as evidenced by the formats of most firms' financial statements. Most firms that reconcile earnings to cash from operations include working capital from operations as the only intermediate subtotal in this reconciliation. (4) Both of these funds items are less correlated with earnings than earnings plus depreciation and are therefore more likely to have incremental information content beyond earnings.[4]

This study finds evidence of an association between stock returns, measured over a nine-day interval centered on the date the annual reports arrive at the SEC, and new information about cash from operations released during this interval. This implies that the cash from operations and total accrual components of earnings, taken together, have information content beyond earnings itself. In contrast, there is insufficient evidence to conclude that the noncurrent accrual and working capital from operations components of earnings have incremental information content beyond earnings.

A related paper by the author [Wilson, 1986] uses returns at both the earnings and funds announcement dates to address the question of whether the accrual component of earnings has incremental information content beyond the funds component. It presents a model which structures the way information about the components is extracted from earnings when earnings are announced. It also links the association between this component information and stock returns at the earnings announcement to the association between stock returns and the common component information released on the date the annual report arrives at the SEC. Although that model also addresses the question studied in this paper, the approach here has five distinct features. First, using a familiar approach, evidence is provided that the annual report release *is* an informational event.[5] The model in the extension is considerably more complex and is estimated using information from both the earnings and funds data simultaneously. Thus, it is not possible to separate the incremental effects of the individual announcements. In particular, in the absence of the results presented here, it could be argued

[4] Bowen, Burgstahler, and Daley [1986a] report mean correlation coefficients between annual earnings and annual earnings plus depreciation of 0.940, annual earnings and annual working capital from operations of 0.754, and annual earnings and annual cash from operations of 0.223. Quarterly measures are used here but the results are comparable. Although the correlation between earnings and earnings plus depreciation was not determined, the correlations between earnings and working capital from operations (0.777) and earnings and cash from operations (0.124) support the Bowen, Burgstahler, and Daley findings.

[5] Foster and Vickrey [1978] also provide evidence that the release of financial statements is an information event. For fiscal 1973 they use a cross-sectional paired difference test ($z=1.45$, $p=0.074$) to demonstrate that the 10-K has incremental information content beyond the annual report. This study can be viewed as an extension of their earlier work, in that it investigates the information content of specific financial statement items and provides detail about the cross-sectional differences in the ways this information is disseminated.

that the findings in the related paper are primarily due to information released at the earnings announcement. Second, other studies concerned with the information content of *any* annual report item can use the approach presented here to control for information released at the earnings announcement. In contrast, the extension model is only applicable to situations where the item of interest is a component of earnings. Third, this study considers the cross-sectional differences in the ways firms release and investors secure financial statement information. This includes an investigation of the items contained in the annual earnings news releases, a discussion of the various ways analysts purchase documents containing financial statements once they are submitted to the SEC, and the results from a questionnaire which asked analysts how they secure information and the extent to which they use it to assess share value. Collectively, these discussions describe institutional features that will be useful in related studies and emphasize the need for additional research to improve the procedure used here to measure the information content of non-earnings items contained in the annual report. Fourth, hold-out tests and resampling procedures are used to compare alternative forecasting models and to assess whether the asymptotic procedures used here are sensitive to the finite sample size limitation. Finally, this paper contains a discussion concerning the tradeoffs between power considerations and scope of inquiry which is applicable in any study which uses the Hotelling T^2 for hypotheses testing.

The paper proceeds as follows. The first section states the hypothesis associated with the question addressed here and establishes the motivation for the study while the second establishes that investors observe earnings and funds at two distinct dates that can be covered by mutually exclusive event intervals. The third section develops a model that addresses the question of whether the components of earnings have incremental information content beyond earnings itself. The fourth section discusses sampling and scaling procedures and controls for outliers and the fifth presents the findings. The final section summarizes these results and suggests future extensions.

Hypothesis and Motivation

The question addressed here can be formulated as the following null hypothesis:

> H_0: The accrual and funds components of earnings, taken together, have *no* incremental information content beyond earnings.

To the extent investors believe earnings is a sufficient statistic relative to its accrual and funds components for assessing share value, it will be difficult to reject this null. Yet, there is some evidence that the demand for information about these components may be quite small relative to the demand for earnings information. For example, analysts' buy/sell reports frequently discuss the potential of a stock only in terms of earnings and price earnings multiples, and the results from an analyst questionnaire indicate some analysts use earnings, but not its components, to assess share value.[6] Other evidence that suggests

[6] The questionnaire was mailed out to 400 members of the Financial Analysts Federation (FAF) randomly selected by FAF from their 19,000 members. Although the response rate was only 15 percent, the survey provides some insight about the extent to which investors use earnings, working capital from operations, and cash from operations in assessing firm value. Sixty of the questionnaires were returned, and 40 of the respondents claimed they had used earnings to assess the value of all the firms they had followed closely over a one-year period, where-

there might be minimal interest in the accrual funds components of earnings includes: the fact that earnings are published in the *Wall Street Journal* shortly after the close of the fiscal year, but component information is generally not available until audited financial statements are released four to eight weeks later; that managers are sometimes criticized for selecting projects based on earnings rather than cash flow; that managers' explicit compensation schemes are typically based on earnings, not funds items; that there are considerably more earnings than cash flow forecasts; and that cash flow forecasts, such as those provided by Value Line, usually use an earnings-plus-depreciation definition of cash flow. Thus, *ex ante*, there are several reasons why H_0 might be difficult to reject.

In contrast, several members of the financial community believe H_0 does not hold. Indeed, there is considerable support among authors of finance texts, financial consultants, and members of the FASB for the view that the components of earnings affect stock price differently. However, this group is divided as to whether accruals are useful for assessing share value. On the one hand, the FASB and the SEC currently support the use of both cash flows and earnings in assessing future cash flows. (In other words, the components of earnings are viewed as having incremental value beyond earnings itself.) On the other hand, some financial analysts have questioned the reliability and relevance of earnings primarily because of their accrual components. To these individuals, the components of earnings have incremental information content beyond earnings because earnings is a noisy signal about funds from operation. For example, the following excerpt from a Chase Financial brochure advocates that investors should abandon concern for earnings-per-share and adopt a cash flow perspective.

> What financial measures do you use when making policy decisions? Earnings per share? Earnings growth rate? Price/earnings multiple? Dilution? Popular as these guidelines are, formulating plans and policies around them could easily result in the misallocation of valuable corporate resources and adversely affect shareholders' values.
>
> We can help you focus on the real issues—the underlying economics rather than accounting data . . .
>
> Empirical evidence has shown that a company's share price is determined primarily by sophisticated, well informed investors. It is their perception of risk/reward trade-offs, as well as their expectations of future cash earnings and expenditures needed to produce those earnings, that largely determine the market price of stocks. It is cash-in minus cash-out, or Free Cash Flow, that counts—not accounting earnings or their growth.

This brochure suggests that sophisticated investors do not find accruals to have incremental information beyond current cash flows for predicting future cash flows (H_0 does not hold), and that managers who gear their policies around earnings data do not understand how this information affects their share price. Moreover, it indicates that results from empirical studies might influence management's perception of how share price

as 14 (22) indicated they had used working capital (cash) from operations for this purpose. Moreover, some analysts do not find funds information to be incrementally useful beyond earnings even though they claim to analyze funds information frequently. When asked to focus on their investment activities during the past year, 11 of the respondents claimed neither working capital nor cash from operations had incremental information beyond earnings for the majority of the firms they followed.

is set. This observation is also supported by Stern [1972].

The Flow of Information

Specifying the Event Interval

The subsequent empirical tests presume it is possible to specify intervals wide enough to include the dates most investors obtain a specific type of information, yet narrow enough so they do not overlap or sacrifice power. This section presents evidence concerning the validity of this assumption and considers the relative merits of several proxies for centering event intervals. In the process of developing these arguments, the investigation presents several facts concerning the flow of information and suggests some controls in the research design.

The date earnings are published in the *Wall Street Journal* is used as a proxy for the first date investors observe earnings and revenues.[7] What makes this proxy particularly appealing is that a single information intermediary, the *Wall Street Journal*, distributes earnings in a timely fashion, for a large number of firms, to a broad audience, at the same low cost to all investors. In contrast to earnings, funds from operations are not published in the *Wall Street Journal* or in any other single medium with a broad audience. Moreover, various documents are used to release funds items, including annual reports, 10-Ks and, in some cases, earnings news releases. Release dates of these documents are candidates for proxies for the first date funds are released.

The extent to which investors have timely access to a firm's funds information depends on whether funds are first released in the annual report or in the 10-K. If funds are first released when a firm mails its annual report to shareholders, then it is reasonable to assume that many investors first see funds close to the date the annual report arrives at the SEC. This argument is based on the belief that most investors who follow a firm closely are probably on the annual report mailing list and that most firms probably mail their annual reports to shareholders and the SEC on the same date.[8] However, if the 10-K is issued before the annual report, some investors may use the 10-K while others may wait for the annual report. The results from the analyst questionnaire substantiate that some investors wait for the annual report even if the 10-K is issued earlier.[9] At first glance this statement seems to suggest that the stock market is inefficient with respect to this component information. However, if information is costly and some investors are informed while others are not, prices may not be fully revealing. Moreover, it may be perfectly rational for some investors to wait and secure their information at a lower cost. In fact, there is evidence that information intermediaries distribute financial statements sequentially to different groups of investors at rates that decline over time. Some investors with relatively large holdings pay for photocopies of documents within two days of

[7] Regardless of whether dates on which firms release and investors observe information coincide, it will be convenient for expositional purposes to act "as if" they do.

[8] This claim is supported by anecdotal evidence. Ten firms in the sample were contacted to ascertain how they distribute annual reports, and all reported that they mail their annual report to shareholders within two days of the date they send it to the SEC.

[9] Results from the FAF questionnaire suggest the dates analysts first see funds from operations are more dispersed (across investors) when the 10-K arrives at the SEC before the annual report than when the annual report arrives first. Some analysts indicate they use the first document released, while others rely on the annual report even if the 10-K is more timely. However, very few analysts claim to know funds from operations prior to either of these dates.

the date they are submitted to the SEC or NYSE, while others pay less for microfiche copies that are available anywhere from two to 15 days later.[10] The length of this adjustment process may, however, be shorter if the annual report is released before the 10-K. In this case, as argued above, many investors will probably receive the annual report shortly after the firm releases it. In addition, at least for the firms sampled here, the 10-K is more likely than the annual report to arrive at the SEC during a peak period.

If the dates that the 10-K and annual report arrive at the SEC are clustered, the event-date proxy choice will not be as important. Moreover, even if these dates are widely separated, it may still be possible to select a suitable proxy if for most firms, the annual report precedes the 10-K. In this case either the annual report or the earliest date (one of these reports arrives at the SEC) is an acceptable choice. However, the 10-K and annual report dates are separated by more than five days for over 60 percent of the observations, and the annual report arrives at the SEC five or more days after the 10-K for more than one-third of the observations. These results may explain why the significance levels of some of the results reported later are affected by the width of the return interval at the funds release date.

In sum, the institutional evidence presented here suggests most firms' earnings and funds information releases are separate events, but that it is considerably easier to identify earnings announcements than it is to specify narrow return intervals that capture the price reactions associated with funds information. Reported results are based on return intervals centered on the date the annual report arrives at the SEC, but many of the tests in this study were repeated using both the date the 10-K arrives and the first date financial statements arrive at the SEC. Although test results are slightly less significant using these alternative proxies, none of the conclusions here are affected. The fact that the results are robust across these alternative event intervals suggests that future studies might improve upon the tests used here by specifying these event intervals more precisely.

Controlling for the Early Release of Component Information

Even if earnings and funds are announced at distinct dates, it will be difficult to distinguish the stock market reaction to the funds announcement from the reaction to the earnings announcement if the dates are close together. For over 90 percent of the observations in this study, the *Wall Street Journal* earnings announcements occurred at least eight trading days before the first date either the annual report or the 10-K arrived at the SEC, and these dates are separated by several weeks for most observations. However, to make certain the earnings and funds event intervals do not overlap, observations with fewer than eight trading days between these dates are eliminated from most tests and all results are checked for sensitivity to this choice.

Because all of the proxies for the

[10] Both Disclosure Inc. and Bechtal provide these services. Prior to 1985 Disclosure Inc. was responsible for providing microfiche to the SEC within 10 days of the SEC arrival date. However, during the peak period at the end of March this requirement was frequently relaxed, and microfiche were not submitted until up to 15 days after the arrival date. When microfiche were sent to the SEC they were also sold to several demand customers. In 1985 Bechtal won the SEC contract to produce microfiche and now guarantees the SEC a turnaround of five days and seven days for non-peak and peak periods, respectively. However, each company provides photocopies to 25–40 clients within two days of the date the firm releases them.

funds announcement date are associated with dates when the firm formally submits audited financial statements to the SEC, there is an implicit assumption that firms do not release funds information earlier. A news release survey was used to classify firms according to the amount of predictive information released prior to the issuance of the audited statements.[11] This classification provides a control which increases the power of tests to detect a stock market reaction at the funds announcement proxy date. Most firms issue news releases shortly after the close of their fiscal years which contain, among other information, annual earnings and revenues. About five to ten weeks later, they release their audited financial statements which contain funds from operations. Some firms issue other news releases between these dates which include additional information useful for predicting funds from operations. Moreover, some earnings news releases provide information more suitable for this purpose than other news releases. Most contain annual corporate revenues and corporate earnings—total, per share, before and after taxes, and extraordinary items; many include segment data for revenues and earnings; some distinguish between operating and nonoperating earnings; and a few contain abbreviated financial statements which are sufficient for determination of both cash and working capital from operations.

Each of the 300 firms used in subsequent tests was requested to submit 1981 and 1982 (test years) news releases containing information about items in their annual financial statements. In all, 63 percent of the final sample of firms used in the subsequent tests sent news releases, and nearly 70 percent of these were from the 1981–82 sample period. All the firms except one that sent news releases for more than one year were classified identically each year in terms of the type of information in the releases. Thus, it seemed reasonable to use a more recent news release as a proxy to classify those firms which did not send a 1981–82 release. The fraction of firms in a given category is the same regardless of whether the news releases from outside the sample period (1981–82) are included. This supports the validity of using the more current news releases as proxies for those from the sample period. Those that sent news releases were classified as follows:

- Seventy-seven percent contained earnings, revenues, and additional information such as segment data but no other information deemed useful for forecasting funds from operations.
- Four percent contained the above plus additional line items on the earnings statement, including depreciation or deferred taxes.
- Thirteen percent contained preliminary earnings statements and balance sheets in either their annual earnings news release or in a subsequent news release issued prior to the date they formally submitted their financial statements to the SEC.
- Six percent issued a fourth-quarter report, at an unknown date subsequent to the earnings release but before the issuance of the audited statements.

Since the sample firms were randomly selected from the manufacturing firms in the 1982 COMPUSTAT file, the survey results are probably representative of

[11] That is, information which is useful for predicting annual funds from operations (other than annual earnings and revenues and items reported in previous interim reports).

large manufacturing firms generally. The results indicate most firms do not officially release funds from operations before they issue their audited financial statements. If more firms had released funds information at the earnings announcement date, it would have been possible to compare stock market reactions, at the date when audited financial statements are released, between the firms that did and did not release funds information at the earlier date. Too few firms issue preliminary abbreviated financial statements to allow formal inferences. However, for those firms that do issue them, there is no evidence of a reaction to the subsequent funds information when audited financial statements are released. There *is* evidence of such a reaction for firms that do not issue abbreviated statements. Moreover, tests concerned with measuring the stock market reaction to funds information at the date when audited financial statements are released may be more powerful if they are restricted to firms that do not issue preliminary abbreviated statements than similar tests that do not have this control.

Econometric Issues

As in previous earnings studies, information content is determined here by examining the association between market model prediction errors averaged over an event period and forecast errors corresponding to accounting items released during this period.[12] Event periods of three and nine days are centered at the date the annual report arrives at the SEC, and funds component information is predicted using linear projections based on information known to investors at the beginning of the period. The closer these projections are to investors' conditional expectations, the more likely information content will be detected if it exists.[13] The suitability of these prediction equations is assessed by comparing their out-of-sample forecasting ability to competing models that resemble those used elsewhere. Information content is measured using regression and portfolio approaches. Both use a two-stage procedure where accounting forecast equations are estimated cross-sectionally in the first stage, and the association between the residuals from the first-stage regression and market model prediction errors is determined in the second stage. In one case, market model prediction errors are regressed cross-sectionally against the first-stage residuals, while in the other case, portfolios are formed according to the magnitude of the first-stage residuals; then their mean returns are compared. Although both procedures are similar to those used elsewhere, each has distinguishing features.

The regression procedure used here is unique in that the first-stage regressions are estimated cross-sectionally rather than over time for each firm. Sufficient

[12] Market model parameters are estimated for each firm-year using 120 consecutive daily returns from the fiscal year prior to the one under consideration. Specifically, if t represents the end of the previous year, then returns from day $t-90$ to $t-210$ were used. If returns were missing, additional ones from before $t-210$ were used. Parameters were also estimated using the procedures suggested in Scholes and Williams [1977] to assess whether the results were affected by nonsynchronous trading; they were not.

[13] The differences between a linear projection and a linear expectation involves the relation between the errors and regressors. For simplicity, assume $X=a+bW+\epsilon$. If $E[\epsilon|W]=0$ so that ϵ is mean independent of W, then $E[X|W]$ is linear. Even if $E[X|W]$ is not linear, it is still possible to form a "best linear" (in a population least-squares sense) predictor of X. The values of a and b that yield this best linear predictor correspond to the ϵ that satisfies the orthogonality condition $E[\epsilon W]=0$. In this case, $a+bW$ is frequently referred to as the linear projection of X onto W and is usually estimated using ordinary least squares. There is no assumption here that investors' conditional expectations are linear, but as Patell [1979] argues, information content is more likely to be detected, if it exists, when $a+bW$ is a good approximation to $E[X|\Phi]$ where Φ is investors' information at the beginning of the event period.

conditions are introduced to ensure that the estimates for the second stage coefficients (which measure information content) are consistent, that the usual OLS t-tests are correct, and that a potential errors-in-variables problem associated with using estimates of the first-stage errors as regressors in the second stage does not occur.[14] Similar conditions have not been established in studies that use separate time-series regressions for each firm in the first stage. Thus, this cross-sectional procedure has a potential advantage, since the errors-in-variables problem could result in inconsistent estimates when (as is typically the case) short time series are used. However, there is a tradeoff: the coefficients in the cross-sectional procedure are assumed constant across firms, while those in the time-series approach are assumed constant across time. In this study the cross-sectional procedure must be used because of data limitations; but even if there were sufficient data, it is not clear that the time-series approach would be preferable. Considering all of the changes in accounting methods over the past 20 years and the problems associated with inflation, trends, and seasonality, the assumption of constant coefficients over time is bound to be violated. Even if these problems are not severe, the coefficient estimates still might be inconsistent because of the errors-in-variable problem.

For the portfolio approach, H_0 is tested by comparing the difference in means across portfolios using a Hotelling T^2-test. However, the tests derived here differ in three ways from those used elsewhere: (1) information content is measured in event time rather than contemporaneously so the approach used by Kaplan and Patell is not appropriate; (2) differences across portfolio means are tested jointly instead of individually; and (3) some tradeoffs between power considerations and scope of inquiry are made explicit.

Cross-Sectional Regression Approach

Let F represent fourth-quarter funds from operations and suppose investors' expectations about F at the earnings announcement can be approximated by a linear projection of F onto W, a vector of information available at the earnings announcement which is useful for predicting F. This prediction equation's forecast error, ϱ, is a proxy for new information about F released after the earnings announcement.[15] Further, let ret be a return metric measured over a short interval covering the funds announcement. Together, the projection of F onto W (hereafter the *accounting prediction equation*) and ret onto ϱ (hereafter the *return equation*) yield the following two-equation model:

$$F = BW + \varrho \qquad (1)$$

$$ret = \Gamma\varrho + v, \text{ and} \qquad (2)$$

$$E[W\varrho] = E[\varrho v] = 0, \qquad (3)$$

where 3 holds because the two equations are projections.

The coefficient, Γ, in equation 2 measures the extent to which market-adjusted returns respond to new information

[14] Wilson [1986] contains a proof that the parameter estimates from this two-stage procedure are equivalent to certain generalized method of moment estimates and, if the error terms are homoscedastic, the usual OLS standard errors are consistent estimates for the asymptotic covariance matrix for the estimator. This implies the estimates of the coefficients in the model are consistent and their OLS t-statistics are correct. In the event the error terms are heteroscedastic, the standard errors in White [1980] are consistent estimates for the asymptotic covariance matrix for the estimator.

[15] For expositional convenience, the subsequent discussion refers to ϱ as new information about the funds component of earnings. However, the reader should keep in mind that ϱ also represents new information about the accrual component. If the accrual component is projected onto W, then B will change, but the regression error will be the same if earnings is included in W.

about accounting variables. For example, if $\Gamma \neq 0$, ϱ has information content, and the components of earnings have incremental information beyond earnings itself.[16] In particular, the t-statistic associated with Γ is used to test H_0.

Before 2 and 3 can be used for prediction, W must be specified and a decision must be made concerning possible restrictions on B. For example, if F is earnings rather than funds from operations; W is the previous year's earnings; and B is restricted to be one, then equation 1 is a random walk. Similarly, Foster's [1977] quarterly-earnings-forecast models can be represented using equation 1 by defining W to be lagged quarterly earnings and restricting B in various ways.

A logical extension here would have been to use univariate prediction models for each of the dependent variables in this study. For example, fourth-quarter cash from operations could have been projected onto cash from operations from the previous four quarters. Each of the resulting forecasts would have been a restricted projection onto the regressors used here, with most of the coefficients restricted to be zero. Yet, without theoretical guidance, it seems inefficient *ex ante* to impose such restrictions. Instead, unrestricted versions of these projections are used here so that W contains fourth-quarter earnings and revenues for the current year, plus three lagged variables for each of the following: revenues; the noncurrent accruals; the difference between the total accruals and noncurrent accruals; and cash from operations. Lagged variables were from the third quarter, the first half of the current year, and the fourth quarter of the previous year.[17] Annual capital expenditures are also included in W to allow for expansions which might have substantial incremental effects.[18] By including the two lagged accrual variables and lagged cash from operations, the model, under suitable restrictions on B, implicitly contains lagged earnings and working capital from operations. Results are reported with and without these restrictions imposed. In addition, the out-of-sample forecasting ability of the unrestricted model is compared to several alternatives where various coefficients in B are restricted to be zero.

The discussion so far has pertained to a single firm. Model estimation requires additional assumptions about the cross-sectional properties of error terms and coefficients. The two-stage estimation method requires independent equation errors across firms and a cross-sectionally constant covariance structure for the accounting variables and returns. To make the first assumption more reasonable, market model prediction errors rather than raw returns are used for the dependent variable. In addition, to help ensure the second assumption, each accounting variable is divided by the total asset value (annual COMPUSTAT item 6) reported in the annual financial statements, at the end of the year in which the accounting variable is measured.[19] For example, third-quarter revenues are divided by total annual

[16] However, if $\Gamma = 0$, ϱ may still have information content since Γ does not reflect the association between the higher order moments of ϱ and *ret*.

[17] For each item, the fourth-quarter measure is the annual number less the aggregate for the first three quarters.

[18] Thus, there is an assumption here that this item is available before annual earnings are published. This may be a reasonable assumption for most firms since capital expansion plans for the current year are frequently included in the previous year's annual report or announced in special news releases. However, all of the tests were repeated using capital expenditures for the first three quarters only and the results were not qualitatively different.

[19] The primary motivation for scaling is to make the constant covariance assumption more reasonable, not to control for heteroscedasticity. The robustness of the results to the homoscedasticity assumption is checked

assets reported at the end of the fourth quarter, so that tests concerning cash flows versus earnings can now be interpreted as tests of cash recovery rate versus return on investment. Since the choice of a scale factor is arbitrary, most of the statistical procedures were repeated using the following alternative scaling factors: total market value of the firm's common shares at the end of the current year; average, over the previous five years, of the total asset value as reported in the financial statements; and average, over the previous five years, of the total market value of the firm's common shares. The conclusions are robust across these alternative scales, so most results are reported for current-year-total-asset scaling only.

Portfolio Approach

The regression model, 1–3, is one way to measure the association between stock returns, *ret*, and components information, ϱ. An alternative approach is to partition returns into portfolios according to the magnitude of ϱ. For two reasons, inference tests based on this approach may have more power to detect information content than the regression approach. First, portfolio-based tests are not as sensitive to outliers in ϱ. Outlier problems can be particularly troublesome for cross-sectional regressions involving returns and accounting variables, since the explanatory power of the regressions is so low. Second, portfolio-based tests are not as sensitive to nonlinearities in the relation between *ret* and ϱ. If these two problems do not exist, the portfolio approach may not be as powerful because it uses less information than the regression approach. For example, differences in mean returns within portfolios are not reflected in the results. The subsequent discussion presents the procedure used to assign observations to portfolios and the inference tests used to address the hypotheses of interest.[20]

Observations are partitioned into three portfolios using a one-way classification, based on the funds forecast errors. Partitions are then determined as follows: The sample mean and standard deviation of the funds forecast error are determined using all available observations. Two cut-off points are used to partition observations into three groups: low, medium, and high according to the magnitude of the forecast error. Forecast errors more than 0.5 standard deviations above the mean (of all observations) are classified as "high." Those forecast errors more than 0.5 standard deviations below the mean are labeled "low" and the remainder are classified as "medium." For each portfolio, $p=1, \ldots P$ and date t, market model prediction errors are averaged across all observations in the portfolio.[21] The results are

---

using a procedure similar to that in White [1980]. In addition, an informal procedure is used to assess whether the covariance between dependent and independent variables is more similar across size after scaling. Five size portfolios are formed based on average market value over the sample period. The stability of the regression coefficients in equation 1 across these portfolios is then examined for both the scaled and unscaled variable cases. As expected, the regressions involving the scaled variables are more stable than those using the unscaled variables. For example, the coefficient estimates for the accounting prediction equation for unscaled cash from operations based on the full sample (462 observations) seem to be primarily determined by the observations in the two portfolios with the largest market values. In contrast, the coefficient estimates for the size portfolios are more stable for the prediction equations for scaled cash from operations.

[20] The approach used by Kaplan and Patell [1977] and Burgstahler and Noreen [1985] is not applicable here because the earnings and funds event dates are not aligned in chronological time.

[21] In this study, P is either three or nine depending on whether portfolios are based on a one-way or two-way classification. Two-way classifications are determined by first forming two one-way classifications based on earnings and funds and then assigning observations to one of nine portfolios according to the two one-way assignments.

then averaged over the event interval and the resulting $P\times 1$ vector is assumed to be distributed $N(\upsilon,\Sigma)$.[22]

The hypotheses in studies using a portfolio approach can be viewed as linear restrictions across the components of υ. For any constant $q\times P$ matrix A the null $A\upsilon=0$ is rejected, at the α level of significance when

$$z'A'(ASA')^{-1}Az>T^2_{\alpha,q,Ne-q}=[(Ne-1)q/(Ne-q)]F_{\alpha,q,Ne-q}, \quad (4)$$

where the probability that a central F-statistic with degrees of freedom $(q,Ne-q)$ exceeds $F_{\alpha,q,Ne-q}$ is α, and where S is an estimate of Σ based on market model prediction errors from an $Ne=81$-day interval starting 170 days before the event date and extending until 90 days before the event date.

Moreover, if $A\upsilon=0$ is rejected, any number of subsequent tests of the form $CA\upsilon=0$, where C is any $1\times q$ vector of constants, can be conducted without increasing the combined type one error, α, for all of these tests.[23] These additional tests are sometimes useful for providing insight as to which components of $A\upsilon$ contributed to the rejection of $A\upsilon=0$. Each test has the same critical value as 4 and a rejection region of the form

$$z'A'C'(CASA'C')^{-1}CAz>T^2_{\alpha,q,Ne-q}. \quad (5)$$

Tests in Gonedes [1978], Kaplan and Patell [1977], and Matolcsy [1984] are a particular case of this approach. Each study begins its inquiry by testing $\upsilon=0$, which is equivalent to setting A equal to the identity. When this null is rejected, subsequent tests are conducted separately to determine if the hypotheses $\upsilon_j=0$ or $\upsilon_i=\upsilon_j$ can be rejected, where the subscripts are L (low), M (medium), or H (high). In contrast, this study defines A by

$$A=\begin{vmatrix}1 & -1 & 0\\ 0 & 1 & -1\end{vmatrix}, \quad (6)$$

and tests $A\upsilon=0$ by using 4, which is equivalent to a joint test of $\upsilon_i=\upsilon_j$ *for all* $i\neq j$. When this hypothesis is rejected, 5 is used to test separately hypotheses such as $\upsilon_L=\upsilon_M$ and $\upsilon_M=\upsilon_H$. There are two advantages of defining A by 6 rather than the identity: (1) it permits the above joint test which cannot be represented as $CA\upsilon=0$ when A is the identity;[24] and (2) for most values of Ne and P the power of the individual tests of $\upsilon_i=\upsilon_j$ is higher when A is defined by 6 rather than the identity.[25] However, to get this increased power it is necessary to narrow the scope of inquiry, for when A is defined by 6 it

[22] More precisely, at each date the $P\times 1$ vector of portfolio prediction errors is assumed to be distributed $N(\upsilon_t,\Sigma)$. Assuming these portfolios are independent over time, their average over the Nu days in the event interval multiplied by the square root of Nu is distributed $N(\upsilon,\Sigma)$ where υ is the corresponding weighted average of the υ_t's. Portfolio prediction errors are also assumed to be independent across portfolios, so Σ is diagonal. This assumption is reasonable here since observations are positioned in event time, but it is not required for any of the following results. These independence assumptions are consistent with those invoked in the regression inferences. However, the normality assumption is not required there.

[23] Additional details concerning simultaneous test procedures can be found in [Anderson, 1958; Johnson and Wichern, 1982; Miller, 1966; Morrison, 1967; Rao, 1973; Roy and Bose, 1953; Roy, 1954; 1956; and 1957].

[24] This means if A is the identity, this joint test cannot be conducted without possibly altering the type one error for the combined tests in some unknown way.

[25] This second result follows because, regardless of whether A is 6 or the identity, there exists a C for which $CA\upsilon=0$ reduces to $\upsilon_i=\upsilon_j=0$, and for both choices of A the left-hand side of 5 is the same, namely, the square of the usual t-test for the difference of two means. But clearly, since q is the number of rows in A, the right-hand side of 5 depends on the choice of A. Thus, tests where A is defined by 6 will be more powerful than those where A is the identity (since q is 2, rather than 3). When Ne is large relative to q, the size of the rejection regions in 4 and 5 can depend substantially on q. For example, if $Ne=80$, and $P=3$, then $T^2_{\alpha,q,Ne-q}$ is either 8.49, 6.32, or 4.00 depending on whether q is 3, 2, or 1, respectively. This indicates the extent of the power gains that can be achieved by limiting the scope of inquiry.

is impossible to represent the hypothesis $\upsilon=0$ in the form $CA\upsilon=0$. At issue, then, is whether tests of $\upsilon=0$ help resolve the basic questions addressed by a study or are presented for completeness. In this study, descriptive statistics concerning mean portfolio returns are presented, but $\upsilon=0$ is not tested.

Sample Selection, Scaling, and Outliers

The estimation method assumes the covariance structure for accounting variables and returns is constant across firms. To make this assumption more reasonable, the sample was restricted to the manufacturing firms (SIC codes 1,000 to 4,800). Initially 1,246 such firms were identified that had COMPUSTAT annual and quarterly records plus a CRSP daily record in the 1982 version of these databases. Of these, 245 were eliminated because specific items required for the subsequent tests were missing from these databases.[26] Three hundred firms were randomly selected from the remaining 1,001, providing 600 firm-year observations for 1981–82. However, 66 of these were dropped from the sample because 33 firms were not included in a later version of the COMPUSTAT data base.[27] In addition, 72 observations were dropped because 10-Qs were not available at Harvard's Baker Library for all of the quarters required for a specific firm-year observation, or because all of the required accounting items were not available. Estimates of the coefficients in the accounting prediction equations are based on the remaining 462 firm-year observations. Tests that required returns from the financial statement release date are based on the 379 firm-year observations for which both the annual report and 10-K SEC filing dates were available and for which the earlier of these dates followed the *Wall Street Journal* earnings announcement date by at least eight days. These firms were further classified into two groups according to the amount of balance sheet information disclosed in their earnings news release. Firms that included abbreviated balance sheets or line items such as depreciation in their earnings news releases are referred to as "early release" firms, while their complements are denoted "late release" firms. Firms that did not submit news releases were classified as late firms; thus some firms may be misclassified. Altogether, there were 322 late release and 57 early release firm-year observations.

To check for outliers and scaling sensitivity, each firm-year observation of each scaled accounting variable was compared to the cross-sectional mean, calculated using all available observations, and was eliminated if it was more than four standard deviations from the cross-sectional mean. On average, across different scaling factors, this procedure eliminated 23 firms.[28] All of the procedures involving estimation and inference were conducted using current-year-total-asset scaling with and without outliers. Most of these procedures were also conducted using all eight of the scaling-outlier combinations. *The major results in this research are robust across these eight combinations. For this reason, unless otherwise noted, results are reported for*

[26] COMPUSTAT availability of the following items for 1978–1981 was required: Annual items—receivables, inventories, total assets, capital expenditures, total funds from operations, extraordinary items, and discontinued operations (COMPUSTAT items 3, 2, 6, 128, 110, and 124 respectively), and quarterly COMPUSTAT item 29—the date earnings and revenues are released. In addition, firms with more than ten missing stock returns over this period also were eliminated.

[27] Many of these firms were removed because of mergers, some of which occurred after the sample period. Thus, some of these observations could be saved by using the 1983 version of CRSP and COMPUSTAT.

[28] Some of the statistical procedures were also run using a three standard deviation cut-off. This eliminated about 20 more firms.

TABLE 1

REGRESSION RESULTS—LATE FIRMS

Table Contents: The first three columns report the Γ-estimates, their related *t*-statistics, and the adjusted R^2's for equation 2 for the case where the regressor is the cash from operations forecast error. For each row the dependent variable is the average market model prediction error over the indicated interval where day zero is the date the annual report arrives at the SEC. Columns four through six contain similar results for working capital from operations. Depending on the availability of returns, the regressions are based on anywhere from 321 to 325 observations.

	Cash From Operations			*Working Capital From Operations*		
Return Interval	*Coefficient Estimate*	*T-statistic*	*Adjusted R^2–%*	*Coefficient Estimate*	*T-statistic*	*Adjusted R^2–%*
(−40,−32)	.011	1.35	.3	.050	1.99	.9
(−31,−23)	.009	0.97	0	−.019	−0.63	−.2
(−22,−14)	.005	0.59	−.2	.005	0.21	−.3
(−13,−5)	−.006	−0.81	−.1	.006	0.25	−.3
(−4,4)	.026	3.26	2.9	.029	1.10	.1
(5,13)	.005	0.48	−.2	.098	2.93	2.3
(14,22)	.012	1.46	.3	.024	0.88	−.1
(23,31)	.011	1.34	.2	.015	0.58	−.2
(32,40)	.017	1.79	.7	.036	1.20	.1

current-year-total-asset scaling only, with no outliers removed.

EMPIRICAL RESULTS

In this section, regression and portfolio results are presented for the late release firms first. Next, some condensed results are given for the early release firms.

Regression Results

The two-stage regression procedure discussed earlier was used to estimate equations 1 and 2. When funds are defined as *cash from operations*, the adjusted R^2 for 1 is 47.3 percent. Although both fourth-quarter earnings (t=2.26) and revenues (t=2.82) are significant, they add little to the overall explanatory power (the adjusted R^2 is 46.1 percent when these variables are excluded).[29] In contrast, when funds are defined as *working capital from operations*, the prediction equations with and without current year fourth-quarter earnings are considerably different from one another. When fourth-quarter earnings (t=22.73) are included, the adjusted R^2 increases from 26.3 percent to 65.7 percent. The fact that fourth-quarter earnings are such a good predictor of working capital from operations may partially explain why there is insignificant evidence of incremental information content at the funds date for working capital from operations. If the magnitude of the forecast error for working capital from operations is insignificant relative to that for cash from operations, then its effect on stock returns at the funds date may be difficult to detect.

Table 1 contains the Γ-estimates, related t-statistics, and adjusted R^2 for

[29] Additional details about the prediction equations' coefficient estimates and t-statistics are in Wilson [1985]. In addition, Wilson [1986] contains similar results for the case where all of the regressors in W are included except fourth-quarter revenues and earnings.

equation 2. For each row the dependent variable is the average market model prediction error over the indicated nine-day interval, and the regressor for all rows is the forecast error associated with the prediction of funds, conditional on information released on or before the earnings release date. A nonzero Γ for the nine-day event interval, (−4,4), is consistent with the hypothesis that the components of earnings have incremental information content over that of earnings itself.[30] Moreover, assuming ideal conditions for this research design, the Γ-estimates over the surrounding intervals should not be significant.[31]

For cash from operations the Γ-estimate is significant (t=3.26) over the nine-day event interval, so H_0 is rejected at the 0.001 level of significance. Evidence from several related tests reflects the robustness of this result. First, as indicated in Table 1, the Γ-estimates are not significant in any of the pre-event or post-event intervals, so the result is probably not induced by measurement error in the cash from operations forecast error. Second, the t-statistic barely decreases (t=3.11) when the homoscedasticity assumption is relaxed and the standard errors are calculated using White's procedure. Third, the Γ-estimate is 0.019 (t=2.70) when nine-day event intervals are centered on the first date the 10-K or annual report arrived at the SEC, which is very close to the estimate for event intervals centered at the annual report arrival date. Fourth, when the variables in the accounting prediction equation, 1, are scaled by current-year-market-value rather than current-year-total-assets, the t-statistic increases to 3.90. Fifth, separate regressions for five portfolios based on market value all have positive Γ-estimates over the event interval. Moreover, this is the only return interval (of those reported in Table 1) where the signs of these five estimates are the same.[32] Sixth, the Γ-estimates over the event interval are quite similar for 1981 and 1982: 0.019 (t=2.01) and 0.031 (t=2.48), respectively. Seventh, the t-statistics over return intervals of various widths centered on the date the annual report

[30] H_0 is also examined using a three-day interval centered on the date the annual report arrives at the SEC. For this shorter interval, the association between stock returns and either of the funds variables is not significant at an acceptable level. The t-statistics for the Γ-estimates are 1.24 and 0.16 for cash and working capital from operations, respectively. However, this outcome is sensitive to outliers. Once outliers are removed (using the procedure discussed in the section on sample selection, scaling, and outliers, the cash from operations coefficient is significant, regardless of the scaling factor used. When 21 outliers were removed, using a four standard deviation cut-off rule, the coefficient and t-statistic for the funds prediction error were .0289 and 3.83, respectively ($t_{399}(.001)=3.09$). In contrast, the coefficient on the working capital from operations variable remains insignificant across all scaling-outlier combinations.

[31] Ideal conditions would include: (1) all investors have common expectations that coincide with the accounting prediction equation used here; (2) no information useful for predicting cash from operations is released between the earnings and funds date; and (3) share prices respond quickly to new information.

[32] Starting with the smallest market value portfolio, the Γ-estimates and their related t-statistics for the (−4,4) return interval are 0.012 (t=0.79), 0.041 (t=2.37), 0.032 (t=1.60), 0.054 (t=1.54), and 0.015 (t=0.62). The t-statistics for the non-event intervals partially explain why the event interval t-statistics are so small for the smallest and largest market value portfolios. For the largest market value portfolio the t-statistic is 3.27 over (−31,−23), and this is the only interval where it is above 1.27. This is consistent with many larger firms' cash from operations information being known earlier, perhaps at the earnings announcement or around the auditor certification date. The t-statistics for regressions based on similar nine-day intervals, where the earnings announcement is day zero, are insignificant for intervals at and after the earnings announcement. Thus, either many large firms have another information event aligned with the annual report arrival date but not with the earnings announcement, or the result is due to random error. For the smallest market value portfolio, the absolute value of the t-statistic is below one for all intervals except (5,13), where it is 1.47, which is close to the values for the three mid-size portfolios for (−4,4). This is consistent with cash from operations information being impounded in price more slowly, perhaps because on average small firms' financial statements are disseminated more slowly among investors.

TABLE 2

DESCRIPTIVE STATISTICS FOR FUNDS PORTFOLIOS—LATE FIRMS

Portfolio Construction Rule: The entries in the first three columns are for a one-way classification based on the magnitude of the forecast errors from the prediction equation for cash from operations (ϱ in equation 1). Similarly, the entries in columns four through six are for a one-way classification based on the forecast errors for working capital from operations (see the discussion in the "Portfolio Approach" section). The means in the seventh column are for the combined portfolio which includes all observations.

Table Contents: The first row contains the average earnings forecast errors for the six portfolios described above, where the earnings forecasts are based on information available prior to the earnings announcement. The second and third rows contain the average cash from operations forecast errors and working capital from operations forecast errors, respectively, where these forecasts also use information in the earnings announcement (equation 1). Accounting variables are scaled by total assets so the low-cash portfolio has an average earnings forecast error of 1.4 cents per dollar of total assets.

Average Forecast Error	*Cash From Operations*			*Working Capital From Operations*			
	Low	*Medium*	*High*	*Low*	*Medium*	*High*	*All*
Earnings	.014	.005	−.016	−.028	.011	.007	.002
CFO	−.206	.004	.231	—	—	—	.008
WCFO	—	—	—	−.068	−.002	.063	−.002
Observations	86	151	85	66	188	68	322

arrived at the SEC are: five-day, 1.56; seven-day, 2.38; 11-day, 3.11; 13-day, 2.22; and 15-day, 2.06. This suggests the results are sensitive to the interval width, but significant for all widths between seven and 15 days. In addition, the results from the resampling procedure presented later provide strong evidence that the result is robust across the sample.

In contrast, the coefficient estimate for the working capital from operations forecast error for (−4,4) is insignificant across all scaling-outlier combinations and sample partitions discussed in the previous paragraph. Although the Γ-estimate is significant over (5,13), it is practically zero for this interval in 1981 (t=.06). Thus, it is determined entirely by observations in 1982 (t=3.16).

In the next section it is argued that this result is probably due to random error. Yet the sensitivity of this t-statistic to random error underscores the importance of checking whether the cash from operations result over (−4,4) is robust across this and other samples. The results from the resampling procedures presented in the section on additional evidence concerning the research design, the diagnostic checks reported earlier for specific sample partitions, and the portfolio tests in the next section all substantiate the cash from operations result for the sample used here.

Portfolio Results

Tables 2 and 3 and Figure 1 present the results from partitioning the sample according to the magnitude of the funds forecast error, where the forecast is conditional on information released on or before the earnings release date (ϱ in equation 1). The observations within both the early and late release subsamples were divided into three groups according to the magnitude of their funds forecast errors. Table 2 presents

TABLE 3

CUMULATIVE MARKET MODEL PREDICTION ERRORS FOR THE FUNDS PORTFOLIOS OVER SELECTED INTERVALS—LATE FIRMS

Portfolio Construction Rule: The cumulative returns in the first three columns are for a one-way classification based on the magnitude of the forecast errors from the prediction equation for cash from operations (ϱ in equation 1). Similarly, the cumulative returns in columns four through six are for a one-way classification based on the forecast errors for working capital from operations (see the discussion in the "Portfolio Approach" section). The cumulative returns in the seventh column are for the combined portfolio which includes all observations.

Table Contents: Cumulative market model prediction errors are provided for each of the above portfolios over the specified intervals where day 0 is the date the annual report arrives at the SEC. The entries are in tenths of a percent. Thus, the high-cash portfolio had a 2.5 percent cumulative market model prediction error over the nine-day interval (−4,4).

Return Interval	*Cash From Operations*			*Working Capital From Operations*			
	Low	*Medium*	*High*	*Low*	*Medium*	*High*	*All*
(−10,−5)	−4	3	3	−10	3	7	1
(−4,4)	−12	0	25	9	0	7	3
(5,10)	11	7	1	−10	6	25	7

descriptive data about the three portfolios for each funds variable, Figure 1 plots these portfolios' cumulative abnormal returns over a 21-day interval centered on the date the annual report arrives at the SEC, and Table 3 presents these portfolios' cumulative abnormal returns for select subintervals of this 21-day period. For comparison purposes, the average earnings forecast errors, conditional on information released prior to the release of earnings, are also reported in the first row of Table 2.[33] Each entry in the first three rows of Table 2 is the average forecast error for an accounting variable scaled by total assets.[34] If there are systematic post-earnings announcement drifts in security returns, as reported in the literature, and funds and earnings forecast errors are positively correlated, then a difference in mean returns across funds levels might be due to the release of earnings information.[35] The results in Table 2 suggest that there may be a positive association between the funds and earnings forecast errors when funds is defined as working capital from operations and a negative association when funds is cash from operations. However, the correlation in these portfolios is probably quite small because, by construction at the individual security level, the funds forecast errors are perfectly uncorrelated with the earnings forecast errors.[36] The results in

[33] The earnings forecasts were based on an equation similar to 1 with fourth-quarter earnings and revenues removed from *W* and *F* replaced by fourth-quarter earnings.

[34] For example, the average earnings forecast error for the low earnings portfolio is .014, indicating 1.4 cents per dollar of assets.

[35] Foster, Olsen, and Shevlin [1984] considered the possibility of post-announcement drift and reviewed the findings in their studies.

[36] This follows because the funds prediction equation includes all of the regressors in the earnings equation plus earnings and revenues, and because the coefficients in both equations are unrestricted. It is also possible that spurious correlation between the market prediction errors at the two event dates could be induced if the parameters in the market model shifted over the interval between the estimation period and event dates. However, the correlation between these return metrics is only 0.029.

FIGURE 1

THE CUMULATIVE MARKET MODEL PREDICTION ERRORS FOR THE FUNDS PORTFOLIOS—LATE FIRMS

Figure Contents: The cumulative prediction errors in the top (bottom) graph are for a one-way classification based on the magnitude of the forecast errors from the prediction equation for cash (working capital) from operations. For each graph, observations are partitioned into three portfolios: low, medium, and high according to the magnitude of the forecast error (see the discussion in the "Portfolio Approach" section). Cumulative market model prediction errors starting ten days before the annual report arrives at the SEC (day 0) are provided for each portfolio.

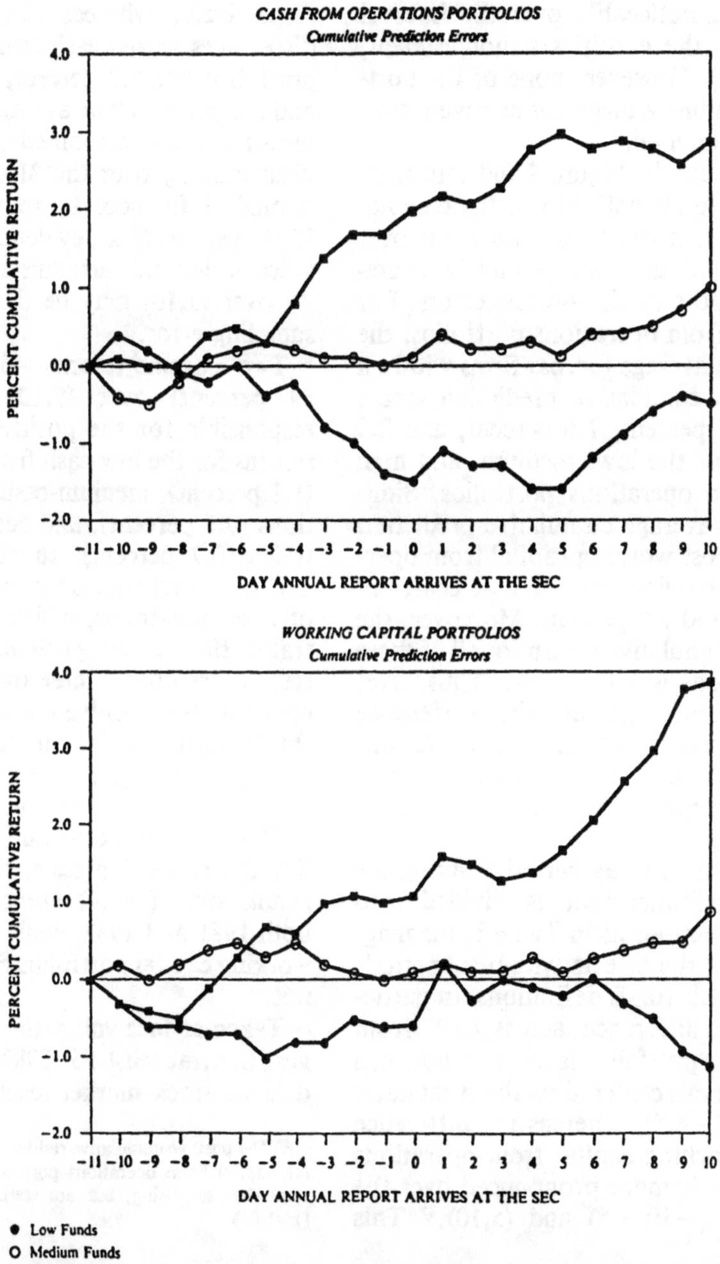

Table 3 also suggest that the differences in mean returns across the cash from operations portfolios are not due to a post-announcement earnings drift. If the cumulative returns of the cash from operations portfolios are nonzero over (−4,4) because of a post-earnings announcement drift, then the effect should be noticeable over the interval closest to the earnings announcement, (−10, −5). However, none of the portfolios exhibits a large cumulative return over this interval.

The results in Figure 1 indicate that, for both funds definitions, the cumulative market model prediction errors over the entire 21 days are positively associated with the funds forecast errors. For the cash from operations portfolios, the respective average (across firms within a portfolio) cumulative prediction errors are −0.5 percent, 1.0 percent, and 2.9 percent for the low, medium, and high cash from operations portfolios. Similarly, the average cumulative prediction errors across working capital from operations portfolios are −1.1 percent, 0.9 percent, and 3.9 percent. Moreover, the average cumulative return for all of these observations is 1.1 percent. Thus, over this extended period the difference across working capital from operations portfolios seems more pronounced than the difference across cash from operations portfolios.

When this 21-day period covering the funds announcement is divided into three subperiods as in Table 3, the magnitudes of the effects within subperiods differ across funds definitions. In particular, the difference across cash from operations portfolios is most pronounced over intervals centered on the event date, such as (−4,4), whereas the difference across working capital from operations portfolios is more pronounced over the intervals (−10, −5) and (5,10).[37] This pattern is consistent with that reported in Table 1 for the Γ-estimate's t-statistics. The differences in average cumulative prediction errors between the high-working capital from operations and low-working capital from operations portfolios at days −5, 4, and 10 are 1.7 percent, 1.5 percent, and 5.0 percent respectively, whereas the comparable differences across cash from operations portfolios are 0.7 percent, 4.4 percent, and 3.4 percent. The average cumulative return for the combined portfolio (all observations) over the 21-day period is strongly influenced by returns over the (5,10) period. Next, evidence will be provided which indicates this unusual activity over (5,10) may be due to random sampling error.

Two extreme returns (43 percent and 54 percent) over (5,10) are largely responsible for the positive cumulative returns for the low-cash from operations (1.1 percent), medium-cash from operations (0.7 percent), and combined portfolios (0.7 percent). In addition, over half of the returns are negative for each of these portfolios, which further illustrates that these positive cumulative returns are due to these two outliers. In contrast, the positive cumulative return for the high-working capital from operations portfolio (2.5 percent) over (5,10) seems to be associated with a positive shift in the return distribution. However, like the regression tests, the cash flow results over (−4,4) are consistent for both 1981 and 1982, while those for the working capital portfolios over (5,10) are not.

Taken at face value, these results suggest that, at least for 1982, there was a delayed stock market reaction to work-

[37] The positive cumulative residual for the low-working capital from operations portfolio over (−4,4) is somewhat surprising, but not statistically significant (t=1.01).

ing capital from operations. Yet it seems unreasonable to believe it would take longer for the working capital from operations information to be assimilated into the stock price than it would for the cash from operations information. If anything, one would expect that analysts find it more difficult to determine cash from operations since it is frequently not a line item on financial statements, whereas working capital from operations is. Alternatively, there may be a cross-sectional dependency in the data or sampling error. For instance, if observations are aligned in real time or there is a common information event over (5,10), such as the first quarter's earnings announcement, then there could be a cross-sectional dependency. The real time alignment problem seems unlikely since the effect is limited to a specific sub-interval and since the annual report release dates are dispersed across years and calendar months.[38] An examination of the *Wall Street Journal Index* over (5,10) for the firms in the high-working capital from operations portfolio indicated that there was no common information event across firms and very little evidence of unusually good news.[39] In summary, the effects over (5,10) remain unexplained but seem to be due to random error.

Additional descriptive evidence based on the quartiles for the cumulative returns within each portfolio over (−4,4) also suggests that there is a more substantial difference across the three cash from operations portfolios' market model prediction errors than across the working capital from operations portfolios'. Within each portfolio the cumulative market prediction error was calculated for the nine-day period. Next, the first quartile, median, etc. of these cumulative returns was determined. For the cash from operations portfolio the measures increase from the low to the high cash from operations portfolios for each quartile. This suggests the subsequent tests are not being driven by outliers. In the working capital from operations case there is no such consistency.

Table 4 presents the T^2-statistics of tests for a difference across means, for each funds variable, across these same subintervals. By inequality 5 in the "Portfolio Approach" section, the null hypothesis $v_i = v_j$, for specific values of $i \neq j$, is rejected at the .05 level whenever $T^2 > 6.32$. The entries in Table 4 indicate that when the rejection regions are properly specified to account for the fact that several tests are being conducted simultaneously, none of the individual differences are significantly different from zero at the 0.05 level. However, several of these differences would have been classified as significant if the rejection regions had not been corrected to account for simultaneous testing. As indicated in the "Portfolio Approach" section, these tests do not test the *joint* hypothesis that there is no difference across the means of all three portfolios. This hypothesis was tested using the T^2-statistic in inequality 4. The value of the T^2-test was 9.36, which indicates a significant difference in mean portfolio returns at the 0.025 level ($T^2_{0.025,2,80} = 7.90$) across portfolios based on cash from operations. In contrast, the value of the T^2 was 1.22 for a similar test using portfolios based on

[38] For example, no calendar month for a specific year contained more than seven of the 68 observations in the high-working capital portfolio. More generally, 20 percent of the observations' annual report arrival dates at the SEC were in March 1982, 19 percent in March 1983, ten percent in April 1982, 11 percent in April 1983, and 40 percent were spread uniformly over the remaining months.

[39] First-quarter earnings announcements were more than 15 days after the annual report for 62 of the observations in the high cash portfolio. Only three firms had earnings announcements during (5,10). Loosely speaking, a few more firms appeared to release good news than bad, but for the majority of firms there was no sign of unusual activity.

TABLE 4

T^2-TESTS FOR COMPARISON OF MEAN RETURNS ACROSS DIFFERENT FUNDS LEVELS—LATE FIRMS

Portfolio Construction Rule: The T^2-statistics in the first three columns are for a one-way classification based on the magnitude of the forecast errors from the prediction equation for cash from operations (ϱ in equation 1). Similarly, the T^2-statistics in columns four through six are for a one-way classification based on the forecast errors for working capital from operations (see the discussion in the "Portfolio Approach" section).

Table Contents: T^2-statistics are provided for a test for a difference of means across the specified portfolio pairs over the specified time intervals (this is an application of inequality 5). Average returns, both across portfolios and time, are measured over intervals specified relative to the date the annual report arrives at the SEC (day 0). For example, the T^2-statistic for the comparison between the high-cash and low-cash portfolios over a six-day interval starting five days after the annual report arrived at the SEC is 0.50. The null hypotheses are rejected at the .05 level of significance whenever $T^2>6.32$.

	Within Cash Flow			*Within Working Capital*		
Return Interval	*Medium Minus Low*	*High Minus Low*	*High Minus Medium*	*Medium Minus Low*	*High Minus Low*	*High Minus Medium*
(−2,2)	0.42	0.79	0.19	0.34	0.00	0.29
(−4,4)	0.72	4.37	2.62	0.22	0.01	0.21
(−10,−5)	0.37	0.25	0.00	1.25	1.21	0.94
(5,10)	0.05	0.50	0.38	1.89	5.20	2.34

working capital from operations.

To validate the regression and portfolio findings, similar tests were conducted using the 57 "early release" firms—those that release significant balance sheet information in their earnings news release. When equation 2 was estimated for this subsample over (−4,4), the Γ-estimate was essentially zero ($t=0.03$). Likewise, the portfolio means for the three portfolios based on the magnitude of the cash from operations forecast errors were also insignificant.[40] Because of the small sample size, these regression and portfolio tests are probably not powerful enough to reject H_0 even if it is false. However, these results are weakly consistent with the premise that cash from operations information for early release firms is assimilated into stock price before the annual report is released.

Additional Evidence Concerning the Research Design

Hold-out tests and resampling procedures are conducted to assess the robustness of the findings to the specification of the accounting prediction equation for cash from operations. They are also used to compare the standard error of the Γ-estimate's sampling distribution to the asymptotically correct standard error used to determine the *t*-statistic reported earlier. In addition, the validity of the research design is checked by com-

[40] The early release firms were partitioned into three cash from operations portfolios using the same cut-off points as the "late release" firms. There were 18, 22, and 17 observations, respectively, in the low, medium, and high cash from operations portfolios and their cumulative returns over a nine-day interval centered at the annual report release date were 0 percent, 2.3 percent, and 1.6 percent. All of the T^2 tests reported above for the late release firms were insignificant for these early release firms.

paring the cash from operations portfolio returns at the earnings and funds announcement dates. According to the assumptions underlying the research design, there should not be an association between ϱ (the regression error in equation 1) and earnings announcement returns. Similarly, returns at both dates are compared for portfolios based on the magnitude of earnings forecast errors, where the forecasts are conditional on information released prior to the earnings announcement. In this case, if the stock market is efficient with respect to earnings, the funds announcement returns on these portfolios should be zero.

Four accounting prediction equation alternatives are considered for cash from operations: the unrestricted version of 1 used to determine the results reported earlier and three restricted versions. The first restricted version's regressors are the three lagged cash from operations items plus the current year's fourth-quarter earnings and revenues. The second includes the lagged cash from operations items only. The third is a random walk based on the previous year's fourth-quarter's cash from operations.

The subsequent comparisons are based on 60 partitions of the 462 observations used to estimate the accounting prediction equations. Each partition is selected using a program which essentially flips a fair coin 462 times and assigns an observation to the estimation (hold-out) subsample if the outcome is heads (tails). Accordingly, the subsamples have varying sizes that average 231 observations. For each partition, the competing prediction models are estimated using the estimation subsample. Their out-of-sample forecasting abilities are compared in the corresponding hold-out subsample. For each partition and competing prediction model, the out-of-sample prediction errors are determined using accounting variables from the holdout subsample, and prediction equation coefficients are estimated using the estimation subsample. Forecasting comparisons are based on the mean absolute error and mean square error criteria suggested in Foster [1986]. For each prediction model and partition, the mean absolute and mean square errors are calculated and their average and standard deviation over the 60 partitions are determined. In addition, for each partition the competing model with the smallest mean absolute error is determined, as is the one with the smallest mean square error. For each criterion, the percent of time each model is ranked first across the 60 partitions is then determined. The first six columns of Table 5 present these findings. Clearly, the random walk model, *RW*, which is based on the previous year's fourth-quarter cash from operations, is inferior relative to the competing models, as an out-of-sample forecaster of the current year's fourth-quarter cash from operations. The average standard deviation of the mean square errors for the random walk is twice as large as its competitors. There is not a single partition where it is ranked first using either criterion. Although the unrestricted version of 1, *UNR*, which is used for the tests reported earlier, is ranked first using the mean square (absolute) criterion for 59 (70) percent of the partitions, the other two models which used three lagged cash from operations terms are close competitors. Indeed, the averages and standard deviations for both criteria are smallest for the unrestricted model, but the margin is very small. Thus, the unrestricted model certainly does no worse at out-of-sample

Table 5

Comparing the Out-of-Sample Forecasting Ability and Information Content Evidence of Competing Cash from Operations Prediction Models

Table Contents: Sixty estimation subsamples and corresponding holdout subsamples were chosen from the 462 observations used to estimate the accounting prediction equations. For each partition, four prediction models were estimated and their out-of-sample prediction errors were determined using estimation sample coefficient estimates and accounting variables from the hold-out sample. These include an unrestricted version of equation 1, *UNR*, which uses the 15 regressors specified in the "Cross-Sectional Regression Approach" section, and three restricted versions: *LAG+* which contains three lagged cash from operations terms plus the current year's fourth-quarter earnings and revenues, *LAG* which contains lagged cash from operations only, and *RW*, a random walk based on the previous year's fourth-quarter cash from operations. For each partition, the out-of-sample mean squared error and mean absolute error are calculated. The first two columns contain the mean and standard deviation of the mean square errors for the 60 samples, and the third column contains the percent of samples where the corresponding model had the smallest mean square error. Columns four through six contain equivalent comparisons based on the mean absolute errors. Columns seven and eight pertain to the 60 hold-out sample estimates of Γ in equation 2. They contain the average *t*-statistics and percent of times these *t*-statistics exceed 2.00.

	Mean Squared Error			*Mean Absolute Error*			*t-statistics for Γ*	
Forecast Equation	*Mean*	*Standard Deviation*	*Percent Ranked First*	*Mean*	*Standard Deviation*	*Percent Ranked First*	*Mean*	*Percent Greater Than 2.0*
UNR	.0042	.0006	59	.044	.002	70	2.22	57
LAG+	.0043	.0007	14	.045	.002	10	1.43	22
LAG	.0043	.0007	27	.045	.002	20	1.12	10
RW	.0080	.0018	0	.052	.004	0	1.98	51

forecasting than alternatives that resemble those used in previous earnings studies, and does significantly better than a random walk model.

These 60 partitions also are used to establish a sampling distribution for the Γ-estimates. For each partition and prediction model, equation 2 is estimated using hold-out subsample returns and out-of-sample prediction errors.[41] The last two columns of Table 5 contain the average *t*-statistics for these Γ-estimates across the 60 partitions and the percent of time these *t*-statistics exceed 2.0, respectively. Nearly 60 percent of the *t*-statistics for the Γ-estimates exceed 2.0 when the cash from operations forecast errors are determined using the unrestricted model and the average *t*-statistic is 2.22. This is strong evidence that the results reported earlier are not driven by outliers. In addition, the average and standard deviation of these 60 Γ-estimates are 0.23 and 0.00959, which are comparable to those for the entire sample (0.26 and 0.00798). This implies that the *t*-statistic reported earlier for the entire sample, 3.26, is only reduced to 2.71 (.026/.00798) when the standard error of the sampling distribution (rather than the asymptotically correct standard error) is used, suggesting the rejection of H_0 is not sensitive to the finite sample size limitation.[42]

Somewhat surprisingly, the out-of-sample forecasting ability of the four

[41] Since only 322 of the 462 observations have returns, these subsamples, on average, contain 161 observations.

[42] Laurentius Marais suggested using the standard error of the estimate's sampling distribution to assess the robustness of the results to the finite sample size limitation.

models is not directly related to the frequency of times the hold-out *t*-statistic exceeded 2.0. The best forecaster, the unrestricted model, also has the largest percent of *t*-statistics over 2.0 and the largest average *t*-statistic (2.22). However, the random walk model, by far the worst forecaster, has a median *t*-statistic of nearly 2.00. This finding is analogous to the Hughes and Ricks [1985] finding that the change in fourth-quarter earnings from one year to the next has incremental information content beyond analyst forecast errors at the earnings announcement. However, here when the returns from the funds announcement are regressed against both forecast errors, using the full sample of 322 observations, the coefficient on the forecast error related to the random walk is not significant ($t=0.94$), while the coefficient related to the unrestricted model is ($t=2.20$).

The small average *t*-statistic reported in Table 5 for the regressions where the forecast errors are based on lagged cash from operations plus current revenues and earnings ($t=1.43$), and lagged cash from operations only ($t=1.12$), suggest that the conclusions here might be sensitive to the forecast model choice. However, these statistics increase ($t=2.11$ and $t=1.68$, respectively) when all 462 observations are used to estimate the prediction equations and 322 observations are used for the return equations. Both these full sample *t*-statistics are smaller than the corresponding regression where the forecast errors are based on the random walk ($t=2.66$). However, the results of the study would have been significant for all of the prediction models except the one whose regressors are lagged cash from operations only.

Assuming that cash from operations has information content, and that ideal conditions for this research design exist: (a) there should *not* be an association between stock returns at the earnings date and ϱ since cash from operations is needed to determine this forecast error and is assumed to be released later at the funds date; and (b) there should *not* be an association between stock returns at the funds date and unexpected earnings. In addition, if positive unexpected earnings and positive unexpected cash from operations (where the expectation is conditional on knowing earnings) are both good news, then portfolios with low (high) unexpected earnings and high (low) unexpected cash from operations should have returns with opposite signs at the earnings and funds date. The results provided next further examine the validity of the two-date research design by considering the extent to which these implications hold.

Table 6 presents the return behavior for both the earnings and cash from operations portfolios over event intervals centered at the *Wall Street Journal* earnings announcement and the date the annual report arrives at the SEC. Clearly the *Wall Street Journal* earnings announcement is more of an earnings event than a cash from operations event, while just the opposite is true at the date the annual report arrives at the SEC. At the earnings announcement the difference between the cumulative market model prediction errors for the high and low earnings portfolios is 3.1 percent as compared to 1.4 percent for the high and low cash from operations portfolios. In contrast, this difference at the funds date is 0.5 percent for the earnings portfolios and 3.7 percent for the cash from operations portfolios. There is some evidence of an early reaction to unexpected cash from operations at the earnings date and of a persistent reaction to unexpected earnings at the funds date, but neither is statistically significant. At the earnings

TABLE 6

COMPARISON OF THE CUMULATIVE MARKET MODEL PREDICTION ERRORS FOR THE EARNINGS AND FUNDS PORTFOLIOS AT BOTH EVENT DATES—LATE FIRMS

Portfolio Construction Rule: The cumulative returns in the first eight rows are for portfolios based on one-way classifications. Cash from operations portfolios are based on the magnitude of the forecast errors from equation 1. The earnings portfolios are based on a similar equation with fourth-quarter earnings and revenues removed from *W*, and *F* defined as fourth-quarter earnings. Two-way classifications are determined by first forming two one-way classifications based on earnings and funds, and then assigning observations to one of nine portfolios according to the two one-way assignments.

Table Contents: Each column contains cumulative market model prediction errors measured over the specified interval. The "earnings announcement" interval includes the day of and the day before the *Wall Street Journal* earnings announcement. The "annual report release date" interval is a nine-day period centered on the date the annual report arrives at the SEC. The entries are in tenths of a percent. For example, the high-cash portfolio had a 2.5 percent cumulative market model prediction error over the annual report release date interval. Some of these results are also in other tables and are provided here for convenience.

	Event Intervals			
	Earnings Announcement 2-Day Interval		*Annual Report Release Period 9-Day Interval*	
Portfolios	*Observations*	*Market Model Prediction Errors*	*Observations*	*Market Model Prediction Errors*
Earnings				
Low	43	−13	43	−4
Medium	209	−2	210	2
High	69	18	69	10
High-Low		31		14
Cash From Operations				
Low	85	0	86	−12
Medium	151	−3	151	0
High	85	5	85	25
High-Low		5		37
Cash From Operations-Low and Earnings-High	20	12	20	−17
Cash From Operations-High and Earnings-Low	19	−19	19	30

announcement, T^2 is 4.71 ($T^2_{0.025,2,80}$= 7.90) for a joint test for a difference in mean market model prediction errors across the cash from operations portfolios and 23.81 for a similar test across the earnings portfolios. For similar tests at the funds date, T^2 was 9.36 for the cash from operations portfolios and 0.872 for the earnings portfolios.[43]

Table 6 also indicates there are return reversals at the funds date for portfolios with unexpected earnings and cash from operations at opposite extremes. Port-

[43] These results are reported here in a descriptive rather than inferential spirit to illustrate the validity of the research design. The combined type one error reported earlier, for the hypotheses tests which are of primary interest in this study, does not cover joint inferences concerning the statistics reported here.

folios with high earnings and low cash from operations have a cumulative market model prediction error of 1.2 percent at the earnings announcement and −1.7 percent at the funds date, while the low-earnings and high cash portfolio returns at these dates are −1.9 percent and 3.0 percent, respectively. Because these portfolios only contain a few observations, the standard errors related to their returns are relatively large. As a result, these returns are not statistically significant. However, these findings support the validity of the two-date design, and they indicate that one of the ways this study could be improved is by using more observations.

Summary and Possible Extensions

This study addressed the question of whether the accrual and funds components of earnings have incremental information content beyond earnings itself. It has provided significant evidence that the answer to this question is affirmative when funds are defined as cash from operations. However, the findings are inconclusive if funds are defined as working capital from operations.

A model was used to determine if the components of earnings have incremental information content beyond earnings itself. It measures the association between market model prediction errors from an event interval covering the date the annual report arrives at the SEC and new information about the accrual and funds components of earnings released at that time. Market model prediction errors were summed over an event interval centered on the date the annual report arrives at the SEC, and the resulting sum was regressed separately against new information about working capital and cash from operations. For a nine-day event interval, the cash from operations regression coefficient was positive and significantly different from zero, whereas the working capital from operations was not significant. A portfolio approach also was used to measure the information content of the components of earnings at the annual report release date. For each funds variable the sample was partitioned according to the magnitude of the funds forecast error. Then, the mean market model prediction errors for the resulting portfolios were compared over various return intervals. When funds were defined as cash from operations and a nine-day event interval was used, there was a significant difference in the mean market model prediction errors across portfolios. In addition, the portfolio ranking based on the magnitude of the cash from operations forecast errors was the same as the rankings based on the mean, median, first quartile, and third quartile of the market model prediction errors across portfolios. These findings indicate that total accruals and cash from operations, taken together, have incremental information content beyond earnings and that there is a positive association between this component information and stock returns. The fact that information content was detected for cash from operations but not for working capital from operations might explain why others, using funds variables which are highly correlated with earnings, have not found evidence that funds have incremental information content.

The evidence here is consistent with the stock market reacting to the new information in the cash from operations and total accrual components of earnings. However, to the extent that there are other correlated items in the annual report, this causality argument is mitigated. One such correlated variable, the current year's capital expenditures, is partly controlled for in this study, but clearly there could be others. Also of interest is whether there are uncorrelated items in the annual report that have information content. A possible extension would be to combine some of the features here with those used by Hoskin, Hughes, and Ricks [1986], who assess the incremental information content of items released concurrently with earnings. Besides addressing these omitted variables issues, such a study should replicate the tests here to see if the results are robust across different firms and years.

One explanation for the results concerning cash from operations is that investors reward firms for being responsive to demand swings in their products. For instance, if during the current period investors believe that demand is going to expand in the near future, they might reward firms that anticipate this demand by expanding their inventories and receivables and, as a result, reduce cash from operations. Similarly, firms which respond to anticipated downturns by reducing inventories and receivables and thus increasing cash flows may also receive a premium from investors. This interpretation is consistent with the findings here, since the association between stock returns and unexpected cash from operations was positive during the two-year sample period when the economy was in a severe downturn (1981–82). Moreover, this perspective suggests that a similar study covering an extended period might find a systematic change in the sign of the correlation between returns and unexpected cash from operations, depending on the state of the economy. This "responsiveness" interpretation is different from the standard "liquidity" argument which would claim that cash from operations has information content because it signals financial distress. Although cash from operations may be useful for assessing credit worthiness, it seems unlikely that there would be a sufficient number of distressed firms in the random sample used here to explain the results.

Some members of the financial community may find these results useful since their decisions are influenced by their perception of how stock price is affected by various accounting variables. Although this study finds that the cash and noncash components of earnings, taken together, have incremental information content beyond earnings, it has no implications for which one of these components (if not both) has information content. After controlling for earnings, incremental information about the cash and noncash components of earnings is precisely the same.

This study has been extended in Wilson [1986], which introduces a model to address the question of whether accruals have incremental information content beyond cash flows. It structures the way information about the components is extracted from earnings when earnings are announced. In addition, it links the association between this component information and stock returns at the earnings announcement to the association between stock returns and the common component information released on the date the annual report arrives at the SEC. This related study confirms the finding here that the cash and total accruals components of earnings have incremental information content beyond earnings itself, and also finds that the total accruals component of earnings has incremental information content beyond the cash component.

REFERENCES

Anderson, T., *An Introduction to Multivariate Statistical Analysis* (John Wiley & Sons, 1958).

Ball, R., and P. Brown, "An Empirical Evaluation of Accounting Income Numbers," *Journal of Accounting Research* (Autumn 1968), pp. 159–178.

Beaver, W., and R. Dukes, "Interperiod Tax Allocation, Earnings Expectations, and the Behavior of Security Prices," THE ACCOUNTING REVIEW (April 1972), pp. 320–332.

———, P. Griffin, and W. Landsman, "The Incremental Information Content of Replacement Cost Earnings," *Journal of Accounting and Economics* (July 1982), pp. 15–39.

Bowen, R., D. Burgstahler, and L. Daley, "Evidence on the Relationships Between Earnings and Various Measures of Cash Flow," THE ACCOUNTING REVIEW (October 1986a), pp. 713–725.

———, ———, and ———, "The Incremental Information Content of Accrual Versus Cash Flows," Unpublished working paper (University of Washington and the University of Minnesota, 1986b).

Burgstahler, D., and E. Noreen, "Two Classes of Statistics for Detecting Contemporaneous Security Market Reactions to a Sequence of Related Events," Unpublished working paper (The University of Washington, 1985).

Easton, P., "Empirical Aspects of an Information Perspective on Accounting," Unpublished doctoral thesis, 1983.

Foster, G., "Quarterly Accounting Data: Time-Series Properties and Predictive-Ability Results," THE ACCOUNTING REVIEW (January 1977), pp. 1–21.

———, *Financial Statement Analysis* (Prentice-Hall, 1986).

———, C. Olsen, and T. Shevlin, "Earnings Releases, Anomalies, and the Behavior of Security Returns," THE ACCOUNTING REVIEW (October 1984), pp. 574–603.

Foster, T., and D. Vickrey, "The Incremental Information Content of the 10-K," THE ACCOUNTING REVIEW (October 1978), pp. 921–934.

Gonedes, N., "Corporate Signalling, External Accounting, and Capital Market Equilibrium: Evidence on Dividends, Income, and Extraordinary Items," *Journal of Accounting Research* 16 (Spring 1978), pp. 26–79.

Hoskin, R., J. Hughes, and W. Ricks, "Analysis of Firm Disclosures Made Concurrently With Earnings Announcements," *Journal of Accounting Research* (Supplement 1986).

Hughes, J., and W. Ricks, "Association Between Forecast Errors and Excess Returns Near to Earnings Announcements," THE ACCOUNTING REVIEW (January 1987), pp. 158–175.

Johnson R., and D. Wichern, *Applied Multivariate Statistical Analysis* (Prentice-Hall, 1982).

Kaplan, R., and J. Patell, "The Information Content of Cash Flow Data Relative to Annual Earnings," Unpublished working paper (Stanford University, 1977).

Matolcsy, Z., "Evidence on the Joint and Marginal Information Content of Inflation-Adjusted Accounting Income Numbers," *Journal of Accounting Research* (Autumn 1984), pp. 555–569.

Miller, R., *Simultaneous Statistical Inference* (McGraw-Hill, 1966).

Morrison, D., *Multivariate Statistical Methods* (McGraw-Hill, 1967).

Patell, J., "The API and the Design of Experiments," *Journal of Accounting Research* (Autumn 1979), pp. 528–549.

Rao, C., *Linear Statistical Inference and Its Applications* (John Wiley & Sons, 1973).

Rayburn, J., "The Association of Operating Cash Flow and Accruals with Security Returns," *Journal of Accounting Research* (Supplement, 1986).

Roy, S., "Some Further Results in Simultaneous Confidence Interval Estimation," *Annals of Mathematical Statistics*, 25 (1954), pp. 752–761.

———, "A Note on Some Further Results in Simultaneous Confidence Interval Estimation," *Annals of Mathematical Statistics*, 27 (1956), pp. 856–858.

———, *Some Aspects of Multivariate Analysis* (John Wiley & Sons, 1957).

———, and R. Bose, "Simultaneous Confidence Interval Estimation," *Annals of Mathematical Statistics*, 24 (1953), pp. 513–536.

Scholes, M., and J. Williams, "Estimating Betas From Nonsynchronous Data," *Journal of Financial Economics*, 5 (1977), pp. 309–327.

Stern, J., "Let's Abandon Earnings Per Share," *Wall Street Journal* (Dec. 18, 1972), p. 14.

White, H., "A Heteroskedasticity-Consistent Covariance Matrix Estimator and A Direct Test for Heteroskedasticity," *Econometrica*, 48 (1980), pp. 817–838.

Wilson, G., "The Incremental Information Content of Accruals and Cash Flows After Controlling for Earnings," Unpublished Ph.D. thesis (Carnegie Mellon University, 1985).

——, "The Relative Information Content of Accruals and Cash Flows: Combined Evidence At The Earnings Announcement and Annual Report Date," *Journal of Accounting Research* (Supplement 1986).

Suggested additional readings

* Arnold, A. J. and Webb, B. J., "Cash, Profits and Pergamon," **The Accountant**, 8 July 1982, pp. 28-30.

* Lawson, G. H., " Was Woolworth Ailing?," **The Accountant**, 4 November 1982, pp. 12-32.

These are both examples of a 'case study' approach to demonstrating the utility of cash flow accounting in relation to the development of a well-known corporate situation.

* Bowen R. M., Burgstahler, D. and Daley, L. A., "Evidence on the Relationships Between Earnings and Various Measures of Cash Flow," **The Accounting Review**, October 1986, pp. 713-25.

Bowen et al is one of the earliest attempts to model and test the predictability of cash flows using both cash flow data and earnings data. The results indicate that earnings may not be a good predictor of future cash flows, but the study is limited by the simplicity of the model.

* Gentry, J. A., Newbold, P. and Whitford, D. T., "Classifying Bankrupt Firms with Funds Flow Components," **Journal of Accounting Research**, Spring 1985, pp. 146-60.

Gentry et al used cash flow-based ratios to determine whether or not they could classify failed and successful companies on the basis of them. They concluded they could, but that they were no better at doing so than accrual-based ratios.

* Lee, T. A., "The Financial Statements of the Hongkong and Shanghai Banking Corporation 1865 - 1980," in King, F. H. H., (ed.), **Eastern Banking: Essays in the History of the Hongkong and Shanghai Banking Corporation** (London: Athlone Press, 1983), pp. 77-92.

An example of the detailed application of Lee's system of cash flow accounting to a well-known commercial entity, revealing aspects of the latter's financial performance which would not have been available from conventional accounting data.

DEBATING THE UTILITY OF CASH FLOW REPORTING

Introduction

The debate on the relative merits of CFA ideas has been small. The first contribution was made by *Ashton* (1976), and this is more of a broad review of the work to that date of Lawson and Lee. In particular, Ashton provides a comparative review, identifying the differences (in theoretical approach and reporting format), and the similarities (user need satisfaction, allocations, price changes, and forecast reports). His one major criticism was the apparent inability of CFA to provide income measures for purposes of entity performance assessment.

This theme appears in the critiques of both *Egginton* (1984) and *Staubus* (1989), but does not appear in *Rutherford* (1982). Rutherford's main concern about the CFA proposals of Lawson and Lee was their claim that cash flow accounting is allocation-free. He articulated an argument, based on the notion of reported accounting data having empirical referents, that such data can never be allocation-free because of the economic inter-actions which take place within reporting entities. In other words, because of such inter-active effects, the empirical referents for accounting data are often difficult to determine, and subjective allocation is necessary.

Egginton and Staubus both concentrate on the potential utility of CFA as a basis for entity performance assessment. Both conclude that, although the system may have considerable utility with respect to assessing entity liquidity, it is deficient regarding profitability and financial position information. Indeed, Egginton and Staubus are particularly concerned at Lee's suggested use of exit prices as cash flow potential, and Staubus argues strongly for the distinguishing of wealth and liquidity.

What each of these critiques represents is an attempt to address apparent weaknesses in the CFA arguments to date. In particular, they are concerned to limit the claims made for CFA by its main proponents, and thereby to constrain the role specified for CFA. Irrespective of the merits of these critiques, it is interesting that none of them condemn CFA outright. Indeed, all of them see a definite if restricted role for CFA systems. Given the nature of this criticism, and its infrequency, it perhaps should not be surprising that CFA ideas have been implemented in recent financial reporting practice.

* Ashton, R.,"Cash Flow Accounting: a Review and Critique," **Journal of Business Finance and Accounting**, Winter 1976, pp. 63-81.

* Egginton, D. A., "In Defence of Profit Measurement: Some Limitations of Cash Flow and Value Added as Performance Measures for External Reporting,'" **Accounting and Business Research**, Spring 1984, pp. 99-111.

* Rutherford, B. A., "The Interpretation of Cash Flow Reports and the Other Allocation Problem," **Abacus**, June 1982, pp. 40-49.

* Staubus, G. J., "Cash Flow Accounting and Liquidity: Cash Flow Potential and Wealth," **Accounting and Business Research**, Spring 1989, pp. 161-69.

CASH FLOW ACCOUNTING: A REVIEW AND CRITIQUE

RAYMOND ASHTON *

As is well known, in recent years, both businessmen and accountants have been increasingly dissatisfied with conventional historic cost accounting and, whilst a Government Committee set up to examine the alternative accounting systems has reported only recently, the aim of this paper is to examine critically one of the suggested alternatives, cash flow accounting. Cash flow accounting is supported by those who feel that the problems of asset valuation and income measuremeant are so formidable that an alternative accounting system must be devised which avoids these problems and yet provides a reliable guide as to how a company has performed in the past and how it is likely to perform in the future. It is claimed by those who support cash flow accounting that this system of accounting satisfies these requirements and that companies should include in their annual report a comprehensive cash flow statement. As implied by its name, under a comprehensive cash flow accounting system, entries would only be made in the books of account when cash was actually received or paid out. This means that fixed assets and materials purchased for either resale or further processing would be charged in full to the year in which they were acquired irrespective of when the benefits from acquiring these assets will accrue. From purely a book–keeping point of view historic cost accounting is very similar to cash flow accounting except that the latter would not incorporate any valuations and would ignore funds items such as debtors and creditors. Having described briefly the main idea underlying cash flow accounting we can now turn to a more detailed review of the related literature.

The development of cash flow accounting in both professional and academic circles is closely associated with the work of Professors Lawson (2) and Lee (3). Whilst their ideas are in many respects similar, in practice there are important and significant differences in their particular systems of cash flow accounting. As a resuit, each author's contribution will be reviewed separately, so that a constrast can be made between their work. In the final section the advantages and disadvantages of cash flow accounting will be discussed and particular reference will be made to what further work needs to be carried out before a comprehensive system of cash flow accounting can be made operational.

THE LAWSON SYSTEM

It has been argued by Lawson that his system of cash flow accounting provides an analytical framework for linking past, present and future financial performance.

**The author is Senior Research Officer at the London Graduate School of Business Studies.* *(Paper received August 1975, revised January 1976)*

TABLE 1

FRAMEWORK FOR A TOTAL CASH-FLOW FINANCIAL SYSTEM

	End Year	1	2	3	etc.	etc.
(1)	Increase or decrease in bank balance or overdraft	+	+	+	+	+
(2)	Net operating cash-flows	+	+	+	+	+
(3)	Corporation taxes on (2)	–	–	–	–	–
(4)	Capital expenditure (including portfolio investment)	–	–	–	–	–
(5)	(i) cash grants; and	+	+	+	+	+
	(ii) tax rebates resulting from tax depreciation allowances on (4)	+	+	+	+	+
(6)	Long term debt flows (in and out) including interest payments on debt	+	+	+	+	+
(7)	Tax rebates on debt interest payments	+	+	+	+	+
(8)	External equity finance	+	+	+	+	+
(9)	Sales of surplus assets	+	+	+	+	+
(10)	Tax rebates on existing assets and losses brought forward	+	+	+	+	+
(11)	Distributable equity cash-flows	$D_1(1-d)$	$D_2(1-d)$	$D_3(1-d)$	etc.	etc.
(12)	*Less* External equity finance	E_1	E_2	E_3	etc.	etc.
(13)	Shareholders' cash-flow stream	$D_1(1-d)$ $-E_1$	$D_2(1-d)$ $-E_2$	$D_3(1-d)$ $-E_3$	etc. etc.	etc. etc.

Operating cash-flow statement (subheading (2))

	End Year	1	2	3	etc.	etc.
(i)	Sales receipts	+	+	+	+	+
(ii)	Materials	–	–	–	–	–
(iii)	Labour	–	–	–	–	–
(iv)	Works overhead	–	–	–	–	–
(v)	Administrative overhead	–	–	–	–	–
(vi)	Selling overhead	–	–	–	–	–
Transfer to (2) above		+	+	+	+	+

$$W_0 = \frac{D_1(1-d)-E_1}{(1+k)} + \frac{D_2(1-d)-E_2}{(1+k)^2} + \ldots$$

Notation. W_0 = objective function. k = cost of capital. d = personal tax rate of shareholders. E1, E2, En = new external equity finance. D1, D2, Dn = distributable equity cash flows.

This ambitious framework is made up of two interlocking cash flow statements which are shown in Table 1.

It is evident from Table 1 that the two sections making up the cash flow statement are similar in form and content to the conventional balance sheet and profit and loss account. The top half of the statement can be likened to the balance sheet and the operating cash flow statement to the profit and loss account. This similarity goes deeper in that both the conventional balance sheet/profit and loss account and the cash flow statement represent outstanding balances at a particular date and that these balances have accrued over the same period of time, i.e. the accounting period. This similarity is more apparent than real because as is well known the conventional statements are a mixture of cash and accruals whilst the balances in the cash flow statement are made up of only the former. Before discussing in detail the reasons for the format suggested in Table 1 it is necessary to clear up a few points which are not made very clear either in the above table or in the author's subsequent writings. The first concerns the time period to be covered by the cash flow statement. At the moment it has been suggested that the statement should cover between five and six years prior to the current period and the forecast for the future should cover between seven and ten years. This point and the problems involved in compiling such a statement will be discussed later in the paper. The next point concerns the shareholders' cash flow stream which is the residual figure remaining after deducting new equity finance raised during the year and retentions from the distributable cash flows attributable to the equity shareholders. This figure is then inserted for each year covered by the statement, into what is referred to in his writings as an objective function and discounted by the company's cost of capital. The author claims that by making an allowance for the time value of money, in the objective function, his cash flow model is consistent with economic and financial theory. This last assertion is justified on the basis that the objective function is a modified application of Gordon's dividend – share price model. Having outlined the basic principles underlying his cash flow accounting statement we must now turn to the deeper question of why such a statement should be prepared and form such an integral part of the financial reports issued to shareholders.

In one of the author's earlier papers on cash flow accounting he justifies the inclusion of a cash flow accounting statement as part of the annual accounts on the following grounds: 1) The information requirements of shareholders, 2) Capital market efficiency.

1) The information needs of shareholders.

The author subdivides these into two further categories:-

(i) The components of the true past and prospective return to the company (and ultimately the shareholders) should be disclosed.

(ii) The annual accounts ought to enable individuals to make investment decisions.

These sentiments are very laudable and extremely difficult to fault. Whether cash flow accounting satisfies these requirements more adequately than conventional accounts (or the suggested alternatives) is an empirical question as yet unresolved either by the author or his opponents. This point together with certain others in this section will be developed further in the critique of the author's work. It is interesting to note that with respect to item (ii) above, the author takes the view that the shareholder will be primarily interested in not only the existing level of dividends but their likely growth in the future. This is because a shareholder who commits capital now forgoes current consumption but obtains the opportunity to consume and/or reinvest an uncertain stream of dividends etc. in the future. In the case of a company, the return to the shareholder will be the stream of dividends likely to be paid in the future and this will also apply to shareholders who invest for a finite time period since they will receive an exit share price based on the market's estimate of the future level of dividend payments.

2) Capital market efficiency.

The author then argues that if companies were obliged to disclose information relating to the amount of dividends to be paid in the future and the expected inflows and outflows of cash from which the dividends are paid, shareholders would be able to assess more accurately and objectively share values. It is then claimed that as a consequence of the latter there would be a more accurate relationship between equity returns and the structure of fixed interest rates. As a result of the foregoing he then concludes that this improvement in capital market efficiency will lead to a more efficient allocation of resources in the economy.

On the basis of premises 1) and 2), the author then argues that the format of the cash flow accounting statement should quantify all the major determinants of a company's future dividend stream. These determinants, which are reproduced from an article by the author, are as follows:–

1. Taxation, investment incentives and additional injections of equity finance.

2. The level of earnings generated by existing assets net of any capital expenditure (which he refers to as replacement expenditure) necessary to maintain the trading and productive capacity of the assets intact.

3. The allocation of earnings between dividends and retentions or in other words the pay out ratio or plough back ratio depending on the viewpoint

taken.

4. New project returns, by which he means the average return or expenditure over and above replacement expenditure. This seems a rather all embracing term in view of 5 below.

5. The time profile of cash flows expected from new projects.

6. The level of debt–financing and debt–raising capacity.

After briefly discussing the dividend implications of points 1 to 6 the author returns to his main theme, that of demonstrating that cash flow accounting is superior to conventional accrual accounting. In an inflationary environment, it is argued, turnover will grow in money terms, and other things being equal the monetary value of debtors and stock will also increase, but unless there is a proportionately greater increase in creditors there is likely to be a significant deviation between accrual earnings and cash flow earnings with the implication that the present system seriously overstates earnings retained for new investment (4). The corollary of this is that at the moment accounts do not provide a reliable measure of earnings and so any appraisal or estimate made by shareholders will be seriously undermined from the start. This deficiency in conventional accrual accounting could be remedied by companies publishing a sources and application of funds statement drawn up on what the author refers to as the "appropriate" basis, i.e. a cash flow basis. It is then pointed out that the problem then is how the investing public might be given sufficient guidance about the "appropriate" basis, i.e. a cash flow basis. This point would also appear valid as regards any form of accounting, whether it was conventional accrual accounting or any of the other variants, including cash flow accounting. Whilst this point is important it should not detract us from the main thrust of the author's argument, that accrual accounting suffers from the drawback that it masks a company's cash position and can lead to a situation where a substantial amount of the company's capital is eroded before its true position becomes apparent.

It is very difficult to criticise the author's cash flow statement since what he is arguing for is additional information (albeit in a special form – cash) over and above what we presently receive from companies. Such a plea for more disclosure and in particular more disclosure about the future of companies rather than less is to be welcomed. A cash flow statement similar to Table 1 would satisfy the first two information requirements of shareholders, that is, to disclose not only true past and future performance but also the main factors contributing to past and future performance. A possible weakness of the author's model is that in relation to past performance it does not distinguish between expected and unexpected changes in cash flows. Examples of the latter being windfall gains or losses attributable to such things as changes in Government legislation, which includes tax and price control policies and sudden changes in the price of raw materials, which might themselves be the result of extraneous factors such as the increased price of oil after the Arab–Israeli war in October 1973. This writer would accept that in many cases it would not only be difficult to identify whether an item was expected or unexpected and even when it could be identified, its magnitude would be very difficult to estimate with any degree of accuracy. Nevertheless, if the model is to be complete, some attempt must be made to incorporate these changes into the cash flow statement. Although any basis for deciding whether a change was expected or unexpected is likely to be in many cases arbitrary, some breakdown, however arbitrary, would at least help the shareholder and capital market to assess more accurately the company's past performance.

The second shareholder information requirement was that annual accounts ought to enable individuals to make investment decisions. The author then argues that shareholders will be interested in future dividends and their likely growth as these will affect their consumption possibilities in the future and those shareholders who invest for a finite time period will also be interested in the level of future dividends, since these will affect the exit share price they receive. Having said this, one suspects the author is really saying that a cash flow forecast covering seven to ten years will more accurately forecast the likelihood of forecasted dividends actually being paid than accrual earnings projected on the same basis. Intuitively the author's argument seems more plausible but it must be said in favour of the alternative hypothesis that there is no reason why forecasted accrual earnings cannot accurately indicate whether the dividends forecasted will actually be paid. The writer agrees that during an inflationary period the sums tied up in working capital might result in a negative cash flow, despite a relatively high accrual earnings per share. In this situation a company is more than likely to be able to meet its dividend forecasts by bank borrowing and so forecasted accrual earnings in many cases are likely to be just as good indicators of ability to pay future dividends as cash flow forecasts. It would seem to this writer that in the absence of empirical evidence which supports either hypothesis, both forecasts should be published, but if a choice has to be made, this writer would favour the cash flow forecast as it is less susceptible to distortion than accrual earnings.

The author's other major argument for including a cash flow statement was that it would improve capital market efficiency. It is very difficult to fault this argument since if the market is provided with additional information vis–a–vis the future, share prices are, in the majority of cases, likely to be more rationally based, unless the expectations of the market prior to the new information are confirmed in some approximate way by the cash flow forecast. No doubt more information about a company's cash flow would be extremely useful, but it should be pointed out that more information per se does not necessarily mean that the market will use it to appraise a particular company's share price or share prices in general. For instance, more information about a company's depreciation rates and bases will not necessarily be of use to the analyst because share prices reflect future cash flows rather than future earnings computed on an accrual basis. In presenting the market with more information, which it is hoped will be used in determining a company's share price it must be borne in mind that no information is costless and it should be established that the benefits from producing this additional information will be greater than the associated costs. However, this writer would accept the main tenor of the author's argument, but would criticise him for not developing this point in more detail.

THE LEE SYSTEM

The next section of this paper will review the work of Lee (3) who together with Lawson, has consistently argued the case for cash flow accounting. Although there are similarities between the work of these writers there are also important differences. Lee argues that utility and relevance should govern the measurement and communication of accounting information. The criteria for deciding the relevance and utility of accounting information is that it should satisfy the information needs of the potential user, or more specifically, it should be capable of influencing his decisions and actions. Users would still receive the conventional historic cost accounts but their role in the financial reports would be that of authenticating management's stewardship. It is then asserted by the author that stewardship information appears less relevant and useful to the investor than cash flow information. This assertion is justified on the grounds that cash is a key resource of the company and is vital to the company's continued existence. In addition, since the value of shareholding or potential interest is linked to the company's continued existence it is argued that users should feceive information about the company's past and future which is cash flow orientated. A stronger argument for users receiving information about future cash flows, which was also put forward by Lawson, is that it would enable users to form an opinion on the level of future dividends. Since both current and future dividends are linked to the availability of cash, information relating to this item would on the surface seem of crucial importance. It is again difficult to fault these arguments and clearly users decisions about alternative investments would be helped considerably if this information were available.

This again raises more fundamental question as to how this information could be provided. The author asserts that the cash flow forecasts should be as formal and credible as possible and that uninformed guess work must be avoided at all times. Whilst the latter statement is true, it is not very helpful, because it does not tell the compiler how forecasts could be made as formal and credible as possible. To be fair, whilst the author does not discuss this latter point in detail, he does suggest general guidelines to be followed by compilers of cash flow forecasts. These statements should satisfy, amongst other things, three main needs which are:–

1) To predict dividends and other benefits receivable by him from the company.

2) To predict its future survival, maintenance or expansion.

3) To predict the degree of risk and uncertainty connected with an existing or potential investment in a company.

Whether cash flow statements based largely on forecasts can satisfy these three needs adequately is an empirical question but given the present state of the fore–casting art it seems very doubtful. On point 3) this writer would take the view that the degree of risk and uncertainty inherent in an investment can be estimated by calculating the company's cost of capital using the capital – asset pricing model. This will give the market's unbiased estimate of the degree of risk involved in investing in a particular equity and so it is now possible to satisfy this need, although this might be more rationally based if forecasts of future cash flows were available.

After discussing user requirements the author then discusses the problem of objectivity and published accounting data based on forecasts. He agrees that mental objectivity on the part of the compiler should be adhered to at all times and makes the point that technical objectivity cannot possibly be achieved in all areas of accounting and that this fact should be recognised and accepted. In applying this to forecasts produced by the company the author asserts that the compiler's criteria should be the relevance and usefulness of the information to the investor. Cash flow information, so the argument runs, satisfies these require–ments since in its historic form it is the most objective information available and is also relevant for the purposes of comparing actual cash flows with forecasted cash flows. Although in the case of forecasted information a degree of uncertainty is introduced, the subjectiveness of accrual judgements and opinions in the case of budgeted accrual profits is avoided and so information relating to a company's future cash flows is less subjective in a total sense than accrual profit forecasts.

As mentioned earlier, in the author's suggested scheme of financial reporting, the conventional historic cost accounts would be retained for the purposes of satisfy–ing the stewardship function. In addition there would be a number of individual cash flow statements, the balances of which would be taken to what the author refers to as a "statement of total cash flow". The separate statements would analyse cash flows relating to specific aspects of the company's business such as operations, taxation, extraordinary items and also financial and capital transactions. These forecasts would eventually cover a four to five year period at the most and the

author suggests that at the moment only a three year forecast would be possible. This information would be subject to continuous reassessment and so account would be taken of significant events which have affected the original forecast. This writer, as he has expressed earlier, is sceptical whether information relating to such a time span could be provided with any degree of accuracy and reliability. His experience with forecasting techniques suggests that at the most only one year's forecast could be currently provided with any degree of accuracy and reliability. Clearly this does not detract from the argument for cash flow accounting but is merely asserting that with current techniques the time period covered by such forecasts should be restricted to a year at the most.
In addition to the cash flow statements mentioned above the author also suggests that there should be a statement which outlines in general terms the assumptions underlying the cash flow forecasts. These would cover such things as the company's sales policy, its pricing policy and the economic, political and social conditions the company expects to face in the period covered by the forecast.
A statement would also be prepared that explained the material variations between actual and forecasted cash flows. This would be further divided into those factors which were outside the company's control, and those factors which were within the company's control. Unfortunately, no guideline is given about the criteria to be used in deciding which category a variance falls into.

It was stated above that separate cash flow statements would be prepared for each aspect of the company's activities. The balances from each of these statements would be then taken to a statement of total cash flow which is reproduced from the author's article and shown in Table 2.

The author argues that these statements, and in particular the total cash flow statement, will enable the user to:

1) Assess whether the company can generate sufficient cash resources to survive in the long run.

2) Judge whether the company will be able to accumulate sufficient cash cash resources to pay satisfactory dividends in addition to its interest obligation.

3) Compute the company's interest and dividend cover which can be calculated by comparing 7 & 8

4) Calculate (from 2) and 3) above) figures for distributable cash per share as well as distributed cash per share. As a performance measure this would enable comparisons to be made with alternative investments. At the moment these figures can be only calculated on a historic basis and it is difficult to deny that such information would be very helpful to users of accounts.

TABLE 2

STATEMENT OF TOTAL CASH FLOW OF COMPANY

Statement of total cash flow – year to 31 July 1971

Cash Flows	Appendix	Year to 31 July 1967 F	1967 A	1968 F	1968 A	1969 F	1969 A	1970 F	1970 A	1971 F	1971 A	Total F	Total A	1972 F	1973 F	1974 F	Total F
1) Bank and Cash Balances Brought Forward		+	+	+	+	+	+	+	+	+	+	+	+	+	+	+	+
		–	–	–	–	–	–	–	–	–	–	–	–	–	–	–	–
2) Operational Transactions Flow	A	+	+	+	+	+	+	+	+	+	+	+	+	+	+	+	+
		–	–	–	–	–	–	–	–	–	–	–	–	–	–	–	–
3) Exceptional Transactions Flow	B	+	+	+	+	+	+	+	+	+	+	+	+	+	+	+	+
		–	–	–	–	–	–	–	–	–	–	–	–	–	–	–	–
4) Financial Transactions Flow	C	+	+	+	+	+	+	+	+	+	+	+	+	+	+	+	+
		–	–	–	–	–	–	–	–	–	–	–	–	–	–	–	–
5) Capital Transactions Flow	D	+	+	+	+	+	+	+	+	+	+	+	+	+	+	+	+
		–	–	–	–	–	–	–	–	–	–	–	–	–	–	–	–
6) Taxation Transactions Flow	E	+	+	+	+	+	+	+	+	+	+	+	+	+	+	+	+
		–	–	–	–	–	–	–	–	–	–	–	–	–	–	–	–
7) Net Distributable Flow		+	+	+	+	+	+	+	+	+	+	+	+	+	+	+	+
		–	–	–	–	–	–	–	–	–	–	–	–	–	–	–	–
8) Interest and Dividends	F	–	–	–	–	–	–	–	–	–	–	–	–	–	–	–	–
9) Undistributed Bank and Cash Balances		+	+	+	+	+	+	+	+	+	+	+	+	+	+	+	+
		–	–	–	–	–	–	–	–	–	–	–	–	–	–	–	–

5) Compare the contribution made by cash generated from operations and externally, to meet capital, tax and dividend requirements.

THE TWO SYSTEMS COMPARED

It is clear from the above that whilst both authors' work is similar there are important differences. This section will compare and contrast these differences and in the final section the advantages and disadvantages of cash flow accounting will be discussed. Whilst both authors' cash flow statements highlight distributable cash flows, Lawson goes further by including what he calls an objective function in his cash flow statement. This is simply the discounted future value of forecasted dividends that the company expects to be paid during the period covered by the forecast. As mentioned earlier in the paper, Lawson's objective function is a modified application of the Gordon–Shapiro dividend share price model. Whilst the Gordon–Shapiro model has been subject to considerable criticism, this detracts from merit of Lawson's work, since unlike Lee, he is attempting to justify his cash flow accounting system within a theoretical framework. Whilst Lee's system emphasises pure cash flows, Lawson sees these as a means to an end, the end being the present value of the company's expected stream of dividend payments. Lawson's system is therefore something more than cash flow accounting since it incorporates the principles of DCF.

A point not unconnected with this is that Lawson's system is more forward looking, by requiring the company's forecast to cover from seven to ten years in contrast to Lee's which, as mentioned above, suggests a three year period initially and after the forecasting art has improved sufficiently, a five year period. Whether the forecasts are feasible is not questioned by either author, but as this writer has stated earlier his personal experience in business forecasting suggests that forecasts covering a time period of more than one year are not only very unreliable but also of very dubious value to say the least. He would concede that for time periods up to one year fairly accurate forecasts can often be made, particularly as regards such things as sales, purchases, capital expenditure and cash, but would suggest that if these forecasts are extended to the time periods suggested by the writers they could be very misleading to users relying on them. The authors do point out that the accuracy of the forecasts diminishes with time but in this writer's view they seriously underestimate this deficiency. Although these would be subject to reassessment every year, at any one moment their utility to the user must be seriously questioned, especially the forecast from year one onwards, particularly if the industry in which the company operates is either rapidly growing or declining. It is important to point out that in no way does this criticism weaken the case for cash flow accounting or for cash flow forecasts but is merely questioning whether the time period to be covered by these forecasts is at the moment too ambitious. If these forecasts covered the twelve to eighteen months which followed the end of the accounting period the chances of investors being misled as a result of spurious forecasts would be considerably reduced. If this modification to the respective authors' cash flow accounting systems is accepted, the importance of the objective function in Lawson's system diminishes and his cash flow statements would become very similar to Lee's.

Another major difference in approach between the authors is in their schemes of financial reporting; Lee favours a series of interlocking cash flow statements, whilst Lawson appears to favour one main statement although this point is not made explicitly in his writings. It is difficult to see what purpose is served by Lee's interlocking cash flow statements except to confuse the user (the intelligent layman) by facing him with a multiplicity of statements which contain lists of cash balances relating to particular individual statements but with no further information or explanation of their significance. Clearly this is an area where improvements in the presentation of cash flow information could, and need, to be made. To be fair to Lee, in one respect his work is an improvement on Lawson's in that provision is made for such things as share issues made by the company for the acquisition of shares in others, the purchase and sale of goods etc. between companies which are settled by contra accounting entries in the respective books of account and the issue of bonus shares to shareholders.

The final point in this section relates to the role of the conventional historic cost accounts. Whilst Lawson favours their abolition, Lee favours their retention for stewardship purposes. This latter suggestion has much to commend it since the balance sheet will contain information about important funds items such as debtors and creditors. It is vital that the investor is given details about these since the immediate liquidity position of the company is of vital importance to management and investors alike. As an economist once remarked, "if there isn't a short run there won't be a long run" and this quotation is especially true in the context of the short run liquidity position of the firm. This point should not be taken too far however, because, if the expected profitability of the firm is sufficiently high, it can always borrow the funds on the market (at least in theory) to fund a short term liquidity crisis. What this discussion highlights is the fact that cash flow accounting, by ignoring fund items such as debtors and creditors, omits information which is of considerable importance to both management and investors alike.

It is clear from the foregoing paragraphs that the assertion made earlier in the paper, to the effect that there were important differences in Lawson and Lee's approach to cash flow accounting is well founded. The next section of this paper will deal with the advantages and disadvantages of cash flow accounting. This aspect is unique to Lee's work as Lawson has largely ignored this aspect, presumably on the grounds that since his cash flow model has a theoretical basis, no further justification was necessary.

ADVANTAGES AND DISADVANTAGES OF CASH FLOW ACCOUNTING

The first advantage claimed by the author for this type of information is that management's view of the future will be projected, which is of considerable importance to investors who are concerned with evaluating the desirability of being part of that future. It is difficult to fault this argument, since what the author is arguing for is information which we do not currently receive. Such a plea for more information about the future is to be welcomed and encouraged.

Perhaps the most important of the advantages claimed, relates to what the author calls the "price/discounted flow" ratio. This is computed by dividing the stockmarket price per share by the discounted cash flow per share. The latter figure would be the net figure which remained after the shareholder had discounted back the projected cash flows to present values at a rate of interest regarded as reasonable for that type of company. It is argued that this rate would be a more reliable investment indicator than the present "price/earnings" ratio because of the arbitrary allocations used to compute the present accrual earnings per share figure. Quite what significance the price/discounted cash flow per share is intended to indicate the author does not discuss and it is difficult to see what purpose would be achieved if this ratio were computed. If the market's expectations and capitalisation rate equalled both the company's estimate of its future cash flow and the rate of interest regarded by the investor as reasonable for the company, this ratio would equal one. Surely a more interesting and meaningful comparison would be between the stockmarket price per share and the discounted cash flow per share of a company. Where there were differences between these two figures, and there almost certainly would be, these would be attributable to:

1) The market's estimate of the company's future cash flows differing from the management's and/or

2) The capitalisation rate used by the market differing from that used by the shareholder.

Clearly where there are differences an identification problem will arise because information about the market's expectations and capitalisation rates is not generally available. Nevertheless, this comparison would be useful as it would give the investor some indication about the likelihood or otherwise of the company meeting its cash flow forecast. It would seem therefore, in the light of the above comments, that this advantage needs modifying.

Another of the advantages claimed by the author which has already been implied is that cash flow accounting would avoid all the arbitrary allocations currently made in historic and replacement cost accounts. Although this is true it solves the problem by walking round it. A correct measure of income is important both from the viewpoint of monitoring the economic progress of a company and also because in a mixed economy there is a need for a yardstick which society can use to judge the success or otherwise of a particular business. Income measures are important because they are a guide to how the company has performed in the past and how it is likely to perform in the future. Cash flow accounting tells the investor very little about profit margins, how quickly assets are being turned over, gearing or how many times interest is covered. These ratios are an important guide to performance and although alternative accounting systems, such as current replacement cost accounting, only enable these ratios to be computed approximately, in most cases they will be indicative of the underlying trend.

To some extent this criticism is a harsh indictment of the author's work since he cites as a separate advantage the fact that if business profitability is regarded as relevant financial information; periodic profits could be computed by comparing the present values of anticipated cash flows at the beginning and end of each accounting period, along the lines suggested by Hicks, using his concept of "well-offness" (6). This is not the paper to discuss income measurement but this writer is puzzled why the author should cite an isolated paragraph in Hicks' book. In the first instance, the chapter which contains this suggestion refers to what a prudent person could consume from his income in any one week and expect to be as well off in terms of consumption in each succeeding week. Later in the chapter Hicks' dismisses this notion of income as an operational concept on the grounds of the assumptions it makes with respect to expectations and future interest rates. In the second instance the chapter in the book which deals with income is a speculative chapter in that it talks generally about income to see whether it has any bearing on the main theme of his book, the theory of value and capital. Since the concept of income which could be calculated, if cash flow accounting replaced the alternative accounting systems which have been suggested, has been found to be theoretically deficient, the author is not justified in claiming that this is an advantage, since in effect, it highlights a major disadvantage of cash flow accounting.

Cash flow accounting retains money as the unit of measurement and so, as with cost current replacement accounting, it has the advantage of automatically incorporating specific price changes. This is quite an important advantage as certain of the suggested alternative accounting systems, for instance current purchasing power (CPP), use different units of measurement. In the case of the CPP accounts general purchasing power units are the unit of measurement. As nearly all transactions, whether business or personal, are conducted in terms of monetary units, a change over to general purchasing power units would involve a major change in how society conducts its financial affairs (10). By retaining the monetary unit as a unit of measurement, cash flow accounting avoids all the problems of changing the unit of measurement and has the advantage of stating amounts in units which people are not only familiar with, but also understand.

At the moment, and indeed with some of the alternative accounting systems which have been suggested, goodwill has not only been separately accounted for but there is also a rather artificial distinction between purchased and created goodwill. By computing the present value of the expected cash flows goodwill no longer becomes a problem, since it recognises the contribution of all the company's resources including goodwill. Whilst this assertion is correct, considerable reliance is placed on management's estimate of future cash flows. What the author should have demonstrated is that this method of valuation is superior to the other alternatives available. For instance, it has been suggested to this writer (7), that for a quoted company, assets and liabilities should be stated in the balance sheet at either their market values or current replacements costs and the residual figure for intangibles, including goodwill, calculated by deducting the market value of the net assets from the stockmarket valuation of its shares. Clearly problems would arise with this type of valuation in the case of private companies and the method suggested by the author may be the only other feasible alternative. Whilst cash flow accounting recognises that all the financial resources of the company contribute to its success or failure, other alternative accounting systems can be adapted to take this factor into account. This advantage, therefore needs qualifying so as to take into account the above comments.

The final advantage claimed by the author (Lee) is that investors could see from the projected cash flows both the ability of the company to pay its way in the future and also its planned financial policy. As was stated earlier, too much emphasis must not be placed on the availability of cash since capital market theory predicts that if the ultimate profitability of the project were sufficiently high, a company can always fund any short term contingency. Having said this, it is clear that such information would be of considerable use to the investor and whilst it is obvious that this is one of the strong points of cash flow accounting, its importance does need modifying along the lines suggested in the previous sentence.

It is clear from the above comments that the main advantages of cash flow accounting are that it provides information about a company's future and that by retaining money as the measuring unit it has substantial advantages over one of the suggested alternative accounting systems, current purchasing power accounting. In addition, by recognising that all resources of the company contribute to its success or failure, cash flow accounting has important advantages. Several of the asserted advantages have however, turned out to be weaknesses. In particular, the "price/discounted flow" ratio has been shown to be a poor investment indicator, although the present writer's suggested modification would to some extent remedy this deficiency. Also the suggestion that a comparison of opening and closing present values anticipated cash flows would be a good indicator of business performance has also been found to be deficient. In the next section of the article the disadvant–vantages listed by the author of cash flow accounting will be considered.

A major problem area which has been discussed earlier in the paper is the ability of management to make accurate forecasts in conditions of rapid technological and economic change. Since this point has been discussed in some detail earlier in the paper no further elaboration seems necessary except to point out that this is a major problem area of cash flow accounting. Another point which has already been discussed in the paper concerns the interest rate to be used for discounting. The author suggests that in order to retain objectivity, management should be required to disclose a rate of interest necessary to at least maintain its financial position. This rate will approximate the anticipated deterioration in the general purchasing power of money. Investors could then make a separate evaluation based on their expectations of the business's potential, over and above the minimum necessary to maintain its financial position. It would seem to this writer that these calcul–ations are unnecessarily complicated . If the company publishes its cost of capital using capital–asset pricing techniques no problem arises. This is because the company's cost of capital will reflect the risk free rate and the risk premium for the project or projects it undertakes. No problem of identification arises because the risk free rate can be obtained from the money market and so reflect the market's view of the anticipated rate of inflation, whilst the risk premium can be calculated from the returns required by the market for the project or projects the company undertakes (8). This technique for calculating the company's cost of capital has the added advantage that it is objective in that it could be verified by any skilled auditor or analyst. It is this writer's view, therefore, that the problem of which discount rate to use is not a disadvantage and would argue by virtue of its theoretical basis and objectivity that it is one of the advantages of cash flow accounting.

Another disadvantage listed and discussed by the author is that there is a danger of giving competitors information concerning the plans of the company. This statement can be turned on its head if it can be established that the overall allocation of resources would be improved. The author implies this in a subsequent sentence but it seems to this writer that an important point has been missed. If all quoted companies were required to disclose this information, our overseas competitors, who would have full access to this information, would be given an unfair advant–age. If cash flow forecasts were introduced there would have to be exemptions for companies, who had substantial overseas interests or who competed with imports on the home market. Apart from the potential harm to the persons referred to in the previous sentence, it is an empirical question whether overall resource allocat–ion would be improved if these forecasts were mandatory and it seems to this writer that arguments could be advanced either way as to whether resource allocation would be improved. Whilst the dangers of publishing this information must be recognised it can hardly be regarded as a major disadvantage and it may in fact be to society's overall benefit.

Another disadvantage of cash flow forecasts which is linked to the first disadvantage discussed above is that management could, and in many cases no doubt would, try to influence their market rating by over or underestimating expected future cash flows. Whilst the market would become aware of systematic over or understanding of future cash flows when reported cash flows became known, in the intervening period it could mislead investors. To some extent the objectivity of the forecast could be verified, as the author states, by experts as regards the non–accounting part and professional accountants as regards the accounting part. There would still however, be a grey area, although this disadvantage should not be overstressed. The information which the market uses to estimate future cash flows comes from a number of sources and so the cash flow forecast, although important, would only be one of the sources used by the market. Whilst the market's rating of a particular share could be altered initially as a result of over or under estimating expected future cash flows, as new information became available to the market the share price would move accordingly. From the available evidence (9) it would seem that a company could only affect its share price in the short run, which at the most would only be six months, and that in the long run it could not alter its market rating by systematically over or underestimating its expected future cash flows. As mentioned above, whilst the dangers of over or underestimating cash flows on the part of management must be recognised, it must also be recognised that other counter–balancing factors are also at work, which though not eradicating the problem, will certainly minimise it.

The final disadvantage which the author discusses has to some extent already been touched on and relates to the difficulty of using this type of financial information to assess managerial efficiency. This is because there is no yard–stick by which to judge whether cash flows are attributable to managerial action or fortuitous circumstances. As mentioned earlier, one of the major weaknesses of cash flow accounting is that it is of very little use in trying to appraise managerial performance and the above case is a good example of this deficiency.

From what has been said in the last few paragraphs cash flow accounting has some formidable disadvantages. The major problem areas fall under four main headings. In the first instance, there is the difficulty of forecasting future cash flows in times of rapid economic and technological change and secondly the related problem of distortions which could arise as a result of management over or underestimating expected cash flows. The third problem area, that of giving overseas competitors an unfair advantage is more tractable, since certain companies could be exempted from publishing information which would be of use to an overseas competitor. Finally and probably the most serious disadvantage is that in using this type of information there is no yardstick by which to judge managerial efficiency.

CONCLUSION

In conclusion it can be said that it is difficult to disagree with the Sandilands Committee (10) comments on cash flow accounting, which were to the effect that they felt there was much of value in the cash flow accounting principle but doubted whether such a fundamental change would be acceptable to British companies at the present time. Further research in this promising area should concentrate on both the theoretical and empirical aspects of cash flow accounting. As has been shown in this paper, the theoretical basis is far from satisfactory and if cash flow accounting is to be made operational one priority must be the development of satisfactory performance measures which would facilitate both inter-firm and inter-period comparisons. Having said this it is difficult to see how such measures could be devised, since cash flow accounting, as implied by its name, focuses on liquidity, rather than on income measurement. As such, cash flow accounting would be of considerable use to investors in helping them assess future performance, but it would be of little use to them in appraising past performance, However, a correct income measurement would enable the investor to make reliable judgements on past and inter–firm performance. Cash flow accounting and income measurement, therefore, answer two different though related questions and should be regarded as complementary to each other rather than as alternatives.

On the empirical side, neither author has to date published any findings on the effects or otherwise of cash flow accounting. To be fair, very little field work has been done on the alternative accounting systems which have been suggested, such as current replacement cost accounting and market value accounting. If cash flow accounting is to become operational, more must be known about the problems of introducing it and how it will affect the decisions of both investors and managers. It is hoped that further research will take place into cash flow accounting, especially on the lines suggested in this paper, since this particular system of accounting has considerable potential as yet unrealised.

REFERENCES

(1) The writer would like to thank Professors Reid, Brealey, Lawson and Perrin for their comments on an earlier version of this paper.

(2) "Cash–Flow Accounting I & II, *The Accountant,* October 28th and November 4 1971; and *The Rationale for Measuring the Cost of Working Capital,* Mimeographed, Manchester Business School, 1974.

(3) A Case for Cash–Flow Reporting, *Journal of Business Finance,* No.2 Vol. 4 1972; "Goodwill - An Example of Will - O' - the - Wisp Accounting, *Accounting and Business Research,* Autumn 1971; and "The Relevance of Accounting information Including Cash Flows," *The Accountant's Magazine, January 1972.*

(4) Later in the paper Lawson points out that for given rates of turnover growth and selling price, the operating cash flow of the business will be permanently negative and that the productive activities of the company can only be maintained at this level be raising additional finance from external sources e.g. long term debt or equity capital. In this situation a company could be earning profits on an accrual basis and yet have a cash deficit although the the existence would be seriously jeopardised if these external sources of finance dried up.

(5) See especially, "Goodwill – An Example of Will - O' - the - Wisp Accounting, *Accounting & Business Research,* Autumn 1971, especially pp. 326–328.

(6) Hicks, J.R., *Value and Capital,* Chapter 14, Oxford University Press, 1946.

(7) By Professor R.A. Brealey.

(8) For a good example of how to calculate this premium see Van Horne, J.C., *Financial Management and Policy,* Chapter 8, Prentice–Hall, 1974.

(9) B. Lev, FINANCIAL STATEMENT ANALYSIS: A new approach, Chapter 15, Prentice–Hall, 1974.

(10) INFLATION ACCOUNTING, REPORT OF THE INFLATION ACCOUNTING COMMITTEE, H.M.S.O. September, 1975.

(11) Professor G. Lawson, in a private communication, has indicated to this writer, that he has installed cash flow accounting in several companies and that the evidence which he has collected is presently under review.

In Defence of Profit Measurement: Some Limitations of Cash Flow and Value Added as Performance Measures for External Reporting*

D. A. Egginton

The problems of profit measurement have been so extensively analysed and debated that there can be few accountants who would be prepared to defend any measure of profit without at least some reservations. Consequently, it is not surprising that proposals should be made for approaches which are intended to displace profit as the central measure of business income in corporate reports. Two such alternatives have received considerable attention in the UK during the past decade, although their possibilities for supplanting profit have not aroused the same level of interest in other countries.[1] Under these approaches corporate reports would give prominence to statements of cash flow (alternatively referred to as 'cash flow accounting' or 'cash flow analysis', henceforth abbreviated to CFA) or to statements of value added (henceforth VA).

CFA and VA differ greatly in their objectives and methodology, but they share three important features which make it legitimate to consider them in association with each other. The first and crucial feature for present purposes is that they have been powerfully advanced as *performance measures* (e.g. Lawson, 1975, p. 3; Lee, 1981a, p. 63; Morley, 1978, p. 2). Performance may have different interpretations, but it will be assumed here that a measure of corporate performance indicates the extent to which a company (and particularly its management) has augmented or depleted the resources entrusted to it. Since performance measurement would be regarded by many people (including the present writer) as the central function of profit in corporate reports, it would seem that the use of CFA and VA as performance measures would make them contenders to usurp rather than to supplement the role of profit. It is with this potential use of CFA and VA, to take over the role of profit measurement in corporate reports, that this paper is particularly concerned.

Another common feature of CFA and VA is that both have been predominantly advocated as flow statements with relatively little attention devoted to the consideration of an interrelated position statement (although proposals of considerable significance for CFA have recently been made by Lee (1981b)). In contrast, the importance of the articulation of the profit statement with the balance sheet is well known.

The third feature which links CFA and VA is that it has been suggested in both cases that they provide a means of reducing the ownership emphasis which is inherent in the profit statement. Whether that is true of the usual presentations of CFA, and whether VA's reduction in ownership emphasis is desirable, are both open to question.

These features provide the focus for this consideration of CFA and VA. The conclusions will suggest that neither CFA nor VA is suitable to displace profit from its central role as a measure of business performance in corporate reports. However, this does not carry any implication that cash flows or value added reports are unsuitable for other roles, and in particular it is recognised that

*This is a revised version of a paper presented to the South West Accounting Group of the Association of University Teachers of Accounting on 17 September 1982. The constructive comments of the discussant Professor R. H. Parker and other participants at the Conference, those of Professor Philip W. Bell and my colleague J. J. Forker, and the helpful suggestions of the anonymous referee for *Accounting and Business Research*, are all gratefully acknowledged.

[1]Of course interest in cash flow information which is intended to be additional to profit statements, rather than a substitute for them, has been widespread. In the USA it has reached the level of official interest (FASB, 1980; Burton, 1981) and has been the subject of proposals for modifying conventional historical cost accounts to integrate cash flow information (Ijiri, 1978; Ferrara, 1981). However, Ijiri (1979) provides a cash flow proposal for 'bypassing the conventional earnings concept'.

In the case of value added statements, there has been a growth in the inclusion of such statements in annual reports or social employee reports in countries of the European Community (Gray and Maunders, 1979).

cash flows might usefully replace the working capital approach to funds flow statements.

CFA systems and profit alternatives

The characteristics of CFA systems have been widely demonstrated in the literature, and Lee (1981a) provides a succinct survey of some 50 articles which have been published on this topic in recent years. For the present purposes it is only necessary to draw attention to certain major aspects of CFA.

In the words of Lee (1981a), p. 68, 'CFA is... conceived as a multipurpose reporting system, compatible with the decision and accountability aims usually associated with conventional allocation-based reporting systems'. CFA essentially summarises the receipts and payments that go through a firm's bank account (although that does not provide an unequivocal definition of cash transactions, since the cash pool could be defined to include a variety of short-term securities).

In the Lawson and Lee systems, cash flows are classified into a number of components, of which the major elements are:

N = net cash flow from operations

R = replacement investment
G = growth investment
} separated by Lawson but a single investment amount in Lee's system

T = taxation

I = interest on borrowings

D = distributions to owners

E = new equity receipts

B = borrowings

C = residual change in cash resources of the period

Lawson (1975, 1981) distinguishes in his system between replacement and growth investment, and emphasises the distributed (or distributable) cash flow to owners along the lines of:

$$N - R - G - T - I + E + B - C = D \quad (1)$$

Considerable importance is attached to the significance of the operating flows element N, thus:

> It is suggested that the financial performance of any organisation, whether publicly or privately owned, ought to be measured in terms of the disposable income or net surplus which it can generate from its trading and productive (or service) activity... (Lawson (1975) p. 3)

Lee does not venture into the distinction between replacement and growth investment; instead capital expenditure comes under a single heading (shown here as [R + G]). His presentation varies but tends to emphasise the cash residual, for example (1972):

$$N - [R + G] - I - T - D + E + B = C \quad (2)$$

or (1981c):

$$N - [R + G] - I - T - D = F \quad (3)$$

where F = C − E − B, representing the residual financing change during the period.[2] Thus F shows the extent to which the firm's transactions were financed from internal activities (positive F) or financed out of cash balances and/or external sources (negative F), and can be regarded as an overall cash surplus or deficit for the period.

In some recent proposals Lee (1981b) links C to a statement of changes in net realisable values of resources. In effect the system is transformed from one which relies solely on cash flows to one which incorporates a profit measure—as a result of which, it will be argued, the system is improved.

In their systems both Lawson and Lee emphasise the importance of reporting both past and forecast cash flows. They adopt 10 years of past data and at least one year of forecasting data, although forecast periods of up to 10 years have been mentioned (Ashton, 1976). A number of other writers have also favoured approaches which would report both past and forecast cash flows, e.g. Briston and Fawthrop (1971), Jones (1975) and Climo (1976).

Lee (1981a) lists nine points that are 'merely a few' of the arguments for CFA, but at the risk of undue condensation the major elements are summarised under five headings below:

1. CFA *avoids dubious accounting allocations* which give rise to correspondingly dubious measures of periodic income.
2. CFA captures the vital factor in decision making and valuation of the *time value of money*; consequently, it is the only proper basis for measuring the value of entities as going concerns.
3. CFA emphasises the most fundamental and vital features of business activity: the *ability of the enterprise to pay its obligations, make distributions and provide for its future continuity.*
4. CFA is *objective, understandable and simple.*
5. CFA *does not require price level adjustments* because cash transactions reflect prices of the period in which they occur (although comparison between different time periods requires some general price level adjustment to a base period).

[2]Any of the elements F, C, E or B may be either positive or negative. Equity capital can, of course, be reduced in a number of ways. For the most recent provisions in the UK see the Companies Act 1981, sections 45–58.

If CFA is to be compared with profit measurement it is necessary to specify which profit concepts are being assumed, since an embarrassingly large number are available. For the present purposes just two extremes need to mentioned. Conventional historical cost occupies the lower end and is in certain respects beyond the bounds of defensibility. Among its disabilities are its disregard for price changes and its questionable bases for allocating costs between periods. At the other end of the spectrum would be those current value accounts which adopt pure market values based on entry or exit prices for assets (second-hand where appropriate). Edwards and Bell (1961) provide the classic entry price system, giving an 'all-inclusive' measure of business profit, although their work also included a measure of realisable profit based on exit prices. Chambers (1966, 1967, 1970, 1974, 1975) provides the classic exit price system, usually referred to as CoCoA. Both of these systems overcome the price change limitations of historical cost profit. Both also offer 'all-inclusive' measures of profit which avoid certain allocation difficulties; in addition, Edwards and Bell provide a measure of current operating profit designed to separate operating profits from holding gains. However, current value accounts still give profit measures which reflect changes in separable asset values (and liability values in the Edwards and Bell scheme) rather than the change in value (in market or subjective terms) for the firm as a total organism.

CFA and the allocation problem

The claim that CFA avoids dubious allocation procedures has been the subject of a recent article by Rutherford (1982) and a riposte by Lee (1982). Rutherford's analysis of the allocation problems of CFA is countered by Lee, who concludes that '... allocation problems do not apply to CFA if proper care and attention is paid to the basics of accounting' (p. 351). Much depends on what is meant by the words 'allocation' and 'problems', but it will be argued that some form of allocation in accounting reports is almost inescapable and CFA is certainly not exempt.

The allocation definitions adopted by Lee will be followed here. Lee starts by quoting Thomas' definitions of allocations with approval and the broadest will be used:

> 'An allocation is any partitioning of a whole into parts, any division of a subject among objects.' (Thomas, 1980, p. 1).

Lee then usefully distinguishes between three types of allocation which will be defined for the present purposes as:

—*time period allocations* which match accounting data to particular periods;

—*classificatory allocations* which classify data under headings (e.g. operating/financing);

—*entity allocations* which assign data to specific entities or subdivisions of an entity.

The present concern is with reports for the entity as a whole. Thus Lee's entity allocations, involving traditional and intractable problems of joint cost allocations, can be conveniently ignored. However, issues of joint cost allocation can still arise in the reports of the entity as a whole, particularly for time-period allocation with regard to stock valuation.

On the question of time-period allocations, any accounting flow statement must allocate data along the time continuum in accordance with some criterion. For a cash basis of accounting the criterion is the point of time at which cash is paid or received. Thus a firm which buys a continuous supply of resources, such as telephone services, electricity or leased assets, would assign cash costs to the points of time (and therefore the time periods) when payment is made. This must qualify as allocation under the Thomas definition, since it involves a 'partitioning of a whole into parts'. Whether the allocation is to be considered dubious is a matter of judgment, and depends on the interpretation to be placed on the results of the allocation. If the purpose is to give information on resources consumed (harking back to the earlier definition to performance measurement) then cash allocation is clearly deficient, since consumption and payment are not identical. The allocation could be determined by events which have nothing to do with the consumption of services, such as postal delays in the delivery of invoices or manipulation of payment dates by management. Similar arguments might be developed for resources which are not supplied on a continuous basis, such as purchased goods, but it is enough for present purposes to have demonstrated that questionable assignments or 'allocations' would occur.

By contrast, accruals accounts, and corresponding profit measures, attempt to reflect the consumption of resources. The resulting time-period allocation problems over matters like stock valuation and depreciation are well known. It is legitimate to compare cash allocation with accruals allocation and argue that one method is more arbitrary (open to error or manipulation) than the other, or that one method yields results which are more informative to users, but it is not valid to suggest that one method can avoid the problem of time-period allocation altogether.

Similarly, CFA must entail classificatory allocations if the whole of a period's expenditure is to be partitioned into parts under different headings. Only if a flow statement showed total outflows as one amount and total inflows as another amount, or perhaps gave full details for every single item of expenditure, could classificatory allocations be said to be avoided. Thus the CFA systems described earlier classified cash flows, and in particular distinguished between operating and investment flows. That distinction also carries implications of time-period allocation, since investment flows must be judged to bring benefits in future time periods (e.g. do research, advertising, or costs of long-term contracts qualify as investment flows?). The Lawson approach went further, and distinguished between replacement and growth investment. Such a division would seem to have potential interest for users, but it represents a classificatory allocation which requires consideration of the same sort of problems as replacement cost accounting for fixed assets (e.g. does replacement investment replace the same physical quantity or the same value of output, and over what time periods, when technology and demand are changing?).

Lee (1982) recognises that classificatory allocation causes problems for CFA, and concludes that the solution may be:

> ... not to treat [capital and revenue expenditure] as essentially different ... but instead ... to deduct all expenditure as one item (other than ... interest, taxation and dividends) from sales revenue and to ensure there are adequate supporting descriptions and explanations of all major expenditure headings within it (for example, raw materials, wages, overheads, plant, vehicles, research and so on). (Lee (1982) pp. 348–9)

In fact this would still not avoid the classification problem, because the suggested list of headings is merely another classification. For example, overheads and research would presumably include some wage payments to employees. If so, why are they not included with wages? The answer is presumably that the suggested classificatory allocation was considered potentially more informative to users. That is perfectly acceptable, and some such judgments on allocations are virtually inescapable if accounting reports are to convey information. It would seem that the only ways of entirely avoiding classification in flow reports would be either to report single totals for inflows and outflows or to give full details of every single item of receipts and expenditure.

Cash flows *ex ante*

The reporting of forecast cash flows is an integral part of the CFA systems outlined earlier. It is presumably the provision of such forecasts that Lee (1981a) has in mind when he suggests that 'CFA captures the vital factor in decision-making and valuation of the time value of money' (p. 72) and that 'CFA is the only proper basis for measuring the value of entities as going concerns because of its attention to the time value of money' (p. 73).

The provision of forecast cash flows could, in principle, permit investors to discount at their personal rates of time preference to obtain a present value. However, it would also be equally possible in principle to discount profit forecasts to a present value. Peasnell (1982) has shown that 'any all-inclusive measure of profit (suitably adjusted) can be discounted back to economic value' (p. 379). Cash flows are not unique in their capacity to be discounted. Moreover, if the forecasts were sufficiently far-reaching, it would only be necessary to give investors dividend forecasts (including any liquidation payments); the detailed intermediate figures for either CFA or profit would be redundant.

The provision of any types of forecast can be valuable to users of accounts, although more as a guide to management perceptions than as a crystal ball. Forecasts couched in terms of alternative scenarios (for different potential economic environments) might be a great deal more informative than the single-valued estimates which are usually implied in CFA discussions. However, a reporting system which relied upon the discounting of forecast cash flows could be effective for valuation only if the forecast stream was both extremely long (i.e. captured all future elements materially affecting value) and the forecasts were regarded by investors as being reasonably reliable. These two conditions are not realistically compatible and that is recognised in the usual assumption of CFA systems that forecasts would be provided for as little as 12 or 18 months. Such a forecast period could not be contemplated as a basis for discounting, unless the initial forecast was quite unjustifiably extrapolated to later periods. Only an horizon of significantly more than a decade could be treated at all seriously *unless* some forecast closure value at the cut-off date is provided. But CFA, as a pure flow system, is not designed to provide such closure values. A forecast share price at the horizon might be an interesting possibility for the listed company, but is hardly appropriate for smaller entities.

The absence of closure values would mean that the comparison of forecasts with outcomes could have no clear significance for performance assessment. Assume, for example, that two companies have the following forecasts and results for cash surplus (residual change in cash resources; no dividends or equity changes):

	Periods				
	1	*2*	*3*	*4*	*5*
Company A					
Forecast	100	100	100	100	100
Outcome	100	100	100	100	100
Company B					
Forecast	150	150	150	150	150
Outcome	99	99	99	99	99

It is evident that A's *forecasts* are more accurate than B's, but the figures provide no basis for judging whether A's *performance* is better—because opening and closing valuations are unstated. In fact, it is relatively easy to think of situations in which A performed worse than B. For example, that would be the case if A had started with a valuation of 500 and ended with 50, whereas B started with 50 and ended with 500.

The adoption of the cash basis of time-period allocations in CFA can also cause difficulties in the interpretation of forecasts against outcomes. The upper section of Table 1 shows forecast and outcome CFA figures for a simple trading company which has no fixed assets or depreciation. It would seem from the CFA statement that the company did particularly well, exceeding the forecast operating flows by 40, doubling the dividend and increasing the cash retentions by 15.

The profit statement in the lower section of Table 1 shows a very different picture.[3] Profit is down on forecast, and it would be very difficult indeed to argue on the evidence of the balance sheet in Table 2 that the company's position had improved compared with the forecast, which is the message of the CFA statement.

Now it may be argued that the result arises from running down debtors and increasing creditors, which could not persist over many periods; all will be revealed when the cash flows for the next year or so are reported. Such a view would ignore the fact that timeliness is crucial to accounting information; the interpretation of this year's figures cannot await next year's results. The basic case for using sales figures (and matched costs) for performance assessment rather than cash receipts is connected with this issue: it is because sales occur before receipts that they give an earlier indication of movements in trading. Such an argument does not carry any implication that the movements should necessarily be extrapolated; they must be interpreted in the context of other information about the company's prospects. Nor is there any suggestion that the collection of cash from sales is unimportant because it is secondary in a chronological sense to selling the goods. Both elements are important and both profit and liquidity information have parts to play in corporate reports.

It is relevant to note that in the USA the SEC is developing policies for disclosure relating to the company's expectations regarding sales, profits *and* liquidity. Thus:

> ... if internal company forecasts show any substantial deviation from the trend line fitted to past year's sales and income from continuing operations, a disclosure obligation exists... (Burton, 1981, p. 56)
>
> ... the ability of an enterprise to generate adequate amounts of cash to meet the enterprise's need for cash... should be discussed on both a long-term and a short-term basis. (Burton, 1981, p. 58)

[3]Price change problems are avoided here. Assets and liabilities are expressed in money terms and it is assumed that there is no difference between the general price level assumed in the forecast and prevailing in the outcome.

Table 1
CFA Statement

	Forecast	*Outcome*
Sales receipts	370	400
Operating payments	(280)	(270)
Operating cash flow surplus	90	130
Taxation paid	(40)	(40)
	50	90
Dividend paid	(25)	(40)
Cash surplus	25	50

Profit Statement

	Forecast	*Outcome*
Sales	380	375
Costs	(285)	(290)
Profit before tax	95	85
Taxation	(40)	(40)
Profit after tax	55	45
Appropriation:		
Opening retained profits	75	75
Profit after tax	55	45
	130	120
Dividend	(25)	(40)
Closing retained profits	105	80

Table 2
Balance Sheet

	Forecast	*Outcome*
Capital	50	50
Retentions	105	80
	155	130
Creditors	75	90
	230	220
Debtors	193	158
Cash	37	62
	230	220

Cash flows *ex post*

Despite the importance attached to cash flow forecasts in discussions of CFA systems, the analysis of *ex post* cash flows provides the main justification for CFA. In a sense the reason is that reported cash flow forecasts are not currently available, but it was seen earlier that explicit and reliable corporate forecasts lengthy enough for company valuation purposes are improbable. Thus, the argument for CFA on grounds of discounting forecast cash flows for valuation purposes disappears, and CFA must be considered on its *ex post* merits.

A central difficulty of employing CFA for *ex post* performance assessment is that CFA ignores non-cash movements in assets and liabilities, as was demonstrated in the simple debtors/creditors example in the previous section. CFA does not adequately register either the consumption or the build-up of non-cash assets, nor is there any recognition of holding gains or losses on assets held by the firm. This may lead to biased performance assessment in two directions: it can flatter the company which liquidates resources accumulated in past years or it can malign the growth company which invests in assets in excess of internally generated cash and finances the resulting cash deficit from borrowing.

When attention is directed to net operating flows, N, there is no estimate in CFA of the extent to which these flows were obtained by consumption of assets (depreciation of equipment or mineral deposits, running down stocks, etc). The Lawson system makes a deduction for estimated replacement investment, R, but this need bear no relationship to the consumption of resources in the period. A company might replace only a small part of its exhausted assets, and in any case those exhausted assets would match fixed asset consumption in a particular period only in unlikely circumstances.[4] Thus separate disclosure of amounts for R and G (growth investment) would not mean that R matched the consumption of the period; consequently, G need not entail an overall increase in the company's resources—although users might be excused for assuming that was so. The Lee system does not separate R and G; instead, the deduction of a single investment figure from N shows the extent to which investment is covered by internally generated funds. The result could quite easily be a surplus for a low-investment company which had not generated enough operating funds to cover the consumption of assets, but a deficit for a high-investment growth company whose operating cash flows covered asset consumption many times over. Such measures are entirely valid in conveying *financing* information but false guides to *performance* assessment.

The issue of non-cash movements of assets is also important in the context of price changes. It is entirely valid to argue that CFA does not require price level adjustments because cash transactions reflect the prices of the period in which they occur (e.g. Lawson (1975), Lee (1981a)). But it does not follow that CFA offers a solution to the price/inflation accounting problem; CFA merely ignores that problem by excluding non-cash movements of assets. If the purpose of accounting reports is to report an enterprise's activities in the context of the prevailing economic environment, then recognition of price changes affecting non-cash assets held and consumed is essential. CFA patently cannot supply this; and suggestions that the problems of price change reporting can be solved by CFA are erroneous.

What CFA undoubtedly does provide is *ex post* financing information showing sources and uses of cash. Perhaps it is this aspect that Lee has in mind in stating (as mentioned earlier) that 'CFA emphasises . . . the ability of the enterprise to pay its obligations, make distributions, and provide for its future continuity (cash needed to reinvest, to expand [etc] . . .)' (Lee, 1981a, p. 72). This is uncontroversial if it means that *ex post* cash flows show that an enterprise was able to make certain payments in past periods.

The matter becomes debatable, however, if 'ability' is taken as meaning that past cash flows can reveal future ability regarding obligations, distributions and continuity. The predictive ability of past operating flows is unproven, although past corporate policy on financing can provide guidance on likely future conduct in the absence of contrary evidence; a company which has followed a policy of not running a cash deficit (to be met by borrowing or new equity) avoids certain financial risks, at the expense of foregoing possible financial rewards. But a company faces many other risks; in particular CFA does not reveal the important financial risk of dependence on trade credit, nor is it more informative than conventional accounting on the whole range of operating risks. Thus CFA may be said to emphasise some, but by no means all, aspects of 'downside risk'; on the other hand it gives sparse indication of the 'upside potential' of externally financed assets.

It is a truism that companies which become insolvent have run out of cash, and therefore it is hardly surprising that CFA can be used to demonstrate that companies which go into liquidation have cash flow deficits. But the reverse certainly does not apply; companies which run cash flow deficits do not necessarily go into liquidation—if they did, corporate financial markets would soon cease to exist.

Many of the points in this section can be illus-

[4]For example, a constant rate of fixed asset consumption, a balanced age structure for fixed assets, no technological change.

Table 3
Royal Dutch/Shell Cash Flow Results

	1975	1976	1977	1978	1979	1980	1981
	£m	*£m*	*£m*	*£m*	*£m*	*£m*	*£m*
Net operating receipts	3,770	4,422	4,777	4,787	5,067	5,601	7,423
Less: capital payments	1,295	1,907	2,223	2,174	3,999	2,953	4,069
	2,475	2,515	2,554	2,613	1,068	2,648	3,354
Less: interest payments	213	275	319	350	358	399	627
	2,262	2,240	2,235	2,263	710	2,249	2,727
Less: tax payments	2,411	2,043	2,150	1,689	1,383	2,468	2,961
	(149)	197	85	574	(673)	(219)	(234)
Less: dividend payments	340	466	546	564	629	681	689
TOTAL CASH SURPLUS (DEFICIT) MET BY BORROWING	(489)	(269)	(461)	10	(1,302)	(900)	(923)
SURPLUS (DEFICITS) IN 1981 PRICES*	(1,070)	(505)	(747)	15	(1,719)	(1,007)	(923)

*Adjusted for General Index of Retail Prices.

trated with the aid of a CFA example. The format adopted follows that used in a *Financial Times* article on the financial weaknesses of BL and its cumulative government backed cash deficit (Lee, 1981c). On this occasion the method will be applied to a very different kind of enterprise, the Royal Dutch/Shell Group (RDS). RDS ran a series of huge cash deficits, financed by borrowing, during the period 1975–81. A cash flow summary for these years appears in Table 3; assumptions have had to be made in deriving the figures from published data,[5] but the table gives a broadly valid approximation of cash flows.

The top line of Table 3 shows that RDS produced vast net operating receipts (excess of sales receipts over operating payments). But even a vast surplus at this stage does not necessarily prove that a company has been performing well in the use of its resources, because no charge has been made for the consumption of assets bought in earlier years. RDS could have been depleting oilfields acquired prior to 1975 and selling the oil at below historical cost. The cash flows cannot reassure the reader to the contrary.

Nor does an operating cash deficit in any year mean that the company must be losing resources; cash payments could be financing the build-up of stocks. Admittedly a *persistent* operating cash deficit is likely to be a warning signal, because it suggests either a net drain of resources or questionable stockpiling. However, the implications can only be gauged by resort to other sources of information—such as the balance sheet.

[5]In particular, it has had to be assumed that payment was made for fixed assets in the year in which they were acquired, and that all interest was paid in the year for which it accrued. For the years 1975 and 1976, for which the amounts of dividends actually *paid* in those years was not available, it was assumed that dividends paid equalled the declared dividend of the time period.

At the next stage the RDS capital payments have been covered handsomely by net receipts. That is informative from a financing viewpoint, but it does not give any indication of how effectively the group's assets were being used. For example, the net operating receipts would be very uninspiring if annual capital consumption proved to be several times the level of capital investment. That is a role in which current operating profit along Edwards and Bell (1961) lines would be of interest.

If the recent suggestion of Lee (1982) were adopted, that allocation problems of CFA might be reduced by ending the distinction between operating and capital payments, interpretation would become even more difficult. It would not be possible to assess which payments were intended to benefit future periods and which related to the current period.

The deductions for interest, tax and dividend payments produce a series of immense cash deficits (financed by borrowing) with only a small surplus in 1978. Naive readers of the CFA statements might well focus on the bottom line and draw unhappy conclusions. In fact, of course, RDS had an enormous asset base and profitable undertakings, which was why it could so readily borrow funds on the market. CFA in isolation provides no sign of this. Whether the investments eventually prove to have been worthwhile is something that obviously cannot be gauged from any current accounting reports, but their present status can be monitored.

CFA, position statements and NRVA

For cash *flow* the corresponding *stock* at the end of the accounting period must be the entity's cash holding. This is clearly inadequate as a representation of resources for a position statement, and this inadequacy is merely a reflection of the narrowness of CFA in ignoring non-cash flows.

Lee (1981b) has proposed a solution to the position statement problem which rescues CFA from some of its limitations. He suggests a system which combines CFA with net realisable value accounting (NRVA). Such a system would contain four statements, the first of which would be a cash flow statement of the sort discussed above, although with some re-ordering of the component items. In addition, there would be a balance sheet and income statement on an NRVA basis, entitled 'statement of net cash and cash equivalent resources' and 'statement of retained income' respectively. Finally, a statement of NRVA changes in financial position would be given the inappropriate title of 'statement of total cash flow movements'.

Thus the importance of profit measurement and of the closure values provided by the position statement would be explicitly recognised. This is to be welcomed to the extent that the profit/income measure is capable of being used for performance measurement, while the cash flow information reports on past liquidity movements. Perhaps rather more is intended by the inclusion in these statements of measures bearing the equivocal titles 'distributable cash flow' and 'distributable income'; if these *ex post* measures are intended to constrain the dividend decision they are no more promising than conventional approaches to distributable profit (see Egginton, 1980).

In any contemplated use of income in Lee's proposed system, the special nature of this measure must be recognised. He states (Lee, 1981b, p. 164) that neither the CFA nor NRVA bases assume the continuity of the activities of the enterprise and its management. Thus the exit values he appears to have in mind are what Edwards and Bell (1961, p. 79) called opportunity costs—'values that could currently be realized if assets . . . were sold . . . at the best prices *immediately* obtainable' (italics added). Such a valuation basis would be consistent with, and necessary for, the cash orientation of Lee's system. It would produce a balance sheet of approximate liquidation values, which could clearly be informative for any users interested in a firm's asset break-up cover (although issues like tax liabilities and redundancy payments are unresolved). There would be corresponding implications for the resulting income figure, which would be equivalent to Edwards and Bell's realisable profit.[6] Such an income figure would estimate, for example, whether a firm teetering on the edge of liquidation had been justified in struggling on for a further year. That is, of course, a very different sort of performance measure from mainstream profit measures which adopt a going concern presumption.

Despite the use of parallel terminology like 'cash equivalent' it would seem that the valuation basis envisaged by Lee is not the same as that adopted by Chambers for CoCoA. For Lee neither CFA nor NRVA assumes continuity, whereas Chambers is at pains to emphasise the going concern intentions of CoCoA, as in the following:

> It was said [in Chambers 1966, p. 218] that 'the current cash equivalents of the assets of a going concern are the sums obtainable in the short run in the ordinary course of business; that is market resale prices in the short run' . . . I was . . . trying to avoid the charge (made by some) that accounting on the basis described was 'liquidation' accounting. That is why the passage refers to 'the ordinary course of business'. The whole of the accounting was intended to be accounting for going concerns. (Chambers 1974, p. 130)

Whether the CoCoA basis is effective in accounting for going concerns is not at issue here, but its adoption of resale prices *in the ordinary course of business* would appear to have a different time focus (and result in higher valuations) than a basis which refrains from any assumption that business will be conducted in the succeeding period. Lee's valuation basis is consistent with the immediate cash emphasis of CFA and such an approach could perform a very useful role in informing users about the firm under a 'liquidation scenario'. It would not, however, provide a measure of performance for a firm as a going concern.

Whatever the features of CFA and NRVA, it is over-optimistic to regard them as 'both allocation-free systems' (Lee, 1981b, p. 164). It was argued earlier for CFA that assignments of data to time periods constitute time-period allocations, and that classificatory allocations can only be avoided by eliminating most of the information content of accounts. As for NRVA, its claim to avoid allocation rests on the fact that a pure market price (whether exit or entry) produces a value at a point in time, which does not require any prior judgments involving time-period allocations. Thus market prices in position statements avoid the need for time-period allocations. However, as soon as a flow statement is added there is an assignment of value changes to a time period. That involves an allocation ('partitioning of a whole into parts') of the entity's continuing activities into time periods, which has more than semantic significance. The amounts allocated depend on the choice which is made between market price bases (e.g. 'ordinary course of business' or 'non-continuity'), and upon considerable judgment in the selection of relevant price data. Thus it does not seem particularly fruitful to attempt to avoid all allocations. What is

[6]Lee's Figure 5 uses the term *realised* income; it is assumed that *realisable* income is intended, since many elements of the income will not have been realised in any usual sense of that word.

important is to consider the extent to which particular bases provide information to assist the economic decisions of users, which in turn gives preference to reports reflecting the market and to reports which have safeguards against manipulative judgments.

In conclusion, Lee's combined CFA/NRVA system would have a cash orientation which would have considerable potential for liquidity assessment. However, it would not provide a measure of performance on a going concern basis for the continuing entity, of the sort which would be provided by a profit measure reflecting accruals and value in use.

Value added as a measure of corporate performance

Whatever the problems of CFA, there are only relatively minor difficulties in defining a cash flow. By contrast, VA presents a minefield of definitional problems; it could be measured on the basis of either cash flows or accruals and it could include or exclude a number of important items like depreciation or interest. However, the motives advanced by *The Corporate Report* (1975) for its original proposals for corporate VA statements are both plain and laudable. Such statements would disclose:

> ...how the benefits of the efforts of the enterprise are shared between employees, providers of capital, the state and reinvestment... [and]... assist users to evaluate the economic performance of the entity. (p. 48)

The intention is to provide a broader perspective to performance than is given by profit alone. Morley (1978) puts the comparison clearly:

> Profit measures the wealth creation which has accrued for the *shareholders* during a period. On the other hand Value Added measures the wealth creation which has been built up by the co-operative efforts of *shareholders, lenders, workers and the Government.*

Accordingly, VA represents sales minus inputs from sources outside the assumed co-operative group. But this leaves considerable scope for interpretation. One possible interpretation would be consistent with a CFA system, as can be shown by returning to the algebraic representation of CFA considered earlier. Net cash flows from operations, N, can be split into the component elements:

S = receipts from sales

W = wage payments

P = purchase payments for goods and services employed in operations

so that

$$S - W - P = N$$

Substituting for N in equation (3) produces:

$$S - W - P - [R + G] - I - T - D = F \quad (4)$$

F shows the extent to which the firm's transactions were financed internally (positive F) or externally (negative F); it is the same as the total cash surplus/deficit used in the example in Table 3.

The elements in formulation (4) can be rearranged as follows:

$$S - P - [R + G] = W + I + D + T + F \quad (5)$$

This gives a cash flow representation of VA. The expression on the left hand side shows the source of the value added flow and the right hand expression shows its application. A formulation of this sort might be expected to be a feature of any CFA system which seeks to emphasise the overall entity view (as opposed to ownership) since it gives explicit recognition to employee rewards as well as payments to other participants. Instead the usual presentations of CFA emphasise residuals which are consistent with a proprietary view of the firm. Distributions to shareholders feature prominently but explicit recognition of employee rewards is notably absent (see equations (1), (2) and (3)), which hardly suggests an overall entity view.

Advocacy of a cash basis for published VA statements has been rare. Worth (1978) provides an exception which is not, however, linked to CFA arguments.

An accruals basis for VA would, at its simplest, merely transform the elements in (5) to a time-period allocation based on legal and contractual relationships rather than on the receipts and payments of cash. This would produce a VA measure (on the left hand side of formulation (5)) which has considerable similarities to the basis adopted for Value Added Tax in the UK and elsewhere in the European Community.

However, the most commonly discussed and published VA statements are those which do not deduct investment expenditures in calculating VA. Instead they are linked to conventional profit calculations in giving recognition to depreciation, either as a deduction in the calculation of VA or as an application. Developing this from the cash flow approach in formulation (5) requires the substitution of two separate elements r_a and g_a for the combined outlays R and G, with r_a representing depreciation and g_a the change in assets (apart from cash) less creditors. Netting off F and g_a to give undistributed profit ($U = F - g_a$) and putting all the other items onto an accruals basis (signified by the subscripts a) produces two alternative views of VA:

$$S_a - P_a = W_a + r_a + I_a + T_a + D_a + U \quad (6)$$

and

$$S_a - P_a - r_a = W_a + I_a + T_a + D_a + U \quad (7)$$

Of these two alternatives, the first method is by far the most popular in UK company reports.[7] Morley (1978) calls the method 'positively dangerous' (pp. 59–60) and argues for the second method on grounds which include the undeniable argument that diminution in value of fixed assets is one of the costs of producing new wealth.

Both formulations (6) and (7) are intrinsically linked to profit measurement, since the elements $D_a \pm U$ will sum to a value for profit. Whether this summation is explicitly shown in the VA statement is a matter of presentation, but the motivation behind the VA statement would suggest playing down the nature of the combined element. Thus, Morley (1978) suggests that '... by the end of the century... the profit statement may have been relegated to a note in the corporate report!' (p. 269)

The VA statement in corporate reports has been the subject of particularly careful analysis by Morley (1978, 1981) and Rutherford (1977, 1980). Both have pointed to significant definitional problems and disadvantages of VA, but Morley sees the balance of advantages as being clearly in favour of the use of VA. His reasons for his conclusions are based on a number of advantages which seem characteristic of the arguments in favour of VA. They can be divided into two main groups, one concerning aspects of economic performance which will be considered here and the other relating to worker involvement which will be examined in the next section.

Morley (1978) suggests that VA would report the company's contribution to national income. Such a hope must be considerably blighted by Rutherford's (1977) analysis. This points among other things to the dangers of double-counting (e.g. if interest were treated as a component of VA by industrial companies and also as a provision of services by financial institutions), the difficulties that tax payments are not merely disbursements but finance the provision of services which can benefit the company (e.g. transport facilities, law and order) and the need for consistent recognition of VA on production or sale which is not present in conventional accounts. (The fact that VA statements can use conventional data is sometimes advanced as an advantage). Moreover, the notion of contribution to the national income of a particular national economy poses problems in respect of companies with international operations.

Quite apart from the measurement difficulties, it is questionable whether a measure of an individual company's contribution to national income on lines consistent with macroeconomic measures for value added would be at all fruitful. At national level such measures ignore asset and liability valuation changes, which are often redistributional (e.g. arising from debt fixed in money terms when prices are changing) but may involve changes in national wealth (e.g.the discovery that a block of the North Sea contains oil). The former type of change cannot be said to involve wealth *creation*, but both types of valuation change are certainly relevant to wealth *accretion* for the individual enterprise. It is wealth accretion that would ideally prove most informative on a firm's financial performance, from the viewpoint of both participators and non-participators. Conventional historical cost profit is not, of course, much help here; an all-inclusive measure of profit which reflects valuation changes affecting both assets and liabilities is the best practicable indicator.

Morley also suggests that VA statements would have the advantage of directing attention to both employee and government shares in value added and to trends in their shares over time. Certainly such trends can be of interest at national level, but whether their use at company level deserves the publication of a VA figure is doubtful. Apart from the measurement problems mentioned above, it would seem better to report statements of sales and individual cost/recipient categories which will allow users to make whatever calculations they desire. There is some evidence (Hussey, 1981) to suggest that, at least for unsophisticated users, the VA approach can cause users to become confused over the significance of bought-in goods and services.

An emphasis on trends in VA in isolation from bought-in goods and services could in fact be quite misleading. For example, assume a company with £100 in sales in successive years. Bought-in goods and services in year 1 were £60, leaving VA of £40 divided equally between wages £20 and owners £20. In year 2, bought-in items were only £50, with wages £28 and owners £22. Wages had increased as a percentage of VA from 50% to 56% but (in the absence of increased investment and price rises) the owners are also better off. Thus percentage shares of VA are misleading; the owners would be better advised to concentrate on rewards in relation to their investment in resources, and it will be seen later that similar arguments apply to employee rewards.

Some other pitfalls in using VA, including the well-known danger of maximising VA rather than profit, are covered by Morley (1978, pp. 26–37) and Rutherford (1981).

VA and the workers

The emphasis of VA on the co-operative nature of a firm's activities is clearly directed primarily at

[7] For example, the 1981–82 *Survey of Published Accounts* (1981) showed that, of the 88 companies providing VA statements, 72 showed VA gross of depreciation, while 9 deducted depreciation. The remaining 7 companies either did not specify the basis or adopted a mixture of methods!

the workforce. Morley (1978) aptly expresses the underlying ambiguity:

> The first advantage is an improvement in the 'team spirit' within the company...
> ...The enthusiasm for Value Added is partly a reaction to the fact that 'profit' is a dirty word to many workers. Amongst the ranks of the Value Added enthusiasts one finds those who sincerely believe that a better educated work force deserves the dignity of explicit recognition as responsible participators in the process of Adding Value. One also finds those who cynically use Value Added in order to de-emphasize the emotive word 'profit', although no change in the attitude or behaviour of management towards the work force is intended. (p. 19)

People's behaviour is not always determined by logic, and it is therefore conceivable that the mere presentation of a symbolic VA statement will enhance the team-spirit of a company's workforce. However, there would seem to be no logical reason to expect such a change on grounds of the VA statement *alone*, and Morley acknowledges the team spirit improvement as 'a hope rather than a promise' (p. 19). In the absence of behavioural evidence it is impossible to resolve this point.

A more material possibility is Morley's suggestion that '... the introduction of productivity schemes based on Value Added is thereby facilitated' (p. 20). However, it would seem that the introduction of such schemes need have only the most tenuous connection with the publication of a corporate VA statement, particularly where different calculation bases apply in different segments of the firm. Many salesmen operated productivity schemes based on sales figures without undue problems long before companies published turnover figures in corporate reports.

There are, of course, other concrete ways of involving workers in the overall financial performance of the firm. One of these is to institute a profit-sharing scheme based on the issue of shares to employees. This approach is not without its problems (e.g. it costs more than a VA statement) but recent tax changes have stimulated a modest number of new schemes of this type (Breakwell, 1980).

In those cases where outside shareholders are eliminated and the firm becomes labour-controlled, it might be thought that VA really comes into its own—because all value after meeting outside commitments belongs to the worker/owners. Yet it is instructive that the renowned Basque Mondragon worker co-operatives maintain a clear distinction between pay and surplus (=profit). Average pay is linked to earnings in local capitalist enterprises (although differentials are very much narrower) and surplus is divided between the individual accounts of participants and collective reserves (Thomas and Logan, 1982). Thus the role of profit is clearly important in the successful Mondragon system, although under the different name (in translation) of surplus. Perhaps a successful change of name needs some help from a change in the underlying system.

One further point of Morley's needs to be considered, and it has some relevance to Mondragon. It is the suggestion that:

> ...union negotiators could compare the proportions of wages to Value Added for each company in the industry... and one could consult the Value Added Statements for prima facie evidence as to which union seemed to achieve the highest share of Value Added for its members. (Morley, 1978, pp. 12–13)

This implies that VA will help employees and trade unions to aim for an increasing share in VA; such an objective could prove in fact to be harmful to the employees' interests. For example, a company with sales of £100 has bought-in goods and services of £30 and its VA is distributed equally between wages £35 and owners £35. The following year, with sales still at £100, the negotiators have managed to raise the wages share of VA to 60%. But the problem is that bought-in goods have risen to £50, with wages £30 and owners £20. The wages proportion of VA has gone up, but fewer workers are employed because bought-in goods have been substituted. The beneficiaries are the suppliers, who may not be operating in the same national economy. Thus, as in the Mondragon case, attention to competitive forces is more important than assuming that VA is some fixed amount to be divided between participants.

VA in search of a position statement

The prospect of finding a position statement for a company which articulates with VA is negligible. The conventional balance sheet records the fundamental position in relation to three groups: shareholders and lenders who are participants and creditors for goods and services who are considered as 'outsiders'. The balance sheet would also record any amounts remaining unpaid to employees or the government. Yet as a measure of value of the interest of these two groups, their balance sheet amounts would be negligible. Whereas the amounts of obligations to shareholders and lenders represent (approximate) capital amounts, the employees and government have no such recognition of their 'stock' position relative to the company. Should the prospective flow of future wages and taxes be discounted to present values?

The possibilities become complicated and unfruitful. In the absence of a workable position statement, VA becomes a *flow* without a corresponding *stock*. It shows movements between two points which remain permanently undefined. That hardly seems a strong candidate to displace profit.

Conclusions

CFA and VA are both measures that have been drafted in from other valid uses to bear an unreasonably heavy burden in the assessment of corporate performance. Cash flows have an undoubted importance for liquidity assessment and VA has important economic applications, but neither is capable of summarising the accretion in corporate resources which is encompassed in an all-inclusive profit measure based on entry or exit values. Nor do they reflect the consumption of resources in operations, as does current operating profit. They do not even compare well in all respects with historical cost profit. Cash flow does have the relative advantage of reflecting prices of the period in which payment and receipts occur but it also has disadvantages like ignoring movements in non-cash elements. VA (in the form envisaged in *The Corporate Report*) could be calculated on a basis consistent with any profit measure, and in that respect would therefore share the advantages or disadvantages of that measure.

In both cases the lack of a satisfactory position statement highlights the inherent weaknesses of the flow statements. Nor do CFA and VA fare well on the issue of avoiding the ownership emphasis of the profit statement; the usual presentations of CFA retain an ownership viewpoint, and there is no evidence that benefits arise from publishing VA statements which do not reflect the realities of control.

The proposal by Lee (1981b) aims at rescuing CFA by reinstating a profit measure of sorts and a corresponding position statement. Thus it would seem that, at least at the theoretical level, advocacy of CFA shows signs of returning to the profit measurement fold. This may have significance for some professional accountants who have been tempted in the direction of CFA in the face of difficulties over 'inflation accounting.'

The VA statement shows some signs that it may have peaked, so far as disclosure in UK corporate reports is concerned. There was considerable growth in the years 1975–78 (Gray and Maunders, 1979; Rutherford, 1980), but the *Survey of Published Accounts* (1982) shows a relatively static situation for the three years to 1980–81. It will be interesting to see whether the new profit formats under the 1981 Companies Act which give the same raw data as VA (but without calculating VA itself) have any influence on the number of VA statements published.

References

Accounting Standards Committee. *The Corporate Report*, Accounting Standards Committee (1975).

Ashton, R., 'Cash flow accounting: a review and critique', *Journal of Business Finance and Accounting*, Winter 1976, pp. 63–82.

Breakwell, B., 'Profit-sharing schemes under the new rules,' *Accountancy*, July 1980, pp. 107–9.

Briston, R. J. and Fawthrop, R. A., 'Accounting principles and investor protection,' *Journal of Business Finance*. Summer 1971, pp. 10–9.

Burton, J. C., 'Emerging trends in financial reporting.' *Journal of Accountancy*, July 1981, pp. 54–66.

Chambers, R. J., *Accounting, Evaluation and Economic Behavior*, Prentice-Hall (1966).

Chambers, R. J., 'Continuously Contemporary Accounting—Additivity and Action,' *Accounting Review*, October 1967, pp. 751–7.

Chambers, R. J., 'Second thoughts on Continuously Contemporary Accounting,' *Abacus*, September 1970. pp. 39–55.

Chambers, R. J., 'Third thoughts,' *Abacus*, December 1974, pp. 129–37.

Chambers, R. J., *Accounting for Inflation (Exposure Draft)*, Department of Accounting, University of Sydney, 1975.

Climo, T. A., 'Cash flow statements for investors,' *Journal of Business Finance and Accounting*, Autumn 1976. pp. 3–14.

Edwards, E. O. and Bell, P. W., *The Theory and Measurement of Business Income*, University of California Press (1961).

Egginton, D. A., 'Distributable profit and the pursuit of prudence,' *Accounting and Business Research*. Winter 1980, pp. 3–14.

FASB Discussion Memorandum. *Reporting Funds Flows, Liquidity and Financial Flexibility*, Financial Accounting Standards Board (1978).

Ferrara, W. L., 'A cash flow model for the future,' *Management Accounting* (USA), June 1981, pp. 12–17.

Gray, S. J. and Maunders, K. T., 'Recent developments in value added disclosures,' *Certified Accountant*. August 1979, pp. 229–236.

Hussey, R., 'Getting the financial message across to employees,' *Accountancy*, May 1981, pp. 109–11.

Ijiri, Y., 'Cash flow accounting and its structure.' *Journal of Accounting, Auditing and Finance*, May 1978, pp. 331–48.

Ijiri, Y., 'A simple system of cash flow accounting.' in R. R. Sterling and A. L. Thomas (eds). *Accounting for a Simplified Firm*, Scholars Book Co., (1979), pp. 57–71.

Jones, C. J., 'Accounting standards: A blind alley?,' *Accounting and Business Research*, Autumn 1975, pp. 273–9.

Lawson, G. H., Memorandum submitted to the Inflation Accounting Committee—July 1974, *Working Paper Series 12*, Manchester Business School (1975).

Lawson, G. H., 'The cash flow performance of UK companies,' in M. Bromwich and A. Hopwood (eds), *Essays in British Accounting Research*, Pitman (1981), pp. 79–100.

Lee, T. A., 'A case for cash flow reporting,' *Journal of Business Finance*, Summer 1972, pp. 27–36.

Lee, T. A., 'Cash flow accounting and corporate financial reporting,' in M. Bromwich and A. Hopwood (eds), *Essays in British Accounting Research*, Pitman (1981a), pp. 63–78.

Lee, T. A., 'Reporting cash flows and net realisable values,' *Accounting and Business Research*, Spring 1981b, pp. 163–170.

Lee, T. A., 'What cash flow analysis says about BL's finances,' *Financial Times* (23 October 1981c).

Lee, T. A., 'Cash flow accounting and the allocation problem,' *Journal of Busines Finance and Accounting*, Autumn 1982, pp. 341–52.

Morley, M. F., *The Value Added Statement: A review of its use in corporate reports*, Institute of Chartered Accountants of Scotland (1978).

Morley, M. F., 'Value added reporting,' in T. A. Lee (ed). *Developments in Financial Reporting*, Philip Allan (1981).

Peasnell, K. V., 'Some formal connections between economic values and yields and accounting numbers', *Journal of Business Finance and Accounting*, Autumn 1982, pp. 361–381.

Rutherford, B. A., 'Value added as a focus of attention for financial reporting: Some conceptual problems', *Accounting and Business Research*, Summer 1977, pp. 215–220.

Rutherford, B. A., 'Published statements of value added: A survey of three years' experience,' *Accounting and Business Research*, Winter, 1980, pp. 15–28.

Rutherford, B. A., 'Five fallacies about value added,' *Management Accounting* (UK), September 1981, pp. 31–33.

Rutherford, B. A., 'The interpretation of cash flow reports and the other allocation problem,' *Abacus*, June 1982, pp. 40–49.

Survey of Published Accounts 1981–82, edited by L. C. L. Skerratt, Institute of Chartered Accountants in England and Wales (1981).

Thomas, A. L., *A Behavioral Analysis of Joint-cost Allocation and Transfer Pricing*, Stipes (1980).

Thomas, H. and Logan, C., *Mondragon: An Economic Analysis*, George Allen and Unwin (1982).

Worth, B., 'Reporting value added,' *Accountant*, 23/30 December 1976, pp. 728–730.

ABACUS, Vol. 18, No. 1, 1982

B. A. RUTHERFORD

The Interpretation of Cash Flow Reports and the Other Allocation Problem

Allocations continue to be a cause of concern to accountants. Allocations may be distributional (i.e. allocation of resources through budgets) or metrical (e.g. overhead costs to departments). Cash flow accounting is often advocated because it avoids metrical allocations. However, the interaction effects of cash flows may nullify their claimed advantages.

Key words: Cash basis accounting; Cost allocation.

Introduction

Accountants use the term 'allocation' in at least two distinctly different ways. In one sense, allocations are decisions about the disposition of resources between alternative applications; these might perhaps be called *distributional* allocations. The essence of a distributional allocation is that it takes place at the discretion of the party or parties concerned: this distinguishes distributional allocations from most resource flows (for example sales revenues or wages) which are determined in part by external factors such as market forces. Perhaps the most familiar example of the process of distributional allocation is the budget-making carried out by public sector bodies.

In another sense, allocation is the apportionment of a measure of an individual phenomenon over more than one locus; this might be called *metrical* allocation. It is metrical allocation that gives rise to the now-famous allocation problem identified by Thomas (1969). According to at least one school of thought (see, for example, Sterling, 1979) the presence of metrical allocations invalidates a financial reporting scheme and cash flow accounting is often advocated on the grounds that it avoids the need to make such allocations.[1] Indeed Thomas himself (1969) was the first to advance this argument.

However, although it is true that cash flows are not tainted by metrical allocation, under normal circumstances cash flow accounting does not overcome the underlying measurement problem caused by economic interaction. The significance of this for the construction and interpretation of cash flow statements is the subject of this paper.

Accounting Numbers and the Empirical Domain

Although Thomas's work is now familiar it is necessary to discuss it briefly here in order to set it in the context of this paper. Metrical allocations, as defined above, do not

[1] It is acknowledged that not all advocates of cash flow reporting regard the absence of metrical allocation as its primary virtue.

B. A. RUTHERFORD is a lecturer in accounting at the University of Kent at Canterbury.

He wishes to thank his colleagues at Kent together with Professor T. A. Lee, Professor M. C. Wells and an anonymous referee for their helpful comments on earlier drafts of this paper.

correspond to any real world events or objects (referents); they are an attempt to impose an analytical framework on the empirical world rather than a reflection of it. Under special circumstances, however, metrical allocations can be given quasi-empirical meaning. This meaning is derived by viewing the allocations as measures of the potentially real events that would have occured had the loci over which the allocation is being performed experienced separate phenomena such that the overall effect was the same as the actual effect of the shared experience. The particular condition which is necessary to allow this device to operate successfully is that there should be no economic interaction between the loci under consideration; if this condition is not met the measures of the separate hypothetical events will not sum to the actual measure of the real event (Thomas, 1974, p. 54).

The device described in the preceding paragraph can be referred to as the decomposition method. This apparently complex procedure can be illustrated by means of a simple example. Suppose I buy two glasses of beer, intending one for myself and one for a colleague, at a total cost of $1. The empirical event is quite simply the purchase of two glasses for $1, but what if I have to produce general purpose financial reports which distinguish between my sustenance and the entertainment of colleagues? I can normally reckon the cost of the latter to be 50c; this measure will not have a direct referent but I can give it quasi-empirical meaning by thinking of it as the event which would have taken place had I purchased only one pint intending it for my colleague's consumption. Now consider the, unhappily rare, case of a bar offering quantity discounts. If one glass costs 50c but two cost 90c, how is the cost of the round to be allocated? The decomposition method will yield measures of 50c for the separate cost of each drink, leaving an interaction effect of 10c. There is no basis for distributing the interaction effect between the two loci which will yield measures having empirical referents; an equal division would no doubt be widely regarded as *equitable* but it would be as arbitrary as any other.[2]

Thus, in the presence of economic interaction, metrical allocations cannot be given meanings which relate to the empirical domain — that is to say, which have empirical or quasi-empirical referents. Since economic interaction pervades the real world, the metrical allocations of orthodox accruals-based financial accounting are incorrigibly arbitrary.

Cash exists in the real world and hence, provided that they are properly carried out, measurements of cash (and thus *ex ante* distributional allocations of cash) will have empirical referents. Further, it will be possible to make *ex post* distributional allocations with quasi-empirical referents. This is because they can be thought of as allocations which could have been made before the event if the parties concerned had desired. For the moment it is assumed that groups of homogeneous cash or near-cash resources (cash pools), flows between those pools (gross and net), and aggregations and disaggregations of those pools can all have empirical or quasi-empirical referents. To take an apparently trivial example which nonetheless has very significant implications for the interpretation

Of course, special purpose reports can be generated utilizing cost data which are designed for the specific purpose in hand and which does not rely on metrical allocation. In some cases (for example tax computations) reports make use of metrical allocation schemes which are externally imposed and are therefore not arbitrary from the standpoint of the entity concerned.

of cash flow statements, suppose that when I come to pay for the round of drinks discussed above I find I have two piles of coins (cash pools). I can contribute towards the cost of the round in whatever proportions I choose and the cash flows and balances on each pool will exist in the empirical domain. If I have only one pool, and therefore pay the total charge from it, the real world contains only the total sum and the overall balance on the pool but I can subdivide them *ex post* and claim a quasi-empirical meaning for the new measurements because I could have performed the subdivision before paying for the round. The subdivision can be carried out in whatever proportions I choose and it is thus a distributional allocation in the sense in which the term was used earlier. Of course it is essential that an *ex post* distributional allocation should be viewed *only* as a statement about what were once potential resource flows and *not* as a measure of, for example, cost.

Distributional Allocation and the Construction of Cash Flow Statements

A bald statement of the net change in cash balances held by an entity over its life can be produced without making distributional allocations; under normal circumstances it will, of course, show 'nil'. If the owners of the enterprise are independent of that enterprise in every respect except their ownership (for example they are not also employees or customers), a similar statement excluding net distributions to owners can also be drawn up without making distributional allocations and such a statement will provide a measure (not necessarily a good one), of the performance of the entity.

It is usually suggested, however, that cash flow statements should provide some breakdown of net lifetime flows, for example between periods or geographical or operational segments. Such statements can be constructed so as to have real world referents. Where there is economic interaction between particular cash flows, however, the design of cash flow statements must inevitably be affected. Reporting schemes for producing cash flow statements with real world referents can be classified according to the way in which interaction is handled:

Type I schemes require that *all* cash flows be disaggregated along some pre-selected dimension (for example by geographical area). It will be shown that, if there is any interaction between flows arising in different elements of the disaggregation, distributional allocations between those elements must be performed.

Type II schemes require that cash flows subject to interaction be excluded from the pre-selected disaggregation and shown separately as one final element which reconciles the total of the disaggregated flows with the overall total for the entity as a whole. The resulting statement will not contain any distributional allocations but it may be difficult to produce and still more difficult to interpret.

Segmental Cash Flows and the Other Allocation Problem[3]

The segmental cash flow statement provides a convenient starting point for considering the problems posed by distribution allocation. One of the best-known cash flow reporting formats is that proposed by Lee. Amongst other breakdowns, he suggested that a firm's

[3] Thomas has recently expressed grave doubts about the use of segmental cash flows to overcome the transfer-pricing problem (1980, p. 220). The argument developed in this section is analogous to his.

'manufacturing and/or trading transactions flow' should be 'analysed according to significant economic unit groupings' (1972, p. 31). He went on to suggest that:

> The main advantage of this [analysis] appears to be that it supplies the investor with information concerning the contribution to total cash flow of each of the company's economic units. It does so without revealing individual profit margins, a point which is often put forward as the reason for not disclosing detailed costs of production in conventional stewardship financial statements. The emphasis of the statement, therefore, is not on the relative profit contribution of each unit, but on the relative contribution each makes to the continuing survival of the company as a whole — a much more fundamental, and in many ways, more important issue to the investor. (pp. 33-4)

This argument conflates two views of cash flows: cash flows as empirical events and cash flows as proxies for something else — in this case, contribution to survival. It is always, of course, possible to provide segmental cash flows having empirical referents. Each segment can be provided with one or more cash pools (for example, bank accounts) and all transactions in which the enterprise engages can then be settled through one or other of these pools. At the worst, however, transactions can be directed between pools entirely at the discretion of head office management: for example segment A might be directed to pay segment B's payroll costs. The resulting cash flow statement would have empirical referents but it would scarcely yield economically significant variables.

In the absence of economic interaction the kind of distributional allocations implicit in the behaviour described above can clearly be avoided by the use of fairly simple rules specifying that when a transaction is entered into in connection with the operations of a particular segment, the cash settlement arising out of that transaction should be made through one of the relevant segment's cash pools. In the face of economic interaction, however, it will not be possible to apportion group cash flows completely using the rule specified above. Thus, for example, where there have been inter-segmental sales giving rise to interaction (i.e. the total cost of the group's output is lower than it would have been had the intermediate good been traded in the market place) this interaction will have an impact on cash flows as well as on costs and the total cash outflows of the group cannot be apportioned between segments without performing distributional allocations. Interaction between segments can arise from a variety of sources including intersegmental transfers, common provision of services, head office expenses, inter-segmental capital flows and other aspects of central management strategy (for example, pricing individual segments' sales so as to avoid the attention of anti-trust authorities).

Thus if there is any economic interaction between flows, a Type I reporting scheme must involve distributional allocation. It is worth stressing that this will not be a result of the manipulation by management of some otherwise 'pure' flow. However, in the absence of specific rules, managers will be able to make allocations which exceed the interaction effects that make them necessary; this is comparable to distributional allocation performed in the absence of economic interaction (discussed earlier) and can be avoided.

Cash flow statements containing distributional allocations must be interpreted with great care. The cash flows which actually take place will determine the liquidity position of individual segments and thus cash flow statements with empirical referents may be interpreted in this light. Further it may be possible to examine, for example, the reasons given by management for making the distributional allocations they have actually carried out. However, it is likely to be extremely difficult to establish any valid interpretation of segmental cash flows in terms of the *performance* of the individual segments. Writers in the area sometimes label particular flows in ways which will not in practice be valid. Careful choice of terminology is essential if lay persons are not to be misled. Thus a segment's cash flows will normally represent neither the cash flows that the segment would generate if it operated independently (its separate effects) nor the reduction in group cash flows that would have occured if the activities of the segment had been discontinued (its separate effects plus attributable interaction effects). This may not be readily apparent to a lay person who is told that a statement shows 'the contribution to total cash flow of each of the company's economic units' (Lee, 1972, p. 34).

Lee himself appears to have recognized the need for allocations of some sort in segmental cash flow statements because in his suggested format he proposes that cash flows expended on 'overheads' should be divided between 'allocable' overheads for each segment and a final category of 'non-allocable' overheads, although he offers no basis on which to distinguish the various flows.

In a Type II reporting scheme flows are distinguished according to whether or not they are subject to interaction. As has been indicated already, such schemes eliminate the need for distributional allocation. They have their own problems of construction and interpretation, however. Some interaction is likely to be very difficult to identify. Conceptually, interaction exists when a flow relating to the activities of an entity which is a segment of a group would have been of a different magnitude if it had occured in an entity which was independent (i.e. not a component of a larger group) but otherwise identical. Thus the identification of interaction involves counterfactual speculation about what would have happened under hypothetical alternative circumstances. This kind of speculation is alien to the tradition of financial reporting.

Assuming that the identification problem can be overcome, it remains difficult to provide any sensible interpretation of segmental flows under a Type II scheme in terms of organizational performance. Such flows will be even further removed from the 'economic' interpretations already ruled out for Type I schemes. They will not normally represent the flows passing through the segment's cash pools and although they can be given empirical (or quasi-empirical) referents by the use of a separate cash pool for flows subject to interaction, this will not yield a useful measure of performance.

It will often be extremely difficult to make comparisons between segments or through time since even small changes in the pattern of interaction (whether brought about by operating decisions or external factors) could have the effect of shifting the whole of the related cash flows into or out of the segmental breakdown. Given the pervasiveness of interaction in the modern economy a large proportion of a group's cash flows are in practice likely to fall 'below the line' (i.e. to be excluded from the segmental breakdown). Thus if central management felt it was desirable that all segments should moderate price increases so as to avoid the appearance of exploiting the group's size, the whole of the group's cash flows from sales would have to be shown below the line.

Economic interaction, then, makes segmental cash flow statements difficult to construct and interpret. But then segmental reporting has proved extremely problematical under traditional methods of financial accounting. Is the rest of cash flow accounting safe? The next sections of this paper demonstrate that the problems discussed above in fact occur in relation to all breakdowns of net lifetime cash flow.

The Capital-Revenue Distinction

The distinction between capital and revenue is, of course, fundamental to accruals-based accounting models, and, although not essential to cash flow reporting, it is carried over into cash flow statements by such writers as Lee, (1972), Lawson, (1975, 1976) and Meyers, (1976). In addition Lawson and Meyers recommend that capital outflows should be divided between replacement and growth expenditure. A number of recent papers have employed variants of the basic distinction; for example, Lee (1981) separates 'investment' flows from 'operating' flows (p. 166).

As in the case of segmental cash flows, the capital-revenue distinction can be given an empirical referent simply by labelling some cash pools as 'revenue' and others as 'capital', but such a method is unlikely to yield useful information. Lee describes capital flows as 'cash movements resulting from the purchase and sale of "profit-contributing" resources by the company, including land, buildings, plant, equipment, investments and sums expended in the area of research and development' (1972, p. 31). Unless the basis for classification as a capital flow is to be simply the type of asset acquired (for example, land), some form of benefit criterion is clearly needed. Such a criterion need not be as refined as that required by the accruals model, since it may not be necessary to allocate flows between periods.

One possible definition would be that capital flows are those which benefit more than one period. A profit-based measure of benefit appears inappropriate in a cash flow framework and it would seem sensible to base the test on cash inflows: thus capital outflows would be those without which future cash inflows would be reduced in more than one period. Several of the problems which plague accruals-based models survive under the definition offered above; for example, the nature of the causal relationship between flows must be established and in some cases (for example, research and development expenditure) this will be very difficult, if not impossible. In addition there is the problem of the level of aggregation at which to apply the test, since, for example, a large single outflow on the acquisition of inventory may benefit several periods, yet it is clear that most writers on cash flow accounting would not regard expenditure on inventory as a capital outflow.

For present purposes, however, the most interesting problem is the economic interaction which will be likely to occur between capital and revenue flows. Examples of such interaction include the purchasing of supplies of raw materials or spare parts at special prices as part of a deal including the acquisition of plant, the purchase of going concerns including inventory as well as fixed assets, and the cost of any department which carries out both capital and revenue work (for example, a maintenance department, or indeed, a research and development department). When Thomas (1969) examined a number of approaches to depreciation as a case of the metrical allocation problem he concluded that 'in most cases examined, the allocation problems discussed . . . have been ones of inability to distinguish depreciable assets . . . from other economic goods' (p. 76), and this difficulty appears to extend to cash flow accounting. Lawson suggested that total capital outflows can be arrived at with 'complete objectivity' (1975, p. 47) but this seems unlikely if objectivity is taken as implying the existence of empirical referents. Meyers accepted that segregating capital and revenue flows 'itself requires an allocation' (1976, p. 55). The degree of interaction between replacement and growth expenditure which, as discussed earlier, some writers suggest should be disclosed separately is likely to be very substantial.

The classification of flows between recurrent and non-recurrent items (or, more properly, between flows from recurrent and non-recurrent events) is proposed by some writers, for example Hendriksen (1970, pp. 241-2) and Lee (1972), usually on the grounds that it will make the prediction of future flows easier. The classification is similar in some ways to that between revenue and capital, and the same problems of aggregation and interaction apply. Consider, for example, payroll outflows during a period in which a work-to-rule has taken place. It is believed that this will not recur. Some output is achieved but it is at an abnormally low level; payroll costs are as for a 'normal' period but obviously high in relation to what would have been incurred in producing the amount of output actually achieved by 'normal' production methods. It would be possible to argue that payroll costs should all be classified as recurrent on the grounds that costs at this level are indeed expected to be incurred in the future although the events with which they are expected to be associated (namely, normal output) will be different. This approach takes a very narrow view of the meaning of the term 'recurrent' and is unlikely to produce information which will be useful by itself although such information may be more valuable if it can be incorporated into a wider framework. If a part of the payroll is to be treated as non-recurrent there is likely to be some degree of economic interaction to be taken into account: thus, for example, total payroll cost for the period will probably be lower than the combined cost of employing one group of part-time workers to produce the output actually achieved and another group to stand about for the rest of the time.

Other Classifications in Cash Flow Statements

Other classifications of cash flows are frequently proposed: examples include nominal and functional classifications and classifications between operating and financing flows and between investment and recovery of investment (Ijiri, 1978). Clearly any of these may be subject to economic interaction and it may thus be necessary to make distributional allocations in order to produce the required figures.

Several other problems which arise in the construction of cash flow statements are also, broadly, questions of disaggregation and classification. Although it is often ignored by advocates of cash flow accounting, the problem of how cash (and, if they are to be included in the system, near-cash) resources are to be demarcated from other monetary assets is a substantial and difficult one. The problem of establishing a cut-off for cash flows through time is really another aspect of the definition of cash. Hendriksen (1970) points out in discussing various concepts of funds flow that:

> A second advantage of the monetary asset concept is that it is consistent with the concept of constructive receipt. An increase in a monetary asset represents a constructive receipt of cash if such asset is readily convertible into cash. A rigid adherence to the cash concept results in the making of arbitrary distinctions between cash and near-cash items. (p. 243)

He cites a similar advantage for the broader concept of net monetary assets. In general, the definition of cash employed will have a major impact on the timing of recognition of the flows associated with individual events. Liquid resources come in such a wide variety that any attempt to produce a definition of near-cash based on differences of substance is likely to involve subjective judgement.

As before, interaction pervades the timing/definition of cash problem. Except in very rare circumstances, the flows associated with a single period in the life of a continuing entity will not be the same as the flows which would arise in the case of an otherwise identical entity operating for one period only. Even amongst operating flows interaction is significant. Closing accounts receivable, for example, *could* no doubt have been collected in the period in which they arose, perhaps by offering a substantial cash discount: the value which would have been received will be the separate effect for the period, and the advantage of not actually having to offer the discount in practice is an interaction effect attributable to the joint existence of the entity in both the period of sale and the period of collection. Any cash flow which arises in connection with a transaction which affects at least one period other than that in which the flow occurs may be subject to interaction. 'Capital expenditure' thus falls into this category by definition.

Lee has expressed concern about the possibility of 'suspicion that company management may be manipulating the figures by delaying or accelerating cash movements' (1974, p. 191). He suggests that an audit may be able to identify such manipulation. Yet in the presence of interaction a Type I reporting scheme seeking to apportion all flows to time periods must leave management with some degree of discretion in the form of distributional allocation through time and it is difficult to see why this should be regarded as manipulation. As before, distributional allocations in excess of interaction effects may be regarded as amounting to manipulation but they can only be detected by comparing actual results for the period with the flows which would have occurred if the entity had existed for that period only and the latter cannot be measured objectively. This has obvious implications for the auditor. A Type II reporting scheme would not avoid this problem since it would rely equally on the identification of interaction. Further, since a fairly high proportion of cash flows would be likely to be subject to interaction, such a scheme would in practice often leave a substantial number of flows unapportioned to time periods.

A further problem concerns transactions which could, and perhaps ordinarily would, have involved cash flows but which have in fact taken place in a form which by-passes cash. Examples include the purchase of non-monetary assets for shares and the netting of accounts payable and receivable. Ijiri (1978) proposes that these transactions, which he calls constructive cash flows, should be reported as if they were actual cash flows, although it is clear that there will be no empirical referents for them. This is not the only possible treatment: Lee (1972 Statement G) suggests that transactions of this kind should be listed elsewhere in the accounts, and it would clearly be possible (and, in a pure system, essential) to ignore them. The decomposition method described earlier can be used to yield quasi-empirical referents for Ijiri's proposed treatment although needless to say, the possibility of economic interaction arises.

The Development of Cash Flow Reporting

Cash flow statements can have empirical or quasi-empirical referents. However economic interaction affects cash flows as well as costs and revenues. Individual cash flows which are subject to interaction are not uniquely determined by the underlying economic events (real resource flows) with which they are associated. When interaction crosses the boundaries between categories in a disaggregated cash flow statement (whatever the basis for the disaggregation), some degree of discretion to make distributional allocations must inevitably reside with management. The further development of a scheme for reporting cash flows should take explicitly into account the existence and impact of cash flow interaction. Reports which apportion *all* flows between the categories of a single-dimensional analysis (including an analysis by time period) must be interpreted bearing in mind the discretion which may have been available to management. Reports which exclude from the analysis flows subject to interaction will be difficult to construct; further, their interpretation will be likely to be hindered by the presence of a large category of unapportioned flows.

One possible development of cash flow reporting might be to use the decomposition method discussed earlier to develop schemes which segregate separate and interaction *effects*, rather than merely separating out flows which are subject to interaction. These might be termed Type III schemes. Alternatively, distributional allocations might be limited to the sum of relevant separate and interaction effects.[4] Unfortunately, as discussed earlier, separate and interaction effects cannot be measured objectively. Highly disaggregated reports are likely to prove very complex in structure since any grouping of two or more categories in a disaggregation can yield an interaction effect.

It has been emphasized throughout this paper that, however distributional allocations are handled, cash flow statements will have empirical referents. It is essential that labels should be selected to give an accurate impression of the nature of those referents. For example, if a segment's operational flows are merely those operational flows accounted for through that segment's cash pools, the flows are not equivalent to the flows which would have occurred had the segment been independent, or the flows which would have been lost if the segment's activities had been terminated, and the labels used and any accompanying narrative should not imply otherwise.

There is a level of meaning at which cash flows are no more a completely 'true' representation of events than historical cost measures and perhaps the terminology of the accounts (including that in the auditor's report) should be selected accordingly. Summary and higher-order statistical measures are not ordinarily thought of as being 'true' or 'false' in the same sense in which individual observations can be true or false; perhaps there is something to be learnt here about accounting terminology.

There is some evidence to suggest (see, for example, Lee and Tweedie, 1977) that lay users of accounts have considerable difficulty in coming to grips with accruals-based accounting; if cash flow concepts are easier to deal with it may well be that lay users will be better able to appreciate the complications of distributional allocation than those of metrical allocation.

Much of this paper may appear to adopt a rather unfriendly attitude towards cash flow

[4] For a discussion of comparable endeavours in joint costing see Thomas (1980).

statements. It is not, however, the intention of the author to undermine the development of cash flow reporting; the construction of measures which have empirical referents would represent a substantial advance in the development of financial accounting. We must be extremely careful, though, not to bring a system of cash flow accounting rapidly and wastefully into disrepute by imposing on its measurements interpretations which they cannot bear.

REFERENCES

Hendriksen, E. S., *Accounting Theory*, rev. edn., Irwin, Homewood, Illinois 1970.

Ijiri, Y., 'Cash-flow Accounting and its Structure', *Journal of Accounting, Auditing and Finance*, Summer 1978.

Lawson, G. H., 'Memorandum Submitted to the Inflation Accounting Committee', Working Paper Number 12, Manchester Business School, Manchester 1975.

——, 'The Rationale of Cash Flow Accounting', *The Investment Analyst*, December 1976.

Lee, T. A., 'A Case for Cash Flow Reporting', *Journal of Business Finance*, Summer 1972.

——, 'Enterprise Income: Survival or Decline and Fall?' *Accounting and Business Research*, Summer 1974.

——, 'Reporting Cash Flows and Net Realisable Values', *Accounting and Business Research*, Spring 1981.

Lee, T. A. and D. P. Tweedie, *The Private Shareholder and the Corporate Report*, Institute of Chartered Accountants in England and Wales, London 1977.

Meyers, S. L., 'A Proposal for Coping with the Allocation Problem', *Journal of Accountancy*, April 1976.

Sterling, R. R., *Toward a Science of Accounting*, Scholars Book Co., Houston, Texas 1979.

Thomas, A. L., *The Allocation Problem in Financial Accounting Theory*, Studies in Accounting Research Number 3, American Accounting Association, Evanston, Illinois 1969.

——, *The Allocation Problem: Part Two*, Studies in Accounting Research Number 9, American Accounting Association, Sarasota, Florida 1974.

——, 'Matching: Up from our Black Hole' in R. R. Sterling and A. L. Thomas (eds), *Accounting for a Simplified Firm Owning Depreciable Assets*, Scholars Book Co., Houston, Texas 1979.

——, *A Behavioural Analysis of Joint-Cost Allocation and Transfer Pricing*, Stipes, Illinois 1980.

Accounting and Business Research, Vol. 19, No. 74, pp. 161-169, 1989.

Cash Flow Accounting and Liquidity: Cash Flow Potential and Wealth

George J. Staubus*

Abstract—The persistence of a minority interest in 'cash flow accounting' alongside the dominant financial reporting pattern that gives cash flow statements a distinctly secondary role in the line-up of flow statements suggests that something is missing from the analyses of the interested parties. The major theme of this paper is that users rely on historical cash flow reporting for information relevant to projecting enterprise liquidity in the short run, and on financial statements based on accrual-deferral accounting for information relevant to their interest in wealth and income. An explicit distinction between the two accounting objectives (providing information for use in assessing future enterprise liquidity and providing information for use in assessing enterprise wealth and income and performance against investors' augmentation-of-wealth objective) is recommended as a basis for clarifying the issues. That distinction suggests the value of two quite different, but related, sets of data: historical cash flows and stocks and flows of cash potentials.

A number of accounting scholars have proposed that 'cash flow accounting' be emphasised more than has been common in conventional financial reporting. Lee (1972, 1981, 1984 and elsewhere) and Lawson (1971, 1978, 1985 and elsewhere) have been prominent among European advocates of cash flow accounting. The works of theorists advocating emphasis on forms of exit values (Chambers, 1966 and elsewhere; Sterling, 1979 and elsewhere) are related to the cash flow accounting proposals through their common concern with enterprise liquidity, or short-term capacity to pay. More recently, several researchers employing econometric techniques have tested securities market responses to flow variables other than conventional earnings; examples include Bowen, Burgstahler and Daley (1986, 1987); Rayburn (1986), and Wilson (1986, 1987). The cash flow issue refuses to go away.

Comparison of cash flow and exit value accounting ideas with more conventional accounting principles reveals deep-seated conflicts. It seems appropriate for one who has long argued for more emphasis on cash flows (Staubus, 1961 and elsewhere) to try once more to put the role of cash flows in financial reporting into perspective. In doing so, the contributions of Egginton (1984, 1985) and the value of his exchange with Lawson (1985) and Lee (1985) are acknowledged.

Most of these comments are intended as generally *descriptive* of pertinent financial and accounting practices observable in Western industrialised democracies, although the impracticality of precisely distinguishing between descriptive and normative statements is granted.

The conclusions, which are believed to be supported by the evidence presented, are (1) that *ex post* and *ex ante* cash flow reporting is valuable to those seeking to assess enterprise liquidity, (2) that liquidity and wealth should be distinguished more clearly, and (3) that the relationships between the key concepts and the role of cash flow potential have been neglected.

Premises

The starting point is a brief review of those features of investment activities and financial reporting that provide the base for an evaluation of the potential roles of reports on historical cash flows and on cash flow potentials.

Investment

The investment relationship is a reasonable place to commence an examination of the role of cash flow accounting in reporting to external parties. The essence of investment is the forgoing of present consumption of wealth for the purpose of enhancing future consumption (including bequests for consumption by beneficiaries). In a fundamental sense, all investors are individuals; business enterprises are only conduits. Investment success is defined as augmentation of the investor's stock of consumption purchasing power. That stock of consumption purchasing power may be under the direct control of the investor, or it may be managed by an agent—a manager of an investee enterprise.

In some cases, investments are divided into homogeneous units (shares, bonds) that are pub-

*George J. Staubus is a professor at the Graduate School of Business Administration, University of California at Berkeley.

licly traded, thus providing direct market price evidence of the investor's stock of consumption purchasing power—the value of the investment. In those cases, many investors seek additional evidence for assessing the value of their investments as a step towards investment decisions. In other cases, no market price for the investment is observable, so again investors seek evidence for assessing values of investments. In either case, the essence of investment value is potential consumption purchasing power, and conversion of that investment value embodied in a business enterprise to direct purchasing power in the hands of the investor depends on the enterprise's future capacity to pay. That dependency presumably explains investors' efforts to predict enterprise cash flows.

An investment analyst's predictions of cash flows may take various forms. First, the direct approach focusing on cash receipts and cash disbursements might be taken. Second, the dividend stream approach is used by many analysts (Hawkins and Campbell, 1978, p. 17). It is based on the idea that the shareholder's direct cash receipts (prior to sale of the shares) is in the form of dividends. Because dividends depend on enterprise cash flows, any well-supported projection of dividends must rest on a projection of the firm's capacity to pay—in cash, with rare exceptions. Third, the analyst may concentrate on predicting earnings (interpreted as cash flows normalised through the accrual-deferral process) and either assume that all revenues and expenses are realised in cash flows in the reporting period plus or minus an immaterial lead or lag, or adjust the predicted earnings for material discrepancies between earnings and cash flows. Any component of earnings that is not related to a recent past, current, or near future cash flow presumably is suspect. For example, if an accountant makes an upward revaluation of goodwill, the analyst is not likely to accept the offsetting entry as a component of earnings. (See Hawkins and Campbell, pp. 97–121, for other examples.) A common interpretation of certain earnings-cash flow discrepancies is as influences on the 'quality of earnings'. For example, if inflation is perceived as requiring expenditures for replacement in excess of reported cost of goods sold and depreciation, the quality of earnings is downgraded. In sum, whether the analyst thinks primarily in terms of earnings, dividends, or direct cash flows, the underlying phenomena of interest are enterprise cash flows. Prospective earnings that are not realisable in cash flows are not important to the investor. Discounting is appropriate in every case.

Many investors, of course, do not make the type of intensive analyses suggested here. They may rely on tips or qualitative judgments, or accept reported earnings without question for use in relative price-earnings assessments. But to the extent that the specific contents of financial statements are used by professional analysts in projecting the firm's capacity to meet investors' objectives, one or more versions of enterprise cash flows are the underlying phenomena of interest (Hawkins and Campbell, 1978; Hawkins *et al.*, 1983). See Exhibit I for a summary of the relationship of earnings to share value that has underlain my own work in this area since 1961.

Financial Reporting

The decision-usefulness objective of financial reporting (Staubus, 1954, 1980) is taken for granted here, although its acceptance probably is not descriptive of practice. Perhaps those most interested in considering the uses of data on historical cash flows and on cash flow potentials are willing to accept that objective. The types of decisions that appear to be most prominent are the basic investment-disinvestment decisions, other contracting decisions, and control-oriented decisions—areas that clearly overlap and that focus on enterprise wealth and liquidity.[1] The investor's interpretation of enterprise wealth—a stock of potential consumption purchasing power—is accepted by those parties engaged in contracting and control decisions. In a money economy, enterprise wealth is interpreted as cash flow potential (Staubus, 1967, p. 660; 1977, p. 163; FASB, 1978, para. 41). The concept of cash flow potential is meant to embody the amount, timing, risk, and cost-of-capital features that determine the market value of a prospective cash flow stream. That interpretation of wealth is generally accepted, often without explicit articulation, in the world of finance (Brealey and Myers, 1984, p. 21; Copeland and Weston, 1979, p. 16). Assets are thought of as positive cash flow potentials; liabilities as negative cash flow potentials. Investors seek information regarding stocks and flows of the entity's cash flow potentials.

Investors and others making investment, contracting, and control-oriented decisions often are said to be concerned with the entity's 'performance' (Egginton, 1984). The meaning of performance is critical. Whether one visualises a corporate version of the medieval master-steward relationship, the principal/agent model, or the conventional owner/manager relationship, performance in the context of reporting to investors means achievement of investors' objectives—enhancement of future consumption—through augmentation of enterprise cash flow potential. Maintenance of liquidity is a means to that end. The cash flow potential interpretation of wealth is

[1]For a different but related view of the 'uses of information', see Butterworth, Gibbons and King (1982, pp. 9–17).

Exhibit I
Relationship Between Accounting Numbers and Share Prices

Earnings are defined as $\Delta(A - L)$*	1 ➔	*A* & *L* are defined as Cash Flow Potentials†	2 ➔	Cash Flow Potentials are realised as Firm Cash Flows‡	3 ➔	Firm's Lifetime Net Cash Flows = Lifetime Dividends	4 ➔	Shares are priced at Present Value of Future Dividends

Link 1 is the Double Entry Tie of Income to Net Assets.
Link 2 is Realisation of Cash Flow Potentials, Subject to Measurement Errors and Omissions.
Link 3 is the Equality of a Firm's Lifetime Net Cash Inflows and Outflows.
Link 4 is the Present Value Model of Share Value.

*Earnings are defined as change in net assets other than in transactions with owners.
†Cash flow potential incorporates the amount, timing, risk, and cost-of-capital features that determine the market value of a prospective cash flow stream.
‡Accounting relies on imperfect evidence of cash flow potential for its measurements: cash at face value, estimated future cash flow, discounted estimated future cash flows, exit prices, current entry prices linked to exit prices in equilibrium, and old entry prices linked to current entry prices by the random walk pattern. Certain assets and liabilities are omitted due to unacceptable measurement weaknesses.

accepted in the world of financial management.[2] *Corporate performance is measured by change in cash flow potential.*

Investors recognise the necessity for trading off risk and return. Information relevant to assessing risks—especially risk of loss of liquidity—is sought by investors. Therefore, information helpful in understanding and predicting the entity's liquidity is valued by investors and investor-oriented users of financial reports. The risk of illiquidity and other risks involve uncertainties of many kinds, so it is difficult to specify standard measures of such risks or proper reporting of risk-relevant information. However, historical cash flow information is widely recognised as helpful in that regard.

Reasons for interest in cash flow accounting

Much attention has been given to the case for historical cash flow accounting in the last 15 years, so it is not necessary to go into great detail in this section. The works of G. H. Lawson and T. A. Lee have been especially prominent, and they extend well beyond the publications listed in the references at the end of this paper. Lee (1981) has argued for a combination of historical cash flow accounting and net realisable values assuming no continuity of enterprise activities (p. 164)—an information set that would appear to provide an excellent basis for 'liquidity management assessment' (p. 170). Staubus (1966, 1977) also deals with arguments pertaining to alternative asset flow concepts, especially flows of cash, net short-term monetary assets, net working capital, and net assets. The discussion in this section, however, is limited to historical cash flow accounting.

Departing from the descriptive mode for the present, the following observations might lead one toward historical cash flow accounting:

1. The entity's stock of cash at the reporting date is of interest because it represents the ultimate liquid asset. Interest in a stock might lead one to the related flows—how the stock arose.
2. Cash serves as the beginning and ending anchor points of sets of related activities viewed as cycles.
3. The role of historical cash flow information as a base on which to build cash flow projections is widely acknowledged. Cash flow projections are used by those who:
   (a) Are concerned about the firm's liquidity, financial flexibility and short-run survival;
   (b) Think of the firm's capacity to pay at any future time as dependent on its cash flows to that time.

[2] In that portion of the world of finance that is oriented to securities markets, descriptive models of securities values clearly focus on the discounting of future cash flows, as they have for several centuries. (See, for example, Isaac Newton (1686) and Eugen von Böhm-Bawerk (1891). The importance of future cash flows to portfolio managers may have increased in recent years as more of those managers have been driven by the responsibility to provide the cash flows necessary to meet pension obligations. In the world of corporate financial management, the net present value model of investment project analysis emphasises management's overriding concern with finding projects that have net positive cash flow potential. Is there any significant evidence to challenge the acceptance of the cash flow potential interpretation of wealth and management performance in the business world?

4. Unreliability and lack of relevance of many measurements of net asset items—e.g., allocations of historical costs—and omission of many valuable resources and obligations from balance sheets, are recognised as weaknesses in the accrual/deferral measurements of wealth and income that make information on alternative stock/flow concepts helpful in assessing the entity's future capacity to pay. The superior reliability (observability, verifiability, representational faithfulness, neutrality) of historical cash flow data surely is a great—perhaps its greatest—strength.

The above considerations, no doubt augmented by others, justify the periodic reporting of a substantial amount of cash-oriented financial information. External reporting practices, for example those required by the Financial Accounting Standards Board's Statement No. 95 (1987), have responded to the indicated need.

The role of cash flow in financial reporting in the 1980s

Returning to the descriptive mode, this section includes observations regarding the roles for which historical cash flow information is widely accepted and a role for which it is not generally accepted, and why.

Acceptance of Historical Cash Flow Data: For Reporting on Liquidity

One can say with some assurance that cash flow reports, or flow reports on some other pool of relatively liquid assets, are widely accepted as helpful to those concerned with an enterprise's past and future liquidity. Information on historical flows is treated as a starting point for projecting cash flows, including dividends, interest payments, and principal payments to creditors. This includes judging the prospect for occurrence of a liquidity crisis. In addition, the information typically provided in cash flow statements regarding investing and financing transactions, operating cash flows, and changes in current asset and current liability items help the reader to understand the firm's activities and management's policies. If the conventional wisdom—that the two major operating objectives of business managers are to maintain liquidity and profitability—is true, cash flow reporting clearly provides information relevant to evaluations and projections of management's performance as measured by the liquidity objective, as noted by Lee (1985, pp. 93, 95).

A curious feature of the widely accepted notion that reporting flows of cash or a similar pool of liquid funds is worthwhile is that those advocating or requiring such reporting give little attention to the concept of liquidity. See, for example, FASB, 1987. An exception is Lee (1981, 1985) who does give considerable attention to the role of cash flow accounting in reporting on liquidity. Liquidity does not, however, tend to be viewed as something that exists, like wealth. Rather, it is seen as an intangible quality of a firm's financial position. The tangible version of liquidity is net liquid assets, which may be defined in relatively narrow or broader terms. Thus, the FASB, which does not define liquidity or liquid assets, calls for cash flow reporting for a pool consisting of 'cash and cash equivalents,' the latter consisting of 'short-term, highly liquid investments that are both: (a) readily convertible to known amounts of cash, and (b) so near their maturity that they present insignificant risk of changes in value because of changes in interest rates. Generally, only investments with original maturities of three months or less qualify under that definition' (1987, para. 7). An earlier view was:

> We believe the essence of the liquidity concept is *short-term capacity to pay*... The primary attribute of a liquid asset is *quickness of convertibility to cash*... A secondary attribute, which we believe most businessmen expect of a liquid asset, is lack of adverse consequences to the entity from the conversion of the asset to cash. The most likely adverse consequences are (a) impairment of operating capacity and (b) the sacrifice of existing wealth, that is, a loss (Staubus, 1977, pp. 366–7).

If cash flow accounting, or any other financial reporting approach, is to be developed further in the interest of reporting on, and contributing to an understanding of liquidity, a more serious investigation of the liquidity concept seems appropriate. Lippman and McCall (1986, p. 48) suggested that 'an asset is liquid if it *can be sold quickly* at a *predictable price*.' But their approach included a 'sales policy that maximizes the expected discounted value of the net proceeds associated with the sale, and defining the asset's liquidity to be the expected time until the asset is sold when following the optimal policy' (p. 44). This position is consistent with Keynes: one asset is more liquid than another if it is 'more certainly realisable at short notice without loss' (1930, p. 67). Liquidity, in this view, is not associated with forced sales.

Three factors appear to determine an asset's liquidity: (1) standardisation of the asset, (2) thickness of the market, and (3) operational efficiency of the market. With regard to standardisation, monetary assets are more objectively classifiable than nonmonetary assets. Accountants have identified three important characteristics of future cash flows: time, amount, and uncertainty. With certainty, the liquidity of money claims is clear. Uncertainty adds a subjective factor, but financial markets are accustomed to dealing with it. The liquidity of many, but not all, money claims is readily assessed.

Turning to nonmonetary assets, those that are graded by well-established standards, as are many agricultural and mineral products, can also 'be sold quickly at a predictable price,' although the degree of predictability varies, especially with the prediction period. Other nonmonetary assets must be recognised as nonstandard and not subject to ready classification. The extreme cases are genuinely unique assets such as real property, specialized assets in process of construction to customers' specifications, and intangibles. It is possible, of course, that a nonmonetary asset could be more liquid than certain monetary assets.

Thin markets are an enemy of liquidity. 'When there are many transactions per day of a homogeneous assets such as wheat or long-term Treasury bonds, the market for the asset is thick' (Lippman and McCall, p. 47). To a prospective seller, the number of buyers in an asset market is most relevant to the asset's liquidity. 'Accordingly, the thickness of the market for an asset is said to increase with the frequency of offers' to buy (Lippman and McCall, p. 47).

Finally, the operational efficiency of the market for an asset affects its liquidity. 'If capital markets are efficient, then purchase or sale of any security at the prevailing market price is a zero-NPV (net present value) transaction' (Brealey and Myers, p. 265). That definition could be extended to other asset markets. Examples of transaction costs that are widely recognised as reducing liquidity are: brokerage commissions, transfer taxes, income taxes triggered by realisation of gains from sale, sales and value-added taxes, and search costs such as advertising, other communication costs, and agents' time. Tax advantages enjoyed when losses are realised are negative transaction costs.

'In view of this discussion, it is clear that financial assets traded in a thick, efficient market will be exceedingly liquid' (Lippman and McCall, p. 50). But that is not enough to define liquidity. With more attention to liquidity, perhaps accountants could develop the concept more fully. For now, the above-quoted 1977 definition may be acceptable.

Note that two related concepts of liquidity are relevant: the liquidity of an individual asset and the liquidity of an enterprise. The latter might involve a time dimension cut-off for both assets and liabilities. Net liquid assets might, for example, include both assets readily convertible to cash in the normal course of business within a week and liabilities due for payment within a week. (In the United States, transactions on major securities markets must be settled in cash within five business days). Dichotomous classification of assets (as either liquid or illiquid) would seem to be a crude application of the liquidity concept to individual assets, but any operational concept for comparing the liquidity of enterprises probably requires a uniform dividing line between liquid items and others, thus defining a pool of 'liquidity'. In practice, that pool of liquidity does not include such nonmonetary cash flow potentials as stocks of merchandise and materials, or real property, at net realisable values. They typically cannot be sold quickly without adverse consequences. It is not unreasonable to propose a concept of liquidity that includes such items, but that does not seem to be a popular view currently. Liquidity of an asset is a matter of degree; empirical evidence of an asset's convertibility to cash quickly and without loss would seem to be the only basis for arguing with current practice.

Rejection of Historical Cash Flow Data: For Reporting on Wealth

Now consider a role for which historical cash flow accounting is not generally accepted as suitable: reporting on wealth and income—and management's performance on the profitability criterion. A review of the status quo may not be satisfying to those committed to change, but the general reasons for preferring accrual-deferral accounting for measuring wealth and income should be acknowledged by all who are interested in the present issue. First, the opportunities for 'operating manipulation' of a cash flow measure of income are substantial. Operating manipulation consists of controlling or influencing the timing of cash transactions so as to affect the operating results of the period. Such opportunities are, of course, permitted by the rules of conventional accrual-deferral accounting, e.g., in the areas of maintenance costs, research and development, training, and other expenditures that are treated as immediate expenses even though they are investments for the benefit of future periods. But the opportunities to control cash transactions with suppliers and customers are generally recognised to be much greater. Those impressed with management's ability to manipulate conventional income by both operating tactics, as mentioned above, and by accounting choices must be even more impressed with the manipulation potential under cash flow accounting.[3] For example, imagine the potential for manipulation by a manager whose bonus is based on the change in cash balance, or on operating cash flow, in a reporting period.

[3]An observation based on experience with respondents to FASB proposals is that when the Board suggested requiring more up-to-date measurements of the values of wealth items, enterprise managers saw more merit in cash flow accounting. Whether that view reflected a preference for the manipulability of cash flows over 'putting themselves at the mercy of the markets' was never stated.

Related to the manipulation weakness of cash flow income are the potential 'economic consequences' of recognising cash transactions as revenues and expenses. In general, the problem is that whenever events are accounted for as having wealth effects that differ from those effects that are important to the 'principals,' agents can be expected to behave so as to maximise what is emphasised in the reports instead of what is sought by the principals. That is the weakness of present conventional accounting for 'intangible investments,' such as research and development, which are, from the point of view of owners, investments but which are treated as expenses by accountants. As between any two 'bases of accounting', the one that is further from that elusive 'economic accounting' that guides principals can be expected to have the less desirable economic consequences in the form of agents' opportunistic behaviour (Williamson, 1985, p. 47). Thus, expensing cash purchases of merchandise or plant assets (or expensing the excess of full acquisition cost over 'as-is' net realisable value) can be expected to discourage otherwise desirable purchases near the end of an accounting period. Conflicts between the measure of operating results that is emphasised in financial reporting and the measure that is of interest to principals is a weakness in any measurement system.

The preceding discussion of economic consequences leads to the third reason for preferring accrual-deferral accounting for the measurement of wealth and income: those noncash items that are recorded by conventional accrual-deferral accounting are important to principals. An owner of a merchandising business views a claim on a customer as valuable. The consumption of services purchased but not yet paid for is an economic sacrifice. The cash purchase of goods for future sale usually is not an unfavorable event. The case for such accruals and deferrals is an overwhelming one from the point of view of the owner of an enterprise who is concerned with measuring his/her own wealth and income, whether an agent is involved or not. That should not be forgotten in the context of discussions of the role of cash flow accounting.

Similarly, the purchase of long-term plant assets is not viewed by principals as sacrificing wealth. Those assets have cash flow potential. The difficulties in measuring such assets after their acquisition are acknowledged, but they are accepted as preferable to reporting acquisitions as declines in wealth—in the full amount of the acquisition cost in the case of strict cash basis accounting, or partially as in the case of a net realisable value system. Nevertheless, treatment of tangible plant assets and certain recognised intangibles contrasts with the conventional treatment of unrecognised intangible investments such as those involving training, systems development, and research and development. In the latter cases, the measurement difficulties have caused accounting to choose immediate expensing. In general, the choices represented in conventional accrual-deferral accounting result in both inclusion of certain items that are measured very crudely and exclusion from enterprise wealth of certain investments measurement of which is judged to be of negative net value. That is conventional accounting's solution to the general problem of measuring wealth and income. If a critic advocates change on the basis of measurement difficulties, should not incremental changes be tried first, rather than giving up on the measurement of wealth and income altogether?

Cash flow potential: a measure of wealth

The objects listed as assets and liabilities on conventional balance sheets have a common property: cash flow potential. Unfortunately, cash flow potential is measured poorly, partly because accounting has not set its measurement as an explicit objective. But that objective is implicit in conventional accounting measurement practices, and all widely used measurement methods, at least in the United States, deal with cash flow potential. That is most obvious in the cases of those contractual receivables and payables that are measured on the basis of future cash flows, present value of future cash flows, or current market prices. Those measurements based on the form of net realisable value that considers the asset's most likely future course—sometimes called completed-cycle NRV—clearly are focused on cash flow potential. In other circumstances, in which the continuity assumption is not justified, 'as-is NRV,' based on sale of the work-in-process, finished goods, accounts receivable, or other assets without proceeding through remaining stages of the operating cycle in the normal course of business, would be consistent with a focus on cash flow potential. 'As-is NRV' under circumstances that justify the continuity assumption clearly is a liquidity-oriented measure (see final section).

Many have not thought of entry prices of assets as being related to cash flow potential, perhaps because completed-cycle NRV is more directly related to it. Nevertheless, it should be clear that in general equilibrium in a competitive economy, the relationships between entry and exit prices make the former relevant surrogates for the latter, and often superior on the reliability and cost criteria (Staubus, 1967, p. 655–6). Lack of equilibrium and market incompleteness certainly can result in gaps between fully loaded (with fringe acquisition costs) current entry prices and completed-cycle exit prices net of remaining costs (including cost of capital), but the validity of current entry prices as a market assessment of cash flow potential surely cannot be denied. Similarly, old entry prices (historical costs) were market assessments of that same property. In sum, conventional accounting practices do measure cash flow potentials, despite not having been purposefully designed to find and use the most relevant, reliable, and economical evidence.

Empirical research employing share prices as a criterion has tested the impact of the manifest 'defects' in conventional accrual-deferral accounting. The general conclusion based on more than a quarter of a century of such research (from Staubus (1967) to Bowen (1986, 1987), Rayburn (1986), and Wilson (1986, 1987)) is that the further the measure tested is from conventional earnings and the closer it is to strict cash flow, the poorer the results, although the value of conventional measurements of depreciation and depletion are still in doubt. Uncertainty regarding the value of depreciation measurements surely does not surprise proponents of serious, value-oriented measurements of plant assets, such as Baxter (1971). It is one thing to question conventional depreciation accounting; it is quite another to extrapolate such concerns to the entire accrual-deferral model.

Conclusions

Three general conclusions follow from the above analysis. First, cash flow information is valuable to users who are concerned with an enterprise's liquidity. That need should not be neglected.

A second conclusion is that liquidity and wealth should be distinguished more clearly. Conventional accounting, and some of the literature, shows confusion on this point. Reporting on liquidity and reporting on wealth/income should be set out as separate objectives of financial reporting.

A third conclusion is that the close relationship between (1) historical cash flows, (2) cash flow projections, (3) cash flow potential, and (4) wealth and income make it easy to confuse liquidity-oriented aspects of past and future cash flows and wealth/income aspects. In particular, more attention should be paid to cash flow potential.

Further comments: liquidity and cash flow potential

An example of failure to make a clear distinction between liquidity and wealth is apparent in certain research focused on a decision situation in which a person needs to know the economic unit's (individual's or firm's) liquidity. For example, an accounting theorist might ask a rhetorical question regarding information needed when one is deciding to sell or hold an asset. The answer clearly includes the asset's selling price. If the asset is shares, the shareholder needs a share market quotation, but that says nothing regarding information the corporation might provide to help the shareholder assess the hold option. Another example: asking a sample of independent professional persons questions regarding 'one's assets' or what makes 'one better off' might induce images of personal and family finances (Chambers, Hopwood and McKeown, 1984). Individuals frequently need to know their liquidity. Can the bills be paid? Can I buy that new automobile or property? They rarely need to know their own net worth in order to make decisions. Their curiosity about their net worth might lead them to think about—to speculate about—such important but not always objectively measurable assets as their retirement plan, their art objects, their potential inheritance, and their personal earning power, but they rarely need to quantify and sum those and other assets for direct decision making. Therefore, if you ask them what information about their assets they use, liquidation values are likely to come to mind. In such circumstances, reports based on historical cash flows and net realisable values, as suggested by Lee (1981), might be quite satisfying. Individuals not immersed in the daily problems of business management are not likely to identify liquidity and profitability as two separate requirements for an ongoing successful business, so may not distinguish between information on liquidity and information on wealth and income.

Individuals do not buy and sell fractional interests in economic units consisting of themselves or their families, so the aggregate values of such economic units need not be known for decision purposes. *Individuals do buy and sell fractional interests in other economic units—business entities—so they do seek information relevant to assessments of the values of such entities.* The liquidity of those entities is not the primary concern of buyers and sellers of ownership interests under typical circumstances. Liquidity and value need to be more explicitly recognised and distinguished.

An observation at the core of these remarks is that cash flow potential is the implicitly accepted concept of enterprise wealth in an exchange economy. Assets have positive cash flow potential; liabilities have negative cash flow potential. Net enterprise wealth is the algebraic sum of positive and negative cash flow potentials, with no time horizon as a limit. Accounting measurements are based on evidence of cash flow potentials—evidence which varies widely in its quality. The omission of many intangible investments is an example of treating as off-balance-sheet assets those items for which the evidence of cash flow potential is unacceptable on the reliability criterion. At the other end of the spectrum, cash balances, then short-turn receivables and payables and publicly traded securities, then current nonmonetary assets, then the various categories of noncurrent, nonmonetary, physical and nonphysical assets—all of these are recognised as having cash flow potential, and are measured by reference to evidence of cash flow potential, primarily market prices. Cash flow potential is, of course, measured very poorly.

Those who have studied economics are acquainted with the perfect competition model, an abstract construct that has been found useful in thinking about the formation of prices in markets. In the theory of finance, another abstract model is widely used: complete markets. In a complete market economy, a price can be observed for anything and everything. Prices for various prospective contributions to enterprise cash flow streams (cash flow potentials), such as the contributions of various assets to the enterprise's cash flows, may be observed. Those prices provide excellent guidance for investors and other economic actors. In equilibrium, all prices in the economy are linked at levels such that no remaining opportunities for arbitrage profits exist.

In the real world, prices for the prospective cash flow streams from particular assets and liabilities, as those are understood in accounting, are not observable and market prices are not in equilibrium. Accountants and managers are not able to find quoted market prices for the 'setting-specific' assets and liabilities of the firm, even though prices for similar assets in other environments may be observed. Consequently, accountants must report imperfect substitutes for the market values of all assets except cash. The conventional accounting measurement system has been called 'market simulation accounting', defined as 'the selection and blending of pertinent observed market prices and other evidence in accordance with accepted principles of market economics to assess the price at which an asset or liability would trade in an active market' (Staubus, 1986, p. 118). Those simulated market prices are for positive or negative cash flow potentials—the generally accepted interpretation of wealth.

Reporting on liquidity—a secondary concern of investors—should not be confused with reporting on wealth. An historical report on cash flows is a useful part of the former. Reporting cash flow potentials and changes therein is the essence of the latter. Explicit recognition and responses to those two separate interests of users might be a big step towards decision-useful financial reporting.

References

Baxter, W. T., *Depreciation* (London: Sweet & Maxwell, 1971).

Böhm-Bawerk, E., *The Positive Theory of Capital*, trans. by W. Smart (New York: G. E. Stechert and Co., 1891).

Bowen, R. M., D. Burgstahler, and L. A. Daley, 'Evidence on the Relationships Between Earnings and Various Measures of Cash Flow,' *Accounting Review*, October 1986, pp. 713–725.

——, 'The Incremental Information Content of Accrual Versus Cash Flows,' *Accounting Review*, October 1987, pp. 723–747.

Brealey, R. and S. Myers, *Principles of Corporate Finance*, 2nd ed. (New York: McGraw-Hill, 1984).

Butterworth, J. E., M. Gibbins, and R. D. King, 'The Structure of Accounting Theory: Some Basic Conceptual and Methodological Issues,' in S. Basu and J. A. Milburn (eds.), *Research to Support Standard Setting in Financial Accounting: A Canadian Perspective* (Toronto: The Clarkson Gordon Foundation, 1982), pp. 1–65.

Chambers, R. J., *Accounting, Evaluation and Economic Behavior* (Englewood Cliffs, NJ: Prentice-Hall, 1966).

Chambers, R. J., W. S. Hopwood, and J. C. McKeown, 'The Relevance of Varieties of Accounting Information: A U.S.A. Survey,' *Abacus*, December 1984, pp. 99–110.

Copeland, T. E. and J. F. Weston, *Financial Theory and Corporate Policy* (Reading, MA: Addison-Wesley, 1979).

Egginton, D. A., 'In Defence of Profit Measurement: Some Limitations of Cash Flow and Value Added as Performance Measures for External Reporting,' *Accounting and Business Research*, Spring 1984, pp. 99–111.

——, 'Cash Flow, Profit and Performance Measures for External Reports: A Rejoinder,' *Accounting and Business Research*, Spring 1985, pp. 109–112.

Financial Accounting Standards Board, *Statements of Financial Accounting Concepts No. 1*, 'Objectives of Financial Reporting by Business Enterprises,' November 1978.

——, *Statement of Financial Accounting Standards No. 95*, 'Statement of Cash Flow', November 1987.

Hawkins, D. F., and W. J. Campbell, *Equity Valuation: Models, Analysis and Implications* (New York: Financial Executives Research Foundation, 1978).

Hawkins, D. F., B. A. Brown, and W. J. Campbell. *Rating Industrial Bonds* (Morristown, NJ: Financial Executives Research Foundation, 1983).

Keynes, J. M., *A Treatise on Money*, Vol. II (New York: Harcourt, Brace, 1930).

Lawson, G. H., 'Cash-Flow Accounting,' *Accountant*, October 18, 1971, pp. 386–389.

——, 'The Rationale of Cash Flow Accounting,' in Cees van Dam (ed.), *Trends in Managerial and Financial Accounting* (Leiden, The Netherlands: Martinus Nijhoff Social Sciences Division, 1978), pp. 85–104.

——, 'The Measurement of Corporate Performance on a Cash Flow Basis: A Reply to Mr. Egginton,' *Accounting and Business Research*, Spring 1985, pp. 99–108.

Lee, T. A., 'A Case for Cash Flow Reporting.' *Journal of Business Finance*, Summer 1972, pp. 27–36.

——, 'Reporting Cash Flows and Net Realisable Values,' *Accounting and Business Research*, Spring 1981, pp. 163–170.

——, *Cash Flow Accounting* (London: Van Nostrand Reinhold, 1984).

——, 'Cash Flow Accounting, Profit and Performance Measurement: A Response to a Challenge,' *Accounting and Business Research*, Spring 1985, pp. 93–97.

Lippman, S. A. and J. J. McCall, 'An Operational Measure of Liquidity.' *American Economic Review*, March 1986, pp. 43–55.

Newton, I., *Tables for Renewing and Purchasing the Leases of Cathedral-Churches and Colleges* (London: Thos. Astley, 1686).

Rayburn, J., 'The Association of Operating Cash Flow and Accruals with Security Returns,' in Studies on Alternative Measures of Accounting Income, *Journal of Accounting Research*, Supplement 1986, pp. 112–133.

Staubus, G. J., *An Accounting Concept of Revenue*, Ph.D. dissertation, University of Chicago, 1954 (New York: Arno Press, 1980).

——, *A Theory of Accounting to Investors* (Berkeley: University of California Press, 1961); republished by (Lawrence, KS: Scholars Book Co., 1971).

——, 'The Association of Financial Accounting Variables with Common Stock Values,' *Accounting Review*, January 1965, pp. 119–134.

——, 'Alternative Asset Flow Concepts,' *Accounting Review*, July 1966, pp. 397–412.

——, 'Statistical Evidence of the Value of Depreciation Accounting,' *Abacus*, August 1967, pp. 3–22.

——, 'Current Cash Equivalent for Assets: A Dissent,' *Accounting Review*, October 1967, pp. 650–661.

——, 'Testing Inventory Accounting,' *Accounting Review*, July 1968, pp. 413–424.

——, *Making Accounting Decisions* (Houston: Scholars Book Co., 1977).

——, 'The Market Simulation Theory of Accounting Measurement,' *Accounting and Business Research*, Spring 1986, pp. 117–132.

Sterling, R. R., *Toward a Science of Accounting* (Houston: Scholars Book Co., 1979).

Williamson, O. E., *The Economic Institutions of Capitalism* (New York: The Free Press, 1985).

Wilson, G. P., 'The Relative Information Content of Accruals and Cash Flows: Combined Evidence at the Earnings Announcement and Annual Report Release Date,' in Studies on Alternative Measures of Accounting Income, *Journal of Accounting Research*, Supplement 1986, pp. 165–200.

——, 'The Incremental Information Content of the Accrual and Funds Components of Earnings After Controlling for Earnings.' *Accounting Review*, April 1987, pp. 293–322.

Suggested additional reading

There is little additional reading to be recommended for this section, other than a small number of responses from researchers debating in the literature. These are stated as follows.

* Egginton, D. A., ' Cash Flow, Profit and Performance Measures for External Reporting: A Rejoinder,' **Accounting and Business Research**, Spring 1985, pp.109-12.

A further reply by Egginton to the responses of Lawson (1985) and Lee (1985) to his 1984 critique.

* Lawson, G. H., 'The Measurement of Corporate Performance on a Cash Flow Basis: A Reply to Mr Egginton,' **Accounting and Business Research**, Spring 1985, pp.99-108.

Lawson's response to Egginton's (1984) criticism of CFA's limitations as a useful reporting system, particularly with respect to the issue of performance assessment using cash flow accounting data.

* Lee, T. A., ' Cash Flow Accounting and the Allocation Problem,' **Journal of Business Finance and Accounting**, Autumn 1982, pp. 341-52.

A response to Rutherford on the nature of allocations in accounting, with specific emphasis on the allocation-free claim for cash flow accounting prescriptions.

* Lee, T. A., 'Cash Flow Accounting, Profit and Performance Measurement: A Response to a Challenge,' **Accounting and Business Research**, Spring 1985, pp. 93-98.

Lee's response to the Egginton (1984) paper.

* Lee, T. A., 'Restricting the Domain and Potential of Cash Flow Accounting,' **Accounting and Business Research**, Autumn 1990, pp. 355-58.

Lee's response to Staubus (1989), again with respect to the issue of the relevance and reliability of CFA for performance assessment.

* Rutherford, B. A., 'Cash Flow Accounting and Distributional Allocations: a Note,' **Journal of Business Finance and Accounting**, Summer 1983, pp. 313-16.

A further clarification of Rutherford's arguments regarding the allocation-free nature of CFA.

INFLUENCING ACCOUNTING POLICY-MAKING

Introduction

The history of CFA ideas has taken a strange twist in recent times. The progression has not been entirely Kuhnian - at least in terms of the normal sequence to be predicted. CFA ideas obviously have some attraction to accounting policy-makers and standard-setters. For example, in 1975, at an early stage in the development of theoretical ideas in CFA, the *Sandilands* committee (1975) on inflation accounting reviewed CFA as a possible solution to the ills of conventional accounting. However, although it saw merit in the idea for liquidity, it saw none for profitability, and recommended further development.

Whether such development has taken place is debatable. Certainly as the earlier sections of this text demonstrate, the CFA theorists have done further work, and empirical research has taken place. In addition, some institutional work has taken place. However, somewhat surprisingly, in 1987, the *FASB* (1987) in the US mandated the reporting of a statement of realised cash flows as a substitute for the conventional funds statement. This requires data relating to operating, investing, and financing flows. It can be produced either on a direct or indirect basis. A similar standard was required in the UK by the *ASB* (1991).

Thus, CFA ideas are no longer the preserve of academe. They have been translated into a working accounting standard. Consequently, academic accounting researchers should have a valuable data base available to test the utility of CFA reports. Such utility has been most recently recognised in an institutional research study by ICAS in the UK (*McMonnies*, 1988). In it, not only are realised cash flows advocated, but so too are forecast cash flows and exit prices. These are deemed to be the most relevant and reliable data for external financial reporting, and are based on ideas consistent with the thinking of Lawson and (particularly) Lee. Obviously, the Kuhnian revolution is still in progress. Equally obviously, it is well under way.

* Accounting Standards Board, "Cash Flow Statements," **Financial Reporting Standard 1** (London: Accounting Standards Board, 1991), 12 pp.

* Financial Accounting Standards Board, "Statement of Cash Flows," **Statement of Financial Accounting Standards 95** (Stamford: Financial Accounting Standards Board, 1987), paras. 1-34.

* Inflation Accounting Committee, "Cash Flow Accounting," in **Inflation Accounting**, Cmnd 6225 (London: HMSO, 1975), pp. 156-58.

* McMonnies, P. N., (ed.), **Making Corporate Reports Valuable** (London: Kogan Page, 1988), pp. 68-80.

FINANCIAL REPORTING STANDARD No 1

CASH FLOW STATEMENTS

SEPTEMBER 1991

Financial Reporting standard No 1 – 'Cash Flow Statements' is issued by the Accounting Standards Board in respect of its application in the United Kingdom and by the Institute of Chartered Accountants in Ireland in respect of its application in the Republic of Ireland.

Summary

a) Financial Reporting Standard No 1 – 'Cash Flow Statements' (the FRS) establishes standards for cash flow reporting. It supersedes Statement of Standard Accounting Practice No 10 – 'Statements of Source and Application of Funds' (SSAP 10) and requires reporting entities which fall within its scope to prepare a cash flow statement as part of their financial statements setting out on a standard basis their cash generation and absorption for a period. The FRS sets out the required structure of the cash flow statement and minimum level of disclosure.

b) The Statement of Principles for Financial Reporting being developed by the Accounting Standards Board (the Board) recognises that users of financial statements need information on the liquidity, viability and financial adaptability of the entity concerned. Deriving this information involves the user in making assessments of the future cash flows of the entity. Accruals accounting, used in producing profit and loss (or income and expenditure) accounts and balance sheets, adjusts cash flows to measure results for a period and this is the primary basis for projections. Nevertheless, long-term provisions and other allocations associated with accruals accounting need to be eliminated in order to reveal the leads and lags in historical cash flows, thereby improving understanding of a reporting entity's cash generating or cash absorption mechanisms and providing a basis for the assessment of future cash flows.

c) In order to promote understanding and to help to achieve the objectives of cash flow reporting by securing the useful presentation of information, the FRS requires that individual cash flows should be classified under certain standard headings according to the activity that gave rise to them. The standard headings required in a cash flow statement are:
operating activities; returns on investments and servicing of finance; taxation; investing activities; and financing.

In addition, the FRS requires that the cash flow statement should show a total giving the net cash inflow or outflow before financing. The FRS specifies particular cash flows to be separately reported under each of the standard headings apart from operating activities. Analysis of net cash flow from operating activities on the so-called 'direct method' is encouraged but not required.

d) In order to ensure that it reflects clearly the substance of a reporting entity's cash management, the cash flow statement deals with flows of cash equivalents as well as with cash flows.

e) A reconciliation between the operating profit reported in the profit and loss (or income and expenditure) account and the net cash flow from operating activities should be given as a note to the cash flow statement. This reconciliation should disclose separately the movements in stocks, debtors and creditors related to operating activities and other differences between cash flows and profits. A reconciliation of the amounts shown in the balance sheet of the reporting entity in respect of items reported within the financing section of the cash flow statement with the equivalent figures in the previous year's balance sheet, disclosing separately the movements resulting from cash flows, differences arising from changes in foreign currency exchange rates and other movements, should also be given as a note to the cash flow statement.

Small reporting entities

f) The FRS exempts most small reporting entities from the requirement to include a cash flow statement as part of their financial statements. The exemption does not extend to public companies, banking companies, insurance companies, authorised persons under the Financial Services Act 1986, or members of a group containing one or more of the above mentioned entities.

Wholly owned subsidiary undertakings

g) A wholly owned subsidiary undertaking of a parent undertaking established under the law of a member State of the European Community is exempt from the requirements of the FRS if:

i) the parent undertaking publishes, in English, consolidated financial statements which include the subsidiary undertaking concerned, drawn up in accordance with United Kingdom or Republic of Ireland companies legislation or the EC Seventh Company Law Directive; and

ii) those consolidated financial statements include a consolidated cash flow statement dealing with the cash flows of the group; and

iii) that cash flow statement gives sufficient information to enable a user of the financial statements to derive the totals of the amounts required to be shown under each of the standard headings set out in the FRS.

Objective

1. The objective of the FRS is to require reporting entities falling within its scope to report on a standard basis their cash generation and cash absorption for a period. To this end reporting entities are required to provide a primary financial statement analysing cash flows under the standard headings of 'operating activities', 'returns on investments and servicing of finance', 'taxation', 'investing activities' and 'financing', disclosed in that sequence, in order to assist users of the financial statements in their assessment of the reporting entity's liquidity, viability and financial adaptability. The objective of the standard headings is to ensure that cash flows are reported in a form that highlights the significant components of cash flow and facilitates comparison of the cash flow performance of different businesses.

Definitions

The following definitions shall apply for the purposes of this FRS and in particular the statement of standard accounting practice set out in paragraphs 7 to 46.

2. *Cash* – Cash in hand and deposits repayable on demand with any bank or other financial institution. Cash includes cash in hand and deposits denominated in foreign currencies.

3. *Cash equivalents* – Short-term, highly liquid investments which are readily convertible into known amounts of cash without notice and which were within three months of maturity when acquired; less advances from banks repayable within three months from the date of the advance. Cash equivalents include investments and advances denominated in foreign currencies provided that they fulfil the above criteria.

4. *Cash flow* – An increase or decrease in an amount of cash or cash equivalent resulting from a transaction.

5. *Companies Act 1985* – Companies Act 1985 as amended by the Companies Act 1989.

6. *Companies (Northern Ireland) Order 1986* – Companies (Northern Ireland) Order 1986 as amended by the Companies (Northern Ireland) Order 1990 and the Companies (No 2) (Northern Ireland) Order 1990.

Statement of Standard Accounting Practice

The statement of standard accounting practice set out in paragraphs 7 to 46 of the FRS should be read together with the Objective of the FRS as stated in paragraph 1, the definitions set out in paragraphs 2 to 6 and also the Foreword to Accounting Standards and the Statement of Principles for Financial Reporting issued from time to time by the Board.

The Explanation section of the FRS, set out in paragraphs 48 to 84, shall be regarded as part of the statement of standard accounting practice insofar as it assists in interpreting that statement.

7. Reporting entities falling within the scope of paragraph 8 of the FRS are required to provide as a primary statement within the reporting entity's financial statements a cash flow statement drawn up in accordance with the standard accounting principles set out in paragraphs 9 to 46 of the FRS.

Scope

8. This FRS applies to all financial statements intended to give a true and fair view of the financial position and profit or loss (or income and expenditure) except those of entities that are:

a) companies incorporated under the Companies Acts and entitled to the exemptions available in Sections 246 to 249 of the Companies Act 1985* for small companies when filing accounts with the Registrar of Companies; or

b) entities which would have come under category (a) above had they been companies incorporated under companies legislation; or

c) wholly owned subsidiary undertakings of a parent undertaking which is established under the law of a member State of the European Community where

i) the parent undertaking publishes, in English, consolidated financial statements which include the subsidiary undertaking concerned, drawn up in accordance with United Kingdom or Republic of Ireland companies legislation or the EC Seventh Company Law Directive; and

ii) those consolidated financial statements include a consolidated cash flow statement dealing with the cash flows of the group; and

iii) that cash flow statement gives sufficient information to enable a user of the financial statements to derive the totals of the amounts required to be shown under each of the standard headings set out in this FRS; or

d) Building Societies, as defined by the Building Societies Act 1986 in the United Kingdom and by the Building Societies Act 1989 in the Republic of Ireland, but only so long as they are required by law to prepare as part of their financial statements a statement of source and application of funds in a prescribed format; or

e) mutual life assurance companies.

9. The cash flow statement provided with group financial statements should reflect the cash flows of the group.

10. Insurance companies, other than mutual life assurance companies to which the FRS does not apply, should include the cash flows of their long term life, pensions and annuity businesses only to the extent that the cash flows are those of the insurance company itself rather than cash flows of the long-term funds.

Preparation of cash flow statements

11. The cash flow statement should include all the reporting entity's inflows and outflows of cash and cash equivalents except those movements within cash and cash equivalents that result from the purchases and sales for cash or cash equivalents of holdings which form part of that entity's cash equivalents. Transactions which do not result in cash flows of the reporting entity should not be reported in the cash flow statement.

Format for cash flow statements

12. The cash flow statement should list the inflows and outflows of cash and cash equivalents for the period classified under the following standard headings:

operating activities; returns on investments and servicing of finance; taxation; investing activities; and financing

in that order and showing a total for each standard heading and a total of the net cash inflow or outflow before financing. Examples of formats for cash flow statements are provided in the illustrative examples annexed to the FRS.

Classification of cash flows

13. The cash flow statement should disclose separately, where material, the individual categories of cash flows under the standard headings set out in paragraphs 15 to 30 except in the extremely rare circumstances where this presentation would not be a fair representation of the activities of the reporting entity. In such cases informed judgement should be used to devise an appropriate alternative treatment. The cash flow classifications may be subdivided further to give a fuller descrpiption of the activities of the reporting entity or to provide segmental information.

14. Where a cash flow is not specified in the categories set out in paragraphs 15 to 30 below then it should be shown under the most appropriate standard heading.

Classification of cash flows by standard heading

Operating activities

15. Cash flows from operating activities are in general the cash effects of transactions and other events relating to operating or trading activities. Net cash flow from operating activities represents the net increase or decrease in cash and cash equivalents resulting from the operations shown in the profit and loss account in arriving at operating profit.

16. Operating cash flows may be reported in the cash flow statement on a net or gross basis.

17. A reconciliation between the operating profit (for non-financial companies normally profit before interest) reported in the profit and loss account and the net cash flow from operating activities should be given as a note to the cash flow statement. This reconciliation should disclose separately the movements in stocks, debtors and creditors related to operating activities and other differences between cash flows and profits.

Returns on investments and servicing of finance

18. 'Returns on investments and servicing of finance' are receipts resulting from the ownership of an investment and payments to providers of finance excluding those items required by paragraphs 15 and 24 to 30 to be classified under operating, investing or financing activities.

19. Cash inflows from returns on investments and servicing of finance include:

a) interest received, including any related tax recovered;

b) dividends received (disclosing separately dividends received from equity accounted entities), net of any tax credits.

20. Cash outflows from returns on investments and servicing of finance include:

a) interest paid (whether or not the charge is capitalised), including any tax deducted and paid to the relevant tax authority;

b) dividends paid, excluding any advance corporation tax;

c) the interest element of finance lease rental payments.

Taxation

21. The cash flows included under the heading taxation are cash flows to or from taxation authorities in respect of the reporting entity's revenue and capital profits. Cash flows in respect of other taxation, including payments and receipts in respect of Value Added Tax, other sales taxes, property taxes and other taxes not assessed on the profits of the reporting entity should be dealt with as set out in paragraphs 34 and 35 of this FRS.

22. Taxation cash inflows include cash receipts from the relevant tax authority of tax rebates, claims or returns of overpayments.

23. Taxation cash outflows include cash payments to the relevant tax authority of tax, including payments of advance corporation tax and purchases of certificates of tax deposit.

Investing activities

24. The cash flows included in investing activities are those related to the acquisition or disposal of any asset held as a fixed asset or as a current asset investment (other than assets included within cash equivalents).

25. Cash inflows from investing activities include:

a) receipts from sales or disposals of fixed assets;

b) receipts from sales of investments in subsidiary undertakings net of any balances of cash and cash equivalents transferred as part of the sale;

c) receipts from sales of investments in other entities with separate disclosure of divestments of equity accounted entities;

d) receipts from repayment or sales of loans made to other entities by the reporting entity or of other entities' debt (other than cash equivalents) which were purchased by the reporting entity.

26. Cash outflows from investing activities include:

a) payments to acquire fixed assets;

b) payments to acquire investments in subsidiary undertakings net of balances of cash and cash equivalents acquired;

c) payments to acquire investments in other entities with separate disclosure of investments in equity accounted entities;

d) loans made by the reporting entity and payments to acquire debt of other entities (other than cash equivalents).

Financing

27. Financing cash flows comprise receipts from or repayments to external providers of finance of amounts in respect of principal amounts of finance.

28. Financing cash inflows include:

a) receipts from issuing shares or other equity instruments;

b) receipts from issuing debentures, loans, notes, and bonds and from other long and short-term borrowings (other than those included within cash equivalents).

29. Financing cash outflows include:

a) repayments of amounts borrowed (other than those included within cash equivalents);

b) the capital element of finance lease

---

* The equivalent references in Northern Ireland legislation are Sections 254 to 257 of the Companies (Northern Ireland) Order 1986.
The equivalent references in Republic of Ireland legislation are Sections 8, 9, 10 and 12 of the Companies (Amendment) Act 1986.

rental payments;
c) payments to re-acquire or redeem the entity's shares;
d) payments of expenses or commissions on any issue of shares, debentures, loans, notes, bonds or other financing.

30. The amounts of any finance cash flows received from or paid to equity accounted entities should be disclosed separately.

Exceptional and extraordinary items

31. Where cash flows relate to items that are classed as exceptional items in the profit and loss account these exceptional cash flows should be shown under the appropriate standard headings, according to the nature of each item. Sufficient disclosure of the nature of cash flows relating to exceptional items should be given in a note to the cash flow statement to allow a user of the financial statements to gain an understanding of the effect on the reporting entity's cash flows of the underlying transactions.
32. Where cash flows relate to items that are classed as extraordinary items in the profit and loss account these extraordinary cash flows should be shown separately under the appropriate standard headings, according to the nature of each item. In the extremely rare circumstances where it is inappropriate to include a cash flow relating to an extraordinary item under one or more of the standard headings within the cash flow statement the cash flows should be shown within a separate section in the cash flow statement.
33. Sufficient disclosure of the nature of cash flows relating to extraordinary items should be given in a note to the cash flow statement to allow a user of the financial statements to gain an understanding of the effect on the reporting entity's cash flows of the underlying transactions.

Value Added Tax and other taxes

34. Cash flows should be shown net of any attributable Value Added Tax or other sales tax unless the tax is irrecoverable by the reporting entity. The net movement on the amount payable to, or receivable from, the taxing authority should be allocated to cash flows from operating activities unless a different treatment is more appropriate in the particular circumstances concerned. In circumstances where sales taxes paid by the reporting entity are irrecoverable cash flows should be shown gross by including the associated sales tax unless this is impracticable, in which case the irrecoverable tax should be included under the most appropriate standard heading.
35. Taxation cash flows excluding those in respect of the reporting entity's revenue and capital profits and Value Added Tax, or other sales tax, should be included within the cash flow statement under the same standard heading as the cash flow which gave rise to the taxation cash flow, unless a different treatment is more appropriate in the particular circumstances concerned.

Foreign currencies

36. Where a portion of a reporting entity's business is undertaken by a foreign entity, the cash flows of that entity are to be included in the cash flow statement on the basis used for translating the results of those activities in the profit and loss account of the reporting entity.

Hedging transactions

37. Cash flows that result from transactions undertaken to hedge another transaction should be reported under the same standard heading as the transaction that is the subject of the hedge.

Groups

38. A group cash flow statement should only deal with flows of cash and cash equivalents external to the group. Accordingly, cash flows that are internal to the group should be eliminated in the preparation of the group cash flow statement. Dividends paid to any minority interests should be reported under the heading returns on investments and servicing of finance, and disclosed separately.
39. The cash flows of any entity which is equity accounted in consolidated financial statements should only be included in the group cash flow statement to the extent of the actual cash flows between the group and the entity concerned.

Acquisitions and disposals

40. Where a group acquires or disposes of a subsidiary undertaking, the amounts of cash and cash equivalents paid or received in respect of the consideration should be shown net of any cash and cash equivalent balances transferred as part of the purchase or sale of the subsidiary undertaking. In addition, a note to the cash flow statement should show a summary of the effects of acquisitions and disposals indicating how much of the consideration comprised cash and cash equivalents and the amounts of cash and cash equivalents transferred as a result of the acquisitions and disposals.
41. Where a subsidiary undertaking joins or leaves a group during a financial year the cash flows of the group should include the cash flows of the subsidiary undertaking concerned for the same period as that for which the group's profit and loss account includes the results of the subsidiary undertaking.
42. Material effects on amounts reported under each of the standard headings reflecting the cash flows of a subsidiary undertaking acquired or disposed of in the period should be disclosed, as far as practicable, as a note to the cash flow statement. This information need only be given in the financial statements for the period in which the acquisition or disposal occurs.

Major non-cash transactions

43. Material transactions not resulting in movements of cash or cash equivalents of the reporting entity should be disclosed in the notes to the cash flow statement if disclosure is necessary for an understanding of the underlying transactions.

Reconciliation with balance sheet figures

44. The movements in cash and cash equivalents and the items shown within the financing section of the cash flow statement should be reconciled to the related items in the opening and closing balance sheets for the period. The reconciliations should disclose separately for cash and cash equivalents and for financing items the movements resulting from cash flows, differences arising from changes in foreign currency exchange rates (those relating to the retranslation of any opening balances of cash and cash equivalents and financing items and those resulting from the translation of the cash flows of foreign entities at exchange rates other than the year end rate) and other movements. Where several balance sheet amounts or parts thereof have to be combined to permit a reconciliation, sufficient detail should be shown to enable the movements to be understood. Possible formats for such reconciliations are provided in the illustrative examples annexed to the FRS.

Comparative figures

45. Comparative figures should be given for all items in the cash flow statement and such notes thereto as are required by the FRS.

Date from which effective

46. The accounting practices set out in this FRS should be adopted as soon as possible and regarded as standard in respect of financial statements relating to accounting periods ending on or after 23 March 1992.

Financial Reporting Standard No 1 – 'Cash Flow Statements' was adopted by the unanimous vote of the nine members of the Accounting Standards Board.

Members of the Accounting Standards Board: David Tweedie (chairman), Sir Bryan Carsberg (vice chairman), Allan Cook (technical director), Robert Bradfield, Elwyn Eilledge, Michael Garner, Donald Main, Roger Munson, Graham Stacy.

Compliance with International Accounting Standards

47. Compliance with the FRS ensures compliance with International Accounting Standard No 7 – 'Statement of Changes in Financial Position'. The FRS is also broadly in line with the exposure draft of a proposed International Accounting Standard – 'Cash Flow Statements' issued by the International Accounting Standards Committee in July 1991.

Explanation

The need for cash flow information

48. Historical cash flow information may assist users of financial statements in making judgements on the amount, timing and degree of certainty of future cash flows; it gives an indication of the relationship between profitability and cash generating ability, and thus of the quality of the profit earned. In addition, analysts and other users of financial information often, formally or informally, develop models to assess and compare the present value of the future cash flows of entities. Historical cash flow information could be useful to check the accuracy of past assessments and indicate the relationship between the entity's

activities and its receipts and payments.

49. A cash flow statement in conjunction with a balance sheet provides information on liquidity, viability and financial adaptability. The balance sheet provides information about an entity's financial position at a particular point in time including assets, liabilities and equity and their relationship with each other at the balance sheet date. The balance sheet is often used to obtain information on liquidity, but the information is incomplete for this purpose as the balance sheet is drawn up at a particular point in time.

50. A cash flow statement shows information about the reporting entity's cash flows in the reporting period, but this provides incomplete information for assessing future cash flows. Some cash flows result from transactions that took place in an earlier period and some cash flows are expected to result in further cash flows in a future period. Accordingly, cash flow statements should normally be used in conjunction with the profit and loss accounts and balance sheets when making an assessment of future cash flows.

Cash instead of working capital

51. The Board believes that the information provided by a cash flow statement has the following advantages over that provided by a working capital based funds flow statement:

a) Funds flow data based on movements in working capital can obscure movements relevant to the liquidity and viability of an entity. For example, a significant decrease in cash available may be masked by an increase in stock or debtors. Entities may, therefore, run out of cash while reporting increases in working capital. Similarly, a decrease in working capital does not necessarily indicate a cash shortage and a danger of failure;

b) As cash flow monitoring is a normal feature of business life and not a specialised accounting technique, cash flow is a concept which is more widely understood than are changes in working capital;

c) Cash flows can be a direct input into a business valuation model and, therefore, historical cash flows may be relevant in a way not possible for funds flow data:

d) A funds flow statement is based largely on the difference between two balance sheets. It reorganises such data, but does not provide new data. The cash flow statement and associated notes required by the FRS may include data not disclosed in a funds flow statement.

Cash and cash equivalents

52. Entities often invest cash in excess of immediate needs in short-term highly liquid investments or borrow on a short-term basis to cover a peak in working capital requirements. Whether an entity's liquid resources comprise cash or a financial instrument that is readily convertible to a known amount of cash is largely irrelevant to users' assessments of liquidity and future cash flows. It is also irrelevant whether a cash flow results in a decrease in a cash balance or results in an increase in an overdraft or short-term bank loan. The Board, therefore, decided that a statement of cash flows should focus on the aggregate of cash and cash equivalents and that cash equivalents should be calculated net of short-term bank advances.

53. Entities' cash management programmes vary in the range of short to medium term deposits and instruments which they manage as a cash or near cash portfolio. In adopting the definition of cash equivalents for the purposes of the FRS the Board distinguished between those deposits and instruments that are effectively available immediately at face value and those that are placed for a longer term and would consequently incur some price risk if they were to be utilised at an earlier date. Thus cash equivalents, apart from any offset of overdrafts and other short-term bank borrowings, must be highly liquid, convertible into known amounts of cash without notice and not have any significant risk of changes in value owing to changes in interest rates.

54. The Board believes that a reasonable cut-off for cash equivalents is represented by a three month maturity threshold on the grounds that instruments within three months of maturity do not have any significant risk of changes in value due to changes in interest rates. The Board believes that the same cut-off point of three months should be used for bank borrowings. An investment purchased with more than three months to maturity does not become a cash equivalent when its remaining maturity is three months. Similarly, bank borrowings with a maturity of more than three months when drawn down do not become cash equivalents when their remaining maturity becomes three months because in these circumstances no transaction has taken place and it would be misleading to represent the approach of maturity as a cash flow.

55. Some entities, particularly banks and other financial institutions, hold highly liquid financial instruments for investment or trading purposes and not as part of their cash management programme. The Board's definition of cash equivalents includes highly liquid instruments only if they had less than three months remaining to maturity when purchased. The Board believes that consistency between the cash flow statements of different reporting entities is desirable, as far as possible, and accordingly highly liquid instruments held by financial institutions for trading purposes should be included as part of their cash equivalents only if they fall within the definition of cash equivalents set out in paragraph 3.

Cash or net debt

56. The Board believes that the focus of the cash flow statement should be not only cash flows but also the movements in a reporting entity's net cash or debt position. By separating the servicing of finance from the movements in principal amounts of finance, by requiring a total giving the net cash inflow or outflow before financing and by requiring disclosure of movements in the reporting entity's financing, the Board believes that information on the movements in the net cash or debt position is given an appropriate degree of prominence. The Board has not specified the form of presentation of the change in cash and cash equivalents because the significance of this item may be expected to differ for individual reporting entities. The illustrative examples show two out of a number of possible forms of presentation.

Scope

57. The Board has examined the circumstances of small reporting entities and has exempted most of them from the requirement to include a cash flow statement as part of their financial statements. This exemption does not extend to public companies that have the powers under their constitutions to offer their shares or debentures to the public and may lawfully exercise that power, or to banking companies, insurance companies, authorised persons under the Financial Services Act 1986, or members of a group containing one or more of the above mentioned entities. The scope of the exemption may be restricted at a later date as part of a wider examination of the reporting requirements of small entities.

58. The Board believes that the small entities exemption is justified because the costs for small entities, which are often owner managed, of producing historical cash flow information in a highly standardised form are likely to be disproportionate to the benefits. The Board has restricted the definition so that entities that are authorised to hold public money or offer securities to the public are required to produce a cash flow statement. However, the Board encourages small reporting entities to include a cash flow statement as part of their financial statements if it would provide useful information to users of those financial statements and the benefits of doing so outweigh the costs of providing the information.

59. The Board recognises that trade and other creditors may be users of financial statements, but has taken into account the fact that small companies or groups of companies as defined by the Companies Act 1985 are able to take advantage of provisions in that Act allowing them to file abbreviated accounts with the Registrar of Companies. These abbreviated accounts need not include a cash flow statement or an equivalent, and thus the information would not necessarily be within the public domain.

60. The Board has examined and rejected the proposition that wholly owned subsidiary undertakings should have to include a cash flow statement as part of their financial statements. Wholly owned subsidiary undertakings are legal entities in their own right and thus have legal obligations to creditors. They are, however, often controlled and managed on a day to day basis by their parent and the group may have a centralised treasury or other cash/debt management operation which results in a wholly owned subsidiary undertaking's cash flow being wholly or partly dependent on the group's overall cash or funding position. In view of the fact that cash balances can be moved around a group rapidly, historial cash flow information of individual group companies

is limited in the information that it can contribute to an assessment of future cash flows. Accordingly, the Board believes that a cash flow statement is not meaningful in relation to wholly owned subsidiary undertakings.

61. The Board has examined the proposition that a cash flow statement would not be particularly useful in respect of financial institutions, particularly banks, insurance companies and building societies.

62. The main reasons advanced for these views in respect of banks are that a bank's cash is its stock in trade and that more useful information would be given by a statement dealing with the capital resources available to the bank. The Board agrees that capital resources are an important indicator of the viability and financial adaptability of financial institutions, but also believes that a cash flow statement provides users of financial statements published by banks with useful information on the sources of cash and how it has been utilised and thus no exemption from the requirements of the FRS is given to banks.

63. The Board does, however, believe that the reporting of gross operating cash flows for a bank would not provide a user of the bank's financial statements with useful information, because many of the gross operating cash flows are essentially cash flows originated as a result of a decision by third parties who hold deposits or have loans with the bank to move funds to or from their accounts with the bank and thus these cash flows are beyond the day-to-day control of the bank's management. However, the FRS allows reporting entities to report cash flows from operations on a net basis (ie gross cash flows after deduction of other cash flows) and the Board believes that the reporting of net operating cash flows, together with cash flow information on a bank's investing and financing activities, provides useful information to users of the bank's financial statements. The illustrative examples annexed to the FRS include an example of a cash flow statement for a bank.

64. The main reason advanced for an exemption from the requirement to publish a cash flow statement as part of financial statements of an insurance company is that the cash inflows for an insurance company, unlike those of a manufacturing company, relate to premiums which by their nature precede the cash outflows in respect of claims, sometimes by a long period of time, and thus a cash flow statement gives little information on the liquidity, viability and financial adaptability of an insurance company. However, the Board believes that cash flow statements are useful to users of insurance company financial statements because, if used in conjunction with profit and loss accounts and balance sheets, they can assist the user of the financial statements to obtain a rounded picture of financial performance, position and adaptability. Accordingly, no general exemption from the requirements of the FRS is given to insurance companies.

65. However, the Board believes that cash flows arising from 'long term assurance' business (life, annuity and pensions) of an insurance company should not be dealt with in the cash flow statement except to the extent that the cash flows are those of the insurance company itself (eg cash withdrawn from the long-term funds by the insurance company) rather than cash flows of the long term funds. The Board believes that this presentation is appropriate, as the shareholders of an insurance company generally have restricted rights to any profits, and associated cash surpluses, made by the long-term funds. In addition, the Board believes that this presentation is consistent with the manner in which many insurance companies currently draw up their profit and loss accounts, balance sheets and statements of source and application of funds. The illustrative examples annexed to the FRS include an example of a cash flow statement for an insurance company. The same considerations apply to mutual life assurance companies that are owned by the policy holders and, accordingly, these companies are exempt from the requirements of the FRS.

66. Users of the financial statements of financial institutions, including insurance companies, may find it useful to have information on total liquid assets when making assessments of liquidity, viability and financial flexibility. In these circumstances the financial institutions concerned may wish to provide additional information on the amounts and flows of those liquid assets not dealt with in the cash flow statement. A possible way of presenting such information is set out in the notes to illustrative example 6 – 'XYZ Insurance Company Limited'.

67. Building Societies in the United Kingdom are required by Section 72(I)(c) of the Building Societies Act 1986 to prepare a statement of source and application of funds as part of their annual financial statements. The format of this statement which is prescribed, is set out in Schedule 3 of the Building Societies (Accounts and Related Provisions) Regulations 1987. The equivalent requirement to prepare a statement of source and application of funds in Republic of Ireland legislation is set out in Section 77 of the Building Societies Act 1989. The Board believes that the cost of Building Societies of including a cash flow statement in addition to the statement of source and application of funds would outweigh the benefits to users of Building Society financial statements. Accordingly, Building Societies are exempt from the provisions of the FRS during the period that they are required by law to include a statement of source and application of funds in their financial statements in a separately prescribed format.

Classification of cash flows

68. The Board believes that, in order to promote understanding and to help achieve the objectives of cash flow reporting by presenting the information in a useful way, individual cash flows should be classified according to the activity which gave rise to them. In order to promote comparability amongst different entities the FRS prescribes certain standard headings. The standard headings to be identified in a cash flow statement are 'operating activities', 'returns on investments and servicing of finance', 'taxation', 'investing activities' and 'financing'. The Board believes that the totals of the amounts within each standard heading provide useful information for general comparison purposes. However, the significance of the components within each standard heading may vary from reporting entity to reporting entity and accordingly the FRS requires sub-division of the amounts shown under each standard heading. In order to provide users of cash flow statements with a standard set of information that they can use in their analyses the FRS specifies certain standard sub-divisions which should be separately disclosed, if material, but reporting entities are encouraged to disclose additional information relevant to their particular circumstances.

Reporting net cash flow from operating activities

69. The Board considered the respective merits of the so-called 'direct' and 'indirect' methods for reporting net cash flow from operating activities. The direct method shows operating cash receipts and payments (including, in particular, cash receipts from customers, cash payments to suppliers and cash payments to and on behalf of employees), aggregating to the net cash flow from operating activities. The indirect method starts with operating profit and adjusts it for non-cash charges and credits to reconcile it to the net cash flow from operating activities.

70. The principal advantage of the direct method is that it shows operating cash receipts and payments. Knowledge of the specific sources of cash receipts and the purposes for which cash payments were made in past periods may be useful in assessing future cash flows. However, the Board does not believe at present that in all cases the benefits to users of this information outweigh the costs to the reporting entity of providing it and, therefore, has not required the information to be given. Nevertheless, in those circumstances where the benefits to users of the information given by the direct method outweigh the costs of providing it the Board encourages reporting entities to provide the relevant information.

71. The principal advantage of the indirect method is that it highlights the differences between operating profit and net cash flow from operating activities. Many users of financial statements believe that such a reconciliation is essential to give an indication of the quality of the reporting entity's earnings. Some investors and creditors assess future cash flows by estimating future income and then allowing for accruals adjustments; thus information about past accruals adjustments may be useful to help estimate future adjustments.

72. The Board believes that it is important that cash flow statements produced by different reporting entities are comparable as far as possible in the circumstances and thus believes that it should prescribe the

Illustrative example 1 – Single company

XYZ LIMITED

Cash flow statement for the year ended 31 March 1992

	£'000	£'000
Net cash inflow from operating activities		6,889
Returns on investments and servicing of finance		
Interest received	3,011	
Interest paid	(12)	
Dividends paid	(2,417)	
Net cash inflow from returns on investments and servicing of finance		582
Taxation		
Corporation tax paid (including advance corporation tax)	2,922	
Tax paid		(2,922)
Investing activities		
Payments to acquire intangible fixed assets	(71)	
Payments to acquire tangible fixed assets	(1,496)	
Receipts from sales of tangible fixed assets	42	
Net cash outflow from investing activities		(1,525)
Net cash inflow before financing		3,024
Financing		
Issue of ordinary share capital	211	
Repurchase of debenture loan	(149)	
Expenses paid in connection with share issues	(5)	
Net cash inflow from financing		57
Increase in cash and cash equivalents		3,081

Notes to the cash flow statement

1 RECONCILIATION OF OPERATING PROFIT TO NET CASH INFLOW FROM OPERATING ACTIVITIES

	£'000
Operating profit	6,022
Depreciation charges	893
Loss on sale of tangible fixed assets	6
Increase in stocks	(194)
Increase in debtors	(72)
Increase in creditors	234
Net cash inflow from operating activities	6,889

2 ANALYSIS OF CHANGES IN CASH AND CASH EQUIVALENTS DURING THE YEAR

	£'000
Balance at 1 April 1991	21,373
Net cash inflow	3,081
Balance at 31 March 1992	24,454

3 ANALYSIS OF THE BALANCES OF CASH AND CASH EQUIVALENTS AS SHOWN IN THE BALANCE SHEET

	1992 £'000	*1991* £'000	*Change in year* £'000
Cash at bank and in hand	529	681	(152)
Short-term investments	23,936	20,700	3,236
Bank overdrafts	(11)	(8)	(3)
	24,454	21,373	3,081

4 ANALYSIS OF CHANGES IN FINANCING DURING THE YEAR

	Share capital £'000	*Debenture loan* £'000
Balance at 1 April 1991	27,411	156
Cash inflow/(outflow) from financing	211	(149)
Profit on repurchase of debenture loan for less than its book value		(7)
Balance at 31 March 1992	27,622	-

outline format of the statement. Accordingly, the FRS requires the cash flow statement to show the net cash flow from operating activities, supplemented by a note reconciling this to the reporting entity's operating profit for the period. This reconciliation should not be given in the primary cash flow statement, in order to avoid confusing operating profit and the reconciling items with cash flows. The result is that reporting entities must give the information required by the indirect method, but may also give the information required by the direct method.

Interest and dividend payments and receipts

73. The Board believes that the presentation of net cash flow from operating activities should not be affected by the capital structure of the reporting entity, that payments resulting from the servicing of finance should be shown together and that the cash flow statement format should be consistent with the other primary statements including the profit and loss account wherever possible. Accordingly, interest and dividends paid are normally required to be classified under a separate heading entitled 'returns on investments and servicing of finance'. Cash flows in relation to interest rate hedging instruments such as interest rate swaps (other than those purchased or sold by a financial institution as part of its operating activities) should also be included under returns on investments and servicing of finance because these cash flows are equivalent to interest or are hedges of interest receipts or payments.

74. Interest and dividends received may result from investment activities, investment of cash and cash equivalents, or in some cases operating activities. The Board believes that, in general, interest received and paid should be shown in the same category within the cash flow statements, that dividends received should be shown under the same heading as interest and that the most appropriate category is returns on investments and servicing of finance. However, investment companies that show interest and dividends received in their profit and loss accounts prior to arriving at their operating profit should include interest and dividends received as part of their operating cash flows. Similarly banks that show interest received and paid in their profit and loss account prior to arriving at their operating profit should include interest received and paid as part of their operating cash flows and insurance companies that include interest and dividends received and certain interest paid in their profit and loss account prior to arriving at their operating profit should include the cash flows relating to those amounts as part of their operating cash flows.

Taxation

75. The taxation cash flows of a reporting entity in relation to revenue and capital profits may result from complex computations that are affected by the operating, investing and financing activities of an entity. The Board believes that it is not

Illustrative example 2 – Group

XYZ GROUP PLC

Cash flow statement for the year ended 31 March 1992

	£'000	£'000
Operating activites		
Cash received from customers	*195,016*	
Cash payments to suppliers	*(109,225)*	
Cash paid to and on behalf of employees	*(56,434)*	
Other cash payments	*(12,345)*	
Net cash inflow from continuing operating activities	*17,012*	
Net cash outflow in respect of discontinued activities and reorganisation costs	*(990)*	
Net cash inflow from operating activities		16,022
Returns on investments and servicing of finance		
Interest received	508	
Interest paid	(2,389)	
Interest element of finance lease rentals payments	(373)	
Dividend received from associated undertaking	15	
Dividends paid	(2,606)	
Net cash outflow from returns on investments and servicing of finance		(4,845)
Taxation		
UK corporation tax paid	(2,880)	
Overseas tax paid	(7)	
Tax paid		(2,887)
Investing activities		
Purchase of tangible fixed assets	(3,512)	
Purchase of subsidiary undertakings (net of cash and cash equivalents acquired) (See note 7)	(18,221)	
Sale of plant and machinery	1,052	
Sale of business (See note 8)	4,208	
Sale of trade investment	1,595	
Net cash outflows in respect of unsuccessful takeover bid	(3,811)	
Net cash outflow from investing activities		(18,689)
Net cash outflow before financing		(10,399)
Financing		
Issue of ordinary share capital	(49)	
New secured loan repayable in 1995	(1,091)	
New unsecured loan repayable in 1993	(1,442)	
New short-term loans	(2,006)	
Repayment of amounts borrowed	847	
Capital element of finance lease rental payments	1,342	
Net cash inflow from financing		(2,399)
Decrease in cash and cash equivalents		(8,000)
		(10,399)

Notes to the cash flow statement

1 RECONCILIATION OF OPERATING PROFIT TO NET CASH INFLOW FROM OPERATING ACTIVITIES

	£'000
Operating profit	20,249
Depreciation charges	3,158
Profit on sale of tangible fixed assets	(50)
Increase in stocks	(12,263)
Increase in debtors	(3,754)
Increase in creditors	9,672
Net cash inflow from continuing operating activities	17,012
Net cash outflow in respect of discontinued activities and reorganisation costs	(990)
Net cash inflow from operating activities	16,022

2 ANALYSIS OF CHANGES IN CASH AND CASH EQUIVALENTS DURING THE YEAR

	£'000
Balance at 1 April 1991	78
Net cash outflow before adjustments for the effect of foreign exchange rate changes	(8,000)
Effect of foreign exchange rate changes	(102)
Balance at 31 March 1992	(8,024)

3 ANALYSIS OF THE BALANCES OF CASH AND CASH EQUIVALENTS AS SHOWN IN THE BALANCE SHEET

	1992 *£'000*	*1991* *£'000*	*Change in year* *£'000*
Cash at bank and in hand	1,041	1,279	(238)
Bank overdrafts	(9,065)	(1,201)	(7,864)
	(8,024)	78	(8,102)

4 ANALYSIS OF CHANGES IN FINANCING DURING THE YEAR

	Share capital (including premium) *£'000*	*Loans and finance lease obligations* *£'000*
Balance at 1 April 1991	10,334	7,589
Cash inflows from financing	49	2,350
Shares issued for non-cash consideration	9,519	
Loans and finance lease obligations of subsidiary undertakings acquired during the year		3,817
Inception of finance lease contracts		2,845
Balance at 31 March 1992	19,902	16,601

[Note to preparers of financial statements

The disclosures set out below in respect of non-cash transactions may be combined with information disclosed elsewhere in the financial statements, eg the disclosure in respect of subsidiary undertakings acquired during the year could be combined with the disclosures required by paragraph 13(5) of Schedule 4A to the Companies Act 1985.]

5 MAJOR NON-CASH TRANSACTIONS

a During the year the group entered into finance lease arrangements in respect of assets with a total capital value at the inception of the leases of £2,845,000.

b Part of the consideration for the purchases of subsidiary undertakings and the sale of a business that occurred during the year comprised shares and loan notes respectively. Further details of the acquisitions and the disposal are set out below:

6 PURCHASE OF SUBSIDIARY UNDERTAKINGS

	£'000
Net assets acquired	
Tangible fixed assets	12,194
Investments	1
Stocks	9,384
Debtors	13,856
Taxation recoverable	1,309
Cash at bank and in hand	1,439
Creditors	(21,715)
Bank overdrafts	(6,955)
Loans and finance leases	(3,817)
Deferred taxation	(165)
Minority shareholders' interests	(9)
	5,522
Goodwill	16,702
	22,224
Satisfied by	
Shares allotted	9,519
Cash	12,705
	22,224

The subsidiary undertakings acquired during the year contributed £1,502,000 to the group's net operating cash flows, paid £1,308,000 in respect of net returns on investments and servicing of finance, paid £522,000 in respect of taxation and utilised £2,208,000 for investing activities.

Continuation of Illustrative example 2 – Group

XYZ GROUP PLC

Cash flow statement for the year ended 31 March 1992

7 ANALYSIS OF THE NET OUTFLOW OF CASH AND CASH EQUIVALENTS IN RESPECT OF THE PURCHASE OF SUBSIDIARY UNDERTAKINGS

	£'000
Cash consideration	12,705
Cash at bank and in hand acquired	(1,439)
Bank overdrafts of acquired subsidiary undertakings	6,955
Net outflow of cash and cash equivalents in respect of the purchase of subsidiaries	18,221

8 SALE OF BUSINESS

	£'000
Net assets disposed of	
Fixed assets	775
Stocks	5,386
Debtors	474
	6,635
Loss on disposal	(1,227)
	5,408
Satisfied by	
Loan notes	1,200
Cash	4,208
	5,408

The business sold during the year contributed £200,000 to the group's net operating cash flows, paid £252,000 in respect of net returns on investments and servicing of finance, paid £145,000 in respect of taxation and utilised £209,000 for investing activities.

useful to divide taxation cash flows into constituent parts relating to the activities that gave rise to them because the apportionment will, in many cases, have to be made on an arbitrary basis. As taxation cash flows generally arise from activities in an earlier period, apportioning the taxation cash flows would not necessarily report the taxation cash flows along with the transactions that gave rise to them. In addition, the Board notes that a taxation cash flow is not normally a collection of individual cash inflows and outflows and thus anlaysing it in this manner would require preparers of financial statements to allocate individual cash flows over the standard headings and would not necessarily give information on the entity's underlying cash flows.

76. Accordingly, the Board believes that taxation cash flows in relation to revenue and capital profits should be disclosed in a separate section within the cash flow statement entitled taxation.

77. The existence of Valued Added Tax (VAT), and other sales taxes, raises the question of whether the relevant cash flows should be reported gross or net of the tax element and how the balance of tax paid to, or repaid by, the taxing authorities should be reported.

78. Generally sales taxes, including VAT, are payable by the ultimate consumer of the goods or services concerned. A business providing goods or services on which VAT is payable (even if at a zero rate) is generally able to reclaim the VAT incurred by it in providing those goods or services. However, businesses that make exempt supplies are unable to reclaim VAT. Between these two categories are partially exempt businesses that can reclaim part of the VAT incurred by them.

79. The cash flows of an entity include VAT where appropriate and thus strictly the various elements of the cash flow statement should include VAT. However, this treatment does not take into account the fact that normally VAT is a short-term timing difference as far as the entity's overall cash flows are concerned and the inclusion of VAT in the cash flows may distort the allocation of cash flows to standard headings. In order to avoid this distortion and to show cash flows attributable to the reporting entity's activities, the Board believes that cash flows should be shown net of sales taxes and the net movement on the amount payable to, or receivable from, the taxing authority should be allocated to cash flows from operating activities unless a different treatment is more appropriate in the particular circumstances concerned.

80. Taxation cash flows excluding those in respect of the reporting entity's revenue and capital profits and Value Added Tax, or other sales tax, should be included within the cash flow statement under the same standard heading as the cash flow that gave rise to the taxation cash flow unless a different treatment is more appropriate in the particular circumstances concerned. This presentation is consistent with the manner in which transactions are presented in profit and loss accounts and balance sheets.

Investing activities

81. Investing activities are sometimes undertaken to maintain an entity's current level of operations and sometimes to expand or contract the level of operations. In addition investing activities may have consequential effects on operating activities, for example by creating a need for further working capital. The Board decided that criteria for distinguishing expenditure to expand the level of operations from expenditure to maintain the level of operations would vary from reporting entity to reporting entity and would distort the comparability provided by the standard headings. Similar problems arise in analysing changes in working capital. Reporting entities that find it useful to make such distinctions are encouraged to do so within the standard headings or by way of note.

Hedging transactions

82. Entities may undertake hedging transactions that result in cash flows. Often the hedging transactions are carried out with investment instruments that would normally be reported as cash flows under investing activities or returns on investments and servicing of finance. However, reporting hedging cash flows separately from the transactions being hedged would not result in the cash flow statement accurately reflecting the commercial effect of the linked transactions. Accordingly, the Board believes that cash flows which result from transactions undertaken to hedge another transaction should be reported under the same standard heading as the transaction that is the subject of the hedge.

Major non-cash transactions

83. Consideration for transactions may be in a form other than cash. The purpose of a cash flow statement is to report cash flows and non-cash transactions should, therefore, not be reported in a cash flow statement. However, to obtain a full picture of the alterations in financial position caused by the transactions for the period, separate disclosure of material non-cash transactions (such as a vendor placing, the exchange of major assets or the inception of a finance lease contract) is also necessary.

Identification with balance sheet figures

84. The amounts of cash and cash equivalents and amounts shown in the financing section of the cash flow statement should be reconciled to the related items in the opening and closing balance sheets for the period in order to facilitate the use of both cash flow and balance sheet information in assessing the liquidity, viability and financial adaptability of the reporting entity.

Illustrative examples

These illustrative examples [pp 134-140] are for general guidance and do not form part of the Financial Reporting Standard. In particular, the analyses of net cash flows from operating activities under the direct method, the subtotalling in the reconciliation of operating profit to net cash flow from operating activity for a bank, and the disclosure of total liquid assets for an insurance company, shown in the examples in italics, are optional disclosures.

This section sets out examples of cash flow statements for six types of reporting entity. The examples, which are for illustrative pruposes only, do not include comparative figures, except where they are required for

Illustrative example 3 – Property investment company

XYZ PROPERTY INVESTMENTS LIMITED

Cash flow statement for the year ended 31 March 1992

	£m	£m
Operating activities		
Cash received from tenants	*263.8*	
Cash payments in respect of direct property costs	*(14.4)*	
Cash paid to and on behalf of employees	*(9.0)*	
Other cash payments	*(8.9)*	
Net cash inflow from operating activities		231.5
Returns on investments and servicing of finance		
Interest received	45.1	
Interest paid	(111.1)	
Dividends paid	(75.7)	
Net cash outflow from returns on investments and servicing of finance		(141.7)
Taxation		
Corporation tax paid	(55.3)	
Tax paid		(55.3)
Investing activities		
Purchase of property	(361.6)	
Sales of property	80.6	
Purchase of plant and machinery and fixtures & fittings	(1.2)	
Sale of plant and machinery and fixtures & fittings	0.1	
Other cash outflows from investing activities	(0.3)	
Net cash outflow from investing activities		(282.4)
Net cash outflow before financing		(247.9)
Financing		
Issue of ordinary share capital	(0.9)	
Issue of Convertible Bonds	(175.0)	
Issue of Unsecured Loan Notes	(3.9)	
Repayments of debenture stocks	11.9	
Amounts paid in respect of the expenses of the issues of Convertible Bonds and Unsecured Loan Notes	3.3	
Net cash inflow from financing		(164.6)
Decrease in cash and cash equivalents		(83.3)
		(247.9)

Notes to the cash flow statement

1 RECONCILIATION OF OPERATING PROFIT TO NET CASH INFLOW FROM OPERATING ACTIVITIES

	£m
Operating profit	241.1
Depreciation charges	1.5
Increase in debtors	(32.5)
Increase in creditors	21.0
Effect of other deferrals and accruals of operating activity cash flow	0.4
Net cash inflow from operating activities	231.5

2 ANALYSIS OF CHANGES IN CASH AND CASH EQUIVALENTS DURING THE YEAR

	£m
Balance at 1 April 1991	350.5
Net cash outflow	(83.3)
Balance at 31 March 1992	267.2

3 ANALYSIS OF THE BALANCES OF CASH AND CASH EQUIVALENTS AS SHOWN IN THE BALANCE SHEET

	1992 £m	*1991* £m	*Change in year* £m
Cash at bank and in hand	0.4	3.4	(3.0)
Short-term deposits	266.8	347.1	(80.3)
	267.2	350.5	(83.3)

4 ANALYSIS OF CHANGES IN FINANCING DURING THE YEAR

	Share capital (including premium) £m	*Loans including convertible bonds* £m
Financing at 1 April 1991	503.7	1,113.5
Cash inflows from financing	0.9	167.0
Financing at 31 March 1992	504.6	1,280.5

a better understanding of the example.

1. Single company
2. Group, including equity accounted entities, with acquisitions and a disposal during the year
3. Property investment company
4. Investment company
5. Bank
6. Insurance company

The development of the standard

This section does not form part of the Financial Reporting Standard.

Summary of the principal changes from statement of Standard Accounting Practice No 10 – 'Statements of source and application of funds'.

1. Statement of Standard Accounting Practice No 10 (SSAP 10), issued July 1975, sought to establish the practice of providing statements of source and application of funds as a part of audited financial statements and to lay down a minimum standard of disclosure in such statements.

2. The objective of the statement of source and application of funds required by SSAP 10 was to show the manner in which the operations of a reporting entity had been financed and in which its financial resources had been used. The information disclosed in the statement is essentially a rearrangement of the information given in the profit and loss (or income and expenditure) account and balance sheet.

3. SSAP 10 was drafted to allow preparers of accounts flexibility in the preparation of funds flow statements. It did not provide a definition of funds or set out a basic structure for a statement. It did, however, specify certain key information which was required to be given in the statement and also provided two examples for general guidance in an appendix, which did not form part of the statement of standard accounting practice.

4. The FRS requires reporting entities to report cash flows rather than accrual based funds flows and the basic structure of the cash flow statement is prescribed.

5. SSAP 10 applied to all financial statements intended to give a true and fair view of the financial position and profit or loss (or income and expenditure) other than those entities with turnover or gross income of less than £25,000 per annum although consideration was to be given to providing the statement for small entities whenever it was desirable. The FRS allows exemptions to a much larger number of reporting entities including most small reporting entities and wholly owned subsidiary undertakings.

6. SSAP 10 allowed the purchase or disposal of subsidiary undertakings to be dealt with either by showing the consideration paid or received as a separate item within the statement of source and application of funds or by reflecting the effects of the acquisition or disposal on the separate assets and liabilities dealt with in the statement. The FRS requires purchase or sales consideration (unless merger accounting is used) to be shown under investing activities and the method reflecting the effects on the separate assets and liabilities, the so-called 'line by line' method, is not permitted.

Summary of the principal changes from Ex-

Illustrative example 4 – Investment company

XYZ INVESTMENT COMPANY PLC

Cash flow statement for the year ended 31 March 1992

	£'000	£'000
Operating activities		
Cash received from investments	*9,491*	
Interest received	*2,870*	
Investment management fees paid	*(1,057)*	
Cash paid to and on behalf of directors	*(35)*	
Other cash payments	*(720)*	
Net cash inflow from operating activities		10,549
Returns on investments and servicing of finance		
Interest paid	(114)	
Dividends paid	(6,642)	
Net cash outflow from returns on investments and servicing of finance		(6,756)
Taxation		
UK corporation tax paid	(1,286)	
Overseas tax paid	(362)	
Total tax paid		(1,648)
Investing activities		
Purchase of investments	(149,770)	
Sales of investments	114,097	
Net cash outflow from investing activities		(35,673)
Net cash outflow before financing		(33,528)
Financing		
Issue of Equity Index Unsecured Loan Stock 2004	(60,000)	
Expenses paid in respect of the loan stock issue	1,162	
Net cash inflow from financing		(58,838)
Increase in cash and cash equivalents		25,310
		(33,528)

Notes to the cash flow statement

1 RECONCILIATION OF OPERATING PROFIT TO NET CASH INFLOW FROM OPERATING ACTIVITIES

	£'000
Income before interest payable and taxation	12,475
Increase in accrued income	(46)
Decrease in other debtors	243
Decrease in creditors	(23)
Tax on franked investment income included within income from UK companies	(2,100)
Net cash inflow from operating activities	10,549

2 ANALYSIS OF CHANGES IN CASH AND CASH EQUIVALENTS DURING THE YEAR

	£'000
Balance at 1 April 1991	10,359
Net cash inflow	25,310
Balance at 31 March 1992	35,669

3 CASH AND CASH EQUIVALENTS

The balance for cash and cash equivalents is shown in the balance sheet as 'Cash at bank and in hand' £35,669,000 (1991 – £10,359,000).

4 ANALYSIS OF CHANGES IN FINANCING DURING THE YEAR

	Share capital £'000	*Loans including equity index loan stock £'000*
Balance at 1 April 1991	55,902	476
Cash inflow from financing		60,000
Change in value of Equity Index Loan Stock		(253)
Balance at 31 March 1992	55,902	60,223

posure Draft No 54 – 'Cash flow statements'

1. The proposed Statement of Standard Accounting Practice set out in Exposure Draft No 54 (ED 54), issued in July 1990 by the ASC, sought to replace the statement of source and application of funds required by SSAP 10 with a cash flow statement and to set out a general format for such a statement.

2. The requirements of the FRS have been based upon ED 54 and the comments received on it together with the Board's own research, consultation and careful deliberation about the benefits and costs of providing the information. The vast majority of commentators on ED 54 were supportive of the overall approach adopted. The principal differences in the requirements of the FRS and ED 54 are set out below.

Scope

3. ED 54 proposed that the standard should apply to all financial statements intended to give a true and fair view of the financial position and profit or loss (or income and expenditure) other than those entities that do not report under the Companies Act and which have turnover or revenue of less than £25,000 per annum. This scope, which allowed fewer exemptions than those allowed by SSAP 10, was criticised by some commentators, who believed that small companies and wholly owned subsidiary undertakings subsidiaries should be exempted in certain circumstances. The FRS allows exemptions from its requirements to a much larger number of reporting entities including most small reporting entities and wholly owned subsidiary undertakings.

Classification of cash flows

4. ED 54 identified the same major classes of activity (ie operating, investing and financing) as the FRS, but the FRS requires certain cash flows to be reported differently from the proposals contained in ED 54 as explained in paragraphs 5 to 8 below. In addition the FRS requires cash flows arising from financing activities to be divided into two separate categories; cash flows resulting from movements of principal amounts of finance, and returns on investments and servicing of finance.

Reporting net cash flow from operating activities

5. ED 54 considered two methods, direct and indirect, for reporting net cash flow from operating activities and allowed either method to be used. The Board notes that many users of financial statements require the reconciliation between operating profit and net cash flow from operating activities. Some respondents to ED 54 stated that they believed that it would be costly to implement the direct method as they did not currently collect information in such a form directly from their accounting systems. Particular problems would be encountered by multinational groups implementing the direct method. Accordingly, the FRS allows the net cash flow from operating activities to be reported on a net or gross basis, but, in addition, a note to the cash flow statement should give a reconciliation between

Illustrative example 5 – Bank

XYZ INTERNATIONAL BANK LIMITED

Cash flow statement for the year ended 31 March 1992

	£m	£m
Net cash inflow from operating activities		1,106.9
Returns on investments and servicing of finance		
Dividends received from associated undertakings	9.9	
Ordinary dividends paid	(57.2)	
Preference dividends paid	(10.4)	
Dividends paid to minority shareholders in subsidiary undertaking	(0.2)	
Net cash outflows from returns on investments and servicing of finance		(57.9)
Taxation		
Corporation tax paid	(73.8)	
Overseas tax paid	(14.2)	
Total tax paid		(88.0)
Investing activities		
Purchase of trade investments	(14.7)	
Sale of trade investments	5.7	
Investment in associated undertaking	(56.1)	
Sale of investment in associated undertaking	71.2	
Purchase of tangible fixed assets	(121.4)	
Sales of tangible fixed assets	40.1	
Net cash outflow from investing activities		(75.2)
Net cash inflow before financing		885.8
Financing		
Issue of ordinary share capital	(6.3)	
Repayments of loan capital	12.3	
Net cash outflow from financing		6.0
Increase in cash and cash equivalents		879.8
		885.8

Notes to the cash flow statement

1 RECONCILIATION OF OPERATING PROFIT TO NET CASH INFLOW FROM OPERATING ACTIVITIES

	£m
Operating profit	241.4
Increase in interest receivable and prepaid expenses	(161.2)
Increase in interest payable and accrued expenses	118.1
Provision for loan losses	20.8
Release of provisions against rescheduled country debt	(50.7)
Depreciation	53.2
Profit on sale of tangible fixed assets	(0.9)
Effect of other deferrals and accruals of operating activity cash flow	1.1
Net cash flow from trading activities c/f	*221.8*
Net cash flow from trading activities b/f	*221.8*
Net increase in deposits and commercial paper	2,542.8
Net increase in loans to customers	(1,419.1)
Net change in finance lease balances receivable	(241.2)
Decrease in securities held (other than those treated as investment activities)	39.9
Increase in collections on other banks	(18.7)
Net increase in placings with banks (repayable beyond 3 months)	(18.6)
Net cash inflow from operating activities	1,106.9

2 ANALYSIS OF CHANGES IN CASH AND CASH EQUIVALENTS DURING THE YEAR

	£m
Balance at 1 April 1991	6,322.9
Net cash inflow before adjustments for the effect of foreign exchange rate changes	879.8
Effect of foreign exchange rate changes	(142.3)
Balance at 31 March 1992	7,060.4

3 ANALYSIS OF THE BALANCES OF CASH AND CASH EQUIVALENTS AS SHOWN IN THE BALANCE SHEET

	1992 £m	*1991* £m	*Change in year* £m
Coin, bank notes and balances with central banks	912.5	736.9	175.6
Money at call and short notice	5,322.4	4,781.6	540.8
Marketable bills of exchange	562.5	584.8	(22.3)
Certificates of deposit	263.0	219.6	43.4
	7,060.4	6,322.9	737.5

The group is required to maintain balances with the Bank of England which, at 31 March 1992, amounted to £54.0 million (1991 – £43.3 million).

Certain subsidiary undertakings of the group are required by law to maintain average reserve balances with the Federal Reserve Bank in the United States of America. Such reserve balances amounted to $30.4 million at 31 March 1992 (1991 – $28.6 million).

4 ANALYSIS OF CHANGES IN FINANCING DURING THE YEAR

	Share capital (including premium) £'000	*Loan capital* £'000
Balance at 1 April 1991	435.3	1,248.1
Effect of foreign exchange differences		(115.7)
Cash inflow/(outflow) from financing	6.3	(12.3)
Other movements	(0.1)	
Balance at 31 March 1992	441.5	1,120.1

the reporting entity's operating profit and the net cash flow from operating activities. Thus reporting entities must give the information required by the indirect method, but may also give the information required by the direct method and the Board encourages reporting entities to give a breakdown of their cash flows under the direct method in those circumstances where the benefits to users of the information outweigh the costs of providing it.

Interest and dividend receipts and payments

6. ED 54 required interest received and paid to be included under operating activities. However, there was no consensus in the comments on ED 54 concerning the treatment of interest received and paid in a cash flow statement and in order to present the cash flow information in a useful way the FRS requires that interest received and paid should normally be shown under returns on investments and servicing of finance.

7. ED 54 drew a distinction between interest paid, which is contractual, and dividends paid, which are discretionary, although both are paid to providers of capital. It proposed that dividends paid be included under the reporting entity's financing activities and dividends received under operating activities. However, there was no consensus in the comments on ED 54 concerning the treatment of dividends received and paid in a cash flow statement and in order to present cash flow information in a useful way that is consistent with the presentation of receipts and payments of interest the FRS does not make such a distinction and requires both dividends received and dividends paid to be shown under returns on investments and servicing of finance.

Taxation

8. ED 54 required taxation cash flows in relation to income and capital gains to be shown as operating activities unless material elements of the cash flows related to another activity, when an apportionment could be made. Many commentators on ED 54 did not agree with this presentation,

Illustrative example 6 – Insurance company

XYZ INSURANCE COMPANY LIMITED

Cash flow statement for the year ended 31 March 1992

	£m	£m
Operating activities		
Premiums received from customers	*2,410.8*	
Reinsurance premiums paid	*(400.3)*	
Claims paid	*(1,634.2)*	
Reinsurance receipts in respect of claims	*350.3*	
Cash received from long term funds	*85.3*	
Cash paid to and on behalf of employees	*(127.5)*	
Interest received	*152.5*	
Dividends received	*166.3*	
Interest paid	*(22.0)*	
Other operating cash payments	*(656.8)*	
Net cash inflow from operating activities		324.4
Returns on investments and servicing of finance		
Interest paid	(20.0)	
Dividends paid	(79.2)	
Net cash outflow from returns on investments and servicing of finance		(99.2)
Taxation		
Corporation tax paid (including advance corporation tax)	(132.5)	
Tax paid		(132.5)
Investing activities		
Purchase of liquid investments (other than cash equivalents)	(382.1)	
Purchase of other investments (other than cash equivalents)	(50.0)	
Sale of liquid investments (other than cash equivalents)	363.8	
Sale of other investments (other than cash equivalents)	48.0	
Purchase of tangible fixed assets	(16.7)	
Net cash outflow from investing activities		(37.0)
Net cash inflow before financing		55.7
Financing		
Issue of ordinary share capital	6.1	
Repayment of long-term loan	(60.1)	
Net cash outflow from financing		(54.0)
Increase in cash and cash equivalents		1.7

Notes to the cash flow statement

1 RECONCILIATION OF OPERATING PROFIT TO NET CASH INFLOW FROM OPERATING ACTIVITIES

	£m
Operating profit	181.8
Depreciation charges	12.0
Increase in debtors	(90.4)
Increase in amount owed by long-term funds	(16.7)
Increase in unearned premiums	47.2
Increase in claims provisions	206.3
Increase in creditors	12.2
Tax on franked investment income included within operating income	(28.0)
Net cash inflow from operating activities	324.4

2 ANALYSIS OF CHANGES IN CASH AND CASH EQUIVALENTS AND OTHER LIQUID INVESTMENTS DURING THE YEAR

	Cash and cash equivalents £m	*Other liquid investments £m*	*Total £m*
Balance at 1 April 1991	23.7	*3,720.4*	*3,744.1*
Net cash inflow	1.7		*1.7*
Purchase of investments		*382.1*	*382.1*
Sale of investments		*(363.8)*	*(363.8)*
Change in market value		*331.3*	*331.3*
Balance at 31 March 1992	25.4	*4,070.0*	*4,095.4*

3 ANALYSIS OF THE BALANCES OF CASH AND CASH EQUIVALENTS AND OTHER LIQUID INVESTMENTS AS SHOWN IN THE BALANCE SHEET

	1992 £m	*1991 £m*	*Change in year £m*
Cash at bank and in hand	59.9	34.6	25.3
Bank overdrafts	(34.5)	(10.9)	(23.6)
Total cash and cash equivalents	25.4	23.7	1.7
Other liquid investments	*4,070.0*	*3,720.4*	*349.6*
	4,095.4	*3,744.1*	*351.3*

4 ANALYSIS OF CHANGES IN FINANCING DURING THE YEAR

	Share capital (including premium) £m	*Long term loan £m*
Financing at 1 April 1991	296.5	346.2
Cash inflow/(outflow) from financing	6.1	(60.1)
Financing at 31 March 1992	302.6	286.1

but preferred that taxation be disclosed separately within its own section in order to present the information in a more useful way or to avoid arbitrary apportionment. The Board agrees with these views and accordingly the FRS requires such cash flows to be shown in a separate section of the statement entitled 'taxation'.

9. ED 54 required cash flows to be disclosed inclusive of any attributable Value Added Tax, or other sales taxes, but the FRS requires cash flows to be reported net of any such taxes unless the tax is not recoverable by the reporting entity, when cash flows should normally include the irrecoverable tax. There was no consensus in the comments on ED 54 on the treatment of Value Added Tax, although some commentators believed that problems would be encountered in the production and interpreatation of tax inclusive cash flows.

Cash or net debt

10. Many commentators on the exposure draft stated that they believed that a statement that analysed the movement in a reporting entity's net cash or debt position would be more useful than one which reported the movement in cash and cash equivalents alone. These commentators noted that the cash position of an entity must be considered along with obligations that the entity may have. The Board agrees with these comments, but believes that the main focus of the cash flow statement should still be cash flows. However, by splitting the servicing of finance from the movements in principal amounts of finance, requiring a total giving the net cash flow before financing and by requiring a reconciliation of the items within the financing section of the statement to the opening and closing balance sheets the Board believes that the information required by these commentators is given.

Sources: FASB Statement 95; FASB Statement 102; FASB Statement 104

Summary

This section presents standards for cash flow reporting. A statement of cash flows is required as part of a full set of financial statements for all business enterprises other than defined benefit pension plans and certain other employee benefit plans and highly liquid investment companies that meet specified conditions. (Not-for-profit organizations are excluded from the scope of this section.)

A statement of cash flows shall classify cash receipts and payments according to whether they stem from operating, investing, or financing activities. This section provides definitions of each category.

Generally, cash flow information about the gross amounts of cash receipts and cash payments during a period is more relevant than information about net amounts of cash receipts and payments. However, because the net amount of related receipts and payments provides sufficient information when the turnover is quick, the amounts are large, and the maturities are short, the reporting of net cash flows for certain items with those characteristics is permitted. Additionally, certain investing and financing activities of banks, savings institutions, and credit unions may be reported as net cash flows.

Enterprises are encouraged to report cash flows from operating activities directly by showing major classes of operating cash receipts and payments (the direct method). Enterprises that choose not to show operating cash receipts and payments are required to report the same amount of net cash flow from operating activities indirectly by adjusting net income to reconcile it to net cash flow from operating activities (the indirect or reconciliation method). If the direct method is used, a reconciliation of net income and net cash flow from operating activities is required to be provided in a separate schedule.

A statement of cash flows shall report the reporting currency equivalent of foreign currency cash flows, using the current exchange rate at the time of the cash flows. The effect of the exchange rate changes on cash held in foreign currencies is reported as a separate item in the reconciliation of beginning and ending balances of cash and cash equivalents.

Information about investing and financing activities not resulting in cash receipts or payments in the period shall be provided separately.

Scope

.101 This section [presents] standards for providing a statement of cash flows in general-purpose financial statements. [FAS95, ¶1] A business enterprise[1] that provides a set of financial statements that reports both financial position and results of operations shall also provide a statement of cash flows for each period for which results of operations are provided. [FAS95, ¶3] [However,] a statement of cash flows is not required for defined benefit pension plans and certain other employee benefit plans or for certain investment companies as provided by paragraphs .135A through .135C. [FAS102, ¶10a]

Purpose of a Statement of Cash Flows

.102 The primary purpose of a statement of cash flows is to provide relevant information about the cash receipts and cash payments of an enterprise during a period. [FAS95, ¶4]

.103 The information provided in a statement of cash flows, if used with related disclosures and information in the other financial statements, should help investors, creditors, and others to (a) assess the enterprise's ability to generate positive future net cash flows; (b) assess the enterprise's ability to meet its obligations, its ability to pay dividends, and its needs for external financing; (c) assess the reasons for differences between net income and associated cash receipts and payments; and (d) assess the effects on an enterprise's financial position of both its cash and noncash investing and financing transactions during the period. [FAS95, ¶5]

[1]Exclusion of not-for-profit organizations from the scope of this section means only that [it] has not yet [been] decided whether not-for-profit organizations should be required to provide a statement of cash flows. [FAS95, ¶69] [On August 29, 1989 the FASB issued the Invitation to Comment, *Financial Reporting by Not-for-Profit Organizations: Form and Content of Financial Statements*. That publication includes the report of the AICPA's Not-for-Profit Organizations Task Force on financial statement display for not-for-profit organizations. After all written comments on the Invitation to Comment are received and analyzed, the FASB expects to develop an Exposure Draft of the proposed reporting requirements for the form and content of financial statements of not-for-profit organizations.]

.104 To achieve its purpose of providing information to help investors, creditors, and others in making those assessments, a statement of cash flows should report the cash effects during a period of an enterprise's operations, its investing transactions, and its financing transactions. Related disclosures should report the effects of investing and financing transactions that affect an enterprise's financial position but do not directly affect cash flows during the period. A reconciliation of net income and net cash flow from operating activities, which generally provides information about the net effects of operating transactions and other events that affect net income and operating cash flows in different periods, also should be provided. [FAS95, ¶6]

Focus on Cash and Cash Equivalents

.105 A statement of cash flows shall explain the change during the period in cash[2] and cash equivalents. The statement shall use descriptive terms such as *cash* or *cash and cash equivalents* rather than ambiguous terms such as *funds.* The total amounts of cash and cash equivalents at the beginning and end of the period shown in the statement of cash flows shall be the same amounts as similarly titled line items or subtotals shown in the statements of financial position as of those dates. [FAS95, ¶7]

[2]Consistent with common usage, *cash* includes not only currency on hand but demand deposits with banks or other financial institutions. *Cash* also includes other kinds of accounts that have the general characteristics of demand deposits in that the customer may deposit additional funds at any time and also effectively may withdraw funds at any time without prior notice or penalty. All charges and credits to those accounts are cash receipts or payments to both the entity owning the account and the bank holding it. For example, a bank's granting of a loan by crediting the proceeds to a customer's demand deposit account is a cash payment by the bank and a cash receipt of the customer when the entry is made. [FAS95, ¶7, fn1]

.106 For purposes of this section, cash equivalents are short-term, highly liquid investments that are both:

a. Readily convertible to known amounts of cash
b. So near their maturity that they present insignificant risk of changes in value because of changes in interest rates.

Generally, only investments with original maturities[3] of three months or less qualify under that definition. [FAS95, ¶8]

.107 Examples of items commonly considered to be cash equivalents are Treasury bills, commercial paper, money market funds, and federal funds sold (for an enterprise with banking operations). Cash purchases and sales of those investments generally are part of the enterprise's cash management activities rather than part of its operating, investing, and financing activities, and details of those transactions need not be reported in a statement of cash flows. [FAS95, ¶9]

.108 Not all investments that qualify [as cash equivalents under paragraph .106] are required to be treated as cash equivalents [in the statement of cash flows]. An enterprise shall establish a policy concerning which short-term, highly liquid investments that satisfy the definition in paragraph .106 are treated as cash equivalents. For example, an enterprise having banking operations might decide that all investments that qualify except for those purchased for its trading account will be treated as cash equivalents, while an enterprise whose operations consist largely of investing in short-term, highly liquid investments might decide that all those items will be treated as investments rather than cash equivalents. An enterprise shall disclose its policy for determining which items are treated as cash equivalents [in the statement of cash flows]. Any change to that policy is a change in accounting principle that shall be effected by restating financial statements for earlier years presented for comparative purposes. [FAS95, ¶10]

---

[3] *Original maturity* [in this paragraph] means original maturity to the entity holding the investment. For example, both a three-month U.S. Treasury bill and a three-year Treasury note purchased three months from maturity qualify as cash equivalents. However, a Treasury note purchased three years ago does not become a cash equivalent when its remaining maturity is three months.[FAS95, ¶8, fn2]

Gross and Net Cash Flows

.109 Generally, information about the gross amounts of cash receipts and cash payments during a period is more relevant than information about the net amounts of cash receipts and payments. However, the net amount of related receipts and payments provides sufficient information not only for cash equivalents, as noted in paragraph .107, but also for certain other classes of cash flows specified in paragraphs .110, .111, [.111A], and .126. [FAS95, ¶11]

.110 For certain items, the turnover is quick, the amounts are large, and the maturities are short. For certain other items, such as demand deposits of a bank and customer accounts payable of a broker-dealer, the enterprise is substantively holding or disbursing cash on behalf of its customers. Only the net changes during the period in assets and liabilities with those characteristics need be reported because knowledge of the gross cash receipts and payments related to them may not be necessary to understand the enterprise's operating, investing, and financing activities. [FAS95, ¶12]

.111 Items that qualify for net reporting because their turnover is quick, their amounts are large, and their maturities are short are cash receipts and payments pertaining to (a) investments (other than cash equivalents), (b) loans receivable, and (c) debt, providing that the original maturity of the asset or liability is three months or less.[4] [FAS95, ¶13]

.111A Banks, savings institutions, and credit unions are not required to report gross amounts of cash receipts and cash payments for (a) deposits placed with other financial institutions and withdrawals of deposits, (b) time deposits accepted and repayments of deposits, and (c) loans made to customers and principal collections of loans. When those enterprises constitute part of a consolidated enterprise, net amounts of cash receipts and cash payments for deposit or lending activities of those enterprises shall be reported separate from gross amounts of cash receipts and cash payments for other investing and financing activities of the consolidated enterprise, including those of a subsidiary of a bank, savings institution, or credit union that is not itself a bank, savings institution, or credit union. [FAS104, ¶7a]

[4]For this purpose, amounts due on demand are considered to have maturities of three months or less. For convenience, credit card receivables of financial services operations—generally, receivables resulting from cardholder charges that may, at the cardholder's option, be paid in full when first billed, usually within one month, without incurring interest charges and that do not stem from the enterprise's sale of goods or services—also are considered to be loans with original maturities of three months or less. [FAS95, ¶13, fn3]

Classification of Cash Receipts and Cash Payments

.112 A statement of cash flows shall classify cash receipts and cash payments as resulting from investing, financing, or operating activities.[5] [FAS95, ¶14]

Cash Flows from Investing Activities

.113 Investing activities include making and collecting loans and acquiring and disposing of debt or equity instruments and property, plant, and equipment and other productive assets, that is, assets held for or used in the production of goods or services by the enterprise (other than materials that are part of the enterprise's inventory). [FAS95, ¶15] Investing activities exclude acquiring and disposing of certain loans or other debt or equity instruments that are acquired specifically for resale, as discussed in paragraphs .122A through .122B. [FAS102, ¶10b]

.114 Cash inflows from investing activities are:[6]

a. Receipts from collections or sales of loans made by the enterprise and of other entities' debt instruments [FAS95, ¶16] (other than cash equivalents and certain debt instruments that are acquired specifically for resale) [FAS102, ¶10c] that were purchased by the enterprise

[5]Generally, each cash receipt or payment is to be classified according to its nature without regard to whether it stems from an item intended as a hedge of another item. For example, the proceeds of a borrowing are a financing cash inflow even though the debt is intended as a hedge of an investment, and the purchase or sale of a futures contract is an investing activity even though the contract is intended as a hedge of a firm commitment to purchase inventory. However, cash flows from futures contracts, forward contracts, option contracts, or swap contracts that are accounted for as hedges of identifiable transactions or events (for example, a cash payment from a futures contract that hedges a purchase or sale of inventory), including anticipatory hedges, may be classified in the same category as the cash flows from the items being hedged provided that accounting policy is disclosed. If for any reason hedge accounting for an instrument that hedges an identifiable transaction or event is discontinued, then any cash flows subsequent to the date of discontinuance shall be classified consistent with the nature of the instrument. [FAS104, ¶7b]

[6]Receipts from disposing of loans, debt or equity instruments, or property, plant, and equipment include directly related proceeds of insurance settlements, such as the proceeds of insurance on a building that is damaged or destroyed. [FAS95, ¶16, fn5]

b. Receipts from sales of equity instruments of other enterprises [FAS95, ¶16] (other than certain equity instruments carried in a trading account) [FAS102, ¶10d] and from returns *of* investment in those instruments
c. Receipts from sales of property, plant, and equipment and other productive assets. [FAS95, ¶16]

.115 Cash outflows for investing activities are:

a. Disbursements for loans made by the enterprise and payments to acquire debt instruments of other entities [FAS95, ¶17] (other than cash equivalents and certain debt instruments that are acquired specifically for resale) [FAS102, ¶10c]
b. Payments to acquire equity instruments of other enterprises [FAS95, ¶17] (other than certain equity instruments carried in a trading account) [FAS102, ¶10d]
c. Payments at the time of purchase or soon before or after purchase[7] to acquire property, plant, and equipment and other productive assets.[8] [FAS95,¶17]

Cash Flows from Financing Activities

.116 Financing activities include obtaining resources from owners and providing them with a return on, and a return of, their investment; borrowing money and repaying amounts borrowed, or otherwise settling the obligation; and obtaining and paying for other resources obtained from creditors on long-term credit. [FAS95, ¶18]

.117 Cash inflows from financing activities are:

a. Proceeds from issuing equity instruments
b. Proceeds from issuing bonds, mortgages, notes, and from other short- or long-term borrowing. [FAS95, ¶19]

.118 Cash outflows for financing activities are:

a. Payments of dividends or other distributions to owners, including outlays to reaquire the enterprise's equity instruments
b. Repayments of amounts borrowed

[7]Generally, only advance payments, the down payment, or other amounts paid at the time of purchase or soon before or after purchase of property, plant, and equipment and other productive assets are investing cash outflows. Incurring directly related debt [payable] to the seller is a financing transaction, and subsequent payments of principal on that debt thus are financing cash outflows. [FAS95, ¶17, fn6]

[8]Enterprises [are not] required to distinguish between expenditures for maintenance and those for expansion. [FAS95, ¶99] Payments to acquire productive assets include interest capitalized as part of the cost of those assets. [FAS95, ¶17, fn7]

c. Other principal payments to creditors who have extended long-term credit.[9] [FAS95, ¶20]

Cash Flows from Operating Activities

.119 Operating activities include all transactions and other events that are not defined as investing or financing activities in paragraphs .113 through .118. Operating activities generally involve producing and delivering goods and providing services. Cash flows from operating activities are generally the cash effects of transactions and other events that enter into the determination of net income. [Refer to paragraphs .122A and .122B for guidance on reporting cash flows from assets in trading accounts and from loans acquired for resale.] [FAS95, ¶21]

.120 Cash inflows from operating activities are:

a. Cash receipts from sales of goods[9a] or services, including receipts from collection or sale of accounts and both short- and long-term notes receivable from customers arising from those sales
b. Cash receipts from returns *on* loans, other debt instruments of other entities, and equity securities—interest and dividends
c. All other cash receipts that do not stem from transactions defined as investing or financing activities, such as amounts received to settle lawsuits; proceeds of insurance settlements except for those that are directly related to investing or financing activities, such as from destruction of a building; and refunds from suppliers. [FAS95, ¶22]

.121 Cash outflows for operating activities are:

a. Cash payments to acquire materials for manufacture or goods[9b] for resale, including principal payments on accounts and both short- and long-term notes payable to suppliers for those materials or goods
b. Cash payments to other suppliers and employees for other goods or services
c. Cash payments to governments for taxes, duties, fines, and other fees or penalties
d. Cash payments to lenders and other creditors for interest
e. All other cash payments that do not stem from transactions defined as investing or financing activities, such as payments to settle lawsuits, cash contributions to charities, and cash refunds to customers. [FAS95, ¶23]

---

[9]Refer to footnote 7, which indicates that most principal payments on seller-financed debt directly related to a purchase of property, plant, and equipment or other productive assets are financing cash outflows. [FAS95, ¶20, fn8]

[9a]The term *goods* includes certain loans and other debt and equity instruments of other enterprises that are acquired specifically for resale, as discussed in paragraph .122B. [FAS102, ¶10e]

[9b][Refer to footnote 9a.] [FAS102, ¶10e]

.122 Certain cash receipts and payments may have aspects of more than one class of cash flows. For example, a cash payment may pertain to an item that could be considered either inventory or a productive asset. If so, the appropriate classification shall depend on the activity that is likely to be the predominant source of cash flows for the item. For example, the acquisition and sale of equipment to be used by the enterprise or rented to others generally are investing activities. However, equipment sometimes is acquired or produced to be used by the enterprise or rented to others for a short period and then sold. In those circumstances, the acquisition or production and subsequent sale of those assets shall be considered operating activities. [FAS95, ¶24] [Similarly,] real estate generally is considered a productive asset, and a cash payment to purchase real estate generally is an investing cash outflow. However, if real estate is acquired by a real estate developer to be subdivided, improved, and sold in individual lots, then the cash payment to purchase that real estate would be classified as an operating cash flow because the real estate is acquired specifically for resale and is similar to inventory in other businesses. [FAS102, ¶25]

Classification of Cash Flows from Acquisitions and Sales of Certain Securities and Other Assets

.122A Banks, brokers and dealers in securities, and other enterprises may carry securities and other assets in a trading account.[9c] Cash receipts and cash payments resulting from purchases and sales of securities and other assets shall be classified as operating cash flows if those assets are acquired specifically for resale and are carried at market value in a trading account. [FAS102, ¶8]

.122B Some loans are similar to securities in a trading account in that they are originated or purchased specifically for resale and are held for short periods of time. Cash receipts and cash payments resulting from acquisitions and sales of loans also shall be classified as operating cash flows if those loans are acquired specifically for resale and are carried at market value or at the lower of cost or market value.[9d] Cash receipts resulting from sales of loans that were not specifically acquired for resale shall be classified as investing cash inflows. That is, if loans were acquired as investments, cash receipts from sales of those loans shall be classified as investing cash inflows regardless of a change in the purpose for holding those loans. [FAS102, ¶9]

[9c]Characteristics of trading account activities are described in Section C28, "Changing Prices: Reporting Their Effects in Financial Reporting," paragraphs .192 and .193, and in the AICPA Industry Audit Guide, *Audits of Banks*, and Audit and Accounting Guide, *Audits of Brokers and Dealers in Securities.* [FAS102, ¶8, fn3]

[9d]Mortgage loans and mortgage-backed securities held for sale are required to be reported at the lower of cost or market value in accordance with Section Mo4, "Mortgage Banking Activities," paragraph .105. [FAS102, ¶9, fn4]

Foreign Currency Cash Flows

.123 A statement of cash flows of an enterprise with foreign currency transactions or foreign operations shall report the reporting currency equivalent of foreign currency cash flows using the exchange rates in effect at the time of the cash flows. An appropriately weighted average exchange rate for the period may be used for translation if the result is substantially the same as if the rates at the dates of the cash flows were used.[10] The statement shall report the effect of exchange rate changes on cash balances held in foreign currencies as a separate part of the reconciliation of the change in cash and cash equivalents during the period. [FAS95, ¶25]

Content and Form of the Statement of Cash Flows

.124 A statement of cash flows for a period shall report net cash provided or used by operating, investing, and financing activities[11] and the net effect of those flows on cash and cash equivalents during the period in a manner that reconciles beginning and ending cash and cash equivalents. [FAS95, ¶26]

.125 In reporting cash flows from operating activities, enterprises are encouraged to report major classes of gross cash receipts and gross cash payments and their arithmetic sum—the net cash flow from operating activities (the direct method). Enterprises that do so should, at a minimum, separately report the following classes of operating cash receipts and payments:[12]

a. Cash collected from customers, including lessees, licensees, and the like
b. Interest and dividends received
c. Other operating cash receipts, if any
d. Cash paid to employees and other suppliers of goods or services, including suppliers of insurance, advertising, and the like
e. Interest paid
f. Income taxes paid
g. Other operating cash payments, if any.

[10]Paragraph .118 of Section F60, "Foreign Currency Translation," recognizes the general impracticality of translating revenues, expenses, gains, and losses at the exchange rates on dates they are recognized and permits an appropriately weighted average exchange rate for the period to be used to translate those elements. This section applies that provision to cash receipts and cash payments. [FAS95, ¶25, fn9]

[11]Separate disclosure of cash flows pertaining to extraordinary items or discontinued operations reflected in those categories is not required. An enterprise that nevertheless chooses to report separately operating cash flows of discontinued operations shall do so consistently for all periods affected, which may include periods long after sale or liquidation of the operation. [FAS95, ¶26, fn10]

[12]Paragraphs .130 through .133 and paragraph .141, respectively, discuss and illustrate a method by which those major classes of gross operating cash receipts and payments generally may be determined indirectly. [FAS95, ¶27, fn11]

Enterprises are encouraged to provide further breakdowns of operating cash receipts and payments that they consider meaningful and feasible. For example, a retailer or manufacturer might decide to further divide cash paid to employees and suppliers (category (d) above) into payments for costs of inventory and payments for selling, general, and administrative expenses. [FAS95, ¶27]

.126 Enterprises that choose not to provide information about major classes of operating cash receipts and payments by the direct method as encouraged in paragraph .125 shall determine and report the same amount for net cash flow from operating activities indirectly by adjusting net income to reconcile it to net cash flow from operating activities (the indirect or reconciliation method). That requires adjusting net income to remove (a) the effects of all deferrals of past operating cash receipts and payments, such as changes during the period in inventory, deferred income, and the like, and all accruals of expected future operating cash receipts and payments, such as changes during the period in receivables and payables,[13] and (b) the effects of all items whose cash effects are investing or financing cash flows, such as depreciation, amortization of goodwill, and gains or losses on sales of property, plant, and equipment and discontinued operations (which relate to investing activities), and gains or losses on extinguishment of debt (which is a financing activity). [FAS95, ¶28]

.127 The reconciliation of net income to net cash flow from operating activities described in paragraph .126 shall be provided regardless of whether the direct or indirect method of reporting net cash flow from operating activities is used. That reconciliation shall separately report all major classes of reconciling items. For example, major classes of deferrals of past operating cash receipts and payments and accruals of expected future operating cash receipts and payments, including at a minimum changes during the period in receivables pertaining to operating activities, in inventory, and in payables pertaining to operating activities, shall be separately reported. Enterprises are encouraged to provide further breakdowns of those categories that they consider meaningful. For example, changes in receivables from customers for an enterprise's sale of goods or services might be reported separately from changes in other operating receivables. In addition, if the indirect method is used, amounts of interest paid (net of amounts capitalized) and income taxes paid during the period shall be provided in related disclosures. [FAS95, ¶29]

.128 If the direct method of reporting net cash flow from operating activities is used, the reconciliation of net income to net cash flow from operating activities shall be provided in a separate schedule. If the indirect method is used, the reconciliation may be either reported within the statement of cash flows or provided in a separate schedule,

---

[13]Adjustments to net income to determine net cash flow from operating activities shall reflect accruals for interest earned but not received and interest incurred but not paid. Those accruals may be reflected in the statement of financial position in changes in assets and liabilities that relate to investing or financing activities, such as loans or deposits. However, interest credited directly to a deposit account that has the general characteristics described in paragraph .105, footnote 2, is a cash outflow of the payor and a cash inflow of the payee when the entry is made. [FAS95, ¶28, fn12]

with the statement of cash flows reporting only the net cash flow from operating activities. If the reconciliation is presented in the statement of cash flows, all adjustments to net income to determine net cash flow from operating activities shall be clearly identified as reconciling items. [FAS95, ¶30]

.129 Except for items described in paragraphs .110 and .111, both investing cash inflows and outflows and financing cash inflows and outflows shall be reported separately in a statement of cash flows—for example, outlays for acquisitions of property, plant, and equipment shall be reported separately from proceeds from sales of property, plant, and equipment; proceeds of borrowings shall be reported separately from repayments of debt; and proceeds from issuing stock shall be reported separately from outlays to reaquire the enterprise's stock. [FAS95, ¶31]

Indirectly Determining Amounts of Operating Cash Receipts and Payments

.130 Given sufficiently detailed information, major classes of operating cash receipts and payments may be determined indirectly by adjusting revenue and expense amounts for the change during the period in related asset and liability accounts. For example, cash collected from customers may be determined indirectly by adjusting sales for the change during the period in receivables from customers for the enterprise's delivery of goods or services. Likewise, cash paid to suppliers and employees may be determined indirectly by adjusting cost of sales and expenses (exclusive of depreciation, interest, and income taxes) for the change during the period in inventories and payables for operating items. That procedure, of course, requires the availability of information concerning the change during the period in the appropriate classes of receivables and payables.[14] The more detailed the categories of operating cash receipts and payments to be reported, the more complex the procedure for determining them. [FAS95, ¶115]

.131 It seems likely that amounts of operating cash receipts and payments at the minimum level of detail specified in paragraph .125 often may be determined indirectly without incurring unduly burdensome costs over those involved in appropriately applying the indirect method. For example, determining net cash flow from operating activities by the indirect method requires the availability of the total amount of operating receivables. That is, any receivables for investing or financing items must be segregated. Within the total amount of operating receivables, information on receivables from customers for an enterprise's delivery of goods or services may well be available separately from those for interest and dividends. Thus, it may be possible to determine indirectly cash collected from customers and interest and dividends received using much the same information needed to determine net cash flow from operating activities using the indirect method. [FAS95, ¶116]

[14]For the resulting operating cash receipts and payments to be accurate, the effects of all noncash entries to accounts receivable and payable, inventory, and other balance sheets accounts used in the calculation must be eliminated. For example, the change in accounts receivable would have to be determined exclusive of any bad debt write-offs and other noncash charges and credits to customer accounts during the period. [FAS95, ¶115, fn17]

.132 The same procedure may be used to determine cash paid to suppliers and employees. Determining net cash flow from operating activities by the direct method requires the availability of the total amount of payables pertaining to operating activities. Within that amount, payables to suppliers and employees may well be available separately from those for interest and taxes. [FAS95, ¶117]

.133 Many enterprises may well be able to determine amounts of operating cash receipts and payments at the minimum level of detail that this section encourages (refer to paragraph .125) indirectly at reasonable cost by the procedure discussed in the foregoing paragraphs. The degree of difficulty encountered in applying it undoubtedly would vary depending on the nature of an enterprise's operations and the features of its current accounting system. [FAS95, ¶118]

Information about Noncash Investing and Financing Activities

.134 Information about all investing and financing activities of an enterprise during a period that affect recognized assets or liabilities but that do not result in cash receipts or cash payments in the period shall be reported in related disclosures. Those disclosures may be either narrative or summarized in a schedule. [FAS95, ¶32] If there are only a few such transactions, it may be convenient to include them on the same page as the statement of cash flows. Otherwise, the transactions may be reported elsewhere in the financial statements, clearly referenced to the statement of cash flows. [FAS95, ¶74] [The disclosures] shall clearly relate the cash and noncash aspects of transactions involving similar items. Examples of noncash investing and financing transactions are converting debt to equity; acquiring assets by assuming directly related liabilities, such as purchasing a building by incurring a mortgage to the seller; obtaining an asset by entering into a capital lease; and exchanging noncash assets or liabilities for other noncash assets or liabilities. Some transactions are part cash and part noncash; only the cash portion shall be reported in the statement of cash flows. [FAS95, ¶32]

Cash Flow per Share

.135 Financial statements shall not report an amount of cash flow per share. Neither cash flow nor any component of it is an alternative to net income as an indicator of an enterprise's performance, as reporting per share amounts might imply.[15] [FAS95, ¶33]

[15]Reporting a contractually determined per unit amount, [such as a] per unit amount of cash flow distributable under the terms of a partnership agreement or other agreement between an enterprise and its owners, is not the same as reporting a cash flow per share amount intended to provide information useful to all investors and creditors and thus is not precluded by this section. [FAS95, ¶125]

CHAPTER 11

Cash flow accounting

Summary

511. Advocates of cash flow accounting believe that there can be no objective 'correct' measure of the income and financial position of a company, and that the traditional profit and loss account and balance sheet of a company should therefore be replaced by a statement of cash flows. Such a system would have many advantages but could not easily be accommodated within the present requirements of the law. In addition users of accounts have a continuing need for a useful measure of the profitability of a company which would not be satisfied by a statement of cash flows alone. Nevertheless, in the Committee's view there is much of value in the cash flow accounting principle. In the light of the recent liquidity crisis statements of companies' cash positions and internal forecasts of cash flows for the forthcoming year merit immediate development.

---

512. The accounting techniques we have so far discussed have had as their objective the measurement of business income on alternative bases within the traditional framework of the annual profit and loss account and balance sheet. This applies equally to historic cost and value accounting, in each of their various forms. There are some who take the view that the debate over the years between these various methods has merely emphasised that there is no such thing as an objective 'correct' measure of income and financial position appropriate to all companies, and that any accounting system based on a particular definition of business income will inevitably allow scope for arbitrary and subjective judgment and lead to inconsistencies between the accounts of different companies. It is argued that as a result of these difficulties the concept of 'income' or 'profit' is unsuitable as a basis for attempting to assess the financial position of a company. Support has, therefore, grown in some quarters for a return to a system of accounting neither in terms of cost nor in terms of value, but in terms of cash.

513. We have already pointed out that a characteristic of historic cost accounting is that profit for the year will not necessarily be related to cash surplus for the year. It is traditional in accounting textbooks, if not actually to make a virtue of this characteristic, at least not to regard it as a drawback, provided it is clearly understood. The same characteristic applies to the techniques of value accounting. Moreover, both historic cost and value accounting are based on the accrual convention under which revenues and expenditures are entered in the accounts when they fall due, not when cash is received or paid out.

514. It is suggested by the supporters of cash flow accounting that the separation of profitability from liquidity is a serious disadvantage of conventional accounting. The liquidity crisis which has forced a number of companies into difficulties in the last year or two seems to lend support to this view. Under a cash flow accounting system, entries would be made in the accounts of a company when cash was received or paid out. Depreciation would be

abandoned for the purpose of published accounts, and the cash spent on acquisition of fixed assets would be charged in full to the year of acquisition. Similarly the cash spent on acquisitions of materials, fuel, stock and all other factors would be charged in full at the point of outgoing. Under a fully comprehensive cash flow system, the conventional profit and loss account would disappear and be replaced by a statement of cash inflow and outflow over a certain period. However, one of the main supporters of cash flow accounting, Professor G H Lawson of the Manchester Business School, has suggested in evidence to us that for an initial period the cash flow accounts might appear as supplementary statements to the conventional accounts of a company.

515. The principle of cash flow accounting is usually based on the dual assumption:

(*a*) that the primary objective of a company is to survive and continue in operation and that in the last resort this means its ability to meet its costs, repay loans and pay dividends; and that the accounts should show how far this aim has been achieved; and

(*b*) that the value of the equity of a company depends on the present value of the expected future cash payments to shareholders in the form of dividends plus any capital payments which might potentially become available for distribution; and that the accounts should be presented in such a way that this information is given.

516. In our view it is difficult to fault these basic assumptions. The advantages of accounting in terms of cash are:

(i) The system is more objective and more easily verified than historic cost or value accounting, particularly the latter. Amounts of cash disbursed can readily be verified by references to invoices, wages records and so on.

(ii) The system automatically deals with the problems of changing costs and prices. All costs and receipts are entered at their cash value when paid or received, so that all the entries in the accounts are automatically at current value when they are made. The problem of calculating the correct depreciation provision, which is significant for other systems of accounting when costs and prices are changing, does not arise under cash flow accounting.

(iii) By entering receipts and expenditures when they are received or paid in cash, not when they fall due, cash flow accounting avoids the problem of gains or losses arising from holding monetary liabilities or assets when costs and prices are changing. The supporters of cash flow accounting argue that it takes true account of the changing value of money through time by entering receipts and expenditures only when they are actually received or paid.

517. However, there are certain disadvantages in this technique which are likely to rule it out as a basis for accounting reform in the foreseeable future. The main difficulty is to accommodate the technique within the conventional form of presentation of annual profit and loss accounts and balance sheets

required by the law. The techniques of historic cost accounting (in particular the accrual convention, the principal of depreciation and the separation of balance sheet and profit and loss accounts) were devised in order to deal with the difficulties of accommodating accounts drawn up solely in terms of cash (which is probably the oldest accounting system of all) with the need to show the annual profit or loss of a company and its financial position on the balance sheet date. We have seen that during a time of changing costs and prices historic cost accounts give rise to difficulties, and these might be avoided by returning to the old system of accounting in terms of cash. However, this would also mean a return to the old difficulties of assessing the profit or loss for the year when the accounting system does not match revenues against costs incurred in their generation. Although we agree with those who advocate cash flow accounting that there can be no 'correct' measure of profit appropriate to all enterprises, we believe that despite its subjectivity users of accounts still require a useful measure of the profitability of a company for practical purposes. As we have seen, historic cost accounts do not meet this requirement at the present time and there is therefore a need for the profit and loss account and balance sheet of a company to be drawn up on a more useful basis. The abandonment of the existing concept of the profit and loss account altogether and its substitution by a statement of cash surplus or deficit over a period of time would not we feel fully meet the requirements for information of users of accounts which we set out in Chapter 5. In addition, to be of most use a cash flow accounting system would need to incorporate cash forecasts possibly based on different assumptions about future changes affecting the company. We doubt whether such a fundamental change would be acceptable to British companies at the present time.

518. Nevertheless, there is in our view much of value in the cash flow accounting principle. Events of the last year have shown that it is essential for companies to consider not only their profitability but also their liquidity position. In the long-term a company which consistently fails to make profits cannot continue, but in the shorter term a company which runs out of cash can collapse overnight. We have already suggested (paragraph 163) that one of the main requirements for information from company accounts is for a statement of the company's cash position, and that directors should prepare internal forecasts of the expected requirements for, and sources of, cash in the forthcoming year (paragraph 229). We believe that in the light of the recent liquidity crisis in industry this aspect of the cash flow accounting method merits immediate development.

from

P. N. McMonnies, ed., *Making Corporate Reports Valuable*
(London: Kogan Page, 1988), pp. 68-80

CHAPTER 7

Meeting the Information Needs of Management and Investors

INTRODUCTION

7.1 In preceding chapters we have outlined what we believe management and external users want to know and we have identified shortcomings of contemporary external reporting. We now go on to suggest the kind of package which we believe would be helpful to both parties.

7.2 We see the annual report to investors of both individual entities and groups as coming directly out of management information, though almost certainly not so full, with the only reductions being those that are essential for reasons that are beneficial to the investors. We believe in principle that the latter need the same sort of information as management, both so that the investors are fully informed in the decisions they have to make in relation to their shares, and also so that they are in a position to judge whether the management they have appointed are managing the affairs of the entity properly. It must be borne in mind, however, that some adjustment to the management figures may be necessary to ensure consistency with previous years and/or comparability with other entities.

7.3 In this chapter we take the needs of both management and external users, as identified in Chapter 3, and propose a package of information which, together with the ideas put forward in Chapter 5, we suggest fulfils these needs. We hope that it will become apparent that this package will largely overcome the weaknesses of the present-day reporting system, discussed in Chapter 4.

7.4 Before going into detail, we should like to make clear our belief that, insofar as our suggestions, if adopted, would have a major effect on the corporate report to the investors, we think the changes should be limited initially to quoted companies.

7.5 We have divided up the information requirements of management, which we define as what management require in order to manage and control the business to the best possible effect, into three main headings, which cover items (a) to (d) of the needs listed in paragraph 3.11 of Chapter 3:

A. Strategy and planning.

B. Information on the present financial status.

C. Information on the probable future financial status.

(Information relating to the environment within which the entity operates is covered in Chapter 5.) Although they should be part of the entire package, we do not in this chapter discuss data on the management of the entity or information about staffing because they should be covered as suggested in Chapter 5. Then there is a further section which gives our views on:

D. The presentation of the information package suggested.

The final section of this chapter refers briefly to the independent assessment of the material published externally.

7.6 Much of the information required under the above headings is available from an entity's internal records but some will have to be obtained externally. We indicate the external material as we come to it.

A. STRATEGY AND PLANNING

7.7 In Chapter 5 we suggested that management needed a statement of the entity's objectives. We also suggested that such a statement should appear in each corporate report.

7.8 In addition, management should have a strategic plan, which will cover several years ahead, a financial plan, which will be for a shorter period, and estimates of future cash flows. These planning documents grow out of each other towards the fulfilment of what have been established as the overall objectives.

7.9 The strategic plan is, we believe, too difficult to "codify" at this stage of development, with very large variations possible, especially in its time scale. Fundamentally, however, it should provide the plan as to how each business sector within the entity will invest, disinvest, market and operate over a certain time scale within the expected economic scenarios to achieve corporate objectives. This plan, unlike the Statement of Objectives, will not normally be made available to external users because of its sensitivity. Knowledge of the overall objectives should provide such users with the ability to judge from the other material in the corporate report what progress is being made towards their achievement.

7.10 The financial plan, which is derived from the strategic plan and will be available to investors in summarised form only, and the estimates of future cash flows are dealt with in more detail later in this chapter.

B. PRESENT FINANCIAL STATUS

7.11 We believe that the ability to judge the wealth of a business at any given time is very necessary for management and would eliminate for external users most of the conceptual problems which afflict present-day accounts and which we discuss in Chapter 4. In Chapter 6 we showed that net realisable value and replacement cost were the best ways of displaying assets in accounts; we also showed that we had chosen NRV because it was a value-based method instead of being cost based and it best met the objective of approximating the financial wealth of a business. The approach to demonstrating financial wealth which we are proposing would involve the preparation of four statements, and we shall discuss them next in this section. These statements are:

(a) Assets and Liabilities Statement;
(b) Operations Statement;
(c) Statement of Changes in Financial Wealth; and
(d) Distributions Statement.

(a) Assets and Liabilities Statement

7.12 The Assets and Liabilities Statement would show the assets and liabilities of the entity at the end of the accounting period, each stated at its net realisable value. Practical considerations about this were discussed in Chapter 6, Section E.

7.13 The normal circumstance will be that the market capitalisation of the entity will be larger than the sum of the net realisable values of the assets shown in the Assets and Liabilities Statement. The difference will be accounted for by the presence in the entity of a host of interacting and complex qualities, such as organisation, corporate culture, staff morale, together with such more obviously measurable (and saleable) items as patents, trademarks, and so on. In addition, there will be variations in the market capitalisation which have nothing to do with the activities of the business. We are not suggesting that it will be possible for each and every one of these items to be identified and assigned a net realisable value. That would be a completely arbitrary exercise at the moment, and we do not think that the computations will become possible in the foreseeable future. We do, however, recommend it as an area for research. The objective of the Assets and Liabilities Statement is to show the total net realisable assets of the entity, and the market capitalisation, and to highlight the difference. We suggest that the movements in that difference should be subject to useful qualitative comment; it should not be expected that a full quantitative reconciliation will ever be feasible.

7.14 If the entity is in financial trouble, the concept of an orderly disposal of the assets may not be the correct one to apply. In such situations, it will be for the management to decide whether there is a more appropriate method of determining the net realisable values (such as "break-up values"). The independent assessors will also have to apply their minds to the matter.

7.15 The market capitalisation of the entity has already been discussed, and we have stated our belief that it represents the only practical, externally verifiable, estimate of the future cash flows of the business. It is true that most current share quotations represent only a small number of shares, and take account of many external variables in addition. But that is a valid reflection of corporate life in a capitalist environment. It is perfectly possible for an entity to do nothing differently from what it has done in the past, and yet have its market value fall below the net realisable value of its assets because of a sudden change in market sentiment. It is our belief that the annual report should tell the shareholders of public companies about this. If the shareholders conclude that the change is temporary, that is their privilege. If they decide that the change is permanent and that they should sell or that the entity should be wound up, that too is their privilege.

7.16 It may be sensible, however, to average the values of the market capitalisation over a period of a few days before and after the year end. Also, the market capitalisation figure should be labelled clearly, so that investors have every reason to understand that the value for which the entire company could be sold might differ from the calculated market capitalisation.

7.17 We also suggest that a statement should be included which indicates the trend in the share price over the last several weeks before the accounting date. It may be possible to carry this trend report forward to the date upon which the accounts are signed by the directors.

7.18 A simple form of Assets and Liabilities Statement for a holding company might look like this:

Market value of property		12,500
Market value of plant		22,170
Market values of subsidiaries		12,984
Market value of other investments		5,468
Market value of vehicles		3,315
Market value of stock and work-in-progress		51,092
Debtors		44,621
Cash		10,471
		162,621
Market value of long loans	(19,231)	
Creditors	(28,008)	
Deferred taxation	(29,304)	
		(76,543)
Net identifiable assets		86,078
Market capitalisation		123,750

Note: There has been a sharp and material increase in the difference between the value of the company as shown by the values of its identifiable individual assets and liabilities, and its market capitalisation as shown by the value of the shares on the London Stock Exchange. The increase is believed to be due to:

(a) The increase in the market for our products, which has made investors regard shares in our sector as growth shares and thus increased the demand.

(b) Rumour of a takeover bid by XYZ plc.

(c) A general rise in the Stock Exchange at a time when the values of our assets less liabilities have risen at a slower rate.

Between the financial year end and the date on which this report was adopted by the Board there was a small rise in the value of our shares (2p per share) on the London Stock Exchange.

7.19 It is assumed that the Assets and Liabilities Statement will be shown for at least one prior period, as is commonplace for balance sheets at present.

7.20 If a business combination were to take place, the assets and liabilities of the two entities would be shown as one after the merger. As these would be aggregated at market value, there would, we suggest, be less room for manipulation than exists in balance sheets at present.

(b) Operations Statement

7.21 The Operations Statement calculates the financial wealth added to the entity by trading and by its operations generally. It differs from the profit and loss account in present use in that:

(a) there would be no depreciation charge,

(b) the stock would be accounted for at net realisable value (assuming orderly markets), and

(c) the only exceptional or extraordinary items would be those arising out of unusual events of a revenue nature; exceptional or extraordinary gains or losses on fixed assets would be dealt with in the Statement of Changes in Financial Wealth outlined below.

7.22 Here is what a simple Operations Statement, which meets the criteria of paragraph 4.9 in Chapter 4, might look like:

Income from continuing activities:		
Sales		307,694
Less Opening stock at market value	(63,535)	
Purchases	(227,677)	
Closing stock at market value	51,092	
	(240,120)	
Operating costs	(31,418)	
		(271,538)
		36,156
Dividend income		920
Income from discontinued operations*		(726)
Income from unusual events*		1,000
Income from prior years not previously accounted for*		(1,716)
		35,634
Less Taxation		(12,760)
Financial wealth added by operations		22,874

* Notes or sub-statements would provide significant details.

(c) Statement of Changes in Financial Wealth

7.23 The Statement of Changes in Financial Wealth which we propose is a statement showing the change in the worth of the business for the period under consideration, such change being split into its main components and indicating how each of these arose.

7.24 A simple Statement of Changes in Financial Wealth would look like this:

Financial wealth added by operations		22,874
Increase in value of quoted investment		1,111
Reduction in debenture liability		4,991
		28,976
Decrease in value of plant	(1,089)	
Decrease in value of subsidiary	(3,000)	
Decrease in value of vehicles	(1,466)	
Decrease in value of stock	(3,456)	
		(9,011)
Distributable change in financial wealth for year		19,965
Distribution		(6,444)
		13,521
New share capital		10,000
Change in financial wealth for year		23,521
Movement in market capitalisation		48,750

7.25 The change in financial wealth is measured in terms of year-end pounds. In times of significant inflation it may be helpful if investors can be given an indication of the real change in financial wealth over the period concerned by applying the retail price index to the figure representing the opening net identifiable assets and deducting the result from the change as brought out in the Statement of Changes. This would indicate how the changes in the entity's portfolio of assets related to the change in prices generally.

7.26 If there has been a sale of fixed assets during the period (not assumed in the example above), the Statement of Changes will include the gain or deficiency which will be calculated on the basis of the previous net realisable values.

(d) Distributions Statement

7.27 The fourth statement which we propose would be a Distributions Statement, in which any dividends would be shown. This statement would look like the following:

Distributable change in financial wealth for the year		19,965
Inflation adjustment		–
		19,965
Undistributed surpluses brought forward		21,449
Surpluses available for distribution		41,414
Interim dividend paid	(2,578)	
Final dividend proposed	(3,866)	
		(6,444)
Undistributed surpluses carried forward		34,970

(The foregoing assumes nil inflation for the year.)

7.28 This statement picks up the changes in financial wealth from the statement of that name, together with any retained surpluses from previous periods. While we envisage the dividends being payable out of the increase in the financial wealth of the entity, we recognise that they should be seen in relation to those values which can be realised and also in relation to the cash resources and obligations of the entity.

7.29 It is clearly possible for an entity to wish to make a distribution in a particular year which exceeds the annual total of change in wealth, and which is quite justified in terms of retentions from prior years.

7.30 In times of stable prices, there is no reason why the shareholders should not be permitted to receive any increase in realisable value over the funds they have contributed, whatever the source of that increase. The shareholders should be entitled to share, by means of cash or scrip dividend, in the net increase in financial wealth which has taken place during the year, whether it arises from operations or from changes in the values of assets or liabilities.

7.31 However, during periods of inflation, we feel that the investors should be aware of maintaining the real value of their capital which they supplied at the outset and the effect of any distribution on that real value. To this end we suggest an inflation adjustment, which is shown in the Distributions Statement above, and which might fairly be computed by applying the retail price index to the value of the shareholders' contributed capital as that stood at the start of the year.

7.32 Entities which wish to maintain their operating capability in physical terms could make a further appropriation, if need be. to maintain the asset portfolio or to provide for the replacement of the services which these assets have been supplying.

(e) Examples

7.33 We think the whole concept of the four statements dealt with above may become clearer if we study some examples at this stage. However, so as not to hold up the reading for those who want to go straight on, we have included them at Annex 1 to this chapter. They deal with two situations which are not unusual but which illustrate the way in which the suggested presentation brings out salient features not ascertainable from the normal profit and loss account and balance sheet. The figures which we have used are not intended to be significant, only to illustrate the effect of the statements.

7.34 The foregoing statements are the means by which the management and the external users can see the state of an entity's financial wealth at a given time and how it has changed since the previous report. However, they do not provide all the information needed to understand the changes that have taken place during the period. We now go on to discuss what is needed in addition to the four basic statements already described.

(f) Cash Flow Statement

7.35 We regard this as essential for any board of directors and for investors. It is something which not all boards see at the moment, and it is not a statement which investors ever see, though the existing source and application of funds statement, which is different in concept, goes some way towards meeting this need. We think much more emphasis requires to be given to this aspect of business management.

7.36 We define the statement as one showing the inflow and outflow of cash broken down into its main components, and usually dealing with the year of the accounts and going three years forward. The figures will normally be shown by months, but for external reporting we suggest that they cover a year, with significant peaks and troughs highlighted and compared with overdraft and other facilities available.

7.37 It is interesting to note that a recent statement by the Financial Accounting Standards Board (FASB) in the USA requires a statement of cash flows as part of a full set of financial statements of all business entities. This statement of cash flows will classify cash receipts and payments by operating, investing and financing cash flows. The FASB is making the statement effective for financial periods ending after 15 July 1988. Such cash flows will be only historical.

7.38 An example of a cash flow statement for external users follows:

Opening Balance	(6,016)
Generated by Operations	18,320
Investments:	
Fixed assets	(16,500)
Quoted shares (trade investment)	(3,333)
New Finance:	
Debentures	8,000
Share capital	10,000
Closing Balance	10,471

(g) Necessary Segments

7.39 We believe that all the statements mentioned above will be inadequate for both managements' and external users' purposes if there is just the one statement for the whole entity. We think they will all need to be split in various ways, as discussed in Chapter 5, and particularly we feel that, provided the amounts are significant, there should be a split:

(i) By product.
(ii) By manufacturing location.
(iii) Geographically.
(iv) By currency.

However, the actual divisions will depend very much on the size and complexity of the entity involved.

7.40 Just to take one example, the geographic split might be by towns, by counties, by countries or even by continents. We think it is impossible to be dogmatic about the type of geographic split required. There may also be particular reasons, for example from the point of view of competition or for political reasons in a country, why some of this information should not be given in public documents, eg to investors. We see it as being part of the role of the new form of audit (the independent assessment) to ensure that as far as the investors are concerned they are given a sensible division for the four categories mentioned above, subject to this not creating serious problems which could affect the health of the business and therefore be to their own detriment.

7.41 Regarding the level of detail, there is no doubt that the systems in use in managing the company would produce far more detail than investors, employees and creditors would want. The level of detail that makes sense for a big corporation (which will normally entail several hierarchical levels of reporting detail) will not usually make sense for smaller enterprises. The amount of detail which should be made available must also depend on the reportee's ability to digest information rather than on the ability of accountants to sub-divide information on an entity into components of various kinds.

7.42 It is likely, however, that certain user groups will want to receive more information than others. It is possible, making use of modern technology, to provide these users with such information. The full detailed figures, broken down as far as can be justified by confidentiality, could be placed in a general access file in an entity's computer and updated as often as required. Those users who need the detail could be provided with a phone number which would link their computer directly to this file, which they could copy on to their own machine and carry out computations as desired. The objective would be to use the information base to enhance the relationship of an entity to the finance markets by making it easier for users to access the data they want. (ICI have made major inroads in the paint and agricultural markets by providing very similar kinds of access to their product selection computers.)

(h) Other necessary information

7.43 Included in the package of information for management and in the one for investors would be the statements which we suggest in Chapter 5 could be introduced in a reasonably short space of time and which are not given externally at present.

7.44 To save looking back, the following is a list of the statements and additional disclosures that we have in mind:
For both directors and external users:

(a) information on related parties (5.16);
(b) information on accounting areas subject to uncertainty (5.17);
(c) statement on relative innovation (5.18);
(d) information on effectiveness and lead-time of research and development (5.19);
(e) information on the economic environment (5.41 – 5.43);
(f) comparative operational statistics (5.44); and
(g) information on staff resources (5.47 – 5.50).

For external users only:

(h) information on ownership, management and their responsibilities (5.35, 5.45, 5.46).

C. FUTURE FINANCIAL STATUS

7.45 We touched in Chapter 5 upon the need for external users to have future-orientated information. We now pursue this idea further, commencing with a review of the normal financial planning practices which managements undertake, before considering what the investors should be provided with.

(a) Financial Plans

7.46 We believe that boards should have, in most cases, a three year financial plan, probably split year by year and possibly in the shorter term into shorter periods of time. It differs from the cash flow statement by dealing with value and not cash. It will therefore embrace figures in the estimated future Operations Statements and movements in the value of the assets and liabilities shown in the Assets and Liabilities Statement. It would not, however, be expected to bring in market capitalisation figures because we do not believe it is realistic to expect management to estimate the market value of their own shares for such a future period.

7.47 The three year period has been chosen because we understand that most businesses find this the optimum period for such plans, but the term should be that most appropriate to the business concerned. The financial plan should not be "cast in stone" but should be subject to regular revision, and we believe that consideration of the need for change in the financial plan, often arising because the original assumptions have proved to be incorrect, is probably of more value to most boards of directors than the current comparison of "actual to budget", which tends to be dealing with history rather than with the future and the planning that has to come from it. The financial plan will need in many cases to be adjustable for sensitivity factors (for example, what is the effect on the plan if parity rates for currency, instead of being as forecast, were to be, say, 10% higher or lower).

7.48 While as stated above we believe that the reasons for changes in the financial plan need more discussion than the actual out-turn compared to the latest financial plan, the comparison of "actual to budget" should not be omitted, but should be regarded as having reduced importance. This comparison of actual to budget would therefore still be used for control purposes, but not for planning purposes.

7.49 Within the financial plan (and also within the cash flow) would be the major projects for expansion or investment and their out-turn.

7.50 A summary of the financial plan should be provided to the investors. This summary should be based upon the current methods used in preparing a prospectus, which normally (depending on the exact date of the proposed share issue) will include a forecast financial report for the coming year. It could, however, be longer if management so decided. Also, we suggest that the major assumptions which have been used by management in preparing the three year financial plan should be disclosed, even though the plan itself is for a shorter period. These major assumptions would be of the type that are fundamental to future-orientated material that has to be published in prospectus or takeover documents today: they would not be required to cover every detail of management's forward thinking.

7.51 Management should provide a discussion of the differences between the financial plan disclosed in last year's report and the actual results for the year. This discussion would enable the investor to:

(a) see the view of the future held by management then and now;
(b) appraise management's ability to forecast;
(c) consider the problems which may have afflicted the entity during the year under review; and
(d) estimate the likely trend of future dividends.

(b) Future Cash Flows

7.52 As well as the statement of cash flows for the current year it will be necessary for the management to have a forecast of the cash flows to come. In paragraph 7.36 three years forward were suggested. These projections should also be available to external users in summarised form, for at least one year forward (but longer if management thought it desirable).

Summary

7.53 We see the information relating to the future which will be before management and investors as comprising:

Suggested additional reading

As in the previous section, there is relatively little additional reading available to meet the needs of this section. The following represents a useful source of early US institutional thinking on the issue of reporting in practice on the basis of cash flow data, and a more recent contribution from the UK.

* Financial Accounting Standards Board, 'Analysis of Issues Related to Reporting Funds, Flows, Liquidity and Financial Flexibility,' **Discussion Memorandum** (Stamford: Financial Accounting Standards Board, 1980).

* Institute of Chartered Accountants in England and Wales, 'The Use of Discounting in Financial Statements,' **Discussion Paper TR 773** (London: Institute of Chartered Accountants in England and Wales, 1989).

For Product Safety Concerns and Information please contact our EU representative GPSR@taylorandfrancis.com
Taylor & Francis Verlag GmbH, Kaufingerstraße 24, 80331 München, Germany

www.ingramcontent.com/pod-product-compliance
Lightning Source LLC
LaVergne TN
LVHW080804011026
849160LV00015B/1530

* 9 7 8 1 1 3 8 9 6 9 9 1 9 *